STUDIES IN BEHAVIOR PATHOLOGY

STUDIES IN

Behavior
Pathology

THE EXPERIMENTAL APPROACH TO THE PSYCHOLOGY OF THE ABNORMAL

Edited by

THEODORE R. SARBIN
University of California, Berkeley

HOLT, RINEHART AND WINSTON
NEW YORK - CHICAGO - SAN FRANCISCO
TORONTO - LONDON

April, 1964

Copyright © 1961 by Holt, Rinehart and Winston, Inc.
All rights reserved

Library of Congress Catalog Card Number: 61-14604

27708-0211

Printed in the United States of America

Acknowledgments

THIS enterprise could not have been completed without the faithful assistance of Messrs. Milton Andersen, Stanley Fong, Kailish Khemka, and Eldred Rutherford. In this public and perhaps too impersonal way, I acknowledge with gratitude their help with the various bibliographical and editorial chores. I am also grateful to Mrs. Rhoda Wolfe who diligently handled the heavy load of correspondence with authors and publishers.

I owe a special debt of gratitude to Vernon Allen who, assisted by his wife, Patricia, carried out the arduous tasks of preparing the index and reading the proofs.

I also wish to acknowledge the courtesy of the publishers and authors for permission to include copyrighted material in this volume. Specific acknowledgements are made on the first page of each contribution.

Berkeley, California   **T. R. S.**
September 1961

Contents

INTRODUCTION

To the Teacher

THIS Reader is specifically designed as a supplementary textbook for undergraduate courses labelled abnormal psychology, behavior disorders, psychopathology, and the like. It is an outgrowth of a pedagogical device that I have used for a number of years, namely to assign undergraduate students the reading of *experimental* articles in contemporary journals. My objective was to acquaint the student with the wide variety of problems in behavior pathology currently being investigated by experimental methods.

From textbooks of abnormal psychology, the student quickly learns that the psychology of the abnormal evolved as a *clinical* enterprise, where the diagnosis of mental illness is made from observations of patient at the bedside, so to speak. We cannot escape the historical fact that the modern psychology of the abnormal began as a subspecialty of clinical medicine. Because certain neurological symptoms were similar to mental symptoms (such as disorientation, confusion, hallucinations), and since the neurological symptoms occurred in persons classified as sick, it was easy to complete the analogy and conclude that persons with mental symptoms were also sick. The humanitarian movement that replaced asylums with hospitals helped to establish the abnormal as ill. Once disordered persons were regarded as sick, then it followed that they be assigned to physicians for care and study.

Working within the context of clinical medicine, physicians formulated taxonomies for the purpose of classifying the mentally ill into diagnostic categories. The most widely used taxonomy was developed by Kraepelin.* The prognostic utility of his classificatory system has been extremely limited, but in spite of these limitations, adaptations of Kraepelin's system still serve as the framework of most textbooks. That is to say, the typical textbook is organized around the *clinically* observed signs and symptoms which comprise a "disease" entity, such as schizophrenia.

Exciting clinical reports and facile dynamic interpretations have their place, of course, but the student's preparation is incomplete if he is not exposed also to the richly varied literature of experimental psychopathology. No science can make progress toward its goal of prediction and control by the exclusive use of clinical observation and anecdotal reporting. Through systematic and controlled observation, behavior pathology,

* E. Kraepelin, *Clinical Psychiatry* (New York: Macmillan, 1902).

no less than other scientific disciplines, can sharpen its concepts and increase its accuracy of prediction and control. A quick perusal of the current history of behavior pathology should convince the reader of the shift from clinical reporting of signs and symptoms to systematic observation of more subtle behaviors. Contrast, for example, the widely quoted book edited in 1944 by Kasanin* on the language and thought if schizophrenia with the recent attempt by Osgood and Walker to analyze the content of suicide notes (reproduced in this volume). Not only are the analytical tools more appropriate to the task, but attention is given to statistical and experimental controls.

Reading and comprehending recent research reports is, in my opinion, the best way for the student to become convinced that systematic and controlled observation not only has a place in our discipline, but is currently creating knowledge of great potential utility. Reading research papers introduces the student to the necessity for statistical and experimental controls, a point not often considered in the standard clinical descriptions of abnormal personalities. In addition, reading contemporary literature affords the opportunity of becoming acquainted with the modern technology employed in behavior pathology research, such as content analysis, electroencephalography, operant conditioning, psychometric scaling, demography, factor analysis, role-taking, and autonomic recording.

Criteria for Selecting Papers

Because research papers suitable for undergraduate reading are scattered throughout the literature, and also because of the limited supply of journals in college and university libraries, I have selected a set of articles that can be assigned as auxiliary reading in courses in abnormal psychology. From an original pool of thousands of papers, I selected and read hundreds of articles and abstracts that, for one reason or another, had been nominated as suitable to the purposes of the reader. The 39 papers finally selected for this reader are *typical,* and to a large degree representative, of contemporary research activity in behavior pathology.

I use the word *typical* advisedly. I do not expect that all or even most of these articles will go down in history as classics or be considered major "breakthroughs" in science. In fact, the alert and conscientious reader could criticize some of the articles in terms of adequacy of controls, propriety of design, representativeness of samples, and so on. However, science may advance on any front. A poorly designed experiment on an important problem may advance the frontiers of behavior pathology more than a meticulously designed experiment on an insignificant problem.

The following criteria were used in deciding which papers to include:

1. *Systematic observation:* All the papers in this collection, save two, contain systematically observed data. I rejected papers that focused exclusively on illustrative case histories or on the presentation of theoretical arguments. This is not to gainsay the importance of such papers for some purposes, but my objective is to acquaint the student with the use of controlled observation and experiment in finding the facts of behavior pathology. The two exceptions to this general requirement are: (a) the paper by Scott reviewing the problems inherent in attempts at defining pathology, and (b) the paper by Farber, Harlow, and West interpreting data on "brainwashing" with the aid of general psychological principles.

2. *Concern with behavior disorders:* To delimit the scope of this book, it was necessary to establish a criterion of *content.* It is impossible in a collection of this size to sample all the content areas that contribute to understanding the abnormal personality. After much deliberation, the criterion finally adopted was this: to be included in the

* J. S. Kasanin, *Language and Thought in Schizophrenia* (Berkeley: University of California Press, 1944).

Reader, a paper must deal explicitly with disordered personalities. I believe that to be most useful to students of behavior pathology the Reader should stress research done with disordered persons as subjects. The temptation was great to include a few papers concerned with the operation of defense mechanisms, a report or two on psychotherapeutic methods, and a sample of the recent literature on the use of drugs. Such a temptation was resisted except for Section 2. Here I have reprinted several papers that deal with possible analogues of pathological processes.

I want to emphasize again that this Reader is intended not to displace but to *supplement* conventional textbooks, lectures, and other pedagogical tools. For this reason it does not present typical experiments dealing with *all* of behavior pathology.

3. *Theoretical bias:* It would be foolish to assume that theoretical bias does not operate in the selection of papers for this or any other anthology. Although I lean toward a "social learning" interpretation of behavior pathology, I tried to see that diverse viewpoints were represented. At the same time that I applied the criteria of "systematic observation" and "concern with behavior disorders" I tried to sample researches done in different theoretical contexts. For example, the reports of Shevrin and Luborsky, Gibson, Beck and Hurvich, and Kepecs, Robin, and Munro were guided by hypotheses drawn from psychoanalytic sources. The social-psychological point of view is reflected in the hypotheses central to the studies of Hesterley and Berg, Sarbin and Hardyck, Phillips and Rabinovich, Medalia and Larsen, and others.

4. *Comprehensibility:* To qualify for inclusion in this Reader, the papers had to be comprehensible to undergraduate students. Increase in comprehensibility of the more technical papers is achieved by some editing, footnoting, and deleting of tabular and text material. Technical terms not defined in conventional textbooks or in the papers are defined in a glossary.

5. *Recency:* Since behavior pathology is a rapidly growing science, I wanted to acquaint the student with current problems and methods. All papers are therefore of recent publication date. The oldest paper has a 1951 dateline; more than half were published since 1955.

Preview

The clustering of papers into meaningful sections presented some problems. No attempt was made to arrange the reports according to standard nosological classifications. Such classifications have outlived their usefulness. Rather, the sorting of papers was done with the aid of conceptions drawn from current research in psychology.

At the beginning of each section I have written a few paragraphs as an aid to the student reader. These *introductory comments* direct the student to particular features of an article, either substantive or methodological. In some cases, specific questions are raised that the student may ponder as he reads the article.

Following this introduction, Section 1 presents four papers that deal with the definitions of behavior disorder. The first of the four is a critical analysis of the problem of determining the criterion of pathology in experimental and field studies. The remaining three arbitrarily adopt commitment to a mental hospital as a criterion and present empirical data to support various notions of deviance.

Section 2 contains four papers, each of which describes behavior under special or extreme conditions, but not in terms of conventional pathology. Each of these papers implicitly presents a model of behavior that is potentially applicable to the study of the etiology of behavior disorders.

Section 3 includes five papers that depend on concepts drawn from learning theories. The approach to behavior pathology from the viewpoint that both ordered and disordered behavior are products of learning illustrates the convergence of clinical psychopathology and the psychology of learning.

Section 4 looks at different forms of pathology from the viewpoint that defective socialization is the key variable. The empirical approach to socialization is obvious.

Section 5 focuses on schizophrenia and illustrates several approaches to the experimental study of this behavior syndrome. Not only the diversity of methods, but the diversity of guiding hypotheses are noteworthy.

Section 6 contains four papers that aim at the clarification of concepts associated with disorders of mood. Demonstration of the psychological antecedents and correlates of mood disturbances deemphasizes the commonly held biological or metabolic interpretations of mood.

Section 7 contains a group of papers that deals with physiological response and responsivity under special psychological conditions. Some experimental approaches to psychosomatic problems are illustrated.

Section 8 has as its focus behavior disorders associated with cerebral damage. Although disordered behavior following brain damage has been repeatedly studied, the research methods reported here are of special interest.

Finally, Section 9 contains three papers dealing with prognosis. The importance of sociological and social psychological variables and the relative insignificance of medical variables in predicting post-hospital performance is underscored.

To the Student

WITH few exceptions, research articles follow a more or less standard format. In the first few paragraphs comprising the *introduction,* the author poses the problem to be investigated. His introductory statement usually outlines the problem in a general way and places it in a historical context by reviewing the theoretical notions or experimental results of other investigators. Having given the reader proper perspective by presenting the general background, the author becomes more specific and presents the particular aspects of the problem in which he is interested. At this juncture, hypotheses, predictions, guesses, or hunches are stated.

The second section of a research article is usually labeled *method* or *procedure.* Here the author describes in detail his apparatus or tests, the selection of subjects, the instructions to the subjects, and the experimental design.

The next section is labeled *results* or *findings.* Here the data are presented, sometimes in expository form, sometimes in the form of tables or graphs, and sometimes by both methods. The results of any statistical tests conducted on the data are also given.

A *discussion* may follow the presentation of the findings. The author tries to link the data to the original hypotheses and may speculate about implications for theory or practice. The results of the study may be compared with the findings of other investigators. At the end of the article, the author writes a condensed version that serves as a *summary.*

The student may read research articles with any one of three aims: (1) acquaintance, (2) comprehension, or (3) critical evaluation. He should approach each article with acquaintance as his first objective, comprehension as his second, and, if he has sufficient background and interest, critical evaluation as his third objective.

To achieve acquaintance with a research paper, the student should first read the introductory paragraphs to determine the nature of the problem under investigation. Then the methods and discussion should be scanned briefly. Finally, the summary statements should be carefully scrutinized. By following this procedure, the student will achieve a cursory acquaintance with the contents of the article.

With this acquaintance as a basis, the student can now concentrate on acquiring comprehension of the work. To do this, it will be necessary to ask a number of questions in the course of the reading. Following are some typical questions that should aid the reader in understanding the substance of research articles.

The *introductory* section will generally provide information to answer the following questions. What is the author trying to do? Is he trying to discover new relations among phenomena? Is his work aimed at testing a hypothesis by systematic observation? Is he trying to confirm findings reported previously? Is he interested in testing the generality of a principle? Is he questioning a widely held conception that has not been subjected to test through controlled experiment or systematic observation? Is he interested in determining the fruitfulness of a method?

The *methods* section will answer questions of this sort: How does the author convert his hunches into testable hypotheses? What operations are employed by the experimenter to answer the questions? In short, how does the author *specify* the variables? How does he select his subjects? What kinds of manipulations or examinations of the subjects does he introduce? What is the nature of the control sample?

The *results* section will answer these questions: What are the raw data from which the results are refined? Are they ratings, scale scores, self-reports, physiological measurements, census data, and so on? Are the original protocols listed, or have the data been processed? And in what ways?

The *discussion* section will provide answers, usually, to these questions: Are the results in line with predictions from the author's initial hypotheses? How does the author relate his findings to conclusions reached by other investigators? How does the author explain differences between his data and the predictions generated by his hypotheses? How are his findings integrated with other current attempts to answer the same or similar questions?

Having achieved comprehension, the student is in a position critically to evaluate the research report by asking a few additional questions. Such questions are based in part on familiarity with research design, statistical methods, the logic of experiment, and last, but not least, common sense.

The following are suggestions: Are the investigator's research hypotheses clearly linked to the questions raised? Are the specifications of the variables reasonable? Is he justified in specifying, for example, that a score on a personality test is equivalent to "ego-control"? Is he concerned with representativeness both in selecting his subjects and in specifying the behaviors to be observed? Are his controls adequate? Are the statistical tests appropriate to the data? May conclusions other than those of the author be derived from the same data? In what way are the findings significant, i.e., do they contribute in any important way to our understanding of behavior pathology? Can the efficiency of prediction and control of behavior be increased as a result of the application of the findings?

The undergraduate student may feel hesitant about critically evaluating a research article. This hesitancy may be eliminated if the student will bear in mind that a research article, simply because it is in print, is not the last word, nor is it perfect. In keeping with one of the purposes of this book—to emphasize that behavior pathology is a science —the student should recognize that any research study provides only tentative and imperfect answers to questions. Let me encourage you, therefore, to be properly skeptical and to doubt and raise questions. By asking penetrating questions, new hypotheses emerge and new research is undertaken. This is as it should be because new research is the hallmark of science.

To summarize: the student should first attain cursory knowledge of an article by scanning the introduction, reading the summary and conclusions, and superficially examining the rest. Reading for comprehension and for critical evaluation may follow. Some suggestive questions have been listed above as an aid to the student seeking comprehensive understanding of research articles. Finally, it is important to caution the student against becoming overinvolved in the fine details of research presentation, lest he lose sight of the general conclusions and their implications.

1 | Problems in Defining Behavior Pathology

T_{HIS} section contains four papers that attempt to deal with problems of defining behavior pathology. Mental illnesses are not so easily defined as their medical counterparts, physical illness and somatic pathology. Criteria for assessing the presence of behavior pathology are more complex, and, in some cases, more subjective than are the criteria of somatic illness and pathology. Psychologists do not in most instances have at their disposal an armamentarium of objective laboratory procedures to detect unequivocally the presence of abnormality as does the physician with X-ray, electrocardiograph, or thermometer. The clinical psychologist frequently must employ instruments that are not independent of his observations. He must make the diagnosis of abnormality through a judgmental process in which his own subjective criteria play an important part.

Definition of behavior pathology is essentially a cultural matter, dependent upon local beliefs and practices. In some cultures, the person who hallucinates or goes into "trance" is highly valued. In our own culture, a person who shows signs of hallucinating is usually declared abnormal and is hospitalized. As the papers in this section argue, even within our own culture, widely divergent definitions of mental illness may be found.

A second complication arises when we try to come to terms with the problem of definition. The distinction between mental illness and mental health is not a qualitative one. Nearly everyone at one time or another shares some of the characteristics of the abnormal personality. There is no simple solution to the problem of defining behavior pathology.

Scott's paper analyzes current definitions of mental health and illness, particularly as used in the context of research, and notes the conceptual and methodological difficulties created by each. Multiple definitions of behavior pathology, some with little overlap, constitute a problem of extreme proportions to the research worker. Difficulties in comparing the work of different experimenters arise because there is no universally accepted set of criteria for mental illness. Moreover, research workers have their own value systems that inevitably play a part in establishing criteria.

The papers by Hesterley and Berg and Sarbin and Hardyck approach the problem of definition from a "deviance" viewpoint. The "deviance" hypothesis asserts that if an individual shows certain responses defined as deviant or abnormal and also as *critical* for a diagnosis of illness, he will also show deviant or abnormal responses in other behavior systems that are not critical for a diagnosis of mental illness.

In the Hesterley and Berg study a simple perceptual task was used. Adult schizophrenics, adult normals, and normal children were tested. The hypothesis under examination asserted that adult schizophrenics and children would be similar, since both are characterized by immature behavior. Note that the objective similarity of immature behavior does not warrant the inference that the same psychological processes are involved.

Sarbin and Hardyck examine the deviance hypothesis through role perception. Hospitalized schizophrenics were compared with normals in their responses to postural cues represented in stick figures. Schizophrenics gave deviant, nonconformant responses. This paper also demonstrates that conformance in role-perception is related to social adjustment in normal subjects.

Phillips and Rabinovitch attack a different aspect of the problem. Reflecting the dissatisfaction of the profession with current nosological schemes based on descriptions of overt signs, they obtained empirical evidence concerning the extent to which symptomatic behaviors occur together. From their data, they devised a system of classification with a conceptual base sounder than that of traditional nosology. Their analysis of how symptoms cluster is illuminating. Use of role theory for conceptualizing the results requires fewer assumptions than do theories concerned with inaccessible mental contents.

Research Definitions of Mental Health and Mental Illness

WILLIAM A. SCOTT

A SERIOUS obstacle to research in the area of mental illness lies in the lack of a clear definition of the phenomenon to be studied. The term "mental ill health" has been used by different researchers to refer to such diverse manifestations as schizophrenia, suicide, unhappiness, juvenile delinquency, and passive acceptance of an intolerable environment. Whether some or all of these various reactions should be included in a single category of "mental illness" is not clear from a survey of the current literature. Theories describing the nature and antecedents of one sort of disturbance rarely relate it to

another, and there is a paucity of research evidence indicating the extent to which such manifestations are empirically intercorrelated.

In the face of such ambiguity it would appear useful to attempt an organized review of the various definitions of mental illness which are explicit or implicit in recent research, with a view toward highlighting their commonalities and discrepancies on both a theoretical and an empirical level. Such a presentation might help students concerned with causative factors to assess the comparability of previous research findings on correlates of "mental illness," and also point toward some next steps in research to discover the degree to

Reprinted by permission from the *Psychological Bulletin*, Vol. 55, No. 1, January 1958.

which these diverse phenomena represent either unitary, or multifold, psychological processes.

The research criteria for mental illness to be reviewed here are subsumed under the following categories: (a) exposure to psychiatric treatment; (b) social maladjustment; (c) psychiatric diagnosis; (d) subjective unhappiness; (e) objective psychological symptoms; and (f) failure of positive adaptation. For each category we shall review studies which appear to have employed the definition, either explicitly or implicitly. This will be accompanied by a critical discussion of the adequacy of each definition, together with an assessment, based on empirical data where possible, of the relation between this and other definitions. Finally, we shall attempt to summarize the differences among the definitions, by indicating their divergent approaches to certain basic problems in the conceptualization of mental illness and health.

MENTAL ILLNESS AS EXPOSURE TO PSYCHIATRIC TREATMENT

The most frequently used operational definition of mental illness, at least in terms of the number of studies employing it, is simply the fact of a person's being under psychiatric treatment. And this definition is usually restricted to hospital treatment, rather than outpatient service. Nearly all the ecological studies (e.g., 3, 16, 22, 30, 35, 50) and most of the studies correlating mental illness with demographic characteristics (e.g., 5, 19, 29, 41, 47) use this as a criterion. They obtain their information from hospital records or, in unusual instances (e.g., 28), from psychiatrists in the area who furnish information about persons treated on an outpatient basis.

Such a definition of mental illness is operational rather than conceptual, but its implicit meaning for the interpretation of research results is that anyone who is regarded by someone (hospital authorities, relatives, neighbors, or himself) as disturbed enough to require hospitalization or outpatient treatment is mentally ill, and people who do not fit into such diagnoses are mentally healthy. Use of hospital records, moreover, requires that the criterion of the nature of the mental illness be the diagnosis which appears on the record.

Shortcomings of such an operational definition are recognized by no one better than its users. The reliability of psychiatric diagnosis is of course open to question, and any attempt to determine correlates of particular kinds of mental disturbance must take into account the large error inherent in the measuring process. (One study of the association between diagnosis at Boston Psychopathic Hospital and previous diagnoses of the patients at other hospitals showed only 51 per cent above-chance agreement between the two [cf. 15, pp. 42–43].)

If "under the care of a psychiatrist" is to be regarded as the criterion of mental illness, one must realize the automatic limitation on the size of the mentally ill population that such a definition imposes. Kramer (34, p. 124) has estimated that the maximum possible number of mentally ill, under such a definition, would be less than 7,000,000, given the present number of available psychiatrists.

It has been suggested by both sociologists (7, 10) and physicians (17) that different rates of hospital admissions for different geographical areas may indicate more than anything else about the areas the relative degree to which the communities tolerate or reject persons with deviant behavior (11). Or as the Chief of the National Institute of Mental Health puts it: researchers using hospital records are dependent on the public's rather uneven willingness to give up its mentally ill members and to support them in institutions (17); this in addition to the admittedly unstandardized and often substandard methods of record-keeping used by the various hospitals is likely to render incomparable prevalence and incidence data from various geographical areas.

The effects of such differential

thresholds for admission in various communities are difficult to estimate, since they cannot be uniform from study to study. In 1938 a house-to-house survey in Williamson County, Tennessee, yielded nearly one person diagnosed as psychotic, but never having been in a mental hospital, for every hospitalized psychotic from the county (48). By contrast, Eaton found in his study of the Hutterites (14) that more intensive canvassing by psychiatrists did not yield a larger number of persons deemed psychotic than did a more superficial count based on community reports.

Eaton's study did yield higher proportions of neurotic diagnoses the more intensive the case finding procedure became, and this observation relates to the finding in New Haven that neurotics under outpatient treatment came disproportionately from the upper socioeconomic strata (28). At first consideration, such differential rates seem readily attributable to the cost of psychiatric treatment, but Hollingshead and Redlich prefer to seek an explanation in the greater social distance between lower-class neurotics and the psychiatrists than in the case of middle- and upper-class neurotics. Whatever the sources of rate differences, it is clear that such correlations as have been reported make one wary of the hospital admissions or outpatient figures as indicative of the "true" incidence of psychiatric disorders. Thus the criterion of exposure to psychiatric treament is at best a rough indicator of any underlying conceptual definition of mental illness.

MALADJUSTMENT AS MENTAL ILLNESS

Adjustment is necessarily determined with reference to norms of the total society or of some more restricted community within the society. Accordingly, one may conceptually define adjustment as adherence to social norms. Such a definition of mental health has an advantage over the preceding in encompassing a range of more-or-less healthy, more-or-less ill behavior, rather than posing a forced dicho-

tomy. The operation for assessing mental health by this criterion might ideally be a community (or other relevant group) consensus concerning a given subject's degree of adjustment. This has been approximated by at least one set of studies (1, 2).

Rather than assess consensus by pooling many divergent individual opinions, it is possible to assume that a law or other visible sign of social norms constitutes the criterion against which adjustment is determined. Such reference is employed in studies of suicide (12, 26) or juvenile delinquency (25) or divorce (39, 53) as indicants of maladjustment. While the operational criterion may become dichotomous in such cases (whether or not the person comes in contact with the law), this is not necessarily so. Gordon (21) has suggested considering the "biologic gradient" of suicide, extending from contemplation of the act to its actual accomplishment.

Finally, it would be possible to assess degree of adjustment with reference to some externally defined set of requirements for a given social system. Thus a work situation might be seen as demanding a high level of productivity from all its members, and the degree of adherence to this standard becomes the criterion of adjustment, without reference to the individual opinions of the group members or to the manifest norms of the group. This criterion of conformity to the requirements of a given social structure has not been explicitly employed by any of the researchers covered in the present review, but it has been hinted at (37) and remains a possibility, provided that the structural requirements of a social system can be determined independently of the members' behaviors.

Theory of social structure suggests that these three criteria of adjustment would tend toward congruence: The demands of a particular social system lead to the development of social norms, which are expressed in laws or customs and also in the individual participants' notions of what is acceptable behavior. Lack of congruence may be taken as evidence of cultural lag, of poor correspondence between manifest and latent function within the social structure, or of defensive psychological processes within the participating individuals. Since all of these factors supporting discrepancy do occur within most social systems, the criteria may be expected to yield somewhat different results.

When maladjustment is assessed by community consensus, one finds considerable divergence of opinion among various segments of the public regarding what constitutes good and poor adjustment. The Minnesota Child Welfare studies (1) showed differences in criteria for assessing adjustment among different occupational groups in the community. Teachers tended to emphasize standards different from those emphasized by ministers, who in turn displayed some differences from a more heterogeneous group of community adults. Beilin concludes that it is meaningless to discuss "adjustment" in the abstract or to contemplate the prediction of "adjustment" in general. One must specify *adjustment to what, adjustment to whose standards* (2). Lindemann reflects this relativistic conception of mental health when he states: "We find it preferable not to talk about a 'case' in psychiatry—rather we try to assess functional impairment in specific situations as viewed by different professional groups in the community. So a 'case' is really a relationship of possibly pathogenic situation and appropriate or inappropriate behavior to that situation. It is often a matter of arbitrary choice whether such a person becomes an object of psychiatric care" (38, p. 130).

Thus, though adjustment appears a more conceptually adequate criterion of mental health than does exposure to treatment, the necessity for considering different personal frames of reference and the demands of different social structures poses seemingly insurmountable obstacles to the establishment of mutually consistent operational definitions. All such difficulties which lie "hidden," as it were, under the psychiatric treatment criterion, come to the fore to plague the researcher trying to establish a criterion for adjustment which applies to the treated and nontreated alike.

PSYCHIATRIC DIAGNOSES AS CRITERION FOR MENTAL ILLNESS

There have been a few studies in which entire communities or samples of them have been systematically screened, either by direct examination (44, 48) or by evidence from community records or hearsay (13, 14, 54). Here the criterion for mental illness or health need not be dichotomous, but can be divided into several gradations. Such intensive case-finding can be expected to increase the yield of persons classified as neurotic (34, p. 124) over that provided by the criterion of exposure to treatment, but whether the psychotic group is thereby increased will depend on the community (34, p. 124; 48) and, of course, on the standards for diagnosis employed by the particular investigator.

The lack of standardization of diagnostic procedures and criteria contributes to the incomparability of mental illness rates derived from such studies (34, p. 139; 55). So long as the criterion of assessment is largely dependent on the psychiatrist's subjective integration of a different set of facts for each subject, nonuniform results can be anticipated. Expensive and unreliable though the method may be, it at least places the judgment regarding mental illness or health in the hands of professionals, which is not the case when adjustment is the criterion. And though hospitalization is in part determined by the judgment of professionals, *who* is sent to the hospitals for psychiatric diagnosis is, for the most part, out of the hands of the psychiatrists. As Felix and Bowers (17) have observed, it is the community rather than the clinician that operates the case-finding process today, and this will continue to be so until diagnostic examinations are given regularly to all people.

MENTAL ILLNESS DEFINED SUBJECTIVELY

It has been maintained by some that a major indication of need for psychotherapy is the person's own feeling of unhappiness or inadequacy. Conversely, the degree of mental health may be assessed by manifestations of subjective happiness, self-confidence, and morale. Lewis (36) quotes Ernest Jones to the effect that the main criterion for effect of therapy is the patient's subjective sense of strength, confidence, and well-being. Terman (52, 53) has used a "marriage happiness" test, composed largely of subjective items, and Pollak (43) has suggested that old-age adjustment be assessed in terms of the person's degree of happiness or well-being in various areas of his life.

That such criteria of mental health correlate somewhat with independent diagnosis by physicians has been indicated in two sorts of studies. In the Baltimore Eastern Health District (9), cases diagnosed psychoneurotic were found to express complaints about their own physical health; it is suggested that persons who report chronic nervousness can be classified as suffering from a psychiatric condition. Rogers has maintained that a marked discrepancy between one's "perceived self" and "ideal self" constitutes evidence of psychiatric disturbance (45), and some empirical studies lend support to this position. When Q sorts of subjects' self concepts are compared with Q sorts of their ideal selves, it is possible to distinguish psychiatric groups from non-psychiatric groups on the basis of the degree of discrepancy between these two measures (4). Furthermore, progress in therapy (as judged by the therapist) tends to be associated with increasing similarity between the patient's self concept and ideal self (46).

Though subjective well-being is an appealing criterion for mental health in ordinary daily living, it might be presumed that under some circumstances psychological defense mechanisms could operate to prevent the person's reporting, or becoming aware of, his own underlying unhappiness and disturbance. Jahoda (33) has rejected happiness as a criterion for mental health on somewhat different grounds: Happiness, she says, is a function not only of the person's behavior patterns, but of the environment in which he moves. If one wants to relate mental health to characteristics of the environment, then one must not take as a criterion of mental health something that already presupposes a benign environment. "There are certain circumstances in which to be happy would make it necessary first to be completely sick" (33, p. 105).

Such objections to this criterion imply that it is possible to find persons who are mentally ill by some other criterion, yet who nevertheless report themselves as happy or self-satisfied. Empirical demonstration of this implication is not available at present. In fact, while one study predicted defensively high Q sorts for the self concept of paranoid psychotics, they were found to have a greater discrepancy between self- and ideal-sorts than normals, and no less discrepancy between these measures than psychoneurotics (4).

MENTAL ILLNESS DEFINED BY OBJECTIVE PSYCHOLOGICAL SYMPTOMS

It is generally accepted almost by definition that mental illness entails both a disordering of psychological processes and a deviation of behavior from social norms (6). The latter aspect of disturbance may be assessed as maladjustment to one's social environment (discussed above); the former aspect can presumably be assessed by psychological inventories aimed at the assumedly critical processes. The distinction between the psychological inventory approach and the subjective assessment procedure discussed above is not really a clear one. Subjective well-being may be regarded as one of the psychological processes which becomes disordered. Yet more "objective" measures of psychological process, which do not require the subject's verbal report of his degree of happiness, are frequently preferred, both to guard against purposeful distortion and to tap areas of disorder which may not be accompanied by subjective counterparts.

Such "objective" psychological inventories may represent various degrees of manifest purpose. For some, the objective of assessment is transparent, and the only reason they are not classed as devices for subjective report is that they stop just short of requiring the subject to report his overall level of well-being. Such a manifest-level inventory is Halmos' questionnaire concerning the respondent's difficulties in social relations (24).

At a somewhat less obvious level are such inventories as the MMPI, the War Department Neuropsychiatric Screening Battery, and the Cornell Medical Index, which require subjects to check the presence of various subjective and objective symptoms (e.g., "I smoke too much."). Once validated against an accepted criterion, such as psychiatric diagnosis, these are frequently used as criteria themselves. Rennie constructed a composite instrument of this type to assess his respondents' levels of mental health in the Yorkville study (44); at the same time, a validity analysis of the index was undertaken, by correlating each item with independent psychiatric diagnosis on a subsample of the respondents. On the basis of their experience with such a composite instrument one of Rennie's colleagues (Langner, personal communication, August 1956) suggests caution in abstracting parts of previously validated batteries, since the item validities are sometimes not maintained when they are used out of context of the total instrument.

An adaptation of the psychiatric screening battery approach for use with children is suggested in the work of the St. Louis County Public Health Department (20). It involves obtaining information about symptoms from the children's mothers rather than from the children themselves. Naturally, the symptoms covered must be of the "objective" type ("Does Johnny wet the bed?") rather than of the "subjective" type ("Does Johnny worry a lot?"). As validated by an outside criterion (teachers' and psychiatric social workers' ratings of the child's level of adjustment), the number of symptoms reported by the mothers appears to be a promising index of the child's mental health.

A general characteristic of the types of psychological inventories reviewed so far is that each item in the battery is assumed, a priori, to involve a "directional" quality, such that one type of answer (e.g., "yes" to "Are you troubled with nightmares?") may be taken as indicative of psychological disorder, and the opposite answer as indicative of normal functioning. Thus the index of disturbance is computed by adding all the positive indicators, weighted equally. That alternative methods of test construction may yield equally, or more, valid indices of mental illness is indicated by the extensive investigations of McQuitty (40).

McQuitty proposes several different methods of diagnostic test scoring, each based on explicit assumptions about the diagnostic procedure which the test is supposed to represent. One of the simplest assumptions, for example, is that an individual is mentally ill to the extent that his psychological processes deviate from the culturally modal processes. Thus, any type of multiple-alternative test may be administered to a group of subjects representing a "normal" population. Each alternative of each item is then scored for its "popularity." The score for a subject is then computed by adding the popularity scores of the items he checks (McQuitty calls this the T method of scoring); a high popularity score is taken as evidence of mental health (by this "typicality" criterion).

An alternative assumption proposed by McQuitty as underlying the diagnostic procedure might be that mental health is manifest to the degree that the subject's responses conform to *any* pattern of answers represented by a significant number of community people, regardless of whether that pattern is the most popular one. Such an assumption leads to a scoring procedure (H method) whereby a subject's index of "cultural harmony" is based on the degree to which his responses to different questions "go together" in the same manner as do the responses of all people in the sample who check the same alternatives he does.

Elaborations on these basic procedures provide for differential weighting of responses depending on their degree of deviance (WH method), and correction for "linkage" between successive pairs of items (WHc method).

The Bernreuter Personality Test and the Strong Vocational Interest Inventory were administered by McQuitty to a group of mental patients and to a group of university students; they were scored by different methods, the scores for the two tests were correlated, and the mean scores of the two groups compared. Results of the comparisons indicate that: (a) when appropriately scored, the Strong can discriminate mental patients from normals, though not so well as the Bernreuter; (b) better results are obtained if, instead of treating each answer as a separate, independent measure, it is evaluated in terms of the pattern of other answers with which it occurs (WHc scoring method); (c) within the Bernreuter, those items which correlated best with the total score (McQuitty's WHc method of scoring) and provided the best discrimination between patients and normals tended to be of the "subjective" type (i.e., they depended on the subject's introspection, as in "Do you often have disturbing thoughts?") rather than the "objective" (items which an observer could report, such as "Do you talk very much?"); (d) different scoring procedures appeared differentially appropriate for the "subjective" and "objective" items; (e) when the "subjective" items were scored by the method most appropriate to them (i.e., the method which best discriminated patients from normals), and the "objective"

items by their most appropriate method, the correlation between the two scores on the same group of subjects was about zero, indicating that two independent dimensions of mental health were being tapped by these two sets of items.

A separate study reported by McQuitty (40) indicated that the simple T method of scoring (based on the popularity of the subject's responses) both subjective and objective items significantly discriminated groups of school children classified on the basis of independent criteria of mental health. There is considerable evidence from these studies that, especially with respect to those traits measured by the "objective" items, the person may be regarded as mentally ill to the extent that he deviates from the dominant community pattern.

The foregoing studies provide a certain amount of evidence that measures of mental illness according to psychometric criteria relate to two of the criteria discussed earlier—maladjustment and psychiatric diagnosis. That such concurrent validation may yield somewhat different results from studies of predictive validity is indicated in Beilin's report of the Nobles County study (2). Two indices of student adjustment predictors were constructed, one (the "pupil index") based on students' responses to five different instruments, and the other (the "teacher index") based on teacher ratings. Both were concurrently validated against juvenile court judges' nominations of delinquent youngsters and against teachers' descriptions of the youngsters. Four years later the mental health of the youth was assessed by a number of different criteria—community reputation, interviewers' ratings, self-assessment, and an adaptation of the Rundquist-Sletto morale scale. The predictors correlated significantly with only some of the subsequent criteria, and all of the correlations were at best moderate. The "pupil index" correlated better with the interviewer's rating than with the community reputation criterion; while the "teacher index" correlated better with the subject's subsequent community reputation than with the interviewer's rating. Or, stated more generally, the psychologist's predictor predicted better to a psychologist's criterion, and a community predictor predicted better to a community criterion. Though the time span (four years) between the predictor and criterion measures may have been such as to allow for considerable change in the subjects, one is nevertheless reminded by these results that various criteria for mental health are not necessarily highly correlated.

In summarizing the various studies of mental health and illness defined by psychological testing batteries, we may note that many of them lack an underlying conception of the nature of mental illness from which to derive items and scoring procedures (a notable exception being McQuitty's measures), that some of them challenge the notion of the unidimensional nature of mental health, and that their degree of correlation with other criteria, such as adjustment or psychiatric diagnosis, depends on the nature of the criterion.

MENTAL HEALTH AS POSITIVE STRIVING

A radically different approach to the assessment of mental health is indicated in the definitions proposed by some writers with a mental hygiene orientation. Gruenberg suggests that, though failure to live up to the expectations of those around him may constitute mental illness, one should also consider the person's failure to live up to his own potentialities (23, p. 131). Frank speaks of the "positive" aspect of mental health—healthy personalities are those who "continue to grow, develop, and mature through life, accepting responsibilities, finding fulfillments, without paying too high a cost personally or socially, as they participate in maintaining the social order and carrying on our culture" (18). In a less exhortative tone, Henry (27) discusses successful adaptation of the person in the "normal stressful situation." He sees many normal situations as situations

of inherent stress. Some individuals in them develop mental disease, while others may develop out of them a more complex, but more successful, personality. It is this successful coping with the "normal stressful situation" that Henry regards as indicative of mental health.

Jahoda has translated this kind of emphasis on the positive, striving, aspects of behavior into a set of criteria amenable to empirical research. She proposes three basic features of mental health (31): (a) The person displays active adjustment, or attempts at mastery of his environment, in contrast to lack of adjustment or indiscriminate adjustment through passive acceptance of social conditions. (b) The person manifests unity of personality—the maintenance of a stable integration which remains intact in spite of the flexibility of behavior which derives from active adjustment. (c) The person perceives the world and himself correctly, independent of his personal needs.

Active mastery of the environment, according to Jahoda, presupposes a deliberate choice of what one does and does not conform to, and consists of the deliberate modification of environmental conditions. "In a society in which regimentation prevails, active adjustment will hardly be possible; in a society where overt regimentation is replaced by the invisible compulsiveness of conformity pressures, active adjustment will be equally rare. Only where there exists social recognition of alternative forms of behavior is there a change for the individual to master his surroundings and attain mental health." (31, p. 563).

Such an approach is quite at odds with the subjective criterion of personal happiness, and with the conformity criterion referred to above as "adjustment." Attempted adjustment does not necessarily result in success, for success is dependent on the environment. The best mode of adjustment only maximizes the chances of success. It is mentally healthy behavior even if the environment does not permit a solution of the problem (*33*). Jahoda proposes that the criterion of happiness be replaced with some more "objective" definition of mental health, based on an explicit set of values.

In an unpublished community study, Jahoda apparently attempted to assess only two of the aspects of mental health incorporated in her definition. Veridicality of perception (actually, of judgment) was determined by asking respondents to estimate certain characteristics of their communities concerning which objective data were available (e.g., proportion of people with only grade-school education), and at the same time inferring needs to distort reality from the respondent's evaluative statements about the problem (e.g., how important *R* believed education to be). This method of assessing need-free perception was regarded as something less than satisfactory (Jahoda, personal communication, August 1956), since the need was so difficult to determine, and it was difficult to establish unambiguously that distortion of judgment was due to the operation of a need rather than simply to lack of valid information.

The degree of attempted active adjustment was assessed by first asking a respondent to mention a particular problem in the community, then determining what he had done, or tried to do, about it, and how he felt about the problem at the time of interview (*33*). Three aspects of respondents' reactions were coded from their replies (*32*): (*a*) the stage of problem solution—mere consideration of the problem, consideration of solutions, or actual implementation; (*b*) the feeling tone associated with the problem—continued worry or improvement in feeling (either through partial solution or through passive acceptance); (*c*) the directness or indirectness of the approach—i.e., whether *R* went to the heart of the problem in his attempted solution or merely dealt temporarily with recurrent nuisances.

In her analysis Jahoda relates her measures of problem-solving and need-free perception to various characteristics of the respondents and of the communities in which they live. The relationships are interesting (e.g., in one of the communities the level of problem-solving was related to the degree of community participation of the respondent), but they appear to leave unanswered a basic question about the appropriateness of the criteria. If one accepts Jahoda's definition of mental health as involving the two components assessed in the study, then the results can be interpreted as showing what patterns of social interaction are associated with mental health. But if one is skeptical about the meaningfulness of the definition, then he is impelled to search for correlations between her two measures and other, more commonly accepted, criteria of mental health. These are not reported, although it would appear to be a fair question to ask about the relation of her concepts to those employed by other researchers.

If one is wedded to the happiness criterion of mental health, for example, one may speculate about the possibility of a negative relation between it and those provided by Jahoda. Unhappiness could conceivably lead to excessive coping behavior (attempted adjustment), or excessive coping behavior might elicit negative reactions from others which, in turn, would increase one's unhappiness. In like fashion, it could be that need-free perception would lead to increased unhappiness, since psychological defenses are not available to bolster one's self image. Though Jahoda might reject the suggestion that happiness is even relevant to her criteria, it would appear useful to explore, both conceptually and empirically, the interrelations among other measures of mental health and the novel one proposed by her.

Clausen (*6*) has maintained that researchers must ultimately face the task of relating mental health defined in positive terms to the individual's ability to resist mental illness under stress. At present it is not known whether they represent a common factor or are independent characteristics. Jahoda (personal communication, August 1956) suspects that positive mental health, as she defines it, may indeed represent a dimension orthogonal to that represented by the conventional psychological symptoms of mental illness. Thus, from a different approach than that employed by McQuitty comes the suggestion that mental health and illness may be a multidimensional phenomenon.

In employing these particular criteria, especially that of active adaptation, Jahoda seems willing to defend the evaluative standards implicit in it. And it may well be that values relating to attempted mastery of problems are every bit as defensible as the values of conformity implied in the adjustment criteria discussed above. Nevertheless, the former appear to exemplify the application of the Protestant ethic to the mental health movement in a manner which might introduce culture and class biases into one's conclusions. Miller and Swanson (42) have hypothesized that lower-class children will show more defeatism than middle-class children, as a result of different interpersonal and environmental experiences. Would they thereby be less mentally healthy by any standards besides those of the middle class? Truly, the problems posed in setting up absolute values from which to judge mental health and illness are perplexing.

BASIC PROBLEMS IN THE DEFINITION OF MENTAL HEALTH AND ILLNESS

Underlying the diversities in definition of mental illness one can discern certain basic differences of viewpoint concerning how the phenomena should be conceptualized. We may abstract certain foci of disagreement by posing the following four points of contention: (a) Does mental illness refer to a unitary concept or to an artificial grouping of basically different specific disorders? (b) Is mental illness an acute or chronic state of the organism? (c) Is maladjustment (or deviance from social norms) an essential concomitant of mental illness? (d) Should mental illness be explicitly defined according to values other than social conformity?

Each of the proposed definitions takes a stand, either explicitly or implicitly, on one or more of these issues. It is likely that resolution of disagreements will depend in part on the outcome of future empirical research. But at least some of the divergence inheres in the theoretical formulation of the problem, and is more a matter of conceptual predilection than of empirical fact. In either case, if one is to arrive at consistent theoretical and operational definitions of mental illness, it would be well to make explicit one's bias concerning each of these issues, and attempt to rationalize it in terms of his conception of the causes of disturbance.

THE UNITARY OR SPECIFIC NATURE OF MENTAL ILLNESS

The position that mental illness is manifest in some rather general form, regardless of the specific diagnostic category in which the patient is placed, would appear to be implicit in the subjective definition of the phenomenon. If the person's feeling of happiness or adequacy is regarded as the crucial indicator of his mental state, this would appear to imply that over-all health or illness can be assessed for a particular person, regardless of the area of functioning referred to. Likewise, the definition of mental health in terms of purposeful striving or active adjustment tends to ignore differences in the underlying bases for such striving or lack thereof. Such a position has been stated explicitly by Stieglitz: "The mensuration of health . . . closely parallels the measurement of biological age as contrasted to chronological age . . . . We are no longer seeking to discover specific disease entities, or even clinical syndromes, but attempting to measure biological effectiveness in adaptation" (51, p. 79). And such a unitary view of the phenomenon is implied in Schneider's comment: "The major 'cause' of mental disease is seen as some form of disorientation between the personality and society" (49, p. 31).

By contrast, the specific view of mental illness is taken by Gordon: "What we choose to call mental disease is an artificial grouping of many morbid processes. The first essential, in my opinion, is to separate the various entities, and in the approach to an epidemiology of mental diseases, to center attention on some one condition, or a few selected conditions, which have functions in common with other mass diseases well understoood in their group relationships" (15, p. 107). McQuitty offers empirical evidence in favor of a specific view, in his isolation of two quite independent measures of mental illness (by psychological testing), both of which correlate with external diagnostic criteria. And he further speculates that the number of areas in which the degree of personality integration varies rather independently is probably greater than the two which he has isolated. "One might expect that mental illness might develop within any one or more patterns. In order to understand the mental illness of a particular subject, we must isolate the pattern, or patterns, of characteristics to which his mental illness pertains" (40, p. 22).

While the weight of opinion and evidence appears to favor the multidimensional view, this may simply be a function of the operational definitions employed (e.g., mental health defined by responses to a battery of tests is bound to turn out multidimensional to the extent that intercorrelations among the test items are low). But there are yet insufficient empirical data collected from the unitary point of view to test whether its assumption is correct. Indeed, it seems quite plausible that both happiness and active adaptation may be partially a function of the situation, hence the concept of mental health implied by them must become multidimensional to the extent that they allow for intersituational variability.

THE ACUTE OR CHRONIC NATURE OF MENTAL ILLNESS

The psychologist's testing approach to assessing mental illness inclines him toward a view of the condition as chronic. That is, the predisposing conditions within the organism are generally presumed to be relatively enduring, though perhaps triggered off into an actual psychotic break by excessively stressful situations. The epidemiological approach, on the other hand, is usually concerned with the counting of actual hospitalized cases, and this may incline one toward a view of mental illness as predominantly acute. Felix has espoused this position explicitly: "Unless the kinds of mental illness are specified, I can't conceive that mental illness is a chronic disease. More mental illnesses by far are acute and even short term than there are mental illnesses which are chronic and long term." (15, p. 163). Of course, the epidemiological approach traditionally considers characteristics of the host, as well as characteristics of the agent and the environment. But the predisposing factors within the organism seem to be regarded, like "low resistance," not as a subliminal state of the disease, but rather as a general susceptibility to any acute attack precipitated by external factors.

It is easier to regard a psychosis as acute than it is similarly to regard a neurosis, since in the former disorder the break with normal behavior appears more precipitate. However, such a judgment, based on easily observable external behaviors, may be unduly superficial. Even in the case of such a discrete disturbance as suicide, at least one writer (21) recommends considering the biologic gradient of the disorder. He distinguishes varying degrees of suicide, with successful accomplishment as merely a possible end product. Where such continuity between morbid and nonmorbid states can be discerned, the possibility of chronic disturbance might well be considered.

THE PROBLEM OF MENTAL HEALTH AS CONFORMITY TO SOCIAL NORMS

The criterion of mental health based on adjustment clearly implies that conformity to the social situation in which the individual is permanently imbedded is a healthy response. And such an assumption would appear to be lurking, in various shapes, behind nearly all of the other definitions considered (with the possible exception of some of the "positive striving" criteria, which stress conformity to a set of standards independent of the person's immediate social group). In fact, McQuitty's methods of scoring psychological inventories are all explicitly based on the assumption that conformity (either to the total community or to a significant subgroup) is healthy.

If the stability of the larger social system be regarded as the final good, or if human development be seen as demanding harmony in relation to that social system, then such an assumption would appear basic and defensible. But one is still impelled to consider the possibility that the social system, or even an entire society, may be sick, and conformity to its norms would constitute mental illness, in some more absolute sense. If any particular behavior pattern is considered both from the standpoint of its adaptability within the social structure to which the individual maintains primary allegiance and from the standpoint of its relation to certain external ideal standards imposed by the observer, perhaps a comparison of the two discrepancy measures would yield information about the degree to which the social system approaches the ideal. On the other hand, such a comparison might be interpreted as merely indicating the degree to which the researcher who sets the external standards is himself adapted to the social system which he is studying. The dilemma appears insoluble.

THE PROBLEM OF VALUES IN CRITERIA FOR MENTAL HEALTH

The mental hygiene movement has traditionally been identified with one or another set of values—ideal standards by which behavior could be assessed as appropriate or inappropriate. The particular set of values adopted probably depends to a considerable degree on who is doing the judging. Such a diversity of evaluative judgments leads to chaos in the popular literature and to considerable confusion in the usage of the term "mental health" in

scientific research. Kingsley Davis (8) presented a rather strong case for the proposition that mental hygiene, being a social movement and source of advice concerning personal conduct, has inevitably been influenced by the Protestant ethic inherent in our culture. The main features of this Protestant ethic, as seen by him, are its democratic, worldly, ascetic, individualistic, rationalistic, and utilitarian orientations.

To the extent that research on mental health is based on criteria devolved from such an ideology, it is middle-class-Protestant biased. To the extent that it is based on some other set of "absolute" norms for behavior, it is probably biased toward some other cultural configuration. At least one researcher, Jahoda (33), has clearly taken the position that mental health criteria must be based on an explicit set of values. There is some advantage in allowing the assumptions to come into full view, but in this case the resulting criteria appear to be rather specialized and not comparable with those used by other researchers. Perhaps the difficulty lies not so much in the existence of explicit assumptions as in their level of generality. If a more basic set of assumptions could be found, from which the diverse criteria for mental health and illness can be derived, then comparability among researches might better be achieved. One would be in a better position to state when mental illness, as defined by psychological tests or by absence of active adjustment, is likely to be displayed in mental illness defined by psychiatric diagnosis or deviance from community standards.

SUMMARY

The various categories of definitions of mental illness discussed here have been distinguished primarily on the basis of their differing operational definitions: the dependent variables employed in empirical research on the phenomena are clearly different. Moreover the conceptualizations of mental illness explicit or implicit in the empirical criteria are often quite divergent

—viz., the radically different viewpoints underlying the "maladjustment," "subjective unhappiness," and "lack of positive striving" definitions.

Certain conceptual and methodological difficulties in each of these types of definition have been noted: "Exposure to treatment" is deficient in that only a limited proportion of those diagnosable as mentally ill ever reach psychiatric treatment. "Social maladjustment" is open to question because of the varying requirements of different social systems and the diversity of criteria for adjustment employed by community members. "Psychiatric diagnosis" provides an expensive, and often unreliable, method of assessing the state of mental health. "Subjective unhappiness" can be criticized as a criterion since it may be a function of intolerable environmental conditions as well as the psychological state of the person, and is subject to distortion by defense mechanisms. The validity of "objective testing procedures" appears to depend considerably on the method by which they are scored, and there is strong evidence that a major component of their score may simply be the degree of conformity of the person to the community average. Finally, criteria included under the heading of "positive striving" are subject to question in that they are inevitably based on disputable value systems of their proponents.

While many of these difficulties would not be considered damaging from the point of view of certain of the definitions of mental illness, they run into conflict with others. Also they suggest certain basic incompatibilities among the various approaches to conceptualization of mental illness. Whether these incompatibilities should be reconciled by further theoretical and empirical exploration, or whether they should be regarded as valid indicators that mental health and illness constitute multidimensional phenomena is still a moot question. We can only note that various studies employing two or more of these different categories of criteria have tended to yield moderate, but not impressive, interrelations.

The criterion of "exposure to psychiatric treatment" has been related to "maladjustment," "psychiatric diagnosis," "subjective unhappiness," and "objective psychometrics." Also "maladjustment" has been related to "psychiatric diagnosis" and to certain "objective" measures; and "psychiatric diagnosis" has been related to both "subjective" and "objective" measures of mental illness. The areas of interrelationship for which no empirical studies have been found are between "subjective" measures and both "maladjustment" and "objective" assessment; also between the "positive striving" criteria and all of the other types of measures.

Two directions for future theory and research are indicated by these results. First, more investigations are needed of the extent of relationship among the various criteria, and of the conditions under which the magnitudes of the intercorrelations vary. Second, assuming absence of high intercorrelations under many conditions, it would be worthwhile to explore the implications of poor congruence between one measure and another—implications both for the person and for the social system in which he lives.

REFERENCES

1. Beilen, H. The effects of social (occupational) role and age upon the criteria of mental health. *J. soc. Psychol.*, in press.

2. Beilin, H. The prediction of adjustment over a four year interval. *J. clin. Psychol.*, 1957, *13*, 270–274.

3. Belknap, I. V., and Jaco, E. G. The epidemiology of mental disorders in a politi-cal-type city, 1946–1952. In *Interrelations between the social environment and psychiatric disorders.* N. Y.: Milbank Memorial Fund, 1953.

4. Chase, P. Concepts of self and concepts of others in adjusted and maladjusted hospital patients. Unpublished doctor's dissertation, Univer. of Colorado, 1956.

5. Clark, R. E. Psychoses, income and occupational prestige. *Amer. J. Sociol.*, 1949, *54*, 433–440.

6. Clausen, J. A. *Sociology and the field of mental health*. N. Y.: Russell Sage Foundation, 1956.

7. Clausen, J. A., and Kohn, M. L. The ecological approach in social psychiatry. *Amer. J. Sociol.*, 1954, *60*, 140–151.

8. Davis, K. Mental hygiene and the class structure. *Psychiatry*, 1938, *1*, 55–65.

9. Downes, Jean, and Simon, Katherine. Characteristics of psychoneurotic patients and their families as revealed in a general morbidity study. *Milbank Memorial Fund Quarterly*, 1954, *32*, 42–64.

10. Dunham, H. W. Current status of ecological research in mental disorder. *Social Forces*, 1947, *25*, 321–326.

11. Dunham, H. W. Some persistent problems in the epidemiology of mental disorders. *Amer. J. Psychiat.*, 1953, *109*, 567–575.

12. Durkheim, E. *Le suicide*. Paris: F. Alcan, 1897. (English translation, Glencoe, Ill.: Free Press, 1951.)

13. Eaton, J. W. *Culture and mental disorders*. Glencoe, Ill.: Free Press, 1955.

14. Eaton, J. W., and Weil, R. J. The mental health of the Hutterites. In A. M. Rose (Ed.), *Mental health and mental disorder*. N. Y.: Norton, 1955.

15. *Epidemiology of mental disorder*. N. Y.: Milbank Memorial Fund, 1950.

16. Faris, R. E. L., and Dunham, H. W. *Mental disorders in urban areas*. Chicago: Chicago Univer. Press, 1939.

17. Felix, R. H., and Bowers, R. V. Mental hygiene and socio-environmental factors. *Milbank Memorial Fund Quarterly*, 1948, *26*, 125–147.

18. Frank, L. K. The promotion of mental health. *Ann. Amer. Acad. of Pol. Soc. Sci.*, 1953, *286*, 167–174.

19. Frumkin, R. M. Occupation and major mental disorders. In A. M. Rose (Ed.), *Mental health and mental disorder*. N. Y.: Norton, 1955.

20. Glidewell, J. C., *et al.* Behavior symptoms in children and degree of sickness. *Amer. J. Psychiat.*, 1957, *114*, 47–53.

21. Gordon, J. E., *et al.* An epidemiologic analysis of suicide. In *Epidemiology of mental disorder*. N. Y.: Milbank Memorial Fund, 1950.

22. Gruenberg, E. M. Community conditions and psychoses of the elderly. *Amer. J. Psychiat.*, 1954, *110*, 888–896.

23. Gruenberg, E. M. Comment in *Interrelations between the social environment and psychiatric disorders*. N. Y.: Milbank Memorial Fund, 1953.

24. Halmos, P. *Solitude and privacy*. London: Routledge and Kegan Paul, 1952.

25. Hathaway, S. R., and Monachesi, E. D. The Minnesota Multiphasic Personality Inventory in the study of juvenile delinquents. In A. M. Rose (Ed.), *Mental health and mental disorder*. N. Y.: Norton, 1955.

26. Henry, A. F., and Short, J. *Suicide and homicide*. Glencoe, Ill.: Free Press, 1954.

27. Henry, W. E. Psychology. In *Interrelations between the social environment and psychiatric disorders*. N. Y.: Milbank Memorial Fund, 1953.

28. Hollingshead, A. B., and Redlich, F. C. Social stratification and psychiatric disorders. *Amer. social. Rev.*, 1953, *18*, 163–169.

29. Hyde, P. W., and Kingsley, L. V. Studies in medical sociology. I: The relation of mental disorders to the community socio-economic level. *New England J. Med.*, 1944, *231*, 543–548.

30. Jaco, E. G. The social isolation hypothesis and schizophrenia. *Amer. social. Rev.*, 1954, *19*, 567–577.

31. Jahoda, Marie. Toward a social psychology of mental health. In A. M. Rose (Ed.), *Mental health and mental disorder*. N. Y.: Norton, 1955.

32. Jahoda, Marie. The meaning of psychological health. *Soc. Casewk*, 1953, *34*, 349–354.

33. Jahoda, Marie. Social psychology. In *Interrelations between the social environment and psychiatric disorders*. N. Y.: Milbank Memorial Fund, 1953.

34. Kramer, M. Comment in *Interrelations between the social environment and psychiatric disorders*. N. Y.: Milbank Memorial Fund, 1953.

35. Lemert, E. M. An exploratory study of mental disorders in a rural problem area. *Rural Sociol.*, 1948, *13*, 48–64.

36. Lewis, A. Social aspects of psychiatry. *Edinburgh med. J.*, 1951, *58*, 241–247.

37. Lindemann, E., *et al.* Minor disorders. In *Epidemiology of mental disorders*. N. Y.: Milbank Memorial Fund, 1950.

38. Lindemann, E. Comment in *Interrelations between the social environment and psychiatric disorders*. N. Y.: Milbank Memorial Fund, 1953.

39. Locke, H. *Predicting adjustment in marriage: a comparison of a divorced and a*

happily married group. N. Y.: Holt, Rinehart and Winston.

40. McQuitty, L. L. Theories and methods in some objective assessments of psychological well-being. *Psychol. Monogr.,* 1954, *68,* No. 14.

41. Malzberg, B. *Social and biological aspects of mental disease.* Utica: State Hosp. Press, 1940.

42. Miller, D. R., and Swanson, G. E. A proposed study of the learning of techniques for resolving conflicts of impulses. In *Interrelations between the social environment and psychiatric disorders.* N. Y.: Milbank Memorial Fund, 1953.

43. Pollak, O. Social adjustment in old age. *Soc. Sci. Res. Council Bull.* No. 59, 1948.

44. Rennie, T. A. C. The Yorkville community mental health research study. In *Interrelations between the social environment and psychiatric disorders.* N. Y.: Milbank Memorial Fund, 1953.

45. Rogers, C. *Client-centered therapy.* Boston: Houghton Mifflin, 1951.

46. Rogers, C. and Dymond, Rosalind. *Psychotherapy and personality change.* Chicago: Univer. of Chicago Press, 1954.

47. Rose, A. M., and Stub, H. R. Summary of studies on the incidence of mental disorders. In A. M. Rose (Ed.), *Mental health and mental disorders.* N. Y.: Norton, 1955.

48. Roth, W. F., and Luton, F. H. The mental health program in Tennessee. *Amer. J. Psychiat.,* 1943, *99,* 662–675.

49. Schneider, E. V. Sociological concepts and psychiatric research. In *Interrelations between the social environment and psychiatric disorders.* N. Y.: Milbank Memorial Fund, 1953.

50. Schroeder, C. W. Mental disorders in cities. *Amer. J. Sociol.,* 1942, *48,* 40–47.

51. Stieglitz, E. J. The integration of clinical and social medicine. In I. Galdston (Ed.), *Social medicine—its derivations and objectives.* N. Y. Acad. of Med., 1947. N. Y.: Commonwealth Fund, 1949.

52. Terman, L. M., *et al. Psychological factors in marital happiness.* N. Y.: McGraw-Hill, 1938.

53. Terman, L. M., and Wallin, P. The validity of marriage prediction and marital adjustment tests. *Amer. sociol. Rev.,* 1949, *14,* 497–505.

54. Tietze, C., *et al.* Personal disorder and spatial mobility. *Amer. J. Sociol.,* 1942, *48,* 29–39.

55. Tietze, C., *et al.* A survey of statistical studies on the prevalance and incidence of mental disorders in sample populations. *Publ. Hlth Rep.,* 1943, *58,* 1909–1927.

Deviant Responses as Indicators of Immaturity and Schizophrenia

S. O. HESTERLY AND IRWIN A. BERG

Wʜᴇɴ patterns of responses to various stimuli are examined, the responses often are biased and do not follow a normal probability distribution. Such "set" or *einstellung* phenomena tend to appear most clearly as the stimulus pattern is unstructured. There are myriad forms of such biased responses, such as the tendency to call "heads" on the first toss of a coin, the tendency to turn right when one may turn left or right, etc. (*8, 14*). In psychological tests, Cronbach (*12,*

Reprinted by permission from the *Journal of Consulting Psychology,* Vol. 22, No. 5, 1958.

13) has identified a large number of such biases and called them *response sets.*

Since there is evidence that such sets or biases are expressions of personality traits (*1, 3, 6, 11, 15, 19, 21, 22, 23, 24*) Berg (*5*) sought to employ these patterns of bias as measures of personality but with only limited success. However, when attention was shifted from the pattern of bias to those responses which departed from the established set or bias, it was found possible to use these departures as measures of personality and other characteristics. Barnes (*2*), for example, was able to construct a series of clinical scales using this concept of deviant responses. Thus the key to the problem of utilizing response bias resides in using, not the pattern of bias itself, but rather, the responses which go counter to the established bias, i.e., the deviant responses. In other words, we should not pay particular attention to the 80% of the population who call "heads" when a coin is flipped, but we would closely scrutinize the 20% who call "tails." The latter response, in our lexicon, is deviant. A fuller account of the problem and its background is given in articles by Berg (*4, 5*).

The present study is one of a series of empirical tests of the Deviation Hypothesis which has been stated as follows: "Deviant response patterns tend to be general; hence those deviant behavior patterns which are significant for abnormality (atypicalness) and thus regarded as symptoms (earmarks or signs) are associated with other deviant response patterns which are in noncritical areas of behavior and which are not regarded as symptoms of personality aberration (nor as symptoms, signs, earmarks)" (*5*, p. 159). In other words, by using deviant responses in a noncritical area, such as a liking for designs, we should be able to measure deviant behavior in a critical area such as psychopathology, chronic organic disease, employee morale, creativeness, etc.

The specific hypothesis of the present study were two:

1. The response patterns of normal, young children to the Perceptual Reaction Test (PTR) (*7*) are significantly different from those of normal adults. As a corollary, older children have response patterns more similar to those of adults than younger children.

2. The response patterns of normal, young children on the PRT more nearly approximate those of adult schizophrenics than those of normal adults.

Thus maturity as a critical area of behavior is assessed by means of deviant response patterns as they occur in the PRT.

Then, since descriptions of schizophrenic behavior (*9, 10, 16, 17, 18, 20*) typically make reference to immaturity as a common feature of the schizophrenic reaction, it is predicted that the deviant response patterns of normal, young children are similar to those found in schizophrenics.

TABLE 1. DISTRIBUTION OF SUBJECTS BY AGE, SEX, AND PLACE OF RESIDENCE

Age and residence	7–0 to 8–11	9–0 to 10–11	11–0 to 12–11	Totals
Male				
Urban	25	25	25	75
Rural	25	25	25	75
Female				
Urban	25	25	25	75
Rural	25	25	25	75
Totals	100	100	100	300

PROCEDURE

In order to elicit deviant response patterns, the PRT was used. This test consists of 60 abstract designs drawn with ruler and compass. The subject is required to mark one of the following options for each design: *like much* (LM), *like slightly* (LS), *dislike slightly* (DS), or *dislike much* (DM). No obvious meaning is inherent in any of the designs; hence, the test is considered to be relatively unstructured, a condition which facilitates the appearance of response biases. It should be noted that other stimulus patterns could be employed. However, the PRT has been used as a research instrument for a number of years and, accordingly, a large body of normative data is available. Also, Barnes' (*2*) data on PRT responses of adult schizophrenics could be used.

Three hundred Louisiana grade-school children were used as *S*s for the present study. See Table 1. The PRT was administered to the *S*s in their regular classrooms during a normal school day. Administration time was approximately 12 minutes. The *S*s' responses were transferred from the PRT booklets to IBM answer sheets for machine scoring. The schizophrenia scales developed by Barnes (called *Sigma Scales* by him) were used to determine each individual's score. Barnes' scales were developed by assigning plus weights to those PRT responses which were significantly characteristic of his schizophrenic group and assigning minus weights to PRT responses which were characteristic of his normal group. The sum of these weights was the schizophrenic score. These scores were compared on the basis of age and place of residence by analysis of variance. The resulting variances for the different groups appeared to be rather heterogeneous [a statistical test confirmed this impression]. Therefore, a nonparametric technique was used to compare the group schizophrenia scores. Specifically, the nonparametric median test seemed to apply to data of the type obtained, as it is not dependent upon homogeneity of variance. The hypothesis tested is that the groups compared are random samples from a population with a common median.

RESULTS

Median schizophrenia scores on the PRT are given for all Ss in Table 2. The result of the nonparametric median tests for male Ss are shown in Table 3. The

fer significantly from those of normal, adult males. The second comparison was between normal, male children and schizo-

TABLE 2. MEDIAN SCHIZOPHRENIA SCORES ON THE PRT FOR 300 NORMAL CHILDREN, 850 NORMAL ADULTS, AND 167 SCHIZOPHRENIC ADULTS TAKEN SEPARATELY AND AS COMBINED FOR NONPARAMETRIC MEDIAN TESTS

| | Median score | | |
Subjects	Group only	Combined with normal adults	Combined with schizophrenic adults
Normal children			
Males ($N = 150$)	+ 8.50	−14.15	+5.80
Females ($N = 150$)	+ 3.25	− 9.62	+3.36
Normal adults[a]			
Males ($N = 500$)	−17.83		
Females ($N = 350$)	−12.81		
Schizophrenic adults[a]			
Males ($N = 99$)	+ 1.40		
Females ($N = 68$)	+ 3.50		

[a] The data for normal adults and schizophrenic adults are from Barnes (2).

TABLE 3. NONPARAMETRIC MEDIAN TEST FOR PRT SCHIZOPHRENIA SCORE DIFFERENCES BETWEEN GROUPS OF MALE SUBJECTS

| | Number | | | | | | |
Subjects	Below median	Above median	Total	Subgroup median	Chi square	df	p
Normal children	10	140	150	+ 8.50	138.14	1	<.0001
Normal adults	309	191	500	−17.83			
Normal children	65	85	150	+ 8.50	3.10	1	>.05
Adult schizophrenics	55	44	99	+ 1.40			
Normal children					7.10	2	<.05
7–10 to 8–11 years	17	33	50	+16.50			
9–0 to 10–11 years	27	23	50	+ 5.50			
11–0 to 12–11 years	31	19	50	+ 2.50			
Normal children					1.71	1	>.05
Urban	33	42	75	+12.00			
Rural	42	33	75	+ 3.25			

first comparisons are between normal, male children and normal, adult males. The resulting chi-square value of 138.14, which is statistically significant at the .0001 level of probability, supports the hypothesis that normal male children attain schizophrenia scores on the PRT that dif-

phrenic adult males. The obtained chi-square value of 3.10 is not statistically significant, supporting the null hypothesis that the two groups are probably samples from a population with a common median.* Next, a comparison was made between three age groups (7-0 to 8-11 years, 9-0 to

[* In the strict statistical sense, the null hypothesis cannot be supported; it can only be rejected. ED.]

10-11 years, 11-0 to 12-11 years) of normal children to determine the possibility of a significant trend in PRT schizophrenia scores as a function of chronological age. The resultant chi-square value of 7.10, which is statistically significant at the .05 level of probability, supports the hypothesis that the schizophrenia scores of normal children decrease significantly with age. The final comparison was made between groups of normal, urban and rural, male children. The obtained chi-square value of 1.71, which is not statistically significant, supports the null hypothesis that the two groups appear to be samples drawn from a population with a common median.

The comparisons made between groups of female Ss were the same as those for male Ss. Although the chi-square values varied somewhat, the probability levels obtained were identical with those obtained for male Ss. Thus, the conclusions reached regarding females were the same as those for males.

DISCUSSION

The results of the present study support the hypothesis, as stated earlier, that the response patterns of normal, young children to the PRT are significantly different from those of normal adults. Their patterns more nearly approximate those of adult schizophrenics than those of normal adults. As normal children mature their response patterns gradually approach the normal adult patterns for the PRT. Thus it appears that these differential response pattern biases may be used to assess maturity, insofar as the evidence of the present study indicates.

Since normal children make responses to the stimulus, patterns of the PRT that are not significantly different from those of adult schizophrenics, it may be inferred that some common factor or factors exist between the two groups. As noted earlier, immaturity of behavior has frequently been used as a phrase characterizing schizophrenics. The results of this investigation support this description,

at least insofar as similarity of performance on the PRT of normal children and adult schizophrenics is concerned. Further, since the schizophrenia scores of normal children decrease significantly with age, gradually approaching the normal adult level, the schizophrenia scale could be used as a crude measure of maturity. In fact, there is every reason to believe that with further investigation, using wider age ranges and larger age samples, a reasonably precise measure of maturity could be developed.

As urban and rural children were not significantly different with reference to schizophrenia scores on the PRT, it would probably be unnecessary to develop separate norms. It should be noted, however, that the actual differences in median scores for the two groups, although not statistically significant, were in the same direction for both males and females. Urban children scored slightly higher than rural children. This difference might possibly be found to be significant for larger groups of children.

SUMMARY

The present investigation was undertaken to determine whether groups differing in chronological age could be shown to differ in response patterns on the PRT, as predicted by Berg's Deviation Hypothesis. In addition, the investigation included a comparison of the response patterns for groups of normal children and schizophrenic adults, both being characterized by immaturity of behavior, to determine whether they might be similar. Groups of normal children were compared, separately, with groups of normal adults and schizophrenic adults. Significant differences were found between the response patterns of normal children and those of normal adults. Normal children and schizophrenic adults did not differ significantly.

A significant trend in response patterns for normal children as a function of chronological age was found when three consecutive age groups were compared. Urban and rural children were found to have response patterns on the PRT which were not significantly different. Thus, it was concluded that response patterns on the PRT are related to chronological age, at least in the case of normal children, and that, since the response patterns of normal children and schizophrenic adults are not significantly different, some common factor or factors such as immaturity must exist between the two groups. Finally, the deviant response patterns of normal children were sufficiently clear-cut that they could be used to assess maturity.

REFERENCES

1. Barnes, E. H. Response bias and the MMPI *J. consult. Psychol.,* 1956, 20, 371–374.

2. Barnes, E. H. The relationship of biased test responses to psychopathology. *J. abnorm. soc. Psychol.,* 1955, 51, 286–290.

3. Bass, B. M. Authoritarianism or acquiescence? *J. abnorm. soc. Psychol.,* 1955, 51, 616–623.

4. Berg, I. A. Response bias and personality: The deviation hypothesis. *J. Psychol.,* 1955, 40, 61–72.

5. Berg, I. A. Deviant responses and deviant people: The formulation of the deviation hypothesis. *J. counsel. Psychol.,* 1957, 4, 154–161.

6. Berg, I. A., & Collier, J. Personality and group differences in extreme response sets. *Educ. psychol. Measmt,* 1953, 13, 164–169.

7. Berg, I. A., & Hunt, W. A. *The perceptual reaction test.* Evanston, Ill.: Author, 1948.

8. Berg, I. A., & Rapaport, G. M. Response bias in an unstructured questionnaire. *J. Psychol.,* 1954, 38, 475–481.

9. Cameron, N. Deterioration and regression in schizophrenic thinking. *J. abnorm. soc. Psychol.,* 1939, 34, 265–270.

10. Cameron, N. The functional psychoses. In J. McV. Hunt (Ed.), *Personality and the behavior disorders.* New York: Ronald Press, 1944. Pp. 861–921.

11. Chapman, L. J., & Campbell, D. T. Response set in the F scale. *J. abnorm. soc. Psychol.,* 1957, 54, 129–132.

12. Cronbach, L. J. Response sets and test validity. *Educ. psychol. Measmt,* 1946, 6, 475–494.

13. Cronbach, L. J. Further evidence on response sets and test designs. *Educ. psychol. Measmt,* 1950, 10, 3–31.

14. Goodfellow, L. D. The human element in probability. *J. gen. Psychol.,* 1940, 33, 201–205.

15. Guilford, J. P. The validation of an "indecision" score for predicting proficiency of foremen. *J. appl. Psychol.,* 1954, 38, 224–226.

16. Hanfmann, E., & Kasanin, J. Conceptual thinking in schizophrenia. *Nerv. Ment. Dis. Monogr.,* 1942, No. 67.

17. Hoskins, R. G. *The biology of schizophrenia.* New York: Norton, 1946.

18. Kasanin, J. S. *Language and thought in schizophrenia.* Berkeley: Univer. California Press, 1944.

19. Lorge, I. Gen-like: Halo or reality? *Psychol. Bull.,* 1937, 34, 545–546.

20. Phillips, L. Developmental theory applied to normal psychopathology percepts. *J. Pers.,* 1954, 22, 464–474.

21. Rapaport, G. M., & Berg, I. A. Response sets in a multiple-choice test. *Educ. psychol. Measmt,* 1955, 15, 58–62.

22. Rubin-Rabson, G. Correlates of the noncommittal test-item response. *J. clin. Psychol.,* 1954, 10, 93–95.

23. Voth, A. C. An experimental study of mental patients through the autokinetic phenomenon. *Amer. J. Psychiat.,* 1947, 103, 793–805.

24. Wallen, R. Food aversions of normal and neurotic males. *J. abnorm. soc. Psychol.,* 1945, 40, 77–81.

Conformance in Role Perception as a Personality Variable

THEODORE R. SARBIN AND CURTIS D. HARDYCK

THIS study, one of a series growing out of a social psychological theory of behavior (5), attempts to clarify "conformance," a perceptual variable, and throw some light on its personological correlates.

Conformance is defined as the modal perceptual response to a social stimulus object. It is parallel to the notion of conformity as applied to overt conduct. When a social object elicits qualitative perceptual responses from members of a specified subculture, a relatively large proportion of the reference population will agree on the quality represented by the object; a small number will differ from the majority but will agree among themselves; and a few will agree with virtually no one. Figure 1 illustrates the notion graphically.

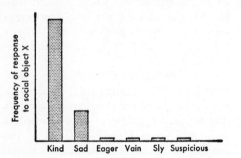

Figure 1. An illustration of conformance.

The stimulus material employed in this study was the same as that developed for a taxonomy of postural cues used in role perception and inference (6). We prepared a set of 44 schematized "stick figures" of humans in various postures. The figures were drawn by an interpretive dancer and represent a wide range of expressive and attitudinal states. The figures were so constructed as to offer no cues

Reprinted by permission from the *Journal of Consulting Psychology*, Vol. 19, 1955.

for interpretation other than posture. Figure 2 is one of the items in the Stick Figures Test.

Figure 2. Illustrative item from the Stick Figures Test.

As a preliminary step the figures were presented on 3×5 lantern slides to a group of 150 upper-division psychology students. The students were given the following instructions:

A number of stick figures, representing people in various postures, will be shown to you. As the figures are shown, you are to write 1 or 2 adjectives which best describe your impression of that figure.

From the data obtained in this sample, a check list of five adjectives, ranging from most frequent to least frequent, was constructed for each figure. As no significant sex differences were found, men and women were combined in preparing the check lists. The reliability of the adjective lists was determined by taking a second sample of 70 upper-division psychology students and repeating the procedure given above. No significant differences in proportion or kind of adjectives were found.

In developing norms for the use of the stick figures, we noted impressionistically that certain persons characteristically selected non-modal, i.e., nonconformant responses. From these impressions and from certain implied postulates of role theory, we were led to the following hypothesis: persons who frequently make nonconformant perceptual responses are characterized by social behavior which is deviant or socially invalid.

The theoretical basis for this hypothesis follows from notions originally advanced by G. H. Mead (4) and more recently developed by the senior author (5). Role perception is the first part of a social act; it is the (usually) silent naming or locating of the position of the other on the basis of available cues. This serves as an aid in locating the position of the self. The motoric response, the role enactment, follows from the perceptual response. Since the perceptual and motoric aspects of the social act are acquired holistically, if the perceptual response is conformant, then there is a high probability of socially valid (though not necessarily conforming) role enactment. Thus, the veridicality of one's role perceptions bears a positive relationship to functional adaptation in the social world.

Following are reports of three experiments which were carried out to test the hypothesis.

SCHIZOPHRENIC VERSUS NORMAL RESPONSES

As an intial check on the validity of our procedure, the stick figures were administered individually to 30 cooperative, undeteriorated, hospitalized schizophrenics. They were given the following instructions:

A number of stick figures, representing people in various postures, will be shown to you. Each figure will be numbered, corresponding to a number on this paper. For the corresponding number on this paper, there is a list of five words, plus a sixth space which is left blank. As the figures are shown to you, you are to check the word which you think best describes your impression of that figure.

If you feel that none of the words on the list adequately describes your impression of the figure, write what you consider to be the best description in the space marked "other."

No time limit was set, and the experimenter was allowed to rephrase the instructions if a subject failed to comprehend the initial instructions.

The distributions of responses for the schizophrenic sample were compared with the norms obtained on our previous samples. For the schizophrenic sample the distributions were all uniformly rectangular, in comparison to the J curves obtained from college normals, thus offering substantial evidence for the usefulness of the technique and for the initial confirmation of the hypothesis.

CONFORMANCE SCORES AND SOCIAL ADJUSTMENT

In the second exploratory study, because of practical limitations, we were unable to obtain direct behavioral rating such as would be obtained in an assessment program. Instead we made use of indirect sources of information on role enactment. The California Psychological Inventory (Gough, 2) has a number of scales, all of which are empirically rooted in social behavior. This instrument was administered to 21 undergraduates who had been subjects for the Stick Figures Test. The Inventory profiles were then ranked by Gough according to a "social adjustment" criterion.

Responses to the stick figures were scored as follows: The modal response to each stick figure for the previous samples was assigned a weight of 1. The subjects were then given a score in terms of the number of modal response choices made. These scores were ranked and a Spearman rho was computed between the stick figure score rankings and the ranking on social adjustment. The correlation was .81 ($p = .01$), a highly significant relationship considering the small number of subjects. On the basis of the second preliminary study, our hypothesis would seem to be further supported. However, a cross validation was indicated owing to the small N and the use of a single judgment of social behavior.

CROSS VALIDATION OF CONFORMANCE AND SOCIAL ADJUSTMENT

The next step involved the presentation of the figures to a sample of 91 upper-division psychology students. The instructions and scoring method were the same as in the two previous studies. For this group the Minnesota Multiphasic Personality Inventory (MMPI) was used as a measure of personality functioning. The MMPI profiles were sorted by each of three judges into a normal distribution on the following criterion of *Adjustment:*

Getting along well in the world as it is. Adequate degree of social conformity; capacity to adapt to a wide range of conditions. Ability to fit in (3).

The results were as follows: The range of scores on the Stick Figures Test was from 11 to 26 (44 stick figures). The correlations of the conformance scores on the Stick Figures Test with the sorts of the MMPI profiles were .32 for Judge A, .68 for Judge B, and .52 for Judge C.

Combining the three sorts to obtain a more stable criterion of social adjustment resulted in a Pearsonian product-moment correlation of .51 with the conformance score. The correlation is unusually high, especially in the absence of a refined method for obtaining the conformance score.[1] The above sorts are done with sex groups combined. Separate sorts for males and females revealed no significant differences among the correlation coefficients.

Interjudge reliabilities on social adjustment were .66 between Judges A and B, .73 between A and C, and .83 between B and C. They are considered adequate for our experimental purposes. The split-half reliability for the Stick Figures Test is .50. Refinement of the test by item analysis will doubtless increase the reliability.

Correlations between conformance score and certain clinical scales provide some additional confirmatory evidence. The F scale on the MMPI indicates the number of "infrequently answered" items in the test. In a sense it is a subtle measure of conformance. Pearsonian r is $-.32$. Subjects who score high on the F scale tend to preceive the postures in a nonconformant way. Another index of social maladjustment is the number of clinical scales on the MMPI on which the subject's score is two sigmas or more above the mean. This index correlates with conformance $-.33$ (and was probably used implicitly by all the judges in making their judgments of social adjustment). An empirically devised scale of ego strength (1) correlates .50 with conformance.[2]

SUMMARY

On the basis of certain postulates derived from role theory, a significant relationship between nonconformant perceptual responses and deviant social behavior is hypothesized. Three experiments were performed to test this hypothesis. The first experiment compared the distribution of responses of normals and schizophrenics to a set of schematized stick figures of humans in various postures. The normal subjects were found to have J-curve distributions as contrasted with the rectangular distribution of the schizophrenic sample.

In a second experiment, the number of conformant responses of a group of normal subjects was found to bear a significant relationship to their social adjustment as judged by test profiles. A third, cross-validational, experiment indicated the stability of the relationship. Correlations with certain empirically derived personality scales offer further confirmation of the hypothesis.

---

[1] In view of the method used to obtain the conformance score, the possibility of curvilinearity should be taken into account. Scatter plots of the correlations revealed no significant tendency toward curvilinearity. It would seem safe to conclude, therefore, that judgments in terms of conformance do bear a significant relationship to level of adjustment as measured by the MMPI profile sorts.

[2] Conformance scores and an indirect measure of kinesthetic inference (empathy) are correlated to the extent of .48. This finding is only peripherally related to the hypothesis and is not discussed in the present paper.

REFERENCES

1. Barron, F. An ego-strength scale which predicts response to therapy. *J. consult. Psychol.,* 1953, *17,* 327–333.

2. Gough, H. G. *The California Psychological Inventory.* Berkeley: Univer. of California Press, 1951.

3. Gough, H. G. Predicting success in graduate training: a progress report. Unpublished manuscript, Univer. of California, Institute of Personality Assessment and Research, 1950.

4. Mead, G. H. *Mind, self and society.* Chicago: Univer. of Chicago Press, 1934.

5. Sarbin, T. R. Role theory. In G. Lindzey (Ed.), *Handbook of social psychology.* Cambridge, Mass.: Addison-Wesley, 1954. Pp. 223–258.

6. Sarbin, T. R., and Taft, R. *An essay on inference in the psychological sciences.* Berkeley: Garden Library Press, 1952.

Social Role and Patterns of Symptomatic Behaviors

LESLIE PHILLIPS AND M. SAM RABINOVITCH

THE present study is a contribution toward a more conceptually oriented system of psychiatric classification than is currently available. The present conventional categories of diagnosis are based primarily on descriptions of overt signs of psychopathology, and are inherently limited in their theoretical base. For example, the precise character of the current diagnostic syndromes themselves is unclear, for these categories sometimes seem to correspond to various (unknown) "disease" processes; sometimes they represent simply "disorders" of "the psychobiological unit"; and sometimes a patient may be "ill primarily in terms of society and of conformity with the prevailing cultural milieu" (*1*).

Further, there is an ambiguous basis for diagnosis in that a single disorder carries the connotation of a variety of disparate symptoms. Various cases carrying a given diagnosis may be classified on quite different grounds, e.g., one patient may be categorized as schizophrenic because of an affective disturbance, another because of cognitive impairment. Thus, in terms of their contribution to a diagnosis, the symptoms of a syndrome are interchangeable. Indeed, the bases of classification shift among cognitive, affective, mood, social, and neuropsychological factors, and there has been relatively little concern with the specific nature of these individual signs of disorder. Because of the ambiguities inherent in the current system of psychiatric diagnosis, it appears more meaningful to deal directly with the raw data of psychopathology, i.e., those explicit symptomatic behaviors which bring patients into institutional contact. Therefore, we studied the statistical relationships occurring among various symptomatic reactions, independent of existing nosologies. Guided by these results, we organized these deviant reactions into symptom clusters or categories. The final phase of the study involved a test of the stability of these categories in another group of subjects.

METHOD

The study was based on an examination of case history data on 604 patients.

Reprinted by permission from *The Journal of Abnormal and Social Psychology,* Vol. 57, No. 2, September 1958.

The Worcester State Hospital Psychology Department keeps detailed case history information on all patients referred for psychological appraisal. The files for approximately a five-year period (1948–52) were screened, and all cases with two or more presenting symptoms were used in the present study. A symptom, in this sense, refers to the description of a patient's behavior by a psychiatrist at the time of initial institutional contact, or the description of behavior presented by referring physicians as the main reason for hospitalization. These symptoms largely represent specific actions, thoughts, or somatic reactions that provide a comprehensive (although not exhaustive) list of those observed in a typical state hospital population, a psychiatric outpatient clinic, and in jail cases.

The investigation proceeded by randomly dividing the total sample into two groups of 302 cases each. The first, or pilot, group provided the initial data on which the symptom categories were based. The other group of subjects was reserved for later use in testing the stability of these devised categories.

Extremely deteriorated individuals, obviously organic cases, and very agitated patients are seldom referred to the psychological service and consequently are not adequately represented in either sample.

Statistical Analysis of Data

Examination of the 604 case records resulted in the tabulation of 46 discrete presenting symptoms. Of these, seven were eliminated from the study because their low frequency of occurrence made them unsuitable for the type of statistical analysis chosen.

The data for the remaining 39 symptoms were independently tabulated and cross-tabulated by IBM procedure. Thus, for each pair of symptoms, the number of patients showing both symptoms, neither symptom, and one of the pair, was determined.

All possible pairings of these 39 symptoms result in 741 different pair-combinations. Each such pair was examined for any tendency for (a) the presence of one symptom to be associated with absence of the other and (b) the simultaneous presence of both symptoms of the pair.

The inference as to whether any such association obtained between paired symptoms was based upon the application of the chi-square test of independence to each of the 741 possible combinations. The .10 significance level was chosen for all tests. A statistically significant result, therefore, indicates that if any two symptoms were indeed independent, the probability is only .10 that the frequency of joint occurrence (or mutual exclusiveness) found in the sample would obtain.

Definition of Symptom Categories

For the pilot group, 31 (out of 39) symptoms evidenced either positive or negative relationships at the .10 level of significance. From an analysis of the relationships, it is possible to organize 25 of these symptoms into three categories according to the following criteria:

(a) Each symptom appears in only one of these categories;

(b) Only positive relations occur among symptoms within each category, whereas no positive relations appear between symptoms in different categories;

(c) For a given symptom, negative relationships occur only with symptoms in the other two categories.

While the three major categories appear quite clear-cut, two exceptions appeared. These were the occurrence of a positive relationship between "perplexed" in Category 1 and 'homosexuality," which was grouped in Category 2. A second is the occurrence of a positive relation between "bizarre ideas" (Category 1) and "headaches" (Category 3). Classification was decided largely on rational grounds for each of these symptoms. No such decision could be made for "fears of own hostile impulses," which showed a statistical relationship with both "drinking" (Category 2) and "depreciatory ideas against the self" (Category 3). Consequently, it was dropped from further consideration. This was true also for "blackouts" and "euphoria," which demonstrated only negative relations and could not therefore be categorized.

Following the formation on statistical grounds of the three symptom categories listed above, a rational analysis of their organization was undertaken. Thus, the first category was taken to represent a withdrawal from others either directly (suspiciousness, withdrawn) or in distorted fantasy (e.g., hallucinations, sexual preoccupation, bizarre ideas). Because "amnesia" may occur on an organic basis, it was deleted from Category 1 and was not further considered. The second category comprises a group of symptoms which were characterized either as actions or thoughts turned against others (e.g., threatens assault, temper outbursts, robbery) or as self-indulgent and socially disapproved behavior patterns (e.g., drinking, perversions). The last of the three categories was interpreted as a turning against the self, either in directly expressive action or thoughts (e.g., suicidal attempt, depreciatory ideas against self) or in suffering expressed somatically (e.g., bodily complaints, insomnia). In essence, this last category appears to represent a group of behaviors which are the opposite of those organized within the second one discussed, in which behavior and bodily expression are so largely turned against others.

On the basis of the rational analysis superimposed on the empirical relationship obtained with the pilot group, the number of symptoms considered for further test was increased. They then also included those deviant reactions which logically belonged in each of the three categories, but for which statistically significant relationships had not been obtained.

The following hypothesis was then formulated: The three categories as described above would be confirmed in the test sample. The specific symptoms in each of these three categories are listed in Table 1.

RESULTS

The results obtained with the test sample ($N = 302$) are in arrgreement with the formulated hypothesis. Positive statistical relationships were found only within each of the symptom categories and negative relationships were established only between symptom categories. The results of this study suggest that for a given individual, if any one of his symptoms falls into one of the categories defined here, his other symptoms (among those listed above) are also likely to fall into that same category. As shown in Table 2, no exceptions to the predicted placement of symptoms occurs in the test sample. As will be seen, the results are so much in conformity with the hypothesis that a statistical test of significance appears superfluous. In any case, it would be difficult to set up any legitimate test of the significance of these findings since there is a lack of statistical independence among the obtained relationships. Table 3 lists those

relationships between symptoms which were actually obtained.

TABLE 1. LIST OF SYMPTOMS OCCURRING IN EACH CATEGORY

	Ideational symptomatology	Mood and affect disturbances	Behavioral symptoms	Somatic disorders
Category 1[a] (Avoidance of others)	withdrawn feels perverted suspiciousness hallucinations bizarre ideas sexual preoccupations	apathetic perplexed		
Category 2 (Self-indulgence and turning against others)	threatens assault		drinking rape (and incest) emotional outbursts irresponsible behavior robbery lying disturbed, destructive perversions (including homosexuality) assaultive	
Category 3 (Self-deprivation and turning against the self)	suicidal ideas depreciatory ideas against self	depressed tense-nervous	suicidal attempt compulsions doesn't eat	bodily complaints insomnia headaches

[a] The symptom of "feels going crazy or mentally sick" would have been included in Category 1, and "accused of murder," "firesetting," "eats a lot," and "all addictions except drinking" would have been included in Category 2, but their incidence in the total sample of 604 Ss was too low for the type of statistical analysis used.

Ideally, one might expect interrelationships among all symptoms within a given category, but this happy state does not obtain. In part, this may be due to the fact that a substantial number of the symptom pairs occur with relatively low frequency. Consequently this precludes the likelihood of obtaining statistically significant relationships with these items. Thus, while in many instances there is insufficient evidence to infer a relationship, this is not to say that we have demonstrated a lack of such relationships. Further, the specific symptom pairs within a category which show positive relationships differ somewhat

TABLE 2. ACTUALLY OCCURRING VERSUS PREDICTED RELATIONSHIPS AMONG CATEGORIES

	Within categories		Between categories	
	Positive	Negative	Positive	Negative
Category 1	8	0	0	19
Category 2	4	0	0	4
Category 3	13	0	0	0
Total	25	0	0	23

between the pilot and test groups, as do some of the negative relationships across categories. For example, in Category 1, "suspiciousness," which was positively associated with "perplexed" in the pilot sample, is not so related in the test group. Similarly, for this same category, in the test group "hallucinations" is positively related to "withdrawn," whereas this relationship does not occur in the pilot study. Nevertheless, such specific incongruities must be interpreted within the context of the general results reported; no negative relationships occur within categories and no positive relationships occur between them.

There are other reasons, however, why a question may be raised as to the clear-cut nature of the obtained results. For example, symptoms assumed to be associated with an observed symptom may have been sought and noted by an interviewer while other symptoms were ignored. Illustratively, it is possible that in an assaultive individual evidence for depression may not have been considered. However, case histories were collected over approximately a five-year period, during which there was a considerable yearly turnover in the psychiatric resident staff at the State hospital, so that there was no opportunity for the biases of a restricted number of

TABLE 3. RELATIONS BETWEEN SYMPTOMS OBTAINED IN TEST SAMPLE
($N = 302$)

Symptom	Joint occurrence with	Mutually exclusive with
1. suspicious	hallucinations sexual preoccupations feels perverted	drinking rape (and incest) other perversions emotional outbursts robbery depressed suicidal ideas suicidal attempt headaches
2. hallucinations	withdrawn perplexed	emotional outbursts depressed headaches
3. bizarre ideas	perplexed	
4. withdrawn	apathetic sexual preoccupations	threatens assault suicidal attempt
5. apathetic		tense-nervous
6. sexual preoccupations		emotional outbursts depressed suicidal ideas
7. drinking	irresponsible behavior	depreciatory ideas vs. self
8. threatens assault	assaultive emotional outbursts	depressed
9. assaultive	emotional outbursts	depressed depreciatory ideas vs. self
10. doesn't eat		depressed
11. depressed	depreciatory ideas vs. self suicidal ideas suicidal attempt tense-nervous bodily complaints	
12. depreciatory ideas vs. self	suicidal attempt tense-nervous	
13. suicidal ideas	suicidal attempt	
14. compulsions	tense-nervous	
15. tense-nervous	insomnia	
16. bodily complaints	headaches insomnia	

individuals to distort the reported case information. Further, the frame of reference at this hospital during the period when these records were accumulated was that of descriptive psychiatry, and thus a minimum of restrictions based on particular theoretical formulations was probably imposed on symptom categorization.

There is a corollary consideration that both psychiatric residents and psychological interns, who recorded the data for the psychology department, may have ignored actually appearing symptoms. Finally, because the original data were not collected for research purposes, there were no definite criteria defining symptoms. Consequently, there were undoubtedly individual differences among the clinical staff in terms of the intensity of disturbance required for reporting the appearance of a symptom. These uncertainties as to the reliability of the raw data attest to the possible incompleteness of results, and the findings should be interpreted within this context. Thus, in this study, we have probably not succeeded in isolating "pure" clusters, but the evidence for their reality is so suggestive that it calls for further investigation directed toward their refinement and clarification.

DISCUSSION

Since the hypothesis about categories was confirmed, one can presume that for a given individual, symptoms tend to fall into only one of the three categories defined here. The deviant forms of social interaction expressed in these categories of symptomatic behaviors may be characterized as (a) avoidance of others, (b) self-indulgence and turning against others, and (c) self-deprivation and turning against the self.

The characteristics of interpersonal relationships delineated here may be compared to those outlined by Fromm (3), Horney (4), and Rosenzweig (7). Fromm speaks of social relationships in terms of "symbiotic relatedness," "destructiveness," and "withdrawal." Horney describes the

neurotic trends of "moving against," "moving away," and "moving towards" other individuals. The formulations of these writers share with each other and with the present findings the general concepts of "avoidance of others" and of "turning against others." Rosenzweig's classification of "extrapunitive" and "intropunitive" types appears to correspond to the interpersonal reactions described here of "turning against others" and "turning against the self." Neither Fromm's "symbiotic relatedness" nor Horney's "moving toward others" can be assessed from our present data, because these behavioral characteristics were not sampled in the admitting interviews of the population used in this study. It may be also that the positive orientation in interpersonal relationships implied by these terms is deficient in a psychopathological population.

The categories proposed on the basis of the present findings may also be formulated within the context of role theory, i.e., symptom patterns may represent a particular mode of relating (albeit inappropriately) to another person. Particular patterns of role-taking may be presumed to represent the individual's implicit assumptions as to the nature of his relations with himself and with others. In themselves, the role orientations described here do not represent psychopathological phenomena, but if attitudes are patterned exclusively in such negative terms toward the self or others, this might provide the basis for the emergence of socially deviant thought and behavior (as well as for such accompanying somatic reactions as headaches and insomnia).

The question may be posed as to how one might conceptually organize the role orientations as represented in the categories. Perhaps a fruitful way of thinking about this problem is in terms of the principles of developmental psychology.

It has been postulated that development proceeds from a relatively global state to one of increasing differentiation and

hierarchization (8). When this formulation is applied to social relationships, it
would suggest a genetically early period in
which the boundaries between the self and
the world are relatively diffuse; a subsequent period of self-centeredness in which
a separation of self and world has occurred
but with little recognition of the rights of
others; and a final phase in which self identity is maintained, but in which relationships on the basis of reciprocity also take
place. In this last stage of development, a
recognition and acceptance of the social
mores has been internalized.

Within a developmental framework,
psychopathology represents a relative dominance of genetically early levels of functioning accompanied by a decreasing emphasis on the higher, more recently
developed, genetic characteristics. On this
basis, the symptom categories described in
this study may be rationally ordered in the
following sequence. The category "avoidance of others" is considered most primitive, for the chronic threat which social
contact implies for the individual may have
prevented an adequate development of self
and object constancy (5) with a consequent vague and amorphous perceptual
structuring of the world. Analogously,
Rapaport (6) considers the motor action
of withdrawal as a primitive form of behavior upon which is built later forms of
reality testing. Recent work by Bexton,
Heron, and Scott (2) has demonstrated
that isolation from environmental stimulation is regularly followed, even in normal
subjects, by hallucinatory experiences.
Their findings are pertinent to this present
study in that they suggest the possibility
that the appearance of hallucinations as
well as of bizarre ideas is a consequence
of the suspiciousness and withdrawal which
characterizes individuals whose deviant behavior falls into the category "avoidance
of others."

In a genetic hierarchy of the proposed three classes of symptoms, the category of "self-indulgence and turning
against others" appears to fall at an intermediate position. First, the category does
not include any symptom indicative of a
formal disturbance of thought. Further,
the behaviors in this group are suggestive
of a self-centered and demanding attitude
without concern for the social mores. The
salient needs of the individuals whose
symptoms fall in this category are of a
concrete bodily nature, such as drinking or
various deviant forms of sexual expression.
From the manner in which these symptoms
cluster, it appears that if his needs are not
met, the individual is likely to retaliate
with behavior carrying an injurious intent.
This aggression may be expressed overtly in
such behaviors as assault or robbery, or
less directly in irresponsible behavior or in
threatening assault.

The third category, "self-deprivation and turning against the self," suggests
an introjection of social standards not implied by the two previous categories. Thus
the individual whose symptoms fall into
this last grouping would appear more socially mature and responsible in that he has
introjected and can take the role of internalized others. The psychopathology represented by this class of symptoms involves
an excessively harsh judgment of the self,
leading to self-deprivation (e.g., not eating) of a turning against the self in either
action or thought (suicidal attempt, suicidal
ideas) or their somatic equivalents (tension, headaches).

Summary

This study has analyzed the tendency of symptomatic behaviors to appear
together or be mutually exclusive in the
deviant behavior of the individual patient.
Thirty-nine symptoms of a sufficiently high
frequency of occurrence for statistical
analysis were considered. The psychiatric
population covered a broad range of diagnostic categories and was drawn largely
from a state hospital, although groups from
an outpatient clinic and from jail were also
liberally represented. A total of 604 patients as studied, distributed randomly into
two groups of 302 subjects each. A statis-

tical analysis of the interrelationships of the 39 symptoms under study was undertaken for the first group. On the basis of this exploratory work, it was hypothesized that symptoms tend to occur in three major groupings, which are assumed to be indicative of "avoidance of others," "self-indul-gence and turning against others," and "self-deprivation and turning against the self." The validity of these categories was supported by the findings on the second group of subjects. Finally, these categories were interpreted within the context of developmental theory.

REFERENCES

1. American Psychiatric Association. Diagnostic and statistical manual of mental disorders. Washington, D. C.: Author, 1952.

2. Bexton, W. H., Heron, W. and Scott, T. H. Effects of decreased variation in the sensory environment. Canad. J. Psychol., 1954, 8, 70–76.

3. Fromm, E. Man for himself. New York: Holt, Rinehart and Winston, 1947.

4. Horney, K. Our inner conflicts. New York: Norton, 1945.

5. Piaget, J. Psychology of intelligence. New York: Harcourt, Brace, 1950.

6. Rapaport, D. Organization and pathology of thought: Selected sources. New York: Columbia Univer. Press, 1951.

7. Rosenzweig, S. An outline of frustration theory. In J. McV. Hunt (Ed.), Personality and the behavior disorders, Vol. 1. New York: Ronald, 1945.

8. Werner, H. The concept of development from a comparative and organismic point of view. In D. B. Harris (Ed.), The concept of development: An issue in the study of human behavior. Minneapolis: Univer. of Minnesota Press, 1957.

2 | Alterations in Behavior under Special Conditions: Possible Analogues of Pathological Processes

MANY features of behavior pathology are observed when persons are placed under extreme or unusual conditions. Introspections of self and observations of others under unusual conditions such as fatigue, fright, fever, hunger, and isolation reveal such pathological symptoms as distorted judgment, delusion, hallucination, apathy, and drowsiness. Such observations may serve a heuristic function by suggesting hypotheses to be tested by experiment or field observation. A condition that regularly produces abnormal behavior manifestations, such as hallucinations, may serve as a model for a theory of behavior pathology.

This section includes four reports of behavior under unusual or extreme conditions. Some of these conditions are produced in the laboratory, others occur naturalistically; some are temporary and transient, others are more persistent and extended in time. Each requires special investigative techniques.

Anecdotal reports have appeared in the literature describing persons who had been isolated from human contact (for example, children reared by wolves) and who had been even more severely isolated from both human contact and sensory stimulation (such as persons confined in dark underground chambers). Until recently, however, reliable information concerning the effect of such isolation was not available. The article by Doane, Mahatoo, Heron, and Scott is one in a series designed to assess the influence on a number of psychological functions of reduction in variation of sensory stimulation. Distortions in perceptual response shown by their subjects are truly remarkable and demonstrate features that are characteristic of psychosis. One might propose for consideration the analogy between experimentally produced stimulus deprivation and the stimulus reduction found in persons displaying apathy, withdrawal, catatonia, and depression.

Shevrin and Luborsky report an investigation of a topic that has all but defied experimentation. They propose a set of hypotheses drawn in part from Freud's exposition on dreams, and subject them to test through the "Poetzl effect." First reported in 1917, the Poetzl effect refers to waking perceptions that one is unable to recall but that influence the content of subsequent dreams. The experimenters used the tachisto-

37

scope, an instrument that permits very brief exposures of visual stimuli under controlled conditions.

By demonstrating the phenomenon of "preconscious" perception, the authors provided a method for studying the unrecognized stimuli that may shape not only dreams and images, but possibly hallucinations as well. The analogy between the influence of preconscious perception on dreams and the construction of hallucinations from unrecognized or preconscious perceptions is not difficult to make. Further experimentation will show whether the analogy has any utility.

The past decade has seen a recognition of the part played by stress in the production of behavior disorders. Many experimental studies of stress are limited, however, because of the unrealistic and the relatively "safe" climate of the laboratory. The stress described in the paper by Strassman, Thaler, and Schein is not limited by lack of realism; it is created by the physical and psychological conditions in a prisoner of war camp. These investigators employed interviews and psychological tests on prisoners of war immediately following repatriation. The use of apathy and withdrawal as an adjustive technique to prolonged stress may be considered as analogous to the withdrawal seen in schizophrenics—who presumably are also seeking ways of reducing distress.

This article should be read in conjunction with another article in this book that deals with the effects of stressful conditions in a prisoner of war camp: "Brainwashing, Conditioning, and DDD (Depression, Debility, Dread)," by Farber, Harlow, and West. The latter paper reviews other studies and treats brainwashing as a phenomenon that can be readily understood with the aid of concepts drawn from general psychology.

The report by Medalia and Larsen on the Seattle windshield-pitting epidemic analyzes a set of unwarranted beliefs held by a large number of people. This study, employing the social survey technique, deals with the phenomenon sometimes called mass hysteria, group suggestibilty, or group contagion.

Such mass delusions occur from time to time under various conditions. One of the most famous was the Orson Welles radio broadcast of 1933, "The Invasion from Mars," which resulted in near panic for many listeners. In the recent past, rumors of flying saucers from outer space have become foci for extended systems of beliefs bordering on delusion. The problem of relative susceptibility to "mass illusions" raised by the authors is parallel to the problem of susceptibility to unwarranted beliefs and actions by psychotic persons.

Changes in Perceptual Function after Isolation

B. K. DOANE, WINSTON MAHATOO, W. HERON, AND T. H. SCOTT

IN AN EARLIER preliminary report (4) we described some of the gross effects of perceptual isolation on visual perception, based on the subjective reports of three sophisticated subjects. In the present paper we provide data from a systematically administered battery of objective tests of visual perception given to thirteen subjects after four days of isolation, and data from a series of tests of somaesthetic perception and spatial orien-

Reprinted from the *Canadian Journal of Psychology*, Vol. 13, No. 3, 1959, by courtesy of the Canadian Psychological Association and the University of Toronto Press.

tation. In addition, we include results from a group of ambulatory subjects who underwent visual isolation, but were not restricted in any other way.

METHOD

The method was that already described (7), with some slight changes in detail: the cubicle in which S was placed was now painted white, he had EEG leads attached throughout the experiment, and the isolation period of four days was agreed upon in advance. We also made certain physiological tests, and two tests of somaesthetic function, which briefly interrupted the isolation (visual perception, however, was occluded throughout). With the time necessary for eating and going to the toilet, S was out of the cubicle for about 4 hrs. out of 24.

The experimental group was made up of 17 male college students. Of these, 13 went through the cubicle procedure and 4 were ambulatory. Two cubicle Ss wore opaque masks, to test the effect of darkness on their hallucinatory activity, until an hour before the end of the experimental period, when they were fitted with the translucent mask worn by the others (this mask admitted light, but did not permit visual perception). The ambulatory Ss wore the translucent mask but not the gloves and cuffs which prevented tactual perception (7), and were not confined to the cubicle. They were worked with in pairs, and allowed to talk with each other, to listen to the radio, to go for walks and, in general, to engage in as much normal activity as was possible in the circumstances. These Ss were given the tests of visual perception only.

Tests of somaesthetic function and spatial orientation were given to 8 Ss, but because of a change of procedure, data are available for the 2-point limen on 5 Ss only.

Twenty normal control Ss were used. All were given the spatial and somaesthetic tests, and 13 were given the visual tests. The tests were given at the same time intervals as for the experimental subjects, S coming into the laboratory at the agreed hour and being, of course, under no restriction at other times.

The tests were first given before S entered the experimental condition. Tests involving somaesthesis and orientation were repeated after 48 and 72 hrs. of isolation only (that is, not after the isolation period was over). Immediately upon coming out of restriction all Ss were asked to examine their visual surroundings and report on their appearance, their reports being recorded. The quantitative visual tests were then administered for the second time.

EFFECTS ON VISUAL PERCEPTION

The tests of perception had to be completed in a short time since the major effects seem to wear off in an hour or two, and this limited our choice of tests to those that could be given quickly. Even so, after allowing about ten minutes for the qualitative description, the test battery took over an hour to administer, and it is likely that some of the later tests showed smaller differences than they would have if they had been given early in the series. The tests are listed below, together with the results, in the same order as given to the subject. Table I shows those in which the mean differences reached or approached significance.

1. No effect on *critical flicker frequency* was found.

2. There was an increase of *figural after-effect*, with the inspection and test figures of Köhler and Wallach's Figure 36 (*6*, p. 292) and the method of measurement described by them (p. 299). The measurement is of the degree of displacement of two test figures.

3. *Size constancy* was decreased. With each of 6 different-sized discs, presented at 3 ft., S made a comparison with a graduated series of 17 discs presented at 12 ft. He was instructed to "pick the far disc that looks the same as the near one," and his score was the difference in diameter between the test disc and the comparison disc that he chose as equal to it. The experimental Ss chose significantly larger comparison discs, showing a decrease in constancy; the control Ss showed no change (the slight difference in their mean scores was in the opposite direction).

4. *Visual acuity* was probably improved by the isolation procedure. A white card was presented at 10 ft., bearing a horizontal row of 14 black vertical lines spaced 1 in. apart. Each line was 1/64 in. wide and 3 in. in vertical extent. There was a gap in each line, decreasing from 3/32 in. at the left to 1/64 at the right. S had to say where the gap was in each line (bottom, middle or top). Three such cards were presented, making a total of 42 trials. Normal control Ss showed no change from first to second test; the experimental Ss improved from a mean score of 35.4 correct identifications, before isolation, to a mean of 36.4 afterwards. Though the result does not reach the usual level of statistical significance ($p < .10$), some weight may possibly be given to the result in view of the significant change of the 2-point limen (see below).

5. In the *phi-phenomenon* no changes were observed in the timing of the stimuli which gave rise to apparent movement.

6. No differences of *brightness contrast* effects were obtained when the method of Thurstone (*9*, p. 53) was used.

7. The *autokinetic effect* was increased. The subject was dark-adapted for 3 min., then seated 10 ft. from a point source of light in a dark room. Two minutes after onset of movement the illumination of the surroundings of the point source was gradually increased up to the point at which movement was abolished. Two such determinations were made. No difference was observed in time of onset of the movement, but movement for the experimental *S*s persisted with a significantly higher level of surrounding brightness.

8. *Colour adaptation* increased. *S* looked with one eye through a 2-in. plain polaroid filter mounted in the front end of a box. Inside the box, 6 in. from the front, was a 2-in. yellow polaroid filter surrounded by a

ception were obtained. A series of black nonsense forms (outlines) were presented one at a time on a white screen for approximately 50 msec. A recognition method of testing was used.

In all these results, data for the ambulatory *S*s are included with those for the more completely isolated *S*s since they showed the same picture and, by increasing the *N*, improved the level of confidence for three of the above results (autokinetic movement, colour adaptation, and the after-image of movement.)

Qualitative Reports

When the mask was first removed, all subjects in the cubicle group and three of the four ambulatory subjects reported gross visual disturbances, which usually disappeared in about half an hour. The effects described were similar to those reported by three subjects earlier (*4*); we are

TABLE I. LEVELS OF CONFIDENCE FOR QUANTITATIVE TESTS SHOWING CHANGES OF VISUAL FUNCTION AFTER ISOLATION

Test name	FAE*	Size constancy	Acuity	Auto-kinetic	Colour adaptation	Shape constancy	After-movement
Test number	2	3	4	7	8	9	12
Value of p	.02	.02	.10	.001	.01	.10	.05

* Figural After-Effect

4-in. white circular field. After fixating a point in the middle of the yellow disc for 90 sec., *S* closed his eyes for 10 sec. and then again looked at the fixation point while the yellow disc was rotated to reduce the saturation. Adaptation was measured by the number of degrees of rotation necessary to make the yellow disc match the surrounding white area.

9. *Shape constancy* may have decreased ($p < .10$). A white equilateral triangle with 3-in. sides was mounted on a grey card attached to supports so that it could be tilted at various angles from the vertical. The card was tilted at 5 different angles, and for each *S* was asked to select from a series of 15 triangles of various altitudes the one which seemed to match best the shape of the tilted triangle.

10. A test of *brightness constancy* showed no apparent effect of isolation.

11. *Necker cube* reversals showed no change of frequency.

12. *Movement after-images* were increased in duration. A 12-in. spiral, 12 ft. from *S*, was rotated at 2 r.p.s. for 30 sec. *S*s report of after-movement was timed on 3 successive trials.

13. No effects on *tachistoscopic per-*

now able to give frequencies of occurrence for the various distortions in a larger group.

Table II includes the results obtained earlier, and thus is based on an *N* of 20. It classifies the distortions under headings which may need some explanation. *Spontaneous movement* includes all apparent activity of the visual field when the observer (including his eyes) was still: shimmering or undulation of surfaces, and drifting, contraction, or expansion of objects. *Induced movement* refers to changes in the position of objects produced by head and eye movements. *Surface distortions* refers to cases in which plane surfaces were described as warped, concave, or convex, or as though folded along an axis in the medial optical plane, and those in which a convex swelling of the central part of the visual field was reported. *Linear distortions: (a)* with fixation on a point between two parallel vertical black lines on a grey background, about two-thirds of the subjects reported that the lines seemed to swell outward near the fixation point, and the remainder that the lines curved inward (toward the fixation point); (b) with fixation above and below a horizontal line, six of the twenty subjects reported that the ends of the line curved downward when fixation was below the line, upward when fixation was above. It should be emphasized that all these linear effects were pronounced: for example, the centres of the parallel lines (¼ in. wide, 3 in. apart, and 3 ft. from the observer) might according to the reports be displaced by one inch or more.

In addition to the distortions summarized in Table II, there were reports of exaggerated contrast, hypersaturation and luminosity of colours, pronounced positive

of the isolation period, both had vivid hallucinations, those of the subject who had already had them becoming stronger.

This result suggested that exposure to diffuse light was a factor in the phenomenon. Accordingly, five subjects who were among the most persistent hallucinators when wearing the translucent mask were put in complete darkness. All reported an immediate increase in vividness of hallucinations; but within two hours there was a decrease of such experiences, three having no more hallucinations and two having them greatly decreased. Exposed again to the diffuse light, all five reported that the hallucinations returned to their original level of intensity.

A further fact of interest is that two of the four ambulatory subjects (with translucent mask) developed hallucina-

TABLE II. INCIDENCE OF VARIOUS DISTURBANCES OF VISUAL PERCEPTION IMMEDIATELY ON COMING OUT OF RESTRICTION: QUALITATIVE OBSERVATIONS BY 20 SUBJECTS

Spontaneous movements*	Induced movements	Surface distortions	Linear distortions
18	12	16	18

* For categories, see text.

and negative after-images, accentuated or diminished depth of perspective, and distortions of human faces. All of the effects described were obtained with both monocular and binocular vision, but were more marked binocularly.

Factors Affecting Hallucination

As an incidental aspect of the visual study, we were also able to obtain some further information on the factors determining the occurrence of the hallucinations which are described elsewhere (5). Of the eleven subjects who wore the translucent mask, and who were thus exposed continuously to diffuse visual stimulation, eight developed hallucinations. Of the two subjects who wore the opaque masks, one developed hallucinations; but when they were given the translucent mask at the end

tions; and further, that these began for one subject while he was being taken for a walk. These results indicate, first, that unpatterned sensory stimulation increases the probability of hallucinatory activity, as Vernon et al. have suggested (10), but is not necessary for its occurrence. Secondly, the hallucinations may be specific to restrictions in the particular sensory mode in which they occur—that is, the probability of visual hallucinations may not be affected by restriction, or lack of restriction, in other senses. It may be noted, however, that visual perception seemed somewhat more grossly disturbed in the cubicle subjects than in the ambulatory ones, which suggests that though the disturbance of function is greatest in the area in which restriction has occurred, there is also some spread of effect to other senses.

SOMAESTHESIS AND SPATIAL ORIENTATION

Two tests of somaesthetic function were made, a tactual form-discrimination test and measurement of the two-point limen. The two tests of orientation, one with paper and pencil and one in which the subject attempted to follow directions in moving about a bare room, might also be considered to be tests mostly of somaesthetic function, since they were done while still wearing the masks which prevented vision. The tests were given before entering the cubicle, after 48 hours of isolation, and after 72 hours. Eight subjects were tested, but data for the two-point limen are available for five subjects only because the procedure used at first was unsatisfactory. Also, one subject felt

his finger for 10 sec. The forms were presented in variable order in the different tests. The second and third tests, after 48 hours and 72 hours of isolation, were made without showing him the forms first. Scores were based on errors (failures of identification).

The results are summarized in Table III: control subjects showed some slight practice effect in the second and third test periods, experimental subjects deteriorated significantly. The statistical analysis was made in terms of difference scores, obtained by subtracting the first test score from the later score, for each subject.

Two-point limens were measured with a standard aesthesiometer on four loci: (1) tip of left index finger, (2) volar surface of left forearm, (3) inner surface

TABLE III. MEAN ERROR SCORES ON FORM DISCRIMINATION, AT THREE TEST PERIODS, FOR 8 EXPERIMENTAL SUBJECTS (7 IN THE 72-HOUR TEST) AND 20 NORMAL CONTROL SUBJECTS

| | Test periods | | | p-values* | (U test) |
Group	Pre-isolation	48 hrs.	72 hrs.	1–2	1–3
Experimental	2.06	3.30	2.70	.001	.02
Control	2.63	2.08	2.03		

* p-values are based on each subject's change in score as between his first and second, and first and third test.

obliged to leave the experiment before the third test was due, so that the results for the third period are based on seven subjects only for form discrimination and orientation tests (Tables III and V), four subjects for the two-point limen (Table IV). In spite of the small *N*, however, significant results were obtained.

Tactual form discrimination was tested with ten figures made by fastening wire to the surface of square cards 6×6 in. Five were familiar geometric forms (circle, triangle, etc.), five were slight variations of such forms (ellipse, rectangle with one curved side.) On the first (pre-isolation) test the subject was shown the forms. He then put on the mask and was required to identify the forms he had been shown, by tracing the outline of each with

of the right upper arm, three inches above the joint, and (4) the forehead one inch above the nasion. To ensure testing the same point on all trials, a line was drawn on the skin with indelible ink. One tip of the aesthesiometer was applied at the end of the line, the other at various points along its extent. The method of limits was used, with modifications, to limit the expenditure of time. At each test period, only one ascending and one descending series of determinations was made until the subject responded correctly three times. Single points were presented at random.

The results (Table IV) showed a decrease of two-point limen for the experimental group in three of the four loci, two of these at conventional levels of significance. The analysis again was based on difference scores, comparing the amount of *change* shown by experimental and by control subjects: this is an important point in understanding the data for the forehead as shown in Table IV, since the limen of one of the experimental subjects was well outside the range for the others, and this gives the experimental group much higher means than the control group.

One peculiar phenomenon was noticed while the experimental subjects were being tested: they were sometimes uncertain whether they were being touched or not, and would frequently respond when no stimulus was being applied. All of them behaved in this way though not on the

and two inches, a left turn and three inches, and so on, with a total of five turns. He was instructed that each turn was to be a right angle, and was warned that at the end he would be required to draw a straight line back to his starting point. The scoring system was based on deviations of distances and angles from the correct ones. Two such tests were given.

The second way in which orientation was tested is the same in principle, but here the subject was placed in an empty room and traced the patterns by walking, and his position and orientation were corrected after each individual response.

TABLE IV. MEAN VALUES FOR TWO-POINT LIMEN FOR 5 EXPERIMENTAL SUBJECTS (4 IN THE 72-HOUR TEST) AND 20 NORMAL CONTROL SUBJECTS

Locus	Group	Test periods			p-values (U test)*	
		Pre-isolation	48 hrs.	72 hrs.	1–2	1–3
Finger	Experimental	1.70	1.70	1.75	NS	
	Control	1.75	1.50	1.60		
Forearm	Experimental	29.6	26.7	24.0	.15	.15
	Control	23.4	23.3	23.7		
Upper arm	Experimental	29.1	21.9	23.8	.002	.05
	Control	32.8	32.8	32.4		
Forehead	Experimental	19.8	16.9	19.2	.02	.02
	Control	9.2	9.2	9.2		

* p-values as in Table III.

pre-isolation tests; only one control subject did so, on one occasion. It seems, then, that they were experiencing some form of "hallucination"; they felt that they were being touched by the aesthesiometer when this was actually not so.

Spatial orientation was tested in two ways, both requiring that the subject follow directions in making a series of movements without vision. The first was a paper-and-pencil test. The pencil held by the subject was placed at the starting point on a sheet of paper, and he was instructed to move left three inches, make a right turn and go two inches, another right turn

In the estimation of distance the experimental subjects did not differ from the control, but they were inferior in the judgment of angles and directions. Table V presents the test results. To these some qualitative observations may be added. In the walking test, when the subject was told to return to his starting point, he sometimes became quite disoriented, without even an approximate idea of the direction in which to move. This was not observed in the control group. Disorientation was also observed at other times. Before the subject entered the cubicle he was shown the layout of the washroom, and during the experiment the procedure for "toilet-ing" was to escort him to the door and then let him find his way to the toilet and back to the door by himself. In the early stages of isolation the subject had no dif-ficulty in doing so, but in later stages he fairly often became lost and would have to call the experimenter to help him find his way out.

SUMMARY AND COMMENT

Quantitative data are provided con-cerning the changes in sensory and per-ceptual processes, both visual and soma-esthetic, that result from the isolation pro-cedure. Some further information is also provided about the factors affecting the occurrence of hallucinations.

It seems possible, further, that vi-sual acuity was improved by the isolation procedure. The 10 per cent level of con-fidence, statistically, can of course justify no final conclusion, and the apparent sup-port from the statistically significant im-provement in the two-point limen must also be regarded cautiously since it is based on data from five subjects only (though in comparison with twenty control sub-jects). However, it is worth noting the similarity of this result to the reports of Haber (3) and Teuber, Krieger, and Ben-der (8) of decrease in the two-point limen in the limb stumps of amputees, results which they interpret in terms of a central reorganization due to reduced sensory in-put.

TABLE V. MEAN TOTAL ANGULAR DEVIATIONS IN SPATIAL ORIENTATION TESTS FOR 8 EXPERIMENTAL SUBJECTS (7 AT THE 72-HR. TEST) AND 20 NORMAL CONTROLS

Test	Group	Test periods			p-values (U test)*	
		Pre-isolation	48 hrs.	72 hrs.	1–2	1–3
Paper and pencil	Experimental	40.6	140.0	56.4	.05	.05
	Control	58.8	57.0	53.3		
Walking	Experimental	112.5	121.3	135.0	.10	.001
	Control	146.5	115.8	102.8		

* p-values as in Table III.

There are certain general areas of perception which seem to be affected by the isolation procedure. Results from the visual tests indicate that the most promi-nent effects are a decrease in the constan-cies and an increase in the after-effects of stimulation (figural after-effect, colour adaptation, and the after-image of move-ment). Size constancy is markedly re-duced, and shape constancy probably re-duced; to these may be added the repeated observation of subjects on first emerging from isolation that the position of objects in the visual field was unstable, moving when the subject moved. As Gibson (2) has pointed out, the stability of objects in the visual world must be regarded as a constancy phenomenon.

Finally, we may note the possibility that the experimental subjects' poorer per-formance in the tactual form-discrimina-tion and spatial orientation tests was in fact caused by visual dysfunction. Some sub-jects remarked that they had lost their ability to visualize the external world. This made it impossible for them to form a mental picture of the route that had been followed in the orientation test, and thus to locate the starting point. One subject who got lost in the confines of the wash-room reported that "One reason why I can't find my way is that when I try to visualize where I am everything seems to be expanding and contracting and waving about." Similar remarks were made by others, and it is relevant to recall that such remarks were typically made by subjects when they were first describing their hallucinatory activity, or the first appearance of the external world when they first emerged from isolation.

These results emphasize again the profound degree of disturbance that is produced by the isolation procedure as observed in this laboratory and elsewhere. Hallucinations of extreme vividness, impairment of thought processes, sensory and perceptual changes, together with significant changes in the EEG, all testify to the widespread effect on central neural function that is induced simply by limiting the normal variation of sensory stimulation.

There is as yet no sign of a satisfactory general explanation of these phenomena, and it is clearly impossible to give one which is plausible and detailed. But one might guess that the functional de-afferentation of the isolation conditions may cause parts of the central nervous system to become hyperexcitable. Evarts (1) has recently shown that such phenomena may take place in the visual system of the cat. Using chronically implanted electrodes, he has demonstrated that the cortical response to electrical stimulation of the optic pathways has a shorter recovery cycle after the animal has worn opaque contact lenses for a few weeks.

In our subjects there was no diminution of total sensory stimulation but, since sensory systems respond most actively to change of stimulation, it is possible that the lack of a varied input results in an inactivity of pathways at some higher levels of the central nervous system. If these pathways consequently became sensitized, it might account for increased figural after-effect, autokinetic movement, colour adaptation, and so on. It would also fit in with the least expected feature of the present experiment, the apparent increase in sensory acuity, visual and somaesthetic (the only example that we have found of an improvement of function after isolation). On the other hand, it would interfere with the integration of the complex patterns of neural activity which must be involved in more complicated tasks such as problem solving and spatial orientation, the constancies being also affected. Finally, it is easy to see how hyperexcitability of parts of the visual system might be related to the occurrence of hallucinations. Until we have more detailed information, however, such ideas must remain speculative.

REFERENCES

1. Evarts, E. The physiological basis of hallucinations. In Jolyon West (ed.), *Hallucinations: A symposium* (in press).

2. Gibson, J. J. The visual perception of objective motion and subjective movement. *Psychol. Rev.*, 1954, *61*, 304–314.

3. Haber, William B. Effects of loss of limb on sensory function. *J. Psychol.*, 1955, *40*, 115–123.

4. Heron, W., Doane, B. K., and Scott, T. H. Visual disturbances after prolonged perceptual isolation. *Canad. J. Psychol.*, 1954, *8*, 70–76.

5. Heron, W., Doane, B. K., and Scott, T. H. Characteristics of hallucinations during perceptual isolation. In Jolyon West (ed.), *Hallucinations: A Symposium* (in press).

6. Köhler, W., and Wallach, H. Figural after-effects: An investigation of visual processes. *Proc. Amer. phil. Soc.*, 1944, *88*, 269–357.

7. Scott, T. H., Bexton, W. H., Heron, W., and Doane, B. K. Cognitive effects of perceptual isolation. *Canad. J. Psychol.*, 1959, *13*, 200–209.

8. Teuber, H. L., Krieger, H. P., and Bender, M.B. Reorganization of sensory function in amputation stumps: Two-point discrimination. *Fed. Proc.*, 1949, *8*, 156.

9. Thurstone, L. L. *A factorial study of perception*. Chicago: Univer. Chicago Press, 1944.

10. Vernon, J., McGill, T. E., and Schiffman, H. Visual hallucinations during perceptual isolation. *Canad. J. Psychol.*, 1958, *12*, 31–34.

The Measurement of Preconscious Perception in Dreams and Images: An Investigation of the Poetzl Phenomenon

HOWARD SHEVRIN AND LESTER LUBORSKY

IN A PIONEER laboratory investigation of dream imagery, Poetzl (16) discovered that his subjects dreamt about the originally unreported parts of a previously exposed picture. He flashed colored slides of everyday scenes at 1/100″ and asked subjects to describe and draw what they saw. He then told them to record any dreams they had that night. When he asked his subjects on the following day to describe and draw their dreams, he observed that the dream imagery borrowed extensively from the unreported portions of the picture. Poetzl's subjects confirmed his observations by identifying elements of the picture of which they were previously unaware as parts of their dream imagery.

Poetzl looked upon his findings as supporting the view that "images of indirect vision, errors of tachistoscopic vision in normal persons, visual dream-images and the visual mistakes of patients with agnosia agree with each other in many qualities regarding form and contents" (16). He attributed these similarities to a functional equivalence between brain damage to visual areas and the impoverishment of normal perception produced by tachistoscopic exposure or peripheral vision. In a brief exposure, involuntary eye movements from the point of fixation to other areas of the stimulus cannot be executed. The time limitation erects a "motoric barrier" that permits a clear perception of only part of the picture; the remainder of the picture registers in the visual apparatus but is not represented in consciousness, analogous to an exposed film that has not been devel-

Reprinted by permission from *The Journal of Abnormal and Social Psychology*, Vol. 56, No. 3, May 1958.

oped. According to a "law of exclusion" formulated by Poetzl, only the registered but consciously unrepresented parts of a stimulus appear in the dream. The fully "developed" perception, or "print," is excluded from the dream process.

Both Poetzl and Freud were aware of the parallel between Poetzl's findings and Freud's theory of dreams. The "indifferent" perceptions that Freud identified as day-residues present in the manifest content of dreams, Poetzl equated with the unreported parts of the picture which were later dreamed about. Poetzl further assumed that there was a functional equivalence between his concept of the "motoric barrier" and the concept of a repressed wish. He maintained that the dream lifted this "motoric barrier" and permitted the successive development of the parts of the picture originally unseen, much as the dream lifted the barrier of repression and permitted the symbolic and disguised expression of unacceptable wishes. The dream work undertook its own kind of "dark room" procedure, developing the exposed but heretofore undeveloped and unprinted "film" according to its own laws rather than the laws of the waking state.

Recently, Fisher (4, 5, 6) revived general interest in Poetzl's work by providing examples of Poetzl's findings on the basis of which he suggested modifications of Freud's theory of dream formation. Klein and his associates (9, 18) felt the need for a more exact method than Poetzl's procedure, and using an ingenious "masking" technique, have attempted to show that an apparently unseen stimulus affects the perception of a simultaneously perceived stimulus. The work of these two investigators provided the immediate stimulus for the present study. Like Fisher, however, we felt the need to use the opportunities offered by the Poetzl method for tracing the vicissitudes of preconscious percepts from the time of their registration to their emergence in dreams. In a previous paper we reported on a preliminary examination of the Poetzl phenomenon together with an attempt to understand it theoretically (12).

If the basic Poetzl observation could be systematically confirmed and if a measure of delayed recall in dreams could be developed, a new approach to the experimental study of unconscious phenomena would be made possible. This method might successfully handle some of the major difficulties encountered in the many studies concerned with measuring unconscious phenomena. These investigations—carried out under such headings as subception (11), and perceptual defense and vigilance (3, 10, 15)—by and large. have utilized indirect indices such as variations in threshold time. As Klein and his associates have pointed out, in these studies ". . . non-conscious perception and the defensive reaction to it [are] both inferred from the deviant recognition times. The threshold technique of these studies . . . [provides] little if any information concerning the processes that determine the threshold measure" (9). These studies focus mainly on "defensive reactions to subliminal perception" and not upon the ways in which "subliminal registration affects conscious thought." (9).

Klein et al. have taken an important step toward dealing with the problem they pose. Their results suggest another question: what is the *fate* of the preconsciously registered impressions after the moment at which they affect simultaneously evoked conscious impressions? The technique discovered by Poetzl and further developed by Fisher is perhaps best designed to answer this question, for the dream would appear to bring to the surface many of these preconscious perceptions.

The Poetzl procedure has been repeated in several studies (1, 4, 5, 6, 13, 14) but thus far no measure of preconscious perception has been developed. Our primary aim in the present report is to construct a reliable measure of preconscious perception as elicited by the Poetzl technique and then to examine evidence bearing on its validity.

METHOD

Our procedure was essentially the same as the one used by Poetzl and Fisher. They varied conditions unsystematically in what were principally clinical approaches (8). We have attempted to collect our data in a systematic fashion, so that statistical procedures could be applied to the data.

We used the same picture for all Ss. It provided a baseline from which could be assessed the nature of the "picture pull," as well as individual differences in response to the same stimulus. None of the other experimenters (1, 4, 5, 6, 13, 14) used one picture for a sizeable number of Ss.

A single description and drawing of a complex picture may not capture all of what the S has consciously perceived. Our instructions therefore emphasize that the S should describe and draw what he saw as fully as possible. In addition, we asked for a second full description and drawing immediately following the first. At the next session (the following day) we obtained a third sample of the conscious memory of the picture. In order to make certain that nothing would be missed, a tape recording was made of the experimental sessions.

We became convinced of the importance of using a complex picture with many objects to assure that even Ss who reported a great deal initially would have a sizeable remainder to recover in their dreams. This would make possible a statistically adequate range of recovered items.

It would be foolhardy to expect dreams to occur and be reported on request. We decided to obtain from those Ss who did not report dreams something similar to a daydream. We asked these Ss to describe and draw the first mental picture that came to mind. A similar technique was employed by Allers and Teler (1) and more recently by Fisher (5).

The 27 Ss who took part in this study

had participated in other experiments on perception at The Menninger Foundation. Our initial explanations of the nature of the experiment could be brief: "This is a study of perception, or how people see the world. It is similar to some of the studies you've taken part in before." The verbatim experimental instructions follow:

Part I (First Session)

1. On the count of three I'm going to flash a picture on the screen. It will appear just about where the x-mark is. [The experimenter also indicates the size of the area in which the picture will appear on the screen.] Ready: one, two, three. [The picture is flashed on the count of three.]

2. Now, describe what you saw as fully as you can. Make a drawing of what you remember seeing and continue to describe it while you draw it.

3. [The S is asked to describe and draw the picture again, as in #2 above. After completing the drawing and description, he is asked,] Is there anything else you remember?

4. Would you remember and write down upon awakening any dreams that you have tonight? Please bring them with you when you come tomorrow. [If the S asks, "What if I don't dream?" he is told, "If you keep a paper and pencil handy we've found that this helps a great deal." If he then asks, "But what if I don't dream at all?" the experimenter replies, "Even people who don't usually dream find that this helps."]

Part II (Second Session)

5. Tell me your dream (dreams). Draw and describe what was pictured in your dream, what you saw in your dream.

Alternate instructions for Ss who do not report dreams:

What were the last thoughts you had before falling asleep last night? [This is followed by instruction #6 below. The remainder of the instructions, from #7 on, apply to these images as if they were dreams.]

6. Close your eyes, let a picture come to mind, let me know when you have one. . . . Fine, tell me about the picture that came to mind. Now draw what you saw and describe it as you draw it. [Two pictures are elicited in this way.]

7. [Associations are obtained to the dreams and images by means of the usual questions, "What comes to mind about the dream?" or "What comes to mind?"—about any part of the dream which the experimenter has reason to think is likely to be important.]

8. Do you see any connection be-

tween your dream (image) and the picture you saw yesterday?

9. Now describe what you saw yesterday as fully as you can. Make a drawing of what you remember seeing and continue to describe it while you draw it.

10. I'm going to expose the picture again. [The experimenter exposes the picture on the screen and lets it stay there for the rest of the session.] What connections do you see between your recall of the picture and the picture on the screen? This time you may inspect it at your leisure.

11. What connections do you see between your dream (image) and the picture on the screen? [After this general inquiry, specific questions are asked about parts of the picture.]

12. Do you see any connections between the dream (image) and anything in the room or anything you might have seen on the way down here yesterday?

13. How does this dream compare with most other dreams you've had?

14. What do you think we have been trying to get at in this experiment?

Apparatus

A slide projector with attached shutter was used. The projector was a La Belle, Model 500 with a 500-watt bulb. The shutter was an Ilex, No. 4 Acme with a range from 1 to $\frac{1}{150}$". Electronic calibration of the shutter was obtained for the exposure time of the experiment, $\frac{1}{50}$".[1] The screen used was a piece of white poster cardboard 44" x 28", and mounted on plyboard. The screen was hung with the long axis parallel to the floor. The room was approximately 9'5" x 10'8". The S sat against the long wall approximately 9' from the screen. The pre-exposure field was measured at .005 foot-candles during the daytime and .000 foot-candles at night. At the moment of exposure the illumination was .200 foot-candles. With the room lights on the illumination was at .800 foot-candles. During the pre-exposure period approximately one minute was allowed for adaptation to the new level of illumination. An electronic photometer, Model 500 with a tube D was used for all measures

[1] We had intended using the same $\frac{1}{100}$" time exposure as Poetzl and Fisher, but found by electronic calibration of our shutter (Ilex, No. 4 Acme, Ilex Optical Co., Rochester, N. Y.) that the actual time exposure when set at $\frac{1}{100}$" was $\frac{1}{50}$". (By courtesy of Charles Snyder.) These types of shutters are inexact, but our time exposure proved consistently to be around $\frac{1}{50}$". Thus, we succeeded in our aim of providing each S with about the same stimulus conditions in terms of length of exposure. This possible difference in time exposure from that of the Poetzl and Fisher experiments (none of the earlier experimenters report on exact calibration) may not be crucial, as is suggested by the work of Fisher (4), and Malamud and Linder (14), both of whom obtained the phenomenon with exposures of half a minute.

of illumination. The size of the slide on exposure was approximately 21" x 15" and appeared on the screen so that the mid-point of the slide was approximately 7½" above eye level. A black and white reproduction of our colored slide, "Inside Ancient Roman Wall," [2] can be found in our earlier article (*12*). A penciled *x*-mark approximately ½" x ½" was drawn on the screen so that it would fall at the exact center point of the picture. *S* was told that the picture would appear "just about where the *x*-mark is" and the approximate size of the exposed picture on the screen was indicated. *S*'s head was not held stationary. On exposure of the picture the *x*-mark did not obscure any objects because it fell on a dark green tree in the center of the picture.

A Measure of Recall of Preconscious Perceptions

Basic to our understanding of the Poetzl phenomenon is the assumption that more of the stimulus registers than the *S* can report to us. We shall refer to those elements of the stimulus that register in the *S*'s perceptual system and are not consciously recalled, but later appear in dreams and images, as preconscious. We say recall rather than perception because in its rigorous meaning perception refers to the experience of a stimulus present to the senses; the stimulus in our experiment is only perceptible for $\frac{1}{50}$". It would be more accurate to refer to our *S*s' reports as the recall of a quite brief perception—a recall in which memory and judgment have already played a role. The dreams and images could also be put in this same frame of reference as another mode of recall, much as we would find in experiments on the hypermnesic character of hypnotic states (*17*). The recall of the stimulus present in the dreams and images differs from the conscious recall of the stimulus in that the *S* does not have the conscious intent to recall parts of the stimulus and is usually not aware that he is recalling something already exposed to his view. We shall refer to recall present in dreams and images as *unintentional recall* in contrast to the *intentional recall* obtained immediately after the exposure of the stimulus and on the *S*'s return the following day. (See Table 1.) (By referring to recall in dreams as "unintentional" we do not imply that there are no intentions other than the conscious intent induced by our instructions.)

The *unintentional recall* in dreams and images consists of at least two different types of elements: (*a*) Parts of the stimulus already reported in *intentional recall* of the stimulus.

We shall refer to these as items *recalled again*. (*b*) Parts of the stimulus previously unreported in *intentional recall*. We shall refer to these items as instances of *preconscious recall*.

As a residual category, we should expect to find in the dreams and images items not present at all in the stimulus. We shall refer to these as *unrelated items*.

Once we view the Poetzl phenomenon as a function of recall we must design the measure of *preconscious recall* to take into account the effects of memory, both as a factor producing a decrement in the amount available to recall and a factor introducing new elements in the form of additions, distortions, assimilations, etc. According to Freud's theory of dreams, we should expect these additive and distorting effects of memory to be more prominent in dreams and images than in *intentional recall*. As a way of taking into account the transformations in perceptual structure produced by memory, we decided to identify instances of *preconscious recall* in terms of a conceptual similarity between dream and picture elements. Thus, if *S* omitted the trucks from his intentional recall of the picture but dreamed about cars, wagons, or bicycles, we would credit him with the preconscious recall of the vehicles in the picture. We assume that the meaning of the percept—in this case "mode of transportation"—is more constant than any of its visual components, which might have been affected by the particular memories of the individual.[3]

The actual score for *preconscious recall* received by the *S* represents the number of elements in his dream or image having a conceptual similarity to elements of the picture which *S* did not describe or draw in his three intentional recalls. The scores for the other measures (amount of intentional recall, number of items recalled again, and number of unrelated items) were also based upon conceptual categories rather than perceptual identities.

[3] Another approach to the problem of identifying instances of *preconscious recall* is to conceive of a preconsciously registered percept as a dissolving photographic image whose fragments become incorporated into the imagery of dreams. From this point of view, there need not be any conceptual similarity between *preconscious recall* and the unreported aspects of the stimulus but only a fragmentary perceptual identity. Fisher relied primarily on this method of identifying *preconscious recall*. There probably is a correlation between these two aspects of *preconscious recall*. In our previous illustration concerning the omitted trucks, the conceptual similarity between the dream and the stimulus is clearly that of a mode of transportation or vehicle; but there is also a perceptual identity present insofar as an *S* usually draws his wagons with wheels, fenders, etc. Our decision in favor of a measure based on conceptual similarity was a first step dictated by the need to achieve adequate reliability, which seemed more readily obtainable by judging conceptual similarities than by judging minute, subtle, and fragmentary perceptual identities.

[2] National Picture Slide Co., N. Y. C., slide #9, Italy, 80.

TABLE 1. TIME SEQUENCE OF EXPERIMENTAL
PROCEDURES

Experimental procedure	Time after exposure
Exposure of picture	0
First intentional recall	immediately following exposure
Second intentional recall	3–5 minutes
Dream (unintentional recall)	10–24 hours
Image (unintentional recall)	24–30 hours
Third intentional recall	24–30 hours

RESULTS

Reliability of the Measure of Preconscious Recall

From the *Ss'* descriptions of the picture, we made up a list of 34 major items. The major elements of the picture to which our *S*s most frequently responded were the sky, the statuary on top of the building, the "tower" (facade of the building), the building itself, the trees and shrubbery on either side of the building, the wall on which the building stood, and three vehicles on a roadway at the base of the wall. A few of the reported items were indistinct and infrequently seen and some of them were subdivisions of these principal elements. For example, the building was not only scored as a building, but windows and doors were scored separately when they were drawn and named by the *S*.

Two judges worked independently in scoring the dreams and images according to the presence or absence of the 34 items. The judge was only required to decide whether a listed item was recognizably present in the descriptions and drawings. "Judge 1" represented the pooled judgments of the two experimenters, and "Judge 2" was the statistician who did most of the analyses reported in this article. We were concerned with three scores for each *S*: (*a*) the amount of *intentional recall;* (*b*) the amount of *preconscious recall;* and (*c*) the amount *recalled again.* The reliability coefficients (Pearson r's) for these three variables were respectively: .92, .84, and .95.[4]

Establishing the Relationship of the Measure to Preconscious Perception

Like Poetzl, we found that parts of the picture which were not reported as seen later appeared in the dreams. Out of an average of about ten items appearing in dreams, three had not been reported previously (see Table 2). We also found that another source of *unintentional recall,* images, was effective in eliciting new picture items. Indeed, the images proved to be significantly more productive of *preconscious recall* than the dreams (see Table 2), a finding that raises some interesting questions beyond the scope of this paper. We have labeled these new items in the dreams (and images) *preconscious recall.* How can we show that this is a proper description?

If we could put "tracers" on the picture items analogous to radioactive isotopes, we could follow them through the mental apparatus and our task would be relatively simple. Until such psychologically radioactive isotopes are discovered, however, we must learn about the validity of the measure by bringing together evidence that it behaves in accordance with our understanding of preconscious perception. We explored hypotheses based on the assumption that preconscious perception occurred and was utilized in dreams and images.

Poetzl's "law of exclusion." Poetzl

[4] The score given each *S* by the two judges could be based on different items. We therefore determined the amount of agreement between Judge 1 and Judge 2 for all *items.* This is the same as asking how well the judges agreed on whether an *S* was drawing and describing, for example, a building, a car, or a tree. The percentage agreement between the two judges for all items, pooling all *S*s, was 68. Almost all the disagreements had to do with one judge scoring an item and another not scoring it. There were two main reasons for these disagreements. Occasionally, one judge noticed an ambiguous item and decided it did not represent the object, while the other judge decided that it did resemble a recognizable object. A more prevalent type of disagreement was essentially one of oversight by one or the other of the judges of an unambiguously represented item. The descriptions were rated more unreliably than the drawings. When oversights were called to the attention of the judges they usually immediately confirmed having overlooked the object.

stated: ". . . out of the total effect of a visual situation the once-performed part [i.e., the part which appeared in consciousness] disappears in the after-effect, but those preconsciously grasped parts, which were not yet developed, continue to be effective. If the grasp of consciousness is at its maximum, the latent after-effects in preconsciousness are at a minimum and vice-versa" (*16*). This "law" might lead one to expect that the more items the *S* reported (*intentional recall*), the smaller the number of items left to be "developed" in the dreams and the images (*preconscious recall*); similarly, the greater the *S*'s "conscious grasp" of the picture (*intentional recall*), the less the number of items *recalled again* in the dreams and images. Our findings indicated otherwise. The correlation between *intentional recall* and *preconscious recall* was not significant (− .06), while the correlation between *intentional recall* and *recalled again* was significant, but in the opposite direction from that predicted (.69, $p < .001$). Poetzl therefore was wrong if the two predictions followed from his "law of exclusion"—the amount one sees initially of a picture is unrelated to the amount one recovers of it in dreams and images; and the more one sees initially, the *more* often the same things will be seen again in the dreams and images.[5]

[5] The relationship between *intentional recall* and *preconscious recall* could be obscured by an uncontrolled factor—we have no way of knowing how much of the picture actually registered in our *Ss*' visual apparatus. There may be wide individual variations in how much a person can "receive," adding together conscious and preconscious perception. Visual acuity might be one such variable which would place a physiological limit upon how much could be perceived at any one time. An analysis which pitted the *S* against himself would control for inter-individual variations in visual acuity and other limiting physiological conditions.
The relationship between *intentional recall* and the number of items *recalled again* in dreams and images is also limited by an uncontrolled factor: on the basis of chance expectations the more things a subject saw in the picture consciously, the greater number of things he could recall again in his dreams or images. If a person reported seeing ten items, he could see again in his dreams a maximum of ten items; but a person who saw only two items could only recall a maximum of two in his dreams. In this sense, a positive correlation was "built into" our measure. If the *S* were compared with himself under the conditions of *intentional* and *unintentional recall,* the amount consciously reported would be eliminated as a source of individual variation.

TABLE 2. MEAN NUMBER OF ITEMS RECALLED IN EACH CATEGORY FOR DREAMERS AND NONDREAMERS

Category of recall	Dreamers (N = 16)	Nondreamers (N = 11)	t
Preconscious recall	2.9	4.7	2.25*
Intentional recall	9.3	9.5	0.17
Items recalled again	2.4	3.6	1.09
Unrelated items in unintentional recall	4.7	5.5	0.44

* $p \leq .05$.

In view of these negative results, one may wonder whether we are measuring the same phenomenon that Poetzl observed. There is, however, another way of testing Poetzl's "law of exclusion" made possible by our obtaining three intentional recalls of the picture, rather than one, as in previous studies. Quite frequently we noted that items not in the first recall emerged in the second or third recalls. We were led to ask whether more new items would appear in the dreams (and images) than in successive intentional recalls. Possibly Poetzl's "law" was intended mainly to emphasize that the dream is a better vehicle than *intentional recall* for *preconscious recall,* rather than to imply that the dream is the exclusive vehicle for preconscious perception. Our definition of *preconscious recall*—the appearance in dreams and image of picture items not previously reported in *intentional recall*—might therefore have been too limiting. Perhaps the new items in successive *intentional recalls* could be viewed as the feeble workings of *preconscious recall* the adverse conditions of the waking state. Similarly, perhaps the dreams and images are relatively inefficient means as compared to *intentional recall* for recalling conscious perceptions. We, therefore, restated our two predictions:

1. Each *S* should recall significantly more new items (*preconscious recall*) in his dreams or images than in his second and third efforts at *intentional recall.*

2. Each *S* should recall significantly fewer old items (*items recalled again*) in his dreams or images than in his

second and third efforts at *intentional recall*.

Both predictions were borne out by our results. For our analyses, a difference score was obtained for each individual between his performances in *intentional* and *unintentional recall*, using the first intentional recall as a baseline. In analyzing *preconscious recall*, for example, the difference was obtained between the number of new items in *unintentional recall* (dreams or images) and the number of new items present in *intentional recall* (second or third recall, or their average, depending on the particular comparison involved). These difference scores were averaged for all *S*s and the significance of the average difference tested. *Intentional recall* was a better vehicle for retaining conscious perceptions, but could not measure to the capacity of *unintentional recall* to activate preconscious perceptions. These relationships applied to dreams and images taken separately or combined. The findings support our restatement of Poetzl's assertion that dreams are prone to "exclude" conscious perceptions in favor of preconscious perceptions. And, our results indicate that this "law" can be generalized to apply to a type of "forced fantasy," the images.

Freud's hypothesis about "indifferent" perceptions. We wondered what characteristics of preconscious perceptions made it possible for them to play a role in dreams and images. In his theory of dreams, Freud identified preconscious perceptions as those which are ". . . indifferent and thus had no attention paid to them; . . . or have been rejected and have thus had attention promptly withdrawn from them" (7). In either case, these preconscious impressions "have not yet been requisitioned by waking thought-activity; and for reasons of censorship . . . [the dream process] transfers psychical intensity from what is important but objectionable to what is indifferent" (7). In this last statement Freud suggested a reason for the operation of Poetzl's "law of exclusion." Fully developed conscious perceptions cannot so easily be used as a "cover" for unacceptable thoughts.

We would predict then that preconscious perceptions, as they emerge in dreams, would be associated with a strong affective charge displaced from ideas originally intensely cathected to ideas having only a weak charge. Moreover, because these intensely cathected ideas are the derivatives of unacceptable unconscious wishes, we should expect the affective charge to be unpleasant in nature. With these considerations in mind, we predicted that *preconscious recall* would be associated with unpleasant affect.

In order to check this prediction, we devised a measure of unpleasantness using a five-point scale in which two judges rated the maximum point of unpleasantness attained (*peak unpleasantness*) within the dreams, images, and the three reports of *intentional recall*. One judge was not aware of the expected relationship between *peak unpleasantness* and *preconscious recall*. We did not get the *S*s' own rating of the dream's unpleasantness. Illustrating a low *peak unpleasantness* rating would be a dream in which there was no more unpleasant part than a man reading a book; illustrating a high rating would be a dream in which a woman was sitting in her car while terribly frightened by a hail storm.

Confirming our prediction that *preconscious recall* would be associated with unpleasant affect, we found a positive correlation between *peak unpleasantness* and the amount preconsciously recalled. Both for our group of *S*s as a whole (.57, $p < .01$) and for the dreamers (.75, $p < .001$) and nondreamers (.60, $p < .05$) the relationship was significant.

It could be argued, however, that the unpleasantness in dreams and images may not be a function of the preconsciously recalled items at all, but a function of other aspects of the dream. With this objection in mind, we correlated *peak unpleasantness* with the number of items that were *recalled again* and the number of *unrelated items* in the dreams and images. The two correlations were, respectively, .01 and .29. These nonsignificant correlations support the assumption that it was the preconsciously recalled items and not the other contents of the dreams and images that were associated with *peak unpleasantness.*

An hypothesis concerning a formal attribute of the picture. Our measure of *preconscious recall* was based on the picture's content. The *formal* attributes of the picture may also be capable of *preconscious recall*. One formal property is the angularity of line produced by the shapes of the picture items.

Each drawing made by an *S* was judged according to its *angularity* (as opposed to roundedness) on a five-point rating scale. For the drawings of the picture a reliability coefficient of .88 was obtained for two judges; the reliability coefficient for the dream and image drawings was .81.

In constructing our measure of *angularity,* we assumed that the average angularity for the group of *S*s would be a good estimate of the angularity of the picture. Statistical analysis indicated that there were no significant differences among the means for *intentional* and *unintentional recall,* a finding in line with the assumption that the mean remained a relatively constant estimate of the angularity of the picture. We can consider individual deviations from the central tendency as errors in reproducing the angularity of the picture. A "z" score was obtained for each *S* representing the difference between the angularity of his *unintentional recall* drawings and the mean angularity of the total group for *unintentional recall.* We would expect that the smaller the "z" score (i.e., the closeness with which the *S* approximates the average angularity of the drawings), the greater the amount of *preconscious recall* of picture contents. The correlation between the "z" scores and *preconscious recall* of picture contents was $- .49$ ($p < .01$). This relationship was stronger for the dreamers ($- .57, p < .05$) than the nondreamers ($- .22$).

Preconscious recall of the picture content was shown to be significantly correlated with *peak unpleasantness*; angularity should similarly be correlated. We found a significant correlation in the expected direction ($- .40, p < .05$).

As with *peak unpleasantness,* however, it could be argued that *angularity* was equally related to other aspects of recall, such as items *recalled again* and *unrelated items.* Our expectation was that there would be no systematic relationship between *angularity* and these two variables. The correlation between angularity of dream and image drawings and the number of items *recalled again* was $- .09$. The correlation between *angularity* and the number of *unrelated items* present in the dreams and images was, however, significant, $- .41$ ($p < .05$), indicating that the nonpicture items appearing in *unintentional recall* are in some way related to the accuracy with which the angularity of the picture is represented in the dream and image drawings.

In view of these findings, the angularity of the picture can perhaps be treated as an aspect of *preconscious recall.* The degree to which this angularity is rendered accurately is related to *peak unpleasantness* and items *recalled again* in the same way as the *preconscious recall* of picture contents. Our measure of *preconscious recall* relied on the conceptual similarities found in the picture content. *Angularity,* on the other hand, would extend our measure of *preconscious recall* to perceptual identities between the dream and picture.

Evidence against the Chance Occurrence of the Picture Items in Dreams and Images

One disadvantage of our measure of *preconscious recall* derives from the range of items that can be included in a conceptual category. How certain can we be that the wagons seen in the dream, for example, are not derived from a source other than the trucks in our picture? And when we note that most of the objects in our picture are commonplace, the strength of this criticism is increased. If we could, however, select from our pictures the items that occur rarely in everyday experience and demonstrate that these rare items are preconsciously recalled more frequently than would be expected by a standard of chance occurrence, we would have presumptive evidence that the source of *preconscious recall* was our picture and not an extraneous stimulus. Comparison data from the literature on extrasensory perception may help establish a standard by which to judge frequency of occurrence of percepts. Catalogues have been constructed to show how frequently an *S* will guess an unseen object, selected at random and without his knowledge. A catalogue has been made for British *Ss* (*2*), and now an unpublished version for American *Ss* by Taves (*19*) (available by courtesy of Gardner Murphy) of 8,164 items produced by 272 *Ss*.

The Taves catalogue can help us answer this question: are the items in our picture that have a low frequency of occurrence in the Taves catalogue and are presumably uncommon in everyday experience recalled preconsciously more frequently than their rare occurrence in the Taves catalogue would lead us to expect? If we find, for example, that an item in our picture which occurs only two per cent of the time in the Taves catalogue, but occurs 20 per cent of the time in our *preconscious recall,* it would seem likely that the picture and not some extraneous source contributed that item. When we selected those items in our picture which made up two per cent or less of the total number of responses in the Taves catalogue, we found that when added together those same items occurred much more frequently in preconscious recall. The chi square was at the .008 level of significance. (If we selected items which occurred .05 per cent or less of the time in the Taves catalogue, the results were even more

significant—the chi square was below the .001 level of significance.)

The comparison with the Taves catalogue supported our assumption that nonexperimental sources alone cannot account for *preconscious recall.* For future work, however, it would be helpful to compile item frequencies for dreams and images, so that the standard of chance occurrence might be more closely related to our data than the ESP catalogues.

DISCUSSION

Our findings form a pattern consistent with the assumption that preconscious perception exists and can be elicited and measured. We have developed a measure, *preconscious recall* in dreams and images, which behaves in accordance with an understanding of preconscious perception. Our *Ss'* dreams and images contain significantly more originally unreported items than do successive efforts at *intentional recall,* while retaining fewer of the originally seen parts of the stimulus. An estimate of unpleasant affect is associated with the new items appearing in the dreams and images. These two findings support Poetzl's "law of exclusion" and Freud's conception of preconscious perception as the raw material "preferred" by the dream. The finding concerning the *angularity* of the drawings indicates that the measure of *preconscious recall* can perhaps be extended to such formal properties of the stimulus as shape and position. A method was successfully applied for assessing the "chance" occurrence of picture items in dreams and images. The rare items in the picture appear significantly more frequently in dreams and images than a standard of expected chance occurrence (i.e., Taves catalogue). Taken together these four findings strengthen the conviction that Poetzl's technique for relating dreams to specific and identifiable daytime stimuli is an effective method for the experimental study of dreams.

Much more remains to be understood about the phenomenon. For example, why are the *unrelated items* unassociated with unpleasant affect? Many of these unrelated items could be day residues stemming from nonpicture sources, and as such should have unpleasant affects associated with them.

It would be desirable if a method could be devised for identifying at what point in the cognitive process the percept acquires anxiety arousing connotations and becomes available as a day residue. Customarily, it has been assumed that anxiety arousing connotations are present at the moment of perception and indeed produce the perceptual omissions or distortions. The process may be the reverse—an initial ambiguity or vagueness in the percept may make it possible for anxiety arousing meaning to adhere to it at some later point.

Lastly, the focus of our measure, preconscious perception, is upon items omitted from conscious report. But many items that were reported as seen appeared again in the dreams and images. Do items that are reported as seen appear in the dream via a different process from omitted items? A thorough study of the *S*'s initial reports may reveal many different types of items which are as likely to appear in dreams and images as initially omitted items. We have preliminary evidence that doubt surrounding items is one of the most significant indications that they will appear in dreams and images.

Among other factors to be taken into account in future experimentation, it would be naive to neglect the fact that what is reproduced in *preconscious recall* is stimulated by much more than the experimenter's picture. Frequently the contents of the experimental room and the building become part of the "experimental stimulation." There was at least one striking example of this. The masonry which was occasionally correctly located in the wall below the building in the picture could as easily refer to the walls of the office in which the experiment took place, which were of unplastered concrete blocks.

It could be argued that the *amount*
of *preconscious recall* is a function of the number of items the person reports in his dreams and images. If the *S* talks long enough he may mention many of the common items included in our picture. The simplest way to test for this is to count the number of items unrelated to the picture appearing in the dreams and images and to correlate this sum with the sum for *preconscious recall*. The correlation for the entire group was not significant. (.29).

Several methods will be profitable for future studies. (*a*) *Prediction study:* By predicting from the *intentional recall* of the picture what items will appear in a dream (or image), we have another way of exploring the phenomenon. By obtaining more than one complete description and drawing of the picture in quick succession, predictions are facilitated. We observed that changes from the first to second set of drawings and descriptions were often predictive of what would appear in the dreams and images. Predictions have been tried on an unsystematic basis with encouraging success (*12*). (*b*) *"Own Control"* method: Images can be elicited both before and after a stimulus picture is exposed. A comparison of the images produced before seeing the picture with those produced afterward can point to the influence of the picture as compared with the readiness for imagining nonpicture items. This procedure has also been tried unsystematically (*6*). (*c*) *Experimental pictures containing unusual objects:* As the Taves frequencies indicated, most of the objects in our picture are common. It is important to use a picture in which many or all of the objects are rare. The frequency with which the objects are commonly associated with each other should also be controlled. Instances of *preconscious recall* might really be commonplace associations—car and street, shrubbery and house, building and windows, etc. The new items in the dreams and images could be *associations* to the originally seen items, dream continuations of thoughts begun in a conscious state. (*d*) *Intra-individual con-*

sistency in response to a number of pictures: By using a number of different pictures for the same person we can separate effects due to individual differences from the effects produced by picture content. The other three methods can be employed with a number of pictures as easily as with one.

SUMMARY

In a pioneer investigation, Poetzl discovered that Ss dreamed about the originally unreported parts of a picture exposed tachistoscopically. If this discovery can be confirmed and a measure developed of preconscious perceptions as they appear in dreams, a new approach becomes available for the experimental study of unconscious phenomena.

A kodachrome slide was exposed at $\frac{1}{50}''$ to 27 Ss. They were asked to describe and draw the picture three times and then to record any dreams they had that night. From Ss who did not report dreams an "image" was obtained by asking them to close their eyes and describe and draw the first picture that came to mind.

High interjudge reliability (.84) was achieved for a measure of preconscious perception (*preconscious recall*) based on the number of new picture items appearing in the dreams and images. The meaning of the measure was explored by testing two hypotheses:

1. Poetzl's law of exclusion: Dream imagery "excludes" conscious perception in favor of preconscious perception.

2. Freud's hypothesis about "indifferent" perceptions: Freud asserted that the neutral or "indifferent" character of preconscious perception permitted it to serve as a "cover" for unconscious ideas which would not otherwise escape dream censorship. If preconscious perceptions were the ones that most often linked up with derivatives of threatening ideas, unpleasant affect would more likely be associated with the recall of preconscious perceptions than with other aspects of the dream.

Our data very significantly supported the Poetzl hypothesis for picture content and also for a formal attribute of the picture, its angularity. Consistent with our inference from Freud's hypothesis, we found a significant correlation of .57 between *preconscious recall* and *peak unpleasantness*.

These findings provide evidence for the Poetzl phenomenon consistent with the assumption that preconscious perception can be elicited and measured both in images and in dreams.

REFERENCES

1. Allers, R., and Telfer, I. "Ueber die Verwertung unbemerkter Eindruecke bei Associatonen." *Ztschr. f. Neurol. und Psychiat.*, 1924, *89*, 492-513.

2. Carington, W. Experiments on the paranormal cognition of drawings, III. *Proc. Amer. Soc. for Psych. Res.*, 1944, *24*, 1–107.

3. Eriksen, C. W. Perceptual defense as a function of unacceptable needs. *J. abnorm. soc. Psychol.*, 1951, *46*, 557–564.

4. Fisher, C. Dreams and perception: The role of preconscious and primary modes of perception in dream formation. *J. Amer. psychoanal. Assn.*, 1954, *2*, 389–445.

5. Fisher, C. Dreams, images, and perception: A study of unconscious-preconscious relationships. *J. Amer. psychoanal. Assn.*, 1956, *4*, 5–48.

6. Fisher, C. A study of the preliminary stages of the construction of dreams and images. *J. Amer. psychoanal. Assn.*, 1957, *5*, 5–60.

7. Freud, S. *The interpretation of dreams.* (Trans. by James Strachey) New York: Basic Books, 1955.

8. Klein, G. Discussion remarks on Charles Fisher's "A study of the preliminary stages of the construction of dreams and images." Unpublished manuscript read at the New York Psychoanalytic Society, 1956.

9. Klein, G., Spence, D. P., Holt, R. R., and Gourevitch, S. Preconscious influences upon conscious cognitive behavior. Paper read at Annual Meeting, American Psychological Association, San Francisco, 1955.

10. Lacy, O. W., Lewinger, N., and Adamson, J. F. Foreknowledge as a factor affecting perceptual defense and alertness. *J. exp. Psychol.*, 1953, *45*, 169–174.

11. Lazarus, R. S., and McCleary, R. A. Autonomic discrimination without awareness: A study of subception. *Psychol. Rev.*, 1951, *48*, 113–122.

12. Luborsky, L., and Shevrin, H. Dreams and day-residues: A study of the Poetzl observation. *Bull. Menninger Clin.*, 1956, *20*, 135–148.

13. Malamud, W. Dream analysis: Its applications in therapy and research in mental diseases. *Arch. Neurol. & Psychiat.*, 1934, *31*, 356–372.

14. Malamud, W., and Linder, F. E. Dreams and their relationship to recent impressions. *Arch. Neurol. & Psychiat.*, 1931, *25*, 1081–1099.

15. McGinnies, E. Emotionality and perceptual defense. *Psychol. Rev.*, 1949, *56*, 244–251.

16. Poetzl, O. Experimentell erregte Traumbilder in ihren Beziehungen zum indirekten Sehen. *Ztschr. f. d. ges. Neurol. und Psychiat.*, 1917, *37*, 278–349.

17. Rosenthal, B. G. Hypnotic recall of material learned under anxiety and non-anxiety producing conditions. *J. exp. Psychol.*, 1944, *34*, 369–389.

18. Smith, G. J. W., and Henriksson, M. The effect on as established percept of a perceptual process beyond awareness. *Acta Psychol.*, 1955, *11*, 346–355.

19. Taves, E. The construction of an American catalogue. *J. Amer. Soc. psych. Res.*, 1945, *39*, 151–156.

A Prisoner of War Syndrome:
Apathy as a Reaction to Severe Stress

HARVEY D. STRASSMAN, MARGARET B. THALER, AND EDGAR H. SCHEIN

PROBLEM AND METHOD

This paper is based on 201 psychiatric interviews and 80 psychological test protocols of United States prisoners of war repatriated by the Chinese and North Koreans in August 1953. Interviews were conducted within 1 to 18 days after repatriation at Inchon, Korea, and on board ship en route home. Rorschach, Thematic Apperception Test (10 cards), and Sacks Sentence Completion Test protocols were obtained on board. All subjects were selected at random and the samples interviewed and tested were subsequently found to be representative of the total population of repatriated POW's with respect to age and length of service, but the sample tested contained a higher percentage of officers than the total group. There is no overlap between the sample of

Reprinted by permission from the *American Journal of Psychiatry*, Vol. 112, 1956.

men interviewed and the sample of men tested.

We attempted to determine: (1) what types of stresses the POW's faced during their internment, (2) what their major psychological reactions to such stresses were, and (3) their reactions following repatriation.

STRESS

Since the end of the Korean conflict, a number of scientific papers and magazine articles have described the ordeal endured by the men captured (*3, 4, 5, 9, 11, 13, 14, 18*). For the purposes of this report we shall list only those constellations of stresses which we viewed as crucial in producing psychological changes. (1) *Cycles of realistic anxiety and their relief:* During combat, the early phases of imprisonment on the marches, and in the temporary camps, the men were chronically being threatened with death, physical maltreatment and nonrepatriation. Fears aroused by such threats were alleviated by concrete events or elaborate promises on the part of the captors, only to be rearoused somewhat later for reasons that seemed irrational or inconsistent to the POW's. Such sycles of fear and their relief continued for months. Hostility toward the captors was aroused by the chronic disappointment and fear but had to be suppressed at all times. (2) *Starvation, disease, and inadequate shelter:* Physical conditions, food, and shelter were so bad in the early days after capture that most men had to concentrate merely on staying alive. Making realistic plans for escape or for the future was impossible when starvation or death from dysentery, pneumonia, or exposure was an immediate and direct threat. (3) *Indoctrination at permanent camps:* In the permanent camps physical conditions improved somewhat, but the POW's then found themselves in a situation where the maintenance of American social and cultural values brought further threat, punishment, and marginal physical conditions, while the acceptance of the communistic ideology, or cooperation with the Chinese in collaborative activities, brought increases in food, physical comforts, privileges in camp, and promises of early repatriation.

REPORTED REACTIONS TO STRESSES OF IMPRISONMENT

As one listened to the POW's relating their experiences, it became apparent that one psychological reaction appeared at some time or another, with varying intensity, in almost every man. This reaction can best be described as a marked withdrawal of involvement with the current situation, accompanied by a paucity of emotion. The men exhibiting this reaction appeared to other POW's to be listless, indifferent, and completely absorbed or preoccupied with themselves. When spoken to, such men would respond rationally and appropriately, but then would quickly re-

turn to their previous state. They took no concerted action toward solving the problems of being a POW, although they could be pushed to action by a leader. Since the content of their speech and their behavior did not suggest depression or psychosis, the reaction seems best characterized by the term "apathy."

According to the accounts of POW's, the reaction occurred in almost every man at some time or another, through the degree and type of stress needed to produce it and the depth and duration of the symptoms varied greatly with different individuals. The severest "apathy" reactions occurred in the winter of 1950, when large numbers of men were captured, marched north, and quartered for weeks on end in inadequately supplied temporary camps. Disease was very prevalent at this time, and many men died of dysentery, pneumonia, or exposure; but, according to a number of observers, including American medical corps officers who were themselves POW's, some of the deaths did not seem warranted by the physical conditions of the men, who seemed to become listless and indifferent to taking care of their bodily needs. They retreated further within themselves, refusing to eat even what food was available, and eventually lay down and curled up, as if waiting for death to overtake them. The reports are emphatic concerning the lucidity and sanity of these men—they seemed simply to give up and accept the prospect of death rather than to continue fighting a severely frustrating and depriving environment.

Two things seemed to save the man close to "apathy" death: getting him on his feet doing something, no matter how trivial, and getting him interested in some current or future problem. It was usually the effort of a friend who maternally and insistently motivated the individual toward realistic goals, or the realization of ties to loved ones at home, that snapped him out of such a state of resignation.

When the men were moved into permanent camps, the food and living conditions improved greatly and the number of such severe "apathy" reactions correspondingly dropped. However, it became clear to the men soon after daily exposure to the Chinese indoctrination efforts, that the only way to keep from either collaborating or resisting to the point of eliciting punishment, was to withdraw as much as possible from any but routine interactions with either the Chinese or other POW's. Withdrawal from other POW's was fostered by the Chinese method of breaking up whatever group ties formed, by changing the membership of groups, and by segregating leaders. It was strongly reinforced by the presence in the groups of known or unknown informers which made the formation of close personal ties difficult.

Most men adopted a pattern of what they called "playing it cool," which involved being aloof, unresponsive, minimally communicative, and noncommittal on everything. They were caught in the conflict between cooperating with the Chinese to a point of arousing the suspicion and hostility of their fellow POW's, on the one hand, and resisting to a point of eliciting the hostility of the Chinese, on the other. To avoid involvement necessitated the continued suppression of most feelings, particularly hostility, and such suppression had to be maintained for 1 to 3 years for most POW's. In this adjustment there was no evidence of resignation or giving up; rather it was a chronic living from day to day without allowing oneself to become dependent on anything or anybody. The men were waiting and watching rather than hoping and planning.

This behavior was heavily reinforced by the feeling of hopelessness concerning their chances of being repatriated. Not until the prisoner of war lists had been exchanged at Panmunjon was there in the majority of men any realistic thinking about the future and returning home. Only in the last months of imprisonment did conditions become sufficiently tolerable to allow men once more to take an active interest in camp activities and to get involved with the Chinese by more active resistance to indoctrination techniques, though by this time the Chinese were making few systematic efforts to indoctrinate.

OBSERVED REACTIONS AFTER REPATRIATION AND PSYCHOLOGICAL TEST RESULTS

The behavior of most of the men immediately following repatriation was somewhat surprising in that they exhibited remarkably little enthusiasm at being free, indicated no strong desires to go home, offered no spontaneous comments on their recent experiences, and verbalized little hostility toward their captors. They seemed preoccupied, quiet, and somewhat listless, though they responded appropriately when interviewed. Their emotional expressions were qualitatively appropriate but very subdued or modulated. Anxiety was not prevalent as a symptom.

This pattern did not last very long. One could observe changes in repatriates even during the 2 or 3 days that they were at Inchon, and on board ship. Those men who were interviewed on board ship, and who had therefore been repatriated for a longer period, could generally not on casual observation be distinguished from other rotating troops. They were more realistic and positively motivated, more enthusiasm and emotion became evident, and some hostility toward the communists began to be verbalized.

This change also showed up in the incidence of the diagnosis of "apathy reaction" in the 201 interviews analyzed. Of those men interviewed within 4 days after repatriation, 28% were diagnosed as being severely apathetic, while of those interviewed within 5 to 18 days, only 7% were so diagnosed. These findings seemed to suggest that the apathetic adjustment which was appropriate to life in prison camp was quickly abandoned once the man was removed from the stressful environment.

However, the psychological test

data and closer observation indicated that underneath the more normal-appearing behavior lay considerable conflict, particularly concerning the expression of hostility. Only 24% of the test records resembled those of "normal" samples of soldiers tested in the U. S. Thirty percent of the records indicated the presence of severe emotional disturbance such as marked acting-out tendencies, strong anxiety or guilt, or trends toward thinking defects. The remaining 46% showed a marked constriction of outlook consistent with varying degrees of "apathy," but combined with strong pent-up aggressive-destructive feelings.

The records of this third group

with its wings ripped off and split open" (card 5).[1]

The content of the 800 TAT stories was grouped under the headings shown in Table 1. In the "apathy" group 98% of the stories were omissions, card description, or depicted actions involving low mood tone and little interaction. Such a high degree of constriction would be expected in only 5-10% of groups of "normal" records (6), whereas it is present in 46% of the POW records.

On the Sentence Completion items dependency needs, passivity feelings, and low mood tone were again evident. The lack of the usual varieties of affect was outstanding in the "apathy" records. Asso-

TABLE 1. RELATIVE FREQUENCY OF THEMES ON TEN TAT CARDS

	Percent of stories					
Type of story	Apathy		Disturbed		Normal	
1. Low mood tone, little interaction or activity	(114)	31.0%	(87)	36.0%	(23)	12.0%
2. Card descriptions	(237)	64.0	(36)	15.0	(9)	4.0
3. Omitted (can't think of a story)	(12)	3.0	(2)	1.0	(0)	0.0
4. Person interacts with environment to receive (eating, drinking, being helped)	(5)	1.0	(67)	28.0	(55)	29.0
5. Future action being planned	(2)	0.5	(48)	20.0	(103)	54.0
Total stories (800)	370	100.0%	240	100.0%	190	100.0%

were arbitrarily delineated from the others on the following basis: Eleven or fewer responses on the Rorschach, mere description of the TAT cards or 1- or 2-sentence remarks enumerating persons or objects, and 1- or 2-words cliches or omissions on the Sacks Sentence Completion items. The content of these records indicated considerable emotional flatness, attenuation of feelings, and an increased dependency on fantasy rather than motor outlets to relieve tension. In the instances where emotion broke through it was of an aggressive-destructive variety such as "two men pulling a man's body apart, they have torn his chest open and ripped out his heart" (to card 3 of the Rorschach), or "a bat

ciations or stories revealing special personal interests, longings, positive drives, creative fantasies, and even the usual indexes of anxiety and hositility were practically absent in this group.

Thus, psychological test data indicate that constriction and "apathy" were still evident 1-2 weeks after repatriation in almost half of the group tested, and that

[1] To check the reliability of the authors' observations, 20 randomly selected test batteries from this group were given to 3 psychologists who were asked to study the records and briefly characterize their outstanding features. The raters were told the age range and that these were service personnel. Each rater emphasized the low productivity, slow reaction time, and generally limited range of affect besides the obvious aggressive-destructive content. Each rater also pointed out that the group might appear emotionally flat and impoverished except for the latent destructive drives.

underlying the "apathy" were excessive pent-up aggressive-destructive drives.

DISCUSSION

The foregoing data indicate that one of the most prevalent reactions of POW's to severe and chronic physical and psychological stress is a withdrawal from involvement with the environment and a constriction of overt behavior and emotional responses. Such a withdrawal does not involve any disintegration of the personality or the development of a psychotic adjustment. The person can maintain his ability to respond appropriately and is capable of distinguishing internal and external reality. He is aware of his surroundings and what is going on but his own responses to it are sharply inhibited and suppressed. It appears that even when such a defensive mechanism brings the person to death, no evidence of frank psychosis can be seen. We have called this pattern of symptoms "apathy" and prefer not to think of it as an absolute state but as a syndrome which can be present in differing degrees.

"Apathy" may be confused with three other psychiatric states. In catatonic stupor there is greater regression and complete withdrawal from reality. In psychosis there are bizarre thoughts and behaviors. In depression, expressions of guilt, worthlessness, inadequacy, and preoccupation with death are verbalized. In "apathy" such verbalizations are absent, thought remains rational, and emotions remain qualitatively appropriate even when they are quantitatively attenuated.

The severity of the syndrome seems to vary with the degree of stress and deprivation in the environment, all the way from the less severe emotional withdrawal seen in POW's after repatriation (the "playing it cool" reaction), to the more severe states reported in the temporary camps which sometimes resulted in death. Severe states such as the latter have been reported by Nardini (*10*) in American prisoners of the Japanese, by Tas (*16*),

Cohen (*2*), and Bettelheim (*1*) in concentration camps, and by Greenson (*7*) in World War II Air Force personnel stationed at isolated outposts.

Greenson postulated a dynamic formulation for the development of "apathy." He states:

The personality structure of the apathetic patient indicates 2 important changes: there is evidence of a regression to a passive oral, narcissistic, libidinal level as well as a severe restriction of ego functioning. . . . In order to understand how deprivation causes apathy it is important to remember the basic needs for food and love in the human infant. In order to survive, food is necessary in the first few days of life. Love and its derivatives seem to be essential already in the first few months of life. Infants who are given the proper amount of physical care but who do not receive an adequate amount of mothering manifest the clinical picture of apathy (*12, 15*). Early in the infant's history the mother's milk serves to gratify both the instinctual and the narcissistic needs. The helpless infant is utterly dependent on some adult for its physical and mental equilibrium. . . . The need to be loved, which was essential for the infant, diminishes with the development of the superego: self-esteem then provides much of the security formerly derived from being loved. To feel loved and cared for, to be needed and wanted, are nevertheless necessary for the maintenance of self-esteem throughout life. . . . It seems that starvation plays a dual role in producing apathy. Physiologically the lack of adequate nourishment brings about a state of marasmus, the physical response to the depletion of the essential bodily needs. Psychologically, the lack of food is felt as loss of love. This loss of love then diminishes the feeling of self-esteem which results in the feeling of having been abandoned (*7*, pp. 295–297).

Captives of the Chinese indicated not only a problem with starvation, but one which came from particularly acute feelings of abandonment because they were not at all sure that they would ever be repatriated. Deliberately fostered legends of banishments to Siberia or summary execution were sufficiently prevalent that many men felt truly without hope for the future. Under such conditions some seemed to return psychologically to a state in which all power and authority were again seen as external to themselves.

Accounts that men survived if a buddy cajoled or forced them into activity and survival behavior, or the man's realization that he had ties to loved ones at home, is generally consistent with Greenson's hypothesis that the regression is to an infantile state where one gains psychological sustenance from the fantasy of being fed by the mother who gives food and love. The buddy replaces the fantasied mother and becomes a reality object who feeds and loves, while the memory of the loved ones at home represents a real object to whom one can return.

The emotional withdrawal observed in the permanent POW camps ("playing it cool") seems to differ both in degree and kind from the more severe "apathy" described above. The more adequate diet and improved living conditions reduced the threat of death from malnutrition and disease. The problem for the men was no longer merely to survive, but rather to avoid involvement in the various Chinese enterprises.

Observations of repatriates after their return from prison camp revealed this syndrome in varying degrees. In effect, many of the repatriates behaved toward members of the psychiatric and medical teams as if they were still in prison camp and must avoid showing any feeling or initiating any action. Spontaneous behavior seemed to return within a few days, but close observation suggested that it was manifested only in situations that allowed streotyped responses or feelings to emerge. The psychological test data strongly suggested that in the majority of repatriates the "apathy" defense was still operating strongly as long as 2 weeks following repatriation.

Part of the explanation for this continued utilization of "apathy" as a defense may be in the fact that the repatriation was itself highly stressful in many ways. Many POW's felt that they would not be welcome, and felt guilty for having been captured and in many cases

for having cooperated with the enemy. They were faced with resuming many of the responsibilities of life back home, yet felt 3 years "behind" in all their relationships. They had the problem of dealing with great quantities of pent-up hostility in an environment where its proper object, the Chinese captor, was no longer present. Some days after repatriation such feeling began to be verbalized. The men expressed intentions of re-enlisting to fight communism on whatever front developed, verbalizing an indiscriminate hatred of anyone or anything associated with communism; they expressed proposals such as "one ought to blow up the *Daily Worker* building," or "all commies should be deported, or sent to North Korea to see what it is like first-hand"; they were going to "slug" anyone who accused them of having collaborated, and they were going to "get the rats" who had.

None of the intentions thus verbalized sounded as if they had been thought through. They sounded immature and as if they were motivated by a kind of indiscriminate need to hit back at anything for all the frustration of the past years. Yet it was clear that the feelings of hostility were so strong that the men were afraid to express them in action, lest they get out of hand. Therefore, the best way to handle them was to keep them bottled up, and to prevent further provocation by remaining withdrawn and uninvolved with the environment.

After these men returned home, anecdotal evidence indicated that problems of expressing hostility continued, since a number of POW's got into difficulty involving indiscriminate outbursts of misdirected aggression. One may also conjecture that one reason for their strongly expressed desire to get together with other former POW's was motivated by the desire to express hostility toward the captors in fantasy, an activity which could be successful only among men who shared the same feelings. Such get-togethers would protect the repatriates from misdirected outbursts by keeping the feelings within safe social bounds. The mutual support which men could give each other in such groups by airing their respective problems and solutions also probably played a key role.

SUMMARY AND CONCLUSIONS

We have pointed out that one defensive adjustment of POW's to stress is withdrawal. If the stresses are not too severe the person will withdraw physically if possible, or in any case will refuse to allow himself to become involved with the environment to as great an extent as possible. Certain kinds of overt behavior will be inhibited and most emotional responses will be suppressed. If the environment is severely stressful and physically depriving as well, the individual may regress into a more complete withdrawal and adopt a maladaptive state of dependency in which he ceases to take care of himself even to

the point of death. We have labelled this type of defense "apathy" and distinguish it from states like catatonic stupor, or depression. "Apathy" appears not to be a single absolute reaction, but a syndrome which can vary markedly in degree. One major symptom in the syndrome is reduced or modulated affect, but only in extreme cases can one speak of true apathy or affectlessness. Other symptoms are listlessness, uncommunicativeness, lack of spontaneity, indifference, slowed reactions, lack of enthusiasm and lack of initiative. It is important to note that underlying the overt lack of emotional spontaneity may lie great quantities of pent-up feelings, and that these will continue to be a problem to the individual when he is no longer in the environment that produced the "apathy syndrome."

The apathy syndrome serves to maintain personality integration in the face of severe reality and psychological stresses.

BIBLIOGRAPHY

1. Bettelheim, B. J., Individual and mass behavior in extreme situations. *J. abnorm. soc. Psychol.*, 1943, *38*, 417.

2. Cohen, E. A., *Human Behavior in the Concentration Camp*. New York: Norton, 1953.

3. Communist War in POW Camps. *Dept. of State Bull.*, 1953, *28*, 273.

4. Dulles, A. W., Brain warfare—Russia's secret weapon. *U.S. News and World Report.*, 1953, *8*, p. 54.

5. Dulles, J. F., *Dept. of State Bull.*, 1953, *29*, 235.

6. Eron, L. D., A Normative Study of the Thematic Apperception Test. *Psychol. Monogr.*, 1950, *64;* 9 (Whole monograph).

7. Greenson, R. R., The psychology of apathy. *Psychoanal. Quart.*, 1949, *18*, 290.

8. Lifton, R. J., Home by ship: reaction patterns of American prisoners of war repatriated from north Korea. *Am. J. Psychiat.*, 1954, *110*, 732.

9. Mayo, C. W., Destroying American minds: Russians made it a science. Text of report to political committee, UN, *U.S. News and World Report*, 1953, *Nov. 6*, p. 35.

10. Nardini, J. E., Survival factors in American prisoners of war of the Japanese. *Am. J. Psychiat.*, 1952, *109*, 241.

11. Release of Anti-communist prisoners from UN camps and correspondence. *Dept. of State Bull.*, 1953, *28*, 905.

12. Ribble, Margaret, *The Rights of Infants*. New York: Columbia University Press, 1944.

13. Schein, E. H., Some observations on the Chinese indoctrination program for prisoners of war. *Psychiatry*. In press.

14. Segal, H. A., Initial psychiatric findings of recently repatriated prisoners of war. *Am. J. Psychiat.*, 1954, *111*, 358.

15. Spitz, R., Hospitalism: An Inquiry into the Genesis of Psychiatric Conditions in Early Childhood. *Psychoanal. Study of the Child*, 1945, *1*, 53.

16. Tas, J., *Psychiat. Quart.*, 1951, *25*, 629.

Diffusion and Belief in a Collective Delusion:
The Seattle Windshield Pitting Epidemic

NAHUM Z. MEDALIA AND OTTO N. LARSEN

WHILE individuals may at times lose touch with reality as their culture defines it, whole communities ordinarily do not. Yet instances are on record when this has very nearly happened: people in Mattoon, Illinois, believed for a few days in September 1945 that a "phantom anesthetist" was prowling their town (3); and a Martian invasion took place in the minds of many persons in the New York City area on October 30, 1938 (2). Russia's Sputniks may be expected to give rise to a wide variety of mass hallucinatory phenomena similar to those that followed our first H-bomb explosions in March, 1954. This paper analyzes one such reaction: the windshield pitting epidemic that broke out in Seattle, Washington, in the Spring of 1954.

Beginning March 23, 1954, Seattle newspapers carried intermittent reports of damage to automobile windshields in a city 80 miles to the north. Police suspected vandalism but were unable to gather proof. On the morning of April 14, newspapers reported windshield damage in a town about 65 miles from Seattle; that afternoon cars in a naval air station only 45 miles from the northern limits of the city were "peppered." On the same evening the first strike occurred in Seattle itself: between April 14 and 15, 242 persons telephoned the Seattle Police Department reporting damage to over 3,000 automobiles. Many of these calls came from parking lots, service stations, and so on. Most commonly, the damage reported to windshields consisted of pitting marks that grew into bubbles in the glass of about the size of a thumbnail. On the evening of the 15th, the Mayor of Seattle declared

Reprinted by permission from the *American Sociological Review*, Vol. 23, 1958.

the damage was no longer a police matter and made an emergency appeal to the Governor and to President Eisenhower for help. Many persons covered their windshields with floor mats or newspaper; others simply kept their automobiles garaged. Conjecture as to cause ranged from meteoric dust to sandflea eggs hatching in the glass, but centered on possible radioactive fallout from the Eniwetok H-bomb tests conducted earlier that year. In support of this view many drivers claimed that they found tiny, metallic-looking particles about the size of a pinhead on their car windows. Newspapers also mentioned the possibility that the concern with pitting might have sprung largely from mass hysteria: people looking *at* their windshields for the first time, instead of *through* them. On April 16, calls to police dropped from 242 to 46; 10 persons called the police on the 17th, but from the 18th on no more calls were received about the subject of pitting.

Another index of the concern with windshield pitting may be seen in the rise and decline in the combined number of column inches of windshield news in the two Seattle daily newspapers during March and April. As the figures in Table 1 shows, the story grew gradually, with only occasional reports, until April 13, reached a peak of interest on April 15, and became newspaper history after the 19th.

On June 10th, the University of Washington Environmental Research Laboratory, assigned by the Governor in April to investigate the pitting, issued its report (1). This report, prepared by a chemist, stated that there was no evidence of pitting that could not be explained by ordinary road damage: "The number of pits increases with the age and mileage of the

TABLE 1. COLUMN INCHES OF NEWS CON-
CERNING WINDSHIELD PHENOMENA IN TWO
SEATTLE DAILY NEWSPAPERS

Date	Column inches
March: 23	2.0
25	2.0
28	2.7
30	5.2
April: 13	14.0
14	22.0
15	248.0
16	210.0
17	109.0
18	62.0
19	11.0

car." The puzzling little black particles found on many automobiles turned out under analysis to be cenospheres, formed by improper combustion of bituminous coal. According to the report, "Cenospheres are not new to Seattle. They have been observed in years past and they can be observed in cars in downtown Seattle today. They are incapable of pitting windshields by impact or otherwise." In its key passage the report concludes:

Although there is a considerable body of testimony from reputable witnesses to the effect that windshields were pitted by some mysterious cause in the space of a few minutes or hours during the "epidemic," it has *not* been possible to substantiate a single one of these statements by scientific observation. Actually, the observed facts tend to contradict such statements (1).

What, then, is the origin of mass delusions such as this? What is the pattern of their initial diffusion in the community? What is the process of their disappearance? How is susceptibility to belief in the delusion distributed? Which persons are most susceptible, which least, and why? The remainder of this paper will deal with these questions. Description and analysis of this case may help us to understand not only events that the common culture labels transient delusions, but also those more persistent hallucinations that take the form of outlandish conceptions of groups other than one's own, for example, to which the culture may give an accent of reality itself.

As a population basis for these in-

quiries, telephone subscribers in Seattle listed as private individuals were selected. The universe consisted of 179,560 names, representing telephones in approximately 84 per cent of the dwelling units located in the city as of April, 1954. Three references were made to a table of random numbers to select each person for the sample. First a page in the telephone book was drawn, then a column on the page, and finally a person in the column. By this procedure, a list of 1,000 names was compiled which constituted about one-half of one per cent of the universe. In common with many samples drawn from telephone subscription lists, the present sample was biased, compared with the Seattle population as a whole, by under-representation of young people, males, and of subjects with less than eleven years of schooling. This bias may simply mean that our findings concerning the collective delusion are a conservative estimate of what transpired in the total population.

The sample was interviewed by telephone between 4 and 10 P.M. on Monday, April 19, and 964 responses were obtained. Since only 4 per cent of the sample failed

TABLE 2. A COMPARISON OF THE CHARACTERISTICS OF THE SURVEY SAMPLE AND THE TOTAL POPULATION OF SEATTLE

Characteristic	Total population* (N = 467,591)	Survey sample (N = 964)
Sex:		
Male	50.0	45.3
Female	50.0	53.5
No response		1.2
Total per cent	100.0	100.0
Education:		
0–11 years	45.2	23.5
12 years	28.2	37.9
13 plus years	23.4	29.9
No response	3.2	8.7
Total per cent	100.0	100.0
Age:		
Below 24	33.9	5.9
25–44	32.1	52.8
45–64	23.8	26.8
Over 65	10.2	8.5
No response		6.0
Total per cent	100.0	100.0

*Source: 1950 Census of Population Bulletin P-D51.

to answer, the possibility of systematic bias due to non-response is small. April 19th was chosen as the interview date because it was close enough to the peak of the pitting epidemic to make possible valid recollections of opinion during that period, yet far enough removed for attitudes relating to extinction of interest in the episode to assert themselves. Interviewers asked open-ended questions directed at the respondent's knowledge or experience of windshield damage; beliefs concerning the cause and duration of the epidemic; initial source of information; and protective action taken, if any.

EXTENT OF DIFFUSION OF PITTING NEWS

How widely diffused was the news of windshield pitting? Interviewers found that 92.6 per cent of the 964 telephone respondents answered "yes" to the question, "Have you heard of any unusual experience with windshields in Seattle recently?" The remainder 7.4 per cent (69 persons), had not heard of the windshield situation. This points to the existence in the urban community of a small core of persons who somehow remain unaware of public events despite extensive and prominent mass media coverage. Compared with the knowers, these non-knowers included fewer car owners, more females, more elderly people, and more people with relatively little education. Thus, 36 per cent of the non-knowers had no car, as against 13 per cent of the knowers; 60 per cent as against 53 per cent were females; 30 per cent as against 11 per cent were over 65 years of age, and 37 per cent of the non-knowers as compared to 22 per cent of the knowers were without a high school diploma.

PATTERN OF INITIAL DIFFUSION OF THE NEWS

To discover how news of the pitting epidemic became diffused, interviewers asked: "How did this windshield situation in Seattle *first* come to your attention?"

The answers to this question were classified into five media categories, as indicated in Table 3.

The report of channel usage suggests that the early stages of the epidemic cannot be characterized as one dominated by word-of-mouth transmission as in a highly charged rumor situation. The tabulation indicates rather that the more formal instruments of mass communication had a considerable direct responsibility in bringing the pitting phenomenon to the attention of a public: three out of four of our respondents claimed they heard the news first over some channel of mass communication.

TABLE 3. CHANNEL OF INITIAL CONTACT WITH WINDSHIELD NEWS

News source	Per cent naming source
Newspapers	51
Interpersonal	19
Radio	18
Television	6
Direct experience	6
Total per cent	100 (N = 895)

This finding of the relative role of mass media and interpersonal communication is consistent with the results of a study made a year earlier in Seattle regarding the diffusion of the news concerning the death of a prominent national political figure (4). Contrary to the findings of the latter study, however, the present results show newspapers rather than radio to be the dominant medium as the initial source of information. What factors might have contributed to the differential prominence of radio and newspapers in the two studies? First, during the windshield event two daily newspapers were being published in the city, while at the time of the story concerning the political figure only one paper was published due to a strike involving the second paper. Perhaps of greater significance are differences in the timing and the content of the news. The windshield news was local, had built up over a longer period of time, and involved a more complex content, whereas the information about the Senator's death was a single item relayed over the radio three hours before it could appear in the first edition of the Seattle newspaper. While radio is generally considered the most adaptable and efficient mass medium for rapid coverage of the news, the windshield situation suggests that for certain kinds of information, the newspapers, without benefit of a head-start, are able to far outdistance other media in giving a public its first remembered contact with the news.

A closer look at the initial pattern of diffusion shows the role of the *newspaper* was about the same for men as for women (52 versus 51 per cent); that women were more apt than men to learn the news via the *radio* (21 versus 15 per cent) and *television* (8 versus 4 per cent); and that men claimed to have *directly observed* damage more frequently than women (8 versus 3 per cent) and also heard the news first via *interpersonal channels* more frequently than women (21 versus 17 per cent).

When these distinctions are qualified by three levels of educational attainment we find that men with college education learned the news first through newspapers to a significantly greater extent (60 per cent) than did any other educational sub-group of either sex (P < .05 for all comparisons);[1] that women of the lowest level of education heard the news first on television to a significantly greater extent (15 per cent) than did any other subgroup; that interpersonal communication did not vary significantly within either sex by education; and that men on the lowest educational level claimed direct experience with pitting significantly more often than any other group (12 per cent). This latter fact may reflect a more personal interest taken in cars by men than by women, either for occupational reasons or in conformance with the culture of the male sex role. We may also speculate that the activities of this latter group of persons,

along with the performance of the mass media, were important in building up the early stages of the epidemic. Having heard on the morning of April 14th that a town 65 miles north had been "peppered," and on that same afternoon that the naval station 45 miles from the city had been hit, men of relatively low educational attainment, particularly bus or truck drivers and parking lot or filling station attendants, may have been looking for pits on the night of April 14th. It may be hypothesized that such men were especially susceptible to belief in pitting, motivated to relay the story to others, and in a good position to do so.

DEFINING THE SITUATION: PATTERNS OF BELIEF

Definition of the windshield pitting situation presents a case of public response to highly contradictory news stimuli. For about three weeks prior to April 15, the police of communities north of Seattle were principally responsible for defining the situation—mainly in terms of vandalism. As police were unable to discover evidence of vandalism, however, the news emphasis changed to the theme of "mystery": *Life* magazine talked of "ghostly little pellets" in its report from a city north of Seattle on April 12; the *Seattle Times* referred to "elusive B-B snipers" on the evening of April 13. When the flood of telephone calls came to the Seattle police between the evenings of the 14th and 15th of April, the situation clearly called for redefinition. News media gave widest publicity to the redefinition supplied by the mayor of Seattle who declared, "The damage to windshields is no longer a police matter," and went on to refer to the Eniwetok H-bomb tests as a possible cause.

Concurrently newspapers began to quote physical scientists, engineers, and automobile glass "experts," as well as police, on the nature and the origin of the pitting. Content analysis of the statements made by these various defining agents shows that the physical scientists, all from the Uni-

[1] Throughout this paper "significant" refers only to differences beyond the .05 level of confidence.

versity of Washington, gave about equal emphasis to ordinary road damage, hysteria, and to air pollution from industrial waste. Engineers, mostly from Boeing Aircraft, without exception propounded some physical cause for the unusual pitting activity; included among these were supercharged particles from the H-bomb explosion, a shifting in the earth's magnetic field, and extremely high frequency electronic waves from a giant new radio transmitter located near Seattle. Automobile experts divided their opinion between atomic ash and vandalism. The police, subsequent to April 15, gave the widest and most contradictory array of causes: atomic ash; air pollution from industrial waste; atmospheric conditions (unspecified); a chemical agent of uncertain origin; ordinary road damage; hysteria; something other than ordinary road damage; and, most frequently, vandalism.

Under these circumstances, what beliefs did our sample of telephone subscribers hold? We asked the question, "What do you think caused this?"—"this" referring to whatever the respondents said they had heard was happening to windshields. Responses yielded the following categories: *Believers, Undecided, Skeptics,* and *Refusals,* distributed as indicated in Table 4.

Four days after the peak presentation of the windshield news in the press, the majority of the respondents in our sample were *Believers.* That is, they were positive in their contention that there had been unusual pitting activity and that this had been caused by some unusual physical agent. The single explanation most frequently mentioned was the H-bomb. Approximately one of three (31 per cent) of the Believers attributed windshield pitting to the after-effects of thermonuclear explosions that had taken place earlier in the Pacific testing grounds. Other explanations offered by the Believers included vandalism, cosmic rays, chemicals, and meteorites.

What were the characteristics of the

TABLE 4. CLASSIFICATION OF RESPONDENTS BY THEIR DEFINITION OF THE CAUSE OF THE SITUATION *

Classification of response	N	Per cent
Believers: Unusual damage caused by unusual physical agent	450	50
Undecided: Had heard many explanations but, even after probing, were unwilling to suggest one most likely cause †	227	26
Skeptics: Dubious of anything other than people noting ordinary road damage	187	21
Refusals: Would not respond to or even consider this particular question	22	3
Totals	886	100

* 69 non-knowers and 9 knowers for whom some background data (age, sex, etc.) are missing are not included in this table.

† Includes 33 respondents (3.7 per cent of total *N*) who gave only a "negative cause"—e.g., "not vandalism"—as explanation of pitting.

persons classified as Believers, Undecided, Skeptics, and Refusals? The four groups did not differ significantly in age distribution, but were distinguished by some significant differences in autmobile ownership, sex, and education.

Automobile ownership was significantly higher among the "Skeptics" than in any other group: 94 per cent ownership versus 84, 84, and 85 per cent. This fact would seem to dispose of the possibility that the skepticism expressed in denying any "unusual" windsheld activity might stem from the lack of possible personal involvement in the threat situation.

The sex distribution of the respondents in the four categories is reported in Table 5. Men and women were about equally apt to be "Believers" and about equally apt to refuse answers to the questions concerning cause of the pitting phenomenon. Men were significantly more skeptical than women, however, while there was a greater but not significant proportion of women in the "Undecided" category than men.

TABLE 5. CLASSIFICATION OF CAUSE BY SEX

Causal category	Male	Female
	(Per cent)	
Believers	49	52
Undecided	20	29
Skeptics	28	15
Refusals	3	4
Total per cent	100	100
	(N = 412)	(N = 474)

The effects of education by sex on the presumed causes of pitting were also determined. When three levels of education (less than high school graduate, high school graduate, some college) are introduced into the analysis, there is a fairly consistent reduction of the proportion of "Undecided" and "Refusals" in both sexes, with an increase in education suggesting a greater decree of opinion structuring. There was also a consistent increase in skepticism among both sexes with an increase in education. The change was particularly marked among men, only 10.2 per cent of whom at the lowest level of education were Skeptics while 34.3 per cent of the men at the highest level of education were in this category. The corresponding range for women is from 11.5 to 16.4 per cent.

A contrasting trend develops between men and women "Believers" when education is considered. With increasing education, the proportion of male "Believers" decreases but the proportion of female "Believers" increases. Thus, 59.3 per cent of the males at the lowest level of education, 48.0 per cent at the middle level, and 40.7 per cent at the college level are "Believers." The corresponding figures for the females are 49.2, 53.3, and 54.8 per cent.

What conclusions do these trends indicate concerning susceptibility to mass illusion? The results are not entirely consistent with the findings of two widely quoted studies in mass hysteria and illusion, "The Phantom Anesthetist of Mattoon" (3), and "The Invasion from Mars" (2). These studies relate belief in collective delusions to an individual psychological factor, suggestibility; and suggestibility in turn to low educational level. The Mattoon research draws an additional inference, that women are more suggestible than men (3). In the present instance, we have seen that, while there was a higher proportion of "Skeptics" among men, there was no significant difference between the proportions of men and women who *believed* in the occurrence of unusual windshield pitting; moreover, in terms of "Believers," the single most "suggestible" group among our respondents consisted of men of low educational level. Finally, education appears to function quite differently for men and women insofar as their susceptibility to collective delusion is concerned. The concomitant of increasing educational level among women was a simple decrease in the number of "Undecided," with a consequent increase in the positively structured but contradictory categories of "Believer" and "Skeptic." The concomitant of increasing educational level among men, on the other hand, was a reduction in both the "Undecided" and the "Believer" categories, increasing thereby only the number of "Skeptics." These facts suggest that the operation of sex role and formal education in susceptibility to collective delusion is more complex than has been hitherto suspected.

EXTINCTION OF INTEREST IN THE WINDSHIELD PITTING EPIDEMIC

Why did interest in the windshield pitting epidemic decline, and decline so rapidly, after the peak of the pitting news on April 15? What implications does this decline suggest for the disappearance of mass delusions generally?

Johnson, in the Mattoon study cited above, draws three conclusions about the extinction of interest in mass delusions. Referring to the mushrooming concern over the "phantom anesthetist," he writes that "such acute outbursts are necessarily self-limiting." (3). The reason given for the self-limiting nature is that "the bizarre details which captured the public imagination at the beginning of the episode became rather ridiculous when studied more leisurely." Finally, Johnson claims that the critical attitude induced by reflection increases and spreads; in consequence "it is proper to say that the wave of suggestibility in Mattoon left a wave of contrasuggestibility in its wage." (3). According to this view, extinction of interest in mass delusions is rationalistically tied to more accurate perception of reality which eventuates ultimately in a wave of contrasuggestibility.

Contrary to Johnson's conclusions, the present study suggests that "acute outbursts" of mass delusion are not necessarily self-limiting. Interest and belief in a phenomenon for which no scientific basis can be found may well persist for periods of time even in a culture presumably committed to science as the ultimate test of reality. Residents of the area north of Seattle maintained a high level of interest in the mystery windshield pitting for almost a month before the pitting reached Seattle. Similarly, sightings of "flying saucers" are reported frequently enough to require a continuing agency for their investigation in the Air Force.[2]

Why then did concern over windshield pitting in Seattle decrease so markedly only four days after the peak outburst of interest expressed in the press and in the telephone calls to the police? The explanation does not seem to lie in a correction of the delusion by scientifically more accurate reality perception, for, as we have shown, on April 19, a majority of our respondents still believed that some physical agency had caused widespread damage to windshields in Seattle; only 21 per cent, the "Skeptics," committed themselves to the conclusion that the whole episode was based on illusion. These facts do not support the connection between interest and belief postulated by Johnson;

[2] For an account of "flying saucer" research carried on in the Air Force "Project Blue Book," see (5, 6).

for they show that *interest* in a mass delusion may very well decline, while *belief* in the delusion persists.

As an alternative hypothesis, we suggest that two considerations may have accounted for the precipitous decline of interest by the press and by the public in the Seattle pitting episode. The first is that the pitting became assimilated to a cause itself regarded as highly transient or episodic: the hydrogen bomb tests at Eniwetok earlier in March. In such a context it became meaningful for people to think that the pitting might have occurred in the space of a few hours or minutes on April 15 rather than over a longer period of time.

The second consideration is that the perception of windshield pitting, and the magical activities associated with this perception, succeeded in bringing to a focus and in reducing diffuse anxieties that may have served to heighten susceptibility to the delusion in the first place. The widespread association of windshield pitting with the H-bomb explosions points again to these as possible sources of the anxiety. During March and April, Seattle papers carried intermittent reports of the tests and the fall-out, hinting darkly at doom and disaster, illustrated by the following headlines:

"3 H-Bomb Victims Face Death: Doctor Reports on Fishermen."
"Witness Says: Hydrogen Test Out of Control."
"Disaster Plan Result of H-Bomb Study."
"AEC Discloses Blast Amid Mounting Concern."
"Atomic Scare Ties Up Japan Fishing Fleet."

The windshield pitting epidemic may have relieved diffuse anxieties built up by this situation in three ways. First, it focused these anxieties on a narrower area of experience, automobile windshields. Phenomena that had long passed unnoticed in the periphery of awareness—cenospheres, or small sooty particles collecting on cars; nicks and pits in windshields—now became charged with new significance.

Second, the pitting epidemic may have loosened the tensions growing out of fixation on an inevitable coming blow: something was bound to happen to *us* as a result of the H-bomb tests—windshields became pitted—it's happened—now *that* threat is over. Third, the magical practices which accompanied the epidemic—for example, calling the police, appealing to the Governor and President for help, covering windshields and cleaning them—all these activities served to give people the sense that they were "doing something" about the danger that threatened.

Extinction of the windshield pitting epidemic, following this interpretation, oc-curred not because of a wave of contrasug-gestibility, but rather because the pitting, as a new, non-institutionalized anxiety-provoking situation, was given symbolic recognition and magical control. To the extent that this type of hypothesis is supported by further research, it follows that to correct mass delusions one should not wait confidently for a wave of contrasug-gestion to gather force. Nor does subsiding public concern with a delusion indicate a rejection of it in favor of reality. Reality itself will be given a magical definition so long as the anxieties that the magic symbolizes are not or cannot be dealt with through rational control.

REFERENCES

1. Bovee, H. H. *Report on the 1954 Windshield Pitting Phenomenon in the State of Washington.* Mimeographed, Environmental Research Laboratory, Univ. Wash., June 10, 1954.

2. Cantril, H. The Invasion from Mars. In, Swanson, G. E., Newcomb, T. M., and Hartley, E. H. (edit.), *Readings in Social Psychology.* New York: Holt, Rinehart and Winston, 1952, 208–219.

3. Johnson, D. M. The Phantom Anesthetist of Mattoon, in Swanson, G. E., Newcomb, T. M., and Hartley, E. H. (edits.), *Read-ings in Social Psychology.* New York: Holt, Rinehart and Winston, 1952, 198–207.

4. Larsen, O. N. and Hill, R. J. Mass Media and Interpersonal Communication in the Diffusion of a News Event. *Amer. Soc. Rev.* 1954, *19,* 426–433.

5. Mandel, S. The Latest on the Flying Saucer. *The Sat. Rev.,* 1956, *39,* 23–29.

6. Ruppelt, E. J. *The Report on Unidentified Flying Objects.* Garden City, New York: Doubleday, 1956.

3 | The Employment of Learning Concepts in the Study of Behavior Disorders: Operant Conditioning and Stimulus Generalization

Concepts from one area of psychological research are often used as explanatory devices in other areas. Learning theory developed primarily in laboratory experiments with lower organisms as subjects.

Three of these articles use *operant conditioning* techniques. Operant conditioning is a type of conditioning in which the response is *emitted* by the subject, as contrasted to classical Pavlovian conditioning where the response is *elicited* by some stimulus. Operant conditioning has been investigated extensively by the use of rats and pigeons in "Skinner boxes." For learning to occur, it is essential that the presentation of a reward follow immediately the proper performance of the response to be learned. Vast amounts of data have been collected from lower organisms by this and other methods.

From such research, general principles of behavior may be derived and either tested with human subjects or employed in the description of human conduct. The widespread interest in this research strategy is reflected in the large number of papers now appearing in the scientific literature directed toward clarifying the acquisition of erratic or pathological behavior. The conclusion should not be drawn, however, that the science of behavior pathology can be reduced to a few learning principles. Behavior may be analyzed simultaneously at different levels, and the appropriate level is determined by the kinds of questions raised by the experimenter.

In the first paper Lindsley applies the free-operant conditioning method to the study of psychotic patients. His paper is a plea for more objective behavioral research with psychotic patients. Emphasis is placed on the paucity of objective data available on psychotic subjects. The sensitivity and usefulness of the free-operant technique is indicated by the agreement found between conditioning records and the subject's psychotic episodes. Use of operant conditioning does not commit one to any particular theory of psychosis. Lindsley prefers first to collect as much data as possible in a "naturalistic" setting before attempting to advance such a theory.

72

The paper by Isaacs, Thomas, and Goldiamond describes an application of operant conditioning to produce a specific result—verbalization in two hospitalized mute psychotics. By controlling the simple renforcement of chewng gum the experimenter was able, after several sessions, to produce verbal behavior in two subjects who had been mute for a number of years.

This paper introduces another important concept in operant conditioning that has many implications for research and for understanding the acquisition of pathological symptoms: shaping behavior. This term describes the method of application of reinforcement. Reinforcement is applied to a particular response only if part of the response is in the direction desired by the experimenter. In this manner—a sort of approximation —a response that was originally not in the subject's behavioral repertoire may be produced by selective reinforcement.

Salzinger and Pisoni also employ operant conditioning in their study of schizophrenics. Such patients have been typically described as being "flat" in affect. The experimenters chose, therefore, affective verbal report as the response class to reinforce. By employing verbal agreement as a reinforcer, the experimenter was able to increase the number of affect responses given by schizophrenics in a series of interviews. Degree of "flatness" of affect is usually a prognostic sign, hence it might be possible to utilize the rate and/or speed of conditioning as a prognostic indicator.

Of special significance is the demonstration that experimental techniques such as are employed in the learning laboratory can be effectively used to study the clinical interview situation.

The article by Knopf and Fager applies two important concepts of learning theory—drive and stimulus generalization—to hypotheses concerning expected differences among neurotics, psychotics, and normals. The potential explanatory power of the concept of stimulus generalization when applied to behavior disorders is great. The essence of most behavior disorders is the failure to discriminate properly among stimuli. The authors expect that because of the assumed higher drive in neurotic and psychotic groups, they will exhibit higher stimulus generalization than controls.

This experiment is an example of a type frequently found in literature dealing with behavior pathology. Certain theoretical notions having been validated in the laboratory, an attempt is made to identify the presence of the variables manifesting these concepts in disordered persons, and differential predictions are made on this basis.

The final paper in this section presents a descriptive analysis of the behavior of prisoners of war under the Communist "brainwashing" program. Much recent publicity concerning the technique of "brainwashing" has tended to consider it a mysterious and effective form of scientific manipulation. Farber, Harlow, and West analyze the process as reported in many recent investigations and suggest that certain explanatory principles from learning theory, plus the realistic facts of the situation, can adequately explain the behavior of individuals in war prisons where indoctrination programs are strenuously implemented. It has not been asserted that this formulation is a model for a general statement of the origins of behavior disorders. One should note, however, the probable resemblance of the stressful setting of the prisoner-of-war camp to the stressful setting of persons who suffer psychotic withdrawal symptoms.

Characteristics of the Behavior of Chronic Psychotics as Revealed by Free-Operant Conditioning Methods

OGDEN R. LINDSLEY

DURING the last sixty years experimental psychology has made great progress in objective behavioral measurement. The most sensitive, objective, and sophisticated of these methodological developments are those of B. F. Skinner and his associates (3, 12, 15). These methods are generally described under the term "free-operant conditioning." The purpose of this research is to attempt to modify and make clinically relevant the methods of free-operant conditioning in order to produce medically useful, objective laboratory measures of the psychoses.

BEHAVIORISTIC APPROACH TO PSYCHOSIS

The general approach to the analysis of psychosis that we are using is behavioristic. Naturalistic or behavioristic approaches to mental illness are rare in psychiatry today, even though the word "behavioral" occurs in many titles and programs. The behaviorist uses behavior as the final criterion of behavior and does not resort to mentalism or physiologism as his final criterion of knowledge or relevance.

At earlier times, naturalistic approaches (2) were briefly tried by men like Kraepelin (5), Pavlov (10), and even earlier by our own Benjamin Rush (11). It is my conviction that early attempts at a behavioristic approach to psychiatry suffered from a lack of popular appeal and sound laboratory techniques of behavioral measurement. I am also convinced that today, even though the approach still suf-

Reprinted by permission from *Diseases of the Nervous System*. Monograph Supplement, Vol. XXI, February 1960.

fers from popular appeal, methods which demonstrate its superiority over introspective approaches are available.

Skinner (13, 14) and Ferster (4) have discussed some of the implications of a behavioral approach to psychiatric problems. However, without objective data such discussions are at best scientific extrapolations, plans or philosophies. The proof of the pudding is not the logical nature of the plans, but the knowledge and control of behavioral deviation produced by research based upon such plans.

To a behaviorist a psychotic is a person in a mental hospital. If psychosis is what makes, or has made this person psychotic, then psychosis is the behavioral deviation that caused this person to be hospitalized, or that is keeping him hospitalized. Looked at from this point of view, very few psychotics are at this moment behaving psychotically. Neither is there any assurance that they will behave psychotically when we wish to evaluate or to sample their behavior in a brief test conducted at irregular intervals. In fact psychosis, defined in terms of the behavior that hospitalizes a person, is most often highly infrequent.

Most patients are hospitalized because the time of occurrence of their infrequent psychotic episodes cannot be predicted. Since the occurrence of these episodes cannot be predicted, the patient must be continuously hospitalized to insure that such episodes do not occur outside of the hospital. Also, many currently hospitalized patients behave psychotically only when they go home. Even though relatively normal in the hospital, they continue to be hospitalized because there is no safe place to send them. There are other patients who once behaved psychotically, but have become institutionalized and do not wish to leave the hospital, and still others who have no home to return to. For these reasons we should not expect all the patients in a mental hospital to exhibit psychotic behavior at any given moment.

Therefore, a few patients should behave relatively normally on all behavioral tasks. In fact, any behavioral measure that clearly separates all hospitalized psychotics from all unhospitalized individuals is merely a correlate of hospitalization and no better a measure of psychosis than the absence of hospital keys, neckties, or some other side effect of the way we care for psychotics.

If we wish to maximize our chances of measuring psychosis, we should evaluate the behavior of patients at the time they are actually doing what they are hospitalized for occasionally doing. This means that we should study our patients long enough to capture a psychotic episode in one of our experimental observation sessions. For, at that moment we would be surely measuring the behavior of a psychotic at the time he is behaving psychotically. This demands that our experimental rooms and recording devices must be indestructible, so that they will not be rendered inoperative by the bizarre behavior of any patient when he has a psychotic episode. Very few of the previously used measurement devices are capable of measuring the behavior of patients while they are behaving maximally psychotic. In this sense the earlier devices are extremely limited.

SELECTION OF PATIENTS AND HABITAT

If we wish to investigate a new phenomenon we should select the ideal conditions for observing it. We should maximize its amplitude and frequency of occurrence and minimize any changes in these properties, whether spontaneous or

caused by agents other than those we can manipulate for investigational purposes. This means that the acutely ill psychotic is a poor research risk. For there is a high probability that his psychosis will change in degree or type while we are endeavoring to analyze it. Also, the natural habitat of the acute psychotic is a dynamic environment in which therapy is maximized and research design usually destroyed. The admissions unit is a model of confounded, rather than isolated and controlled behavioral variables.

However, the chronic psychotic has a maximized form of psychosis and the lowest probability of spontaneously changing during the course of study. Also, the chronic psychotic's natural habitat (the back wards of large state hospitals), although far from the research ideal of full experimental control, more closely approximates this research ideal of full control than does an admissions ward. Moving chronic patients to admissions units or research wards, takes them from their natural habitat which reduces the probability that their psychosis will remain stable, and places them in an environment full of uncontrolled behavioral variables.

Therefore, in order to maximize our phenomenon and its stability we selected a group of approximately 50 chronic psychotics for intensive investigation, who would continue to live on the back wards in their natural habitat. They were hospitalized a median of 18 years, insuring that their behavioral deviations were maximum and stable. Males were selected to eliminate any behavioral fluctuations that might be correlated with menstrual cycles. Patients were selected independently of psychiatric diagnosis in order to eliminate any theoretical bias, and to approach our subject matter with a maximized degree of freedom, limited only by our methods of observation and creative ability in adopting the methods to the measurement of clinically relevant behaviors. The clinical relevance was sought in clinical practice and experience, rather than in formal theory or diagnosis.

RESEARCH DESIGN

The research design is frankly Darwinian rather than Newtonian. It is our feeling that there is not enough experimental data on the behavior of psychotics in finely controlled situations to draw exact and meaningful generalizations at this time. Since the behavioral properties of psychosis are highly individual, each experiment must be conducted in such a fashion that each patient serves as his own control. We must not have to resort to the behavior of any other individual in order to determine the significance of the effects of any agent upon the behavior of our experimental subject.

The experimental observations are conducted in continuous experimental sessions of one or more hours duration each week-day, until we have exhausted our ability to obtain further important experimental information concerning the behavioral abilities and symptoms in a given patient. Although psychosis is clinically known as an oscillating, dynamic process, and patients are clinically known to be timid, afraid and nervous in novel situations, the majority of previous experimental studies of psychosis have investigated psychotics in novel situations. It is important to remember that we often evaluate a psychotic in 15 minutes, a secretary in one month, and an executive in one year. It seems to me that we might do better by reversing this order—at least until we develop reliable and exact methods of evaluation.

In our own research, we have found that the behavior of many psychotics is modifiable by manipulating properties of the immediate physical environment. However, their behavior is so slowly modified that experimental manipulation and observation must be continued over a period of years in order to disclose such slowly developing laws of psychotic behavior. Shorter periods of observation would show no lawful modification in the patient's behavior, and lead us to conclude that it was not modifiable, and the law of psychotic behavior would remain hidden.

Intensive investigation of single psychotics is the only way that a number of different behavioral deficits may be catalogued with respect to individual psychotics in attempts to locate and define syndromes of behavioral deficits which could define sub-types of psychosis.

Then again the currently used therapeutic variables (tranquilizing drugs, insulin, and psychotherapy) appear to take weeks, months and even years to reach their maximum effect. Experiments must be conducted over a period of years in order to provide a continuous measure of the effects of such variables on the behavior of individual patients. This intensive and continuous study of single individuals also permits a comparison of the effects of several different therapeutic agents upon the same individual as the experimental case history grows. I know of no other way to adequately control for placebo effects without confounding the results with individual variability in reaction.

APPARATUS AND TECHNIQUES

The theoretical and historical background and the modifications of the method of free-operant conditioning for use with chronic psychotics, including its advantages and disadvantages have been discussed elsewhere (6, 16). In brief, a volunteer patient is conducted, or conditioned to approach a small six-foot square experimental room. In this room there is only a chair and a manipulandum panel on one wall. On the panel is a plunger that can be pulled and a small aperture through which small objects can be automatically presented. Such a controlled environment can be used to measure the simplest operant or "volitional" behavior known—pulling a plunger for an unconditioned reinforcement or reward.

However, by manipulating the objects or events used as reinforcers, a wide variety of different motivations or "interests" can be studied (7). By manipulating the contingencies of these reinforcers upon the plunger-pulling responses, a wide variety of discriminations and other behavioral processes can be studied. For example, with such a simple experimental environment, motivations ranging from food to social altruism, and discriminations ranging from simple visual to time estimation and complicated concept formation can be studied (8).

By permitting visual communication between such rooms (opening windows at the sides of the room) social interaction from the most primitive facilitation and imitation to complicated leader-follower relationships in cooperation and

free-operant conditioning can be modified to the objective and exact measurement of behaviors as clinically relevant as vocal hallucinatory symptoms in chronic psychotics.

BEHAVIORAL RECORDS

Since the response recorded by the operation of the manipulandum is free to occur at any moment during the experimental session, maximum information is obtained if responses are recorded as they occur in time. Graphs of the distribution of the responses in time are automatically made on cumulative response recorders. The operation of such a recorder is schematically shown in Figure 1. The paper

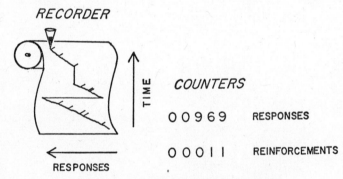

Figure 1. Schematic diagram of operation of a cumulative response recorder. Described in text.

competition teams can be controlled and objectively measured. (1)

By changing the form of the manipulandum or plunger, a wide variety of different response topographies ranging from simple manual to complex vocal responses can be studied. If the manipulandum is carefully designed, peripheral response properties (fatigue, frequency limitation, etc.) can be overcome and will not confound the interpretation of the data.

By making intelligent and creative changes of the types described above, and making these one at a time so that variables are not confounded, the method of

is driven under the pen at a constant rate. The pen makes one small movement up the paper when each response is made. In this way a graph of cumulated responses plotted against time is automatically produced. The slope of the pen tracing gives an index of the rate of response. If the slope is almost vertical, the rate is high and even. If the slope is horizontal, no responses were made. Events, such as the presentation of reinforcements can be marked on the record by a downward deflection of the pen. After 500 responses have been made, the pen is automatically reset from the top to the bottom of the paper where it is ready to draw another segment of a cumulative response record.

Clinical records of the patients' behavior on the wards and in psychiatric and psychological evaluations are periodically made in the usual manner. Also, the patients can be observed within the experimental rooms through a hidden periscopic system. Important changes in their symptoms and other demeanor are written down and used for correlation with the operant response records. The non-operant records

CHARACTERISTICS OF THE OPERANT BEHAVIOR OF CHRONIC PSYCHOTICS

The first and most striking characteristic of the free-operant behavior of chronic psychotics is the extreme degree of behavioral debilitation found in the majority of patients. For example, approximately 90% of the patients are unable to respond normally in the simple situation described above. Also surprising is the unpredictability of the patients' operant abil-

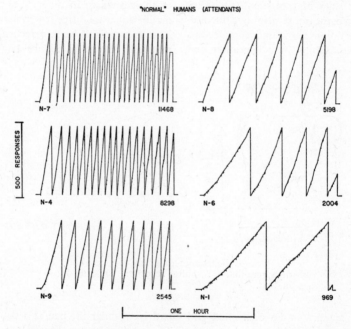

Figure 2. Cumulative response records for six unhospitalized normal adults, responding on a one-minute variable-interval schedule of intermittent reinforcement with five-cent coins. Each record is of the fifth hour of responding on this schedule. Under each record is printed the number of the subject on the left, and on the right the number of responses made during the hour.

are useful in making plans for developing new manipulanda to bring clinically relevant response topographies out on an electrical switch for automatic recording and programming. The non-operant records are also useful for correlation with the operant records in demonstrations of the validity and meaning of the operant data.

ity from observations of the patients' ward behavior and general appearance. Remember, that we are talking here of dynamic behavioral ability—the ability to develop and to maintain new behavioral repertories, as distinguished from the behavioral repertoire that a patient may have acquired before he became ill.

For example, Patient No. 48 has a much greater current behavioral repertoire, but a much lower current behavioral modifiability than Patient No. 46. The first patient was an acute depressive and now is a chronic schizophrenic with an operant response rate (candy reinforcement on a 1'VI schedule) of zero responses per hour. The second patient has always been a psychotic idiot, but he now

even rates of response on variable-interval schedules of reinforcement. Figure 2 shows six records of normal humans responding on that schedule for five-cent coins as reinforcers. Note that although reliable individual differences in rate of response exists, all the rates are above 800 responses per hour and are relatively even. These reliable individual differences in rate of response have not been extensively studied,

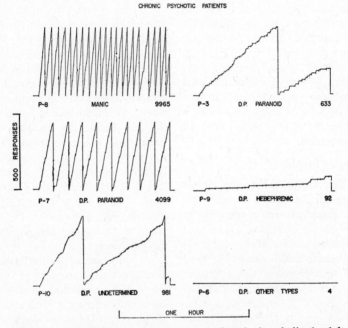

Figure 3. Cumulative response records for six hospitalized adult chronic psychotics, responding on a one-minute variable-interval schedule of intermittent reinforcement for small assorted pieces of candy. Each record is of the fifth hour of responding on this schedule. Under each record is printed the number of each patient to the left, the most recent psychiatric diagnosis, and to the right the number of responses made during the hour.

has an operant response rate of over 1,000 responses per hour and he can form primitive counting discriminations. Both patients are currently untestable by psychometric procedures.

1. *Low, Erratic Operant Response Rates.*

Normal humans and lower organisms respond at moderately high (above 800 responses per hour) and remarkably

and could probably be related to personality differences in preferences for certain work tempos. Perhaps they might be even related to accident proneness, with the high rate person going through doors before he opened them, and the low rate person going through doors after he had closed them.

Figure 3 shows six records of chronic psychotics responding on the variable-interval schedule for candy reinforcement. Note that the majority of the patients respond intermittently. Aproximately 50% of those patients with a normally high number of responses per hour show an abnormally high number of pauses in responding greater than ten seconds. During these pauses patients that have readily observable psychotic symptoms can be observed displaying these symptoms.

Summarizing the debilities in simple operant responding on a one-minute variable interval schedule of intermittent reinforcement with candy, we find that only 20% of our unselected group of 50 chronic psychotics are capable of responding at the normal rates above 800 responses per hour; 50% of these, or only 10% of the total group of patients responded at normally high and even rates of responses, with no pauses in their responding greater than 10 seconds in duration.

II. Psychotic Incidents

We have termed these small pauses in responding on a schedule of reinforcement which produces even responding in normals, "psychotic incidents." They have been successfully quantified by using, 1) automatic counters which record the total number of inter-response times greater than ten seconds that occur in each experimental session, and 2) automatic time indicators which record the total amount of time spent in inter-response times greater than ten seconds. These two quantities give a record of the number and total duration of psychotic incidents within a given experimental session. The average duration can be computed from the two. These measures correlate highly with clinical measures of ward behavior, and ward assignment, and with the ability to work in hospital industry (9). However, they do not correlate with psychiatric diagnosis nor with years of hospitalization. Therefore they indicate the general degree of psychosis or psychotic debilitation rather than the presence of a particular form of psychosis from which a given patient suffers. In other words, these measures have the dis-

advantage of being non-specific measures of the different types of psychosis, but the distinct advantage of permitting a direct comparison of the effects of a given therapy on the severity of psychosis in several different patients with different types of psychosis. Therefore, the measures are useful in the evaluation of therapies on patients with different types of phychosis, once non-psychotic causes of intermittent responding have been ruled out.

Since low, erratic rates of response on variable-interval schedules occur in non-psychotic individuals under certain unusual conditions, erratic response rates do not indicate psychosis unless these other potential causes are ruled out. Low, erratic response rates occur in normal individuals when: 1) inappropriate reinforcement is used, 2) before the response is fully acquired and the experimental situation is still novel, 3) when a competing response system is present, and 4) in acute psysiological illness or under the action of certain drugs. These are a difficult, but not impossible, set of variables to rule out in order to make our measures specific to the psychoses.

In order to further investigate and to rule out the *possibility of inappropriate reinforcement,* several different reinforcing stimuli were tried with a large number of patients (7). Reinforcers used were: money, food, candy, cigarettes, male and female nude pictures, bursts of music, tokens, escape from loud noise, and escape from a dark room. Although significant differences in rate of response for these different reinforcers were found in most of the patients, no patient was restored to a normal rate of responding by any of these reinforcers. The different reinforcers could be used to develop motivation profiles for diagnostic use, but were not useful in providing high, even rates of response for the maintenance of behavior for further investigation. Therefore, the low rates of response did not appear to be due to inappropriate reinforcement.

To investigate the *possibility of*

slow acquisition causing the low, erratic rates of response, patients with extremely low rates were held on the variable-interval schedule with candy reinforcement for over a year of one hour experimental sessions each week-day. Only three of these patients (approximately 10%) showed a gradual increase in rate of response. The experimental history of one of these patients is shown in Figure 4. Responses per hour are plotted in thousands (10-day

maintained by the candy reinforcement, and not by the patient's activation, visits to the laboratory, or personal attention in the waiting room and during the daily physical examination. When the responses were again reinforced, the rate immediately increased to over 4,000 responses per hour. This immediate re-acquisition showed that a permanent change had been made in the patients' behavior, and that he did not have to go through another

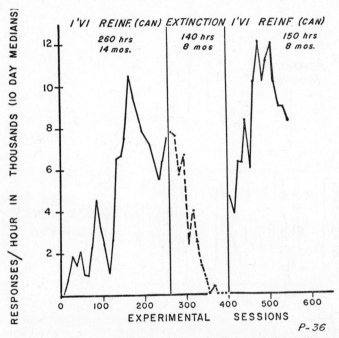

Figure 4. Slow acquisition, slow extinction, and immediate re-acquisition of a high rate of plunger-pulling reinforced with candy on a 1' VI schedule in a chronic psychotic. Patient No. 36.

medians) against experimental sessions on the abscissa. The rate of response gradually increased from less than 10 responses per hour to over 6,000 responses per hour in 260 hours, or 14 months. When the response was no longer reinforced (extinguished), it slowly declined in rate to less than 10 responses per hour within 140 experimental hours, or 8 months of calendar time. This decrease in rate during extinction shows that the rate increase during reinforcement was produced and

long drawn-out re-acquisition process.

However, the patients that showed this slow acquisition did not develop completely normal rates of response. Even though their rates of response were well above the lowest normal rate of 800 responses per hour, their responding was still erratic with an abnormally high number of pauses greater than ten seconds in duration. These three patients differed from the majority of the patients that did not show slow acquisition because the manual plunger-pulling response mechanically completed with their psychotic symptoms which were primarily manual in nature. In other words, these data suggest that slow acquisition of a high rate of response is possible in some patients with candy reinforcement, if a non-symptomatic response is reinforced which *mechanically* competes with the patient's most characteristic motor symptom.

Since slow acquisition only occurs with a very small number of patients, it

ceived can be ruled out as a cause of the pauses in responding or psychotic incidents. The records of the non-psychotic individuals shown in Figure 2 attest to the fact that no stimuli were present in the rooms which would produce competing responses in non-psychotic individuals. However, our more recent analyses strongly suggest that many forms of psychosis act as a competing response system does on the free-operant behavior of non-psychotics. In other words, many psychotics behave simi-

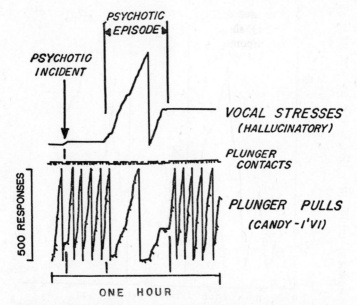

Figure 5. A psychotic incident and episode appearing in simultaneous cumulative response records of vocal stresses with psychotic or hallucinatory origin and manual plunger-pulls reinforced with candy on a I-VI schedule. Manual contacts with the plunger are recorded on the event marker between the cumulative records.

is more probably a form of restricted occupational therapy, rather than a general property of the behavior of chronic psychotics. Therefore, the possibility that the low rates of response of the majority of the patients were due to slow acquisition was ruled out.

Since each patient was in a finely controlled environment during each experimental session, the *possibility of a competing response system* as normally con-

larly to non-psychotics who are being intermittently bombarded with behavioral stimuli.

Our physiological controls (the daily physical and weekly laboratory examinations) and therapeutic controls adequately rule out the *possibility that acute physiological illness and drug action* caused the pauses in responding. It is important to note that in careful behavioral investigation such physiological controls are absolutely necessary in order to attribute any recorded behavioral deviations to other causes.

III. Psychotic Episodes

Occasionally certain patients who usually respond at higher, more even rates of response, will have a period of very low, erratic responding which lasts for a period of 20 or 30 minutes up to several hours. During these periods of lowered response rate, they can be observed dis-

of such episodes that keeps many chronic patients in the hospital, off parole, or on the disturbed ward.

Such periods of temporarily lowered response rate, and increased duration and/or frequency of psychotic incidents, we have termed *psychotic episodes*. Cumulative response records of a single psychotic incident, and a psychotic episode in the behavior of patient No. 7 are shown in Figure 5. This figure will be described in more detail in a later section of this

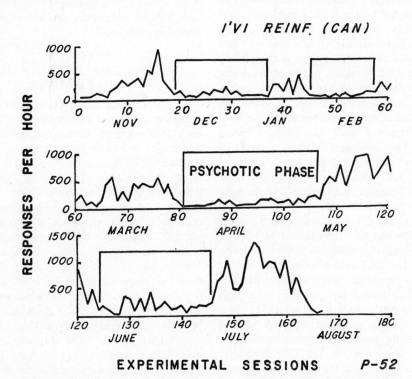

Figure 6. Psychotic phases or rhythms in rate of response of a chronic psychotic responding on a 1' VI schedule of candy reinforcement. Each experimental session lasted one hour and was conducted on successive week-days. The months of the year are printed below the experimental session closest to the first of each month to indicate calendar time. Patient No. 52.

playing hallucinatory, disturbed, destructive, or other more extremely psychotic symptoms than they usually display. Psychiatric aides usually say a patient "went high" when such episodes occur on the wards. It is the unpredictable occurrence

paper. Here, we wish only to point out that such psychotic episodes occur, and that they are the truly psychotic behavior which keeps many patients hospitalized, and that they can be automatically and objectively recorded. Some drugs, for example Benactyzine at high dosages, increase the frequency and duration of psychotic incidents and produce one of these psychotic episodes in many patients.

IV. Psychotic Phases

In the intensive, longitudinal studies several of the patients showed marked rhythms in their rate of response. These rhythms characteristically occur over relatively long periods of time. For a few weeks the rate of response will be consistently high. Then, for a few weeks or months the rate will be consistently low. Then the rhythm will repeat. We have called these periods of low response rate *Psychotic Phases*. They are not related to temperature, humidity, phases of the moon, home visits, or changes in ward assignments or hospital social environment. They are related to ratings of the patients' ward behavior until the behavior rating scales lose their sensitivity as a result of repeated administration.

An example of these psychotic phases is shown in Figure 6. At the start of the experiment the patient was hospitalized for 20 years and was 52 years old. He was first hospitalized at the age of 18 and diagnosed as a manic-depressive. The diagnosis at admission for his current period of hospitalization was dementia praecox, hebephrenic type. His last hospital diagnosis (in 1951) was schizophrenia, paranoid type. A current "blind" diagnosis was organic psychosis.

It is easy to see how long-term hospitalization and the loss of social reinforcement could suppress the socially observable behavior of a patient to such a low level that such behavioral rhythms, which were originally easily observed without instrumentation and used to diagnose a manic-depressive psychosis, could later only be recorded by sensitive, and highly quantified behavioral recording devices.

It is important to note the havoc than can be wrought by including such a patient in a drug evaluation study of the type that would run a 30-day placebo control while the patient happened to be in a psychotic phase, and a 30-day drug run when the patient was in his following more normal phase. The drug would be interpreted as therapeutic. It is also important to note that such patients could be of great value in attempts to show physiological or biochemical correlates of psychosis. For, here in a single physiological system we have a naturally oscillating amount of psychosis, which could be correlated with samples of biochemical materials in order to determine correlations without confounding the data with inter-patient differences in behavior or chemical quantity.

SPECIFIC CHARACTERISTICS OF PSYCHOTIC BEHAVIOR

More complicated behavioral processes are debilitated by fewer agents than the rate of a simple operant response. For this reason debilities in these more complicated behaviors more specifically indicate the presence of psychosis and the type of psychosis than do debilities in the simple rate of response. However, in order to determine debilities in more complicated behavior, the scientist needs enough behavior to study. Only about 50% of the chronic patients have useful rates of response above 100 responses per hour, so specific debilities cannot be determined in the other 50% of the patients who are extremely debilitated.

Due to our lack of time, I will only briefly summarize the more complicated, and hence more specific behavioral characteristics of the psychoses that we have located to date. The majority of the patients have extremely slow extinction processes. We have located one patient in which there appears to be a complete lack of extinction. In counting discriminations as measured on fixed-ratio schedules of reinforcement, approximately 50% of the patients have deficits. In more complicated discriminations based upon differential responding to two manipulanda and two lights, 90% of the patients show deficits. These discriminatory deficits have diagnostic utility in separating seniles and true mental defectives from the social mental defectives.

SIMULTANEOUS RECORDING OF VOCAL SYMPTOMS AND NON-SYMPTOMATIC RESPONSES

Visual observation of patients through the hidden periscopic viewing system has shown that most patients with abnormally long pauses in their operant responding engage in their particular individualistic symptoms during these pauses. The development of keys or switches to automatically and electrically record the occurrence of these symptoms would facilitate their further analysis.

Simultaneously recorded cumulative records of both the psychotic symptoms and the reinforced operant responses would permit an exact and objective analysis of their competition. Such simultaneous records would also permit an objective search for sympto-specific drugs which should decrease the frequency of symptoms without decreasing the frequency of reinforced operant, normal, or non-symptomatic behavior.

Also, the symptom key could be used to automatically schedule the presentation of environmental stimuli contingent upon the psychotic symptoms. The differential reinforcement of symptomatic responses would show whether they are or are not affected by environmental changes in the same way as are non-symptomatic responses.

In Figure 5 simultaneously recorded cumulative records of vocal stresses and manual plunger-pulls are shown for the 747th experimental session with a chronic psychotic patient. The vocal responses were never experimentally reinforced and can be considered to have a psychotic origin. Their content was identical with that in the vocal behavior of the patient whenever he "went high" on the wards.

Patient No. 7 is male, 58 years old and he has been continuously hospitalized for 29 years. His experimental behavior has been under study for five years. Admitted in 1930 at the age of 29 he was diagnosed dementia praecox, paranoid type. The recent "blind" diagnoses were simple schizophrenia (by the clinical psychologist), and schizophrenia, mixed (by the psychiatrist). His recent Wechsler-Bellevue I.Q. was 60 and he scored in the 3rd percentile on the Hospital Adjustment Scale and lives on a locked ward. His personality picture is "that of a withdrawn, colorless patient who shows little evidence of acting-out and whose general defense is that of compulsivity in terms of wanting a fixed routine, his own things, and to be left alone." He is very untidy, but not incontinent. He collects worthless objects and eats cigarette butts. He cleans the hospital basement floors but needs almost constant supervision. He is a good worker unless provoked, when he has tantrums and runs about, yelling, biting his fists, and pounding the walls. He behaved in this fashion during the psychotic episode shown in Figure 5 and it is this behavior which keeps him on a locked ward.

Consider Figure 5 and note the exact nature of the functional competition between the patient's vocal symptoms and his manual operant responses. The manual responses were reinforced on a 1' VI schedule with candy. The rate of reinforced manual non-symptomatic responses was reduced about 75% for two periods by competition from a moderate rate of never-reinforced vocal symptomatic responses.

The first period of symptom display and reduced rate of normal or non-symptomatic behavior lasted only about one minute and might be properly called a "psychotic incident." The second period lasted about 20 minutes and appears to be composed of a long series of psychotic incidents. Such sustained periods of psychotic display are often called "psychotic episodes."

Note that in the psychotic episode the vocal symptoms began about two minutes before the manual response rate dropped. This delay in the reduction of the non-symptomatic responding by the symptomatic responding shows that the competitive effect of the symptoms takes a minute or two to build up. The delay also demonstrates the physical independence of the two responses and their recording systems.

Note also that at the end of the episode there was a period of about two minutes with no vocal responding before the non-symptomatic responses returned to their pre-incident rate. This delay in the recovery of the non-symptomatic responding shows that the competitive effect of the symptoms lasts longer than their display. These delays in onset and recovery of the competitive effect of the symptoms suggest that the competition is a higher-order behavioral effect than the symptoms. The delays also show that symptoms can occur without the competition.

Note also that a relatively even rate of vocal symptoms and manual responses was maintained throughout the episode. These even episodic rates indicated that the severity of the psychotic episode and its competition with the normal behavior was maintained at about the same intensity throughout.

Also shown in Figure 5 is a record of the time that the patient's hand was in contact with the manipulandum (plunger contacts). The contacts were recorded by a capacitative relay circuit. The event pen on one recorder was in the "up" position whenever the patient's hand was on the manipulandum. Note that the patient usually took his hand off the manipulandum when a reinforcement was delivered. At this time he placed the candy in a paper bag that he carried. But also note that his hand was off the manipulandum during the psychotic incident and much of the time during the psychotic episode. This record of contacts shows that the symptomatic vocalizations not only compete with the recorded manual responding, but also compete with non-recorded responses necessary to the performance of the recorded responses.

In summary, a voice key to automatically record the competition between symptomatic vocalizations and the normal non-symptomatic behavior of patients within an experimental setting was developed. Its use has clearly shown that the pauses in the operant responding of patients with vocal hallucinatory symptoms are due to functional competition from these symptoms. The opportunity to record the exact nature of this competition will be useful in further research into the basic nature of psychosis. Objective recording of these vocal symptoms and their competitive effect will also be useful in the evaluation of therapeutic agents. Such a high degree of exactitude in the observation of the competition between the psychotic symptoms and normal behavior of a patient can be obtained by no other currently available psychiatric research device.

FUNCTIONAL DEFINITION OF A PSYCHOSIS

In order to show that Darwinian, naturalistic observations can lead to what might be called theories, lastly I shall present a way of defining a certain type of psychosis. This definition is functional because it describes the psychosis in terms of its effects on and interaction with non-psychotic behavior.

This notion is a direct outgrowth of the simultaneous measurement of symptomatic and non-symptomatic behavior. When normal individuals are placed in this two-channel recording situation the only vocal responses they emit, when alone and being reinforced for their manual responses, are occasional bursts of singing and whistling. This singing and whistling can be readily separated from most psychotic hallucinating by the pattern of response emission which is regular for singing and whistling, and irregular for one-sided conversations with no one. Also, the singing and whistling does not compete with, but rather seems to "pace" along with the plunger-pulling responses.

However, if non-psychotic individuals are given an hallucinogenic drug (i.e., Benactyzine in high dosages) and their name is called over a hidden microphone, they will carry on a "psychotic-like" one sided conversation with no one. When questioned afterwards they report having had auditory hallucinations. The interesting fact is that the drug-induced vocal hallucinatory symptoms in the non-psychotics do not compete with their plunger-pulling responses. The non-psychotics pull the plunger for nickles without reduction in rate through their hallucinatory episode.

Also, the non-psychotics do not hallucinate for as long a period after their name is called over the hidden speaker as do the psychotics. The after-discharge of the drug-induced and experimentally stimulated hallucinatory episodes in the non-psychotic is much shorter than the after-discharge of the "spontaneous," or experimentally stimulated hallucinatory episodes in the psychotic.

To date we have run very few psychotic and non-psychotic subjects under these conditions, but the data collected are amazingly uniform. Therefore we tentatively venture the hypothesis that one property of one form of psychosis is its symptoms have an abnormally long after-discharge and an abnormally high degree of competition with strongly reinforced non-symptomatic behavior. In other words, it is not the symptom (talking to no one) that defines this form of psychosis. Neither is it the stimulus that produced the symptom ("hearing" your name called when no one is there) that defines the psychosis. Rather, it is having the symptomatic response (talking to no one) last long after a non-psychotic would stop, and more importantly being unable to do anything else demanded of him while this talking is going on, that defines the psychotic.

I think this definition of psychotic symptoms has a lot of clinical relevance.

We are all familiar with the old lady walking down the street, obeying traffic signals, nodding and occasionally speaking to friends along the way. She is not hospitalized as a psychotic, because she is walking down the street and only talks to no one when there is nothing else to do with her mouth. She just "talks to herself."

And again, if a person goes to a psychiatrist and says, "I worry all the time, I think I am going to die, please help me." The psychiatrist will probably ask, "Do you sleep well? Do you eat well? Are you getting your work done?" If the answers to all of these questions are honestly in the affirmative, the patient is not diagnosed as psychotic and hospitalized. Rather he is classified as an interesting and compensated neurotic. On the other hand, if a man is located who has been talking to no one in a closet for three days, and has done nothing else, he stands a high probability of being immediately hospitalized if he won't even stop talking to his "friend" for the police.

SUMMARY

Much of what we have learned from our carefully controlled experiments appears in retrospect to be composed of things that skilled, experienced clinicians "knew" all the time. But, that is as it should be, for the business of science is to separate the wisdom of casual and field observation from its superstition, and then to quantify and to make this wisdom practically useful. For the first time we have brought a few facts of psychosis into the body of natural science. In so doing much of what we have brought in looks just as the clinicians always said it did. But remember that we now have the advantage of measuring these things automatically in the laboratory. And also remember that we have left many things that clinicians say in the clinic.

REFERENCES

1. Azrin, N. H., and Lindsley, O. R., The reinforcement of cooperation between children. *J. Abnorm. Soc. Psychol.*, 1956, *52*, 100-102.

2. Bernard, C., *An Introduction to the Study of Experimental Medicine*, 1865. Reprinted, Henry Schuman, 1949.

3. Ferster, C. B., and Skinner, B. F., *Schedules of Reinforcement*. New York, Appleton-Century-Crofts, 1957.

4. Forster, C. B., *Psychiat. Res. Reports.* 1958, *10*, 101-118.

5. Kraepelin, E., The Psychological Experiment in Psychiatry. *Psychol. Arbeit*, Leipzig. Engelmann, 1896.

6. Lindsley, O. R., Operant conditioning method applied to research in chronic schizophrenia. *Psych. Res. Repts.*, 1956 *5*, 118-193, 140-153.

7. Lindsley, Ogden R., Skinner, B. F., and Solomon, H. C., *Periodic Project Reports*, Metropolitan State Hospital, Waltham, Mass., June, 1953-August 1956. Microcard No. FO-57-524-527, L. C. No. MicP 57-30.

8. Lindsley, O. R., Symposium on Cerebral Dysfunction and Mental Disturbance. Chicago, Ill., June 6, 1959. To be published in *Amer. Psychiat. Assoc. Monogr.*, 1959.

9. Mednick, M. T., and Lindsley, O. R., Some correlates of operant behavior. *J. Abnorm. Soc. Psychol.*, 1958, *57*, 13–16.

10. Pavlov, I. P., *Lectures on Conditioned Reflexes*, Volume Two, *Conditioned Reflexes and Psychiatry*. Translated by W. Horsley Gantt, New York. International, 1941.

11. Rush, B., *Medical Inquiries and Observations on the Diseases of the Mind*, 1835.

12. Skinner, B. F., *The Behavior of Organisms*. New York, Appleton-Century, 1938.

13. Skinner, B. F., *Science and Human Behavior*, New York, Macmillan, 1953.

14. Skinner, B. F., *Theory and Treatment of the Psychoses*. St. Louis. Washington University Studies, 1956.

15. Skinner, B. F., The experimental analysis of behavior. *Amer. Scientist*, 1957 *45*, 343-371.

16. Skinner, B. F., Solomon, H. C., and Lindsley, O. R., Mass. Soc. for Res. in Psychiatry I. A new method for the experimental analysis of the behavior of psychotic patients. *J. Nerv. Ment. Dist.*, 1954, *120*, 403-406.

Application of Operant Conditioning to Reinstate Verbal Behavior in Psychotics

WAYNE ISAACS, JAMES THOMAS, AND ISRAEL GOLDIAMOND

IN OPERANT conditioning, behavior is controlled by explicitly arranging the consequences of the response, the explicit consequence being termed reinforcement. For example, a lever-press by a rat activates a mechanism which releases food. If the rat has been deprived of food, lever-pressing responses will increase in frequency. If this relationship between food and response holds only when a light

Reprinted by permission from the *Journal of Speech and Hearing Disorders*, Vol. 25, No. 1, February 1960.

is on, the organism may discriminate between light on and light off, that is, there will be no lever-pressing responses when the light is turned off, but turning it on will occasion such responses. From this simple case, extensions can be made to more complicated cases which may involve control of schedules of reinforcement. These procedures have recently been extended to the study of psychopharmacology (5), controlled production of stomach ulcers (4), obtaining psycho-physical curves from pigeons (3), conditioning cooperative behavior in children (2), programming machines which teach academic subjects (11), analyzing the effects of noise on human behavior (1), and decreasing stuttering (7), to mention a few examples.

The following account is a preliminary report of the use of operant conditioning to reinstate verbal behavior in two hospitalized mute psychotics. Patient A, classified as a catatonic schizophrenic, 40, became completely mute almost immediately upon commitment 19 years ago. He was recorded as withdrawn and exhibiting little psychomotor activity. Patient B, classified as schizophrenic, mixed type, with catatonic features predominating, was 43, and was committed after a psychotic break in 1942, when he was combative. He completely stopped verbalizing 14 years ago. Each S was handled by a different E (experimenter). The E's were ignorant of each other's activities until pressed to report their cases. This study covers the period prior to such report.

CASE HISTORIES

Patient A

The S was brought to a group therapy session with other chronic schizophrenics (who were verbal), but he sat in the position in which he was placed and continued the withdrawal behaviors which characterized him. He remained impassive and stared ahead even when cigarettes, which other members accepted, were offered to him and were waved before his face. At one session, when E removed cigarettes from his pocket, a package of chewing gum accidentally fell out. The S's eyes moved toward the gum and then returned to their usual position. This response was chosen by E as one with which he would start to work, using the method of successive approximation (9). (This method finds use where E desires to produce responses which are not present in the current repertoire of the organism and which are considerably removed from those which are available. The E then attempts to "shape" the available behaviors into the desired form, capitalizing upon both the variability and regularity of successive behaviors. The shaping process involves the reinforcement of those parts of a selected response which are successively in the desired direction and the nonreinforcement of those which are not.

For example, a pigeon may be initially reinforced when it moves its head. When this movement occurs regularly, only an upward movement may be reinforced, with downward movement not reinforced. The pigeon may now stretch its neck, with this movement reinforced. Eventually the pigeon may be trained to peck at a disc which was initially high above its head and at which it would normally never peck. In the case of the psychotic under discussion, the succession was eye movement, which brought into play occasional facial movements, including those of the mouth, lip movements, vocalizations, word utterance, and finally, verbal behavior.)

The S met individually with E three times a week. Group sessions also continued. The following sequence of procedures was introduced in the private sessions. Although the weeks are numbered consecutively, they did not follow at regular intervals since other duties kept E from seeing S every week.

Weeks 1, 2. A stick of gum was held before S's face, and E waited until S's eyes moved toward it. When this response occurred, E as a consequence gave him the gum. By the end of the second week, response probability in the presence of the gum was increased to such an extent that S's eyes moved toward the gum as soon as it was held up.

Weeks 3, 4. The E now held the gum before S, waiting until he noticed movement in S's lips before giving it to him. Toward the end of the first session of the third week, a lip movement spontaneously occurred, which E promptly reinforced. By the end of this week, both lip movement and eye movement occurred when the gum was held up. The E then withheld giving S the gum until S spontaneously made a vocalization, at which time E gave S the gum. By the end of this week, holding up the gum readily occasioned eye movement toward it, lip movement, and a vocalization resembling a croak.

Weeks 5, 6. The E held up the gum, and said, 'Say *gum, gum,*' repeating these words each time S vocalized. Giving S the gum was made contingent upon vocalizations increasingly approximating *gum.* At the sixth session (at the end of Week 6), when E said, 'Say *gum, gum,*' S suddenly said, 'Gum, please.' This response was accompanied by reinstatement of other responses of this class, that is, S answered questions regarding his name and age.

Thereafter, he responded to questions by E both in individual sessions and in group sessions, but answered no one else. Responses to the discriminative stimuli of the room generalized to E on the ward; he greeted E on two occasions in the group room. He read from signs in *E*'s office upon request by *E*.

Since the response now seemed to be under the strong stimulus control of *E, the person,* attempt was made to generalize the stimulus to other people. Accordingly, a nurse was brought into the private room; *S* smiled at her. After a month, he began answering her questions. Later, when he brought his coat to a volunteer worker on the ward, she interpreted the gesture as a desire to go outdoors and conducted him there. Upon informing *E* of the incident, she was instructed to obey *S* only as a consequence of explicit verbal requests by him. The *S* thereafter vocalized requests. These instructions have now been given to other hospital personnel, and *S* regularly initiates verbal requests when nonverbal requests have no reinforcing consequences. Upon being taken to the commissary, he said, 'Ping pong,' to the volunteer worker and played a game with her. Other patients, visitors, and members of hospital-society-at-large continue, however, to interpret nonverbal requests and to reinforce them by obeying *S*.

Patient B

This patient, with a combative history prior to mutism, habitually lay on a bench in the day room in the same position, rising only for meals and for bed. Weekly visits were begun by *E* and an attendant. During these visits, *E* urged *S* to attend group therapy sessions which were being held elsewhere in the hospital. The *E* offered *S* chewing gum. This was not accepted during the first two visits, but was accepted on the third visit and thereafter. On the sixth visit, *E* made receipt of the gum contingent upon *S*'s going to the group room and so informed *S*. The *S* then altered his posture to look at *E* and accompanied him to the group room, where he seated himself in a chair and was given the gum. Thereafter, he came to this room when the attendants called for him.

Group Sessions 1–4. Gum reinforcement was provided for coming to the first two weekly sessions, but starting with the third, it was made contingent upon *S*'s participation in the announced group activity. The group (whose other members were verbal) was arranged in a semicircle. The *E* announced that each *S* would, when his turn came, give the name of an animal. The *E* immediately provided gum to each *S* who did so. The *S* did not respond and skipped his turn three times around. The same response occurred during the fourth session.

Group Session 5. The activity announced was drawing a person; *E* provided paper and colored chalk and visited each *S* in turn to examine the paper. The *S* had drawn a stick figure and was reinforced with gum. Two of the other patients, spontaneously and without prior prompting by *E*, asked to see the drawing and complimented *S*. Attendants reported that on the following day, *S*, when introduced to two ward visitors, smiled and said, 'I'm glad to see you.' The incident was followed by no particular explicit consequences.

Group Session 6. The announced activity was to give the name of a city or town in Illinois. The *S*, in his turn, said, 'Chicago.' He was reinforced by *E*, who gave him chewing gum, and again two members of the group congratulated him for responding Thereafter, he responded whenever his turn came.

After the tenth session in the group, gum reinforcement was discontinued. The *S* has continued to respond vocally in the situations in which he was reinforced by *E* but not in others. He never initiates conversations, but he will answer various direct questions in the *group sessions*. He will not, however, respond vocally to questions asked *on the ward,* even when put by *E*.

DISCUSSION

Both *S*'s came from special therapy wards of patients selected because of depressed verbal behavior and long stay in the hospital; tranquilizing drugs were not used. The extent to which reinstatement of verbal behavior was related to the special treatment offered the patients in the special wards set up for them cannot readily be assayed. Among the special treatments accorded them were group therapy sessions. Nevertheless, the similarities between the pattern of reacquisition of verbal behavior by the patients and the patterns of learning encountered in laboratory studies suggest that the conditioning procedures themselves were involved in the reinstatement of verbal behavior.

In the case of Patient A, the speaking response itself was gradually shaped. The anatomical relation between the muscles of chewing and speaking probably had some part in *E*'s effectiveness. When a word was finally produced, the response was reinstated along with other response members of its class, which had not been reinforced. The economy of this process is apparent, since it eliminates the necessity of getting S to produce *every* desired response in order to increase his repertoire. In this case, E concentrated on one verbal response, and in reinstating it, reinstated verbal responses in general. On the stimulus side, when the response came under the stimulus control of E, the stimulus could be generalized to other members of E's class of discriminative *stimuli,* namely, people. This may have relevance for the clinical inference of the importance for future interpersonal relations of prior identification with some person. In the case of Patient B, the stimulus control involved a *given setting,* the rooms where he had been reinforced. The discrimination of E in one case, and not in the other, may be explained in terms of the establishment of operant discrimination, which also involves extinction (9). Operant discrimination is established when a response in the presence of S^D, a discriminative stimulus, is reinforced, and a response in the presence of $S\Delta$, a stimulus other than S^D, is not. After some time, the response will occur when S^D is presented, but not when $S\Delta$ is presented; the response discriminates S^D from $S\Delta$, it having been extinguished when $S\Delta$ was presented. In the case of Patient A, E was with S on the ward, in the group room, and privately. Reinforcement occurred in all occasions. But S was on the ward (and other rooms) without E, and therefore without reinforcement for those responses which were occasioned by the ward and which only E reinforced. Hence, these responses would extinguish in the ward alone, but would continue in the presence of E, defining discrimination of E from other stimuli. In the case of Patient B, this process may have been delayed by the fact that E and the other patients reinforced only in a specific room. It will be recalled that attendants rather than E brought S to the group room.

Interestingly, in the group sessions, when Patient B emitted the responses which E reinforced, other psychotic patients also reinforced Patient B. They were thereby responding, on the occasion of S's responses (discriminative stimuli for them), in the same way that E did. The term *identification,* used as a label here, shares some behavioral referents with the term as used in the preceding paragraph and might be explained behaviorally in terms of the *generalized reinforcer (10).* These behaviors by the patients are similar to behaviors reported in client-centered group sessions, where clients increase in reflective behaviors as counseling progresses, and in psychoanalytic group sessions, where patients increasingly make analytic interpretations of each other. Here, the patients are also behaving like the therapist. While this parallel lends itself to the facetious thought that operant group sessions may produce operant conditioners, it does suggest that psychotics are behaving, with regard to responses by the major source of reinforcement in the group, according to the same laws which govern such group behaviors of non-hospitalized S's.

The various diagnostic labels applied to psychotics are based to a considerable extent upon differences between responses considered abnormal, for example, hallucinations, delusions of persecution, and the like. The therapeutic process is accordingly at times seen in terms of eliminating the abnormal behaviors or states. Experimental laboratory work indicates that it is often extremely difficult to *eliminate* behavior; extinction is extremely difficult where the schedule of reinforcement has been a variable interval schedule (6), that is, reinforcement has been irregular, as it is in most of our behaviors. Such behaviors persist for considerable periods without reinforcement. Experimental laboratory work has provided us quite readily with procedures to *increase* responses. In the case of psychotics, this would suggest focusing attention on whatever *normal* behaviors S has; an appropriate operant, no matter how small or insignificant, even if it is confined to an eye movement, may possibly be raised to greater probability, and shaped to normal behavior (8). Stated otherwise, abnormal behaviors and normal behaviors can be viewed as reciprocally related, and psychotics as exhibiting considerable abnormal behavior, or little normal behavior. Normal behavior probability can be increased by decreasing probability of abnormal behaviors, or abnormal behaviors can be decreased by the controlled increase of normal behaviors. This preliminary report suggests that a plan of attack based upon the latter approach may be worth further investigation.

SUMMARY

Verbal behavior was reinstated in two psychotics, classified as schizophrenics, who had been mute for 19 and 14 years. The procedures utilized involved application of operant conditioning. The relationship of such procedures, based on controlled laboratory investigations with men and animals, to procedures based on clinical practice with human patients was discussed and was considered as directing our attention to shaping and increasing the probability of what normal behaviors the psychotic possesses.

REFERENCES

1. Azrin, N. H., Some effects of noise on human behavior. *J. exp. Anal. Behavior,* 1958, *1*, 183–200.
2. Azrin, N. H., and Lindsley, O. R., The reinforcement of cooperation between children. *J. abnorm. (soc.) Psychol.,* 52, 1956, 100–102.
3. Blough, D. S., A method for obtaining psycholphysical thresholds from the pigeon. *J. exp. Anal. Behavior,* 1958, *1*, 31–44.
4. Brady, J. V., Ulcers in 'executive' monkeys. *Sci. Amer.,* 1958 *199(4),* 95–100.
5. Dews, P. B., The effects of chlorpromazine and promazine on performance on a mixed schedule of reinforcement. *J. exp. Anal. Behavior,* 1958, *1,* 73–82.
6. Ferster, C. B., and Skinner, B. F., *Schedules of Reinforcement.* New York: Appleton-Century-Crofts, 1957.
7. Flanagan, B., Goldiamond, I., and Azrin, N. H., Operant stuttering: the control of stuttering behavior through response-contingent consequences. *J. exp. Anal. Behavior,* 1958, *1,* 173–178.
8. Goldiamond, I., Research which can be done in a mental hospital. Address delivered to Illinois State Mental Hospitals Conference, Giant City State Park, Illinois, 1958.
9. Keller, F., and Schoenfeld, W., *Principles of Psychology.* New York: Appleton-Century-Crofts, 1950.
10. Skinner, B. F., *Science and Human Behavior.* New York: Macmillan, 1953.
11. Skinner, B. F., Teaching machines. *Science,* 1958, *128,* 969–977.

Reinforcement of Affect Responses of Schizophrenics during the Clinical Interview

KURT SALZINGER AND STEPHANIE PISONI

BEHAVIOR theory has recently expanded its scope to deal with verbal behavior (6). Greenspoon (1) demonstrated the effectiveness of verbal reinforcers upon a subject's rate of utterance

Reprinted by permission from *The Journal of Abnormal and Social Psychology,* Vol. 57, No. 1, July 1958.

of plural vs. non-plural words. Hildum and Brown (2) showed the effect of verbal reinforcement upon attitude statements. Verplanck (7) used verbal reinforcers during conversations to condition opinion statements. Finally, Salzinger (5) investigated the conditioning process in clinical interviews with schizophrenics.

While these studies have supplied evidence for the validity of the application of reinforcement theory to verbal behavior, a good deal of research is still necessary. The present experiment is designed to study (a) reliability of response unit isolation, i.e., to what extent the interviewer can respond reliably with reinforcement to the patient's verbal behavior, (b) the effect of different sources of reinforcements (different interviewers) upon the verbal behavior of the interviewee, and (c) the relationship between the number of reinforcements and the number of responses in extinction.

Since a patient's ability to express affect is usually evaluated through the interview and is considered an important criterion both for diagnosis and prognosis of schizophrenia, the conditions under which affect is evoked by the interviewer might have theoretical importance for arriving at laws describing interview behavior and practical importance in furnishing an objective method for the evaluation of "flatness" of affect. An attempt was made, therefore, to examine the effect of reinforcement upon schizophrenics' output of affect responses in an interview.

METHOD

Subjects

Twenty-four female and twelve male hospitalized schizophrenics from the age of 18 to 50, with a median of 34.3 years, were selected from the admissions to Brooklyn State Hospital. Patients were classified as schizophrenic upon their current admission to the hospital distribution center. One was later rediagnosed as manic-depressive. Nineteen had been previously hospitalized, and 17 had no history of previous hospitalization.

None of the patients received any somatotherapy such as insulin, electric shock, or tranquillizing drugs for a least one week before the first interview or during their participation in the study.

The first 20 patients interviewed were placed in the experimental group. Fourteen were females and six males, with a median age of 32.0 years and a median number of years of education of 10.3. The other 16 patients were placed in the control group. Twelve were females and 4 males with a median age of 34.5 years and a median number of years of education of 11.5.

Experimental Procedure

All patients were interviewed one week after their arrival in the hospital. The Ss in the experimental group were interviewed once by a female E and once by a male E on two consecutive days for a period of 30 minutes each. Eleven of the patients were first interviewed by the male; nine were first interviewed by the female E. The Ss in the control group were interviewed once only, nine by the female and seven by the male E. All interviews were recorded with the apparatus in full sight of both patient and interviewer.

The interview was presented to the patients as a routine mental hospital procedure. For the first interview, E brought the patient into the experimental room and explained that the interview was being conducted to help him. The second interview was introduced by telling the patient that it is helpful to patients to be interviewed more than once despite the fact that this might mean a repetition of their story. All other interview procedures were the same for the second as for the first interview.

The E questioned the patient about the following items: name, age, marital status, children, and siblings. The patients answered these questions with little hesitation, thus making it possible for E to begin the interview by repeating the answer given, by writing it down, and by saying such words as "mmm-humm," "uhhuh," "I see," etc. This procedure was adopted in an effort to obtain factual information upon which subsequent interview questions could be based and to establish E as a source of reinforcement, in this way encouraging the patient to speak in the presence of E. The main part of the interview was then initiated with the question, "Would you tell me why you are here in this hospital?"

Interviews with the experimental group were conducted in the following manner: During the first 10 minutes (operant level), the base rate of spontaneous affect responses (see definition below) was determined. The E asked questions but did not reinforce any statement made by the patient. Reinforcement was defined as E's verbal agreement through the use of such words as "mmm-hum," "I see," "yeah," etc., with statements made by the patient.

During the second 10 minutes (conditioning), E continued to question the patient and reinforced each affect response by immediately following each expression of affect with verbal agreement.

During the third 10-minute period (extinction), E withheld all reinforcement but continued asking questions.

Interviews with the control group also lasted 30 minutes, during which time E asked questions but did not reinforce any of the patient's responses. This procedure was identical with the operant level phase of the experimental group procedure.

Definition of Response

The response class of affect for this experiment was defined as any statement describing or evaluating the state (other than intellectual or physiological) of the patient by himself. The response class therefore included all statements beginning with the pronouns "I" or "we" and followed by an expression of affect. Examples include such expressions as: I am satisfied, I'm happy, We enjoyed it, I like him, I'm very close to him, I was mad at him, We hated her, I'll always be jealous of him, I am upset, I am a lonely person, I was so ashamed, I'm sorry for him, I feel . . . (followed by any words), I was frightened, We couldn't take it, I always suffer, I had a fright, etc.

Quotations in which affect is referred to the speaker, although fitting all other criteria, were excluded on the basis of not being direct expressions of the patient's affect. An example of this was, "My husband said I didn't feel good." Statements like "I am happy and excited" were considered as one affect statement only, since the pronouns "I" or "we" did not precede the second affective word. On the other hand, incomplete (in the sense that the object of the affect is not mentioned) statements like "I love. . ." or "We feared. . ." were viewed as separate responses.

Certain types of private events or internal states were excluded from the response class of affect because they referred primarily to intellectual processes, to actions which are sometimes but not always associated with affect, or to desires which appear to constitute a class of responses different from the affect class as defined here. I am confused, I am confident, I would like to. . ., I want, I was surprised, I am not well, We forgave him, I threaten her constantly, I didn't trust them, etc., are examples.

A count per minute was taken of statements belonging to the general class of self-references (statements beginning with "I" or "We") in order to compare changes in the occurrence of this class with those of the class of self-referred affect statements. In other words, self-referred statements included both self-referred affect statements as well as self-referred nonaffect statements.

Interviewer Questions

After the initial question, "Why are you here?" E asked additional questions only when the patient ceased talking for at least two seconds. Some or all of the following topics were discussed during each interview: reasons for being in the hospital and causes for illness; patient's relationships to his parents, siblings, fellow employees, employers, fellow students and teachers, wife or husband, children, friends; patient's activities during free time, and plans for the future. The E made an attempt to balance these topics over the different conditions. For instance, if the patient discussed the symptoms of his illness in the operant level condition, E asked questions regarding the possible causes of the illness during conditioning and brought the patient back to these topics during extinction. As long as the topics were approximately balanced over the three conditions, however, E took his cues as to topic from the content of the patient's statements. Both the number of topics and the order in which they were discussed varied from interview to interview.

Questions asking directly for affect such as, "How did you feel about that?" or "Were you happy?" were not used.

RESULTS

Reliability of Response Unit Isolation

A sample of 15 recorded interviews was coded independently for self-referred affect by the two interviewers. Proportions of agreement based on the number of affect statements counted were computed separately for each condition of each interview and ranged from .79 to 1.00. Examination of the disagreements revealed that they were primarily due to poor recording. It was therefore concluded that the affect responses as defined in this experiment can be objectively isolated and counted.

Interviewer Differences

The adequacy of the definition of the response was examined by having the two Es who served as interviewers in the experiment independently code the affect responses of the same 15 recorded interviews. This procedure made it possible to test whether both Es would have reinforced the same responses in identical interviews.

In order to determine whether the two interviewers evoked a different number of affect statements, comparisons were made between the two interviewers on each condition of the initial interviews of the experimental group and the control group interviews. The Mann-Whitney test yielded no statistically significant differences ($p > .05$), suggesting that the two interviewers evoked approximately the same number of affect statements in their respective interviews. The exact p levels for the experimental group interviews were .79 for the operant level, .54 for the conditioning period, and .52 for the extinction period. For the control interviews, the p levels were considerably lower, although still not significant. The p level for the first 10-minute

ferences was not statistically significant ($p = .37$) by the Mann-Whitney test (4).

Conditioning Effect

The difference between operant level, conditioning, and extinction for the initial interviews of the experimental group was tested by Wilcoxon's nonparametric analysis of variance (8) and found to be statistically significant ($p < .01$). The greatest number of affect statements was emitted during conditioning (sum of ranks = 51.0), the next greatest during the operant level (sum of ranks = 39.5), and

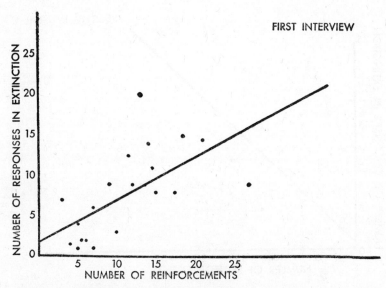

Figure 1. Number of affect responses during extinction as a function of number of reinforcements in the first interview.

period was .07, for the second .06, and for the third .22.

Base Level of Affect

In order to determine whether the experimental and control groups differed initially in the amount of affect spontaneously emitted, a statistical comparison of the number of affect statements given in the first 10 minutes of the control interviews with the number of such statements given during the operant level of the experimental interviews was made. The dif-

the least during extinction (sum of ranks = 29.5). The difference between the three conditions of the second interviews of the experimental group was not statistically significant ($.2 > p > .1$). Inspection of the sums of ranks for the three conditions, however, still revealed the greatest number of affect statements in the conditioning period (sum of ranks = 45.0), the next greatest number of affect statements in extinction (sum of ranks = 41.5), and the smallest number during operant level (sum of ranks = 33.5). The fact that the second interview did not yield a statistically significant difference between the conditions appears to be due largely to the greater number of responses emitted during extinction in the second interview in contrast to the first. This is also evident in the comparison of Figs. 1 and 2, where responses during extinction were plotted as a function of number of reinforcements, from which one can see the steeper slope in the second than in the first interview. In other words, this result does not indicate a lack of reliability over time but, rather, that apparently fewer reinforcements were

during the first 10 minutes (sum of ranks = 32.0).

The Mann-Whitney test was used to compare each 10-minute period of the experimental group interviews to its corresponding period in the control interviews. Comparison of the first 10 minutes of the experimental with the control interviews yielded no significant difference ($p = .37$). Comparison of the last 10 minutes also yielded no significant difference ($p = .92$). The difference between the second 10-minute period of the control-group interviews and the conditioning period of the experi-

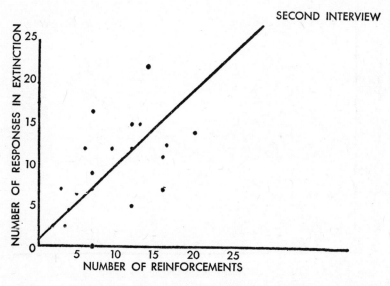

Figure 2. Number of affect responses during extinction as a function of number of reinforcements in the second interview.

necessary for the same number of extinction responses in the second than in the initial interview. This effect is generally reported for reconditioning.

When the same test was used to compare the three 10-minute periods of control group interviews, no significant difference was found ($p = .75$). The greatest number of affect responses was emitted during the last 10 minutes of the interview (sum of ranks = 36.0), the next greatest during the second 10 minutes (sum of ranks = 34.0), and the smallest number

mental-group interviews was statistically significant ($p = .03$), using the one-tailed test hypothesis that the experimental group would emit more affect than the control group.

Figs. 3 and 4 represent individual cumulative curves of affect responses over the three conditions of the experimental group interviews. Fig. 3 shows the curves of three individuals whose rate of response was modified by reinforcement. These individuals were selected on the basis of being representative of low, medium, and high rates of response in operant level. Fig. 4 shows the curves of three individuals whose rates of response were not modified by reinforcement. These individuals were also representative of their group.

In order to gauge the lawfulness of the process of conditioning in the experimental group, the number of responses of each patient during extinction was plotted against the number of reinforcements in conditioning. It was found that the relationship could be described by a linear equation, i.e., the greater the number of

In order to investigate further the effects of reinforcement, rank-order correlation coefficients were computed between every pair of conditions, separately for the first and second experimental interviews and the control interviews. As expected for the experimental group, the highest correlations were found between the number of reinforcements and the number of extinction responses for both the first (.73) and second (.60) interviews. The correlations between all other pairs of conditions were much lower, varying within a

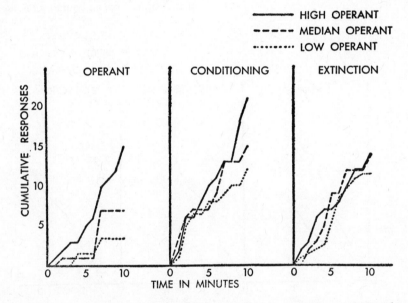

Figure 3. Individual cumulative response curves for three patients who showed the conditioning effect.

reinforcements administered, the greater the number of responses emitted during extinction. The goodness of fit can be seen by examining Figs. 1 and 2. Two patients appear to deviate markedly from the rest of the sample. The diagnosis of one of these patients was changed from schizo-affective to manic-depressive psychosis. She received 13 reinforcements and gave 20 extinction responses. The other deviate from the group, who received 27 reinforcements and gave only 9 extinction responses, was later found to be hard of hearing.

restricted range from .41 to .50 (see Table 1). The correlation between the two extinction periods of Interviews 1 and 2 was .41 ($p < .05$) and that between extinction of Interview 1 and conditioning of Interview 2 was .44 ($p < .05$).

In direct contrast to the results of the experimental group, the correlations between the conditions in the control group were all evenly high, ranging, from .70 to .85.

Since every affect statement in the second period of the experimental group

TABLE 1

Rank-Order Correlations Between the Three Ten-Minute Periods of the Interviews

Conditions	Experimental		Control
	First interview	Second interview	
Conditioning vs. Extinction (2nd vs. 3rd 10 minutes)	.73**	.60**	.74**
Operant level vs. Conditioning (1st vs. 2nd 10 minutes)	.46*	.47*	.85**
Operant level vs. Extinction (1st vs. 3rd 10 minutes)	.41*	.50*	.70**

* $p < .05$.
** $p < .01$.

experimental group. The tau of .58 ($p = .0002$) between number of reinforcements and extinction responses for the fist interview became .53, and the tau of .45 ($p = .002$) for the second interview became .37. When the first 10-minute period of the control interviews was partialed out of the correlation between the second and third 10-minute periods, the tau of .59 ($p = .002$) became .38, a drop of .21, whereas the corresponding drop in the experimental group was only .05.

This indicates that only a small part of the correlation between number of reinforcements and number of responses

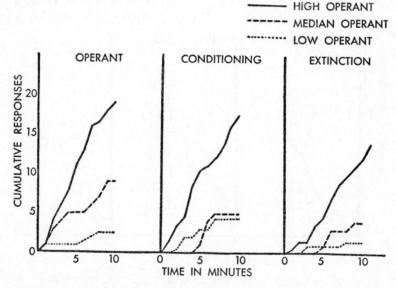

Figure 4. Individual cumulative response curves for three patients who showed little or no evidence for conditioning.

was reinforced, the question arises whether the correlation between number of reinforcements and number of responses in extinction merely reflects a correlation between the affect statements in different parts of the interview.

Kendall's tau (3) was computed in order to partial out the correlations between operant level and conditioning and operant level and extinction from the reinforcement-extinction correlation in the

in extinction can be accounted for by the correlation between operant level and number of reinforcements; the correlation between the second and third parts of the control group, on the other hand, can be accounted for in larger part by the correlation between the first and second part of the interview.

The rate of making self-referred statements was found to be invariant over the three conditions of the first and second interviews of the experimental group as well as the interviews of the control group. This was tested by Wilcoxon's *(8)* nonparametric analysis of variance ($p > .05$). Inspection of the sums of ranks for the first experimental interview (based on an N of 20) indicated a trend toward decreasing frequency of self-referred statements from operant level (sum of ranks = 48.0) to conditioning (sum of ranks = 37.0) to extinction (sum of ranks = 35.0), while in the second interview, the greatest number of self-referred statements appeared in conditioning (sum of ranks = 46.0), the next greatest in extinction (sum of ranks = 39.0), and the smallest in operant level (sum of ranks = 35.0). In the control group (based on an N of 16), the greatest number of self-referred statements was emitted during the first 10 minutes (sum of ranks = 38.5), the next greatest during the third 10 minutes (sum of ranks = 3.5), and the smallest during the second 10 minutes (sum of ranks = 30.0).

DISCUSSION

While it is true that two different interviewers evoked the same number of affect statements within the margin of random error, the fact that two of the comparisons approached the .05 level of significance would seem to indicate that there is still room for greater control of interviewer behavior or that such interviewer characteristics as sex, age, appearance, etc., play an important role in controlling the interviewee's behavior.

While Verplanck *(7)* was unable to test the constancy of the response used during any one conversation or among different conversations, the recording done in this experiment made it possible to demonstrate that a response class decided upon prior to the interview can be reliably reacted to by different interviewers and coders.

Although this experiment gave definite evidence for conditioning, there was much variability among individuals. This

was not surprising in view of the fact that the interviewing was carried out with schizophrenics and the response conditioned one of affect statements. This variability, both in operant level and in susceptibility to reinforcement, might well provide an objective prognostic measure of degree of flatness of affect. Such a measure would be of value since there are strong indications *(10)* that marked flatness of affect augurs badly for the outcome of schizophrenia. Follow-up of the patients interviewed in this sample may allow an exact test of the relationship between outcome of illness and flatness of affect.

Perhaps one of the most interesting findings of this study was the linear relationship between number of reinforcements and number of responses in extinction. In a similar study, Williams *(9)* found that the relationship between number of reinforcements and number of responses during extinction for food-deprived rats was also linear up to about 30 reinforcements. Since fewer reinforcements were administered in the present study, it will certainly be of interest to try to duplicate the rest of Williams' curve for verbal behavior. The results become even more dramatic when account is taken of the fact that flatness of affect, as defined here by frequency of affect statements, appears to vary directly as a function of the interviewer's reinforcing behavior. The implications for the regular psychiatric interview are self evident.

The two patients in the experimental group who showed atypical relationships between reinforcement and extinction, are noteworthy because both deviated in directions that seem sensible on a *post hoc* basis. The hard-of-hearing individual got more reinforcements for the number of responses she emitted in extinction than the *S*s in the rest of the sample. This, of course, is exactly what one might expect if *S* could not hear all the verbal reinforcements given her. The patient whose diagnosis was changed from schizophrenic to manic-depressive psychosis, manic stage, gave many more affect statements in extinction than might be expected from the number of reinforcements she received. This observation suggests the possibility that if a sample of manic-depressives was administered the same number of reinforcements as the schizophrenic group, a linear relationship might similarly be found but with a steeper slope. Manic-depressives may require a smaller number of reinforcements than schizophrenics for the same number of responses in extinction.

The correlation coefficients between all possible combinations of conditions were computed in an attempt to see whether the relationship between number of reinforcements and number of responses during extinction could be explained simply as a correlation that might be obtained between any two 10-minute periods of the same interviews. Table 1 shows that while correlations occurred between all conditions, the highest were between the number of reinforcements and number of responses during extinction in the experimental group. Furthermore, upon partialing out the operant level correlation to study the relationship to be expected between any two 10-minute periods, no substantial change occurred in the correlation between number of reinforcements and frequency of response in extinction. The correlations between the conditions in the control group yield further evidence for the conditioning effect in the experimental group. The fact that they are all approximately equally high, whereas the reinforcement-extinction correlations in the experimental group are outstandingly high by comparison to the operant-extinction and operant-reinforcement correlations, argues strongly for the effect of reinforcement.

A final control on the effect of reinforcement in the interview, that of the rate of self-referred statements, was used in order to check on the possibility that the reinforcement functioned merely to make the patient feel more at ease and therefore talk more about himself. This analysis indicated that the conditioning effect was specific in producing an increase in self-referred affect statements and not in increasing the general class of self-referred statements.

SUMMARY

Thirty-six hospitalized schizophrenics were included in this study. Twenty of them (the experimental group) were interviewed for a period of 30 minutes each on two consecutive days by two interviewers. The other 16 (the control group) were given one interview only, which lasted for 30 minutes. Each interview in the experimental group consisted of a 10-minute operant level, during which E only asked questions necessary to keep up the patient's talk but did not respond to the patient's speech; 10 minutes of conditioning, during which E reinforced by agreement all self-referred affect statements; and, finally, 10 minutes of extinction, during which E withheld all further reinforcement. Each interview in the control group consisted of 30 minutes of operant level only.

It was demonstrated that a difference in interviewers or sources of reinforcement per se need not produce discrepant results during an interview when utilizing a standard procedure for interviewing. It was further shown that a verbal response class can be reliably isolated and reacted to. Conditioning of the response class of self-referred affect statements was found to be possible with schizophrenics during an otherwise usual clinical interview. The relationship between number of reinforcements and number of responses in extinction was described by means of a straight line, i.e., the greater the number of reinforcements, the greater the number of extinction responses.

The lawfulness of these findings indicates that the clinical interview is subject to investigation by experimental techniques. Furthermore, a controlled interview may prove useful as a research tool.

REFERENCES

1. Greenspoon, J. The reinforcing effect of two spoken sounds on the frequency of two responses. *Amer. J. Psychol.*, 1955, *68*, 409–416.

2. Hildum, D. C., and Brown, R. W. Verbal reinforcement and interviewer bias. *J. abnorm. soc. Psychol.*, 1956, *53*, 108–111.

3. Kendall, M. G. *Rank correlation methods.* London: Griffin, 1948.

4. Mann, H. B., and Whitney, D. R. On a test of whether one of two random variables in stochastically larger than the other. *Ann. math. Stat.*, 1947, *18*, 50–60.

5. Salzinger, Suzanne. Rate of affect response in schizophrenics as a function of three types of interviewer verbal behavior. Paper read at East. Psychol. Ass., Atlantic City, March, 1956.

6. Skinner, B. F. *Verbal behavior.* New York: Appleton-Century-Crofts, 1957.

7. Verplanck, W. S. The control of the content of conversation: Reinforcement of statements of opinion. *J. abnorm. soc. Psychol.*, 1955, *51*, 668–676.

8. Wilcoxon, F. *Some rapid approximate statistical procedures.* New York: American Cyanamid, 1949.

9. Williams, S. B. Resistance to extinction as a function of the number of reinforcements. *J. exp. Psychol.*, 1938, *23*, 506–521.

10. Zubin, J. Role of prognostic indicators in the evaluation of therapy. Paper read at Conference on the Evaluation of Pharmacotherapy in Mental Illness, Washington, D. C., 1956.

Differences in Gradients of Stimulus Generalization as a Function of Psychiatric Disorder

IRWIN J. KNOPF AND ROBERT E. FAGER

STIMULUS generalization (SG) is well recognized as an important explanatory concept in both infrahuman and human learning. Dollard and Miller (*2*), Miller and Kraeling (*11*), and Miller and Murray (*12*), among others, have been instrumental in highlighting the significant role SG has come to play in personality theory, psychopathology, and psychotherapy. In the area of psychopathology, Dollard and Miller utilize the principle that "increasing the strength of the drive raises the entire gradient of generalization, increasing the strength of all generalized responses and the range of stimuli that will elicit them" (p. 178) for the purpose of explaining the development of symptoms and defense mechanisms. They also indicate that such emotional states as

Reprinted by permission from the *Journal of Abnormal and Social Psychology*, Vol. 59, 1959.

fear, anxiety, and guilt can acquire the properties of a drive. From this it may be postulated that increments in these emotional states raise the gradients of generalization. If one could infer from clinical observations a broad relationship between the intensity of such emotional state and severity of psychopathology, then it seems reasonable to hypothesize a relationship between severity of psychopathology and SG.

The present research investigates the hypotheses that there are differences in the shape of SG gradients among psychotic, neurotic and control Ss. The specific predictions are as follows:

1. Psychotics show more generalization than either neurotics or control Ss.

2. Neurotics show less generalization than psychotics but more generalization than controls.

We were also interested in the relative performance of a brain-damaged group, but this was a side issue, and no attempt was made to account for the performance of this group on the basis of our theoretical formulation.

METHOD

Subjects

The population included 106 psychiatric Ss (32 psychotically depressed, 24 schizophrenics, 26 neurotics, and 24 brain-damaged) and 32 controls who were nonprofessional hospital employees. None of the psychiatric Ss was on any treatment other than psychotherapy. With the exception of the brain-damaged group, only those psychiatric Ss who received identical diagnoses at both admission and discharge staff conferences were selected for study. Because of the importance of laboratory data and neurological consultation in arriving at a diagnosis of brain damage, the diagnosis of many of these Ss was deferred on admission, so the discharge diagnosis was accepted as the criterion for this group. The S characteristics are presented in Table 1. Statistical analysis among the five groups showed significant differences ($p < .001$) in both age and education. The controls, schizophrenics, and neurotics were younger ($p < .001$) than both the depressed and brain-injured Ss. The controls were better educated than the other four groups ($p <.001$), while the schizophrenics had more schooling than the depressives ($p < .02$) and brain-injured Ss ($p. < .01$), and the neurotics more than the brain-injured ($p < .02$). No differences in either age or education were found between the schizophrenics and neurotics or between the depressed and brain-injured; the neurotics and depressed patients had similar educational levels. With the exception of the brain-damaged group, the number of males and females in each of the other groups was approximately equal.

Apparatus

The apparatus was similar to that developed by Brown, Clarke, and Stein (1). It consisted of seven stimulus lamps mounted in a horizontal row on a black plywood panel and spaced at eight-degree intervals. The panel was curved so that all lamps were five feet from S, who was seated in front of a stand on which was mounted a spring-return toggle switch. When S moved the switch forward or backward, the words "win" or "lose" would light up in the upper or lower *left* quadrants of a small box below the central lamp. The upper

and lower *right* quadrants also contained the words "win" and "lose," and were activated by E to give S information as to the actual outcome of each trial.

Procedure

The S was told that each of the seven lamps represented a race horse. When a lamp was lighted, it indicated that this horse was running a race against other horses not represented on the stimulus panel. The seven horses on the panel were not competing against each other. Each time a light went on, it was a new

TABLE 1. AGE, EDUCATION, AND SEX CHARACTERISTICS FOR THE FIVE GROUPS

Group		Mean age	Mean education	Sex	
				M	F
Control	32	26.03	15.28	17	15
Schizophrenic	24	26.00	12.43	12	12
Neurotic	26	27.54	11.96	14	12
Depression	32	48.59	10.53	15	17
Brain damage	24	45.21	10.08	15	9

race, and S was supposed to guess whether the horse would win or lose that race. If S thought the horse would win, he was to push the switch forward. If he thought it would lose, he was to pull the switch toward him. S was told to remember how well each horse did in order to increase the accuracy of his bets.

Each trial (or race) consisted of the presentation of a stimulus light by E. S's response automatically terminated the stimulus, at which time E activated the appropriate light to indicate the actual outcome of the race. Unknown to S, a predetermined schedule of 80% win for the central lamp but only 20% win for the other six lamps was used. There were 210 randomly ordered races. The response measure was the frequency of win responses to each stimulus lamp.

A Lindquist Type I trend analysis (8) was used to test the difference in the shape of the gradients elicited from the five groups.

RESULTS

The percentages of win responses to the stimulus lights for the five groups are shown in Fig. 1. For greater clarity, this figure combines the responses to peripheral lights spaced at 8, 16, and 24 degrees from the center light. It will be noted that the percentage of win responses decreases progressively as the angle separating a given light from the center increases. This result is in keeping with those of Brown, Clarke, and Stein (1) and of Fager and Knopf (3), who found that gradients of generalization could be elicited on this task. The over-all analysis among the five groups indicates significant differences at the .01 level in both height and slope of the gradients. In order to determine whether the schizophrenic and the from the psychotics and above the controls, comparisons were made between the neurotics vs. the controls and the neurotics vs. the combined psychotic group. These analyses indicated no difference between the neurotics and the controls, but a significant difference at the .001 level in the slope of the gradients between the neurotics and the psychotics. To the extent that the gradient for the neurotics falls significantly below

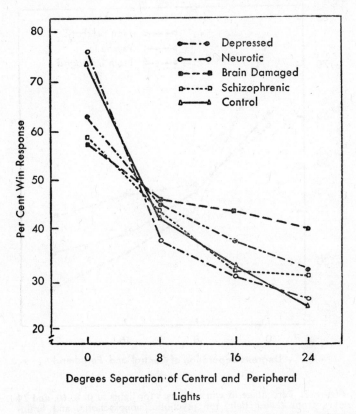

Figure 1. Percentage of win response for lights at 0, 8, 16, and 24 degrees from center light for psychiatric and control groups.

psychotically depressed groups could be combined in view of their differences in age, education, and diagnosis, an analysis of the gradients for these groups was made. No differences in either height or slope of the gradients were found.

With respect to the prediction that the SG gradient obtained from a neurotic group would fall below the gradient elicited that of the psychotics, the hypothesized relationship between severity of psychopathology and SG is supported. However, this relationship is not substantiated by the null finding in gradients between neurotics and control Ss. Perhaps the difference in severity of psychopathology between the neurotics and the controls was too small to be significantly manifested in generalization, or the task used to elicit gradients of SG was not sufficiently sensitive to reflect the difference.

Fig. 2 presents the percentage of win responses plotted for the brain-damaged group, the psychotic group (schizophrenic and depressed), and the nonpsychotic group (neurotic and control). The difference in the slope of the gradients between the psychotics and the

The brain-damaged group showed significantly more generalization than the control group at the .001 level. However, there was no evidence of differences between them and the psychotics. It is of interest to note that the findings for the brain-damaged Ss are at variance with those reported by Mednick (9). He found that brain-damaged Ss showed significantly less generalization than a nonpsychiatric

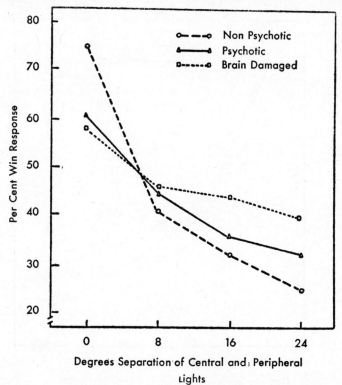

Figure 2. Percentage of win responses for lights at 0, 8, 16, and 24 degrees from center light for psychotic, nonpsychotic, and brain-damaged groups.

non-psychotics is significant at the .001 level. The psychotics showed a greater deviation from the predetermined schedule of 80% win to the center light and 20% win to the peripheral lights than the nonpsychotics. This finding supports the hypothesis predicting that psychotics show more generalization than nonpsychotic Ss. Here, again, the hypothesized relationship between severity of psychopathology and SG seems to be substantiated.

control and a schizophrenic group. Although the differences in sampling, experimental design, and the SG task between the two studies makes direct comparisons difficult, the apparent polarity of these findings requires definitive investigation.

DISCUSSION

Except for the null finding between the neurotics and the controls, our results confirm the hypotheses under study and support the posited relationship between severity of psychopathology and SG. It might appear, at first blush, that age and education differences among the groups could account for a large portion of the variance in our findings. While it was not possible to control for these differences, there are some indications in the data which tend to argue against such an interpretation. For example, if age was an important contributor, then we would expect to find similar gradients among the schizophrenics, neurotics, and controls, and differences in the gradients between the schizophrenics and depressives. These expectancies are not borne out in the results. Similarly, if education was an important factor, then we would expect to find no differences in gradients between the neurotics and schizophrenics or between the neurotics and depressives, but differences in gradients between the neurotics and controls and the schizophrenics and depressives. Here, again, none of these expectations were substantiated. The data reflect no consistent relationship between gradients of SG and either age or education.

The results may plausibly be attributed to the greater amount of behavior disorganization typically observed in the more severely ill. This interpretation suggests that increments in disorganization are associated with the greater number of errors (heightened gradients of SG) obtained in the psychotics as contrasted to the neurotics and controls. Such an interpretation is consistent with our application of drive theory in that there is considerable evidence which indicates that under conditions of heightened drive and emotionality, Ss make more errors (become more disorgagnized) on complex tasks (4, 5, 6, 7, 13). Thus, the concept of drive level may have some utility in further understanding the behavior of psychopathological groups. However, the ultimate utility of this concept rests upon further extensions of the relationship between degree of psychopathology and a wide variety of performances from which drive level may be inferred.

The performance of the brain-damaged Ss is quite interesting in that these individuals show elevated gradients comparable to those of the psychotics. This finding suggests that the brain-damaged group, at least with respect to this SG task, is as disorganized as the psychotics. While it seems reasonable to attribute this disorganization to neurological deficits, Miller (10) recently referred to a growing body of literature which indicates that brain lesions can modify emotionality, and brain stimulation can produce states from which drives can be inferred. Thus, future research may demonstrate that the disorganized behavior of the drain-damaged group may be in part a function of changes in drive level associated with neurophysiological impairment.

SUMMARY

On the basis of a postulated relationship between severity of psychopathology and SG, it was hypothesized that psychotics would show more generalization than nonpsychotic Ss and neurotics would should an SG gradient falling below that of the psychotics and above that of the controls. An SG task was administered to a total of 138 Ss (32 nonprofessional hospital employees, 26 neurotics, 32 psychotically depressed, 24 schizophrenics, and 24 brain-damaged). The results indicate that (a) the psychotics showed more generalization than the nonpsychotics; (b) the neurotics showed less generalization than the psychotics, but did not differ from the controls; and (c) the brain-damaged Ss showed more generalization than the nonpsychotics, but they did not differ from the psychotics.

Except for the finding of no difference in SG between the neurotics and the controls, these results confirm the hypotheses under study and support the posited relationship between severity of psychopathology and SG.

REFERENCES

1. Brown, J. S., Clarke, F. C., and Stein, L. A new technique for studying spatial generalization with voluntary responses. *J. exp. Psychol.*, 1958, *55*, 359–362.

2. Dollard, J., and Miller, N. E. *Personality and psychotherapy.* New York: McGraw-Hill, 1950.

3. Fager, R. E., and Knopf, I. J. Relationship of manifest anxiety to stimulus generalization. *J. abnorm. soc. Psychol.*, 1958, *57*, 125–126.

4. Farber, I. E., and Spence, K. W. Complex learning and conditioning as a function of anxiety. *J. exp. Psychol.*, 1953, *45*, 120–125.

5. Knopf, I. J., Worell, Judith, and Wolff, H. D. The effect of an "anxiety reducing" drug on stimulus generalization under experimental stress. *Amer. Psychologist*, 1958, *13*, 343. (Abstract)

6. Kohn, H. The effect of variations of intensity of experimentally induced stress upon certain aspects of perception and performance. *J. genet. Psychol.*, 1954, *85*, 289–304.

7. Korchin, S. Perceptual adequacy in life stress. *J. Psychol.*, 1955, *39*, 109–116.

8. Lindquist, E. F. *Design and analysis of experiments in psychology and education.* Boston: Houghton Mifflin, 1953.

9. Mednick, S. A. Distortions in the gradient of stimulus generalization related to cortical brain damage and schizophrenia. *J. abnorm. soc. Psychol.*, 1955, *51*, 536–542.

10. Miller, N. E. Central stimulation and other new approaches to motivation and reward. *Amer. Psychologist*, 1958, *13*, 100–108.

11. Miller, N. E., and Kraeling, Doris. Displacement: Greater generalization of approach than avoidance in a generalized approach-avoidance conflict. *J. exp. Psychol.*, 1952, *43*, 217–221.

12. Miller, N. E., and Murray, E. J. Displacement and conflict: Learnable drive as a basis for the steeper gradient of avoidance than of approach. *J. exp. Psychol.*, 1952, *43*, 227–231.

13. Taylor, Janet A., and Spence, K. W. Relationship of anxiety level to performance in serial learning. *J. exp. Psychol.*, 1952, *44*, 61–64.

Brainwashing, Conditioning and DDD (Debility, Dependency, and Dread)

I. E. FARBER, HARRY F. HARLOW, AND LOUIS JOLYON WEST

Few aspects of Communism have been more puzzling and disturbing to the Western world than the widely publicized collaboration, conversion, and self-denunciation in individuals—communist and noncommunist, innocent and guilty alike—who have suffered Communist imprisonment. Such behavior in persons whose intelligence, integrity, or patriotism can scarcely be doubted has suggested to many a mysterious power or knowledge that enables Communists to manipulate the thoughts and actions of

Reprinted by permission from *Sociometry*, Vol. 20, 1957.

others in a manner ordinarily reserved to characters in the more lurid sorts of science fiction. Accordingly, such terms as "brainwashing," "thought control," "menticide," and so on, have been applied to the process or product of this manipulation. To lend some degree of scientific respectability to such concepts, attempts have been made (e.g., *12, 16*) to relate them to the psychiatric implications of Pavlovian conditioning procedures.

While these speculations have an undeniable romantic appeal, more sober analyses (*1, 2, 7*) of factors influencing the behavior of prisoners under Communist control indicate that they are neither mysterious nor indicative of any unusual amount of psychiatric sophistication on the part of Communists. Indeed, considering the extraordinary degree of control the Communists maintain over the physical and social environments of their prisoners, it is rather surprising that their efforts to indoctrinate and convert have not been more successful. Contrary to the views of some writers in popular media, the record indicates that most American prisoners in Korea, for instance, showed remarkable "sales resistance," even under profound duress.

It is a fact that the Communist Chinese in Korea achieved considerable success in stimulating cooperative behavior in a large number of United Nations prisoners of war through a combination of threats, propaganda, group pressures, and group manipulation. By Segal's criteria, 15 per cent of American army prisoners cooperated unduly. And if it can be considered that it was every man's duty to exercise active resistance to the enemy and his propaganda during the period of captivity, then fully 95 per cent failed to meet the most stringent criteria for commendable behavior (18, 28, p. 80). Nevertheless, the Chinese induced only 21 American prisoners to remain under Communism (13), and it is doubtful whether all these were truly "converted." Most authorities agree that despite occasional lapses the vast majority of American prisoners of war performed well and honorably. As the Secretary of Defense's advisory committee on POW's has reported, "the record seems fine indeed" (30).

In the light of these findings, a complete analysis would concentrate more heavily on the factors that enabled the large majority of POW's to resist in some degree. However, it is not with these phenomena that the present discussion is primarily concerned. Rather, we wish to discuss the basis for the success of techniques whereby false confessions, self-denunciations, and participation in propaganda activities were brought about. The Communists made special efforts to elicit these behaviors in flying personnel, particularly with regard to confessions of participation in bacteriological warfare. After their world-wide propaganda campaign went into high gear with accusations of "germ warfare" in Korea, beginning on February 21, 1952, a vigorous policy of coercive pressure was applied to a large number of American flying personnel captured during the Korean conflict. As a result, a number of flyers from the Air Force and Marine Corps signed false confessions of bacteriological warfare and participated to various extents in enemy propaganda activities. A detailed account of those events may be found elsewhere (24, 28).

The objective intensity of noxious stimulation, injury, disease, malnutrition, deprivation, sleeplessness, fatigue, isolation, and threat suffered by many prisoners for a greater or lesser period was extreme. There were few, if any, who were not subjected to some of these conditions. Accounts of observations and experiments related to these various types of stress are now appearing in the literature in increasing number (e.g., 11, 29). The present discussion is concerned with the theoretical analysis of the psychological states and processes resulting from such objective conditions of stress.

DDD

Although the specific components of these states vary in intensity and pattern, in the case of the prisoner of war they contain at least three important elements: debility, dependency, and dread. They refer to the fact that individuals subjected to the kinds of environmental conditions listed above have reduced viability, are helplessly dependent on their captors for the satisfaction of many basic needs, and experience the emotional and motivational reactions of intense fear and anxiety. These components are separable, but it is evident that they also interact. Consequently it seems appropriate as well as convenient to conceive of these states and processes as though they were an entity or syndrome including debility, dependency, and dread, to be referred to as *DDD*. Among the POW's pressured by the Chinese Communists, the *DDD* syndrome in its full-blown form constituted a state of discomfort that was well-nigh intolerable.

Debility was induced by semi-starvation, fatigue, and disease. Chronic physical pain was a common feature. Loss of energy and inability to resist minor abuse, combined with the lack of proper facilities for the maintenance of personal hygiene, led to inanition and a sense of terrible weariness and weakness.

Dependency, produced by the prolonged deprivation of many of the factors, such as sleep and food, needed to maintain sanity and life itself, was made more poignant by occasional unpredictable brief respites, reminding the prisoner that it was possible for the captor to relieve the misery if he wished. If an individual was placed in prolonged isolation, as was so often the case with flyers pressed to confess to the bacteriological warfare charges, the deprivation of ordinary social stimulation and relations markedly strengthened the dependency. Although we shall not dwell on this aspect of the situation, the effectiveness of Communist methods was undoubtedly greatly enhanced by their control of the means for satisfying nuclear social needs for recognition, status, communication, and so on. The captors' condemnation and misunderstanding of American social values, in connection with the withdrawal of accustomed social supports, e.g., reliable sources of information and communication with others as a means of testing reality and of appraising moral standards, played a significant part in the dependency relationship (2, 7, 10, 17).

Dread is the most expressive term to indicate the chronic fear the Communists attempted to induce. Fear of death, fear of pain, fear of nonrepatriation, fear of deformity or permanent disability through neglect or inadequate medical treatment, fear of Communist violence against loved ones at home, and even fear of one's own inability to satisfy the demands of insatiable interrogators—these and many other nagging despairs constituted the final component of the *DDD* syndrome (2).

The interrelations of these factors, carefully contrived and nurtured by the Communists, were of great importance in determining the total effect of *DDD*. Although there were some individuals who acceded to the demands of their captors fairly early in the game, it is clear that the Chinese realized the importance of preparing the resistant prisoner, through *DDD*, for the long, drawn-out process designed to bring about the desired goal—complete compliance.

Before considering in greater detail the specific mechanisms underlying the role of *DDD* in accomplishing this aim, three prefatory comments are in order. First, the present analysis lays no claim to comprehensiveness. It deals with only a few aspects of *DDD* occurring under certain conditions. We believe these aspects to be important, but they are not all that is important. In this connection, the present paper may be considered as an elaboration of portions of the comprehensive discussion of Communist "thought reform" by Hinkle and Wolff (7). It is gratifying that our conclusions, arrived at independently and on somewhat more theoretical grounds, are essentially in agreement with theirs.

Secondly, our use of the terminology of learning theory, broadly conceived, and our use of concepts derived from conditioning, does not imply that we consider learning theory uniquely competent to explain the effects of *DDD*. On the other hand, we do consider factors influencing behavior in *DDD* to have something in common with factors affecting behavior in learning situations generally, and, therefore, that it may be worth while attempting to analyze some aspects of behavior associated with *DDD* in terms of principles of classical and instrumental conditioning. But, as an eminent conditioning theorist has recently noted (*20*), the view that principles derived from conditioning might apply to more complex behavior does not at all imply that complex behavior can be explained solely in terms of the variables affecting conditioning. In this instance, it is particularly doubtful that the procedures used to influence the behavior of prisoners under Communism derived from the methods of Pavlov, or that the prisoners' reactions are generally understandable in purely Pavlovian terms. On the contrary, to the extent that such concepts apply at all, selective or instrumental (Thorndikean) learning was a more prominent feature than classical (Pavlovian) conditioning. Certainly, only limited aspects of the behavior of prisoners under Communism bear any resemblance to the generalized inhibitory or excitatory states characterizing some of Pavlov's dogs (*14*).

Finally, we should beware of the "psychologist's error." Although some of the behavior of prisoners under Communism may be susceptible to analysis in terms of learning and conditioning principles, it does not follow that the application of these principles by Communist captors was deliberate and self-conscious. Animal trainers and side-show barkers are often extremely competent manipulators of behavior; this does not mean they are comparative or social psychologists.

DDD, SELF-PERCEPTION, AND THINKING

By providing a radically changed context *DDD* might be expected to produce new responses that actively compete or interfere with wonted behavior. It may also produce a condition of markedly reduced responsiveness, not unlike the generalized inhibitory states described by Pavlov (*14*) and Liddell (*8*), due to the reduced or monotonous stimulation associated with isolation and confinement, or to reduced energy, or to the frustration of previously successful techniques for achieving goals. Whenever individuals show extremely selective responsiveness to only a few situational elements, or become generally unresponsive, there is a disruption of the orderliness, i.e., sequence and arrangement of experienced events, the process underlying time spanning and long-term perspective. By disorganizing the perception of those experiential continuities constituting the self-concept and impoverishing the basis for judging self-consistency, *DDD* affects one's habitual ways of looking at and dealing with oneself.

This effect, which has elsewhere been related to the collapse of certain ego functions (*22*), bears an interesting resemblance to some aspects of the post-lobotomy syndrome. The latter, too, is characterized by apathy and the disturbance of the self-concept or self-regarding tendency (*15*). The frequency and degree of flattened affect and self-deprecation in the confessions of prisoners under Communism have probably been overestimated, but to the extent they have occurred, the observed behavior has much in common with that of some brain-damaged individuals.

Closely related to the foregoing consequence of *DDD* is a disturbance of association and a concreteness of thinking similar to that sometimes seen in schizophrenia. The retention of recent experiences and habit patterns may be impaired, with consequent regression, i.e., primitivization, in language, thought, and those integretative and mediating symbolic processes essential to reasoning and foresight. Conditioning performance in human subjects is impaired by some kinds of symbolic activity, and conversely, the impoverishment of thinking may increase susceptibility to arbitrary and unsubtle training procedures (cf. *3*) leading to relatively automatic and uncritical imitative responses. This susceptibility may be further enhanced by anxiety and emotionality (5, 21, 23).[1]

REINFORCEMENT OF SOCIAL COMMUNICATION

On the assumption that conditioning principles apply in part to the behavior of prisoners of war, it is important to analyze further the nature of the conditioned stimuli and the responses elicited by them. Careful consideration would seem to indicate that the situation contains features both of selective or instrumental learning and of classical conditioning (20). The instrumental (i.e., Thorndikean rather than Pavlovian) aspect is emphasized by the fact that an individual must acquire a particular set of responses in order to bring about a reinforcing state of affairs. It is our thesis that an alleviation in the state of DDD provides the reinforcement for much of the behavior desired by the enemy. In other words, DDD does not, in and of itself, produce the desired behavior. DDD merely provides the occasion for the selective reinforcement of certain modes of response.

The role of DDD in the reinforcement process depends on the fact that it is not constant. Instead, it may be assumed to fluctuate in time, partly as a result of spontaneous psychophysiological processes, and partly as a result of deliberate manipulations designed to maintain its intermittent nature (2), thus preventing its fall

to a baseline of permanent depression and hopelessness. Those individuals who were reduced to complete apathy undoubtedly represented failures from the point of view of their Communist captors.

At the risk of considerable oversimplification, one may conceive of two consequences of the occasional mitigation of DDD. First is the conditioning of the "expectancy" that DDD will be alleviated. (This constitutes the actual classically conditioned anticipatory goal response.) Relief, whether due to spontaneous factors or deliberate manipulations, is intermittent, temporary, and unpredictable. Far from weakening the expectancy of relief, however, this tends to maintain the expectancy and renders it less susceptible to extinction. In nontechnical terms, this process serves to keep hope alive, permitting some degree of adaptive behavior, and inhibiting self-destructive tendencies, which would frustrate the enemy's purpose.

This aspect of the learning process throws some light on the frequent practice in Communist prisons of having prisoners "punish themselves." Thus, a captive might be instructed to stand or kneel in a certain position until he should decide to cooperate. This emphasis on the self-inflicted nature of the prisoner's punishment, and his ability to mitigate his condition "voluntarily," is clearly calculated to increase the intensity of expectancies of the possibility of relief. At the same time, it is evident that the prisoner's belief that he actually exercises control is delusory. so far as the objective facts are concerned, since the captor may select any behavior he chooses as the condition for relieving a prisoner's distress.

The alleviation of DDD at the time of occurrence of the desired behavior leads to the second consequence—the learning of instrumental acts. This is not so difficult to arrange as one might suppose and is certainly not the result of any mysterious power of the manipulator. Very often, the desired behavior is verbal in nature. Verbal behavior is in a general way al-

[1] These assumptions do not imply a negative correlation between intelligence and conditioning in normal subjects, nor better conditioning in feeble-minded or brain-damaged subjects than in normal individuals. The empirical evidence does not support any such views. The suggested effect of impoverished thinking relates only to that produced by debility, isolation, and such factors. One may speculate, in this connection, on the relation between this putative effect of DDD and the kinds of hypersuggestibility and automatism reported among primitive peoples suffering from prolonged physical stress and privation. Whether these symptoms result from some state of hyperconditionability is a moot question. Arctic hysteria and latah, for instance, are presumably dissociative and therefore hysteroid in nature (25), and the relation between hysteria and conditioning is as yet uncertain (4, 5, 6). Thus it is not possible at present to identify the effects of DDD with any particular psychiatric state.

ready strongly conditioned to *DDD* in all human adults. One learns from infancy to use verbal behavior as a means of relieving or avoiding many of the components of *DDD*. And, as the foregoing discussion indicates, the aperiodic and unpredictable nature of the selective reward of particular language responses may be one of its chief strengths. If one may extrapolate from the results of numerous laboratory experiments, this is the very procedure calculated to produce the maximum number of responses and also to make them highly resistant to extinction, even in the absence of rewards (*19*).

The nature of the rewards used needs no elaboration. Relief of hunger, fatigue, isolation, or pain, even temporarily, serves as an automatic reward. Even the verbal and empty promise of alleviation of *DDD* leads to appropriate anticipatory goal responses, keeping hope alive. Paradoxically, interrogation, harangues, threats, and contumely may also have a rewarding aspect, so great is the acquired reinforcement value of social communication and speech, under conditions of isolation, dependency, and physical debility.

Since the habits of social communication associated with *DDD* are initially strong, and are further strengthened by selective reinforcement, it is not strange that prisoners often show considerable social responsiveness in the presence of their captors. Despite the impoverishment of the self-concept and primitivization of thinking referred to earlier, prisoners could enjoy in some degree a much needed social relationship in the interrogation and indoctrination situations. It may be hypothesized that some prisoners became the victims of the very socialization process that under ordinary circumstances is regarded as a desirable and, indeed, essential aspect of civilized living. It is of interest in this connection to record the finding of Lifton, who explicitly noted among a group of repatriated prisoners who had most aggressively resisted collaboration with the Communists, a large portion of individuals with significant antisocial tendencies (*9*). We do not suggest that collaboration and confession by prisoners under Communism are signs of desirable social attitudes. We do suggest that socialization training facilitates the tendency to engage in social communication, even with a recognized enemy, particularly under conditions in which the behavior is reinforced by the satisfaction of powerful drives while at the same time interfering or inhibitory tendencies are markedly reduced.

There are some analogies between the condition of an individual under such circumstances and that of a hypnotized subject. The hypnotized subject also tends to respond automatically, especially to verbal stimuli, to be greatly influenced by the attitude of the hypnotist, and to be highly selective in his social responsiveness. Furthermore, there is general agreement regarding the susceptibility of most normal individuals to hypnosis, except in the case of strong deliberate resistance. Under conditions of *DDD*, the possibility of resistance over a very long period may be vanishingly small. As soon as resistance appears, the intensity of *DDD* can be increased, thus at one and the same time punishing resistance and increasing the influence of the reward when relief occurs. It must be remembered that the strengthening effects of rewards—in this instance the alleviation of an intensely unpleasant emotional state—are fundamentally automatic. They occur because of the kind of nervous system we have, and not in any essential way because of the mediation of conscious thought processes.

RETENTION OF PRISON EXPERIENCES AND BEHAVIOR

What is the aftermath of such experiences? The evidence clearly indicates that, except in the case of organic brain damage such as might result from avitaminosis, the behavior of the typical returnee from Communist prisons is "normal," in the special and important sense that he behaves in a manner that would be predicted on the basis of ordinary laws of behavior. There is not the slightest evidence for the necessity of postulating new or unknown factors or conditions. This does not mean the experience of imprisonment leaves no trace. Such a circumstance would in itself be abnormal, i.e., inconsistent with the known principles of behavior. In terms of normative criteria, many ex-prisoners are more than ordinarily anxious, defensive, dependent, suspicious, insecure. Pressed to explain any possibly discreditable acts, they often exhibit a very considerable degree of hesitancy, vagueness, paramnesia, and rationalization. In a word, they behave exactly as one would expect of any individual required to explain and defend his behavior, many determinants of which he is not aware.

Most returnees remember a great deal of what occurred during their imprisonment. They do not remember everything and may be unable to give a very clear account of their own behavior. Some behavior may appear as strange and inexplicable to the person concerned as to anyone else. The explanation of whatever impairment of memory occurs may be found in the laws of forgetting, deriving from both clinic and laboratory. There is no need to expatiate here on the role of repression in forgetting when the material to be recalled elicits anxiety and guilt. But it may be useful to note briefly some of the factors that would influence retention even in the absence of these emotions.

In an earlier section, it was pointed out that the state of *DDD* produces responses that actively compete with ordinary responses to environmental stimuli. By the same process, the comforting and familiar stimuli of home and friends are associated with a wholly different set of responses from those produced by *DDD*. The changed context may actively inhibit recall of the prison experiences. This phenomenon is nothing more than the familiar psychological explanation of forgetting in terms of associative interference.

Among the most important of these competing responses are the affective ones. The returnee simply does not feel as he did as a prisoner. He may be able to talk about how he felt, although this too offers difficulties because our terminology for describing emotional states is woefully inadequate and vague (*3*), but he does not currently respond affectively in the same way. Similarly, the familiar stimuli of home reinstate different verbal responses, both overt and implicit, that affect recall. The returnee feels different, talks differently, and thinks differently than he did in the former context. Since, like all of us, he is unaware of many of the cues to his former behavior (as well as his current behavior), it is as useless to ask him to explain his earlier reactions as it is to ask a person why he once disliked olives or is for the moment unable to recall the name of an old acquaintance.

The particular reactions and attitudes constituting patriotism, bravery, loyalty, and so on, depend on the appearance of particular cues, symbolic or other. Such qualities are tendencies to respond positively or negatively, in varying degrees and combinations, in the presence of certain combinations of cues. From this point of view, unwonted reactions occurring under *DDD* do not represent a different attitude; rather, the habitual attitude does not appear because the appropriate cues have been removed. Back home in the presence of adequate cues, the returnee tends to act and feel as he did prior to imprisonment.

Finally, one must consider the effect on retention of the adequacy of the original impression. Occasionally the returnee does not remember much because he did not observe much. The impoverished stimulation, impaired responsiveness, reduced symbolic activity, and disorganization of time-spanning characteristic of *DDD* reduce the clarity and strength of impressions at the time of the original experience, and thus decrease ability to recall.

In the light of all these factors, whose pejorative influence on retention is well known by students of human learning, it is clearly to be expected that the recall of returnees would be something less than complete and wholly accurate as regards their actual prison experiences and behavior.

RESISTANCE TO EFFECTS OF DDD

Despite our opinion that the most undesirable effects of *DDD* are not necessarily permanent, or, given appropriate social conditions after repatriation, even particularly long-lived, the general picture of *DDD* presented in the foregoing discussion is rather gloomy. This is in part because we have emphasized its stressful aspects rather than the considerable resources most persons can muster to oppose them. The many environmental, social, and motivational variables that produce resistance to these effects have not been discussed, but their potency should certainly not be underestimated. As we have observed earlier, the resistance of American prisoners under Communism, in the face of the objective circumstances detailed above, was in most instances notable, and in some nothing less than heroic (*2, 24, 28*).

It is evident that there are great individual differences in susceptibility to *DDD* even under conditions in which the level of *DDD* itself could reasonably be regarded as constant, i.e., not a differential factor. To state the point somewhat differently, there are unquestionably a number of variables, whose values differ from person to person, affecting the degree of resistance to the effects of *DDD*. The question may then be raised whether the potency of these variables might not be increased in any given individual. We believe they can.

The statement, "Every man has his breaking point," contains a germ of truth, but like other bromides, is liable to misinterpretation. It does not mean the "breaking point" is fixed for any given individual, so that nothing can affect it. Such a view is scientifically indefensible, if not meaningless, since it implies that some kinds of behavior are unlawful, i.e., not affected by variations in any kinds of antecedent conditions. Furthermore, the term "breaking point" is itself misleading. Susceptibility to *DDD* or any other stressful condition is not an all-or-none affair. We are discussing behavior, and behavior varies in degree and in kind. It may be possible to define "breaking" in the manner that one defines a right or wrong response in arithmetic, but it should be recognized that such a definition would be arbitrary at best and of doubtful conceptual significance. As Biderman has pointed out, a prisoner's physical and moral strength may be sapped by Communist coercive methods to a degree that resistance appears insignificant. But, however feeble his performance, motivation to resist usually persists and shows itself as circumstances permit (*2*).

It is not the purpose of the present discussion to consider all the possible personal or social variables of which resistance to the effects of *DDD* may be a function, or indeed to consider any of them in detail. We mention two, not because they are necessarily of particular importance, but because they throw further light on the nature of the *DDD* state. First, there is the factor of physical health. Other things equal, there is probably a negative relation between degree of physical health and vigor on the one hand and susceptibility to *DDD* on the other. Debility can be postponed longer, dependency fought against, and the self-concept maintained more easily if bodily well-being obtains. Second, there is the factor of initial or chronic anxiety. No matter what anxiety is due to, the higher the anxiety level, the greater is the possibility of rewarding behavior by its momentary reduction. Contrariwise, a low level of initial anxiety should retard the growth of the "dread" component of *DDD*, and at least indirectly affect some of its antecedents, e.g., the reactivity to pain (*27*).

Thus, techniques for promoting health and decreasing anxiety in those who may become prisoners are probably of great importance. Nevertheless, one should not expect factors such as these to block the effects of *DDD* indefinitely. Physical health, for instance, may be of utmost value over in short haul, e.g., during early interrogation. But on a long-term basis it may be relatively insignificant. Health can be broken down by a determined and informed enemy in a very short time. And although a healthy individual can better resist the effects of debilitating variables, there is no evidence that, once illness and physical debility occur, previously healthy individuals can tolerate this condition better than those who might have become habituated to it. In some cases, indeed, the reverse might obtain.

A somewhat similar reservation may be expressed concerning procedures calculated to reduce initial anxiety, i.e., training individuals to be generally non-anxious. The fear component of *DDD*, unlike neurotic anxiety or neurotic fears (phobias), is quite realistic for the most part. Realistic fears are not easily extinguishable and, if they were, the desirability of extinguishing such fears is not altogether certain. For instance, fear of punishment for displaying hostility toward one's captors is adaptive. Wolf and Ripley (26) quote one prisoner of the Japanese in World War II in this regard: "I had to make a conscious effort not to resent things because I realized that my bones are brittle."

On the other hand, certain anticipatory fears may be modified through training procedures. Alleviation of unrealistic fears of the unknown (through accurate indoctrination regarding enemy methods) undoubtedly improves the ability of the individual to deal with those fears that are realistic. It may make it possible for him to admit his fear to himself, as a reasonable and expected reaction, thus modifying its influence as a covert force toward compliance. Furthermore, an expectation of the probable psychophysiological effects of stress may rob them of some of their "shock" value. Finally, a certain amount of transfer may be expected from stressful training experiences in which adaptive modalities have been learned, thus permitting the prisoner to conceptualize his current stressful experience in terms of previous (and at least partly successful) transactions under stress.

Still, it would be foolish to disregard the fact that some of the elements of *DDD* represent a pathological organic state, some consequences of which are probably innately determined. To the extent this is true, one cannot expect to achieve a great degree of phophylactic success in regard to the effects of *DDD*, any more than one can reasonably expect at the present state of knowledge to prevent some of the undesirable consequences of lobotomy.

Though many of the behavioral consequences of *DDD* are not innately determined, the conditioning of certain types of responses desired by the enemy may eventually occur, even in the face of superlative resistance. One of the conclusions that may legitimately be drawn from the present analysis of the circumstances of imprisonment under Communism is that, if a prisoner's state of *DDD* reaches a truly extreme degree of severity (and it cannot now be predicted whose ability to resist will be the most effective in combating *DDD*), and *if he lives,* he probably cannot be expected to resist indefinitely. This prediction does not require the assumption that Communists have mysterious powers, or that their prisoners are subjected to some strange process of "brainwashing" negating the effects of their previous training and attitudes. It is based, rather, on the assumption that under the physical, social, and emotional conditions of extreme *DDD*, some degree of ultimate compliance may be considered a natural consequence of the operation of ordinary principles of human behavior.

SUMMARY

Although the behavior of some prisoners under Communism, including collaboration, conversion, and self-denunciation, appears to suggest that Communists are able to "brainwash" their prisoners in a mysterious way, a consideration of the physical, emotional, and social conditions of the prisoner in conjunction with the ordinary principles of human behavior reveals that such behavior may be readily explained. The state of the prisoner may be described in terms of the concepts of debility, dependency, and dread (DDD), and some of the behavioral principles explaining the effects of the DDD state derive from learning and conditioning phenomena.

It is assumed that DDD operates in part to produce a generalized state of hyporesponsiveness, disrupting time-spanning processes and disorganizing the self-concept. Another consequence of DDD is the impairment of symbolic processes, perhaps rendering the prisoner susceptible to relatively simple conditioning techniques. The intermittent nature of DDD leads both to the expectancy of relief (i.e., hope) and to the reinforcement of specific kinds of verbal behavior. The latter effect is facilitated by the fact that social communication is already strongly conditioned to cues such as those produced by DDD, as a result of normal socialization training.

The typical prisoner returnee exhibits no extraordinary peculiarities of memory. The degree of forgetting of prison experiences is such as would be expected as a result of the inhibition of anxiety-producing thoughts (repression), change of situational context during recall, and the inadequacies of original impressions during imprisonment.

Resistance to the undesirable consequences of DDD is a matter of degree and may be modified by such factors as physical health and level of initial anxiety. Nevertheless, factors such as these cannot reasonably be expected to provide more than temporary respite. Through various defenses, a prisoner may postpone the development of extreme DDD for a long time, perhaps indefinitely. But if a prisoner's state of DDD is extreme, and if he lives, he probably cannot resist indefinitely. Far from furnishing proof of the operation of some unnatural process of "brainwashing," this eventuality is a predictable consequence of the operation of laws of normal human behavior.

REFERENCES

1. Bauer, R. A., "Brainwashing—Psychology or Demonology," American Psychological Association Symposium, September 3, 1956.

2. Biderman, A. D., "Communist Techniques of Coercive Interrogation," Air Force Personnel and Training Research Center Development Report TN-56-132, Lackland Air Force Base, Texas, 1956.

3. Dollard, J., and N. E. Miller, Personality and psychotherapy, New York: McGraw-Hill, 1950.

4. Eysenck, H. J., "Cortical Inhibition, Figural After Effect, and Theory of Personality," Journal of Abnormal and Social Psychology, 1955, 51, 94–106.

5. Farber, I. E., K. W. Spence, and H. P. Bechtoldt, "Emotionality, Introversion-Extraversion, and Conditioning," Midwestern Psychological Association, May 3, 1957.

6. Franks, C. M., "Conditioning and Personality: a Study of Normal and Neurotic Subjects," Journal of Abnormal and Social Psychology, 1956, 52, 143–150.

7. Hinkle, L. E., and H. G. Wolff, "Communist Interrogation and Indoctrination of 'Enemies of the State,' " Archives of Neurology and Psychiatry, 1956, 76, 115–174.

8. Liddell, H. S., "Conditioned Reflex Methods and Experimental Neurosis," in J. McV. Hunt (ed.), Personality and the Behavior Disorders, New York: Ronald, 1944.

9. Lifton, R. J., "Home by Ship: Reaction Patterns of American Prisoners of War Repatriated from North Korea," American Journal of Psychiatry, 1954, 110, 732–739.

10. Lifton, R. J., " 'Thought Reform' of Western Civilians in Chinese Communist Prisons," Psychiatry, 1956, 19, 173–196.

11. Lilly, J. C., "Effects of Physical Restraint and of Reduction of Ordinary Levels of Physical Stimuli on Intact, Healthy Persons," Group for the Advancement of Psy-

chiatry, *Symposium No. 2, Illustrative Strategies for Research on Psychopathology in Mental Health,* New York: GAP Publication Office, 1790 Broadway.

12. Meerloo, J. A. M., "Pavlovian Strategy as a Weapon of Menticide," *American Journal of Psychiatry,* 1954, *110,* 809–813.

13. Pasley, V., *21 Stayed,* New York: American Book—Stratford Press, 1955.

14. Pavlov, I. P., *Conditioned Reflexes and Psychiatry,* W. H. Gantt (trans.), New York: International, 1941.

15. Robinson, M. F., and W. Freeman, *Psychosurgery and the Self,* New York: Grune and Stratton, 1954.

16. Santucci, P. S., and G. Winokur, "Brainwashing as a Factor in Psychiatric Illness," *Archives of Neurology and Psychiatry,* 1955, *74,* 11–16.

17. Schein, E. H., "The Chinese Indoctrination Program for Prisoners of War," *Psychiatry,* 1956, *19,* 149–172.

18. Segal, J., "Factors Related to the Collaboration and Resistance Behavior of U. S. Army PW's in Korea," *Technical Report 33, Human Resources Research Office,* The George Washington University, Washington, D. C., 1956.

19. Skinner, B. F., *Behavior of Organisms,* New York: Appleton-Century, 1938.

20. Spence, K. W., *Behavior Theory and Conditioning,* New Haven, Conn.: Yale University Press, 1956.

21. Spence, K. W., and I. E. Farber, "Conditioning and Extinction as a Function of Anxiety," *Journal of Experimental Psychology,* 1953, *45,* 116–119.

22. Strassman, H. D., M. B. Thaler, and E. H. Schein, "A Prisoner of War Syndrome: Apathy as a Reaction to Severe Stress,"

American Journal of Psychiatry, 1956, *112,* 998–1003.

23. Taylor, J. A., "The Relationship of Anxiety to the Conditioned Eyelid Response," *Journal of Experimental Psychology,* 1951, *41,* 81–92.

24. West, L. J., "U. S. Air Force Prisoners of the Chinese Communists," Group for the Advancement of Psychiatry Symposium on Prisoners of War, Nov. 11, 1956.

25. West, L. J., "Hypnosis and the Dissociative Reactions," *Journal of Clinical and Experimental Hypnosis* (in press).

26. Wolf, S., and H. S. Ripley, "Reactions among Allied Prisoners Subjected to 3 Years of Imprisonment and Torture by Japanese," *American Journal of Psychiatry,* 1947, *104,* 180–193.

27. Wolff, H. G., and S. Wolf, *Pain* (3d ed., 1952), New York: Charles C. Thomas, 1952.

28. "Communist Interrogation, Indoctrination and Exploitation of American Military and Civilian Prisoners," *Hearings Before the Permanent Subcommittee on Investigations of the Committee on Government Operations, U. S. Senate, 84th Congress, 2nd Session,* Washington, D. C.: U. S. Government Printing Office, 1956.

29. "Factors Used to Increase the Susceptibility of Individuals to Forceful Indoctrination: Observations and Experiments," *Group for the Advancement of Psychiatry, Symposium No. 3,* New York: GAP Publications Office, 1790 Broadway.

30. "POW: The Fight Continues After the Battle," *Report of the Secretary of Defense's Advisory Committee on Prisoners of War,* Washington, D. C.: U. S. Government Printing Office, 1955.

4 | *Socialization Variables in Relation to Behavior Disorders*

M<small>ANY</small> forms of behavior pathology appear to be the products of defective socialization. This conception lies at the base of the case history method in clinical work. To be properly "socialized" or enculturated means to have acquired the habits and attitudes that are considered appropriate to one's age, sex, occupational, and other roles.

The studies included in this section illustrate several aproaches to the study of defective socialization. Greenfield, using the method of retrospective self-report, focuses on types of discipline in childhood. The association between discipline and the acquisition of appropriate behavior is part of every person's theory of child rearing. But the specification of what *kinds* of discipline favor pathological behavior has received little attention in systematic studies. Greenfield shows how "indirect" methods of discipline are more frequently associated with disordered personalities than "direct" methods. A further analysis of discipline with the aid of concepts drawn from learning theory poses a new frontier for research workers. Another analysis of discipline might relate the experience of "shame" to direct discipline and the experience of guilt to indirect discipline.

Kohn and Clausen, also using retrospection by subjects as their raw data, offer some unsettling findings about a hypothesis that most behavior pathologists regard as true. Countless clinical studies have led to the inference that social isolation in adolescence is an important etiological factor in schizophrenia. Limiting their data to retrospections of the ages 13-14, the answers to questions posed during structured research interviews allowed the construction of an Index of Social Isolation. About two-thirds of the patients showed no differences on this index when compared with controls, thus challenging the long-standing hypothesis that links schizophrenia with one aspect of adolescent socialization.

Schofield and Balian also addressed themselves to differential socialization as the important etiological variable in schizophrenia. They approached the problem through the systematic analysis of life histories. Their recognition of the biases that go into "psychiatric histories" is worth an extra reading.

117

A common criticism of research in which life-history methods are used is the absence of control groups. Of 300 reported studies of life histories of mental patients, fewer than 10 employed a comparable control group. Schofield and Balian attempted to meet this criticism by taking life histories of nonpsychiatric patients, using the categories of the psychiatric history. Their aim was to discover in what ways, if any, psychiatric and nonpsychiatric patients differ. Their results question the validity of many hypotheses about the relationship between early socialization variables and pathology. Poverty, for example, differentiated between the two groups, but in the direction opposite to that predicted by the folklore. The overlap between normals and schizophrenics was so great that one must question the notion that schizophrenic disorganization follows from socialization practices and settings that at the gross level, at least, deviate from the normal. The results direct us to the question: what *subtle* factors in socialization (or in constitution) operate to mitigate the effects of uncertainty, isolation, lack of affection, and so on? Or stated in an alternate way, is there a suppressor variable that insulates or immunizes the person from a pathological environment?

The remaining two studies in this section focus on psychopathic deviates. Gough reports a number of studies which were guided by a theory of socialization having had its origin in the writings of George Herbert Mead and other role theorists. Antisocial behavior is construed as symptomatic of defective socialization. His analysis of defective socialization is in terms of inadequate or inept role-taking.

Gough adds to this reader a description of an important method in behavior science. He reports the construction of a scale that differentiates between and within groups of antisocial persons and "normals." He also offers some compelling data and arguments for regarding socialization as a measurable continuum.

The research report by Lykken might just as readily have been included in Section 7 because of the use of psychophysiological methods, or in Section 3 because of the employment of learning concepts. We place it here because of its continuity of subject-matter with Gough's paper. The sociopaths described by Lykken are persons who would score at the low end of Gough's socialization scale.

The locus of interest in Lykken's paper is different from Gough's. While the latter draws his conclusions exclusively from scale scores of criterion groups calculated on the basis of yes-or-no answers to self-revealing questions, the former turns his attention to the concept of *anxiety* as measured by physiological indicants and learning variables as well as scores on various scales. The finding that psychopaths do not condition to an anxiety situation points to enormous possibilities for an experimental analysis of the socialization process.

The Relationship between Recalled Forms of Childhood Discipline and Psychopathology

NORMAN S. GREENFIELD

IN RECENT years, many articles have appeared in both the lay and professional literature with the primary in-

Reprinted by permission from the *Journal of Consulting Psychology*, Vol. 23, No. 2, 1959.

tent of advising parents to stop worrying so much about pseudoexpertness in parenthood. In general, the drift of informed opinion—vintage 1958—is in the direction of minimizing the rigidity of old authority accentuating the fallibility of contemporary authority and, in essence, urging the anxious parent to relax and enjoy herself (himself) with her children. Doing what comes naturally is the current fashion and has been advocated by such spokesmen as Spock (8), Baruch (2) and Bruch (3).

The advocacy of the principle of "doing what comes naturally" with one's children is but a single facet of a much larger problem relating to the inhibition of feeling expression in general. There is a growing body of clinical opinion which suggests that one of the primary dimensions of psychopathology is an inability to freely express feeling at subsequent cost to the individual. The literature of psychosomatic medicine is replete with illustrations of some of the cost in terms of structural changes within the individual which lead to organic illness.

Rogers (6) is one of many who have emphasized the importance of accessibility of feelings to the self in maintaining adjustment. Advocates of the "doing what cames naturally" school of child rearing practice recognize the crucial importance of expressing genuine feeling in the parent-child relationship. Kanner (4), in describing the parents of a series of very seriously disturbed children diagnosed as suffering from early infantile autism, emphasized the coldness and formality of these people and their inability to behave in a spontaneous or demonstrative manner.

The central focus of this paper is not on discipline as a learning experience. Such an approach is well represented in Sears, Maccoby, and Levin (7). In the present study, discipline is viewed as an index of the kinds of feeling communication which may exist between parent and child. Spock (9) has noted that the mode of discipline expression may serve as a sensitive indicator of the parent's feelings toward the child. After espousing the salutary effect of ". . . an occasional swift slap on the behind . . .," Spock (9) notes that "The inhibition against this and other brisk, direct, impulsive methods has played a part in pushing parents into more civil-ized and more damaging techniques" (p. 76).

Within this frame of reference the present study reflects an attempt to investigate the relationship between recalled forms of childhood discipline practices and psychopathology. If indeed the parent-child relationship is crucial to personality functioning and malfunctioning, and if discipline practice is an indicator of a broader set of behaviors and attitudes, then the hypothesis suggested is that psychiatric patients will report a greater incidence of indirect discipline forms, while a control group will report a greater percentage of direct expressions of discipline.

METHOD

The subjects (Ss) were 58 outpatients of a university student phychiatric clinic whose diagnoses ranged from relatively mild adjustment reactions to longstanding schizophrenic reactions. There were 26 females and 32 males. The technique of matched control was employed and for each patient a control S matched for sex, age, father's occupational level, and size of home town community was selected from the university population. The average age of the patient group was 22.69 years with a range from 18 to 38, while the average for the control group was 22.48 years with a range from 18 to 37 years. On a scale from one to seven, the mean socioeconomic status of the patients was 2.78 and for the controls 2.71, indicating a generally middleclass background. The average S from both groups came from home town communities of between 10,000 and 100,000 populations. Each S was given a questionnaire which contained nine of the usual forms of punishment the parents employed. This questionnaire had previously been used by MacKinnon (5) in a study which demonstrated differences in recalled forms of discipline among violators and nonviolators of prohibitions. In the present study, S was asked to check the forms most usually employed by the mother, the father, or by both. The forms of discipline were: being scolded or reasoned with; being spanked; being sent away from the group; being denied some pleasure; being made to feel that the S is not as good as his brother, sister, or other children; being made to feel that the child had hurt the mother or father; being made to feel that the child had fallen short of what was expected of him; being denied any demonstration of affection by mother or father; and being told by the mother or father that they cannot love the child when he is bad.

These items fall roughly into two groups of treatments: the first four items represent a relatively direct, "physical," unambiguous means of discipline expression, while the second group represents a more subtle expression of "psychological" discipline. Here the emphasis falls upon the

forms of "indirect" discipline was computed for each S, and between-group difference for the various parent-child relationships were analyzed. The results permitted rejection of the null hypothesis in all instances except in the case of fathers of girls wherein no significant difference was found (see Table 1).

DISCUSSION

It should be emphasized that no known selective factor influenced the choice of experimental Ss other than their status as psychiatric outpatients. For a period of several weeks the questionnaire was administered to all patients coming to the clinic.

At first sight, the data which indicates that the Ss in both groups reported

TABLE 1. COMPARISON OF MEAN PERCENTAGES FOR "INDIRECT" FORMS OF DISCIPLINE FOR 58 PATIENTS AND MATCHED CONTROLS

	Patients		Controls			
Source	Mean	SD	Mean	SD	z	p
Parents	54.3	26.40	70.6	20.70	2.57	.005
Mothers	56.2	25.49	72.4	26.09	3.00	.001
Fathers	58.8	38.37	71.3	34.58	1.81	.035
Parents of males	54.7	21.92	71.8	23.09	2.49	.006
Parents of females	55.4	20.76	72.8	18.07	2.55	.005
Mothers of males	58.8	33.75	73.4	27.07	2.10	.017
Mothers of females	51.9	26.65	71.9	25.24	2.50	.006
Fathers of males	48.3	40.29	73.4	32.34	1.81	.035
Fathers of females	73.3	30.00	68.8	34.74	1.93	.052*

* Two-tailed test.

arousal of guilt feelings in the child and the expression of disappointment or denial of love by the parent. For purposes of the present study the first group was thought of as "direct" discipline practice, while the second group was labeled "indirect" discipline practice.

RESULTS

In evaluating the results it was first thought necessary to establish the fact that any difference found would be a function of differing emphases in method rather than of total number of items responded to, and thus a comparison of total responses for both groups was made with the finding that no significant differences exist.

The percentage of the reported

that their parents relied more on physical than indirect discipline seem at odds with the generally held belief that parents of middle-class children use less physical discipline than do the parents of the lower class. This may well be the case in an absolute sense, but with regard to the ratio of "direct" to "indirect" discipline the present results are entirely consistent with a previous study (5), which utilized the same questionnaire with a group of Harvard students. The data presented by Sears, Maccoby, and Levin (7), on the reported use of physical discipline add further confirmation to the impression that the present findings in this regard are probably representative.

To the extent that we can assume

a relationship between recalled and practiced discipline, what are some of the implications of these results?

Implicit in the hypothesis is the belief that direct and indirect forms of discipline are related to more general modes of direct and indirect expressions of feeling or, more properly, to the relative ability or inability of the parent to express genuine feelings toward the child. It is assumed that the inability to come to terms with one's own feelings regarding discipline-provoking situations is but one aspect of a more generalized emotional suppression. It is this inhibition of expression which may be transferred to the child and thus give rise to emotional difficulties. In effect, the child learns to respond as he has been responded to.

The concept of limits becomes relevant in terms of the mechanism of this learning process. The setting of limits by the parent in the direct method frees the situation of much of its fearful ambiguity and permits the child to express feelings which could not be expressed in a less well defined context which necessarily is fraught with all the dangers of the unknown. Phenomenologically, the child must first know where he stands before he can permit himself the risk.

Another factor in this learning not to express feelings is what Baldwin (1) has called the parental technique of visible suffering. Baldwin pointed out that what MacKinnon (5) called "psychological" discipline and what the present investigator termed "indirect" discipline is, in fact, the parental expression of pain and shame which has a guilt-inducing effect on the child. In the present formulation we need take this only one step further and point out that the guilt feelings become prominent inhibitors of feeling expression.

This interpretation does not imply a single cause for all the behavior pathology encountered at the clinic wherein the study was carried out. However, the present formulation is presented with the belief that inhibition of affective expression is a common nuclear correlate. Studies are currently in progress to test this relationship with regard to the recalled expression of parents' positive feelings.

The problem raised by the inconsistency in the results with regard to fathers of females will be left unanswered. It is tempting to discuss some of the possible implications of the cultural role of the father of the female in this context, but these pages have little room for sheer speculation.

SUMMARY

The hypothesis that psychiatric patients will report a greater incidence of indirect or "psychological" forms of childhood discipline, while a control group will report a greater percentage of direct or "physical" discipline, was tested in a university population. The results indicate general confirmation of the hypothesis. Theoretical implications in terms of viewing methods of discipline as behavior samples representative of more generalized attitudes of feeling expression in the parent-child relationship are discussed.

REFERENCES

1. Baldwin, A. L. *Behavior and development in childhood*. New York: Holt, Rinehart and Winston, 1955.

2. Baruch, Dorothy W. *New ways in discipline*. New York: McGraw-Hill, 1949.

3. Bruch, Hilde. *Don't be afraid of your child*. New York: Farrar, Straus & Young, 1953.

4. Kanner, L. Early infantile autism. *J. Pediat.*, 1944, 25, 211–217.

5. MacKinnon, D. W. Violation of prohibitions. In H. A. Murray, *Explorations in personality*. New York: Oxford Univer. Press, 1938. Pp. 491–501.

6. Rogers, C. *Client-centered therapy*. Boston: Houghton Mifflin, 1951.

7. Sears, R., Maccoby, Eleanor, and Levin, H. *Patterns of child rearing.* Evanston, Ill.: Row, Peterson, 1957.

8. Spock, B. *The pocket book of baby and child care.* New York: Pocket Books, 1946.

9. Spock, B. Symposium on the healthy personality. In M. J. Senn (Ed.), *Transactions of special meetings of conference on infancy and childhood.* Supp. 2, New York: Josiah Macy, Jr., 1950.

Social Isolation and Schizophrenia

MELVIN S. KOHN AND JOHN A. CLAUSEN

OF THE several hypotheses relating the frequency of mental disorders to social conditions, none has been more persistently enunciated than that which proposes that schizophrenia is the outgrowth of social isolation. First stated by Faris in 1934 (*3*), this hypothesis subsequently seemed consistent with, and indeed explanatory of, the findings of Faris and Dunham's classic ecological study of mental disorder. Faris and Dunham ascertained that high rates of first hospital admissions for schizophrenia are found in areas of the city characterized by high residential mobility and low socio-economic status, among ethnic group persons living in non-ethnic areas, and among the foreign-born populations of the slums (*5*). All of these indices were regarded as reflecting tendencies toward the social isolation of certain segments of the population.

In early statements of the hypothesis, Faris suggested that "any form of isolation that cuts the person off from intimate social relations for an extended period of time may possibly lead to this form of mental disorder" (*3*). More recent statements have suggested that isolation is a result of incongruent intra-familial and extra-familial orientations toward the child and represents a stage in a "typical process" for schizophrenics. Briefly this typical process is said to involve the following stages:

(1) "Parental oversolicitude produces the 'spoiled child' type of personality," and leads to

(2) "a certain isolation from all but the intimates within the family."

(3) "The next stage is persecution, discrimination or exclusion by children outside the family."

(4) "The most usual reaction to this persecution is to feel unhappy but with no immediate depreciation of establishing friendships."

(5) "Often the children try for years to make friends. . . . Eventually there is a resignation—a withdrawal from a hopeless goal. . . . From this time on their interest in sociability declines and they slowly develop the seclusive personality that is characteristic of the schizophrenic."

(6) Finally, the symptoms of schizophrenia are ascribed to the lack of social experience in the person so isolated: "Not being experienced in intimate personal contacts with a larger number of other persons he is deficient in his understanding of the reactions of others, and responds unconventionally and inappropriately to them" (*4*).

This view holds that social isolation —that is, the diminution or total absence of social interaction with peers—enters the schizophrenic process as a directly predisposing or "causative" factor. The bizarre behavior of the schizophrenic is attributed to social inexperience stemming from isolation. Presumably then, such isolation should underlie all schizophrenic disorders. Supporting evidence for this hypothesis was provided in a study by Dunham of the early social experience of catatonic schizophrenes who grew up in areas of high delinquency rates (*2*). On the other hand, Weinberg found little evidence of social isolation in the childhood histories of a sample of acute schizophrenics (called by him transient schizophrenics), more than half of whom were catatonics (*6*).

Reprinted by permission from the *American Sociological Review*, Vol. 20, No. 3, June 1955.

The present paper reports findings of a study designed to ascertain the extent and significance of social isolation in adolescence in a sample group of schizophrenic patients and a matched group of normal controls. A small group of manic-depressive patients, together with controls for these patients, was also studied.

SAMPLE AND METHOD OF DATA COLLECTION

The sample of patients interviewed consists of 45 schizophrenic and 13 manic-depressive patients who were first admitted to mental hospitals in Maryland during the period 1940-1952. These comprise 58 out of a total of 79 first admissions from Hagerstown, Maryland, who were diagnosed either schizophrenic or manic-depressive during this period. Of the 21 patients not interviewed, at the time of the research, 11 were too ill, 6 had moved too far from the site of the research, and 4 refused to be interviewed. Thus interviews were secured with 73 per cent of the total sample and 94 per cent of those patients who can be regarded as having been physically and psychologically accessible. In 15 of the 21 cases where an interview with the patient was not possible, we were able to interview a close relative. Analysis of these interviews demonstrates that the non-interviewed patients do not differ appreciably from the interviewed patients with respect to their social participation as adolescents.

Controls were individually paired with the patients on the basis of age, sex, and occupation (or father's occupation), using records derived from Public Health Service morbidity studies conducted periodically in Hagerstown since 1921. By this method it was possible to accomplish matching as of a period well before the onset of illness—on the average, 16 years before hospitalization. In roughly half of the cases the patient and his control had attended the same class in public school. In addition to individual matching on the characteristics mentioned, over-all frequencies were balanced with respect to family composition and area of residence.[1]

The interview schedule covered the following topics: residential and occupational history, relationships in the parental family, friendship and activity patterns in early adolescence, dating patterns, social participation as an adult, and a brief psychosomatic inventory.

All interviews with patients were conducted by one of the authors, as were approximately one-fifth of the interviews with controls. The balance of the controls were interviewed by another staff member after a period of training and with careful check to insure comparability of approach.

EXTENT OF SOCIAL ISOLATION AMONG SCHIZOPHRENICS

Assessment of social isolation was accomplished by the use of an index of social participation based upon the respondents' answers to two types of questions.

TABLE 1. USUAL PLAY PATTERNS OF PATIENTS AND CONTROLS IN ADOLESCENTS

Usually played	Schiz.	Con-trols	Manic-dep.	Con-trols
With crowd or close friends	20	37	6	11
With siblings	5	6	1	2
Alone	8	1	4	....
Primarily alone, but occasionally with crowd, close friends, or siblings	12	1	2	....
Total	45	45	13	13

The first ascertained *with whom* the respondent played when he was 13-14 years old, the second *what types* of activities he

[1] Our intent in pairing patients and controls on some variables and balancing frequencies on others was to hold constant several variables known to relate significantly to the frequency of schizophrenia, and then to examine the relationship between presence or absence of this illness and other characteristics or experiences of the two groups, especially with reference to social isolation. This is, of course, quite different from the intent and assumptions involved in matching for an experimental design entailing "before" and "after" measures.

engaged in at that age.[2] We first asked:

"(When you were 13 or 14 years old) did you usually hang out with a crowd, with one or two close friends, with your brothers or sisters, or did you stay by yourself most of the time?"

Both schizophrenic and manic-depressive patients more frequently than their controls replied that they stayed by themselves, controls that they played with a crowd or with close friends.[3]

To determine the *types* of social activities in which respondents engaged, we asked a series of questions:

(1) What were your favorite activities or pastimes when you were 13 or 14 years old?
(2) What sorts of things did you and your friends do together?
(3) What were the types of things you most enjoyed doing *alone* when you were 13 or 14?
(4) Did you enjoy (the things you did alone) as much as you enjoyed playing with other children?
(5) Thinking back to whomever it was you considered your closest friend about the time you were 13 or 14, can you tell me what sorts of things you most enjoyed doing together?
(6) Did you belong to the scouts, the "Y," or any clubs in school, or Sunday School? Which clubs?

[2] It was necessary to delimit the time period about which we asked in order to secure reasonably comparable data from all respondents. It was difficult to determine, however, which time period was most important. In all probability the crucial phases of personality development do not occur at the same age for all persons. It is also probable that some important events in the individual's relations with his peers occur at so early an age that we cannot expect an adult to remember them. Thus, our selection had to be to some degree arbitrary. Age 13-14 had the two virtues of being a period of high peer-group activity and of being quite definitely marked in the respondent's memory by virtue of the transition from grade school to high school.
We shall show, later in this paper, that the age range selected affects the number of isolates we distinguish in a group of patients, but that it does not affect the question of the possible etiological importance of isolation.

[3] The significance of differences between the patient and control groups has been tested by the method suggested by McNemar for comparisons between samples whose means are intercorrelated See Quinn McNemar, *Psychological Statistics,* New York: John Wiley and Sons, 1949, pp. 71-82. The chi-square test was used for testing the significance of differences between the proportions of isolated and non-isolated patient groups. The five per cent level has been used as the criterion of significance.

This material was then coded without knowledge of any respondent's replies to other questions, or whether the respondent was a patient or a control.[4] Four categories were used: (a) activities primarily social, with few or no solitary activities; (b) both social and solitary activities; (c) activities primarily solitary, with few or no social activities; and (d) ambiguous cases.

TABLE 2. TYPES OF ACTIVITIES PARTICIPATED
IN BY PATIENTS AND
CONTROLS IN ADOLESCENCE

	Schiz.	Con-trols	Manic-dep.	Con-trols
Activities primarily social, few or no solitary activities	15	21	4	5
Both social and solitary activities	19	20	6	6
Activities primarily solitary, few or no social activities	9	3	3	1
Ambiguous cases	2	1	0	1
Total	45	45	13	13

Finally, these two aspects of social participation—*with whom* the individual played and the *types* of activities in which he engaged—were combined to form a single index. In schematic form, this *Index of Social Participation*[5] is as follows:

[4] The answers to these particular questions were transcribed onto separate sheets of paper, without identifying information and without the answers to any other questions. Patients and controls were randomly interspersed. Two coders working independently agreed 94 per cent of the time on the categories in which they would place respondents. We attempted to code this same material along several other continua (for example, physical-sedentary, competitive-non-competitive, structured-non-structured) but coding reliability was too low, approximating only 60 per cent. Interviewing specifications had not been drawn up with such dimensions clearly envisaged.

[5] Evidence on the consistency of responses to items in this index with related items not included in the index is provided by the answers to the question, "(At the age of 13-14) did you spend more or less time alone than most other children your age did (or did you spend the same amount of time alone?)" The isolates without exception replied, "more time alone." Nine of the eleven partial-isolates replied "more time alone" and the other two replied, "The same amount of time as the average." Among the non-isolates, eight replied that they spent more time alone, 35 that they spent the average time alone, and 27 that they spent less time alone than other children their age.

PATTERN OF ASSOCIATION IN PLAY ACTIVITIES (AT AGE 13-14)

Types of activities	"Alone"	"Alone, but occasionally with friends or crowd"	"With siblings," or "alone, but occasionally with siblings"	"With close friends" or "crowd"
Social	X	X	Played only with siblings	Non-isolates
Both social and solitary	X	Partial isolates		
Solitary	Isolates	X	X	X

(X = Ambiguous classification)

Comparing patients to controls on the basis of this Index, we find a significantly larger proportion of both the schizophrenics and the manic-depressive than of the controls have been isolates or partial-isolates. However, this is by no means true of all patients—only one-third of the schizophrenics and one-third of the manic-depressives had been isolated or partially-isolated at this age. Finally, patients and controls do *not* differ with respect to the proportion who played only with siblings.[6] For two-thirds of the patients, then, ret-

patients were not isolated as adolescents, there remains the possibility that isolation was a predisposing factor for the remaining one-third; these may constitute a distinct sub-group whose etiology differs from that of other patients. If so, this sub-group cannot be defined according to the usual diagnostic criteria. Schizophrenics are no more likely to have been isolates than are manic-depressives: the proportion of manic-depressives who were classified as having been isolates or partial isolates is 38 per cent, the proportion of schizophrenics 34

TABLE 3. CLASSIFICATION OF SOCIAL PARTICIPATION OF PATIENTS AND CONTROLS

	Schizophrenics		Controls		Manic-depres.		Controls	
	Number	Per Cent	Number	Per Cent	Number	Per Cent	Number	Per Cent
Isolates	7	16	1	2	3	23	0	0
Partial-isolates	8	18	1	2	2	15	0	0
Played only with siblings	9	20	6	14	1	8	2	15
Non-isolates	19	42	36	80	6	46	9	70
Ambiguous cases	2	4	1	2	1	8	2	15
Total	45	100	45	100	13	100	13	100

rospective reports show no discernible social isolation in early adolescence.

In the present state of psychiatric knowledge, there is considerable question whether either schizophrenia or manic-depressive psychosis is a single disease of common etiology or a group of similar appearing diseases of differing etiology. For this reason, even though two-thirds of the

per cent. Similarly, within the schizophrenic group the proportion of isolates is approximately the same among paranoids (42 per cent) as it is among catatonics (31 per cent).[7]

6 The most important fact about the persons who played only with siblings is that all of the patients and all but one of the controls in this category are female.

7 Though the number of cases on which these percentages are based is small, the consistency is so striking that it seems justified to conclude that there are no appreciable differences in the proportion of isolates and partial-isolates in these diagnostic groups. (These percentages are based on 26 cases of paranoid schizophrenia and 16 cases of catatonic schizophrenia.) Nor is isolation a sex-linked phenomenon: the proportion of females among isolates is 55 per cent, among non-isolates, 64 per cent. (Based on 20 male cases and 38 female cases.)

Therefore, it appears that, for the cases here studied, social isolation in early adolescence is not a necessary condition for any subtype of schizophrenia. There remains, however, the task of examining the conditions leading up to isolation and the consequences of isolation. We turn to a direct comparison of the adolescent social experiences of the isolated and the non-isolated patients. Because the proportion of isolates and partial-isolates among the manic-depressives is so similar to the proportion among schizophrenics, the two diagnostic groups will be considered together. The results that will be presented are almost precisely the same as those for the schizophrenic group alone, because empirically the manic-depressive isolates and partial-isolates behaved similarly to the schizophrenic isolates and partial-isolates, and the manic-depressive non-isolates behaved similarly to the schizophrenic non-isolates.

Conditions Leading to Isolation

There are several possible reasons why the isolates might have been prevented from playing with other children—for example, childhood illness, living on out-of-the-way farms, great residential mobility. But a systematic comparison shows that

these factors were no more applicable to the isolated and partially isolated patients than to the non-isolated patients. A slightly higher proportion of the isolates report fewer than five available playmates, but the difference does not approach statistical significance and even among the isolates 14 in 20 report there were five or more children of their age living in the neighborhood.

The isolates were not prevented by serious illness from playing with other children: isolates and partial-isolates do not differ significantly from non-isolates with respect to the proportion who report having been very sickly or rather sickly, either in the first decade of life or as a teenager.[8]

Finally, the isolates were not prevented by excessive residential mobility from interacting with other children: isolates and partial-isolates do not differ significantly from non-isolates with respect to the proportions who lived in five or more residences, four or more neighborhoods, or four or more cities up to the age of fifteen.[9]

These factors, then, do not explain why the isolates became isolated. Non-isolates and controls who lived on out-of-the-way farms apparently managed to play in the school yard after school hours or to have their classmates visit them at home. The isolates did not do this. Non-isolates and controls whose families moved around frequently nevertheless managed to find playmates where they moved; isolates did not.

Nor is social isolation the result of parental restrictions upon the activities of the child: no greater proportion of isolates and partial-isolates than of non-isolates report parental restrictions either on physical activities or on choice of friends.

TABLE 4. NUMBER OF CHILDREN OF SIMILAR AGE REPORTED TO HAVE BEEN LIVING IN THE NEIGHBORHOOD WHEN PATIENT WAS 13-14 YEARS OLD

	Isolated and partially-isolated patients* (20) Per cent	Non-isolated patients† (25) Per cent
None	5	0
One or two	10	4
Three to five	15	4
More than five	70	88
Can't say	0	4
	100	100

* Isolated and partially-isolated patients have been combined in all tables because empirically they behaved almost identically.

† Ambiguous cases and persons who played only with their siblings are excluded from these comparisons. The isolates and partial-isolates are compared only to the clear-cut non-isolated cases.

[8] Furthermore, those patients who had been included in the Public Health morbidity records did not differ from their controls with respect to the number of days they were absent from school.

[9] Comparisons of residential mobility are based upon complete residential histories secured from all patients. These histories were checked against past Hagerstown City Directories and found to be highly consistent with Directory listings.

ISOLATION AND FAMILY RELATIONSHIPS

How about the patterning of familial relationships? Let us state, first, that a larger proportion of *patients* than of *controls* recalled their mothers as having been more easily angered, more dominating, more anxious for the children to get ahead, less likely to be satisfied with the children's behavior, and more restrictive than their fathers. Correspondingly, a larger proportion of patients recall their fathers as having been more likely in case of disagreement to give in, less certain of themselves and less strict than their mothers.

TABLE 5. RECOLLECTIONS OF PARENTAL BEHAVIOR BY PATIENTS AND CONTROLS*

Respondent recalls mother as	Patients (52) Per cent	Controls (52) Per cent
More easily angered than father	50	17
More dominating than father	46	19
More likely to restrict the children's freedom than father	38	6

* Excludes those patients and controls raised by only one parent.

We present a comparison of patients to controls on three of these items as an illustration: a larger proportion of patients than of controls recall their mothers as having been more easily angered, more dominating, and more restrictive than their fathers.

But *isolated* and *partially-isolated* patients do not differ significantly from *non-isolated* patients in their comparisons of mother to father on these same items. (See Table 6.)

The same is true of all other aspects of family functioning that the patients report differently from the controls: in no case do the isolated and partially-isolated patients differ from the non-isolated patients. This is true, for example, of their perceptions of how well their parents got along; how close they felt to each of their parents; to which parent they turned when in trouble; and which parent made the day-

to-day decisions, the major decisions, and the decisions that particularly affected the children. Nor do isolated patients differ from non-isolated patients on a number of other aspects of family structure and func-

TABLE 6. RECOLLECTIONS OF PARENTAL BEHAVIOR BY ISOLATED AND NON-ISOLATED PATIENTS

Respondent recalls mother as	Isolated and partially-isolated patients (18) Per cent	Non-isolated patients (23) Per cent
More easily angered than father	44	48
More dominating than father	49	40
More likely to restrict the children's freedom than father	32	43

tioning with respect to which patients do not differ from controls—such as family composition; deaths, illnesses, or divorce of parents; occupations of parents; parental aspirations for the children; or the respondents' relations with their siblings. In summary we find no evidence that the social isolation of one third of the patients was a resultant of, or even a correlate of, the familial relationships studied.

ISOLATION AND WITHDRAWAL

We have been unable to find any evidence that the isolates have been prevented from social participation because of lack of available playmates, residential mobility, illness, or parental restrictions. Nor have we been able to find any evidence that the isolation of one third of the patients resulted from the particular nature of their family relationships. Did the isolates and partial-isolates become isolated, then, because they withdrew from social relationships? Here our primary sources of information are the hospital case-records, based on interviews with family respondents, together with supplementary research interviews that we have conducted with the siblings of still hospitalized patients.

Information indicating that the patient's isolation could be viewed as an expression of his shy, timid, or fearful personality was reported for seven of the ten persons whom we have classified as *isolates*. The pattern is quite different for those patients classified as partial-isolates: family respondents almost uniformly stated that these patients appeared normal and sociable at age 13 or 14. This was true also of the patients classified as *non-isolates,* none of whose case-records gives evidence that his relatives considered him shy, withdrawn, or at all disturbed at age 13–14. But relatives of three of these patients state that subsequent to that age the patients definitely withdrew from normal social participation.

It would seem, then, that the patients whom we have classified as *isolates* had already manifested signs of personality disturbance sufficient to be noted by family respondents by the time they were 13 or 14 years old. Patients whom we have classified as *partial-isolates* appeared normal to their relatives at that age, even though they report that they had already begun to withdraw from social activities by that age. Presumably the isolation process had not proceeded as far. This process had proceeded least far for the patients classified as *non-isolates.*

THE SIGNIFICANCE OF SOCIAL ISOLATION

We had anticipated that patients who had been isolated from an early age would either have been hospitalized earlier than other patients or would have suffered a more long-lasting illness. Neither of these is the case. Isolates and partial-isolates were hospitalized at approximately the same ages as were non-isolates.

Nor did the isolates and partial-isolates require longer hospitalization, or respond less adequately to hospitalization, than did the non-isolates.

At the time of the research interview, we were unable to discern any important differences in the current functioning of the two groups of patients. Furthermore the two groups do not differ with respect to their current patterns of social relationships—how they spend leisure time, whether or not they belong to formal groups, and how frequently they get together informally with friends. These data all lead to the conclusion that social isolation in this early period does not seem to have appreciably influenced the development of the illness.

SUMMARY AND THEORETICAL IMPLICATIONS

We may summarize our findings as follows: (a) approximately one-third of the schizophrenic and manic-depressive patients give evidence of having been socially-isolated at age 13–14, whereas appreciably none of the normal controls gives evidence of having been isolated at that age; (b) we

TABLE 7. AGE AT FIRST HOSPITALIZATION

	Isolated and partially-isolated patients (20) Per cent	Non-isolated patients (25) Per cent
Under 25	15	28
25–34	40	28
35–44	40	36
45–49	5	8
	100	100

have been unable to find any evidence that the isolated patients had been prevented from interacting with their peers because of a lack of available playmates, excessive residential mobility, severe illness, or parental restrictions; (c) we have been unable to find any evidence of a correlation between social isolation and familial relationships—that is, we have been unable to ascertain any appreciable difference between the perceptions of their relationships with parents and siblings held by the isolated patients and those held by the non-isolated patients.

These data, it must be recognized, are based on the retrospective impressions of a group of persons who have undergone the severely disorienting experience of psychosis. But a systematic comparison of the research interviews with the patients to prior hospital interviews with their relatives shows a high level of consistency for 26 of the 30 patients whose hospital records contain data on this topic.

Our general conclusion must be, then, that for the group here studied the data do not support the hypothesis that social isolation in adolescence is a predisposing factor in either schizophrenia or manic-depressive psychosis. Only a third of the patients were isolated in adolescent

One wonders why, if this complex series of events is seen as necessary to the schizophrenic process, isolation is seized upon as the crucial element that leads to schizophrenia. Why was the individual rebuffed in the first place? Why did he react so extremely to rebuff as to withdraw from all social interaction? Does not his behavior before he became isolated indicate that his personality development was already quite abnormal? A far simpler explanation of the isolation experience was afforded by Bleuler as long ago as 1908 in his classic volume on schizophrenia: "The overt

TABLE 8. STATUS OF ISOLATED AND NON-ISOLATED PATIENTS AT YEARLY INTERVALS FOLLOWING DATE OF FIRST ADMISSION*

	One year		Two years		Three years	
	Isolated and partially-isolated patients (20) Per cent	Non-isolated patients (25) Per cent	Isolated and partially-isolated patients (19) Per cent	Non-isolated patients (22) Per cent	Isolated and partially-isolated patients (17) Per cent	Non-isolated patients (18) Per cent
Patient resident in a mental hospital	30	16	26	22	18	22
Patient discharged, occupation similar to that prior to illness	45	60	48	60	47	56
Patient discharged, functioning at markedly reduced level	20	24	26	18	29	22
Patient discharged, but no data available as to level on which he is operating	5	0	0	0	6	0
	100	100	100	100	100	100

* The number of patients included beyond the first year decreases because some of the patients had been admitted to the hospital less than two years prior to the time of data collection.

life, and even for them isolation does not seem to have been instrumental in predisposing them to psychosis. Nor does it seem to increase the duration of hospitalization.

In early statements of the social isolation hypothesis, it was posited that isolation of any person for an extended period of time results in schizophrenia. Later the process was seen as far more complex: a particular type of person, living in a particular social setting, becomes rebuffed and rejected by his peers; after fruitless attempts to gain acceptance, he finally withdraws into a shell of isolation.

symptomatology certainly represents the expression of a more or less successful attempt to find a way out of an intolerable situation" (1).

An interpretation in harmony with the findings of this study is that as a result of inadequacies in their social relationships, both within and outside the family, certain individuals come to feel that they do not really belong to their peer-groups—that is, they become *alienated* from their peers. Under severe enough conditions, alienation may lead to a withdrawal from social interaction, that is, to isolation. But it need not do so; it might lead, for example, to compulsive interaction such as that engaged in by some manic patients, or it might not lead to abnormal behavior at all. In any case, isolation does not seem to be the crucial experience in predisposing the individual to illness.

Thus, in terms of process, social isolation is to be viewed as a sign that the individual's interpersonal difficulties have become so great that he is no longer capable of functioning in interpersonal relationships. The question of how he got that way is not a question of social isolation, *per se*. It is rather a series of problems, starting with the question of what are the conditions that produce alienation, and continuing with the processes by which subsequent interpersonal experiences transform this base of interpersonal difficulty into interpersonal failure.

REFERENCES

1. Bleuler, Eugen, *Dementia Praecox, or the Group of Schizophrenias*. English edition translated by Joseph Zinken. New York: International Universities Press, 1950. p. 460.
2. Dunham, H. Warren, "The Social Personality of the Catatonic Schizophrene," *Amer. J. Soc.* 1944, *49*, 508–518.
3. Faris, Robert E. L., "Cultural Isolation and the Schizophrenic Personality." *Amer. J. Soc.* 1934, *40*, 155–164.
4. Faris, Robert E. L., "Ecological Factors in Human Personality," In Hunt, J. McV. (ed). *Personality and the Behavior Disorders*. New York: Ronald Press, 1944, II, 736–757.
5. Faris, Robert E. L., and Dunham, H. Warren, *Mental Disorders in Urban Areas*. Chicago: University of Chicago Press, 1939.
6. Weinberg, S. Kirson, "A Sociological Analysis of a Schizophrenic Type," *Amer. Soc. Rev.* 1950, 600–610.

A Comparative Study of the Personal Histories of Schizophrenic and Nonpsychiatric Patients

WILLIAM SCHOFIELD AND LUCY BALIAN

ONE of the currently popular views of the etiology of severe personality disruption holds that the seeds of mental illness are to be found in the life experiences of the individual. In particular, the childhood is conceived as a critical period, and certain areas, such as parent-child relationships and psychosexual development, are viewed as crucial determiners of or prodromal to later adjustment or psychopathology. Three possible forms of "historical" or biographic etiology may be distinguished: (*a*) the traumatic incident (e.g., witnessing in childhood the "primal scene"), (*b*) sequential traumata (i.e., a concatenation of emotional blows resulting finally in disintegration of the ego), and (*c*) acquired predisposition (i.e., the learning of a pattern of maladaptive response). Writing in 1893, Breuer and Freud (*2*) noted that:

The causal relation between the determining psychical trauma and the hysterical phenomenon is not of a kind implying that the trauma merely acts like an "agent provocateur" in releasing the symptom, which thereafter leads a separate existence. We must presume rather that the psychical trauma—or more precisely the memory of the trauma—acts like a foreign body which long after its

Reprinted by permission from *The Journal of Abnormal and Social Psychology*, Vol. 59, No. 2, September 1959.

entry must continue to be regarded as an agent that is still at work (p. 6).

Freud (2), in describing the case of Elizabeth von R., observes:

Almost invariably when I have observed the determinants of such conditions what I have come upon has not been a *single* traumatic cause but a group of similar ones. . . . In some of these instances it could be established that the symptom in question had already appeared for a short time after the first trauma and had then passed off, till it was brought on again and stabilized by a succeeding trauma (p. 173).

Finally, we have a succinct expression of the learning hypothesis in Shaffer and Shoben (7):

An evident conclusion is that our distinctive attributes, even our most fundamentally human qualities, are products of our experience with other human beings. *Personality* [underlining ours] is learned as a result of the events in one's history (p. 402).

The significance of the once-occurring trauma in production of later sympomatology is given less prominence now than it held during the heyday of "la grande hysterie" and when public-compulsive symptoms were viewed as more circumscribed phenomena. Likewise, a simple additive notion about accumulations of emotional "shocks" is retained today chiefly by the laity, who express this notion in the "straw and camel's back" allegory. It is currently more common to view the patient's history as either having deprived him of an opportunity to learn normal patterns of socialization or as "overtraining" him in some repertoire of abnormal responses. If varying patterns of psychopathology are differentiated, and if the biography, or certain ages or elements in the biography, are believed to have pathogenic potential, it is reasonable to assume that differential patterns of personal history might be found which are demonstrably associated with various behavioral syndromes. Research in this realm immediately involves the investigator in difficult methodological problems with respect to

definition and recording of the life history.

What is a life history? As the concept is widely and loosely used in much psychological writing, it is implicitly a theoretical abstraction. It may be conceived as inclusive of all *events* in the total sequence of time-space displacements of the individual from the moment of his birth up to some time at which a summary is prepared. It may be conceived as the complete sequence of *experiences* had by the individual over such a period. It may be thought of as a "complete" collection of the events *and* experiences of the individual. Unless one wishes to assume perfect recording (and retention?) characteristics for the nervous apparatus, it is unlikely that the individual's population of events, as observable time-space dispositions, has isomorphic representation in his population of experiences or subjective events.

Without much formal attention to the theory of the life history, most of the research into biographical factors in mental illness has been content to use the framework or part of the structure of the so-called "psychiatric history." This is essentially a relatively uniform selection of significant events and experiences in the histories of research subjects. What determines the selection and what defines significance? Selection is determined in part by what data are obtainable as a function of accuracy of records and integrity of memory. Significance is expressed through clinical judgment, largely as a result of observations of apparent association between certain factors and specific outcomes (e.g., broken homes and delinquency). Significance may be also determined on the grounds of currently (and locally) popular theory. Recognizing these constraints upon the adequacy of the typical psychiatric history as a representative sampling from the theoretical population of events and experiences constituting the true life history, it is incumbent upon the investigator into the contribution of life history factors to psychogenesis of emotional disturbance to seek at least minimal insurance against these sources of error. Such safeguards are afforded in the utilization of history outlines and recording forms and in the collection of data for control samples. The development and application of detailed history schedules helps to assure uniformity and thoroughness of coverage. The study of control groups serves as a check on the associations and hypotheses of etiological factors suggested by the study of exclusively pathological samples.

The obviousness of these experimental caveats encourages an expectation that they have been well respected in researches into the life history as a source of psychopathology. A search of the literature reveals over 300 studies of life histories of psychiatric patients. Fewer than ten of these included data on a reasonably comparable control group (1, 5, 6, 9). The bulk of the studies report simply the frequency of such items as patient's age at death of a parent as recorded in mental hospital records. Frequently, only selected items are tabulated without any attempt at a comprehensive history. When more extensive coverage of history data has been undertaken, a variety of procedures for collection has been used and efforts to study a control sample have been rare. When studied, control groups have seemed mostly to be determined by accessibility rather than appropriateness (3).

PURPOSE AND PREMISES

The purpose of this study was (a) to determine what the life histories of "normal" persons look like if examined through the spectroscope of a comprehensive psychiatric history interview as conducted and recorded by a skilled clinician and (b) to determine in what ways such histories may be distinguishable from those of such psychiatric patients as schizophrenics.

The basic hypothesis of this research simply stated was: the life histories of "normal," i.e., nonpsychiatric patients, will be readily and clearly differentiated from those of psychiatric patients if equally complete and carefully collected history data are available for both. More specifically, the hypothesis is that the histories of normals will reveal markedly less occurrence of those events or experiences (trauma, deprivations, frustrations, conflicts, etc.) which have been commonly considered to have a psychogenic or prodromal role in schizophrenia. This is a formal statement of the assumption which is made, usually implicitly, in those clinical and uncontrolled studies which derive from the absolute frequency of given events in the histories of certain patients the conclusion that the event has causal import. In the absence of comparative data on the frequency of these same events in appropriate control subjects, there is not only room but need to be doubtful of such conclusions.

SAMPLE AND PROCEDURE

The selection of the "normal" subjects (Ss) for this study was determined primarily by the nature of the 178 schizophrenics with whom comparison was to be made. These patients were hospitalized at the University of Minnesota Hospitals, and comprehensive personal history statistics have been previously reported (8) for them. To assure comparability of the normal and psychiatric samples, the former were drawn primarily from the same population which yielded the latter, i.e., the general group of persons referred to the University hospitals for diagnosis and treatment. Of the total, 105, or 70% were University patients. An additional 14 cases were obtained from Minneapolis General Hospital. Finally, 31 physically and psychiatrically negative cases were obtained from sources including hospital employees, students, employees of a large industrial firm, and office workers. The term "normal" as applied to this sample specifies the absence of psychiatric disturbances under treatment at the time the histories were recorded *and* the absence of any previous mental disorder. The nonpsychiatric patients were drawn from all but the psychiatric wards and psychiatric clinics of both the University hospitals and Minneapolis General Hospital. The medical diagnoses represented covered a wide range, and no type of illness or defect was predominant.

To assure further comparability of the two groups, selection of the normals was made so as to achieve matching with the schizophrenics for age, sex, and marital status. Success of the matching is indicated in Table 1. As a further reflection of the comparability of the two samples, data on education, rural–urban origin, and religious affiliation are recorded in Table 1. The mean number of years of formal education for the normals is reliably higher than that of the schizophrenics; however, the overlap between the two distributions is approximately 50%. Also, the higher average educational level of the normals undoubtedly reflects the general increment in average educational level of the public, since they were hospitalized in 1956–1957 (of school age in 1904–1956), in contrast to the schizophrenics who were hospitalized between 1938–1944 (of school age in 1886–1944). No basic difference is indicated in the intellectual or general socioeconomic character of the two samples. The comparability of the two samples is further supported by the data on number of sibs and number of children in the married Ss as reported in Table 1.

The life histories of the normals were collected through the medium of a comprehensive clinical interview requiring from 45 to 90 minutes. Only two of the patients who were approached refused to cooperate. Satisfactory rapport was achieved in most cases, and the Ss appeared to give reliable accounts of their backgrounds. Many of them were interested in the nature of the study, and this was briefly discussed with them at the close of the interview. Also, at the end of the interview each S was administered an MMPI as a further check on his psychiatric status.

Immediately after each interview, the interviewer transcribed her notes and

TABLE 1. GROSS DESCRIPTIVE DATA FOR NORMALS AND SCHIZOPHRENICS

	Normal (N = 150)	Schizophrenic (N = 178)
Age	M = 28.6 yrs. SD = 9.7	M = 28.7 yrs. SD = 9.6
Sex		
Male	44.7%	44.4%
Female	55.3	55.6
Marital Status		
Married	33.3%	26.9%
Single	64.7	69.1
Divorced	1.3	1.7
Widowed	0.6	1.7
Separated	0.0	0.6
Education	M = 12.0 yrs. SD = 3.4	M = 9.9 yrs. SD = 2.5
Home		
Urban	44.7%	50.8%
Rural	55.3	49.2
Religion		
Lutheran	38.0%	35.7%
Other Prot.	31.7	31.0
Catholic	24.0	27.0
Jewish	0.6	6.2
Moslem	0.6	0.0
No. of Siblings	M = 4.1 SD = 2.8	M = 4.2 SD = 3.4
No. of Children	(N = 53) M = 2.4 SD = 2.1	(N = 50) M = 2.8 SD = 2.4

further observations onto a detailed schedule covering over 100 distinct items pertaining to developmental, personal, social, and medical history. This was the same schedule which had been used in recording the history data for the schizophrenic sample.

RESULTS

The major findings of the study are reported in Tables 2–7, which show the percentage frequency of occurrence in the two samples of various psychological relationships and adjustment variables. These range from the quality of the relationship between the Ss parents to the degree of manifestation of a life plan and initiative in the pursuit of that plan. The reliability of the differences between the distributions of the two samples are reported in the tables. Generally more notable than the

TABLE 2. INTERPERSONAL RELATIONSHIPS, HOME FACTORS, AND SCHOOL ADJUSTMENT IN THE EARLY HISTORIES OF NORMALS AND SCHIZOPHRENICS

	Normal	Schizo-phrenic	χ^2	P
Interparental Re-lationship	(N = 144)	(N = 101)		
Affection	75.7%	76.2%	0.14	>0.98
Ambivalence	6.3	5.9		
Indifference	0.7	1.9		
Hostility	17.4	15.8		
Paternal Relation-ship	(N = 143)	(N = 127)		
Affection	76.2%	65.3%	13.02	<.05
Ambivalence	9.8	5.5		
Indifference	4.2	3.1		
Rejection	7.7	11.8	3.91	<.05
Overprotection	0.7	1.5		
Domination	1.4	11.8		
Maternal Relation-ship	(N = 150)	(N = 128)		
Affection	81.3%	64.8%	32.90	<.01
Ambivalence	8.0	2.3		
Indifference	2.7	1.5		
Rejection	6.0	6.2	9.72	<.01
Overprotection	0.7	13.2		
Domination	0.7	10.9		
Neglect	0.7	0.7		
Sibling Relation-ship	(N = 178)	(N = 126)		
None	3.4%	3.9%	4.43	<.50
Affection	70.8	76.1		
Indifference	2.2	4.7		
Rivalry	16.3	13.4		
Domination	2.8	0.7		
Submission	4.5	0.7		
Home Conditions				
Poverty	20.7%	9.0%	8.00	<.01
Alcoholism	6.0	6.8	0.19	<.70
Invalid	12.7	0.6	18.67	<.01
Divorce	6.0	1.6	3.14	<.10
Separation	2.7	1.1	0.38	<.70
Death of parent	14.7	10.7	0.82	<.50
School Acceptance	(N = 155)	(N = 159)		
Marked hostility	7.1%	3.8%	13.64	<.01
Mild dislike	17.4	11.3		
Indifference	11.0	25.8		
Agreeable	54.8	54.7		
Keen enjoyment	10.0	4.4		
School Achieve-ment	(N = 150)	(N = 163)		
Repeated failure	7.3%	4.9%	21.49	<.01
Work difficult	6.0	19.6		
Average per-formance	42.0	50.2		
Easily earned good grades	38.7	19.6		
Accelerated	6.0	4.4		

	Normal	Schizo-phrenic	χ^2	P
School Deport-ment				
Poor record	9.3%	7.9%	22.92	<.01
Usual no. of es-capades	36.0	10.6		
Excellent record	54.7	31.6		

Note.—In this and subsequent tables, where two χ^2 values appear for a given factor, one is based on all categories and the second is for comparison of bracketed versus unbracketed categories.

TABLE 3. OCCUPATIONAL HISTORIES AND RELIGIOUS ORIENTATION OF NORMALS AND SCHIZOPHRENICS

	Normal	Schizo-phrenic	χ^2	P
Occupation	(N = 150)	(N = 177)		
None	15.3%	21.1%	0.72	<.50
Occupational Suc-cess	(N = 127)	(N = 127)		
Poor	0.0%	14.9%	1.60	<.30
Average	38.6	31.5		
Good	61.4	53.5	18.66	<.01
Occupational Sat-isfaction	(N = 127)	(N = 126)		
Dislike	7.9%	9.5%	21.74	<.01
Indifference	17.3	43.6		
Enjoyment	74.8	46.8		
Church Attend-ance	(N = 150)	(N = 147)		
Very infrequent	22.0%	38.3%	4.77	<.10
Occasionally	36.7	31.2		
Steady	41.3	35.3		
Religiousness	(N = 142)	(N = 121)		
Intellectualized, ritualistic	18.3%	4.1%	12.31	<.01
Occasional sol-ace	42.3	55.4		
Dominant source of balance	39.4	40.5		

presence or absence of statistical reliability of the differences are the marked *overlaps* in the distributions for the schizophrenic and normal samples.

Table 2 reveals that the relationship between the parents of *both* the normal Ss and schizophrenic patients was predominantly one of affection. Relationships characterized as ambivalent, indifferent, or hostile were slightly more frequent between the parents of the normals. In their relationships with their fathers, the schizophrenics experienced a reliably higher frequency of unfavorable attitudes. However, two-thirds of these patients apparently received affection from their fathers, and less than one-fourth were the recipients of either rejection or domination. The maternal relationship more clearly differentiates the two samples. Again, however, it is to be noted that nearly two-thirds of the schizophrenics enjoyed the affection of their mothers. Of the various undesirable relationships which were recorded, overprotection and domination were most prominent in the schizophrenics. This is slight support for the current belief of some experts in the existence of the so-called "schizophrenogenic mother":

Psychoanalytic students are uniform in the opinion that maternal rejection and domination are regularly found in the histories of those who are found later to have been predisposed to the development of schizophrenia. The mother of the schizophrenic is variously described as cold, dominating, narcissistic, lacking love for the child, having death wishes toward it ... (Woolley, 1953).

However, domination or overprotection characterized the relationship of *less than one-fourth* of the mothers of the schizophrenics in the present study.

Table 2 also reports the relationships between the two samples and their respective sibs and the frequency of six factors of physical and/or psychological deprivation or trauma. The intersib relationships do not differentiate the two groups. While none of the home conditions noted occurred in more than a fifth of the homes of either sample, two of the factors, namely, poverty and invalidism, did have a reliably different rate in the two groups, and the rate of divorce approached a reliable difference. All three of these more frequently characterized the childhood homes of the normals.

The attitudes, adjustment, and achievement of the two groups in their school experiences are recorded in Table 2. All three factors show reliably different distributions for the two samples. General attitude toward the school situation was less different for the normals and schizophrenics than were achievement and deportment. Three times as many schizophrenics as normals found their school work difficult, and twice as many normals as schizophrenics easily earned good grades. The passivity of the prepsychotic schizophrenic in the school room, which has been commonly observed by clinicians, is suggested in their clear preponderance of excellent deportment records. While nearly one-fourth of the schizophrenics experienced failure or difficulty with their school work, less than one-tenth of them had poor deportment. By contrast, while better than 85% of the normals had satisfactory or superior achievement, only half of them had excellent deportment records.

Occupational success and satisfaction distinguishes the normals from the schizophrenics as revealed in Table 3. The proportion of the two groups without any history of occupation is not reliably different. While poor occupational achievement was recorded for none of the normals with an occupational history, this rating was assigned to one-fifth of the schizophrenics. Overlap is again notable, with 85% of the schizophrenics manifesting average or good occupational success. Satisfaction with their occupations also differentiated the two groups. Over half of the schizophrenics disliked or were indifferent to their work, while three-fourths of the normals apparently enjoyed their occupations.

Table 3 indicates that the two groups were not differentiated with regard to frequency of church attendance, although the role of religion or attitude toward it was different in the two. While there was no difference in the frequency with which religion afforded as dominant source of balance to the lives of the two groups, an intellectualized or ritualistic approach to religion was found four times as frequently among the normals as among the schizophrenics. Table 3 also reports the occurrence of delinquency and criminal records; the rates are very small and not different for the two samples.

Table 4 records the dating history and marital adjustment of the two samples. Frequency of dating is not reliably different in the two groups if the "average" and "very popular" categories are combined for contrast with the "none or little" category. Although there were no schizophrenics rated as "very popular" in terms of frequency of dating, less than 5% of the normals fell into this category. Approximately a third of both samples were married (Table 1). The marital adjustment of the two groups was not different, and a third of both groups experienced frustration or conflict in their marriages. Although the normals tended to derive distinct pleasure from their marriages with somewhat higher frequency than the schizophrenics, a third of both groups evinced attitudes of affection toward their spouses.

TABLE 4. DATING HISTORY, MARITAL AND HETEROSEXUAL ADJUSTMENT OF NORMALS AND SCHIZOPHRENICS

	Normal	Schizo-phrenic	χ^2	P
Dating	(N = 150)	(N = 145)		
None or little	49.3%	57.2%	5.98	<.10
Average	46.0	42.8	1.83	<.20
Very popular	4.7	0.0		
Marital Adjustment	(N = 53)	(N = 50)		
Extreme frustration	18.9%	16.0%	6.73	<.20
Continual conflict	15.1	14.0		
Compatibility	17.0	42.0		
Pleasure	41.5	24.0		
Chief pleasure	7.5	4.0		
Affection to Mate	(N = 53)	(N = 51)		
	62.3%	64.7%		
Heterosexual Adjustment	(N = 150)	(N = 171)		
Poor	36.7%	22.2%	10.49	<.01
Fair	20.7	33.3		
Good	42.7	44.4		
Adequacy of Outlet	(N = 150)	(N = 170)		
Poor	38.6%	24.7%	11.18	<.01
Fair	33.3	30.5		
Good	28.0	44.7		

TABLE 5. SOCIAL SKILL AND ADJUSTMENT OF SCHIZOPHRENICS AND NORMALS

	Normal	Schizo-phrenic	χ^2	P
Social Adjustment	(N = 150)	(N = 85)		
Withdrawal	10.0%	61.2%	78.60	<.01
Ambivalence	7.3	14.1		
Membership	82.7	24.7		
Social Intelligence	(N = 150)	(N = 167)		
Inept and clumsy	8.7%	8.9%	29.66	<.01
Moderate skill	68.7	88.8		
Adept	22.7	2.3		
Poise	(N = 150)	(N = 170)		
Retiring and sensitive	22.7	37.4%	12.99	<.01
Fairly articulate	51.3	49.7		
Confident	26.0	12.8		
Recreation	(N = 150)	(N = 163)		
Solitary	27.3%	40.5%	6.51	<.05
Mixed	66.0	52.2		
Social	6.7	7.3		

The quality of sexual adjustment and adequacy of outlet are shown in Table 4. Sexual adjustment is reliably different in the two samples. Surprisingly, the difference appears primarily in the greater frequency of poor sexual adjustment in the normal Ss. Likewise, the schizophrenics were rated twice as frequently as the normals as enjoying "good sexual outlets."

The quality of social adjustment and of factors affecting interpersonal relationships are shown in Table 5. The adequacy of social adjustment is clearly different for the two samples, with the schizophrenics showing a high frequency of withdrawal and a low rate of active group membership. Likewise, both the variables of social intelligence and poise show reliably inferior distributions for the schizophrenics. The overlaps between the two groups are considerable, however. Nearly 90% of the schizophrenics were rated as having at least moderate skill in interpersonal relations, and only a third of them were characterized as retiring and sensitive. Pursuit of solitary recreation was more characteristic of the schizophrenics than the normals, but over half of the former had a history of mixed or social recreation.

In Table 6 are reported five areas of

TABLE 6. INTERESTS, ASPIRATIONS, AND INITIATIVE OF NORMALS AND SCHIZOPHRENICS

	Normal	Schizo-phrenic	χ^2	P
Breadth of Interest	(N = 150)	(N = 173)		
Narrow	20.7%	35.2%	44.30	<.01
Some outside	46.0	60.2		
Broad	33.3	4.6		
Level of Aspiration	(N = 150)	(N = 170)		
Limited	16.0%	34.7%	17.79	<.01
Interested in improving	61.3	55.3		
High	22.7	10.0		
Life Plan	(N = 150)	(N = 164)		
Vague	22.7%	46.4%	56.63	<.01
Confused	9.3	28.0		
Clear	68.0	25.6		
Stability	(N = 150)	(N = 172)		
Constant fluctuation	10.7%	13.9%	47.17	<.01
Moderate variability	78.7	42.7		
Stolid	10.7	43.4		
Initiative	(N = 150)	(N =169)		
Apathetic	8.0%	16.0%	4.12	<.20
Appropriate	57.3	53.2		
Energetic	34.7	30.8		

early personal attitude and expression which might be broadly classed as manifestations of individual perspective and morale. Four of these variables show reliably different distributions in the two groups. Summarizing for these variables, it may be said that the schizophrenics less frequently had broad interests, a high level of aspiration, and a clear life plan; more frequently than the normals they were characterized by a stolid, nonvarying temperament and by absence of initiative.

DISCUSSION

The single most impressive feature of the data presented in Tables 2–6 is the sizable overlap of the normal Ss and schizophrenic patients in the distributions of the various personal history variables. Of the 35 separate tests which were run, 13 (or 37%) failed to reveal a reliable difference between the two samples. Further, on 5 of the remaining 22 variables, the distributions showed a reliably greater presence in the normals of negative or undesirable con-

ditions. In those instances where the statistical tests did indicate a reliable characterization of the schizophrenics by prevalence of a pathogenic variable, the normals generally also showed a closely approximating degree of the same factor. Before discussing the implications of the findings, it will be well to review facets of the data collection and recording which might have had biasing effects.

The history data for the schizophrenics were abstracted from the material routinely collected and recorded clinically in the hospital charts of these patients as they were admitted, diagnosed, treated, and discharged. A variety of persons, including social workers, junior medical students, psychiatric residents, and staff psychiatrists, contributed to the recording of these data. No single person was charged with the collection of comprehensive history nor was a detailed research schedule applied as a reference in collecting the material. These facts suggest the possible underestimation of the actual frequency of certain variables in the histories of the schizophrenics. However, in abstracting the clinical material and recording it on the research schedule, no attempt was made to force the rating of a variable when clear information was not available; free use was made of an "unknown" category. This tactic has the effect of enhancing the reliability of the frequencies reported at the expense of having a varying size of sample (for example, "paternal relationships" was rated for only 127 of the 178 schizophrenics).

Reliability of the ratings of the various factors is an important consideration. This is especially true with respect to the data on the schizophrenics for whom the original clinical records were not uniform and from which, without any other source of information or contact with the patient, the rater had to abstract the material pertinent to a given variable and then assign it a rating. The definitions of the various scales were made as objective and nonambiguous as possible, and the number of steps to each scale was generally small. As reported previously, independent abstractors-and-raters achieved an 80–95% agreement over a small sample of trial cases (8).

The reliability of the data for the normals was enhanced by providing for an immediate recording and rating of information which had been collected in an extended interview conducted with the research schedule as an implicit guide to insure coverage. Failure to find distinguishing features for the two groups might be the result of a "contamination effect" if the same person or persons had been responsible for the study and rating of both the schizophrenics and normals. Actually, two researchers working quite independently and at different periods of time collected and rated the schizophrenic and normal material respectively. This avoids an artificial overlap in the distributions as a function of a common rater projecting implicit "base rate" standards from one sample to another. There remains the question of interrater reliability and the possibility of stable but different interpretations of the criteria for various ratings leading to Type I errors (10). This possibility was particularly suggested, for example, by the surprising distributions of the "heterosexual" adjustment variable (see Table 4). As a check on the possibility that relatively different criteria had been applied by the two raters (both single females) in assessing this variable, they were asked to give independent, free accounts of their respective interpretations of the steps on this scale and of the criteria they utilized in assigning the cases. They appeared to be in essential agreement in these respects. In short, within the limits of the inequalities imposed by the differences in the nature of the raw data for the two samples and the methods by which the basic history material was obtained, it would seem that the ratings of the various history factors were reasonably reliable and no obviously biasing and unbalanced factor operated which would serve to either exaggerate or diminish true differences between the two groups.

Consideration must also be given to the possibility that such differences as were obtained between the two samples might be a function of the different periods of time from which they were sampled. As pointed out in discussing the difference in mean educational level of the two groups, the schizophrenic patients were hospitalized between 1938–1944. Approximately 80% of these patients were between the ages of 20–50 when hospitalized. Using these ages as a reference point for the sample and defining childhood and early adolescence as encompassing the first 15 years of life, this period occurred for the bulk of the schizophrenics between 1890–1940. By contrast, the normals (with the same age distributions as the schizophrenics) were evaluated in 1956–1957. For these Ss, the period of childhood and early adolescence would fall predominantly in the years 1910–1950. It would be difficult to ascertain the degree to which these two periods would be characterized by distinctive patterns of parental attitude, child-rearing practices, major social upheaval, and other potential sources of psychological effects in the early life histories of individuals. Such contrast could be best drawn for the earliest period represented in the schizophrenics (1890–1910) and the most recent period sampled in the normals (1940–1950), but these periods would account for the "formative years" of only a small portion of each of the groups. The overlap in childhood years for the two samples is great, and such significant factors as the impact of Freudian psychology, the first World War, and the Great Depression occurred in the time interval common to both. It seems unlikely that broad differences in the sociopsychological cultures from which the schizophrenics and normals were drawn can be used to account for their respective distributions on the personal history variables analyzed in this study. In any event, if significant social and cultural factors did indeed differentiate the periods 1890–1910 and 1940–1950, and such factors had causal potency for personality development, they should contribute to more and larger differences between the schizophrenics and normals. The restricted number of differences obtained and the impressive amount of overlap between the two groups suggests limited existence and/or potency of differential sociological factors.

Finally, the lack of more extensive and clear-cut differences between the backgrounds of the two samples might be attributed to the fact that they did not actually represent distinct populations of the psychiatrically ill and the psychiatrically negative. No quarrel can be made with the diagnoses of the schizophrenics. They clearly suffered psychotic disturbance of sufficient magnitude to necessitate hospitalization. Furthermore, they received their specific diagnoses at a time when schizophrenia was not being used as a synonym for all psychosis without obvious brain pathology.

Some clinicians undoubtedly would take exception to the "normality" of our control group. It should be iterated that they denied any history of mental illness or psychiatric consultation, and they manifested no evidence of gross emotional disturbance at the time they were interviewed

TABLE 7. MMPI SCORES OBTAINED BY NORMAL CONTROLS

			Mean T scores		
Scale	*Female (N = 75)*	*Male (N = 57)*	*"Traumatized" (N = 37)*	*"Nontraumatized" (N = 95)*	*t Ratio*
?	50	50			
L	53	50	4.27 ± 1.98	4.01 ± 2.21	0.6
F	50	53	3.78 ± 2.98	2.88 ± 2.13	1.66
K	59	59	14.43 ± 5.47	17.56 ± 4.00	4.35*
Hs	56	57	57.73 ± 9.41	55.88 ± 10.30	1.0
D	57	58	62.27 ± 11.11	54.38 ± 9.74	3.75*
Hy	59	60	59.95 ± 8.21	59.26 ± 8.43	0.43
Pd	55	60	57.46 ± 11.53	57.69 ± 9.08	0.11
Mf	51	55	51.76 ± 10.21	52.46 ± 8.55	0.37
Pa	56	53	54.43 ± 7.87	53.77 ± 7.93	0.44
Pt	55	56	56.62 ± 8.86	55.48 ± 8.61	0.67
Sc	55	57	56.81 ± 9.64	55.83 ± 6.86	0.56
Ma	53	55	53.68 ± 9.64	53.94 ± 10.41	0.13

* Exceeds the .01 level.

in spite of the fact that they were currently under study or treatment for serious physical illnesses. The MMPIs administered as an objective check on psychiatric status supported the clinical impression of essential normality. As shown in Table 7, the mean scores on this psychiatric screening test were well within normal limits. A further analysis of the quality of the normal group was made by identifying those Ss whose histories included one or more of the events or experiences which are generally regarded as psychic trauma. The MMPIs of this group of 37 persons (nearly one-fourth of the normal sample) were compared with those of the remaining "nontraumatized" sample. Mean profiles of the two subgroups are reported in Table 7. Only the K and D scales distinguish these cases. The "traumatized" group had a lower mean K score ($t = 4.35$; $P < .01$) and a higher mean D score ($t = 3.75$; $P < .01$). These observations suggest a less defensive and somewhat more depressive orientation in the Ss with the traumatic histories. The lack of more extensive differentiation of these two subgroups throws a further doubt on the hypothesis that early trauma per se are significant predisposing factors in later mental illness.

The data of this study seem to cast serious doubt on the etiological significance of certain early life factors for which such import has been frequently claimed. These factors may in fact play a causal role in the development of personality disturbance, but not as solitary pathogenic elements. It would appear that it is the patterning or chaining of experiences rather than occurrence or absence which must be examined. While the notion of multiple causation is well established, it is more frequently stated in the context of types of etiological agent—the physical and the psychological—rather than in terms of multiplicity within a given area—personal relationships.

The surprising frequency with which certain forms of pathogenic experiences or circumstances were found in the life histories of the normal Ss suggests the need to think in terms of "suppressor" experiences or control variables in the development of personality. Woolley (*11*) found cold, rejecting, or dominating and exploiting mothers to be "regularly" present in 100 cases selected only for the adequacy of their histories, but stipulated:

These factors constitute the background for the children who escape as well as for their schizophrenic siblings. Moreover, there are families in which no schizophrenic denouements occur. Evidently, there must be factors concerning the degree of rejection, its time of occurrence, its differential distribution among the siblings or the occurrence of reinforcing or ameliorating experiences.

May it not be that the development of serious mental disorder will be less well understood if we concentrate solely on examination of pathological processes and injurious agents, rather than examining for the nature and extent of "immunizing" experiences? It seems necessary that we turn some of our research energies toward a discovery of those circumstances or experiences of life which either contribute directly to mental health and emotional stability or which serve to delimit or erase the effects of pathogenic events. For this purpose, we will need to make extensive psychological study of the biographies of normal persons as well as of patients, with such biographies recorded so that their coverage and uniformity facilitate analysis.

SUMMARY AND CONCLUSIONS

Through the medium of extended clinical interviews the life histories of 150 psychiatrically normal subjects were collected and subsequently recorded in detail on a research schedule which had been used previously in a study of the histories of 178 hospitalized schizophrenics. Of the 150 normals, 119 were hospital or clinic patients being studied and treated for a wide range of serious physical illnesses. Selection of the normals was made so that they were drawn from the same general population as the psychiatric patients, and they were matched with the schizophrenics for age, sex, and marital status.

Separate statistical analyses were made of the reliability of the differences between the distributions of the normals and schizophrenics on 35 major aspects of early history and adjustment. Of these 35 variables, 13 (or 37%) failed to reveal a reliable difference between the two samples. On 5 of the 22 variables which yielded reliable differences, the normals were characterized by greater frequency of the undesirable or pathogenic factor. Specifically, the normals had a greater frequency of poverty and invalidism in their childhood homes, poorer heterosexual adjustment and adequacy of sexual outlet, and a greater incidence of an intellectualized, ritualized orientation toward religion. Additionally, the greater frequency of divorce in the childhood homes of the normals approached reliability.

The schizophrenics were characterized by reliably higher incidence of unfavorable relationships with mothers and fathers, poorer attitudes toward and achievement in school, less occupational success and satisfaction, higher rates of social withdrawal, lack of social adeptness and poise, narrow interests, limited aspiration, vague life plans, and lack of initiative. These personal history characteristics which are predominant in the schizophrenics are in line with the general description which has been made of the preschizophrenic personality and lend some support to the central concept of withdrawal. However, the extent to which these same characteristics were found in closely approximate proportions in the histories of the normals suggests the need for great reservation in interpreting the isolated schizophrenogenic potency of such factors as the mother-child relationship.

The notion that any single circumstance, deprivation, or trauma contributes uniformly and inevitably to the etiology of schizophrenia is called into serious question. The necessity of studying the incidence of such factors in appropriate samples is exemplified. It is suggested that the patterning of life experiences may be more crucial than occurrence or absence of specific psychic stresses. The finding of "traumatic" histories in nearly a fourth of the normal subjects suggests the operation of "suppressor" experiences or psychological processes of immunization. It is suggested that improved insights into mental illness may be afforded by careful, intensive studies of the life histories of normals.

REFERENCES

1. Aldrich, C. K., and Coffin, M. Clinical studies of psychoses in the Navy. I. Prediction values of social histories and the Harrower-Erickson Test. *J. nerv. ment. Dis.,* 1948, *108,* 36–44.

2. Breuer, J., and Freud, S. *Studies on hysteria.* J. Strachey (Trans.) New York: Basic Books, 1957.

3. Brockway, A. L., Gleser, G., Winakur, G., and Ulett, G. A. The use of a control population in neuropsychiatric research (psychiatric, psychological, and EEG evaluation of heterogeneous sample). *Amer. J. Psychiat.,* 1954, *3,* 248–262.

4. Dahlstrom, W. G. An exploration of mental status syndromes by factor analytic techniques. Unpublished doctoral dissertation, Univer. of Minnesota, 1949.

5. Lane, Robert C. Familial attitudes of paranoid schizophrenic and normal individuals of different socioeconomic levels. Unpublished doctoral dissertation, New York Univ., 1955.

6. Nielsen, G. K. The childhood of schizophrenics. *Acta psychiat. neurol. Kbh.,* 1954, *29,* 281–290.

7. Shaffer, L. F., and Shoben, E. J., Jr. *The psychology of adjustment.* (2nd ed.) New York: Houghton Mifflin, 1956.

8. Schofield, W., Hathaway, S. R., Hastings, D. W., and Bell, Dorothy. Prognostic factors in schizophrenia. *J. consult. Psychol.,* 1954, *18,* 155–166.

9. Steinberg, D. L., and Wittman, M. P. Etiologic factors in the adjustment of men in the Armed Forces. *War Med.,* 1943, *4,* 129–139.

10. Walker, H. M., and Lev, J. *Statistical inference.* New York: Holt, Rinehart and Winston, 1953.

11. Woolley, L. F. Experimental factors essential to the development of schizophrenia. In P. Hoch, and J. Zubin (Eds.), *Current problems in psychiatric diagnosis.* New York: Grune & Stratton, 1953.

Theory and Measurement of Socialization

HARRISON G. GOUGH

A SOCIOLOGICAL conception of a continuum of socialization, running from persons of exemplary probity and rectitude at one end, through persons of more typical and less beneficent coadunations of positive and negative propensities, to persons of frankly errant and wayward impulse can easily be delineated. The precise location of a particular individual or group along this continuum may pose something of a problem, but the existential nature of the continuum itself and the fact that persons can and do make ready and reliable judgments in reference to it cannot be gainsaid.

An adequate theory of socialization must pay attention to this continuum and be in consonance with it. This admonition also applies to any procedures of measurement employed in behalf of the theory. That is, a scale of measurement for "socialization" should position individuals in the "asocial," "normal," and "supernormal" zones of the continuum in general accordance with the verdict which the sociocultural environment has handed down concerning them.

If the scale of measurement is psy-

Reprinted by permission from the *Journal of Consulting Psychology,* Vol. 24, No. 1, 1960.

chological, appealing to factors of individual response and calibrated on such reactions, then the problem is a psychosociological one, as it were, requiring the scaling of the psychological dimension in such a way as to covary with the sociological one. Discrepancies are of course to be expected in individual instances between the sociological baseline and the psychological measurement, if for no other reason than that the culture will occasionally make mistakes in putting some men in prisons and others in positions of trust and responsibility. One of the benefits to be derived from a psychological method for assessing the socialization continuum is that errors of this kind can be identified.

For a number of years the author has been concerned with a theoretical formulation of the socialization problem which attempts to do justice to this notion of the continuous nature of the function (5, 6, 8). Perhaps a brief summary of the theoretical position would be in order here. Socialized behavior is behavior based on a proper viewing of the self as a social object, where the terms self and social object are used in the sense defined by Mead (9). That part of the personality which links an individual to the social community is the "self." The sense of self, or view of self, is a product of social interaction and of the capacity of the individual to view himself as an object; that is, from the standpoint of the other. The self, therefore, has its roots in role taking, in a developing objectification of the critiques and evaluations of oneself. In early life these views of self (called "me's" by Mead) may be discrete and unintegrated, but in time a certain communality and consistency in the patterns permits the evolvement of a conception of the "generalized other" which represents social reality as witnessed by the self.

Such a process of introjection of societal standards is always coupled with a degree of uncertainty or independence in the expression of the self. This unpredictable element in the self is called the "I" by Mead. On the other hand, social adaptability, cooperation, and socialization itself are functions of the "me's," that is, of the role-taking experiences and the role-taking capacities. Thus the degree to which the person will be able to govern internally his thought and behavior in accordance with the imperatives of his culture will be a consequence of the depth and validity of the role taking experiences that he has enacted.

In an earlier paper (5) the author tried to show how this theoretical position could be brought to bear on the problem of psychopathy, and how the various symptomatic expressions of psychopathy could be deduced from the fundamental propositions of role theory. Later (8) an attempt was made to develop a measuring instrument for asocial behavior using questionnaire materials derived on the basis of the role theory and focusing on the domain of social interaction and role taking experiences. Diagnostic items pertaining to the self view and role psychology were assembled and then administered to experimental samples, male and female. These included high school students, nondelinquent disciplinary problems in high school, and institutionalized delinquents. Statistical analysis permitted the identification of 64 items (from some 200 evaluated) having significant correlations with the socialization criterion.

These 64 items were grouped into a scale which was then cross-validated on a military sample of 1,092 inductees vs. 99 stockade prisoners, and a second military sample in which 144 prisoners with two or more offenses were compared with 209 first offenders. The difference between the mean of the inductees and that of the prisoners was 7.26, critical ratio 11.52. For the first offenders vs. recidivists the difference between means was 2.45, critical ratio 3.31. The signs in each instance were in the predicted direction, but even with use of the two-tailed test both critical ratios give probabilities well under .01.

However, these two cross-validational citations cover only two points on the socialization continuum: delinquents vs. nondelinquents and first offenders vs. repeaters. It must also be shown that *socialized* behavior can be brought under the purview of the theory and its scale of measurement to the same extent as *asocial* behavior. A scale or theory which would apply only to the distinction between delinquents and nondelinquents would be a limited one indeed. The goal of the theory, on the contrary, is to encompass the full range of phenomena implied by the continuum and the goal of the scale is to locate persons and groups in their proper places in any of its zones.

To test the validity of the scale in making such differentiations, a greater variety of samples was needed than reported in the 1952 paper, especially samples in the "more socialized" regions of the continuum. Such samples have gradually been obtained over the past seven years, in a sufficient number it would now seem to warrant analysis and reporting.

Shortening of the Scale

As a first step, the 64-item scale developed in the 1952 study was item analyzed against the first offender vs. repeater dichotomy. Such an analysis follows logically from the theoretical conception of socialization-asocialization as a continuum, and from the contention that individual items as well as the full scale should possess validity at different regions of this continuum. Ten items were eliminated by the analysis, leaving 54 in the shortened scale.[1] The following are representative of those retained (shown with the scored response for socialization).

1. Before I do something I try to consider how my friends will react to it. (true)
2. I often think about how I look and what impression I am making upon others. (true)
3. I would rather go without something than ask for a favor. (false)
4. I find it easy to "drop" or "break with" a friend. (false)

[1] This 54-item version is the one included in the California Psychological Inventory (7). The CPI Manual gives a great deal of clinical and psychometric information about the scale.

Because the purpose of the scale is to position either individuals or groups along the basic underlying socialization continuum, it has been designated "So" for socialization. A definition of the psychological implication of the scale can be given as follows: "To indicate the degree of social maturity, integrity, and rectitude which the individual has attained."

New Samples

The present findings are based upon an entirely new series of 41 research samples, totalling 1,295 male delinquents and 9,001 non-delinquents, and for females 784 delinquents and 9,776 controls. The samples cover a wide spectrum of the socialization continuum, ranging from nominated "best citizens" through various occupational and professional groups, through disciplinary samples, to known delinquents and prison inmates.

Tables 1 lists the male samples tested and presents summary statistics on the 54-item So scale. The samples are ranked by mean score on So, with "more socialized" or nondelinquent groups on the left, "less socialized" or delinquent on the right. The highest mean score among the 25 samples is observed in that on the nominated best citizens, and the lowest in the sample of federal reformatory inmates. In general, the rank ordering of samples by the So scale seems to accord quite well with what would occur if they were ranked sociologically for socialization. It should be noted that all seven of the samples carrying some explicit designation of asocial behavior score below the mean of the lowest scoring of those samples not so designated. Comparison of the 9,001 cases in the more socialized group of samples with the 1,295 cases in the less socialized group gives a difference between the means of 8.76, critical ratio 48.94, $P < .001$. The biserial correlation with the So scale for this same dichotomy is $+ .73$.

Quite clearly, the So scale locates male samples along the socialization continuum in the way required by the underlying theory. The question now is, can this same differentiation be demonstrated for women? Table 2 presents summary statistics of the CPI So scale for sixteen female samples. The progression of mean scores for the female samples in Table 2 shows the same correspondence to the underlying socialization continuum as was previously observed for the male samples. There is

psychometric ordering and the sociological hierarchy is remarkable. The statistical tests are also significant for the female samples, with a difference between the means of the more vs. less socialized cases of 9.52, critical ratio 37.83 ($P < .001$), and a biserial r of $+ .78$.

If one is willing to accept these results as indicating the validity of the So

TABLE 1. MEANS AND STANDARD DEVIATIONS ON THE CALIFORNIA PSYCHOLOGICAL INVENTORY So (SOCIALIZATION) SCALE FOR MALE SAMPLES INDICATED

More socialized				Less socialized			
Sample	N	M	SD	Sample	N	M	SD
1. Nominated high school "best citizens"	90	39.44	4.95	1. High school disciplinary problems	91	31.25	5.40
2. Medical school applicants	70	39.27	4.82	2. County jail inmates	177	29.27	6.44
3. Banking executives	121	39.00	4.59	3. Prison inmates, New York	94	28.28	5.80
4. Regional wholesale flour salesmen	85	38.31	4.37	4. Young delinquents, California	426	28.07	5.72
5. City school officials	200	37.58	4.19	5. Prison inmates, California	177	27.76	6.03
6. Psychiatric aides	132	37.57	4.37	6. Training school inmates, New York	100	26.53	4.89
7. Business executives	116	37.47	4.72	7. Inmates, federal reformatory	230	26.23	6.53
8. College students	1745	37.41	5.28				
9. Civil Service supervisory personnel	122	37.25	4.98				
10. Electronic technicians	55	36.93	5.66				
11. Correctional officers	620	36.72	5.47				
12. Semiskilled workers	108	36.62	5.17				
13. High school students	4474	36.46	5.95				
14. Social work graduate students	182	36.40	4.62				
15. Military officers	495	36.38	4.74				
16. Machine operators	105	35.99	4.98				
17. Psychology graduate students	142	34.60	4.13				
18. Selective service inductees	139	32.83	6.71				
Total	9001	36.74	5.61		1295	27.98	6.08

Note.—$M_1 - M_2 = 8.76$; CR $= 48.94$; $P < .001$; $r_{bis} = +.73$.

again a perfect separation between the nine samples in the more socialized column and the seven less socialized samples manifestly designated, in one way or another, for some defection from the socialization norms. For both the male and female samples the validity of the specific placement of a sample on the socialization continuum by the average So score might be disputed, but the general correspondence between the

scale as a measure of socialization, some interesting observations can be made about the relative standings of the groups tested. For example, there is the bemusing finding that psychologists (University of California, Berkeley, psychologists, it might be cautioned) tend to rank rather low on the socialization continuum, although fortunately not quite so low as to fall into the outrightly troublesome region of the dimension. The sample of unmarried mothers stands midway in socialization between high school disciplinary problems and county jail inmates. In both male and female rankings incarcerated persons score at the low end of the scale. It should also be noted that female samples in nearly all instances score significantly higher than their male counterparts.

The grouping of cases in Tables 1 and 2 into more socialized and less socialized is maintained in Table 3, where percentage frequency distributions are presented. Some indication of possible cutting scores and their screening efficiencies for

dicting a dichotomous criterion (delinquent vs. nondelinquent here) from a continuous variable (the So scale) is the point of intersection of the smoothed frequency distributions of the two classes on the predictor variable, where the areas of the two distributions are proportional to the base rates.

The question in our case is what base rate frequencies to use? As an example, suppose it is assumed that the true incidence of delinquent personalities is 10% of the population. Using Cureton's method for smoothing the distribution curves for the four samples in Table 3 and checking

TABLE 2. MEANS AND STANDARD DEVIATIONS ON THE CALIFORNIA PSYCHOLOGICAL INVENTORY So (SOCIALIZATION) SCALE FOR THE FEMALE SAMPLES INDICATED

More socialized				Less socialized			
Sample	N	M	SD	Sample	N	M	SD
1. Nominated high school "best citizens"	90	41.51	4.55	1. High school disciplinary problems	87	34.79	7.00
2. High school students	5295	39.69	5.55	2. Unmarried mothers	213	32.92	6.24
3. College students	3452	39.37	5.05	3. County jail inmates	51	29.61	5.86
4. Factory workers	291	38.99	4.76	4. Prison inmates, Indiana	127	28.37	6.24
5. Psychiatric aides	67	38.70	3.91	5. Prison inmates, California	135	28.36	5.68
6. Nurses	142	38.24	4.89	6. Prison inmates, Wisconsin	76	26.83	7.04
7. Airline hostesses	60	38.07	4.51	7. Young delinquents, California	95	25.83	5.13
8. Social work graduate students	320	37.99	4.38				
9. Psychology graduate students	59	36.44	3.93				
Total	9776	39.46	5.30		784	29.94	6.89

Note.—$M_1 - M_2 = 9.52$; CR $= 37.83$; $P < .001$; $r_{bis} = +.78$.

the usual delinquent vs. nondelinquent dichotomy can be gained from this table.

However, one might still ask whether any practical validity of the So scale for making the two-category classification in mass testing might not be vitiated by a base-rate limitation. That is, if Category A (delinquency) is quite rare, the rules of inverse probability might make it more valid (accurate) in the long run simply to predict that everyone tested will be non-A. As Cureton (2) has shown, this problem can be handled by proper setting of cutting scores so as to allow for base-rate asymmetries. The optimal cutting score for pre-

for the defined intersections leads to the specification of a cutting score of 23 (and below) for delinquency in males, and of 26 (and below) in females. If the true incidence of individuals sufficiently asocial to be classed as delinquent personalities is at least 1 in 10, then diagnostic classifications of all men with scores of 23 and below as delinquent types, and as nondelinquent types those with scores of 24 and above, will be more accurate than the 90% accuracy level which would automatically follow from classifying everyone tested as a nondelinquent.

With a more misanthropic view that

TABLE 3. PROPORTION OF CASES SCORING AT OR ABOVE THE INDICATED SCORES OF THE CALIFORNIA PSYCHOLOGICAL INVENTORY So (SOCIALIZATION) SCALE FOR Ss CLASSIFIED AS MORE SOCIALIZED AND LESS SOCIALIZED

So scale score	Males		Females	
	More socialized N = 9001	Less socialized N = 1295	More socialized N = 9776	Less socialized N = 784
42	21	1	40	4
41	28	2	47	6
40	34	3	55	9
39	41	4	62	11
38	48	6	68	15
29	91	47	97	58
28	94	53	98	64
27	95	60	98	68
26	97	65	99	72
25	98	70	99	76
24	98	75	99	81
23	99	81	99	85
22	99	86	99+	88

delinquent personalities in reality constitute as much as 20% of the population, the optimum So cutting score for males is at 25 or below for delinquency. For females, the one in five assumption determines a cutting score of 28 (and below).

Perhaps two comments should be interjected before closing this section. The first is that the possibility of deriving dichotomies of the above type does not in any way alter the fundamental theory of the scale and of its psychosociology as representing a continuous socialization function. The second is that specifications for optimum use of the scale in other categorization problems could just as easily be made, for example, for super-citizens vs. all others.

WORK OF OTHERS

A number of other investigators have carried out studies using the CPI So scale which help to illuminate the relationship between the measure and the theoretical continuum of socialization hypothesized to underlie it. One of these studies is that by Clark Vincent of unwed mothers. The So scale data were gathered for 232 subjects (Ss), tested in several public and private maternal care centers. For this sample the mean So score was 32.25, SD 6.58.

These figures closely approximate those for the smaller sample of 213 reported in Table 2 earlier.

The theoretical rationale for the So scale however, requires a more detailed analysis of this sample, an analysis attentive to the gradations of the continuum. In the present instance socialization gradations can be reflected by the number of pregnancies of each S. Classification on this basis gave the following So results:

Group	N	M	SD
1. One child	201	33.60	5.65
2. Two children	18	24.39	5.98
3. Three or more children	13	22.23	4.16

The progression of means here is that specified by the theory of the scale, and is supported statistically by the significance of the F test over the three means. Groups 2 and 3 can be combined into a sample of 31 Ss having had two or more illegitimate children. The biserial correlation for this sample vs. the 201 females having only one child is + .83. This coefficient offers rather striking evidence of the power of the So scale to discriminate within a certain range of the continuum.

The mean scores listed above can also be reviewed for hypotheses about the proper location of each sample on the socialization continuum. The Ss having one child score at about the same point as high school disciplinary problems; Ss having two or more children fall into a distinctly lower region of the dimension, into the range populated by the delinquent and criminal samples.

The next study to be considered is that of Donald (4). He administered the So scale to 230 consecutively admitted federal reformatory inmates. The mean of 27.77 (SD 6.53) places the total sample in its proper position on the continuum. The question for analysis is again that of differentiation within the total sample. Five of Donald's comparisons can be reported. The first is one in which socialization theory would not predict a difference, a comparison between white and Negro inmates. This expectation was confirmed, as the two part-samples did not differ significantly. The mean for 56 Negro inmates was 29.39, for 174 white inmates 27.75; however, the t test of the difference was not significant.

A second of Donald's comparisons was between 135 Dyer Act commitments, $M = 25.96$, $SD = 6.14$, and the remaining 95 cases, $M = 30.34$, $SD = 6.19$. Dyer Act offenses are in general more serious, and this difference is therefore in the predicted direction; the t ratio of 5.3 is significant well beyond the .01 level.

Comparison 3 pitted 111 boys with zero or one previous commitment vs. 119 boys with two or more. The means and standard deviations were 29.72 and 6.27 vs. 25.95 and 6.23. The difference is in the expected direction, and the t ratio of 4.5 is again statistically significant.

The fourth contrast was between boys whose first commitment occurred at age 15 or before vs. those whose first commitment came at age 16 or later. Socialization theory would predict lower So scores for the former group. Findings were in accord with these expectations; for the 96 boys in the first group $M = 24.76$, $SD = 5.89$, and for the 134 in the second $M = 29.93$, $SD = 6.09$. The t ratio for this difference was 6.4, $P < .01$.

The last comparison is a novel one, contrasting boys committed for "moonshining" infractions vs. all others. Federal liquor law violations lead to federal institution commitment, but from a socialization standpoint seem more akin to troublesome or moderately wayward behavior than to the asocial nature of most felonies. Therefore, one would expect higher So scores for this special sample. Such indeed was the case, for the 18 "moonshiners" had a mean score of 32.44, SD 6.99, and the 212 remaining inmates had a mean of 27.37, SD 6.33. This difference is also statistically significant, the t ratio being 2.9. The absolute level of the So mean, 32.44, should also be noted. It would rank the "moonshiners" just above "high school disciplinary problems" on the socialization hierarchy (see Table 1).

The third study to be mentioned is

that of the Pilot Intensive Counseling Organization Project (1) being conducted at the Deuel Vocational Institution in California under the auspices of the California Youth Authority and the California State Department of Corrections. In the PICO project, youth authority wards are assigned on a random basis at intake to experimental and control samples, the experimental cases participating in an intensive counseling program. The aim of the project is to discover the effects of this counseling program, hoping to find that the experimental cases will show better parole and postinstitutional records. The data reported here are all drawn from cases in the control sample.

The CPI is administered to all Ss in the study at the time of admission to the training school. From the project records three samples were established for our use: (1) parolees receiving suspensions during the first four months of parole; (2) parolees suspended during the fifth or a later month; and (3) parolees still free of suspension after five or more months on parole. The presumed socialization gradient is from lowest (1) to highest (3). CPI So scale statistics for these samples are as follows:

Sample	N	M	SD
1. Suspended within four months	90	27.26	5.10
2. Suspended after four months	90	28.18	5.36
3. Five or more months of parole without suspension	226	28.25	5.78

The progression of mean scores is in the direction specified, but the F test falls short of statistical significance. The follow-up period in the PICO project was not far enough along at the time of this writing to permit designation of a "successful discharge from parole" sample; the third group above is only an approximation of such a sample. If comparison is limited to early suspensions on parole (Sample 1) vs. later suspensions on parole (Sample 2), a critical ratio of 1.18 for the difference between the two means is obtained. Using the one-tailed test of significance, appropriate here because the difference is in the predicted direction, the probability level is between .05 and .10.

The fourth reference to the work of other investigators concerns the program of studies being conducted by Reckless and Dinitz and their associates at the Ohio State University (*3, 10, 11*). In the Reckless, Dinitz, and Murray study, 125 boys living in high delinquency areas in Columbus, Ohio, were nominated by teachers as being "insulated" against delinquency. These nominations were confirmed by a brief social service check of school and police records. The mean So scale score for this sample was 39.43, *SD* 6.42. Only one sample in Table 1, the high school best citizens, had a higher average score. In another study (*10*), these 125 boys were compared with 101 boys from the same high delinquency areas nominated by their teachers as being delinquency prone. The So scale statistics for this second sample were $M = 31.40$, $SD = 7.99$. The difference between this and the earlier mean was highly significant.

The paper by Reckless, Dinitz, and Murray (*11*) also contains a comment bearing directly on the view of socialization as a continuous dimension and on the capacity of the So scale to differentiate within regions of this dimension:

The delinquency vulnerability [socialization] and social responsibility scales did more than differentiate between the potentially delinquent and non-delinquent nominees. The scales also discriminated significantly, within the sample of potential delinquents, between those who had and those who had not experienced previous police and court contact.

The "delinquency vulnerability" scale referred to in the quotation is the CPI So scale discussed throughout the present papare. The "social responsibility" scale is another one of the scales included in the full set of 18 in the California Psychological Inventory.

SUMMARY

Arguments in behalf of viewing socialization as a continuous dimension rather than as merely a dichotomy of social vs. asocial behavior were presented. A theory of socialization was summarized, and a method of psychological measurement consonant with this theory was described.

The greater portion of the paper was then taken up with findings seeking to demonstrate the validity of the measuring scale along the full range of the socialization continuum.

Evidence from the writer's inquiries as well as from those of other investigators gave strong support to the systematic validity of the scale.

REFERENCES

1. California Youth Authority and State Department of Corrections. Technical Report Series, Pilot Intensive Counseling Organization Project. Deuel Vocational Institute, Tracy, California, 1956, 1958.
2. Cureton, E. E. Recipe for a cookbook. *Psychol. Bull.*, 1957, *54*, 494–497.
3. Dinitz, S., Kay, Barbara, and Reckless, W. C. Delinquency proneness and school achievement. *Educ. res. Bull.*, 1957, *36*, 131–136.
4. Donald, E. *Personality scale analysis of new admission to a reformatory.* Unpublished master's thesis, Ohio State Univer., 1955.
5. Gough, H. G. A sociological theory of psychopathy. *Amer. J. Sociol.*, 1948, *53*, 359–366.
6. Gough, H. G. Systematic validation of a test for delinquency. *Amer. Psychologist*, 1954, *9*, 381. (Abstract)
7. Gough, H. G. *Manual for the California psychological inventory.* Palo Alto, Calif.: Consulting Psychologists Press, 1957.
8. Gough, H. G., and Peterson, D. R. The identification and measurement of predispositional factors in crime and delinquency. *J. consult. Psychol.*, 1952, *16*, 207–212.

9. Mead, G. H. *Mind, self, and society.* Chicago: Univer. Chicago Press, 1934.
10. Reckless, W. C., Dinitz, S., and Kay, Barbara. The self component in potential delinquency and potential non-delin-

quency. *Amer. sociol. Rev.,* 1957, *22,* 566–570.
11. Reckless, W. C., Dinitz, S., and Murray, Ellen. The "good" boy in a high delinquency area. *J. crimin. Law Criminol.,* 1957, *48,* 18–25.

A Study of Anxiety in the Sociopathic Personality

DAVID T. LYKKEN

THE concept of the psychopathic personality includes so heterogeneous a group of behavior disorders as to be at least two steps removed from the level of useful psychiatric diagnosis. Sociopathic personality is a more recent designation (*1*) which refers to a subgroup of these disorders in which the pathognomic characteristics are impulsiveness, antisocial tendencies, immorality, and a seemingly self-destructive failure to modify this pattern of behavior in spite of repeated painful consequences. This category may be regarded as a genus composed of phenotypically similar, but etiologically distinct, subtypes such as the dissocial and the neurotic sociopaths.

A third species has been described (*3, 12, 13, 14, 17*), which may be called *primary sociopathy*, in which neither neurotic motivations, hereditary taint, nor dissocial nurture seem to be determining factors. Cleckley (*3*) has reported the chief clinical characteristic of this group as a lack of the normal affective accompaniments of experience. If this observation is correct, it would point the way toward accurate diagnostic isolation of primary sociopathy as well as guiding research into the question of its etiology. Classification according to the presence or absence of defective emotional reactivity, therefore, satisfies one criterion of useful diagnosis in that it shows promise of relationship to the as yet unknown origins of the disorders to be distinguished.

The other requirement for useful diagnosis is that the criteria of classification must be objective. Clinical assessment of the "normality of the affective accompaniments of experience" is subjective and unreliable. In consequence, Cleckley's work has had as yet little real impact on psychiatric practice. By expressing this putative defect of the primary sociopath in terms of the anxiety construct of experimental psychology (*18, 19, 20, 21, 22*), it becomes susceptible to quantification and empirical test.

An experimental hypothesis may now be formulated. Among persons conventionally diagnosed as psychopathic personality, those who closely resemble the syndrome described by Cleckley are (*a*) clearly defective as compared to normals in their ability to develop (i.e. *condition*) anxiety, in the sense of an anticipatory emotional response to warning signals previously associated with nociceptive stimulation. Persons with such a defect would also be expected to show (*b*) abnormally little *manifest anxiety* in life situations normally conducive to this response, and to be (*c*) relatively incapable of *avoidance learning* under circumstances where such learning can only be effected through the mediation of the anxiety response.

METHOD

The Sample

The extreme heterogeneity, even on the crudest descriptive level, of persons diagnosed as psychopathic personalities in various clinical or institutional settings complicated the selection of an appropriate experimental sample. The institution psychologists were given a list of 14 criteria drawn from Cleckley (*3,* pp. 355–392) and were asked to compare against these criteria those inmates diagnosed as psychopathic personality. Inmates who, in their opinion, best fitted the Cleckley prototype were listed as candidates for experimental Group I, the primary sociopathic group. Inmates who they felt did *not* meet the criteria in important respects were listed as candidates for experimental Group II, designated as the neurotic sociopathic group. In this selection process, the psychologists were asked to reaffirm the original diagnosis, discarding from consideration for either group those inmates who, in their present opinion, would not be diagnosed as psychopathic personality at all.

A control Group III of 15 "normals," roughly comparable in age, intelligence, and socioeconomic background, was selected from the University General College and a local high school.

Group I, composed of 12 males and 7 females, had a mean age of 21.6 years ($SD =$ 4.3), and a mean IQ of 109.2 ($SD = 10.7$). Group II included 13 males and 7 females, had a mean age of 24.5 years ($SD = 5.4$), and a mean IQ of 104.5 ($SD = 8.8$). For the 10 male and 5 female normals, the mean age was 19.07 ($SD = 3.2$), and the mean IQ 100.4 ($SD = 10.2$). None of these group differences was significant.

The Measures and Testing Procedure

It was necessary to do the testing at the several institutions under varying conditions. In all cases, however, the apparatus was arranged on a large table, the experimenter on one side and the subject (S) seated comfortably opposite. The S was told that he was assisting in a psychological experiment having no bearing on his personal record and that his performance would be treated with strict anonymity. An attempt was made throughout to keep the testing on an informal basis.

As an indicant of manifest anxiety as referred to in hypothesis b, an "Anxiety Scale" was constructed expressly for this study to supplement the Taylor scale and Anxiety Index which appear to be more strongly loaded on a factor of neurotic self-description. In this new scale, each of the thirty-three items involves two statements of activities or occurrences, matched for general unpleasantness or undesirability according to a modified Thurstone scaling procedure utilizing 15 college student judges. One activity of each pair is unpleasant, presumably because of its frightening or embarrassing character (e.g., "making a parachute jump" or "knocking over a glass in a restaurant"). The paired activity is intended to be onerous but not frightening (e.g., "digging a big rubbish pit"

or "cleaning up a spilled bottle of syrup"). The S is required to choose that member of each pair which he would prefer as a lesser of evils. The degree to which the "frightening" alternatives are rejected is interpreted as an index of the extent to which anxiety determines behavior choices within the range of life situations sampled by this test.

The booklet form of the MMPI was used and the answer sheets scored and K-corrected in the usual way (*10*). The Anxiety Index, or AI, was calculated according to the formula given by Welsh (*23*). The Heineman form (*11*) of the Taylor scale was given and scored by subtracting the number of "anxiety" items rejected as "least applies to me" from the number endorsed as "most applies to me."

An avoidance learning test was given to determine whether there were group differences in capacity to learn on the basis of anxiety reduction (hypothesis c). It involved an elaborate, electrically operated mental maze which the S was given 20 trials to learn (the "manifest task"). At each of the 20 choice points in this maze, choice of one of the 4 possible alternatives (always an error alternative) gave an electric shock. It was intended that social and ego rewards should reinforce performance in the manifest task. Performance on the "latent task," which was to avoid the shocked alternatives—to err instead on the unshocked alternatives—was presumably reinforced only through anxiety reduction.

The measure of anxiety conditionability (hypothesis c) employed the GSR [Galvanic Skin Response] as the dependent variable. A shocking electrode was attached to S's nondominant hand, the GSR electrodes being already in place on the dominant hand. The S was told that after the blindfold had been replaced, he was to sit as quietly as possible for the next 30 to 40 minutes, during which time he would periodically hear a buzzer (which was then demonstrated) and occasionally receive a brief electric shock. When the S was seated comfortably and relaxed insofar as possible, the recording apparatus was started and the conditioning series begun.

Two buzzers were used which were distinguishably different in timbre rather than in pitch, the difference being one not easily labeled (to minimize verbal mediation of a discrimination between them). Buzzer No. 1 was used as the CS [conditional stimulus] and was the only one reinforced; buzzer No. 2 was used to test for generalization effects. In all cases, stimuli of the conditioning series were presented as soon as GSR activity from preceding stimuli had subsided, the intertrial interval being therefore not constant within or between Ss, but averaging between 20 and 60 seconds. (This method of stimulus timing automatically eliminates temporal conditioning.) When turned on, the buzzers sounded for a period of 5 seconds, controlled by an automatic timer.

The reinforcing stimulus or UnCS [unconditional stimulus], was an electric shock from a 700-volt AC supply through two 68,000-ohm series resistors, presented automatically for about 100 milliseconds just before the termination of the CS (buzzer No. 1). The shock was applied between an electrode on the palm of one hand and the GSR *ground* electrode on the palmar tip of the middle finger of the opposite hand. The shock sensation was felt mainly on the richly innervated finger tip and was a decidedly unpleasant stimulus, producing in most cases a pronounced startle reaction and in all cases a strong GSR.

The sequence of trials or stimulus presentations was as follows:

1. To permit the adaptation of unconditioned GSR to the buzzers themselves, stimuli were first presented without shock reinforcement for a total of 10 trials in the order 2, 1, 2, 1, S, 2, 2, 1, 1, 1, 1. A single preliminary shock was given in the series at the point S, separated by at least 30 seconds from the buzzers occurring before and after it.

2. Seven consecutive shock-reinforced presentations of the CS were given as the conditioning series, followed by four more reinforcements interspersed with four unreinforced trials with buzzer No. 2 in the order 1, 1, 1, 1, 1, 1, 1, 2, 1, 2, 2, 1, 2, 1, 1.

3. A total of 24 extinction trials was then given, the two buzzer stimuli being presented in the order 1, 2, 1, 1, 2, 1, 2, 1, 1, 1, 2, 1, 1, 1, 1, 2, 2, 1, 2, 1, 1, 2, 1, 1, 1. Considering only the CS, buzzer No. 1, the series therefore consisted of 6 prereinforcement trials, 11 reinforced conditioning trials, and 16 extinction trials.

Skin resistance was measured by a modification of a circuit suggested by Flanders (6).

All GSRs were recorded in terms of resistance change. A variety of transformations was then applied and tested against the usual criteria of normality of distribution, correlation with basal resistance, and homogeneity of variance across people with respect to several test stimuli (2, 8, 9, 16). The result of this analysis was that each resistance change was expressed as the logarithm of the ratio of that change to the mean resistance change produced by the first six electric

shocks. This unit expresses the galvanic CR as a proportion of the individual's UnCR and, for a conditioning study, seems quite appropriate for individual comparisons.

Three GSR indices were derived from the protocols of the conditioning series: (a) GSR Reactivity, which is the mean GSR to the CS during the fourth through seventh conditioning trials; (b) GSR Conditioning, which is equal to (a) minus the mean GSR to the last three preconditioning trials and the last three extinction trials (this index measures essentially the slope of the conditioning curve or the increment actually produced by the reinforced trials); (c) GSR Generalization, the ratio of the mean GSR to buzzer No. 2 during early extinction trials 18, 20, 21, 23 to the mean GSR to buzzer No. 1 during trials 17, 19, 22, 24.

The testing sequence was as follows: (a) Anxiety scale; (b) GSR Conditioning series; (c) Avoidance Learning test; (d) MMPI (given during the week following the foregoing individual testing); (e) Taylor Manifest Anxiety Scale, forced-choice form given later with the MMPI.

RESULTS AND DISCUSSION

Scores on all measures were converted for easier comparison to a standard score form with each distribution having

TABLE 1. GROUP MEANS ON ALL MEASURES: SIGNIFICANCE TESTS *

Measure	Group			d-Test
	I	II	III	prob.†
Taylor Scale	471	556	462	.01
Anxiety Index	472	557	464	.01
Anxiety Scale	470	511	529	.05
MMPI Pd-Scale	532	547	395	.05
Avoidance Learning	461	501	558	.01
GSR Reactivity	498	494	534	.05
GSR Conditioning	478	483	551	.05
Generalization	473	542	490	—

* All measures converted to a scale having an over-all mean of 500 and SD of 100.

† Probabilities given are for significance of largest difference (e.g., III − I for GSR Conditioning). Significance test was Festinger's distribution-free 'd' test (5).

a grand mean of 500 and a standard deviation of 100. Group means on all measures, together with significance test results, are given in Table 1.

It would clearly be too much to expect of the judgments based upon the

Cleckley criteria that they should have perfectly separated the psychopathic sample into a "primary" species in Group I, and a neurotic or dissocial species in Group II. That the separation was reasonably good, however, is supported by the finding that Group II scored significantly higher than the normals on the Taylor scale, a great deal of evidence having accumulated (4, 7, 15) to indicate that this scale is primarily a measure of neurotic maladjustment or neuroticism rather than of anxiety level or anxiety reactivity *per se*. On the MMPI Anxiety Index, which like the Taylor scale is unquestionably polydimensional with a heavy loading on neuroticism, Group II again has the highest mean, with Group I again only slightly higher than Group III.

In contrast, the Anxiety scale, which was designed for this study and which is not loaded on neuroticism and only negligibly correlated with the Taylor scale or the AI, separated the groups in a different order. On this test, the primary types of Group I show the least anxiety reactivity, significantly less than the normals, with Group II falling in between but rather nearer to the Group III mean. This result appears to support hypothesis *b* of this study, that the subset of primary sociopaths show abnormally little manifest anxiety, i.e., anxiety reactivity to the real-life anxiety stimuli referred to in the questionnaire.

Both sociopathic groups scored significantly higher than the normals on the *Pd* [psychopathic deviate] scale of the MMPI, but this measure, which differentiates at the phenotypic or genus level, does not distinguish between the types or species of sociopathy represented in Groups I and II.

Schedule difficulties unfortunately led to a reduction in the number of *S*s to whom the avoidance learning test could be given. With nearly half of the total group, the available testing time was too short to cover all of the procedures; in such cases the avoidance test, requiring nearly an hour to give, was passed over. Even on the residual sample of 34 *S*s, however, rather clear-cut differences exist. As a crude, over-all index of avoidance learning, the avoidance scores (shock errors divided by unshocked errors) were averaged for all but the first of the 20 trials; this is the basis of the mean scores entered under "avoidance" in Table 1. The distribution was reversed to make high values represent greater avoidance of the shock. It is impossible, of course, to summarize adequately a complex learning process by a single numerical index of this sort, but in spite of these limitations, it is striking that Group I (primaries) shows the least avoidance as expected, Group II (neurotics) next, and Group III (normals) the most. The Group I versus Group III, and Group II versus Group III differences are significant by Festinger's *d*-test (5), and the actual distribution of scores shows the groups to be remarkably well separated (only 17 per cent overlap between Groups I and III). This result supports hypothesis *c* of this study, that the primary sociopath demonstrates defective avoidance learning.

Results of the GSR Conditioning Series

Of all the tests employed here, principal emphasis should be laid on GSR conditioning. The various difficulties attending the interpretation of GSR data are well known, but one fact stands out with relative certainty: given certain necessary conditions, if an *S* does *not* produce a GSR to a stimulus, one can be sure that he has not "reacted emotionally" to that stimulus.

The two numerical indices which were derived as alternative ways of representing in a single value the conditioning indicated by the GSR protocols (anticipatory GSR to the buzzer after several pairings with shock) have already been described. As shown in Table 1, the group means are in the expected order on both indicants, with Group I significantly lower than Group III on GSR Reactivity and GSR Conditioning (.05 level, *d*-test).

A somewhat more meaningful comparison is obtained by contrasting the reactivity by trials for the three groups. Group I shows the least GSR reaction to the CS in 14 out of the 16 double trials. Group II is significantly higher (.02 level) than Group I at the end of the extinction trials. The positions of Group II and Group III interchange during the series with Group II beginning to show greater reactivity during the extinction trials, suggesting a perseveration (failure of extinction) of the anxiety response in the neurotic group. This trend was tested for statistical reliability by correlating the differences between Group II and Group III with the ordinal position in the conditioning series at which the difference was taken. The quadrant sign test (24) shows this association to be significant at the .01 level. This result supports hypothesis a of this study, that the primary sociopath is defective in his ability to condition the anxiety response.

The generalization scores were leptokurtically distributed, the group differences being determined by a few deviant Ss. Group II shows the highest mean generalization score, but the differences are not significant.

SUMMARY

Forty-nine diagnosed psychopaths were divided into two groups according to the descriptive criteria of Cleckley. Fifteen normals served as controls. A battery of tests related to anxiety reactivity or anxiety conditionability were administered. As compared with normals, the Cleckley, or "primary" sociopaths, showed significantly less "anxiety" on a questionnaire device, less GSR reactivity to a "conditioned" stimulus associated with shock, and less avoidance of punished responses on a test of avoidance learning. The "neurotic" sociopaths scored significantly higher on the Taylor Anxiety Scale and on the Welsh Anxiety Index.

REFERENCES

1. Amer. Psychiatric Assoc. *Diagnostic and statistical manual: mental disorders.* Washington, D.C.: American Psychiatric Assn., 1952.

2. Bitterman, M. E., and Holtzman, W. H. Development of psychiatric screening of flying personnel. III. Conditioning and extinction of the GSR in relation to clinical evidence of anxiety. *USAF Sch. Aviat. Med.*, 1952, Proj. No. 21-37-002, Rep. No. 3, N. 232 p.

3. Cleckley, H. *The mask of sanity.* (2nd ed.) St. Louis: C. V. Mosby, 1950.

4. Eriksen, C. W., and Davids, A. The meaning and clinical validity of the Taylor Anxiety Scale and the hysteria-psychasthenia scales from the MMPI. *J. abnorm. soc. Psychol.*, 1955, 50, 135–137.

5. Festinger, L. The significance of the difference between means without reference to the frequency distribution function. *Psychometrika*, 1945, 11, 97–105.

6. Flanders, N. A. A circuit for the continuous measurement of palmar resistance. *Amer. J. Psychol.*, 1953, 66, 295–299.

7. Franks, C. Conditioning and personality: a study of normal and neurotic subjects. *J. abnorm. soc. Psychol.*, 1956, 52, 143–150.

8. Haggard, E. A. Experimental studies in affective processes. II. On the quantification and evaluation of "measured" changes in skin resistance. *J. exp. Psychol.*, 1945, 33, 46–56.

9. Haggard, E. A. On the application of analysis of variance to GSR data. I. The selection of an appropriate measure. *J. exp. Psychol.*, 1949, 39, 378-392.

10. Hathaway, S. R. *Supplementary manual for the MMPI. Part I, The K scale and its use.* New York: Psychological Corp., 1946.

11. Heineman, C. E. A forced choice form of the Taylor Anxiety Scale. *J. consult. Psychol.*, 1953, 17, 447–454.

12. Karpman, B. Psychopathic types: the symptomatic and the ideopathic. *J. crim Psychopathol.*, 1941, 3, 112–124.

13. Karpman, B. The myth of the psychopathic personality. *Amer. J. Psychiat.*, 1948, 104, 523–534.

14. Karpman, B. Conscience in the psychopath: another version. *Amer. J. Orthopsychiat.*, 1948, *18*, 455–491.
15. Kerrick, Jean S. Some correlates of the Taylor Manifest Anxiety Scale. *J. abnorm. soc. Psychol.*, 1955, *50*, 75–77.
16. Lacey, O. L., and Siegel, P. S. An analysis of the unit of measurement of the galvanic skin responses. *J. exp. Psychol.*, 1949, *39*, 122–123.
17. Lippman, H. S. Psychopathic behavior in infants and children: a critical survey of existing concepts. *Amer. J. Orthopsychiat.*, 1951, *21*, 227–231.
18. May, M. A. Experimentally acquired drives, *J. exp. Psychol.*, 1948, *38*, 66–77.
19. Miller, N. E. Studies of fear as an acquirable drive. I. Fear as motivation and fear-reduction as reinforcement in the learning of new responses. *J. exp. Psychol.*, 1948, *38*, 89–101.
20. Miller, N. E. Learnable drives and rewards. In S. S. Stevens (Ed.), *Handbook of experimental psychology.* New York· Wiley, 1951. Pp. 435–472.
21. Mowrer, O. H. A stimulus-response analysis of anxiety. *Psychol. Rev.*, 1939, *46*, 553–565.
22. Mowrer, O. H. Anxiety reduction and learning. *J. exp. Psychol.*, 1940, 27, 497–516.
23. Welsh, G. S. An anxiety index and an internationalization radio for the MMPI. *J. consult. Psychol.*, 1952, *16*, 65–72.
24. Wilcoxon, F. *Some rapid approximate statistical procedures.* New York: American Cyanamid Co., 1949.

5 | Six Approaches to the Study of Schizophrenic Disorders

IN THIS section we present some typical research studies focused on schizophrenia. In the past, research investigators have been interested primarily in how the language and thought processes of schizophrenics differ from those of normals. Today the range of interest has broadened to include such phenomena as the influence of subcultural factors on the development of the schizophrenic disorder, social organization of schizophrenics, the role-taking abilities, perceptual function, and autonomic responsiveness of schizophrenic patients, and stimulus generalization and conditionability as an indication of severity of pathology. (Articles illustrative of the use of conditioning and stimulus generalization concepts in the study of schizophrenia are included in Section 3.)

The use of anthropological concepts in the study of behavior pathology is relatively new. Singer and Opler obtained two groups of schizophrenic patients, differing only in cultural background, and studied their performances on tests of fantasy and mobility. Although all the patients were American citizens, had been subject to the standardizing influence of the New York City metropolitan area, and were undergoing severe emotional crises, the pattern of their behavior could be predicted from a knowledge of the prevailing characteristics of the culture in which they had participated. The conclusion that schizophrenia is the resultant of unsuccessful attempts to resolve culturally generated conflicts is a natural one. Not only does this study illustrate a provocative set of concepts for analyzing behavior pathology, it raises some real questions about the usefulness of standard psychiatric classifications. Here we have two groups of patients both formally diagnosed as schizophrenics, yet their performances on certain relevant tests are significantly different, and are predictably so from a knowledge of certain cultural orientations.

According to recent behavior pathologists, the disorder labeled schizophrenia is essentially a syndrome in which role-taking is inept, distorted, ineffective, and unnecessarily labile or rigid. The observer of a schizophrenic patient is quickly impressed with his failure to take the "role of the other" in interactional settings. Helfand's study was conducted from this orientation. His subjects were given an autobiography and asked to predict the test performances of the subject in the autobiography. The generalized-

155

other, or general frame of reference for predicting the behavior of others, served as a guide to the normal subjects. Such a generalized-other framework was absent from the responses of the schizophrenics. A pertinent question to consider in this connection is the following: what are the conditions of socialization that interfere with a person's developing a generalized frame of reference congruent with that of others in his society?

Although Grayson and Olinger do not tie their experiment to the language of role-taking, their methods and conclusions may be interpreted in such a context. When psychiatric patients are required to answer a questionnaire as a normal person would, they are being asked to take a role. Performances of patients on such a task give us information on how they define the normal. But more important, the ability to take the role of the normal person is linked to favorable prognosis. The results generate a further hypothesis: Those disordered persons who, in fact, can simulate the performance of normals have the skills required for social participation. Having such skills—even latently—is a necessary prerequisite to improvement.

In recent years there has been a pronounced shift from the medical orientation to the social-psychological in the study of behavior pathology. In the latter orientation, the severity of mental illness as determined by conventional criteria would be tied to the degree of disturbance in social interaction. Sociometrics, a method for assessing social relationships, was employed in the Murray and Cohen study. The relationship between severity of illness and sociometric choices shows the usefulness of looking at behavior pathology from the social-psychological viewpoint. From this viewpoint, one would predict that attempts at increasing readiness for, and practice in, social interaction would reverse the pathological process. Murray and Cohen, through the use of *milieu* therapy, offer some data that lend support to this hypothesis.

The papers by Becker and by King make use of an increasingly useful conception in the study of schizophrenia. In the simplest terms, this conception recognizes two qualitatively different schizophrenias: process and reactive. On admission to a psychiatric hospital, the presenting symptoms of schizophrenics do not allow any precise differentiation. An analysis of the history of the patient, together with an intensive "mental status" examination, permits a diagnosis of reactive or process. This distinction has prognostic utility: reactive schizophrenics tend to return to the community; process schizophrenics tend toward chronicity.

The paper by Becker combines this distinction with the conception of genetic levels proposed by Werner,* and suggests a continuum of pathology, rather than a dual typology. For the purposes of his research, Becker used the Rorschach test and the Benjamin Proverbs. Both of these instruments tap perceptual-cognitive performances. By establishing scoring procedures based on the "levels of development" notion, Becker was able to demonstrate the fruitfulness of the genetic (i.e., developmental) approach to the study of schizophrenia.

King approached the problem of discovering correlates of the process-reactive typology through the study of the responsiveness of the autonomic nervous system to the injection of a drug, mecholyl. This research procedure has been fruitfully used in recent times: for example, it has been shown that blood pressure changes after the injection of mecholyl are related to such dimensions as levels of abstract thinking.

By sorting his patients according to the criteria of reactive or process schizophrenia, King was able to demonstrate that the autonomic responsiveness of the process

* Werner, H. *Comparative Psychology of Mental Development.* Chicago: Follett & Company, 1948.

schizophrenics (those with poor prognosis for recovery) more closely resembled that of normals. This finding requires interpretation: why should the process schizophrenics (who for the most part are headed toward chronicity) react as normals do, while the reactives were different, in that they showed greater responsiveness? King's interpretation of these findings is penetrating. He sees both the normal subjects and the process schizophrenics as having a high degree of stability of response. The reactive schizophrenics, on the other hand, are struggling with their problems and their equilibratory controls are more readily activated.

Contrasting Patterns of Fantasy and Motility in Irish and Italian Schizophrenics

JEROME L. SINGER AND MARVIN K. OPLER

THE occurrence of differential patterns and manifestations of psychiatric illness in various cultures has long been documented by anthropologists and sociologists (2, 3, 10, 16, 17). There have been, however, relatively few studies employing psychological testing techniques to evaluate evidence of variations in personality characteristics of mental patients within American subcultural groups. The present study. part of a broader comparison of the psychopathology of two such subcultural groups, represents an initial effort to test certain hypotheses within a sample of schizophrenics stemming from Italian and Irish backgrounds. Underlying this study is the assumption that certain factors in early family structures and subsequent cultural conditionings have led to different modes of energy distribution and interpersonal orientation in Americans of Irish and Italian background and that these divergencies persist even when serious emotional disturbance is in evidence.

The specific focus of the present investigation is upon an aspect of personality tentatively designated as *fantasy-motility*. A considerable body of research has suggested that motor and fantasy behavior may be viewed to some extent as function-ing vicariously, the inhibition of motor activity leading to heightened fantasy or motion perception or the characteristic resort to fantasy being linked in many individuals with tendencies or capacities for motor inhibition (18, 21). The theoretical significance of this dimension stems from its relationship to a number of important theories of ego-development and the genesis and function of thought in human behavior (4, 8, 21). Much of the empirical work in this field has resulted from studies with the Rorschach inkblots and there is evidence that normals and schizophrenics who see relatively more Human Movement percepts (M) on the inkblots tend to show less overt movement, on the one hand, and to be more disposed to imaginative thought, on the other (4, 21, 22). To the extent that Rorschach's M response and its correlates may be taken as measures of basic ego functions involving the capacity to defer gratification and to resort to thought as "experimental action" (8), their employment in studies of subjects with differing cultural backgrounds has practical as well as theoretical implications.

There are suggestions in the literature that early identifications with significant family figures may be basic to the development of delaying capacities or fantasy (9, 12, 17, 21, 23). There is also evidence which points to differences in cogni-

Reprinted by permisson from *The Journal of Abnormal and Social Psychology*, Vol. 53, No. 1, July 1956.

tive attitudes respecting time that seem to stem from differing family constellations in middle- and lower-class normals and schizophrenics (11, 13, 15, 20). These socioeconomic class differences cut across the normal-pathological dichotomy and it seems clear that, at least in response to projective test situations, the adult schizophrenic's pattern of "time perspective" and parental attitudes reflects in part cultural influence on family constellations as well as specific pathogenic childhood identifications. It is reasonable, therefore, to anticipate persisting personality differences among schizophrenic adults who come from cultural backgrounds in which early family structures differ and in which adult values and customs continue to stress divergent patterns of inhibition or deferment of gratification. Within the crude nosology of severe emotional disturbance, one may still expect to observe characteristic patterns of fantasy and motility that reflect cultural origins and that incorporate the gross symptomatology of schizophrenia, the hallucinations, delusions, the relative flattening of affect, and thought disorders within the context of these culturally-conditioned ego functions.

The selection of Irish- and Italian-Americans as subjects for the study was based on accumulating anthropological and sociological indications of marked differences in their cultural patterns, family constellation, and male social and sexual role positions (1, 2, 3, 5, 16, 17). The clinical experience of the authors based on intensive study with individuals from these cultural groups further amplified the general picture as did considerable evidence from the existing literature. In the Irish family an oft-observed central and controlling maternal role contrasts with that of the Italian mother who, despite warmth and protectiveness, often represents a reflection of greater paternal authority. Sexuality in the two traditions differs as do attitudes towards their common religion. In the Italian family sexuality is often em-

phasized as part of the expressive and emotional life and is accepted as an assertion of maleness. Among the Irish, known for their mild and protracted courtships, delayed marriages, and celibate emphases, sexuality is clearly subordinated to procreation and, apart from this framework or from the marital setting, is more likely to be regarded as guilt-producing and sinful. In brief, the Irish family constellation with the relatively powerful mother-figure and female siblings tends to emphasize inhibition and delay of gratification with ambivalence toward the female and difficulty in establishing an identification with a father-figure who is psychologically neutral and frequently absent from the home.

In the Italian family, fairly common practice permits use of the normative cultural pattern for an expressive acting out of feelings. Thus, the emphasis is on direct expression of emotions resulting from conflicts with the relatively powerful father and older male siblings. Such emotions may tend in their pathological extremes to be built more readily into hostile patterns of reaction, often self-destructive as well as destructive of the male parental image. A previous anthropological survey by Opler of milder forms of mental illness among Irish and Italians in another hospital had suggested that the Irish male schizophrenic may be seen as beset with fear and guilt, controlling deeply repressed hostility towards female images chiefly through repression and fantasy. The Italian male model for schizophrenia seemed, on the contrary, given to more destructive and overtly hostile impulses, aimed chiefly at the male parental image but built up to uncontrollable dimensions in accordance with a cultural value of emotional expression at all costs.

In proceeding toward an operational formulation of hypotheses derived from the cultural differences between the Irish and Italian, it was decided to employ a battery of evaluative procedures with fairly well known properties. Rorschach's

Human Movement response (M) seemed a logical variable for study as well as the Thematic Apperception Test Transcendence Index (22), both measures of fantasy disposition. A time-estimation task involving delaying ability for accuracy as well as a slow-writing task were included as measures of inhibition. Similarly, the Porteus Mazes, involving as they do a combination of motor restraint and foresight for successful performance, were included in the battery. The resort to fantasy and greater obsessional tendencies of the Irish might be expected to lead to more ready *admission of disturbance* following failure in a frustration-tolerance situation. Finally, in order to obtain something approximating a longitudinal section of behavior in the motor area, ratings of ward behavior with respect to cooperativeness and aggression or assaultiveness were employed (14).

HYPOTHESES

1. Irish schizophrenic patients differ from Italian schizophrenics by showing greater evidence of fantasy-tendency. Specifically, they show more Human Movement responses on the Rorschach inkblots, lower threshold for Human Movement on Barron's inkblots, and higher scores in Transcendence on Thematic Apperception Test stories.

2. Irish patients show greater evidence of inhibition, motor inhibition, and restraint on tasks calling for delaying capacity. They require longer times in a slow-writing motor inhibition task, score higher Test Quotients on the Porteus Mazes, and achieve greater accuracy in Time Estimation in a situation involving delay in response.

3. Irish patients more readily admit to disturbance following failure in a frustration-tolerance test.

4. In ratings by personnel of their ward behavior, Irish patients are less aggressive, less overtly assaultive, and more cooperative in ward routines than are Italian schizophrenics.

METHOD

Subjects

A total of 60 male veteran patients diagnosed as schizophrenic were chosen from the wards of the hospital so as to constitute two samples of thirty patients each from Irish-American and Italian-American cultural backgrounds. Criteria for inclusion of patients involved (a) use only of clearly diagnosed schizophrenics without known organic brain damage, (b) first to third generation from both ethnic groups with residence in the New York City metropolitan area, (c) ages 18–45 inclusive, (d) patients sufficiently in contact to undergo the test battery and anthropological interview. Table 1 presents pertinent data comparing the two samples for age, education, date of first hospitalization, and Wechsler-Bellevue IQ. An evaluation of socioeconomic status was also carried out, using as indices parents' education and occupation, income, and housing as well as Ss' standing on these variables. Socioeconomic status and religion (all Ss were professed Roman Catholics) did not differ for the two samples. Within the Irish group, all families originated in the poorer Southwest counties while the Italian Ss with two exceptions were of South Italian or Sicilian origin. Generation level was approximately equated in each group, thus limiting differential effects of acculturation, a factor of considerable significance for motor patterns in Efron's work (7).

Procedure

All Ss received an assessment battery administered in standard fashion. The following is a brief description of the procedures and the measures employed to test experimental hypotheses:

Rorschach Inkblots. All Rorschachs were scored by Klopfer's method. The primary variable derived from the Rorschach was the Human Movement response (M). Only frequency of occurrence was considered in this study. Statistical analysis of other Rorschach data was limited to those variables in which a sufficient range of scores emerged.

Barron's Movement-Threshold Inkblots. These blots were included in order to evaluate their suitability as a measure of Rorschach M more easily obtained and more suitable for quantification. Barron's inkblot series (4) consists of a series of black-and-white inkblots arranged in a sequence which elicits increasing numbers of M responses over the range of 30 cards. The score employed was the card number on which the initial Human Movement response was offered by S.

Thematic Apperception Test. Four

cards, 1, 6, 7, and 12, of the Murray series were administered. Weisskopf's Transcendence Index as employed in an earlier study (22) was applied to the content of the stories. This index, a measure of the extent to which S's story introduces characters, activities, and emotions not actually present on the stimulus card, may be thought of as a reasonable operational definition of fantasy disposition. The actual score employed was the total number of transcendent items over the four cards.

Porteus Mazes. This instrument was administered in standard fashion. Test Quotients were computed in accordance with norms available from Porteus (*19*). Qualitative notes on mode of approach were kept.

Time Estimation. As a fairly direct measure of delaying capacity, the Ss were asked to indicate when they thought a given time interval had elapsed. Three times were used, 15, 30, and 60 seconds. The E started a stop watch and recorded the actual time passed when S signaled that he thought the stated interval had passed. The score was the sum of the three estimations subtracted from absolute times. Since almost all Ss indicated that the time had passed before it actually had, accuracy and delaying ability were practically identical.

Motor Inhibition. This task, adapted from Downey's Will-Temperament scale, required Ss to write a simple phrase as slowly as possible without stopping the motion of their pencils. Time in seconds taken to write the phrase was the basic score.

Admission-Denial of Frustration. This variable was derived from response to a simple experimentally induced failure experience devised by Wilensky (*24*). Following a period of nine successive failures on digit series, Ss almost invariably showed impairment in retention of digit series previously within their scope. Despite this apparent evidence of disturbed performance following failure, many Ss denied conscious distress upon direct inquiry. In this study each S was asked if he had been disturbed by his failures. Responses were categorized as *admissions* or *denials* of disturbance following failure. Some cases were lost in this technique because of bizarre verbalization or refusals to comment.

Behavior Ratings. To obtain some evaluation of a longitudinal nature, two groups of items from the Multidimensional Rating Scales for Ward Behavior of Psychiatric Patients (*14*) were employed. These items, grouped into scales for Aggression and Cooperation, were rated by a staff clinical psychologist during interviews with ward personnel, aides, nurses, and physicians, all of whom had observed the patients for approximately six months on their wards. The emphasis in these scales is on actual incidents and overt behavior rather than on interpretations of underlying trends. Items on the Aggression Scale included instances of overt destructive behavior, assaultiveness, and verbal outbursts, while items on the Cooperation Scale involved such factors as willingness to follow ward therapeutic routines, assisting in ward chores, and accepting authority of ward

TABLE 1. MEANS OF IRISH AND ITALIAN SCHIZOPHRENICS ON PERTINENT BACKGROUND FACTORS, RORSCHACH DETERMINANTS, AND EXPERIMENTAL VARIABLES

Variables	Irish (N=30)	Italian (N=30)
Background Factors		
Age	32.0	30.5
Educational Grade Level	10.5	10.9
Year of First Hospitalization	1949.8	1949.5
Wechsler-Bellevue IQ	108.4	105.5
Rorschach Variables		
Total Responses (R)	21.1	20.7
Human Movement (M)	2.2	1.3
Animal Movement (FM)	3.4	2.8
Form-Color (FC)	0.8	0.7
Color-Form (CF)	1.5	1.4
Weighted Color Sum (Sum C)	2.5	2.6
Experimental Variables		
Movement-Threshold Inkblots	14.3	20.8
TAT Transcendence Index	19.3	14.3
Porteus Mazes TQ	87.2	86.7
Time Estimation (dev. in secs. from absolute times)	38.8	44.0
Motor Inhibition Time (secs.)	147.0	106.5
Admit Frustration	67%	42%
Aggressive Ward Behavior Rating	1.60	2.30
Cooperation Behavior Rating	1.87	0.67

personnel. As employed here, high scores on these scales imply considerable aggressive behavior and minimal cooperation.

RESULTS

Table 1 presents a comparison of Irish and Italian group means for background variables, Rorschach determinants, and experimental variables. The groups do not differ significantly in age, years of education, date of first hospitalization (an estimate of chronicity), Wechsler-Bellevue IQ, or in the representation from various socioeconomic levels.

The Irish and Italian Ss do not differ in frequency of the Rorschach determinants except for the M responses, which are definitely more numerous among the

Irish. The Irish patients, as hypothesized, show lower thresholds for Human Movement responses in Barron's inkblots, greater transcendence in their TAT stories, lower deviation from absolute times in Time Estimation, longer inhibition times in the slow-writing task, greater tendency to admit distress following failure, and, in their ward behavior, less aggression and greater cooperativeness. Only the Porteus Maze scores reveal no differences and fail to support the relevant hypothesis. A qualitative difference in performance on the mazes was evident, however. While both groups obtained similar scores, the Irish, according to qualitative notes, were far more often reported to be deliberate and cautious in performance, whereas the Italian Ss were more often described as impulsive and rapid. Why this difference did not affect ultimate outcome in maze score could not be ascertained.

In connection with the ward ratings, it should be noted that ward personnel who provided the data and the raters were ignorant of the purposes of the experiment. Similarly, the difference between the groups in ward cooperation could not account for test score differences since, in the actual testing situation, the Italian Ss proved to be somewhat more genial and amenable to examination.

DISCUSSION

There seems little question that the test performance of these two groups reflects clearly a difference in fantasy and motility that is strikingly in accord with anticipations based on anthropological evaluations of cultural frameworks and family constellations. When it is kept in mind that both the Italian and Irish patients are American citizens, most of them native born, that they have participated in the same urban culture and have also undergone the standardization of military service, then the persistence of differences rooted in subcultural group participation is highly noteworthy. When it is further recognized that both groups of patients were grossly psychotic, the emergence of the differential fantasy-motility pattern is indeed a remarkable demonstration of the hypothesized group differences. The patients in this study all showed many symptoms of schizophrenia, although such symptoms as "flattening of affect" were less apparent in the Italian and "catatonic excitements" were not characteristic of the Irish. At the same time, despite the obvious fact that thinking disorders and hallucinations were present in most cases, wide variations in personality structure emerged. As James S. Plant, Fromm-Reichman, and Horney have suggested, however, these data and other materials from the same larger study (18) suggest that schizophrenias and other personality disorders highlight culturally engendered conflicts. This view poses serious questions about the validity and usefulness of current psychiatric nomenclature (16). Should study with further samples confirm the findings of this report, extensive familiarity with subcultural patterns may be increasingly essential for effective psychiatric diagnosis and personality evaluation. The need for further work using test batteries like the one reported here with normal Ss from various subcultural groups is obvious.

Pending further exploration it seems reasonable to conclude that schizophrenics stemming from Irish and Italian cultural backgrounds do show markedly different patterns of fantasy and motility. The results seem best interpreted as suggesting the possibilty that because of the limitation on variability in family constellation imposed by cultural background, as well as the recurrent influences of cultural values during development, characteristic differences in modal personalities (9) from different subcultural groups persist through adulthood and are in evidence even during a period of severe emotional disturbance. To the extent that such modal personality patterns may be derived from differing family constellations and cultural values, an extensive exploration of fantasy and motor activity as well as of other relevant personality dimensions by means of joint psychological testing and anthropological survey with many other subcultural groups appears to be desirable. Such explorations might go beyond traditional cultural stereotypes toward an understanding of variables underlying the relationships between patterns in family life and cultural standards as they interact to mold the adult personality in its normal and pathological manifestations.

SUMMARY

This study represented a portion of a larger investigation involving a comparison of the psychological test performance and psychopathological manifestations of schizophrenic subjects from different American subcultural groups. Based on anthropological evaluation of cultural patterns and child-rearing practices in families of Irish and Italian ethnic background, certain hypotheses concerning differences in fantasy and motor activity were developed. The Irish were expected to prove more given to imaginative behavior and motor control when compared with Italian Ss. When comparable samples of Irish and Italian schizophrenic males were studied by psychological tests and ward behavior ratings, these hypotheses were essentially confirmed. In the test results, no differences emerged in Rorschach variables except for the Human Movement responses, more of which were produced by the Irish. The Irish showed lower threshold for perception of Human Movement on Barron's inkblots, greater transcendence of stimulus content in their TAT stories, longer motor inhibition times on a slow-writing task, longer delay in time estimation, greater tendency to admit distress following frustration. Ratings of ward behavior indicated the Irish as more cooperative in therapeutic routines and less overtly aggressive than the Italian patients. No differences in Porteus Maze Test Quotients emerged, although a qualitative tendency for the Irish to work more slowly and hesitantly compared with the impulsivity and haste of the Italian Ss was clearly apparent. In general, the results appear to support the hypothesis of persistent differences in motor and fantasy activity between patients from the two ethnic groups. Implications for review of psychiatric nosology, personality research, and interdisciplinary collaboration are manifold.

REFERENCES

1. Arensberg, C., and Kimball, S. T. *Family and community in Ireland*. Cambridge: Harvard Univer. Press, 1948.
2. Bales, R. F. Cultural differences in rates of alcoholism. *Quart. J. Stud. Alcohol,* 1946, *6*, 480–493.
3. Barrabee, P., and Von Mering, O. Ethnic variations in mental stress in families with psychotic children. *Soc. Problems,* 1953, *1*, 48–53.
4. Barron, F. Threshold for the perception of Human Movement in inkblots. *J. consult. Psychol.,* 1955, *19*, 33–38.
5. Child, I. L. *Italian or American?* New Haven: Yale Univer. Press, 1943.
6. Edwards, A. *Statistical analysis for students in psychology and education.* New York: Holt, Rinehart and Winston, 1946.
7. Efron, D. *Gesture and environment.* New York· Kings Crown Press, 1941.
8. Freud, S. Formulations regarding the two principles in mental functioning. *Collected Papers,* Vol. IV. London: Hogarth, 1946.
9. Inkeles, A., and Levinson, D. J. National character: the study of modal personality and sociocultural systems. In G. Lindzey (Ed.), *Handbook of social psychology.* Vol. II. Cambridge: Addison Wesley, 1954. Pp. 977–1020.
10. Kluckhohn, C. Culture and behavior. In G. Lindzey (Ed.), *Handbook of social psychology.* Vol. II. Cambridge: Addison-Wesley, 1954. Pp. 921–976.
11. Kohn, M. L., and Clausen, J. A. Parental authority behavior and schizophrenia. *Amer. J. Orthopsychiat.,* in press.
12. Lair, W. S. *The psychoanalytic theory of identification.* Unpublished doctor's dissertation, Harvard Univer., 1949.

13. Le Shan, L. L. Time orientation and social class. *J. abnorm. soc. Psychol.*, 1952, *47*, 589–592.

14. Lorr, M. Multidimensional scale for rating psychiatric patients. Hospital form. *VA tech. Bull.*, No. 10-507, Nov. 16, 1953.

15. Mitchell, H. E. Social class and race as factors affecting the role of the family in Thematic Apperception Test stories of males. Unpublished doctor's dissertation, Univer. of Pennsylvania, 1950.

16. Opler, M. K. Cultural anthropology and social psychiatry. *Amer. J. Psychiat.*, in press.

17. Opler, M. K. Cultural perspectives in mental health research. *Amer. J. Orthopsychiat.*, 1955, *25*, 51–59.

18. Opler, M. K., and Singer, J. L. Ethnic behavior and psychopathology: Italian and Irish. *Int. J. soc. Psychiat.*, 1956, *2*, 11–23.

19. Porteus, S. D. *The Porteus Maze test and intelligence.* Palo Alto: Pacific Books, 1950.

20. Singer, J. L. Projected familial attitudes as a function of socioeconomic status and psychopathology. *J. consult. Psychol.*, 1954, *18*, 99–104.

21. Singer, J. L. Delayed gratification and ego-development: implications for clinical and experimental research. *J. consult. Psychol.*, 1955, *19*, 259–266.

22. Singer, J. L., and Herman, J. Motor and fantasy correlates of Rorschach Human Movement responses. *J. consult. Psychol.*, 1954, *18*, 325–331.

23. Singer, J. L., and Sugarman, D. A note on some projected familial attitudes associated with Rorschach movement responses. *J. consult. Psychol.*, 1955, *19*, 117–119.

24. Wilensky, H. The performance of schizophrenic and normal individuals following frustration. *Psychol. Monogr.*, 1952, *66*, No. 12 (Whole No. 344).

Role Taking in Schizophrenia

ISIDORE HELFAND

EXPERIMENTAL investigations of role taking or the empathic process have been primarily conducted with "normal" Ss, especially college students. The results of these investigations, notably the studies of Dymond (*3, 4, 5*) and McClelland (*8*), suggest that the greater the degree of emotional instability, the poorer the ability of the Ss to take the role of another. These findings are consistent with the hypotheses offered by Cameron (*1, 2*) who suggested that a disturbance in role-taking skills is crucial to the development of schizophrenia.

The present experiment was designed to explore role-taking characteristics in schizophrenia. In addition, it was hoped that some light would be cast upon the characteristics of empathic ability, not only in schizophrenia, but in the normal individual. Specifically, two major hypotheses were tested:

1. Schizophrenics, when compared with nonpsychotic individuals, show poorer role-taking skills.

2. Nonpsychotic individuals, when compared to schizophrenics, are more homogeneous in their agreement with one another as to the characteristics of the individual whose roles they are instructed to take.

PROCEDURE

Studies in role taking have used what might be termed the method of personal acquaintanceship. Students sharing a common course in college are asked to rate one another. In a study which seeks to compare schizophrenics and normal individuals, such a procedure becomes impractical. It is especially so when it is desired that the degree of familiarity as

Reprinted by permission from the *Journal of Consulting Psychology*, Vol. 20, No. 1, 1956.

well as the type of relationship be controlled.

In the present study, therefore, an autobiography obtained from a former hospital patient was used as a common stimulus. The patient had been hospitalized briefly for one of a series of minor recurring depressions. He was frank, honest, and, in the opinion of the hospital staff, someone with whom one could readily empathize. He was asked to discuss his life with reference to parents, siblings, courtship, marriage, sex, education, and vocation. From this material, an 80 item Q sort was constructed. Items were selected which minimized reactions on the basis of fact; rather, they emphasized the need for infer-

is concerned with this second or Simulated sort and its relationship to the Criterion.

Subjects

All 64 Ss were given screening tests consisting of the Wechsler-Bellevue Vocabulary Test (12) as an estimate of verbal abilities and a reading test (10). The aim here was to eliminate illiterates, functional mental defectives, and those too uncooperative or inattentive to manage the tasks adequately.

Of the 200 male schizophrenic patients at a chronic treatment center between the ages of 20–45 who had been hospitalized for two to five years, 25 remained after screening. These 25 patients fell into two

TABLE 1. SUMMARY OF BACKGROUND DATA

	C's	P's	T.B.	Normal	F Ratio†
Age in years	35.9	38.2	37.9	33.4	.99
School grade completed	10.6	11.5	10.1	12.2	3.61*
Reading grade level	8+	8+	8+	8+	
Reading score	14.9	17.4	18.5	19.6	17.14**
Vocabulary raw score	23.2	26.5	23.6	25.1	1.3
Hospitalization months	43.9	37.2	37.8		1.06

† The F ratios are the results of the analyses of variance on each of the five factors indicated.
* Significant at the .05 level of confidence ($F_{.05}=2.76$).
** Significant at the .01 level of confidence ($F_{.01}=4.13$).

ence on the part of the S. This procedure also reduced the likelihood of the sort's being a mere reading task.

The Q sort was then administered to the author of the autobiography with instructions to distribute the items so as to reflect most accurately his feelings and attitudes. The result is referred to hereafter as the Criterion sort.

Each of the Ss was asked to take the Q sort twice: First, they sorted the items to reflect their own attitudes and feelings. The second time, they were read the autobiography. They also had a copy which they could read and refer to. They were then asked to take the Q sort again, but this time as it reflected the ideas of the author of the autobiography. They were to act like him when they took the test. The present paper

groups, a chronic group of 15 patients, and a privileged group of 10 patients. Chronic patients are confined to the wards and have a poor prognosis. Their activities are limited to simple routine ward chores. Privileged patients have made a sufficient recovery to be permitted freedom of the grounds. They worked in the hospital shops and some were being considered for discharge.

A group of 19 tuberculous patients were included as a control for any possible deterioration due to hospitalization. They were nonpsychotic and had never required consultation for a mental disorder. They had been hospitalized for a period ranging from twenty months to five years.

The normal group included 20 individuals who were functioning members of their community. None had been hospitalized for a mental disorder or had ever sought professional help for such a disturbance. They were firemen, machine operators, clerks and the like. All were gainfully employed.

Table 1 provides a summary of the background data of the subjects employed. An analysis of variance indicated that the groups differed significantly on two factors: Education (at the .05 level of confidence) and reading ability (at the .01 level of confidence). Chronic schizphrenics and tuberculous patients appear to be less well educated than the other two groups. While all groups were able to surpass requirements for an eighth grade reading level, chronic schizophrenics show a marked impairment in these skills, possibly as a function of a concentrative difficulty. Age, length of hospitalization, and verbal abilities do not differ significantly among the groups.

The influence of education and reading ability was considered in the analysis of the results.

RESULTS

Empathic ability was determined by comparing the Simulated sort with the Criterion sort. The individual correlations were converted to z scores since correlations are not normally distributed. The resulting array was subjected to an analysis of variance. The F ratio obtained ($F = 11.05$) indicates that the between-group variance was greater than the within-group variance to a degree in excess of that which might be anticipated by chance ($F_{.01} = 4.13$). The analysis was continued using a t test, the results of which can be seen in Table 2.

As can be seen, all groups differ significantly from the chronic schizophrenic group in their ability to empathize. The privileged schizophrenic group is superior to all others. This superiority is particularly striking when the privileged patients are compared with normal individuals. Tuberculous patients, while sig-

TABLE 2. MEAN EMPATHY SCORES OF ALL GROUPS AND THE SIGNIFICANCE OF THE DIFFERENCES BETWEEN MEANS

	C's	P's	T.B.	Normal
Mean	.050	.437	.356	.290
SD	.236	.165	.149	.153
C's t		4.61**	4.25**	3.33**
P's t			1.2	2.22*
Normal t			1.3	

* Significance at or better than the .05 level of confidence.

** Significance at or better than the .01 level of confidence.

nificantly different from the chronic schizphrenics, stand between the privileged and normal groups and are significantly different from neither.

To determine whether these results were influenced either by reading ability or education, an analysis of these two factors was carried out using the Mann-Whitney U test. The entire group was split in two, a high and low empathic group. A comparison was then made between poorer readers and more proficient readers. A similar analysis was made comparing education. A critical ratio of .49 for reading ability and .36 for education suggested that these factors had little bearing on empathic ability.

The second hypothesis was tested by correlating the Simulated sort of each individual with the sort of every other individual in his group.

From these data, it would appear, inspectionally, that the differences between the chronic schizophrenics and other three categories are particularly pronounced. Normals, it would appear, are superior to all groups, and, as was the case with role-taking measures, privileged schizophrenics most closely resemble tuberculous patients. The tuberculous appear to have greater homogeneity than the psychotics. Consequently, there seems to be an increasing degree of homogeneity in going from the chronic schizophrenics through the privileged and tuberculous Ss to the normals.

The fact that each individual was correlated with everyone else within his group makes for a lack of independence in observation that precludes the application of a statistical analysis or any conclusive tests of homogeneity among the groups. While, therefore, it appears that normal individuals are more homogeneous in their agreements and that schizophrenics agree less among themselves concerning the individual whose roles they take, this conclusion must be taken only as suggestive in view of the inapplicability of rigorous tests of significance.

DISCUSSION

The findings tend to confirm certain aspects of the hypotheses. Others remain moot and unsupported. The normal individual's reaction appears to be more consistent with the hypothesis offered by Lindgren and Robinson (7). Rather than responding with any marked degree of sensitivity, normals appear to respond more in terms of a preconceived and more universally shared idea of what another should be like. It seems likely that "well-adjusted" individuals of Dymond's studies had a good appreciation of cultural norms and expectancies from which their judgments were derived. In any event, this factor of conventionality appears to be more important in the normal individual's reaction to another than does the other's idiosyncrasies.

The chronic schizophrenic is apparently deficient in both areas. He is indeed the individual, responding on the basis of his own fantasies and ideas, with little concern for either the accuracy of what he perceives or whether his ideas are shared with others. One limitation of this study is the lack of certainty as to whether the chronic schizophrenic patient responded because of a basic impairment of role-taking skills or because of disinterest in the task. It was hoped that this latter was minimized by screening. Following an analysis of the results, the question appeared to remain unanswered. Because of practical considerations due to the lapse of time, the reliability of the sorts could not be obtained.

Some suggestion that role taking may not be deficient in the chronic schizophrenic, but merely not utilized, is offered by the results of the privileged patients. Assuming that the latter were once as severely disturbed (requiring custodial treatment) as were the chronic schizophrenics, partial remission from the disease appears to be characterized by a hypersensitivity to the feelings of others, a phenomenon Fromm-Reichman aptly titled "emotional eavesdropping" (6). In contrast to normal individuals, however, they appear to lack a conventional frame of reference. Despite their relative accuracy in role taking, each responded to the cues given in a very individual manner.

The results pose at least two problems: *What* is it that permits, or enables the schizophrenic to respond with such sensitivity? Secondly, *why* do they respond with such sensitivity?

In reviewing the method, the task appears to be not unlike a projective or semistructured situation. An opportunity was provided for interpretation rather than a repetition of facts, as so much of the behavior of the Ss might be characterized as projective in the psychometric sense of the term. The behavior of the normal individual was to project a preconceived set of ideas based primarily on a commonly shared cultural stereotype. The privileged patients, responding to the same information, made better use of it, although their reactions were highly idiosyncratic. Sarbin's description of the schizophrenic as lacking a "generalized other" concept seems appropriate to the results here (11). The schizophrenic, possibly because of this lack, responded to the cues as he perceived them.

The normal individual, on the other hand, may have received the same cues, tested or evaluated them, and, in the absence of corroborating data, rejected many of the hypotheses. The schizophrenic appears to be much less critical. In all probabilities, both this lack of criticalness and a lack of a conventional frame of reference, or what Mead has termed a "generalized other" (9), serve to contribute to the hyperacuity noted.

Assuming that schizophrenics lack this generalized other, such an impairment, with resultant hyperacuity, should be found in younger children, and in emotionally disturbed children as compared to well-adjusted children of the same age. Since such concepts as a generalized other are predicated on the transition from concern with particular people, via interpersonal relationships, disturbances in such relationships, as is indicated in schizophrenia, would contribute to a failure to make the transition. If inconsistency, rejection, and hostility characterize the history of the individual with a predisposition to the development of schizophrenia, he would look on each individual not unlike a sentry on a hostile frontier, carefully evaluating and appraising each one, and never, as do normal individuals, taking others for granted, and relying on generalized norms of what others are like.

Concerning the tuberculous group, the findings offer only equivocal suggestions. In terms of the results, these Ss appear to most closely resemble the privileged schizophrenic. Whether this is a function of the debilitating social consequences of long hospitalization and the nature of the routine, or of some "tuberculous personality," awaits further research. It is interesting to note that one would expect a higher degree of homogeneity than appeared to characterize these individuals, since they are sequestered together for a long period of time, and have an excellent opportunity to know one another.

SUMMARY AND CONCLUSIONS

Schizophrenics, tuberculous, non-psychotic patients, and normal individuals were tested on their ability to take roles. Empathy was determined by their ability to simulate the test performance of an author of an autobiography which was provided them. In addition, the relative agreement with one another, within each group, was determined. The results suggest the following:

1. Chronic schizophrenics have impaired role-taking skills and are relatively individual in their perception.

2. Normal individuals, while superior to chronic schizophrenics in role-taking skills, are more inclined to rely on a conventional frame of reference, rather than demonstrating marked role-taking skills.

3. Privileged patients show a marked sensitivity to others, but appear to respond in a highly idiosyncratic manner.

4. A suggestion was offered that schizophrenics appear to lack a concept of a "generalized other," and that they never make the transition in role-taking skills, from empathy with particular people to a more conventional—universally shared—frame of reference.

5. Tuberculous patients appear to be more like the privileged or partially remitted schizophrenics. The findings here, however, can only be suggestive in the absence of statistical significance.

6. The autobiography appears to be a useful tool in the measurement of empathic ability.

REFERENCES

1. Cameron, N. The paranoid pseudo-community. *Amer. J. Sociol.*, 1943, *49*, 32–38.

2. Cameron, N. *The psychology of behavior disorders.* Boston: Houghton Mifflin, 1947.

3. Dymond, Rosalind F. A preliminary investigation of the relations of insight and empathy. *J. consult. Psychol.*, 1948, *12*, 228–233.

4. Dymond, Rosalind F. A scale for the measurement of empathic ability. *J. consult. Psychol.*, 1949, *13*, 127–133.

5. Dymond, Rosalind F. Personality and empathy. *J. consult. Psychol.*, 1950, *14*, 343–350.

6. Fromm-Reichman, Frieda. *Principles of intensive psychotherapy.* Chicago: Univer. of Chicago Press, 1950.

7. Lindgren, H. C., and Robinson, Jacqueline. An evaluation of Dymond's test of insight and empathy. *J. consult. Psychol.,* 1953, *17,* 172–176.

8. McClelland, W. A. A preliminary test of role-playing ability. *J. consult. Psychol.,* 1951, *15,* 102–108.

9. Mead, G. H. *Mind, self and society.* Chicago: Univer. of Chicago Press, 1934.

10. Monroe, W. S. *Monroe standardized silent reading test, revised, test II, grades 6–8.* Bloomington, Ill.: Public School Publishing, 1920.

11. Sarbin, T. R. The concept of role taking. *Sociometry,* 1943, *6,* 273–285.

12. Wechsler, D. *The measurement of adult intelligence.* Baltimore: Williams & Wilkins, 1944.

Simulation of "Normalcy" by Psychiatric Patients on the MMPI

HARRY M. GRAYSON AND LEONARD B. OLINGER

Studies on simulation of normal or abnormal adjustment on psychological tests have been conducted by a number of techniques including the Rorschach (*1, 2, 4, 11*), sentence completion test (*9*), and objective personality schedules (*3, 6, 7, 8, 10*). However, studies on simulation of "normalcy" by psychiatric patients are, to our knowledge, nonexistent. Such studies would appear to be justified by the following considerations: they may throw light on the concepts of normal adjustment which are held by different kinds of psychiatric patients; they may yield important implications for psychotherapy, based upon the nature of the differences between the patient's self concept and his ego ideal, as inferred from differences between his original and simulated test performances; they may prove of value in predicting length of hospitalization or outcome of therapy, since the ability to "improve" on the tests may reflect a degree of reality orientation or ego-strength suggestive of a favorable prognosis.

The present paper, which is part of a larger study involving tests tapping different levels of personality, presents preliminary findings based on the Minnesota Multiphasic Personality Inventory (MMPI). In undertaking this investigation, answers were sought to the following questions:

1. To what extent can psychiatric patients produce "normal" test performance when requested to do so?

2. What other kinds of changes in test performance occur; and are these different for patients of different diagnostic categories?

3. May ability to give improved performance when simulating normalcy be predictive of shorter hospitalization?

PROCEDURE AND RESULTS

The experimental procedure was as follows: Patients took the MMPI routinely, on entering the hospital. The next day the test was repeated, but with instructions to answer it "the way a typical, well-adjusted person on the outside, would do." Upon completing the test, each patient was asked to describe how he did it, what his method was; and his comments were noted. Forty-five consecutively hospitalized male patients participated in the study. In each case, the psychiatric admissions-diagnosis was obtained from the patient's clinical folder.

In order to see how many patients actually improved their performance, the authors independently made blind sortings

Reprinted by permission from the *Journal of Consulting Psychology,* Vol. 21, No. 1, 1957.

of the pairs of original and simulated profiles for each patient, based on the expectation of improvement in the simulated profile. Where both investigators correctly sorted the patient's profiles, and where this coincided with a reduction in the Total T score based on the sum of the nine clinical scales, the case was considered as improved. On this basis, 33 out of the 45 cases (73%) were judged as improved in performance when simulating normalcy. The rest either did not improve, or became worse. Figure 1 shows the change in the over-all pattern for these 33 improved patients.

The changes in the direction of the $F*$ and K scales are of interest, the patients

Statistical analysis of the differences in the profiles of the nine clinical variables was undertaken, based on a method recently devised by Gengerelli and Butler (5). This method, which takes into account the absolute magnitude of each individual's score on each variable, revealed the profiles to be significantly different at beyond the one per cent level of confidence, with a t value of 5.4 for 32 degrees of freedom.[1]

The kinds of diagnostic changes actually produced in the profiles of all 45 patients, improved and unimproved, are shown in Table 1. The table reveals that 28 of the 45 cases (62%) showed no change in diagnostic category, although many of these showed improvement in

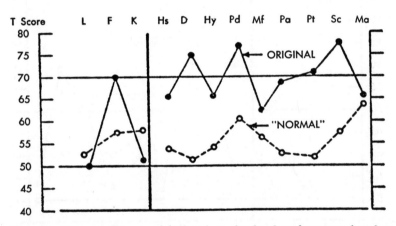

Figure 1. Mean profiles on original and on simulated performance, based on 33 "improved" cases.

showing increased defensiveness, K, and decreased confusion, F. (If the F scale is considered simply as a validity indicator, the simulated performance would appear to be more valid than the original!) It will be noted that the profile changes from that of a highly disturbed incipient paranoid schizophrenic to the double-spike curve of the "anxiety-free psychopath." It is as though the typical, disturbed schizophrenic patient were to say, "If only I could lose my anxiety and guilt feelings, and my feelings of personal inadequacy, and if I felt less inhibited in accepting and acting on my impulses, then I would not be the harrassed, mentally-ill person that I am."

terms of a "softening" or reduction in the deviancy of the personality pattern. Only five cases (11%) became "normal." The remaining 27 per cent underwent a "diagnostic shift" to another category.

Of the 24 schizophrenics, exactly half remained unchanged, while the rest

[1] Two *profile-numbers* were computed for each individual (one representing his original performance and the other his simulated performance) by multiplying his standard T score on each variable by constants according to the following equation: $Pi = 8.11(Mf) + 6.13(Ma) + 4.19(Hy) + 2.11(Hs) + O(Pa) - 2.23(Pt) - 4.21(Pd) - 6.17(D) - 8.21(Sc)$. The resulting pairs of profile numbers were treated, with due regard to signs, as two separate distributions. Means and variances were computed and the usual t test made.

* The conventional labels for all the scales are indicated in Table 2.

TABLE 1. "DIAGNOSTIC SHIFTS" BETWEEN ORIGINAL AND SIMULATED MMPI PROFILES

Original diagnosis	Simulated diagnosis	Number
Schizophrenia (N = 24)	Schizophrenia	12*
	Character disorder	6
	Psychoneurosis	2
	Psychosomatic syndrome	1
	Normal	3
Character disorder (N = 13)	Character disorder	11*
	Normal	2
Manic depressive (N = 4)	Manic depressive	2*
	Schizophrenia	1
	Character disorder	1
Psychoneurosis (N = 4)	Psychoneurosis	3*
	Schizophrenia	1

* Diagnosis remained unchanged.

gree of severity or the nature of the behavior disorder. Figures 2 and 3 show examples of two kinds of changes which occurred. Space considerations preclude the showing of other interesting examples.

Figure 2 illustrates a "softened" deviancy pattern, and indicates a diagnostic shift from an incipient schizophrenic reaction to one of anxiety neurosis. Figure 3 illustrates a "mirror image" or reaction-formation pattern which sometimes results when the patient strives hard to deny unacceptable feelings or impulses. This figure exemplifies a diagnostic shift from a de-

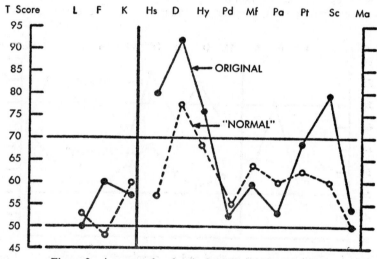

Figure 2. An example of a "softened" deviancy pattern.

converted to character disorders, psychoneurotics, psychosomatic, and "normal." Of the 13 character disorders, 11 remained unchanged, while two became "normal." Of the four manic-depressives, two remained unchanged; one became schizophrenic; and one a character disorder. And of the four psychoneurotics, three remained unchanged although less deviant, while one gave a schizophrenic profile.

Thus, although in general the simulated profile was better than the original, most patients, under the conditions of the experiment, did not produce a "normal" performance, but rather changed the de-

compensating obsessive-compulsive neurosis to an acting-out type of character disorder.

The patients' comments were frequently of interest, as evidenced by the following examples: "It was pretty hard at first but when you just think: I'm Superman, there's nothing wrong with me."; "Well, I was thinking of my dad, for example. He's always been my ideal."; "Well, I just put down the opposite to what I did yesterday."; "Through books and things you get to understand the average person."; "I have answered these questions as a so-called normal person would (if there is such a person). What is a normal person?"; "I answered these questions as I hope to answer truthfully in the near future."

The degree and nature of the changes have possible diagnostic and therapeutic implications. For example, in some cases, especially in the character-disorder class, the similarity of the two profiles, along with the verbalizations, indicates that the patients do not feel there is anything wrong with them. As one patient put it, "I *am* well adjusted. I have no nervous problems." Other patients, by the very mild softening of their deviant profiles, express that they are essentially normal. In the words of one patient, "What would you say

nine clinical scales, the critical ratio being 4.6. This means that most psychiatric patients were capable of recognizing and avoiding many of the individual deviant responses, even though they were still largely unable to produce normal profile patterns. For the 33 "improved" cases, the critical ratio rose, as one would expect, to 6.3. There was also a significant reduction in the number of scales at or above the critical T score of 70.

As Table 2 shows, significant improvement took place on all scales except

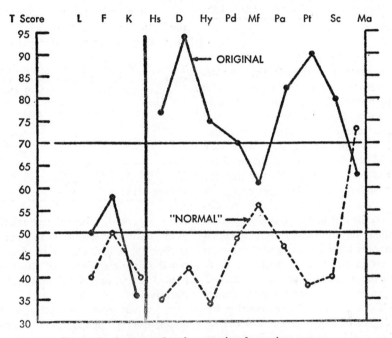

Figure 3. An example of a reaction-formation pattern.

if I told you I wouldn't have to change mine a whole lot to be typically well adjusted?" Others feel quite hopeless. For example, one patient said, "How can we answer as a typical, well-adjusted person if we're not?" The cases of "diagnostic shift" suggest that, for some patients, being normal involves the use of different (usually less deviant) adjustment patterns, including the elimination of bizarre symptoms.

There was a significant reduction in Total T score for all 45 patients on the

the Lie scale and the Mf and Ma scales.

Apparently, the "improved" patients did not feel it necessary to present more of a socially acceptable front on the obvious items of the Lie scale, although defensiveness increased significantly on the more subtle K and K-F scales. Furthermore, the patients did not seem to consider the Mf and Ma scale items as indicative of pathology. All of the other scales, however, underwent significant change, the greatest mean differences in T score taking place on

TABLE 2. CHANGES IN T SCORE ON THE
MMPI SCALES

Scale		Mean change	SE_M	Critical ratio
L	(Lie)	− 0.4	0.47	0.9*
F	(Validity)	− 5.6	1.50	3.7
K	(Suppressor)	+ 3.5	0.74	4.7
K-F		+ 9.1	2.10	4.3
Hs	(Hypochondiasis)	−13.1	3.30	3.9
D	(Depression)	−22.6	4.00	5.6
Hy	(Hysteria)	−11.0	2.40	4.6
Pd	(Psychopathic deviate)	−14.0	2.36	5.9
Mf	(Masculinity)	− 5.9	15.10	0.4*
Pa	(Paranoid)	−14.8	2.90	5.1
Pt	(Psychasthenia)	−16.9	3.06	5.4
Sc	(Schizophrenia)	−20.9	3.50	6.0
Ma	(Hypomania)	− 1.0	1.80	0.6*

* Not significant

the D, Sc, and Pt scales.

It seemed reasonable that the degree of test improvement might be a useful index of potentiality for clinical improvement. It was, therefore, hypothesized that the greater the improvement shown when the original and simulated profiles were compared, the less would be the need for prolonged hospitalization. To test this, the number and corresponding percentage of correct identifications (trial visit or discharge, on the one hand, vs. continued hospitalization, on the other) were obtained three months after testing against criterion reductions in the total T score of more than 90, more than 65, and more than 45 on the grand T score for the nine clinical scales. Table 3 shows the relationship between degree of improvement when simulating "normalcy" and status (hospitalized or nonhospitalized) three months later.

At each criterion level, the discharged patients who equalled or exceeded the criterion measure, and the hospitalized patients who did not equal the criterion measure, were considered correctly identified by the application of that criterion.

It will be seen from the table that the higher the criterion value, the greater the accuracy of prediction for patients remaining in the hospital. (That is, these patients were less capable of producing that much change.) On the other hand, the lower the criterion value, the greater the

accuracy of prediction for patients who were out on trial visit or discharge status. (That is, more of these patients could meet this less stringent criterion.)

Since a criterion change of 65 or more gave the least number of false negative identifications for either group of patients, a 2 by 2 chi-square test was performed. This yielded a chi-square value of 5.0 which proved significant, for 1 degree of freedom, at the .025 level of confidence, indicating a significant relationship between ability to improve and early trial visit or discharge.

It is of interest to note that neither the Total T score on the original performance, nor on the simulated performance,

TABLE 3. CORRECT IDENTIFICATIONS OF DISCHARGED VS. HOSPITALIZED STATUS AT THREE REDUCTION LEVELS OF MMPI CHANGE

Reduction in total T score	Correctly identified	
	Discharged pts.	Hospitalized pts.
90 or more (=1 sigma per scale)	47%	81%
65 or more (=0.7 sigma per scale)	68%	65%
45 or more (=0.5 sigma per scale)	74%	58%

taken separately, showed any relationship to length of hospitalization. In other words, neither the initial degree of disturbance, nor the simulated degree of disturbance, is predictive; but only the change in degree of disturbance.

Apart from predictive value, the double-testing approach herein employed seems to offer another advantage, namely that of highlighting the subject's problem areas. Such problem areas are not always immediately apparent either to the therapist or to the patient. The kind of clear and immediate focus which this approach seems capable of yielding could be of real use to the diagnostician or therapist. For example, the patient whose altered profile declares, in effect: "I would be normal if I could accept my passive tendencies and feminine interests more comfortably," or "If I had fewer doubts about my manhood, I could be less anxious," may be helped early in the therapeutic process to view these feelings and attitudes in a perspective which minimizes any seriously disruptive effects they might have on treatment. The psychotherapist is thus enabled to correct the patient's gross misconceptions early and, by helping the patient to make a more realistic appraisal of his strengths as well as his limitations, to clear the way for further psychotherapeutic endeavors.

Perhaps a word of caution is in order lest the data lead to unduly optimistic interpretations of the changes observed in the "improved" cases. It might be well to distinguish between favorable prognosis for early discharge from the hospital as against psychotherapeutic accessibility. Many patients capable of simulating normalcy on a lip-service basis might also be capable of producing superficial changes in their outward behavior which would enable them to be rated much improved and ready for release. Some of these patients may merely have gained temporary control of their erratic and frequently unmanageable impulses without any new basic understanding or mastery of these impulses. Others, who may recognize how much they are at variance with the rest of the world, may be unable to effect the basic changes which psychotherapy hopes to achieve.

SUMMARY

In summary, this study revealed marked individual differences in the ability of psychiatric patients to simulate "normalcy" on the MMPI. Although most of the patients (73%) gave an improved performance, very few (11%) became "normal" and some became worse. Ability to improve differed for patients in different diagnostic categories. Improvement was manifested, in many cases, by a reduction in the deviancy of the same diagnostic pattern; in other cases, by a "diagnostic shift" to a less seriously disturbed category. Areas of emotional disturbance appeared to be highlighted in terms of differences between the patient's self concept and his ego ideal, as these could be inferred from the changes that took place in the profiles. Improvability on the test appears to be a favorable prognostic indication for early hospital discharge. Some diagnostic and therapeutic implications of the double-testing approach used in this study were briefly discussed.

REFERENCES

1. Benton, A. L. Rorschach performance of suspected malingerers. *J. abnorm. soc. Psychol.*, 1945, *40*, 94–96.
2. Carp, A. L., and Shavzin, A. R. The susceptibility to falsification of the Rorschach Psychodiagnostic Technique. *J. consult. Psychol.*, 1952, *16*, 265–267.
3. Cofer, C. N., Chance, J., and Judson, A. J. A study of malingering on the Minnesota Multiphasic Personality Inventory. *J. Psychol.*, 1949, *27*, 491–499.
4. Feldman, M. J., and Graley, J. The effects of an experimental set to stimulate abnormality on group Rorschach performance. *J. proj. Tech.*, 1954, *18*, 326–334.
5. Gengerelli, J. A., and Butler, B. V. A method for comparing the profiles of several population samples. *J. Psychol.*, 1955, *40*, 247–268.
6. Gough, H. G. Simulated patterns on the MMPI. *J. abnorm. soc. Psychol.*, 1947, *42*, 215–225.
7. Gough, H. G. The *F* minus *K* dissimulation index on the Minnesota Multiphasic Personality Inventory. *J. consult. Psychol.*, 1950, *14*, 408–413.
8. Hunt, H. F. The effect of deliberate deception on MMPI performance. *J. consult. Psychol.*, 1948, *12*, 396–402.
9. Meltzoff, J. The effect of mental set and item structure upon response to a projective test. *J. abnorm. soc. Psychol.*, 1951, *46*, 177–189.
10. Noll, V. H. Simulation by college students of a prescribed pattern on a personality scale. *Educ. psychol. Measmt*, 1951, *11*, 478–488.
11. Rosenberg, S. J., and Feldberg, T. M. Rorschach characteristics of a group of malingerers. *Rorschach Res. Exch.*, 1944, *8*, 46–70.

Mental Illness, Milieu Therapy, and Social Organization in Ward Groups

EDWARD J. MURRAY AND MELVIN COHEN

CULTURALLY oriented personality theorists such as Sullivan have suggested that mental illness, broadly conceived, is related to difficulties in interpersonal relations (6). Fromm-Reichmann (2) views mental illness as a condition involving a withdrawal from social relationships because of fears of rejection and feelings of inadequacy which can be alleviated by a therapeutic process involving insight, emotional discharge, and respect by the therapist. This general theory of mental illness would lead one to predict that the greater the degree of mental illness of a patient the more his social relationships with his fellow patients in a mental hospital will show various disturbances such as withdrawal. McMillan and Silverberg (3) have presented evidence which generally supports this prediction.

A continuum of degree of mental illness was obtained by McMillan and Silverberg by ranking five wards according to decreasing level of adjustment: (a) neurological, (b) gastrointestinal medical, (c) open psychiatric, with neurotics and psychotics, (d) insulin therapy, with anxiety neurotics, and (e) closed psychiatric, with psychotics. Sociometric choice patterns were then compared with three results. First, there was a trend suggesting that the greater the degree of mental illness, the fewer reciprocal choices, which was, however, significant only for the insulin ward. Second, there was a slight but not significant trend suggesting that the more disturbed patients concentrated their negative choices on fewer people. Third, there was a striking tendency for patients on all

Reprinted by permission from *The Journal of Abnormal and Social Psychology*, Vol. 58, No. I, January 1959.

wards to have more positive than negative reciprocations. While these results generally tend to support the hypothesis, they are not all as clear and consistent as one would expect.

The purpose of the present study was to apply the McMillan and Silverberg technique to a somewhat more easily ranked group of wards and to employ somewhat simpler measures in the hope of obtaining a more clear-cut test of the hypothesis that the greater the degree of mental illness, the greater the disturbance of social relationships. An additional purpose was to take an initial step in determining the effect of milieu therapy on group organization in psychiatric wards.

METHOD

Major Ward Groups

A total of 132 patients in three wards at a large army hospital was used in the main part of the study. Nearly all of the patients were enlisted men. The *control medical ward* was a large orthopedic ward with a total of 40 patients, 5 of whom were omitted from the study because of absence or language difficulty. The majority of these patients had limb fractures or amputations but were ambulatory and able to socialize. The ward could be conveniently divided into front, back, and porch areas. The *open psychiatric ward* contained 51 patients, of whom 2 were omitted and 15 refused to participate. The diagnosis of the patients included various neuroses, nonacute psychoses, and character disorders. The men in this ward were considered by the staff to be almost well-adjusted enough to be returned to duty or discharged to their own care. If they became disturbed they were returned to the locked ward. The men had ground privileges and frequent weekend passes. There were common eating and recreational facilities, but the men slept in three separate areas. The *locked psychiatric ward* contained 41 patients, 13 of whom were omitted because of language difficulties or because they were not in contact enough to fill in their own names and identifying data on the questionnaire. This ward contained more acute psychotics and severe neurotics as well as patients who had not been fully diagnosed. The staff felt that these patients were considerably more disturbed than the patients in the open psychiatric ward. The patients were locked in the ward and escorted to all activities and examinations. They were not allowed passes. The ward had three sleeping areas as well as a central day room.

Additional Ward Groups

In addition to the three wards used in the main part of the study, three smaller wards were also used to study the effects of milieu therapy on group organization. The *nonpsychiatric control ward* was an experimental ward used for long-term studies of metabolic diseases. At the time of the initial sociometric questionnaire administration, there were eight patients on the ward. These patients were ambulatory but were restricted to the ward in order to control diet rigidly and to measure bodily waste materials. The *milieu therapy ward* was an experimental psychiatric ward for the long-term treatment and study of schizophrenia. The patients all had been hospitalized during basic training. On the ward, the patients were put in a therapeutically oriented milieu *(4)*, including group therapy three times a week, varying hours of individual therapy with the psychiatrist, and frequent therapeutically oriented contacts with the nurse, social workers, and psychiatric aides all coordinated by weekly staff conferences. The staff was especially selected for empathic attitudes and high motivation. None of the patients received drugs, shock, or other somatic therapy. There were nine patients on the ward at the time of the first administration of the sociometric questionnaire. The *somatic therapy ward* was a typical closed psychiatric ward for disturbed patients. The patients were referred from smaller army hospitals and showed a greater age, rank, and diagnostic range than the ward just described. However, most of the patients were schizophrenic and all were confined to the locked ward. The patients were being treated with a long series of electroconvulsive shocks, a series of insulin comas, or massive daily doses of tranquilizing drugs. Very little psychotherapy was employed. The staff was competent and pleasant but not oriented towards milieu therapy. There were 15 patients on the ward at the time of the first sociometric questionnaire.

From four to eight months after the first administration of the sociometric questionnaire, the questionnaire was given again to the same three wards. By this time, all of the patients on the milieu therapy ward and the somatic therapy ward and all but three of the patients on the control ward had been replaced by new patients. At this time there were seven patients on the control ward, six on the milieu therapy ward, and eight on the somatic therapy ward. A few patients on all wards were omitted both times because they were on the ward for less than a week. The average length of stay was about equal on all wards.

Sociometric Questionnaire

The questionnaire was mimeographed in a booklet clearly marked confidential. The patients were asked to give their name, ward number, and other identifying data and were omitted if they could not reasonably fill out this section. Then, the patients were asked simply to list all of the names of the patients on the ward that they could remember. First names and nicknames were accepted as well as last names. Finally, the patients were asked to make choices on twelve sociometric items. They were asked to select at least one person for each item but allowed to write in as many more as they wished. There were four spaces for names under each item but the patients were allowed to write in more if they wished to. The sociometric questionnaire included: four positive items—like most, at ease with most, like to eat with most, like to work with most; four negative items—like least, ill-at-ease with, like to eat with least, like to work with least; and four neutral items—tallest patients, heaviest patients, most intelligent patients, and best-liked patients. Later evidence suggested that the neutral items, particularly the last two, were influenced by the patients' likes and dislikes. The 12 sociometric items were mimeographed in a random order.

PROCEDURE

Arrangements were made with the staff ahead of time to insure maximum attendance at a group administration of the questionnaire on each ward. The senior author explained the general nature of the questionnaire and emphasized its confidential nature. The booklet and pencils were handed out, and the patients worked at their beds or in the day room. Communications between the patients were kept to a minimum. All patients who were absent at the group meeting or who had refused to fill out the questionnaire were contacted individually and asked again to cooperate.

Social Background Factors

After the administration of the sociometric questionnaire, the hospital records of each patient were examined and information obtained about age, race, rank, length of service, marital status, education, population area of origin, branch of service, and religion. In formation was also obtained about the length of time in the hospital and on the ward, diag nosis, and ward bed assignment.

RESULTS AND DISCUSSION

Degree of Mental Illness and Sociometric Choice

A number of sociometric measures were directly related to the degree of mental illness represented by the three major

reciprocals shows a significant variation over all wards ($p < .01$). (Unless otherwise stated, significance levels in this study are based on a one-tail chi-square test.) There are fairly significant decreases from the control medical to the open psychiatric ($p < .07$) and from the open psychiatric to the locked psychiatric ward ($p < .05$). The percentage of patients who had one or more negative reciprocals was significantly lower than for positive reciprocals for all wards ($p < .01$). However, the same trend as with positive reciprocals was evident with fewer people with negative reciprocals as degree of mental illness increased ($p < .02$). This suggests a general withdrawal rather than a differential effect

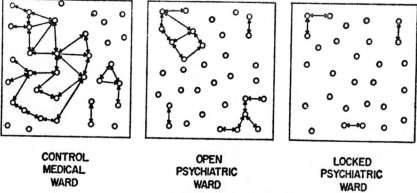

CONTROL
MEDICAL
WARD

OPEN
PSYCHIATRIC
WARD

LOCKED
PSYCHIATRIC
WARD

Figure 1. Positive reciprocal choices for three Ward Groups representing a continuum of degree of mental illness

wards. This can be seen graphically in Fig. 1 where the sociograms based on positive reciprocal choices are shown for the control medical, open psychiatric, and locked psychiatric wards. Reciprocals are based on a mutual positive choice regardless of which of the four items was involved. These three wards form a continuum of degree of mental illness about which there can be very little disagreement. The sociograms indicate that as degree of mental illness increases there is a decrease in the complexity of the social organization as well as a decrease in the number of reciprocals. As Table 1 shows, the percentage of patients with one or more

of mental illness on positive and negative aspects of interpersonal relationships.

It is of interest to examine the number of reciprocal choices as well as the number of patients involved, since the number of reciprocal choices may reflect the complexity of the social organization more faithfully. For example, there may be a reciprocal choice between A and B and between B and C involving three patients altogether. However, this is a simpler organization than if there were also a reciprocal choice between A and C, which would increase the number of reciprocals but not the number of patients with one or more reciprocals. But in making such a comparison, it must be kept in mind that generalizations are limited to a population

TABLE 1. VARIOUS SOCIOMETRIC MEASURES IN WARDS REPRESENTING A CONTINUUM OF DEGREE OF MENTAL ILLNESS

Sociometric measure	Degree of mental illness		
	Control medical ward	Open psychiatric ward	Locked psychiatric ward
Percentage of patients with one or more positive reciprocal	74	50	25
Percentage of patients with one or more negative reciprocal	26	6	0
Percentage of positive choices reciprocated	44	38	22
Percentage of negative choices reciprocated	6	4	0
Average number of names known	14.2	8.8	7.2
Average number of positive choices	4.1	2.8	2.3
Average number of negative choices	2.5	1.5	1.0
Average number of neutral choices	4.3	2.2	2.2
Percentage of patients receiving no choices at all (total isolates)	0	18	21

of not fully independent choices. It is felt that in this case such a comparison is useful and legitimate since the finding has already been established for a population of patients. The percentages of both positive and negative choices which were reciprocated in the control medical, open psychiatric, and locked psychiatric wards are shown in Table 1. As degree of mental illness increases there are fewer reciprocal choices on either positive or negative items. The over-all decrease of the percentages of positive reciprocals was significant ($p < .001$). The difference between the locked psychiatric and the open psychiatric wards was significant ($p < .01$) as was the difference between the locked psychiatric and the control medical wards ($p < .001$), but the difference between the open psychiatric and the control medical wards failed to reach significance on this measure. The percentages of the negative reciprocals showed an over-all decrease with degree of maladjustment ($p < .01$). The over-all difference between percentage of positive and negative reciprocals is significant ($p < .001$) but appears to be about equal for all wards.

Another way of showing this relationship is to simply compare the average number of names known on each ward. Table 1 makes this comparison; the more disturbed the ward, the fewer the names known. The over-all difference is significant ($p < .01$) as well as the difference between the control medical ward and the open psychiatric ward ($p < .05$) and the difference between the control medical ward and the locked psychiatric ward ($p < .01$). The difference between the open and locked wards did not reach significance.

Similarly, the average absolute number of choices on the sociometric items decreases with degree of mental illness. Table 1 shows over-all decreases in average positive, negative, and neutral choices which are all significant ($p < .05$). The over-all average number of negative choices is significantly less ($p < .01$) than the average number of positive or neutral choices.

The number of social isolates increases with degree of maladjustment (Table 1). There is a significant difference in percentage of patients receiving no choices between the control medical ward and the two psychiatric wards combined ($p < .01$). The difference is accounted for almost entirely by a difference in the number of isolates on positive sociometric items, since from 40 to 60% of patients on all wards had no negative or neutral choices, a value that is significantly higher ($p < .001$) than the 20% who had no positive choices.

An analysis of variance showed that the three groups did not differ significantly in average length of time on the ward or in the hospital. Furthermore, the various measures showed almost zero correlations with number of weeks on the ward or in the hospital. This result would indicate that the decrease in interpersonal relationships from control medical to open psychiatric to locked psychiatric wards was not due to different opportunities for socialization.

It is also of interest to examine the degree to which the same person was chosen on several positive items or negative items. A score analogous to the criteria overlap score used by McMillan and Silverberg was obtained for each patient. There was no significant difference between the three ward groups on either positive or negative items. However, there was an over-all tendency for greater overlap on positive than negative items ($p < .01$). These results are in agreement with those of McMillan and Silverberg.

An acceptability score was also adapted from McMillan and Silverberg, consisting of the percentages of patients from all wards who were chosen various numbers of times on positive, negative, or neutral items. As would be expected, most patients were chosen very few times if at all on any of the items, while a few people were chosen very often. But is was also found that fewer people received no choices at all on positive items than nega

tive or neutral items. This result is contrary to McMillan and Silverberg's finding of fewer patients with zero neutral choices. Other differences between positive, negative, and neutral choices were not significant. McMillan and Silberberg's finding that more people had two positive choices was not confirmed. Except for the differences already noted, there were no significant differences between wards.

Sociometric Choice and Similarity of Social Background

Another way of getting at the relationship between mental illness and interpersonal relations is to examine the extent to which patients on different wards choose fellow patients with social backgrounds similar to themselves. A number of social background variables that might be expected to influence sociometric choices are listed in Table 2. Each variable is dichotomized at some convenient point so that a 2×2 table could be set up to measure the degree to which patients made choices of fellow patients in the same category. In the control medical ward, for example, 80 of the 86 choices made by Caucasians were for Caucasians, and 8 of the 11 choices made by Negroes were for Negroes. Therefore, 88 out of 97 or 91% of the choices were for persons similar to self on the racial variable. The distribution of patients with these characteristics was about the same in the three wards. The general pattern of results in Table 2 suggests that as mental illness increases, similarity in social background variables plays less of a role in determining sociometric choices. On the control medical ward, four social background variables yielded significant percentages—age ($p < .03$), race ($p < .01$), rank ($p < .02$), and length of service ($p < .04$). On the open psychiatric ward, only three background variables yielded significant percentages—age ($p < .01$), race ($p < .01$), and population area of origin ($p < .01$). On the locked psychiatric ward, no social background variables were significant. The locked ward percent-

TABLE 2. PERCENTAGE OF SOCIOMETRIC CHOICES FOR INDIVIDUALS SIMILAR TO SELF IN SOCIAL BACKGROUND VARIABLES

	Degree of mental illness		
Social background variable	Control medical ward	Open psychiatric ward	Locked psychiatric ward
Age (within ± 5 years)	65	64	46
Race (Caucasian vs. Negro)	91	92	72
Population area (metropolitan vs. other)	63	71	47
Rank (Sgt. vs. Cpl. or Pvt.)	66	61	50
Length of service (under or over 3 years)	60	55	50
Marital Status (single vs. married)	61	56	44
Education (under or over ninth grade)	50	50	44
Geographical area (north vs. south)	55	68	56
Service (Army vs. Air Force)	68	52	64
Religion (Prot. vs. Catholic)	56	59	59

age is significantly lower ($p < .07$ or better) than the other two wards for age, race, and population area of origin. Rank, length of service, marital status, and education show similar trends, but these are not significant. The results suggest several additional aspects of social behavior that might be influenced by mental illness. Caudill et al. (1) also report that on an intensively studied ward there was a ". . . muting of outer-world distinctions on the basis of race, ethnic group, or social class. . . ."

Sociometric Choice and Similarity of Diagnosis

An effort was also made to evaluate sociometric choices in terms of similarity in diagnosis. When the data for the control medical ward were analyzed by amputation, fracture, and other groups it was found that 20% of the sociometric choices were within groups. The psychiatric wards

TABLE 3. PROPINQUITY AS A FACTOR IN SOCIOMETRIC CHOICES AND DEGREE OF MENTAL ILLNESS

	Degree of mental illness			
Sociometric measure	Control medical ward	Open psychiatric ward	Locked psychiatric ward	All wards
Percentage of positive choices within own section of ward	44	45	54	46
Percentage of negative choices within own section of ward	42	32	38	39

were subdivided into paranoid schizophrenic, other schizophrenic, character disorder, neurotic, and other groups. On the open psychiatric ward, 40% of the choices were within groups, a value somewhat higher than the 21% on the locked psychiatric ward. When the psychiatric wards were categorized as schizophrenic and nonschizophrenic, 62% of the choices on the open ward and 46% on the locked ward were within groups. These differences are not significant, and these diagnostic factors

appear to be less important than some of the social background variables. On the other hand, Shipman's finding (5) that paranoids tend to choose one another while schizoids do not was supported. When the choices of schizophrenics from both psychiatric wards were examined it was found that 64% of the choices by paranoid schizophrenics were for other paranoid schizophrenics as opposed to all other patients. Only 33% of the nonparanoid schizophrenic choices were for nonparanoid schizophrenics. This difference is significant ($p < .05$).

Sociometric Choice and Propinquity

A somewhat different kind of variable that might be related to mental illness is propinquity, defined as the degree to which patients made sociometric choices from among those patients who slept in the same area as they. It will be recalled that each ward was divided into three sleeping areas. Table 3 shows the percentage of choices within the patient's own sleeping area on positive and negative items for the three ward groups. The percentage that would be expected if the choices were randomly distributed throughout the ward is $33\frac{1}{3}$. There are no significant differences between the wards on either positive or negative items. However, over all wards more positive choices are made within the patient's sleeping area than would be expected by chance ($p < .001$). On the other hand, the percentages of negative choices are what would be expected by chance. The difference for all wards between the percentage of positive and negative choices within the area approaches significance ($p < .06$). There is an insignificant trend for this difference to increase with degree of mental illness.

Milieu Therapy and Ward Organization

An initial indication of the effect of milieu therapy on social relationships can be seen in Fig. 2 where the sociograms for the three smaller wards are compared. The social organization on the nonpsychiatric control ward, as indicated by reciprocal choices on the "like-best" item, is fairly complex and involves 75% of the group. On the other hand, the somatic therapy ward shows little social organization with reciprocal choices on the "like-best" item limited to 27% of the group. The critical ward is the milieu therapy one shown in the center of Fig. 2. It can be seen that the milieu therapy ward has a complex organization involving 78% of the group and therefore resembles the nonpsychiatric control ward much more than the typical closed psychiatric ward. The difference between these percentages in the control

the somatic therapy ward is due to a direct effect of the treatment. But this is not likely. An examination of the treatment history of each individual patient on the ward failed to reveal a relationship between type or length of somatic therapy and sociometric results. For example, the three patients with reciprocal choices in Fig. 3 included a patient who had just completed 20 electroconvulsive shocks, a patient getting heavy doses of a transquilizing drug, and a patient who had had 50 insulin coma treatments. These patients can be compared with the three most isolated patients of whom one had just completed 24 electroconvulsive shocks, one was getting heavy

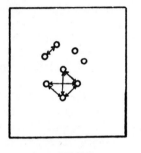
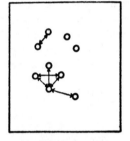
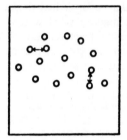

| NON-PSYCHIATRIC (METABOLIC DISEASE) CONTROL WARD | EXPERIMENTAL SCHIZOPHRENIC WARD EMPHASIZING MILIEU AND GROUP THERAPY | TYPICAL CLOSED PSYCHIATRIC WARD EMPHASIZING SOMATIC THERAPY |

Figure 2. Positive reciprocal choices for a control medical ward, a locked psychiatric ward emphasizing milieu and group therapy, and a locked psychiatric ward emphasizing somatic treatment

and milieu therapy wards is not statistically significant, while the difference between the milieu therapy and somatic therapy wards is ($p < .05$). The number of patients on these wards is too small to justify an elaborate statistical analysis. More reliance is placed on the fact that the same over-all, qualitative result was obtained when the study was replicated with the same wards after a patient turnover. This is shown in Fig. 3: the nonpsychiatric control and the milieu therapy wards show a complex social organization, while there is much less interaction and social patterning on the somatic therapy ward. It is conceivable that the lack of social organization on

doses of a tranquilizing drug, and another had just had six electroconvulsive shocks. While the results suggest that milieu therapy improves group organization on the ward, other evidence is needed to evaluate the long-term effects of the milieu therapy on the patient's illness and adaptive capacities.

Summary and Conclusions

The study was designed to test the hypothesis that the greater the degree of mental illness in a patient, the more disturbed are his social relationships. A sociometric questionnaire was administered to three wards arranged along a continuum of degree of mental illness—a control medical, an open psychiatric, and a locked psychiatric ward.

A sociogram showed that the complexity of ward social organization decreased as degree of mental illness increased. Percentage of patients with one or more reciprocal choice, percentage of choices reciprocated, absolute number of names known, and the absolute number of choices made decreased as degree of mental illness increased. The percentage of social isolates increased in the more disturbed wards.

The results suggest that as mental illness increases, sociometric choices are influenced less by similarities in social background variables such as age, race, and population area of origin. Except for paranoid schizophrenics, similarities in diagnostic variables have little effect on sociometric choices.

There were fewer reciprocals, number of choices, etc., on negative sociometric items than on positive ones for all wards. Negative reciprocals, choices, etc., decreased as degree of mental illness increased but proportionally to the decrease in positive items.

Sociograms from three additional wards showed a degree of social interaction and organization on a psychiatric ward emphasizing milieu and group therapy which was quite comparable to that of a control medical ward. In contrast, a psychiatric ward emphasizing somatic therapy showed much less interaction and organization. After a patient turnover, the study was replicated with similar results.

It was concluded that as degree of mental illness increases, there is a decrease in social organization and social relationships involving positive or negative feelings. This process appears to be reversed by milieu therapy.

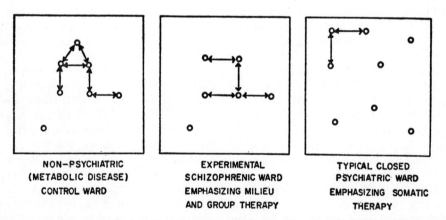

| NON–PSYCHIATRIC (METABOLIC DISEASE) CONTROL WARD | EXPERIMENTAL SCHIZOPHRENIC WARD EMPHASIZING MILIEU AND GROUP THERAPY | TYPICAL CLOSED PSYCHIATRIC WARD EMPHASIZING SOMATIC THERAPY |

Figure 3. Positive reciprocal choices for a control medical ward, a locked psychiatric ward emphasizing milieu and group therapy, and a locked psychiatric ward emphasizing somatic treatment (based on a second sociometric questionnaire after a patient turnover)

REFERENCES

1. Caudill, W., Redlich, F. C., Gilmore, H. R., and Brody, E. B. Social structure and interaction processes on a psychiatric ward. *Amer. J. Orthopsychiat.,* 1952, 22, 314–334.

2. Fromm-Reichmann, Frieda. *Principles of intensive psychotherapy.* Chicago: Univer. Chicago Press, 1950.

3. McMillan, J. J., and Silverberg, J. Sociometric choice patterns in hospital ward

groups with varying degrees of interpersonal disturbances. *J. abnorm. soc. Psychol.*, 1955, *50*, 168–172.

4. Rioch, D. McK., and Stanton, A. H. Milieu therapy. *Psychiatry*, 1953, *16*, 65–72.

5. Shipman, W. G. Similarity of personality in the sociometric preferences of mental patients. *J. clin. Psychol.*, 1957, *13*, 292–294.

6. Sullivan, H. S. *Conceptions of modern psychiatry*. Washington, D. C.: William Alanson White Psychiatric Foundation, 1947.

A Genetic Approach to the Interpretation and Evaluation of the Process-Reactive Distinction in Schizophrenia

WESLEY C. BECKER

T HE behavior disorders currently labeled "schizophrenia" pose some of the most complex problems psychologists and psychiatrists have yet to unravel. The problem facing the investigator in this area remains an overwhelming one. If controlled research is to be undertaken, some meaningful ways of organizing and understanding the gross individual differences among schizophrenics is necessary.

One compelling suggestion comes from the many prognostic investigations by such people as Hunt and Appel (*13*), Langfeldt (*16*), Kant (*14*), Becker and McFarland (*5*), Kantor, Wallner, and Winder (*15*), Stotsky (*25*), Benjamin (*9*), and Wittman (*26, 27, 28*). All of these prognostic studies have led to the conclusion that remitting schizophrenics have a better personality adjustment before and during illness than nonremitting schizophrenics. In addition, these and other studies[1] have suggested two consistent clusters of signs having differential prognostic significance. Briefly, the signs related to poor prognosis, which for convenience have been termed the "process syndrome," are (*a*) a "shut-in," withdrawn, inadequate prepsychotic personality, (*b*) slow, insidious development of psychosis, (*c*) relative absense of precipitating factors, and (*d*) presence of dull, rigid, or inappropriate affect. The signs related to good prognosis and termed the "reactive syndrome" are (*a*) relatively normal prepsychotic personality, (*b*) acute onset of psychosis, (*c*) presence of identifiable precipitating factors, and (*d*) presence of strong emotionality or tension. One implication of these findings is that a variable of severity of illness or level of adjustment is important to understanding individual differences among schizophrenics.

The consistency of the prognostic findings has led some to postulate the possibility of two kinds of schizophrenia with possible different etiologies. The process syndrome is most frequently assumed to have an "organic" basis, and the reactive syndrome is assumed to have a "psychological" basis (*7*). However, there are many reasons for rejecting such a conclusion. First, examination of the research data reveals considerable group overlap. Consequently, any attempt to force all schizophrenics into one group or the other would be clinically difficult and arbitrary. Also, if one recognizes with Bellak that schizophrenia is a deficit reaction which may be brought about by any combination of 40 or more etiological factors (*8*), and if one accepts the fact that twenty years of research have failed to find clear etiological differences between any subgroupings, then the conception of two types of schizophrenia loses usefulness.

Reprinted by permission from *The Journal of Abnormal and Sociol Psychology*, Vol. 53, 1956.

[1] The reader is referred to Bellak (*7*) and Kantor *et al.* (*15*) for reviews of these studies.

An alternative assumption is that the process-reaction syndromes are best thought of as end points on a continuum of levels of personality organization. "Levels of personality organization" is a difficult concept to define succinctly. It is concerned with changes in the content and structure of mental organization as the human organism develops toward psychological maturity. A complete definition would encompass such factors as objectivity in perception (constancy), differentiation of needs, interests, and other aspects of personal motivation, and the degree of emotional control or adaptive functioning under stress. Lewin (*17*), Baldwin (*2*), and especially Werner (*29*) have all attempted to deal with this construct. Common to most attempts to conceptualize levels of personality is the general idea that "the development of biological forms is expressed in an *increasing differentiation* of parts and increasing *subordination,* or *hierarchization*" of the parts with respect to the whole (*29*). While space does not permit a detailed analysis of the parallel, the general proposition that the process syndrome reflects a very primitive, undifferentiated personality structure and the reactive syndrome a more highly organized one offers a potentially fruitful point of departure.[2]

To demonstrate the organizing value of this interpretation of the process-reaction concept, and to facilitate measurement of the dimension of personality levels, the following hypothesis was generated and tested: Schizophrenic patients who more nearly approximate the process syndrome show more regressive and immature thinking processes than schizophrenics who more nearly approximate the reactive syndrome. The argument here involves taking a prognostic rating as the criterion measure, placing each schizophrenic S along a process-reaction dimension. If this measure is essentially a measure of level of personality organization, and if the hypothesis is sound,

then maturity of thought processes should be predictable from the ratings.

METHOD

Newly admitted schizophrenics were interviewed and their clinical records examined in order to gather social history data. This information was then evaluated in terms of the process-reaction dimension. Thinking processes were evaluated from psychological test results. Finally, interrelations between history and test data were explored.

Subjects

The Ss were 51 diagnosed schizophrenics selected at time of admission to a California state hospital (Agnews) on the basis of their being testable, non-Negro, under 41 years of age, without complicating neurological or other physical disorder, and on the basis of their being either a first admission case or a second admission case where the first admission was under four months duration. Twenty-four Ss were male, 27 female. Average age for the men was 29.4 and for the women, 31.1. Twenty per cent had attended college, and over 60 per cent had been graduated from high school. About half were married. All but seven cases were first admissions. Twenty-four were diagnosed as paranoid type, nine as acute undifferentiated type, eight as chronic undifferentiated type, eight as schizo-affective type, and one each as catatonic and hebephrenic.

Evaluation of Thinking Processes

The independent variable to be evaluated is degree of regressive and immature thinking. In the literature one finds many definitions of schizophrenic thinking disorder, but few, if any, of such definitions contain the possibility of scaled quantification. The conceptual structure taken in this paper, however, suggests both theoretical and empirical (i.e., studies with children) methods of scaling severity of thinking disorder by initially equating it with immaturity of thinking.[3] To dem-

---

[2] A more detailed theoretical exposition can be found in Becker (6). Reference to Werner (29) will also help to make this parallel more explicit for the reader not familiar with Werner's work.

[3] To avoid misunderstanding, elaboration of this point is needed. What is asserted here is that the *formal organization* of mental processes of severe schizophrenics and young children, or of less severe schizophrenics and slightly older children is quite similar. The assumed basis for this similarity is that the schizophrenic has been fixated at an immature level of personality organization and/or has reverted to simpler levels of organization under stress. This approach provides a rational framework for the initial scaling of schizophrenic mental productions. Empirical findings, such as those by Friedman (10), can then be used to refine such a scale and to take into account any *differences* which may exist in the mental productions of children and schizophrenics of a given organizational level.

onstrate the method and to test the hypothesis given above, the Rorschach and Benjamin Proverbs were used to evaluate thinking processes. The 1937 Stanford-Binet Vocabulary test was included in order to estimate verbal intelligence.

Rorschach. Administration of the Rorschach followed the procedure proposed by Beck *(3, 4)*. The method of analyzing the Rorschach was derived most directly from Werner's developmental theories *(29)* and the empirical studies by Friedman *(10)*, Siegel *(23)*, and Hemmendinger *(12)*. In studying the problem of perceptual regression in schizophrenia, Friedman developed a scoring system for the Rorschach which would presumably reflect levels of perceptual development as suggested by Werner's theory. In comparing adult normals, schizophrenics, and children of various ages on his measures, he found strong support for the hypothesis that the structural aspects of schizophrenic perception were in many ways similar to, though not identical with those of children. Werner's conceptual structure and these supporting studies encouraged the notion that a scale could be devised which would differentiate levels of mental organization within the schizophrenic population.

In quantifying his data, Friedman used two gross categories—genetic-early and genetic-late perceptions. Each genetic group was further divided into three progressive levels, giving a total of six levels. The empirical findings of Friedman and Siegel, as well as Werner's theories were employed in making these differentiations. In order to derive an over-all score to reflect average level of mental organization, each response was given a weight from one to six, corresponding to the genetic level of response, and the sum of the weights was divided by the number of responses.

A summary outline of the Rorschach scoring system with examples is given in Table 1.[4] Rationale for placement of categories is discussed below.

Level one is characterized by diffuse, global, undifferentiated perceptions. *Wa* is a direct indicator of the diffuse, global nature of perception at this level. *W*—indicates the lack of differentiation of inner and outer

[4] The reader is referred to Friedman *(10)* and Siegel *(23)* for more complete definitions of scoring categories, with the exception of Unusual Details and Perseveration. The Unusual Detail scores are discussed in the text. Friedman's use of a perseveration score based on Beck's content classes did not prove to be discriminatory between age groups. For this reason the writer adopted Piotrowski's *(21)* more severe criterion for perseveration. Examples in the table are from Friedman *(10)*, Phillips and Smith *(20)*, and the author's own experience.

worlds and the syncretism in mental organization. *DW* is a clear example of a type of diffuse perception Werner has described by the phrase *"pars pro toto"*—any part has the quality of the whole *(29)*. The contaminated and fabulized responses reflect both the concrete and syncretic nature of primitive perception. In these responses there is an absurd fusion of percepts on the basis of spatial identity and spatial contiguity. Perseveration is assumed to reflect the dynamic rigidity of the personality at this level. Empirically, Friedman, Siegel, and Hemmendinger found these perceptual classifications most characteristic of children under five years of age and of severely regressed schizophrenics.

Level two is characterized by attempted differentiation in which the diffuse and syncretic nature of perception is still apparent. Friedman found the *Da, DdD,* and *Dv* responses all relatively rare in children, suggesting that where perceptual organization is so advanced as to permit discreteness (*D*), the diffuse and syncretic modes of perception have already begun to wane. In psychopathology, however, one might expect to find a greater frequency of this combination of discreteness with diffusion and syncretism where there is regression from higher levels of perceptual differentiation. A similar explanation is offered by Friedman to account for the differences in relative frequencies of the *Wv* and *Dv* responses. The greater frequency of vague responses in the schizophrenic group may be the result of regressive diffuseness and vagueness interfering with percepts which might have been *Wm* responses. Because *Wv* shows some integrative effort with consideration of the formal aspects of the blot it is placed at level three. *Dv* lacks integrative effort and is therefore placed at level two. *D*— and *Dd*— again are indicative of an unsuccessful attempt at differentiated perception.

Level three is characterized by the achievement of fair differentiation with only rudimentary integrative efforts. Developmentally, the scores at this level (with the exception of *Wv*) are most characteristic of children from ages seven to ten. In some ways *Adx-Hdx* responses are like the *Dm* of the next level. However, they are placed at this lower level because they clearly indicate a failure at integration where integration is usually easily achieved. *Dd* responses were omitted from Friedman's schema. However, Hemmendinger *(12)* and Siegel *(23)* indicate that *Dd*'s are found most frequently between the ages of six and ten. Within this age range, an average of 13 per cent of the responses were of the *Dd* variety. None was found before the age of six, and normal adults gave but 4 per cent Dd. Siegel's less severe paranoid group gave 15 per cent Dd, whereas his more severe hebephrenics and catatonics gave but 3 per cent. These data are consistent with the interpretation that Dd is most characteristic of a level of development where the primary focus is analytical. With Beck's tables as a guide (3, 4) $Dd+$ was placed at level three,

while the more immature $Dd-$ was placed at level two.

Level four is a stage of accurate differentiation with the ability to make simple integrations. The Mediocre responses scored at this level indicate the ability to meet certain constant typical requirements in form necessary for adult perception.

Level five is indicative of clearly inte-

TABLE 1. DEFINITIONS AND EXAMPLES FOR THE RORSCHACH GENETIC-LEVEL SCORING SYSTEM

Level	Classification	Definition	Examples
1	Amorphous Whole (Wa)	Shape plays no determinable role.	I. "Black paint" II. "Fire and smoke"
	Minus Whole ($W-$)	Content requires specific form not provided by blot.*	I. "A fly" IV. "Starfish"
	Confabulatory Response (DW)	A single detail is basis for interpretation of the whole.	VI. "Cat," because of "whiskers"
	Contaminated Response ($Con R$)	Fusing of two interpretations of the same blot area.	VI. "Turtle-skin rug"
	Fabulized Combination ($Fab C$)	Absurd combination on basis of spatial contiguity.	X. "Rabbit with worms coming out of eyes"
	Perseveration (Per)	Same content to 3 or more cards with little regard to form requirements.	I, IV, V. "Spider" VIII, IX, X. "Internal organs"
2	Amorphous Detail (Da)	Analogous to Wa.	II. (D 2) "Fire" VIII. (D 6) "Flesh"
	Confabulatory Detail (DdD)	Analogous to DW.	VI. (D 3) "Cat's head," solely on "whiskers"
	Minus Detail ($D-$)	Analogous to $W-$.*	II. (D 2) "Kittens"
	Vague Detail (Dv)	Form element is so unspecific that almost any blot area could encompass content.	II. (D 2, 3) "Blood stains" X. (D 9) "Island"
	Minus Unusual Detail ($Dd-$)	Analogous to $W-$.*	VI. (Dd 25) "Pig's foot"
3	Vague Whole (Wv)	Analogous to Dv.	I. "Piece of a puzzle" X. "Design," "Map"
	Oligophrenic Detail (Adx-Hdx)	Response to part of an A or H percept usually seen as a completed figure.	III. (D 6) "Head of a person" V. (D 4) "Wing"
	Plus Unusual Detail ($Dd+$)	Content is a reasonable match to blot area isolated.*	X. (D 26) "Funny face"
4	Mediocre Detail (Dm)	Form implied in outline and articulation matches blot area. At level of "populars."	III. (D 3) "Bow tie" X. (D 15) "Little bird"
	Mediocre Whole (Wm)	Analogous to Dm, but applies only to unbroken blots.†	I. "Bat," "fox's head" VI. "Mud turtle"
5	Plus Detail ($D+$)	Two or more D areas are combined into one "good form" percept.*	II. (D 1's) "Bears fighting"
	Plus Whole ($W+$)	All D portions of a broken plot are combined into one "good form" percept.*†	II. "Two fellows at a bar toasting each other"
6	Plus-Plus Whole ($W++$)	An unbroken blot is perceptually articulated and reintegrated into a "good form" percept.†	IV. "A giant sitting on a stump"
	Plus-Plus Detail ($D++$)	A D area is articulated and reintegrated into a "good form" percept.	X. (D 8, left) "Guy riding a horse"

* Beck's tables (3, 4) are used as a guide in scoring.
† Unbroken blots are I, IV, V, VI, and IX; broken blots are II, III, VII, VIII, and X.

grative activity with the ability to subordinate differentiated parts to the whole.

Level six is characterized by the highest form of differentiation and hierarchic integration which is found only in mature perception.

In scoring, additional responses given during the inquiry were included. If *S* rejected a response on inquiry, it was excluded. If *S* improved a response on inquiry, he was given appropriate credit. The focus was on how well *S* could do rather than on how poorly. Beck's locations (*3, 4*) were used for *D* and *Dd* areas.

Siegel (*23*) found the mean percentage of agreement among three judges to be 93.9 per cent, using all of the above scoring categories with the exception of perseveration and the distinction between *Dd+* and *Dd—*. His findings indicated that the definitions are clear enough to be used by other Rorschach examiners. No further reliability studies were made at this time.

Proverbs test. Benjamin (*9*) was one of the first to apply proverbs in a systematic way to the study of schizophrenic thinking. As Werner's theories would suggest, the poorly differentiated schizophrenic and the child tend to take a literal or concrete approach to proverb interpretation. In administering the test, *S* was given an example and told to "interpret the proverb, to try to give a general meaning." Thirteen of the 14 proverbs were then given in the order originally used by Benjamin (*9*). Proverb 13 (an absurd phrase and not a proverb) was omitted. While Benjamin has never published a systematic scoring system for his test, he has described the types of thinking pathology exhibited through proverb interpretation (*9*). In developing the scoring system, both Benjamin's analysis and Werner's theories were taken into consideration. The following general scoring classifications were used:

Abstract III: A correct generalized interpretation without detracting elements. (Weight of 6.) Example: "Brooding over past mistakes is futile."

Abstract II: A correct example with reference to human behavior; another proverb meaning the same thing; a response partly generalized, partly restricted to a specific example; a lower level generalization. (Weight of 5.) Example: "What's done is done."

Abstract I: A response tinged with the literal; a response which would be acceptable at Abstract II but for some minor inaccuracy, overstatement, or alternative explanation which is false. (Weight of 4.) Example: *"Don't cry over* something that's happened; can't be helped" (literal tinge).

Vague Response: An attempt at interpretation which is on the right track, but is left too vague to be adequate, or fails to account for part of the proverb. (Weight of 3.) Example: "It's too late, in other words."

False Interpretation: The interpretation is very inaccurate, yet an attempt was made to interpret. The error is usually due to faulty desymbolization or faulty generalization. (Weight of 2.) Example: "Don't let defeat stop you."

General Literal: The interpretation is literal in effect, though stated in general terms. At first glance these responses do not appear to be literal, but they can only be understood as stemming from a literal interpretation. (Weight of 2.) Example: "What is wasted is wasted; no tears."

Literal: The proverb is interpreted literally. (Weight of 2.) Example: "Don't cry when you spill some milk."

Absurd: The response indicates a failure to interpret and/or is logically absurd in terms of the task at hand. These responses are usually based on concrete associations to some aspects of the stimulus. (Weight of 1.) Example: "The milk is on the floor and the horses will drink the water."

Literal abstract: A response which gives both a literal and an abstract interpretation. The tendency to be drawn into a literal interpretation is strong, but the subject is able to counteract it. (Weight at best abstract level reached.) Example: "Call the cat to lick it up, or what is happened has happened; let's look ahead."

To determine rater reliability, 25 cases were rescored by a fourth-year clinical psychology student. This second rater used the general definitions given above, plus examples drawn from the cases not rescored. The two-rater reliability was found to be .98. Odd-even reliability for 50 cases was found to be .83. It would appear that the scoring system is reliable and that the different parts of the Proverbs test define a similar function.

Because of a high relationship between ability to interpret proverbs and verbal intelligence in normals (*18*), it was assumed that a more sensitive index of thinking disturbance would be a discrepancy score based on the standard-score difference between a vocabulary estimate of verbal intelligence and the Proverbs score.

EVALUATION OF PROCESS-REACTION FROM CASE HISTORIES

The method of qualifying the social history data so as to reflect the process-

reaction dimension was adapted from Wittman (26, 27). Wittman has made repeated
studies of the prognostic value of case history data and formalized her findings as the
Elgin Prognostic Scale. The scale consists of
20 variables, weighted according to prognostic
significance. Included in the subscales are
evaluations of prepsychotic personality, nature
of onset, and typicality of the psychosis relative to Kraepelin's definition. These are the
same factors on which the process-reaction
distinction was made, so that Wittman's scale
is an adequate summary of what has typically
been included in the process-reaction distinction.

Three primary sources of data were
used in rating the Elgin scale: (a) direct
interview with the patient, (b) anamnesis,
and (c) psychiatric history obtained by the
examining psychiatrist. Using her scale with
similar sources of information, Wittman found
a two-rater reliability of .87 for 61 cases (26).
In several studies of the prognostic validity of
the scale, Wittman (26, 27, 28) found the
scale to predict outcome, with or without
shock therapy, in 80 to 85 per cent of the
cases. These data indicate that this is a
moderately reliable instrument for assessing
the process-reaction dimension.

Wittman has defined only the end
points of each subscale. To add precision to
the ratings, definitions were developed for
intermediate points. The added definitions
adhered closely to Wittman's original intent
as to subscale meaning. Though a check of
the reliability of the modified scale was not
possible, it is doubtful if it would be less than
that reported by Wittman.

PREDICTIONS

The following specifications of the
hypothesis were made: Those schizophrenics with more process-like case histories
(higher scores on the Elgin scale) receive significantly lower mean-genetic-level
scores on the Rorschach and significantly
lower Proverbs-minus-vocabulary discrepancy scores than those schizophrenics with
more reactive-like case histories.

RESULTS

The distribution of scores on the
Elgin scale were first normalized by use of
McCall's T-scored method (11). Analysis
showed a significant difference (.02 level)
in the means for the men and women on
the Elgin scale. The mean for the men

was 52.9 and for the women 46.2. This
difference suggests that on the average the
women in this sample were less severe
cases. A possible selective factor is the
care given a large portion of the less severe
males by the Veterans Administration hospitals in the San Francisco area. Because
of this significant difference in means on
the Elgin scale, the hypotheses were first
examined separately by sex group. If the
relationships did not differ significantly, the
correlations were then averaged to obtain
an estimate of the population r independent
of the sex difference in means on the Elgin
scale.

Main Results

The Rorschach hypothesis was confirmed for both sex groups. The Rorschach mean-genetic-level score and the
Elgin Prognostic Scale correlated $-.599$
($p < .01$) for the men, and $-.679$ ($p
< .001$) for the women. Since these cor-
relations did not differ significantly, an
averaged r was computed and found to be
$-.641$ ($p < .001$). These results indicate
that there is a meaningful relationship between the process-reaction dimension, as
evaluated from case-history data, and disturbances of thought processes as measured
by the Rorschach genetic-level scoring
system.

The hypothesis concerning the Proverbs test was confirmed only for male
schizophrenics. The correlation between
the Proverbs discrepancy score and the
Elgin scale was $-.682$ ($p < .001$) for
men, and .048 (obviously insignificant) for
the women. The difference between these
two correlations is significant beyond the
.01 level. These results indicate that the
Proverbs-vocabulary discrepancy score is
significantly related to the process-reaction
dimension for men, but not for women.

Further Analyses

In making further analyses, certain
inter-relations of the data were explored.
First, it was found that the Rorschach and
Proverbs-vocabulary discrepancy scores

measured a similar function for the men ($r = .599$; $p < .01$) but not for the women ($r = -.210$). Second, the adequacy of the assumptions about vocabulary corrections was tested, using a multiple correlation technique. No predictive gain was found when vocabulary was used in the regression equation to predict Elgin-scale placement from the Rorschach. This result is consistent with the initial assumption. A similiar analysis for the Proverbs test (meaningful only for the men) showed an increase in correlation from $-.603$ for Proverbs alone to .690 (corrected for "shrinkage") when both Proverbs and vocabulary were used to predict the Elgin scale. The multiple R gives about the same result as was reported earlier for discrepancy scores ($-.682$) and supports the value of a vocabulary correction. Finally, the effectiveness of the best linear combination of the Rorschach, Proverbs, and vocabulary scores in predicting the Elgin scale was investigated. For the men, the multiple R was .768 after correction for "shrinkage." All three tests contributed substantially to the prediction with vocabulary acting as a suppressor variable. For the women, the multiple R showed no increase over a direct prediction from the Rorschach, since the Proverbs test carries no weight for this group.

DISCUSSION

The results in part support the central hypothesis and demonstrate the value of a levels-of-personality interpretation of the process-reaction construct. A number of questions, however, were raised by the findings. Most difficult to understand is the sex difference in the meaning of the Proverbs test. Elaborate statistical analyses of the data failed to clarify this situation. A possible clue may lie in the fact that predictions were confirmed as long as the focus was on perceptual organization (Rorschach) but failed to be confirmed for women with the shift to conceptual organization (Proverbs). Possibly conceptual functioning in schizophrenic women

is more easily disrupted than perceptual functioning by momentary emotional factors independent of severity of illness. However one interprets these results, if supported by future research, they imply a need either to control for the "interfering factor" or to develop different types of instruments for the evaluation of degree of pathology in male and female schizophrenics.

Two further implications should be mentioned. First, the Rorschach findings may be interpreted as evidence for the validity of the Rorschach in reflecting levels of personality organization. In addition, a theoretical framework (seldom found in the Rorschach literature) is offered for why the Rorschach should be able to perform such a task. Second, the coherence of the findings suggests the feasibility of developing a diagnostic system similar to the stanine system used by the Air Force. On the basis of history and test data, schizophrenics could be classified as Level One's, Level Two's, etc., and the diagnosis would have genuinely prognostic value. In addition, such a classification would provide a sounder basis for distinguishing subgroups for etiological research, an important control variable for research on the effectiveness of therapy, and a frame of reference for evaluating the course of the disturbance over time.

SUMMARY

The Elgin Prognostic Scale was used to evaluate the case records of 24 male and 27 female schizophrenics in terms of a process-reaction continuum on the assumption of its equivalence to a measure of level of personality organization. Werner's developmental theories and certain empirical studies were used to score Rorschach and Benjamin Proverbs responses in terms of levels of differentiation and integration. It was then predicted that more process-like schizophrenics obtain lower Rorschach genetic-level scores and lower Proverbs-minus-vocabulary scores than more reactive-like schizophrenics. Because of a significant difference between men and women on the Elgin scale, the hypotheses were examined separately for the sex groups.

The Rorschach hypothesis was confirmed for both sex groups. The r between the Rorschach genetic-level score and the Elgin Prognostic Scale was $-.599$ ($p < .01$) for the men and $-.679$ ($p < .001$) for the women. The hypothesis for the Proverbs test was confirmed only for male schizophrenics. The r between the Proverbs discrepancy score and the Elgin scale was $-.682$ ($p < .001$) for the men and .048 for the women. No adequate explanation for this sex difference was found.

The general conclusion is drawn that the results in part support the central hypothesis. There is evidence for a measurable dimension of regressive and immature thinking which is related to the process-reaction dimension. In addition, the value of a levels-of-personality-organization interpretation of the process-reaction dimension is supported.

REFERENCES

1. Babcock, Harriet. *Dementia praecox, a psychological study.* Lancaster, Pa.: Science Press, 1933.

2. Baldwin, A. L. *Behavior and development in childhood.* New York: Holt, Rinehart and Winston, 1955.

3. Beck, S. J. *Rorschach's test.* Vol. I. *Basic processes.* New York: Grune & Stratton, 1944.

4. Beck, S. J. *Rorschach's test.* Vol. I. *Basic processes.* (2nd Ed.) New York: Grune & Stratton, 1949.

5. Becker, W. C., and McFarland, R. L. A lobotomy prognosis scale. *J. consult. Psychol.,* 1955, *19,* 157–162.

6. Becker, W. C. The relation of severity of thinking disorder to the process-reactive concept of schizophrenia. Unpublished doctor's dissertation, Stanford Univer., 1955.

7. Bellak, L. *Dementia praecox.* New York: Grune & Stratton, 1948.

8. Bellak, L. A multiple-factor psychosomatic theory of schizophrenia. *Psychiat. quart.,* 1949, *23,* 738–755.

9. Benjamin, J. D. A method for distinguishing and evaluating formal thinking disorders in schizophrenia. In J. S. Kasanin (Ed.), *Language and thought in schizophrenia.* Berkeley: Univer. of California Press, 1946. Pp. 66–71.

10. Friedman, H. Perpetual regression in schizophrenia. An hypothesis suggested by use of the Rorschach test. *J. proj. Tech.,* 1953, *17,* 171–185.

11. Guilford, J. P. *Fundamental statistics in psychology and education.* (2nd Ed.) New York: McGraw-Hill, 1950.

12. Hemmendinger, L. Perceptual organization and development as reflected in the structure of Rorschach test responses. *J. proj. Tech.,* 1953, *17,* 162–170.

13. Hunt, R. C., and Appel, K. E. Prognosis in psychoses lying midway between schizophrenia and manic-depressive psychoses. *Amer. J. Psychiat.,* 1936, *93,* 313–339.

14. Kant, O. Differential diagnosis of schizophrenia in the light of concepts of personality stratification. *Amer. J. Psychiat.,* 1940, *97,* 342–357.

15. Kantor, R. E., Wallner, J. M., and Winder, C. L. Process and reactive schizophrenia. *J. consult. Psychol.,* 1953, *17,* 157–162.

16. Langfeldt, G. Prognosis in schizoprhenia and factors influencing course of disease: catamnestic study, including individual re-examinations in 1936 with some considerations regarding diagnosis, pathogenesis and therapy. *Acta Psychiat. Neurol.,* 1937, Suppl. 13. Pp. 1–228.

17. Lewin, K. *A dynamic theory of personality.* D. K. Adams and K. E. Zener (Trans.). New York: McGraw-Hill, 1935.

18. McNemar, Q. *The revision of the Stanford-Binet scale.* New York: Houghton Mifflin, 1942.

19. McNemar, Q. *Psychological statistics.* New York: Wiley, 1949.

20. Phillips, L. and Smith, J. G. *Rorschach interpretation: advanced technique.* New York: Grune & Stratton, 1953.

21. Piotrowski, Z. A. On the Rorschach method and its application in organic

disturbances of the central nervous system. *Rorschach Res. Exch.*, 1936–1937, *1*, 65–77.

22. Shipley, W. C. A self-administering scale for measuring intellectual impairment and deterioration. *J. Psychol.*, 1940, *9*, 371–377.

23. Siegel, E. L. Genetic parellels of perceptual structuralization in paranoid schizophrenia: an analysis by means of the Rorschach technique. *J. proj. Tech.*, 1953, *17*, 151–161.

24. Simmins, C. Studies in experimental psychiatry: IV. Deterioration of 'G' in in psychotic patients. *J. ment. Sci.*, 1933, *79*, 704–734.

25. Stotsky, B. A. A comparison of remitting and nonremitting schizophrenics on psychological tests. *J. abnorm. soc. Psychol.*, 1952, *47*, 489–496.

26. Wittman, Phyllis. Scale for measuring prognosis in schizophrenic patients. *Elgin State Hosp. Papers*, 1941, *4*, 20–33.

27. Wittman, Phyllis. Follow-up on Elgin prognosis scale results. *Illinois psychiat. J.*, 1944, *4*, 56–59.

28. Wittman, Phyllis, and Steinberg, D. L. Follow-up of objective evaluation. *Elgin State Hosp. Papers*, 1944, *5*, 216–227.

29. Werner, H. *The comparative psychology of mental development.* (Rev. Ed.) Chicago: Follet, 1948.

Differential Autonomic Responsiveness in the Process-Reactive Classification of Schizophrenia

GERALD F. KING

CONSIDERABLE research attention has recently been focused on the relationship between autonomic nervous system (ANS) activity and schizophrenic behavior. Funkenstein and collaborators (*9, 10, 11, 12*) have been able to predict prognosis to electric shock and other forms of therapy with a variety of neuropsychiatric patients on the basis of ANS reactivity to certain drugs. Confirmatory evidence for the relationship between ANS activity and prognosis in schizophrenia has been provided in studies by Geocaris and Kooiker (*14*) and Hirschstein (*15*). In the initial method of analyzing ANS activity (*9*), changes in the systolic blood pressure after adrenergic stimulation (intravenous epinephrine) and cholinergic stimulation (intramuscular mecholyl) were classified into seven patterns of response. The number of blood pressure patterns has been reduced from seven to three in subsequent research (*23*). Further modifications have been introduced in regard to mecholyl; response to this drug has been expressed in quantitative terms, with meas-

ures of the extent and duration of blood pressure changes being employed (*13, 24*).

In attempting an integration of physiological and psychological processes, Meadow and Funkenstein (*23*) found a relationship between the ANS response patterns of schizophrenics and impairment in abstract thinking. Such a relationship was predictable on the basis of earlier studies by Bolles *et al.* (*4*) and others, who concluded that poor prognosis was associated with low performance on tests of abstract thinking. An investigation by Ficca (*8*) revealed that neuropsychiatric patients with "unfavorable" ANS patterns of response, in terms of prognosis, produced significantly more "schizophrenic" signs on the Rorschach than patients with "favorable" ANS responses. In a later study by Meadow and his associates (*24*), in which only mecholyl stimulation was used, measurements of ANS activity were obtained on what might be called a "level of autonomic responsiveness" dimension (e.g., maximum fall in systolic blood pressure). A significant positive relationship was found between level of autonomic responsiveness and level of abstract thinking with schizo-

Reprinted by permission from *The Journal of Abnormal and Social Psychology*, Vol. 56, No. 2, 1958.

phrenic subjects. The authors interpret the results as suggesting two polar types of schizophrenia, with the descriptions corresponding closely to the so-called "process" and "reactive" syndromes. The purpose of the present research was to explore further the relationship between level of autonomic responsiveness and the process-reactive classification.

The following gives a brief delineation of the process-reactive concept, which is usually viewed as a dichotomy: process schizophrenia is indicated by a gradual onset of psychosis and a relatively inadequate prepsychotic personality, whereas reactive schizophrenia is characterized by sudden onset of illness in a relatively normal prepsychotic personality. Additional criteria are given by Kantor, Wallner, and Winder (18). The distinction, for a particular patient, is commonly made on the basis of personal history information.

A number of investigators (17, 20, 25, 27) have presented evidence showing that schizophrenics with process characteristics have lower rates of recovery than patients more reactive in nature. In a study by Kantor, Wallner, and Winder (18), the Rorschach protocols of process schizophrenics were judged as being more "psychotic" than those of reactive schizophrenics. Brackbill and Fine (6) found that process schizophrenics could not be differentiated from organics on the basis of Rorschach indices of organicity, but that reactive schizophrenics showed significantly fewer signs of organic involvement than both groups. Becker (3), conceiving of a process-reactive continuum, found a significant relationship between this continuum and "genetic" scores derived from the Rorschach. The data also revealed a relationship between the process-reactive dimension and the conceptual level of the responses to a proverbs test, but the relationship was restricted to male patients, not appearing in females. It can be summarized that, in comparison with process schizophrenics, reactives (a) have a more favorable prognosis, (b) produce Rorschach records which are less apt to be judged as "psychotic," (c) respond with fewer organic signs on the Rorschach, (d) give responses of a higher genetic level on the Rorschach, and (e) possibly interpret proverbs on a higher conceptual level.

The available physiological and psychological evidence suggests that the process-reactive concept can be used as a frame of reference for predicting ANS responsiveness. The following hypothesis is offered: Predominantly reactive schizophrenics exhibit a higher level of autonomic responsiveness after the injection of mecholyl than predominantly process schizophrenics. The modifying adverb "predominantly" makes the hypothesis more congruent with Becker's method of analysis (3). The variety of criteria used in making the process-reactive distinction permits patients to display a mixture of both characteristics. What is involved is a typology of personal history incidents but not a typology of patients. Thus, a given patient may fall anywhere on a scale from "purely process" to "purely reactive." To be presented in this paper are two studies which bear on the hypothesis indicated.

STUDY I

Subjects

The basic group of Ss consisted of 136 recently hospitalized neuropsychiatric patients, all being given the diagnosis of schizophrenia. A variety of diagnostic subtypes and symptoms were represented. None of the patients showed any evidence of neurological complications from routine examination. Ages ranged from 20 to 42 years. All patients had been hospitalized eight weeks or less when the physiological measures were obtained.

Physiological Measures

The method of securing the physiological measures of ANS activity was a modification of that used by Funkenstein, Greenblatt, and Solomon (9). While the patient was lying in bed shortly after awaking in the morning, the resting systolic blood pressure was determined by a cuff manometer. The patient then received 10 mg. of mecholyl intramuscularly, and the systolic blood pressure was recorded at intervals of 2, 5, 7, 10,

12, 15, and 20 minutes. The following two measures of level of autonomic responsiveness, as derived from Meadow *et al*, (*24*), were obtained: (*a*) maximum fall in systolic blood pressure below the resting blood pressure following the injection of mecholyl and (*b*) area under the base-line (projection of the resting blood pressure) demarcated by blood pressure readings following mecholyl. A graphic illustration of these measures is given in Fig. 1.

The correlation between the two measures of autonomic responsiveness was found to be .82 ($N = 28$), indicating a high degree of commonality. Of the two measures, maxi-

classified on the basis of case histories as either "process" or "reactive" by the present investigator, using the frame of reference provided by Kantor, Wallner, and Winder (*18*). Independent classification of all *S*s was accomplished by either one of two other raters. None of the raters had knowledge of the physiological measures. The percentage of agreement between the two judgments was 76.7. Analysis of the agreement between the judgments with a fourfold table yielded a chi square of 17.47, which is significant at the .001 level of confidence. This is essentially of the same order of interrater agreement reported previously (*18*). Discussion among

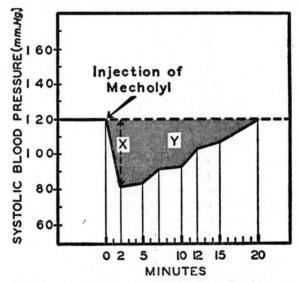

Figure 1. Diagrammic illustration of response of stystolic blood pressure to mecholyl (adapted from Meadow *et al*. [24]).
Maximum fall in blood pressure is indicated by X. Area under baseline of resting blood pressure is indicated by Y.

mum fall in systolic blood pressure (MFBP) was much easier to tabulate, involving merely the subtraction of the lowest systolic blood pressure reading from the basal reading. In the present research, only MFBP was employed as a measure of level of autonomic responsiveness. Indirect evidence of the reliability of this measure is indicated by its being positively correlated with level of abstract thinking in two independent samples (*24*).

Procedure

A sample of 60 was drawn from the basic group of schizophrenic *S*s. All *S*s were

the raters revealed that at least two factors probably lowered reliability: (*a*) instances of inadequate case histories and (*b*) case histories that indicated process and reactive characteristics to an almost equal degree.

Using only *S*s on which there was classificatory agreement resulted in process and reactive groups consisting of 22 and 24 *S*s, respectively. A comparison of the groups revealed no significant difference in age. Further, in considering the process-reactive concept as a continuum, 16 *S*s were randomly selected from the two groups and ranked accordingly by two independent raters. Rank 1 was assigned to the *S* judged to be the most process in nature, with rank 16 being occupied by the S being most clearly reactive. Agreement between the raters is indicated by a rho of .89.

Results

The mean MFBP score of the reactive schizophrenics was 24.41 $(SD = 8.25)$, as compared to 18.50 $(SD = 7.71)$ for the process schizophrenics.[1] The usual t test gives a value of 2.51, which indicates that this difference is significant at the .01 level (one-tailed test). For the 16 Ss, the rho between the sets of ranks on the process-reactive dimension and MFBP is —.58 $(p < .01$, one-tailed test). In accordance with the hypothesis, the reactive schizophrenics displayed a higher level of autonomic responsiveness following the injection of mecholyl than the process schizophrenics. The results also indicate that it is feasible to order the process and reactive syndromes on a continuum.

STUDY II

Subjects

With the elimination of the 46 Ss who participated in Study I, the basic group of Ss was reduced to 90.

Physiological Measures

The same method as in Study I was employed.

Procedure

The following modification was introduced in the classificatory procedure: all 90 Ss were classified as either "process," "process-reactive," or "reactive." The process-reactive category was designed to be an intermediate one, representing schizophrenics with both types of characteristics to an almost equal degree. Otherwise, the same rating procedure was followed as in Study I. The percentage of agreement between the independent judgments was 87.8. The corresponding chi square, using a 3-by-3 contingency table, was 121.53, which is significant considerably beyond the .001 level. Groups representing the three categories were formed from the Ss on which there was classificatory agreement. Balanced for N, each group consisted of 24 Ss. A comparison for age yielded no significant differences among the groups.

In addition, scores on the Elgin Prognostic Scale (31) were obtained for 22 Ss. This

scale consists of ratings on factors which are based on the process-reactive differentiation, Data for the ratings were secured from interviews and clinical folders (case histories, etc.) Higher scores on the scale represent a greater incidence of process elements. Wittman (31) reports an interrater reliability coefficient of .87 for an N of 61. In the present research, 12 Ss were rated independently by two raters, the interrater rho being .94.

Results

Treating the MFBP scores of the three groups by analysis of variance yielded an F ratio that is significant beyond the .01 level. The mean MFBP scores were of ascending magnitude, with the process schizophrenics being lowest $(M = 17.04)$, the process-reactives intermediate $(M = 22.79)$, and the reactives highest $(M = 26.62)$. This trend is in accordance with the hypothesis and the conception of a process-reactive continuum. Since this is not a *post hoc* analysis, there is justification for computing t tests between the individual means. Using one-tailed tests, the results show that the process schizophrenics were significantly lower than the process-reactives $(t = 2.39, p < .025)$, who in turn approached being significantly lower than the reactive schizophrenics $(t = 1.54, p < .07)$. The rho between the Elgin scale and the MFBP scores $(N = 22)$ was —.49 $(p < .025$, one-tailed test). The findings thus indicate that the reactive schizophrenics exhibited a a greater autonomic response to mecholyl than the process schizophrenics; or, in other words, the process-reactive dimension is inversely related to level of autonomic responsiveness. As in Study I, the hypothesis is supported.

DISCUSSION

The results provide a basis for discussing and speculating about some of the past research dealing with physiological aspects of schizophrenia. Citing a variety of supporting studies, Angyal, Freeman, and Hoskins (2) and Hoskins (16) characterize schizophrenics, in comparison with normals, as showing reduced physiological responsiveness. However, confirmation of this position has not been obtained in a number of other studies (1, 7, 26). As suggested by Sands and Rodnick (29) and as illustrated by Malmo, Shagass, and Smith (22), contradictory results in this

---

[1] In comparison with the distribution reported by Funkenstein *et al.* (13), the MFBP scores obtained in the present research seem to be depressed.

area are undoubtedly due in part to variations in the types of experimental stimulation and the nature of the physiological measures. Variations in the schizophrenic samples employed in different studies is another likely factor. According to the present research, responsiveness is related to the process-reactive make-up of the schizophrenic sample. If we consider pure cases of "process" and "reactive" patients for the sake of discussion, the evidence points to diminished physiological responsiveness in process but not in reactive schizophrenia. Thus, reduced responsiveness would not be found in studies where the schizophrenic subjects were predominantly reactive in character.

One possible reaction to the preceding discussion is that it moves in the direction of a two-factor theory of schizophrenia. Process characteristics are associated with a physiological "impairment," at least implicitly. What remains, it would seem, is to tie the disturbance in the reactive syndrome to interpersonal factors. This notion is compatible with the contention of Brackbill (5), who, after reviewing the studies of brain dysfunction in schizophrenia, postulates the existence of central nervous system pathology in process but not in reactive patients. In this context, the question arises as to whether autonomic disturbances are primary or secondary to cortical defect.

If the information on normal responsiveness is given more consideration, it is possible to cast the problem in a different light. Although the data on the reactivity of normals to mecholyl are meagre (10, 14), it seems to indicate that their blood pressure responses are very similar to what can be expected from process schizophrenics. In graphic terms, if level of autonomic responsiveness represents the ordinate and normals, reactives, and process schizophrenics lie on the abscissa in that order, the relationship can be described as curvilinear. In accordance with this hypothetical graph, the reactives would be high in autonomic responsiveness, whereas the normals and process patients would be relatively low. Such a relationship offers a more adequate account of studies which have found that schizophrenics, especially patients in the early stages of illness, are physiologically even more reactive than normals (e.g., 21, 30). A study by Pfister (28) gives a more complete illustration of the curvilinear relationship: Early schizophrenics were hyperreactive on cardiovascular measures; if the illness persisted, however, the same Ss dropped toward or even below the normal level. Although a loose interchange of concepts is sometimes necessary, a good deal of the available data can be fitted to the curve. A possible explanation lies in viewing both normals and process schizophrenics as representing relatively uniform, stable adjustments over a period of time. It is suggested that the corresponding physiological homeostasis is indicated by a low autonomic responsiveness. A heightened autonomic reactivity then would reflect a disruption of homeostasis, which corresponds with the more transient, precipitous nature of the reactive adjustment.

Although problems of interpretation are posed, the results in general provide additional evidence of the meaningful nature of the process-reactive classification, or dimension, of schizophrenia. Using this concept of schizophrenia, which cuts across symptomatology, evidence has been compiled from this and other studies revealing interrelationships among several classes of variables: case history information, psychological dimensions, physiological measures, and prognosis. The numerous failures of past studies dealing with schizophrenia seem to give this classification even more significance. When samples of undifferentiated schizophrenics, or even ones based on the standard diagnostic subtypes, have been employed in research, the findings have typically been either negative, not readily interpretable, or not reproducible (19). Pending the development of a better schema for delineating the heterogeneous category of schizophrenia, the process-reactive classification seems to offer a productive orientation for research.

SUMMARY

This investigation consisted of two studies which were concerned with the relationship between the process-reactive classification of schizophrenia and autonomic nervous system activity. On the basis of psychological and physiological findings, it was hypothesized that predominately reactive schizophrenics display a higher level of autonomic responsiveness after the injection of mecholyl than predominantly process schizophrenics. Similar in nature, the two studies had the following methodological features in common: (a) The process-reactive classification of schizophrenic Ss was made on the basis of case history information, (b) a small sample of the total N was ranked on a process-reactive continuum, and (c) maximum fall in systolic blood pressure constituted the measure of autonomic responsiveness.

In accordance with the hypothesis, the results of both studies revealed that the patients classified as "reactive" exhibited a significantly greater fall in blood pressure after the administration of mecholyl than the process patients. Significant rank-order correlations were also obtained between the process-reactive dimensions employed in each sudy and maximum fall in blood pressure, indicating that it is feasible to order the process and reactive syndromes on a continuum. Some implications of the findings in regard to physiological responsiveness in schizophrenia were discussed. It was concluded that the process-reactive classification seems to provide a fruitful frame of reference for research in schizophrenia.

REFERENCES

1. Altschule, M. D., and Sulzbach, W. M. Effect of carbon dioxide on acrocyanosis in schizophrenia. *Arch. Neurol. Psychiat.*, 1949, *61*, 44–55.

2. Angyal, A., Freeman, H., and Hoskins, R. G. Physiologic aspects of schizophrenic withdrawal. *Arch. Neurol. Psychiat.*, 1940, *44*, 621–626.

3. Becker, W. C. A genetic approach to the interpretation and evaluation of the process-reactive distinction in schizophrenia. *J. abnorm. soc. Psychol.*, 1956, *53*, 229–236.

4. Bolles, M. M., Rosen, G. P., and Landis, C. Psychological performance tests as prognostic agents for the effiicacy of insulin therapy in schizophrenia. *Psychiat., Quart.*, 1938, *12*, 733–737.

5. Brackbill, G. A. Studies on brain dysfunction in schizophrenia, *Psychol. Bull.*, 1956, *53*, 210–226.

6. Brackbill, G. A., and Fine, H. J. Schizophrenia and central nervous system pathology. *J. abnorm. soc. Psychol.*, 1956, *52*, 310–313.

7. Cameron, D. E. Heat production and heat control in the schizophrenic reaction. *Arch. Neurol. Psychiat.*, 1934, *32*, 704–711.

8. Ficca, S. C. Relationship of "autonomic" blood pressure pattern types and subjects' performance on the Wechsler-Bellevue and the Rorschach test. Unpublished doctoral dissertation, Pennsylvania State Univer., 1950.

9. Funkenstein, D. H., Greenblatt, M., and Solomon, H. C. Autonomic nervous system changes following electric shock treatment. *J. nerv. ment. Dis.*, 1948, *108*, 409–422.

10. Funkenstein, D. H., Greenblatt, M., and Solomon, H. C. Psycho-physiological study of mentally ill patients. *Amer. J. Psychiat.*, 1949, *106*, 16–28.

11. Funkenstein, D. H., Greenblatt, M., and Solomon, H. C. Autonomic changes paralleling psychologic changes in mentally ill patients. *J. nerv. ment. Dis.*, 1951, *114*, 1–18.

12. Funkenstein, D. H., Greenblatt, M., and Solomon, H. C. An autonomic nervous system test of prognostic significance in relation to electro-shock treatment. *Psychosom. Med.*, 1952, *14*, 347–362.

13. Funkenstein, D. H., Greenblatt, M., and Solomon, H. C. Nor-epinephrine-like and epinephrine-like substances in psychotic and psychoneurotic patients. *Amer. J. Psychiat.*, 1952, *108*, 652–662.

14. Geocaris, K. H., and Kooiker, J. E. Blood

pressure responses of chronic schizophrenic patients to epinephrine and mecholyl. *Amer. J. Psychiat.*, 1956, *112*, 808–813.

15. Hirschstein, R. The significance of characteristic autonomic nervous system responses in the adjustment, change and outcome in schizophrenia. *J. nerv. ment. Dis.*, 1955, *122*, 254–262.

16. Hoskins, R. G. *The biology of schizophrenia.* New York: Norton, 1946.

17. Kant, O. Differential diagnosis of schizophrenia in light of concepts of personality-stratification. *Amer. J. Psychiat.*, 1940, *97*, 342–357.

18. Kantor, R. E., Wallner, J. M., and Winder, C. L. Process and reactive schizophrenia. *J. consult. Psychol.*, 1953, *17*, 157–162.

19. King, G. F. Research with neuropsychiatric samples, *J. Psychol.*, 1954, *38*, 383–387.

20. Langfeldt, G. The diagnosis of schizophrenia. *Amer. J. Psychiat.*, 1951, *108*, 123–125.

21. Malmo, R. B., and Shagass, C. Physiologic studies of reaction to stress in anxiety and early schizophrenia. *Psychosom. Med.*, 1949, *11*, 9–24.

22. Malmo, R. B., Shagass, C., and Smith, A. A. Responsiveness in chronic schizophrenia. *J. Pers.* 1951, *19*, 359–375.

23. Meadow, A., and Funkenstein, D. H. The relationship of abstract thinking to the autonomic nervous system in schizophrenia. In P. Hoch & J. Zubin (Eds.), *Relation of psychological tests to psychi-*

atry. New York: Grune & Stratton, 1952. Pp. 131-149.

24. Meadow, A., Greenblatt, M., Funkenstein, D. H., and Solomon, H. C. Relationship between capacity for abstraction in schizophrenia and physiologic response to autonomic drugs. *J. nerv. ment. Dis.*, 1953, *118*, 332–338.

25. Milici, P. Postemotive schizophrenia. *Psychiat. Quart.*, 1939, *13*, 278–293.

26. Parsons, E. H., Gildea, E. F., Ronzoni, E., and Hulbert, S. Z. Comparative lymphocytic and biochemical responses of patients with schizophrenia and affective disorders to electroshock, insulin shock, and epinephrine. *Amer. J. Psychiat.*, 1949, *105*, 573–580.

27. Paskind, H. A., and Brown, M. Psychoses resembling schizophrenia occurring with emotional stress and ending in recovery. *Amer. J. Psychiat.*, 1940, *96*, 1379–1388.

28. Pfister, H. O. Disturbances of the autonomic nervous system in schizophrenia and their relations to the insulin, cardiazol and sleep treatments. *Amer. J. Psychiat. Suppl.*, 1938, *109*, 94–118.

29. Sands, S. L., and Rodnick, E. H. Concept and experimental design in the study of stress and personality. *Amer. J. Psychiat.*, 1950, *106*, 673–679.

30. Williams, M. Psychophysiological responsiveness to psychological stress in early chronic schizophrenic reactions. *Psychosom. Med.*, 1953, *15*, 456–462.

31. Wittman, Phyllis. Scale for measuring prognosis in schizophrenic patients. *Elgin State Hosp. Papers*, 1941, *4*, 20–33.

6 | *The Investigation of Mood Disorders*

STANDARD textbooks in abnormal psychology include at least one chapter on mood aberrations, sometimes called manic-depressive psychoses or affective disorders. The basic questions for research in this area are the same as those in the study of other forms of pathology, namely: What are the antecedents, the causative factors? What are the symptoms, the characteristics of thought and action that are specific to this disorder? What are the features in the history or present status of the patient that may be used to predict outcomes? What therapeutic or management measures lead to recovery? The four papers in this section deal with some of these questions.

In general, the depressed patient in the clinical setting is assessed in terms of potential for suicide. Although other disturbed persons sometimes commit suicide, it is generally regarded as the most extreme resultant of depression. The paper by Osgood and Walker, although theoretically oriented to communication theory, also contributes to an understanding of suicide. A significant and unusual feature of their research is the use of suicide notes written by persons just before they took their own lives. Content analysis, a method by which communications are analyzed according to standard content classifications, is the research method employed to analyze the notes. Comparison of these notes with nonsuicidal letters illustrates the kinds of inferences that may be drawn from painstaking analysis of written communications. Certain correspondences were found in the content categories when comparisons were made between genuine suicidal notes and simulated or faked suicidal notes. The following interpretation of this finding is worth careful study: The correspondences reflect the enactment of a role that is subtly defined by certain cultural standards.

The paper by Gibson is probably the most intensive study of the effect of family background and early experience on the development of manic-depressive psychosis. Informants were interviewed and the records of these interviews were rated on a number of scales. The data are compared with data from a sample of schizophrenic patients. It is important to note that this investigation repeats many aspects of an earlier study which was guided by the same interpersonal theory. Some of the conclusions of the earlier study were confirmed, thus strengthening the confidence of the investigator in the utility of interpersonal theory. The real value of this research cannot be assessed until the same data are collected on nonpatient controls. If, let us say, the manic-depressive patients are not significantly different from normals on such items as striving for social prestige, envy, competitiveness, and so on, then the search must be directed toward discovering what suppressor factor was responsible for sparing normals from the disorder.

The paper by Beck and Hurvich illustrates the use of dreams as the raw data for inferences about the psychological correlates of depression. The paper further illustrates how clinical data may be used for research purposes. The records of the dreams are systematically analyzed according to a pre-established set of categories. Such a method removes some of the ambiguities from the raw clinical data. Although the number of subjects is small, and the sample of patients is hardly representative of the general population, the findings give some preliminary validity to the concept of inverted hostility as an important mechanism in depression.

Few professional workers are content with present schemes for classifying disordered persons. Most current nosological systems have their origin in nineteenth-century psychiatry. The effect of retaining these descriptive labels is to bias both the examination procedure and the disposition of the patient. One classification—usually discussed in connection with mood disorders—is "involutional psychosis." Wittenborn and Bailey attack the problem of diagnosis by using factor-analytic techniques. They describe a quantitative method for establishing multiple diagnosis. While some of the technical details may elude the general reader, the paper can be understood as an attempt to make the process of diagnosis more exact and reliable. Substantively, the study shows that the concept "involutional psychosis" is composed of a heterogeneous array of factors. The method of diagnosis developed by Wittenborn and Bailey yields a classificatory statement which has a higher reliability than that produced through traditional clinical diagnosis.

Motivation and Language Behavior
A Content Analysis of Suicide Notes

CHARLES E. OSGOOD and EVELYN G. WALKER

Whenever a person produces a message, whether it be conversation, an ordinary letter to a relative, or a suicide note, he employs a complex set of encoding habits. It seems reasonable to assume that these language habits are organized in much the same way as the habits underlying nonlanguage behavior and that the general principles of learning and performance therefore apply equivalently in both cases. This paper is concerned with the effects of motivation upon language behavior. It is assumed that the author of a suicide note—presumably written shortly before he takes his own life—is functioning under heightened motivation. Therefore, the structure and content of suicide notes should differ from both ordinary letters and from simulated suicide notes in certain ways predictable from a general theory of behavior. Following a brief theoretical discussion, we describe the application of a number of relevant content measures to a comparison, first, of suicide notes with ordinary letters to relatives and, second, of suicide notes with faked notes. Many of

Reprinted by permission from *The Journal of Abnormal and Social Psychology*, Vol. 59, No. 1, 1959.

these measures differentiate in predicted ways suicide notes from normal control notes; a smaller number differentiate suicide from simulated suicide notes, suggesting that nonsuicidal individuals are able to adopt the state of the suicidal person in some respects but not in others.

Language habits, like habits in general, appear to be organized into hierarchies of alternatives. We shall assume that increased drive has two distinct effects upon selection within such hierarchies: generalized energizing effects and specific cue effects (cf., Osgood, 6, for a more complete analysis).

The generalized energizing effects of drives are characterized by a nonspecific facilitation of all habits. Following the views expressed by Hebb (3) one may identify the generalized energizing effects of drives with arousal of a neural system in the brainstem from which there is diffuse, nonspecific projection into the cortex, these impulses having a summative, "tuning-up" function. Assuming a multiplicative relation between habit strength and drive in producing reaction potential (10), the effect of increasing drive should be to make the dominant alternatives within all hierarchies even more probable relatively. Our first prediction, therefore: (A) *Suicide notes will be characterized by greater stereotypy than messages produced under lower degrees of motivation.* Suicide notes should therefore be more repetitious, less diversified in lexical content, use fewer adjectival and adverbial qualifiers, more familiar words and phrases, and so on. However, since the maximum strengths of habits are assumed to be asymptotic, extreme increase in drive should force many competing habits toward a common maximum and hence produce interference and blocking. Therefore: (B) *If extremely high levels of drive can be assumed, suicide notes should display greater disorganization of language behavior.* This would include various kinds of errors, breaking up of messages into shorter units, and similar phenomena.

To the extent that drive states are accompanied by distinctive sensations— e.g., thirst sensations, feelings of anxiety, sensations of pain—these distinctive cues can become associated with certain alternatives within habit hierarchies through the operation of ordinary learning principles. The presence of such cues, as directive states, will have the effect of modifying the probability structure of behavioral hierarchies, increasing the probability of some alternatives, decreasing the probability of others. This leads to the following prediction: (C) *Suicide notes should be characterized by increased frequency of those grammatical and lexical choices associated with the motives leading to self-destruction.* On a rather mundane level, this means that suicide notes should contain a relatively high frequency of self- and other-critical statements. Less obviously, they should contain a high frequency of what Skinner (9) calls "mands"—constructions of the demand, command, request type that express needs of the speaker and require some behavior on the part of the listener for their satisfaction. Finally, if two or more motives are operating, and their cues are associated with selection of different alternatives within hierarchies, one may expect oscillation between the responses associated with each state. Since it seems reasonable to assume that suicidal people will often be functioning under competing motives, e.g., self-criticism vs. self-protection, spouse-aggression vs. spouse-affection, etc., we may predict that: (D) *Suicide notes should be characterized by more evidence of conflict than messages produced under nonsuicidal states.* Among indices of conflict would be use of constructions with *but, however, if,* and the like, qualification of verb phrases, and ambivalence in the assertions made about significant persons.

METHOD

The suicide materials for this study consisted of two samples. The first was a set of 100 genuine suicide notes, 50 written by men and 50 written by women just prior to taking their own lives. These were obtained from Edwin S. Shneidman from his Los Angeles files. For comparison purposes, we obtained a sample of ordinary letters written to 100 members of a panel of Ss in the Champaign-Urbana area; this panel had been used for other purposes in connection with research on the communication of mental health information. Since many of the quantitative measures we wished to make made it desirable that the messages include at least 100 words or so, the total sample was reduced to the following: 40 male suicide; 29 female suicide; 13 male control; 59 female control. The second set of materials received from Edwin S. Shneidman consisted of 33 paired notes, one of each pair being a genuine suicide note and the other a simulated suicide note; a key to which was which accompanied this set in a sealed envelope. We decided to use this set as a final test of our measures, after trying them out against the known suicide and normal letters. It was expected, however, that certain measures that would discriminate between suicide notes and ordinary letters probably would not do so between genuine and deliberately faked suicide notes—particularly measures reflecting the specific content of the message.

Quantitative measures designed to test the four general predictions—intended indices of *stereotypy*, of *disorganization*, of *directive state*, and of *conflict*—were devised and applied to the samples of known suicide notes and control letters. Sixteen measures were applied, along with certain additional analyses. Some of the measures are standard and well known in content analysis work; others were developed by us for this purpose. These were probably not the best measures that could have been devised, and they certainly do not exhaust the possibilities, but they do represent a considerable variety of quantitative estimates. The two investigators worked together in devising the measures, stabilizing the rules, and applying them to a small sample of notes. Each measure was then applied as consistently as possible to the total materials by one of us, not by both. We therefore have no direct evidence on the reliability of our measures across coders. For some of the measures, the objectivity of what was counted (e.g., number of *repetitions, number of syllables per word*) reduced the seriousness of this problem. Several of the less objective measures (e.g., *evaluative assertion analysis, distress-relief quotient, type/token ratios, cloze procedure*) have been checked for reliability by their authors, and these reports are in our references. To avoid redundancy, the detailed description of the measures will be given in connection with the results obtained with them.

RESULTS

Suicide Notes vs. Ordinary Letters to Friends and Relatives

The differences between scores of males and females were tested for statistical significance separately within suicide and control groups. If no sex difference was found, the male and female letters within groups were combined and the total suicide vs. control samples were then compared statistically. If a sex difference did appear, separate analyses for differences between suicide notes and controls were made for each sex. Nonparametric tests of significance were used, generally the median test, and occasionally chi square. In the former case, levels of significance were evaluated by reference to the Mainland and Murray tables (5). Conservative estimates of the significance of the differences are given since a two-sided hypothesis was tested in spite of the fact that the direction of the difference was predicted in all cases.

Stereotype Measures

1. *Average number of syllables per word.* We would expect a person functioning under high drive to select words in terms of his strongest habits, i.e., familiar high-frequency words. Since, as Zipf (*12*) has shown, there is an inverse relation between length of words and their frequency, and since longer, rarer words typically have more syllables, it follows that ordinary letters should have more syllables per word on the average than suicide notes. The total number of syllables per message, as estimated from breath pulses, was divided by the total number of words per message to obtain this index. There were no sex differences on this measure. Differences between suicide notes and control letters did not reach statistical significance but were in the expected direction.

2. *Type/token ratio* (TTR). This measure is obtained by dividing the number

of *different* words by the total number of words in each message. It has been shown to be a good index of lexical diversity, differentiating between educational levels, telephone vs. ordinary conversation, and so on (*4*). If high drive increases stereotypy, we would expect suicide notes to display lower TTRs than ordinary letters to friends and relatives. There were no sex differences on this measure, and differences between suicides and controls were significant at the .01 level in the predicted direction.

3. *Repetitions.* Another index of stereotypy in messages is redundancy in what is talked about. We would expect people under high drive to repeat phrases more often than people under low drive. Here repetition of single words did not count (cf. TTR above), but phrases and parts of phrases of more than one word did. For example, in ". . . I really love you very much . . . and *I really* do *love you* . . .," the part phrase *I really love you* would count as repetition of 4 words. For each message, the number of words repeated in this fashion was divided by the total number of words as an index of repetitiousness. Here, again, there were no differences between sexes, but the difference between suicide notes and ordinary letters was significant at the .01 level.

4. *Noun-verb/adjective-adverb ratio.* This measure—a modification of the familiar verb/adjective ratio (*1*)—was obtained by dividing the total number of nouns and verbs contained in the message by the total number of adjectives and adverbs. Definition of nouns, verbs, adjectives, and adverbs was done on the basis of whether the words could be substituted in linguistic test frames characteristic of the particular grammatical form. The rationale for the analysis is that under high drive states there should be less tendency toward modification of noun and verb forms, toward discriminative qualification of simple assertions, in line with our assumptions about the generalized energizing effects of drives. The prediction therefore follows that the ratio should be higher in the sui-

cide than in the normal letters. The results bore out this prediction at the .01 level of confidence.

5. *Cloze measures.* Taylor (*11*) has devised a method of estimating redundancy or stereotypy in which a message is "mutilated" by substituting a blank for every *n*th word (say, every fifth word, as used here) and *S*s try to fill in these missing items. Presumably, the more predictable the message as a whole, the more accurately *S*s can perform this task and, hence, the higher will be the cloze score. It follows that suicide notes should generate higher cloze scores than control notes. Subsamples of 10 male suicide, 10 male control, 10 female suicide, and 10 female control notes were mutilated by substituting blanks for every fifth word. Because sex differences in content might be significant here, we had 34 male *S*s fill in the male notes and 31 female *S*s fill in the female notes; suicide and control letters were alternated in order of presentation. Each *S*'s mean cloze score for the 10 suicide notes and the 10 control letters was computed. A chi square test was used to determine whether the proportion of *S*s having mean suicide cloze scores higher than their control scores deviated significantly from chance. For male *S*s completing male materials, differences were significant at the .01 level in the expected direction; for females completing female material, however, there were no differences whatsoever.

6. *Allness terms.* People speaking or writing under high drive or emotion could be expected to be more extreme or polarized in their assertions. They should use more terms that permit no exception, e.g., *always, never, forever, no one, no more, everything, everyone, completely, perfectly,* and so on. Strictly speaking, this is not a measure of stereotypy, but it should be affected by generalized drive level. The number of such terms in each message was divided by total words and expressed as a rate per 100 words. Suicide notes yielded significantly more allness terms (.01 level), and there were no sex differences.

Disorganization Measures

1. *Structural disturbances.* Extremely high levels of drive should result in disruption of the myriad of delicately balanced language encoding habits, according to theoretical analysis. To obtain a disturbance measure, the coder took the attitude of an English composition teacher, noting all grammatical, syntactical, spelling, and punctuation errors, and even clearly awkward constructions. Points where material was obviously omitted, e.g., "I don't ( ) him any more," were also counted. The index was the number of such errors expressed as a rate per 100 words. There were no sex differences here and no significant differences between suicide and control notes, although the latter difference was clearly in the expected direction.

2. *Average length of independent segments.* We assume that people encoding under stress will tend to break their utterances into short, explosive units. Here we are interested in sentence length, but must correct for compound sentences joined together by conjunctions like *and* and *but*. The coder divided each message into the number of segments that could stand by themselves as sentences. The index was the total number of words in each message divided by the number of such segments, yielding the average number of words per independent segment. Although there were no sex differences for control letters, there were for suicide notes, male suicides using significantly longer segments (.05 level). Comparing suicides with normals, we find no differences for females but a difference significant at the .05 level for males—male suicide notes used significantly *longer* independent segments than ordinary letters written by males, a finding that is contrary to the direction predicted.

Directive State Measures

1. *Distress/Relief Quotient (DRQ).* This well-known measure developed by Dollard and Mowrer (*2*) is the ratio of distress-expressing phrases to the sum of these plus relief-expressing phrases, the former being indicative of disturbing drive states and the latter of the reduction of such states. This measure obviously depends to a considerable degree on the judgment of the coder. Here we found definite sex differences for both control and suicide messages; females yielded higher ratios (more distress-expression), in both cases significant at the .05 level. This difference may reflect a trait of masculine reticence in our culture. And, as might be expected from the nature of the suicide situation, both male and female suicide notes displayed higher DRQs than ordinary letters to friends and relatives (.01 level in both cases).

2. *Number of evaluative common-meaning terms.* Common-meaning terms in a language are those upon whose denotation and connotation people must agree if they are to understand one another. Examples would be *sweet, round, table, thunder, run, eat,* and so on. They are in contrast to attitude objects, like *labor union* and *ex-Senator McCarthy,* upon whose connotative meanings, at least, communicators need not agree. *Evaluative* common-meaning terms are those, like *unfair, dangerous, sweetheart,* and *drunkard,* which can be judged as clearly related to either *good* or *bad.* Our index here is simply the total number of such terms in each message divided by the total number of words in the message. There are no differences between sexes for either suicides or normals in the simple *number* of evaluative common-meaning terms (in contrast to the distress/relief measure above and percentage of positive evaluative assertions below), but differences between suicides and normals are significant at the .01 level, with suicides having more evaluative terms.

3. *Positive evaluative assertions.* Evaluative Assertion Analysis has been described in detail elsewhere (*7, 8*). In essence, it involves the linguistic isolation of statements that assert a relation between an attitude object and either another attitude object or an evaluative common-

meaning term. Examples: *I* (EGO)/*have always respected/you* (FATHER); *You* (SPOUSE)/*could never stand being/simply a loyal helpmate.* Assertive relations can be either associative (*have always respected*) or dissociative (*could never stand being*). For present purposes, analysis was restricted to those attitude objects representing the significant persons in Ego's life and their relation to Ego; e.g., EGO, ALTER (person written to when not spouse, parent, or child), SPOUSE, CHILD, MOTHER, FATHER. The index with which we are presently concerned was obtained by dividing the number of positive evaluative assertions by the total number of evaluative assertions, positive and negative, i.e., the proportion of positive evaluations. It would be expected that this measure would correlate highly and negatively with the Distress/Relief Quotient, and it does. Although sex differences were not significant, they were in the direction of greater negative evaluation by females in both suicide and normal letters. Differences between suicide and ordinary letters home were significant at the .01 level and in the expected direction.

4. *Time orientation.* It was expected that the motivational state characteristic of suicide might direct interest of the writer away from the present toward the past. Therefore, suicide notes should contain fewer statements referring to the present and the future but more referring to the past. Examples: present reference— *I love you, I'm afraid that . . .*; past references—*I have tried . . . Everything you've done . . .*; future reference—*. . . who will always love you, Tell my parents. . . .* We measured both the proportion of total references which were to present time and the imbalance of nonpresent references toward past vs. future. Contrary to our expectations, there were neither significant differences between sexes nor between suicides and controls.

5. *Mands.* According to Skinner (*9*), a *mand* is an utterance which (*a*) expresses a need of the speaker and which (*b*) requires some reaction from another person for its satisfaction. It is usually expressed in the form of an imperative, where the verb comes early in the utterance (e.g., *Don't feel too bad about this* or *Please understand me*), but is not restricted to this form (e.g., *I wish I could see you, I hope you understand,* or *May God forgive me*). Our index was the number of such constructions, expressed as a rate per hundred words. This proved to be one of the most useful measures in our arsenal. In the present test situation, differences between sexes were not significant, but differences between suicide notes and ordinary letters to friends and relatives were significant at the .01 level in the predicted direction.

Conflict Measures

1. *Qualification of verb phrases.* When a speaker or writer is in conflict about the topics being discussed, it seems likely that he will modify or qualify his assertions away from the flat, direct present or past tense, e.g., from *I was good to you* to something like *I used to be good to you,* or *I tried to be good to you.* To quantify this characteristic of messages, the coder first bracketed each complete verb phrase for which a single verb could be substituted, e.g., for *I* (*could have helped*) *you more* we can substitute *I* (*loved*) *you more,* where the one word *loved* substitutes structurally for the three words *could have helped;* then the coder totaled the number of words in these brackets and divided by the number of such brackets. The larger this ratio, the greater the amount of excess, qualifying material. There were no sex differences on this measure, but differences between suicide and normal letters were significant at the .01 level in the expected direction.

2. *Ambivalence constructions.* There are a number of syntactical constructions in English that may directly express ambivalence, conflict, and doubt on the part of the speaker: *but, if, would, should, because (for, since), well, however, maybe, probably, possibly, seems, appears, guess,*

surely, really, except, etc. Certain question forms also express the same indecisive state, e.g., *Must I do it? Why do I try at all?* The coder determined the number of such forms in each message and expressed it as a rate per 100 words. Differences between sexes were not significant; differences between suicide notes and ordinary letters were significant at the .01 level.

3. *Percentage of ambivalence evaluative assertions.* The essential nature of evaluative assertion analysis has already been described (see Directive State Measures numbered 2 and 3). If a speaker displays perfect consistency or lack of ambivalence, then all of the assertions relating to each attitude object or association between each pair of attitude objects will have the same sign. For example, assertions concerning the self would be either consistently positive or consistently negative—*I am no good; I have been a failure; Luck has not been on my side;* or for the relation of Ego to Spouse, *I have always loved you; You relied on me; I tried to help you; My Darling Wife.* Ambivalence, on the other hand, is indicated by assertions of different signs in the same set, e.g., *I love you, Honey; You never trusted me; I quarreled with you; You stuck by our marriage, though.* Our index of assertion ambivalence was the total number of deviant assertions (i.e., the number of least frequent signs in each set, summing over sets) expressed as a proportion of total assertions. For this conflict measure, also, there were no sex differences, but suicide vs. control differences were significant at the .01 level and in the predicted direction.

Genuine vs. Simulated Suicide Notes

We had originally planned to apply the measures that had successfully differentiated suicide from control letters blindly to the entire set of 33 paired suicide and simulated notes. Unfortunately only 13 of these pairs included both suicide and faked notes of sufficient length to make most of our measures meaningful. In attempting to predict which of these 13 pairs were the genuine suicide notes, we eliminated those measures which had failed to differentiate suicides from normal controls (*structural disturbances, average length of independent segments, time orientation*), those which obviously and nonsubtly reflected the suicide topic and hence would be readily faked (*distress-relief quotient, evaluative terms, positive evaluative assertions*), and the *cloze procedure* (too few messages of sufficient length). A prediction of suicide vs. simulated was made for each of the 13 paired notes on the basis of each of the remaining nine measures, and the final prediction was based on which note in each pair garnered the most suicide votes. Our quantitative predictions proved to be correct in 10 out of 13 cases, a value significant at the .05 level.

However, before checking the accuracy of these quantitative predictions against the key in the sealed envelope, both authors independently assigned all 33 pairs to suicide or fake categories on an intuitive basis. One of us got 31/33 correct and the other 26/33. To check on the possibility that we had actually been employing cues derived from our previous quantitative coding, we had eight graduate students with no prior experience with these notes assign the pairs to genuine suicide and fake categories. They were successful on the average in 16.5/33 cases, exactly chance. So it would appear that familiarity with a large sample of known suicide vs. nonsuicide notes, or sensitivity to cues derived from quantitative measures, or both, contributes to successful identification of genuine suicide notes.

Knowing which of the 33 pairs are genuine suicide notes, we may now ask which of our quantitative measures, successful in differentiating suicide from ordinary leters home, are also successful in differentiating genuine suicide from pseudo notes. This analysis should indicate which encoding characteristics of the suicidal individual can be intuited and, hence, faked by the nonsuicidal person, and which cannot. We may look first at the very small sample of 13 pairs where both genuine and pseudo notes could be coded.

Stereotypy Measures: Of these measures, three (*syllables per word, repetitions,* and *allness terms*) were clearly in the expected direction but not significantly so. One, *noun-verb/adjective-adverb ratio* was significant at the .05 level in the predicted direction.

Directive State Measures: Of the directive state measures, *DRQ, frequency of evaluative terms,* and *proportion of positive evaluative assertions* did not differ-

Stereotypy measures tend in the right direction, but only the *noun-verb/adjective-adverb ratio* significantly so; *mands* just miss significance at the .05 level; *proportion of ambivalent assertions* approaches significance in the expected direction, but the other *conflict measures* are either non-differential or significant in the wrong direction. Interestingly, the two disorganization measures, which were computed for this larger sample, approach (*structural disturbances*) or reach (*length of independent segments*) significance at the .05

TABLE 1. WORDS INCLUDED IN FIVE OR MORE OF THE GENUINE AND SIMULATED SUICIDE NOTES

Nouns		Verbs		Adjectives and Adverbs	
Genuine	Simulated	Genuine	Simulated	Genuine	Simulated
everything (9)	life (13)	love (19)	know (10)	good (15)	good (9)
way (out) (9)	way (11)	tell (13)	leave (9)	sorry (11)	sorry (8)
wife (9)	way (out) (8)	know (12)	think (9)	only (7)	happy (6)
love (8)	thing (8)	hope (11)	have (8)	dear (6)	all (5)
mother (8)	wife (7)	please (11)	please (8)	bad (5)	
thing (8)	all (8)	think (11)	love (7)		
God (6)	love (5)	do (10)	forgive (6)		
time(s) (6)	insurance (5)	get (9)	hope (5)		
darling (5)		say (9)	seem (5)		
dear (5)		take (9)	see (5)		
honey (5)		give (8)	tell (5)		
life (5)		want (8)			
one (5)		feel (7)			
person (5)		goodbye (7)			
something (5)		have (7)			
trouble (5)		make (7)			
way (5)		go (6)			
years(s) (5)		help (6)			
		see (6)			
		forgive (5)			
		try (5)			
		take care of (5)			

entiate (as expected), but *mands* did differentiate significantly at the .05 level.

Conflict Measures: Of the three conflict measures, one was not significant (*qualification of verb phrases*), one was significant at the .05 level, but in *the wrong direction* (*ambivalence constructions*) and one was barely significant in the predicted direction at the .10 level (*proportion of ambivalence assertions*).

If we enlarge our sample to 24 suicide and 18 faked notes by scoring all notes of sufficient length, regardless of their pairing, about the same results appear:

level and in the predicted direction.

Although gross measures of "what is talked about" like the DRQ and negative evaluative assertions may not differentiate genuine from pseudo suicide notes, we may ask if a more detailed content analysis might reveal differences. Accordingly, the frequency with which lexical words (nouns, verbs, adjectives, and adverbs) were used in the 33 genuine and facsimile suicide notes was analyzed. Since the sample of Ss was small, and hence liable to bias by discussion of a particular topic by a single S, subject-frequencies rather than word-frequencies per se were counted, i.e., the use of a given word by a given S was only counted once no matter how often he used it.

Table 1 gives the words included in five or more of the 33 suicide notes and in five or more of the simulated notes. Again, we note evidence for greater stereotopy in the suicide group; in every category, suicide notes display a greater sharing of common lexical items than do simulated notes. Some of the differences in choice of most frequently used lexical items are interesting: Suicide notes are more heavily loaded with terms of endearment (*darling, dear, honey*) and references to *mother*, whereas faked notes have more abstractions (*life, way, all*) and references to *insurance*. Whereas genuine suicide notes are replete with verbs referring to simple action (*tell, do, get, say, take, give*), faked suicide notes include relatively more verbs referring to mental states (*know, think, seem, see*). The genuine suicides have more stress on positive states (*love* 19 and *hope* 12 vs. 7 and 5 for the same words in pseudo notes), whereas the simulated notes have 9 references to *leave* vs. only 3 for suicides. To summarize this rough content comparison, genuine suicide notes reflect ambivalence toward loved ones through higher frequency of *positive evaluative terms* (cf., *ambivalent assertions* above) and they reflect greater *concreteness*.

Finally, a contingency analysis of some of the major content categories in suicide and pseudocide notes was made in an attempt to get at the association structures characteristic of the two groups. The content categories given in Table 2 were used. Before discussing the results of the contingency analysis, some of the differences in relative frequency of reference to these categories in the genuine and spurious suicide notes are worth noting: Suicide notes have relatively higher frequencies of reference to *self praise and defense, goodbyes* and *farewells, criticism of the spouse*, references to *parents, God and religion*,

TABLE 2. RELATIVE FREQUENCY OF CASES REFLECTING VARIOUS CONTENT CATEGORIES

Categories	Genuine	Simulated
Spouse praise, defense, love	.69	.42
Self criticism	.48	.39
I'm sorry; forgive me	.45	.36
Self praise, defense	.39	.06
Children	.36	.33
Goodbye, farewell, etc.	.30	.12
Feelings of confusion, being tired, etc.	.27	.42
Spouse criticism	.24	.03
"Way out"	.24	.39
Physical disabilities, symptoms	.21	.18
Parents	.21	.06
God and religion	.21	.06
Material possessions	.21	.00
Reference to suicidal pact	.18	.33
Money, bills, debts	.15	.06
Notify, tell someone	.15	.03
Isolation, loneliness	.15	.00
Insurance, etc.	.12	.21
Reference to suicide note	.12	.06
Instructions about own remains	.12	.03
Job	.09	.03
Love triangles (other man, woman)	.09	.06
"Fate," "Life," "World," etc.	.03	.33
Sex relations	.03	.00

and *material possessions;* simulated notes refer relatively more frequently to *feelings of confusion, being tired,* and the like, to the *suicidal act* itself, to *insurance,* and to abstractions like *Fate, Life,* and *The World.*

Expected and obtained contingencies among these categories (for genuine suicide and simulated notes separately) were obtained in the following way: Letting A and B represent two content categories, the *expected contingency* is p_{AB}, i.e., the probability of both A and B being present in notes of a given type, based on their separate rates of occurrence. The *obtained contingency* is simply the relative frequency of actual co-occurrence, i.e., the percentage of notes of a given type in which contents A and B are actually both present. The obtained contingency may be either greater than (association) or less than (dissociation) the expected or chance contingencies. Significances of deviations from chance expectancies are estimated in terms of the standard error of the expected percentage. Because of the crude nature of this analysis and the rather small N, significances at the .10 level or better were used as the basis for the following summary statements; they should be considered to be merely suggestive.

In the genuine suicide notes we find *criticism of the spouse* associated with references to *insurance, money, bills and debts,* and *requests to notify* someone of his death. As might be expected, *requests to notify* are associated with references to the *suicide note* itself and with *instructions about handling one's remains.* Expressions of feeling *isolated and lonesome* are associated with references to *money, bills and debts,* and to *love triangles.* References to the *parents* appear with statements about taking a *"way out"* and with references to *material possessions.* References to *own children* appear with *instructions about handling remains.* Again as would be expected, references to *money, bills and debts* co-occur with references to *material possessions.* Less obviously, references to *the job* are contingent upon references to the *suicide note* itself; *self praise* is contingent upon references to *insurance.*

In the simulated notes, references to *own children* are associated with references to *God and religion,* while references to *parents* are associated with stereotyped abstractions, *Fate, Life, the World.* When people write "make-believe" suicide notes, references to *the suicide act* itself tend to be accompanied by references to *God and religion,* and talking about a *"way out"* appears with comments about *money, bills and debts.* Expressions of *sorrow, regret, and asking for forgiveness* appear with saying *goodbye* and *farewell* in these faked notes. There are also two significant dissociations (co-occurrence *less* than chance at the .10 level)—faked notes that speak of *physical disabilities* do not express *feelings of confusion and being tired,* and the notes which refer to *insurance* do not include expressions of *sorrow, regret, and asking for forgiveness.*

In viewing the total evidence on as-sociation structures, one gets the following general impression: When geople produce fake suicide notes "on demand," they generally embroider a few standard themes available in our folklore—taking a "way out" of financial and other problems, asking forgiveness and saying "farewell," pondering on the moral and religious implications of taking one's own life, and so on. The patterns of association in genuine suicide notes suggest more mundane connections—for example, criticism of the spouse being connected in the suicidal person's mind with his financial problems, with being insured and the like, or references to being insured being coupled with self-praise.

DISCUSSION

Of the four general predictions about the effects of heightened motivation upon encoding, three are borne out clearly in the comparison of suicide notes with ordinary letters to friends and relatives. Suicide notes display greater *stereotypy*— the writer of a suicide note tends to use shorter, simpler words, his vocabulary is less diversified, he is more repetitious, he uses more simple action expressions (nouns and verbs) and fewer discriminative qualifiers (adjectives and adverbs), and his messages are more easily filled in (*cloze* procedure) by others. He also uses more polarized "allness" terms. The effects of the suicidal *directive state* are also clearly evident—in higher distress-relief quotients, in the greater frequency of evaluative terms, and in the smaller proportion of evaluative assertions that are positive in direction. Suicide notes also display the demanding, commanding, pleading nature of this state by higher frequency of *mands.* Suicide notes yield evidence of greater *conflict* of motives—by greater qualification of verb phrases, more ambivalence constructions, and a larger percentage of evaluative asserations about Ego and significant others that are ambivalent in sign. Most of these differences were significant at the .01 level.

and they substantiate our general hypotheses about the effects of heightened drive level upon language encoding.

One major prediction was not borne out: there was no evidence for greater *disorganization* of encoding behavior in suicide notes as compared with ordinary letters to friends and relatives. We conclude that the suicide state, at least at the time a note is penned, does not represent a sufficiently high degree of motivation to cause disruption of language skills, but the negative result could also indicate that our measures of disorganization were inadequate or that the hypothesis was wrong. The failure of the time orientation measure to yield any differences may also mean that our notions were wrong. It is also possible that this measure was confounded with that for *mands;* mands usually have future reference and are significantly more frequent for suicide notes.

The comparison of genuine suicide notes with simulated suicide notes, matched for age, education, and general social status, can be considered, on the one hand, a more stringent test of the hypotheses or, on the other hand, an indication of the degree to which a nonsuicidal person can intuit and adopt the encoding content and style of the suicidal person. From the former point of view, we would have to conclude that most of our measures fail to distinguish significantly between the genuine and pseudo notes (excepting the *noun-verb/adjective-adverb ratio, mands, length of independent segments,* and perhaps the *proportion of ambivalent assertions*). Nevertheless, the quantitative indices that differentiated suicide from ordinary letters, and which might be expected to differentiate genuine from faked notes, did so for 10 out of the 13 matched pairs to which they could be applied.

How well can nonsuicidal writers adopt the encoding content and style of the suicide state? First, nonsuicidal people can obviously intuit the superficial *content* of suicide notes—the distress-expression, the

use of evaluative terms, and the decrease in positive evaluative assertions. Less superficially, however, we note interesting differences in the words used (more positively toned terms, expressing the ambivalence of the true suicidal state, and more concrete terms generally) and in the contingencies among content categories (less stereotyped, "story-book" associations in the true suicide cases). Second, although the over-all reduction in significance of differences, as compared with the suicide vs. control analysis, shows that the *style* of the suicidal person can be adopted to some degree by a person merely instructed to write such a note, there are certain exceptions. The person faking a suicide note fails to reflect the demanding, commanding, pleading style (*mands*), the reduced qualification (*noun-verb/adjective-adverb ratio*), and the evaluative ambivalence toward self and others of the genuine suicide notes.

One criticism that could be leveled at this study is that other determinants than motivation might be responsible for the results. It is known that many of the indices used here as tests of motivational effects can be affected by other source characteristics as well. For example, stereotypy measures like length of words and TTR are influenced by the education and IQ level of the source. Our control sample of ordinary letters to friends and relatives could be matched with the suicide notes in terms of sex and age, but that was all. Could the differences we found be accounted for simply on the basis that our suicide note writers were less intelligent and/or less well educated? If we explain the differences in stereotypy in this way, we are unable to explain why the same notes showed no differences in structural disturbances (ordinary English composition, for the most part) and, in fact, for males showed *longer* integrated sentence segments. Furthermore, this would not explain the directive-state differences (e.g., in *mands*). Also, in the genuine-pseudo comparison, where these factors were controlled by matching, differences for the most part were in the same direction, although not as large.

SUMMARY

Theoretical analysis of the effects of of motivation level upon language encoding led to several hypotheses. Messages produced under heightened drive level should (a) be more stereotyped, (b) be more disorganized, if the motivation level is extremely high, (c) reflect the specific nature of the motives operating, and (d) reflect conflict of responses if two or more competing motives are operating. These hypotheses were tested by (a) a comparison of suicide notes with ordinary letters to friends and relatives and (b) a comparison of genuine suicide notes with stimulated suicide notes, written by nonsuicidal people. In the first comparison, all of the hypotheses were clearly borne out except that concerning disorganization of encoding skills. In the second comparison, differences were smaller, only certain measures, the noun-verb/ adjective-adverb ratio, Skinner's mands, length of sentence segments, and proportion of ambivalent evaluative assertions still discriminating significantly. Implications of these results for psycholinguistic theory and for stylistics are considered in the discussion, along with certain criticisms that could be made of the study.

REFERENCES

1. Boder, D. P. The adjective-verb quotient. A contribution to the psychology of language. *Psychol. Rev.,* 1940, *3,* 309–343.

2. Dollard, J., and Mowrer, O. H. A method of measuring tension in written documents. *J. abnorm. soc. Psychol.,* 1947, *42,* 3–32.

3. Hebb, D. O. Drives and the C. N. S. (conceptual nervous system). *Psychol. Rev.,* 1955, *62,* 243–254.

4. Johnson, W., Fairbanks, Helen, Mann, Mary Bachman, and Chotlos, J. W. Studies in language behavior. *Psychol. Monogr,.* 1944, *56,* No. 2 (Whole No. 255).

5. Mainland, D., and Murray, I. M. Tables for use in fourfold contingency tests. *Science,* 1952, *116,* 591–594.

6. Osgood, C. E. *Motivational dynamics of language behavior.* In M. R. Jones (Ed.), *Nebraska symposium on motivation.* Lincoln: Univer. Nebraska Press, 1957.

7. Osgood, C. E., Saporta, S., and Nunally, J. C. Evaluative assertion analysis. *Litera,* 1956, *3,* 47–102.

8. Pool, I. (Ed.) *Contemporary trends in content analysis.* Urbana: Univer. Illinois Press, in press.

9. Skinner, B. F. *Verbal behavior.* New York: Appleton-Century-Crofts, 1957.

10. Spence, K. W., Farber, I. E., and McFann, H. H. The relation of anxiety (drive) level to performance in competitional and noncompetitional paired-associates learning. *J. exp. Psychol.,* 1956, *52,* 296–305.

11. Taylor, W. L. Recent developments in the use of "Cloze Procedure." *Journalism Quart.,* 1956, *33,* No. 1.

12. Zipf, G. K. *Human behavior and the principle of least effort.* Cambridge, Mass.: Addison-Wesley, 1949.

The Family Background and Early Life Experience of the Manic-Depressive Patient

A Comparison with the Schizophrenic Patient

ROBERT W. GIBSON

THE CURRENT STUDY is a continuation of work done by a research group composed of Frieda Fromm-Reichmann, Mabel Blake Cohen, Robert A. Cohen, Grace Baker, and Edith V. Weigert (4). The previous study indicated that the early interpersonal experiences of a group of twelve manic-depressive patients showed certain common features. These features will be discussed below in greater detail, but, in brief, they were such as to cause the adult manic-depressive patient to see relationships as all-or-none propositions and to lack the ability to deal with interpersonal subtleties. It was felt by the research group that these findings should have further validation by the investigation of a greater number of patients and the use of a control group.

This study was designed to replicate the original study using a briefer and therefore a more readily available technique. A control group of schizophrenic patients was studied by this same technique, so that the findings from the two groups of patients could be tested against each other. Thus the primary purpose was to test the ability of the concepts of the research group to differentiate between manic-depressive and schizophrenic patients. The secondary purpose was to attempt further the clarification and elaboration of the picture of the family patterns and early life history of the manic-depressive patient.

REVIEW OF THE WORK OF THE ORIGINAL RESEARCH GROUP

To provide some background, those parts of the work of the research group which pertain to the family background and early life experience of the manic-depressive patient will be reviewed in some detail (1).

Family Background

The families of manic-depressive patients were found to have been set apart in some way from their environment. In

Reprinted by permission from *Psychiatry*, Vol. 21, No. 1, February 1958.

some cases this was because they were members of a minority group; in others it was because of financial reverses; in still others it was because of some aberrant behavior by a member of the family group.

The families had attempted to counteract this situation in two major ways. First, they had placed a high premium on conforming to the expectations of the community. Second, they had made a prodigious effort to raise the economic level of the family. This led to a situation in which the status of the family was of primary importance, while each member was important only in terms of the contribution he could make to the family.

Children in these families were used as instruments for achieving prestige. Considerable attention and interest might be focused upon the child, but mainly in terms of his role as the carrier of prestige for the family. Thus, there was a devaluation of the child's importance as a person in his own right. It was commonly noted that the manic-depressive patient had borne the brunt of this situation by being the chief carrier of prestige.

The need for winning prestige was frequently inculcated by the mother, who in most cases was the dominant parent, and was looked upon as strong and reliable.

She commonly blamed the father for the family's ill fortune. The child usually thought of the mother as the moral authority in the family, and his attitude toward her was usually cold and unloving, but fearful and desirous of approval.

By contrast, the fathers were thought of as weak but lovable. They were thought of as failures because of their inability to achieve the degree of success they *should* have achieved. Sometimes they engaged in futile rebellious gestures, but on the whole they accepted the blame and thus conveyed to their children the attitude, "Don't be like me."

Thus, the child faced the dilemma of finding one parent lovable but weak and unreliable, and the other strong and reliable but unlovable. In addition, the attitude of the mother toward the father served as a dramatic example of what might happen to the child should he fail to achieve the high goal set by the mother.

Early Development

It is postulated that the major anxiety-provoking experiences of the manic-depressive occur at a later perior than do those of the schizophrenic. This hypothesis is based on the concept that the capacity for object relations goes through three successive stages: (1) At and soon after birth other persons—chiefly the mother—are hardly recognized as such and although interpersonal closeness is great, it is based upon the intense dependency of the infant upon his mother. (2) As relationships develop, the primary closeness based upon identification diminishes. (3) Later a more mature closeness begins to develop in which the self is at last perceived as distinct and separate from other persons.

It is believed that the major unresolved anxiety-provoking experiences of the schizophrenic occur in this first phase of personality development when closeness is based upon identification and relationships are partial in character. In the manic-depressive these experiences occur in the second phase, when identification is less frequently used and the ability to relate to others as persons distinct from oneself is in the earliest stage of development. Consequently, although relationships in the second phase are more mature than in the first, the person in another sense is in a more isolated position, since he no longer employs the mechanism of identification to the degree that he did in earlier infancy, but has yet to develop the capacity for a higher level of interpersonal relatedness. At this time, therefore, the developing child could be expected to feel peculiarly alone and consequently vulnerable to any threat of abandonment.

The impression is that the mothers of manic-depressive patients experience the utter dependency of the infant as pleasurable, but that the growing independence and rebelliousness of the early stage of childhood are threatening to her. Thus the loving, tender mother abruptly changes into a harsh and punishing figure at about the end of the first year. This leads to a difficulty in integrating the good and the bad mother that remains with the manic-depressive for life unless interrupted by treatment or life experience. Thus, for these patients, there is a tendency to look upon an important authority as the source of all good things provided he is pleased, but as a tyrannical, punishing figure if he is not pleased.

Later Development

The manic-depressive patient is frequently the best endowed member of the family. He often occupies a special position in the family as a result of his own striving, or because of some fortuitous circumstance such as being the eldest child or an only son. This leads him to guard his special position enviously and subjects him to the envy of the other siblings and the parents. By and large neither the patient nor the parents are aware of the envy. As has already been indicated, the manic-depressive patient is raised in a prestige-conscious family where the emphasis has been to cling together in the face of an adverse world, providing a background in which neither the active nor passive participants are aware of the development of envy. A great deal of energy is devoted to counter-acting such feelings; for instance, the patient frequently attempts to deny his full capabilities through underselling himself. This is often seen in the patient's excessive concern for the siblings and apparent sacrifice of his own ambitions to help his siblings.

Often the child is brought up not only by his parents but also by other important members of the clan. Despite this, there is rarely any one person in whom he can have confidence. He is frequently burdened by the family's expectation that he will do better than the parents in the service of raising the family's prestige. His accomplishments are not recognized in their own right but only in terms of their value to the family. The lack of close interpersonal relatedness often leaves the patient quite isolated and lonely, although such feelings are often not in awareness because of the family emphasis on the feeling that the members "belong together."

Adult Character

During the 'healthy' intervals between attacks adult persons with cyclothymic personalities appear to be superficially well adjusted and at ease. They show a certain social facility and have many acquaintances with whom they seem to be on cordial terms. Actually, there is little communicative exchange in these relationships because the hypomanic is carrying out a social performance that takes little or no account of the other person's traits and characteristics. Both hypomanic and depressed patients have one or a few extremely dependent relationships. This is obvious in the depressed patient but may be concealed in the hypomanic by his apparent aggressiveness. Demands are made for love, but the concept of reciprocity is missing. The failure to recognize the needs of the other does cause unconscious guilt, which the manic-depressive deals with by

devaluing and underselling himself. This failure to use his full potentialities serves to counteract the old unconscious fears of envy and competition and may reach a point where creative abilities are paralyzed. His inner feeling is one of emptiness and need, with the principal anxiety being the fear of abandonment.

This character structure can be seen to have a clear-cut relationship to the infantile development which we have hypothesized for the manic-depressive. According to this hypothesis, interpersonal relations have been arrested in their development at the point where the child recognizes himself as being separate from others, but does not yet see others as being full-sized human beings: rather he sees them as entities who are now good, now bad, and must be manipulated. If this is the case, then the adult's poorness of discrimination about others is understandable. His life and welfare depend upon the other's goodness, as he sees it, and he is unable to recognize that one and the same person may be accepting today, rejecting tomorrow, and then accepting again on the following day. Nor can he recognize that certain aspects of his behavior may be acceptable while others are not; instead, he sees relationships as all-or-none propositions. The lack of interest in and ability to deal with interpersonal subtleties is probably also due to the fact that the important persons in the child's environment themselves deal in conventional stereotypes. The child, therefore, has little opportunity at home to acquire skill in this form of communication (1).

The Psychotic Attack

It is well known that the depressive attack may be precipitated by a loss, but many cases have occurred in which there has been no apparent loss. In this latter group the loss has occurred in the patient's appraisal of the situation; for example, a promotion may mean the loss of a relatively stable dependency relationship with a superior.

After each attack the depressive patient tries to recapture this dependency relationship. When the object does not fulfill his need a vicious circle is set in motion: he uses depressive techniques such as whining or complaining; these become offensive to the other person, who becomes less gratifying; the patient redoubles his efforts and receives less. Finally, he loses hope and then there is a psychotic attack.

The manic attack occurs in a similar way and is seen as a defense against the more intolerable discomfort of the guilt feelings in the depression. Thus, manic attacks are to be differentiated psychodynamically from depressive attacks only on the basis of what makes the manic defense available to some and not to others. The basic psychotic pattern is the depressive one, and it is only an exaggeration of the type of appeal the manic-depressive makes to important figures during 'healthy' intervals.

REVIEW OF THE LITERATURE

The current study is concerned primarily with the early life experience of the manic-depressive patient, and a review of the literature will be limited to the few reports that deal explicitly with this aspect.

From 1928 to 1930 Pollock and others made an intensive study of the family backgrounds of 155 manic-depressive and 175 dementia-praecox patients (6, 7, 8). In their studies of the families of manic-depressive patients they found that as a group these families were in better economic condition than the over-all hospital population, with only one family being classified as dependent, 99 as marginal, and 55 as comfortable. The social life of the parents was restricted, but this was not a striking finding. Both parents had been in the home during the developmental years of 129 of the 155 patients. In 20 cases the household included other adults besides the parents, or in place of the parents. Family dissension was noted in 43 of the 155 cases. In the cases for which information was available, 131 fathers and 139 mothers were considered affectionate, while 14 fathers and 6 mothers were antagonistic. For the 132 patients having siblings, the relationships were harmonious in 129 cases. A detailed study was made of the order of birth for both the female and male patients with the conclusion that there was no sig-

nificant deviation from the expected findings.

Witmer and others studied the family backgrounds of 40 manic-depressive and 68 dementia-praecox patients (9). These patients had all been hospitalized, and the diagnoses were agreed upon by the hospital's staff. Interviews were conducted with several informants in all cases. The study was primarily focused on: (1) the emotional tone of the family; (2) the behavior of the parents toward the children; (3) the overt relationships of the patients to their parents. Findings of general interest arising from this study were that the homes of one third to two thirds of the patients were close-knit and harmonious for both groups. One quarter of the homes in both groups had outstanding friction. Overprotection was extreme and common especially for the manic-depressive patients. In one third of the cases of both groups the mother was dominant and the father weak.

In the discussion of a paper by English, Fromm-Reichmann made some observations regarding the biographical data of manic-depressive patients. She noticed that it was common in these families to have multiple parental figures share responsibilities for guidance of the infant and child. Despite this, there was little interest in the child in his own right, but only as he served the needs of the family. Frequently these families were in some way isolated from the community. In some cases the patient, even in childhood, was held responsible for any calamities that befell the family.[1]

These observations by Fromm-Reichmann are quoted in two papers by Wilson reporting on an extensive study of 12 manic-depressive patients and a review of the case records of 75 more (3.) He did not find the presence of the mixed dominance described by Fromm-Reichmann nor did he find any evidence that

---

[1] These findings were greatly expanded and to some degree modified in her later work, (1, 4). See also (2, 5).

those who became ill felt guilty because of injury to the family code.

It was found that families containing those with manic-depressive psychoses felt more pressure to conform to the attitude of the parents and had less freedom than those families without the disease. . . . They were found to have a tendency to remain in the same location, to maintain the same culture pattern which had become traditional. There was evidence of a strong focus of dominance and an obvious family motive to which the members had to conform. The results were conformity, manic-depressive psychosis, alcoholism, or flight (3).

METHOD

Research Design

The family patterns and early life experiences of three groups of patients were compared by means of a questionnaire, especially designed to represent the concepts of the research group, to determine whether manic-depressive and schizophrenic patients can be differentiated on the basis of these concepts. These three groups were the original manic-depressive study group, or criterion group; a group of manic-depressive patients from St. Elizabeths Hospital; and a group of schizophrenic patients from St. Elizabeths Hospital.

Description of the Sample

The group of manic-depressive patients was selected by studying the records of the 120 patients diagnosed as manic-depressive and admitted to St. Elizabeths in 1953 and 1954. The only requirements for inclusion within the final study group were an unequivocal diagnosis of manic-depressive psychosis and the availability of reliable informants to supplement the history in the charts. Forty patients were eliminated on the basis of diagnosis, with the most common reasons being atypical symptomatology and complicating organic or toxic factors. Fifty-three more were eliminated because reliable informants were not available.

The final group of manic-depressive patients totaled 27; 13 were male, and 14 were female. Twenty-three were white and 4 were Negro. Twelve had had manic attacks only, 2 depressions only, and 13 both manic attacks and depressions. Tests were made to see if any differences between patients on the questionnaire could be attributed to sex, race, or the diagnostic subtypes—manic, depressed, or mixed. Since no such differences were found, it was concluded that the manic-depressive group could be considered as homogeneous.

The schizophrenic patients were selected by studying charts of patients admitted within the same approximate time span. The requirements for inclusion within this group were an unequivocal diagnosis of catatonic schizophrenia or paranoid schizophrenia and the availability of reliable informants.

The final group of schizophrenic patients studied totaled 17; there were 9 males and 8 females. There were 10 whites and 7 Negroes. Ten were diagnosed as paranoid and 7 as catatonic. Tests were made to see if any differences between the patients on the questionnaire could be attributed to sex, race, or the paranoid and catatonic diagnostic subtypes. Since no such differences could be found, it was concluded that the schizophrenic group could be considered as homogeneous.

In the original research design it was planned to match the manic-depressive and schizophrenic groups for sex and race. However, this was done only approximately because, as already indicated, no differences were found within the groups on the basis of sex or race.

The mean age of the MD St. Elizabeths Group was 49, while the mean age of the Schizophrenic St. Elizabeths Group was 35. A difference in age at the time of the study would not, of course, alter the family pattern in early life experience of the patients, but it might possibly influence the reports of the informants, since the older patients would have had a longer time to forget. This was not considered to be a valid objection to the difference in mean age, because the manic-depressive patients were older, and therefore any tendency on the part of the informants to forget would diminish rather than increase the frequency of findings in accord with the concepts of the research group.

Measurement of the Research Variables

A questionnaire was designed so that the information collected on each patient could be evaluated in a uniform way. It was designed by collecting all the findings of the research group and stating them in the form of 16 questions, referred to as items, that were grouped under 5 major categories, referred to as scales. The questions of each item are so stated that a high rating would indicate the closest possible conformity to the pattern described by the research group, and a low rating would indicate the greatest possible deviation from this pattern. This questionnaire was discussed with several members of the original research group, and they were in agreement that it represented an accurate statement of their findings. The questionnaire itself is reproduced below:

QUESTIONNAIRE FOR MANIC-DEPRESSIVE
RESEARCH PROJECT

Please circle appropriate answer under each category which most closely describes the situation from the patient's birth to the age of 18:

(I) *Relation to Community*
   (A) The incidence of factors that would tend to interfere with acceptance of the family (especially as relates to the children) in the community was:
      High
      Moderate
      Low
   (B) Efforts to raise or maintain social prestige were:
      High
      Moderate
      Low
   (C) The family's aspirations for the patient to raise the prestige of the family were:
      High
      Moderate
      Low

(II) *Envy*
   (A) The incidence of envy and competitiveness in the family was:
      High
      Moderate
      Low
   (B) The degree of envy to which the patient was subjected was:
      High
      Moderate
      Low
   (C) The patient's tendency to be self-defeating or failing to utilize the full extent of his qualifications was:
      High
      Moderate
      Low

(III) *Role of Parents*
   (A) The difference between the parents in terms of reliability and forcefulness was (note which parent more reliable):
      High
      Moderate
      Low
   (B) The difference between the parents in terms of warmth and affection was (note which parent more affectionate):
      High
      Moderate
      Low
   (C) The degree to which the child was "used" by the parents in their conflict was:
      High
      Moderate
      Low

(IV) *Authority in the Home*
   (A) The amount of dissension in the family was:
      High
      Moderate
      Low
   (B) The incidence of inconsistent discipline in the family was:
      High
      Moderate
      Low
   (C) The incidence of inconsistent indulgence in the family was:
      High
      Moderate
      Low
   (D) Multiple parental figures were, were not, present in the home.

(V) *Conventionality*
  (A) The degree to which the family adhered to generally accepted conventional values was:
      High
      Moderate
      Low
  (B) The degree to which conventional values were impressed on the child was:
      High
      Moderate
      Low
  (C) The parents' concern about social approval by other groups (what "they" think) was:
      High
      Moderate
      Low

The questionnaire included 16 items; however, Item IV-D, "Multiple parental figures were, were not, present in the home," was considered separately, and therefore in the actual analyses of the questionnaires there were just 15 items that were classified into 5 scales. Each of these scales was composed of 3 items, so designed that the responses to them could be rated on a 3-point scale as high, moderate, or low. In making statistical comparisons a rating of high was given a score of 3; a rating of moderate was given a score of 2; and a rating of low was given a score of 1. Thus, it can be seen that the possible range in scoring for each scale would be from 3 to 9 and the possible range of scoring for the questionnaire as a whole would be from 15 to 45. In all instances where comparisons were made of the questionnaire this scoring system was used. Certain of the data did not lend themselves to questionnaire technique and were analyzed in a different fashion, which will be described in each case.

Using the questionnaire, ratings on 11 of the 12 patients in the original manic-depressive study group were obtained from the therapist who had treated the patients. In one case it was not possible to obtain a rating from the therapist, but extensive clinical records were available on this patient, permitting the author to make a rating.

Ratings on the two St. Elizabeths groups were obtained in the following manner. Each informant was interviewed by a trained social worker who then wrote up each interview in detail and rated it. The written report was then submitted to the author, who made an independent rating. The social worker and the author then discussed the interview with special reference to any differences in rating. With experience the disagreements decreased and those that did occur generally resulted from different interpretations of the written reports and were not the results of any basic disagreement in the assessment of the patient's history. When all the interviews on a given patient were completed and evaluated they were considered as a whole, and an over-all evaluation was made by the social worker and the author. This final rating was the one used in the various statistical comparisons.

In an effort to minimize bias in the collection of data, a number of precautions were taken. The social workers were instructed to focus on certain areas in conducting their interviews, but were given no direct information regarding the expected findings. Thus they were not influenced by preconceived opinions about the patients under study. However, as the study proceeded and differences between the groups were noted, they did develop a partial picture of the findings. Some of the interviews by the social workers were recorded. In this way it was possible to compare the written report with recordings of the interviews, to be certain of the adequacy of the interviewing technique. Every interview was discussed by the social worker with the author as soon after its completion as possible. In this way it was possible to amplify the written reports and pick out those areas requiring additional study by further interviews.

Reliability of Measurement

The use of the questionnaire raises two crucial questions. First, can the original raters—the social worker and the author—repeat the ratings? In other words, how stable are the ratings on the questionnaire? Second, can another person be trained to rate clinical material using this questionnaire?

To answer these questions four cases were selected for re-rating more than a year after the original rating by the social worker and the author. Without referring to the original ratings, the social worker, the author, and a psychiatrist from St. Elizabeths Hospital read and discussed the clinical material on these cases. The psychiatrist was familiar in a general way with the study but had not participated in the collection of the clinical material and had not attempted to rate it before. Independent ratings were then made on each of the four cases by the three raters.

The technique of comparison was that of determining the number of instances in which the pair of ratings being compared were: (1) in complete agreement—that is, 0 discrepancy between ratings; (2) in partial agreement—a discrepancy of 1 between ratings; or (3) in disagreement—a discrepancy of 2 between ratings. Since the ratings on four patients for each of the 15 items were analyzed, the total of possible agreements for any pair of ratings was 60.

The over-all agreement between the joint ratings and each rater's independent rating of the four patients is sufficiently high to warrant the acceptance of the combined ratings made by the author and social worker as adequate, stable judgments for the purposes of this study. The inter-rater agreement between the three independent ratings of the four patients is sufficiently high to warrant the conclusion that the technique of rating can be communicated to people outside of the research group.

The frequency of partial agreement and the frequency of disagreement between ratings on each scale were computed. This showed that the highest frequency of disagreement occurred on Scale IV, Authority in the Home, while the lowest frequency of disagreement occurred in Scale V, Conventionality. This finding suggests that Scale IV may need some revision or more explicit definition.

PRESENTATION OF FINDINGS
Analyses of the Questionnaire

The primary purpose of this study was to test the ability of the concepts of the research-group study to differentiate between manic-depressive and schizophrenic patients. To determine this, mean-scale ratings and mean-item ratings were computed from the questionnaires for the 3 groups of patients, the Criterion Manic-Depressive Group, the St. Elizabeths Manic-Depressive Group, and the St. Elizabeths Schizophrenic Group. The results of these tabulations are presented in Table 1 and Figure 1.

Having tabulated the mean-scale ratings and the mean-item ratings for each, an analysis-of-variance technique was employed to test the variance due to differences among the three groups of patients. It was found that the three groups of patients could be differentiated on the basis of scale and item ratings; therefore, more detailed statistical analyses were carried out.

Comparison of the Manic-Depressive Criterion Group and the St. Elizabeths Schizophrenic Group.—The conclusions of the original study regarding the characteristics of manic-depressive patients were based on detailed analyses of 12 manic-depressive patients; however, no systematic comparison with a control group was made. Although it is not possible to determine the comparability of the Schizophrenic St. Elizabeths Group with the schizophrenic sample the research group had used, it is reasonable to utilize the latter as a control. This comparison is undertaken to determine the differences between the two groups of patients without assuming any a priori hypothesis. Therefore, it is necessary to consider chance sampling deviations in both directions, and a two-tailed test of significance is appropriate.

A total of 13 out of the 15 items show higher scores for the Manic-Depressive Criterion Group than the St. Elizabeths

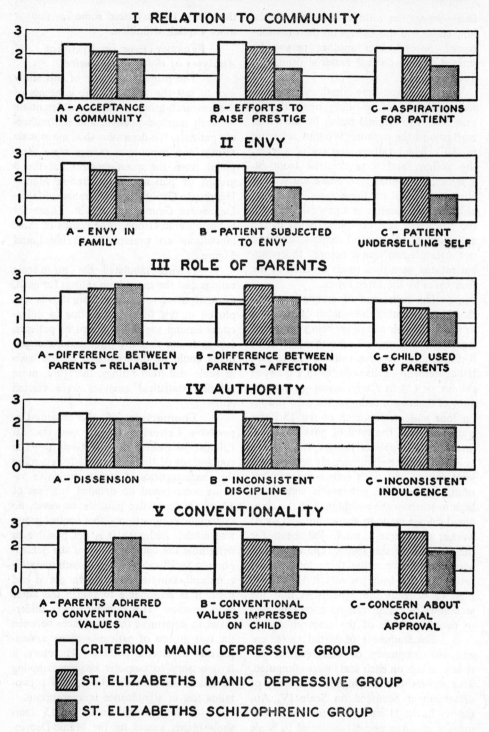

Figure 1. Comparison if item scores from Table 1A.

Schizophrenic Group; see Tables 2 and 3. However, only 7 of these item differences —all higher—reach an acceptable level of statistical significance. It is to be noted that only items under Scale I, Relation to the Community, Scale II, Envy, and Scale V, Conventionality, can distinguish between the two groups.

On Scale I, Item B, Efforts to Raise Prestige, and Item C, Aspirations for Patient, reach statistical significance. On Scale II, the differences between groups reach an acceptable level of statistical significance on all three items. None of the items under Scale III or Scale IV reach an acceptable level of significance. On Scale V, Item B, Conventional Values Impressed on Child, and Item C, Concern about Social Approval, showed significant differences between the two groups.

The over-all effect of the three items of Scale I differentiates the two groups of patients at better than the .001 level of confidence. The over-all effect of the three items of Scale II differentiates the two groups of patients at better than the .001 level of confidence. The over-all effect of the three items of Scale V differentiates the two groups of patients at better than the .001 level of confidence.

Comparison of the St. Elizabeths Manic-Depressive Group with the St. Elizabeths Schizophrenic Group. —The comparison between the Criterion Manic-Depressive Group and the Schizophrenic St. Elizabeths Group demonstrates that the research group's concepts do differentiate between the two groups of patients. It also indicates the direction of these differences, and therefore a one-tailed test of significance may be used in the comparison between the St. Elizabeths Manic-Depressive Group and the St. Elizabeths Schizophrenic Group. This comparison was undertaken as a further test of the hypothesis that the findings of the original study, as represented by the questionnaire, can differentiate between manic-depressive and schizophrenic patients.

A total of 12 out of the 15 items

show differences in favor of the hypothesized differences between the St. Elizabeths Manic-Depressive Group and the St. Elizabeths Schizophrenic Group; see Tables 2 and 3. However, only 6 of these item differences reach an acceptable level of statistical significance.

It is to be noted that just as in the comparison between the Manic-Depressive Criterion Group and the St. Elizabeths Schizophrenic Group, only items under Scale I, Relation to the Community, Scale II, Envy, and Scale V, Conventionality, revealed significant differences between the groups being compared. The items that reached an acceptable level of significance in differentiating between the two groups were the following; I-B, I-C, II-A, II-B, II-C, and V-C.

The over-all effect of the three items of Scale I differentiates the St. Elizabeths Manic-Depressive Group and the St. Elizabeths Schizophrenic Group at better than the .001 level of confidence. The over-all effect of the three items of Scale II differentiates the two groups at better than the .001 level of confidence. The over-all effect of the three items of Scale V does not differentiate between the groups, because of the fact that Item A, Parents Adhere to Conventional Values, and Item B, Conventional Values Impressed on Child, tend to obscure the differentiating power of Item C, Concern about Social Approval.

Comparison of the Manic-Depressive Criterion Group and the St. Elizabeths Manic-Depressive Group.— The purpose of this comparison is to determine whether findings comparable to those of the research group would be found when a different group of manic-depressive patients was investigated.

The Manic-Depressive Criterion Group scores exceeded those of the St. Elizabeths Manic-Depressive Group on 12 of the 15 items, but only 1 of these item differences reaches an acceptable level of statistical significance; see Table 1 and 1-A.

Differences between the two groups on Scale V, Item B, Conventional Values

TABLE 1. MEAN SCALE RATINGS FOR THREE SAMPLES

	I Relation to community	II Envy	III Role of parents	IV Authority	V Conventionality
Criterion Manic-Depressive n = 12	7.25*	7.08	6.08	7.17	8.50
St. Elizabeths Manic-Depressive n = 27	6.44	6.48	6.22	5.93	7.07
St. Elizabeths Schizophrenic n = 17	4.82	4.71	5.88	5.71	6.12

* Possible range for each scale is 3.00 to 9.00.

1-A. MEAN ITEM RATINGS FOR EACH SAMPLE

	I			II			III			IV			V		
	A	B	C	A	B	C	A	B	C	A	B	C	A	B	C
Criterion Manic-Depressive n = 12	2.50**	2.50	2.25	2.58	2.50	2.00	2.25	1.83	2.00	2.42	2.42	2.33	2.67	2.83	3.00
St. Elizabeths Manic-Depressive n = 27	2.11	2.33	2.00	2.41	2.07	2.00	2.33	2.26	1.63	2.07	2.07	1.78	2.22	2.30	2.56
St. Elizabeths Schizophrenic n = 17	1.88	1.41	1.53	1.94	1.53	1.24	2.35	2.12	1.41	2.06	1.82	1.82	2.29	2.00	1.82

** Possible range for each item is 1.00 to 3.00.

Impressed on Child, just reach the level of statistical significance. None of the other scales or items reaches an acceptable level of statistical significance.

The over-all effect of the three items of Scale V differentiates the Manic-Depressive Criterion Group and the Manic-

of the Parents, and Scale IV, Authority, led to a further study of these areas.

The mean-item ratings for Item III-A, Differences between Parents in Terms of Reliability, and Item III-B, Difference between Parents in Terms of Warmth and Affection, reflect the degree of difference

TABLE 2. MEAN DIFFERENCES BETWEEN SCALE SCORES

Scale	Criterion manic-depressives minus St. E. schizophrenics			St. E. manic-depressives minus St. E. schizophrenics			Criterion manic-depressives minus St. E. manic-depressives		
	Mean difference	t	p	Mean difference	t	p	Mean difference	t	p
I	2.43	3.47	<.001	1.62	3.31	<.001	.81	—	NS
II	2.37	3.34	<.001	1.77	3.05	.001	.60	—	NS
III	.20	—	NS	.34	—	NS	—.14	—	NS
IV	1.46	1.78	NS	.22	—	NS	1.24	—	NS
V	2.38	3.50	<.001	.95	1.38	NS	1.43	2.10	<.05

TABLE 3. MEAN DIFFERENCES BETWEEN ITEM SCORES OF THE THREE SAMPLES

Item	Criterion manic-depressives minus St. E. schizophrenics			St. E. manic-depressives minus St. E. schizophrenics			Criterion manic-depressives minus St. E. manic-depressives		
	Mean difference	t	p	Mean difference	t	p	Mean difference	t	p
I-A	.62	1.88	NS	.23	.85	NS	.39	—	NS
B	1.09	4.19	<.001	.92	4.18	<.001	.17	—	NS
C	.72	2.18	<.05	.47	1.88	.03	.25	—	NS
II-A	.64	2.06	.05	.47	1.88	.03	.17	—	NS
B	.97	3.23	<.001	.54	2.25	.01	.43	—	NS
C	.76	2.53	.05	.76	3.30	<.001	—	—	NS
III-A	—.10	—	NS	—.02	—	NS	—.08	—	NS
B	—.29	—	NS	.14	—	NS	—.43	—	NS
C	.59	1.84	NS	.21	—	NS	.37	—	NS
IV-A	.36	1.16	NS	.01	—	NS	.35	—	NS
B	.60	1.76	NS	.25	—	NS	.35	—	NS
C	.51	1.59	NS	—.04	—	NS	.55	—	NS
V-A	.38	1.31	NS	—.07	—	NS	.45	—	NS
B	.83	3.07	.01	.30	1.15	NS	.53	2.12	<.05
C	1.18	5.13	<.001	.74	3.08	.001	.44	2.00	NS

Depressive St. Elizabeths Group at only the .05 level of confidence.

Additional Findings

The failure of the questionnaire to differentiate between the two groups of manic-depressive patients and the group of schizophrenic patients on Scale III, Role

between the parents as well as the frequency that such differences were found. Further analysis of the three groups of patients was made for Item III-A to determine simply how often the mother was considered to be more reliable, the father was considered to be more reliable, or there was no difference in reliability between the parents. A similar analysis for Item III-B was made to determine how often the mother was considered to be warmer, the father was considered to be warmer, or there was no difference in warmth between the parents. A further analysis was made to see how often it occurred in a given case both that the mother was more reliable and the father warmer. Table 4 shows these findings in terms of percentage figures for the three groups of patients studied.

It will be noted from Table 4 that in all instances the St. Elizabeths Manic-Depressive Group approaches the concepts of the original study to a higher degree than did the Criterion Manic-Depressive Group. In most instances the St. Elizabeths Schizophrenic Group approaches the con-

TABLE 4. RESPECTIVE RELIABILITY AND
WARMTH OF PARENTS

	Criterion md	St. E. md	St. E. schizo-phrenic
Mother more reliable	42%	63%	53%
Father more reliable	33	18.5	29
No difference between parents	25	18.5	18
Mother warmer	8	30	12
Father warmer	42	55	53
No difference between parents	50	15	35
More reliable mother and warmer father	33	41	29

cepts to a higher degree than did the Criterion Manic-Depressive Group. However, there are no statistically significant differences among the three groups of patients. Therefore, this analysis of Scale III, Role of the Parents, does not lend support to this finding of the research group.

It is of interest here to recall Witmer's finding that the mother was dominant and the father weak in one third of the schizophrenic cases as well as one third of the manic-depressive cases (9). These findings are approximately the same as those of the present study.

Items III-A and III-B of the questionnaire were designed to show the differ-

ences between the parents, but they did not give information about the mothers as a class or the fathers as a class. It is obvious that valuable information might have been lost by examining only the differences between the parents. For example, two parents might be considered equally reliable because they were both seen as weak, irresponsible, and undependable, but two parents might also be considered equally reliable because they were both seen as strong, responsible, and dependable. The effect on the child might be expected to be quite different in these two instances, but the method of analyzing the data would not show this, since in both cases the report would show no difference between the parents in terms of reliability. Therefore, an evaluation was made of each parent separately in regard to reliability and warmth. This was an easy matter because the original work-ups had all aimed at first building a picture of each parent and then comparing them. This revealed in the St. Elizabeths Manic-Depressive Group that the mothers as a class were considered to be more reliable than the fathers as a class. the St. Elizabeths Schizophrenic Group there was essentially no difference between the mothers as a class and the fathers as a class in terms of reliability. In both the St. Elizabeths Manic-Depressive Group and the St. Elizabeths Schizophrenic Group the fathers as a class were warmer than the mothers as a class. The degree of difference in regard to warmth and affection was approximately the same for each of the two groups of patients. A comparable analysis of the Criterion Manic-Depressive Group could not be made, because in the study of this group the focus had been on the interaction between parents.

Item III-C, Child Used by Parents, was further analyzed by studying the raw data on the case work-ups. It was noted that a child might be used in a rather impersonal way to raise family prestige. The findings on the questionnaire under Items I-B, Effort to Raise Prestige, and Item I-C, Aspirations for Patient to Raise Prestige, indicate this to be the case for the two groups of manic-depressive patients. It was also noted that a child might be used through an intense emotional involvement which satisfied the quite personal needs of one or both parents. This seems to fit the pattern of the symbiotic relationship that has been described as existing between the schizophrenic patient and the parent. This pattern occurred in 7 out of the 17 schizophrenic cases, and occurred in only 3 out of the 27 manic-depressive patients. This finding differentiates the St. Elizabeths Manic-Depressive Group from the St. Elizabeths Schizophrenic Group at the .06 level of confidence.

A finding of the original study was that manic-depressive patients were often brought up in families in which there were multiple parental figures. Where this occurred it might lead the child to feel that there were inconsistencies in the authority figures in the home, since so many were present that confusion and disagreement would be bound to occur. In checking this point it was found that 6 of 17—35 percent—of the schizophrenic patients had had multiple parental figures, while 10 of 27—37 percent—of the manic-depressive patients had had multiple parental figures. This indicates that there is no significant difference between the St. Elizabeths Schizophrenic Group and the St. Elizabeths Manic-Depressive Group on this point. It is of interest to recall here that in the study by Pollock and others, there were multiple parental figures in 20 of 155— 13 percent—of the manic-depressive patients studied (8).

In attempting a further study of Scale IV, Authority, the raw data of the original case work-ups were restudied to see if any qualitative differences in the patterns of tension in the home, in the types of inconsistent discipline, or in the types of inconsistent indulgence could be found. While no differences in the patterns of tension could be found between the St. Elizabeths Schizophrenic Group and the St. Elizabeths Manic-Depressive Group, it

was noted that inconsistencies of discipline took a variety of forms. In some families the inconsistencies occurred between parents in the sense that one parent treated the child in one way and the other parent in another way. In other families the inconsistency was present in the sense that one child was treated differently from another. In still other families a given parent might be inconsistent in that his behavior varied drastically from one time to another. This would be particularly true in the case of alcoholic or psychotic parents.

When the case material of the St. Elizabeths Schizophrenic Group and the St. Elizabeths Manic-Depressive Group was evaluated in terms of the specific types of the inconsistency that occurred, it was found that inconsistencies of discipline and indulgence by the parents of the manic-depressive patients most often took the form of one child's being treated differently from another. However, this finding did not reach an acceptable level of statistical significance.

DISCUSSION OF FINDINGS
General Considerations

As already indicated, the conclusions of the original study regarding the characteristics of manic-depressive patients were based on detailed analyses of 12 manic-depressive patients; however, no systematic comparison with a control group was made. The current study attempts to confirm these findings and also to test them against a control group. Differences have been demonstrated between the two groups of patients. The ultimate goal would be to determine whether these findings are specific for manic-depressive patients and no other group. However, the current study is limited to manic-depressive and schizophrenic patients and, therefore, it is impossible to say in any given instance whether it is the manic-depressive patient or the schizophrenic patient who differs from the norm, or whether both do. To determine this, further studies will have to be made of additional groups of patients, as well as of a group without psychiatric disease.

The Criterion Manic-Depressive Group and the St. Elizabeths Manic-Depressive Group approximate each other very closely with a statistically significant difference occurring in only one out of the 15 items on the questionnaire. The scores of the Criterion Manic-Depressive Group generally run higher than those of the St. Elizabeths Manic-Depressive Group. This is not surprising in view of the fact that the concepts being tested were derived from the Criterion Group, and it is very common for the findings of an original study to be more pronounced than those of a replicate study. It should also be noted that the Criterion Group came from a different socioeconomic level and was drawn from patients who sought private psychiatric treatment. Thus, several factors were operative that might have affected the sampling of the Criterion Group and accounted for the slightly higher scores on the questionnaire.

The two manic-depressive groups can be differentiated from the schizophrenic groups on 3 of the 5 scales of the questionnaire. It is significant that the same 6 items which differentiate the St. Elizabeths Manic-Depressive Group from the St. Elizabeths Schizophrenic Group also differentiate the Criterion Manic-Depressive Group from the St. Elizabeths Schizophrenic Group. Only one other item differentiates the Criterion Manic-Depressive Group from the St. Elizabeths Manic-Depressive Group, and this is the weakest one, which just barely reaches the level of statistical significance.

On those items where both manic-depressive groups show significant variation from the schizophrenic group, there is confirmatory evidence that this particular finding of the original research group's study can be used to differentiate between groups of manic-depressive and schizophrenic patients. Nevertheless, it is still necessary to evaluate such findings very

carefully to be sure that they are not artifacts of the method of study. In those instances where the manic-depressive groups and the schizophrenic groups do not show any significant difference, the findings do not support the hypothesis that the concepts of the original study will differentiate between the manic-depressive and schizophrenic patient. However, before accepting this, at least two other possible explanations must be considered. First, the present method of study may not be sensitive enough to detect differences in these areas. Second, the particular findings as presented by the research group may require more precise definition to be specific for the manic-depressive patient. The purpose of this discussion is to evaluate all of the scales studied along the lines of the various considerations that have just been described.

Relation to Community

The findings of the current study support the hypothesis that the manic-depressive patient can be differentiated from the schizophrenic patient in that the former comes from a family in which there is marked striving for prestige and that he has borne the brunt of this. The research group suggested that these strivings might be an effort by the family to compensate for conditions, most commonly low-prestige producing, that set them apart from the community. The current study does not support this last concept. Rather it seems that the strivings for prestige come from the personality makeup of one or both parents.

It has already been noted that manic-depressive patients bear the brunt of high aspirations of the family more often than schizophrenic patients. A study of the raw data of the case work-ups suggests a further qualitative difference. The high aspirations for the patient by the families of the manic-depressive patients were regularly concerned with strivings for prestige. No such pattern occurred for those schizophrenic patients whose families had high aspirations for them. Instead, one or both parents were involved in an intense emotional relationship with the patient through which they tried to realize a wide variety of goals and to gratify various needs. This picture again seems to fit the symbiotic relationship described for the schizophrenic patient and his parent.

Envy

On this scale both manic-depressive groups were clearly differentiated from the schizophrenic group. It should be emphasized here that for the purposes of this study envy was not considered as occurring only in those cases in which the objective performance of the patient would seem to warrant such a reaction.

Quite the contrary point of view was utilized, because it was often found that siblings were highly envious of special considerations that the patient might reveive as a result of illness or poor performance. It had been expected that patients and their families might be reluctant to acknowledge feelings that would be conventionally considered undesirable. However, some of the manic-depressive patients and many of their siblings spoke directly about feelings of envy and competitiveness, or at least gave illustrative incidents from which such feelings could be inferred. It was true that as a rule the parents did not appear to have been aware of the feelings experienced by the children.

The results of this scale are confirmatory evidence for the finding that the manic-depressive patient is subjected to the envy of siblings. However, it does not fully support the statement, "This, then, is a background in which neither the active nor the passive participants in developments of envy and competition are aware of these developments." (1) Rather, it seems that the active participants, namely the siblings, are generally quite aware of the feelings of envy, while the passive participants, namely the patients, some-times—although less often than the siblings—are aware of the feelings of envy.

Item II-C, Tendency of Patient to Undersell Self, revealed a remarkable difference between the manic-depressive sample group and the schizophrenic sample group. A careful analysis of this finding casts considerable doubt on its significance. In order that a patient may undersell himself or fail to live up to his potentialities, he must have demonstrated that he is capable in some field. Characteristically, the manic-depressive patients show great promise but in one way or another fail to use their abilities effectively. On the other hand, 10 of 17 schizophrenic patients had histories of repeated failures from early childhood. This is a well-known and fairly common finding in the history of schizophrenic patients. Thus, it would be impossible to say that these patients had undersold themselves in the same way that the manic-depressive patients had, since they had never shown any great promise. This does not invalidate the observations made concerning the manic-depressive group, but it does mean that the schizophrenic group does not provide a suitable control for this particular point. Nevertheless, the findings regarding the manic-depressive patients are so consistent that even without adequate control they lend convincing support to the concepts of the research group that most manic-depressive patients undersell themselves and fail to live up to their potentialities. However, one qualification must be made. The patients of the Criterion Manic-Depressive Group were studied through intensive psychotherapy, which would allow the therapist to conclude with considerable certainty that the patient's self-defeating behavior arose as a defense against guilt feelings engendered by the envy of his siblings. The current study could simply show in a given case that the patient had engaged in self-defeating behavior, but the case work-ups were not sufficiently intensive to permit a dynamic formulation as to the cause of this behavior.

Role of Parents

The findings on this scale of the questionnaire and the additional methods of analysis do not support the concepts of the research group. The technique of gathering data for the current study seems to be sensitive enough, since the scores of the St. Elizabeths Manic-Depressive Group actually exceed those of the Criterion Manic-Depressive Group. It seems most likely that any differences between the manic-depressive patient and the schizophrenic patient in this area will be related to the way in which the child is used by the parents. Findings of the current study suggest that the manic-depressive patient is used in the interest of achieving prestige, while the schizophrenic patient is used through a symbiotic relationship to gratify a variety of needs of the parents; these points need further elaboration and confirmation.

In the current study, the mothers of the manic-depressive patients as a class were found to be more reliable than the fathers as a class, a situation which was not true of the parents of the schizophrenic patients. The significance of this finding is unclear. It is important to note that in arriving at this finding the interaction of the parents in the family groups was ignored. Therefore, this finding is in a different frame of reference from the rest of the study, which focuses on the interpersonal relationships within the family group.

Authority in the Home

This scale of the questionnaire fails to support the concepts of the research group. In the test of reliability, described under *Method,* it was found that raters showed the greatest disagreement in the items of this scale. It was believed that this indicated a need for better definition of the concepts. When this was attempted, it was found that inconsistencies and indulgence in the families of manic-depressive patients most often took the form of

different treatment of one child as against another. This is additional confirmation of the findings of Scale II, Envy, since inconsistencies of this sort between children would in all probability encourage feelings of envy and competitiveness.

Conventionality

This scale is based on the following theoretical reasoning. It was first noted that the parents of manic-depressive patients showed a high degree of concern about social approval—Item V-C of the questionnaire. This observation was primarily made from the statements by patients to the effect that conventional values had been strongly impressed on them—Item V-B. This was felt to be the result of highly conventional values of the parent—Item V-A.

It would seem that the most important point is the first one, namely that the parents of manic-depressive patients show a high degree of concern about social approval. The findings on Item V-C, Concern about Social Approval, support this concept.

The next point, having to do with the patients' feeling that conventional values were impressed upon them, when measured by Item V-B, Degree to which Conventional Values were Impressed upon Child, was the only instance in which there was a significant statistical difference—at the .05 level of confidence—between the St. Elizabeths Manic-Depressive Group and the Criterion Manic-Depressive Group. It seems probable that this results from the difference of data-gathering technique of the two studies. Patients in intensive psychotherapy generally study their relationship to their parents in minute detail so that they become highly aware of subtle pressures that might previously have been unnoticed. However, in the current study the relatively brief series of interviews could not be expected to elicit material of this same depth on this point. Thus, it is felt that the difference between the two manic-depressive groups is an artifact of method rather than a real difference.

The findings of Item V-A, Degree to which Parents Adhere to Conventional Values, do not support the final point that the parents' concern about social approval resulted from their highly conventional values. Rather, it seems that the excessive concern about social approval comes from the personality make-up of one or both parents.

Aside from the work of the research group reviewed here, few studies have dealt with the family background and early life history of the manic-depressive patient. Thus the present study has focused upon testing the hypotheses of this research group—in particular, the hypothesis that certain characteristics of early life history and family background may be differentiated for manic-depressive and schizophrenic patients.

In order to do this, a group of 27 manic-depressive patients and 17 schizophrenic patients were studied by means of a review of hospital records and interviews with families, and the data were evaluated by means of a questionnaire designed in the light of the concepts of the earlier research group. The 12 patients of the original study were also evaluated according to this questionnaire.

An analysis of the questionnaire results showed only minor differences between the two manic-depressive groups, but certain significant differences in the hypothesized direction between the two manic-depressive groups and the schizophrenic group.

Thus the present study supports certain of the concepts of the original study—namely, that the manic-depressive patient can be distinguished from the schizophrenic patient in that he more commonly, although not always, fits the following pattern: He comes from a family in which there has been special concern about social approval. As a consequence, there has been a marked striving for social prestige, with the patient having borne the brunt of these strivings. This provides a background in which there has been intense envy and competitiveness. The patient has commonly been the object of this envy and in later life, presumably to counteract this envy, has developed a pattern of underselling himself to hide the full extent of his qualifications.

It will be necessary to study additional groups of patients* to determine whether these findings will distinguish the manic-depressive patient from those in diagnostic categories other than the schizophrenic.

* as well as normals. Ed.

REFERENCES

1. Cohen, G. B., Cohen, R. A., Fromm-Reichmann, F., and Weigert, E. V., An Intensive Study of Twelve Cases of Manic-Depressive Psychosis, *Psychiatry*, 1954, *17*, 103–137.

2. English, O. S., Observations of Trends on Manic-Depressive Psychosis, *Psychiatry*, 1949, *12*, 133–134.

3. Finley, C. B., and Wilson, D. C., The Relation of the Family to Manic-Depressive Psychosis, *Diseases of the Nervous System*, 1951, *12*, 362–369.

4. Fromm-Reichmann, F., Baker, G., Cohen, M. B., Cohen, R. A., and Weigert, E. V., *An Intensive Study of Twelve Cases of Manic Depressive Psychosis*. Final Report, Nav. Res. Contr. Nonr-751 (00); Wash., D. C., Wash. Sch. Psychiatry, Sept. 30, 1953.

5. Fromm-Reichmann, F., Discussion, *Psychiatry*, 1949, *12*, 133–134.

6. Pollock, H. M., Prevalence of Manic-Depressive Psychoses in Relation to Sex, Age, Environment, Nativity, and Race. *Manic-Depressive Psychosis, Vol. II*. Baltimore Md., Assoc. Research N. and M. Disease, 1931.

7. Pollock, H. M., Malzberg, B., and Fuller, R.G., Heredity and Environmental Factors in the Causation of Dementia Prae-

cox and Manic-Depressive Psychoses. *Psychiatric Quart.*, 1933, *7,* 450–479; 1936, *10,* 110-126; 1936, *10,* 495-509; 1937, *11,* 131-162; *Amer. J. Psychiatry,* 1940, *96,* 1227-1244.

8. Pollock, H. M., Malzberg, B., and Fuller, R. G., *Heredity and Environmental Factors in the Causation of Manic-Depressive Psychoses and Dementia Praecox.* Utica N.Y., State Hospitals Press, 1939.

9. Witmer, H. L., *et al.,* The Childhood Personality and Parent-Child Relationships of Dementia Praecox and Manic-Depressive Patients. *Smith Coll. Studies in Soc. Work.* 1934, *4,* 289–377.

Psychological Correlates of Depression

1. Frequency of "Masochistic" Dream Content in a Private Practice Sample

AARON T. BECK AND MARVIN S. HURVICH

DEPRESSION has been regarded by many writers as a psychosomatic disorder. (*10*) On the basis of an extensive review of the literature on manic-depressive psychoses and allied states, Bellak (*3*) posits a multifactor psychosomatic theory. He holds that there are several differing syndromes and etiologic factors grouped under the depressive heading and that any combination of physiological and psychological factors may be operative in a given case.

The present report is derived from an attempt to test some observations on the psychological aspects of neurotic-depressive conditions. This study is part of a broad investigation of the psychological and physiological correlates of depression.

The psychological aspects of depression have engaged the attention of psychoanalytic writers since Abraham's first paper on manic-depressive psychosis published in 1911. (*1*) The mechanisms of inverted hostility and self-punishment were underscored by Freud in his classic paper "Mourning and Melancholia" (*6*) and many subsequent psychoanalytic papers have reiterated the importance of these mechanisms in the psychodynamics of depressed patients. (*7, 9, 10*)

Since these clinical studies failed to include control groups, it is not possible to establish with a high degree of certainty the *specificity* of these mechanisms for depression. A recent systematic study of depressives by Gibson (*8*) included a comparison with a control group of schizophrenics. This study supported certain formulations made by Fromm-Reichmann and her coworkers (*4*) regarding the family background and early life history of the manic-depressive patient; the mechanisms of inverted hostility and self-punitiveness, however, were not investigated.

The senior author, who has concentrated on the psychoanalytic therapy of depressive conditions for the past 5 years, made an observation that appeared to be consistent with the formulation of inverted hostility and self-punitive wishes. The dreams of his neurotic-depressive patients showed a relatively high frequency of unpleasant content or affect. Previous work has revealed that unpleasant dreams outnumber pleasant ones in both psychopathological and nonpsychopathological groups. (*5*) However, the content of the unpleasantness in the dreams of these neurotic-depressive patients appeared to be of a particular kind; namely, the dreamer was rejected, disappointed, thwarted, or criticized in the dream action. The affect, when reported, was frequently described as a feeling of sadness, guilt, or humiliation.

Reprinted by permission from *Psychosomatic Medicine,* Vol. 21, No. 1, 1959.

These unpleasant occurrences seemed related to the self-abasement and self-reproaches that Freud described in "Mourning and Melancholia." (6)

The term "masochistic" has been selected to designate the characteristic unpleasantness of these dreams, since in the manifest content the dreamer "makes" himself the recipient of criticism, rejection, or other types of discomfort. As currently used, the word masochism has the meaning of a *need to suffer,* and it is in this sense that we have applied the term to the dreams that we are describing. It should be emphasized, however, that the term is used here for purposes of identification. Whether or not the "masochistic" dream content is related to masochism as observed in clinical behavior remains to be demonstrated.

The data for this investigation have been limited to the manifest content of the dreams; the free assocations, the associations to the dreams, the day residue, and the latent dream thoughts have been excluded from consideration for methodologic reasons. Moreover, it was not feasible to investigate the operations of the dream work, such as "reversal of affect." As Saul has pointed out, however, the manifest dream itself is an important subject of research (11). He stated that focusing on the manifest content of consecutive dreams of patients will reveal the characteristic patterns and themes in their lives.

The systematic application of quantitative techniques to the manifest dreams of patients for the purpose of evaluating psychoanalytic material was reported in 1935 by Alexander and Wilson (2). More recently, Saul and Sheppard have described a rating scale for the quantification of hostility in the manifest dream (12). In another paper they outlined a comprehensive rating system for estimating ego function in dreams (13). These studies provided a stimulus for the present investigation.

The hypothesis of this study was: Consecutive dreams of neurotic-depressed patients in psychoanalytic therapy show a greater incidence of manifest dreams with "masochistic" content than a series of dreams of a matched group of nondepressed patients.

PROCEDURE

In order to subject this hypothesis to test, a scoring manual was developed by a combined theoretical and empirical approach. On the basis of the original observation, a number of categories reflecting a need to suffer were listed. Several hundred dreams of patients diagnosed as depressed and non-depressed (from the files of the senior author and from other analytic therapists) were then studied. Examples of unpleasant content in these dreams that appeared to reflect a need to suffer, and which were found often in dreams of the depressed patients and infrequently in dreams of the nondepressed patients, provided the basis for expanding and refining the scoring categories. It should be stressed that the dreams of the 6 matched pairs of subjects reported on below were not part of the series of dreams used in the construction and refinement of the scoring manual.

An abbreviation of the scoring manual used in the present study follows.*

The dream will score positive (+) "masochistic" if it falls into one of the following three categories.

A. The dreamer explicitly reports one of the following unpleasant affects accompanying the dream: bad, guilty, sad, hurt, disappointed, sorrow, unhappy, lonely, deserted, unwanted, worthless, rejected, humiliated, inferior, or inadequate.

B. The dreamer is crying or sobbing.

C. The dream action or the appearance of the dreamer is indicative of an unpleasant experience for the dreamer. In order to score positive in this category the unpleasant experience must fall into one of the following subcategories.

* The unabridged scoring manual is available on request from the authors.

1. *Deprived, disappointed, or mistreated.* Examples: "I was in a restaurant but the waiters would not serve me." "I put a nickel in a coke machine but all I got was fizz, no syrup." "I got a hamburger but it was made of rubber." "The professor sprang an exam on us. He had told the other students about it but not me."

2. *Thwarted.* Examples: "I ran to make my appointment with you. I was one minute late and the door was locked." "I put some bottles of wine in the refrigerator. The corks fell out and the wine spilled over and spoiled everything." "I tried as hard as I could on the exam but I flunked it."

3. *Excluded, superseded, or displaced.* Examples: "Everybody was invited to the party but me." "My fiancée married

unless there is a specific "masochistic element" or theme as described above. No score is given for affects classified as "frightened," "anxious," "worried," or "apprehensive," or where there is a danger or threat but the dreamer is not actually harmed.*

Examples of dreams that do *not* score: "There was some dangerous force in the building." "I fell off a cliff but I don't remember hitting bottom." "There was a monster chasing me. I woke up before he caught me."

After the scoring system as described above was developed and the authors had attained a high degree of agreement in scoring dreams, the system was applied to our experimental and con-

TABLE 1. IDENTIFYING DATA ON DEPRESSED AND NONDEPRESSED PATIENTS

Pair	Age		Marital Status		Diagnosis nondep.
	Dep.	Nondep.	Dep.	Nondep.	
A	23	20	S	M	Anxiety reaction
B	28	28	M	M	Character neurosis
C	31	29	M	M	Spastic colitis
D	31	33	M	M	Cardiac neurosis
E	36	36	M	M	Character neurosis

somebody else." "My husband was making love to another woman."

4. *Rejected or deserted.* Examples: "You said, 'Get out. I don't want to see you any more!'" "I was waiting for my friends all night but they never showed up."

5. *Blamed, criticized, or ridiculed.* Example: "He said I was a cry baby."

6. *Legal punishment.*

7. *Physical discomfort or injury.* Examples: "Leeches were crawling all over me." "Blood was coming out of my nose."

8. *Distortion of body image.* Examples: "My hair fell out." "I was large and fat."

9. *Being lost or losing something.*

No score is given for dreams with "threat," "anxiety," or "shame" content

trol groups. Six female patients with the diagnosis of neurotic depression were selected from the senior author's files. The nondepressed (control) group was matched patient-for-patient as closely as possible on the basis of sex, age, marital status, and an estimate of severity of illness.

The criteria for establishing the diagnosis of neurotic depressive reaction in these patients were as follows: depressed mood, feelings of discouragement, unwarranted pessimism, feelings of unworthiness, self-criticism and self-reproaches, inertia or apathy, sleep disturbance, anorexia, and suicidal fantasies. The following diagnostic signs were also present: psychomotor retardation, weight loss, and melancholic

* A more detailed description of the exclusions is contained in the scoring manual.

facies associated with weeping and crying. Each patient showed at least 11 of these 13 diagnostic signs and symptoms. The absence of any evidence of a thought disorder, inappropriate affect, and inappropriate behavior ruled out a psychotic process.

The estimate of severity of illness was based on the intensity of the symptoms and the degree of impairment of social adjustment. An informal estimate of socioeconomic standing suggested that all subjects would likely be labelled upper-middle or lower-upper class. A rough clinical estimate of intelligence suggested that both groups were of at least bright average intelligence. The range of social class and intelligence thus appeared to be somewhat restricted, and there did not seem to be any systematic differences between the 2 groups on either continuum. The relevant identifying data on all patients is listed in Table 1.

The first 20 dreams in treatment were abstracted by the senior author from each case record and typed on individual sheets of paper. The total sample of 240 dreams (20 per patient for 12 patients) was then arranged in random order and presented to the junior author to rate on the "masochistic elements" scale. He had no knowledge of any of the patients or of their associations to the dreams; this insured an unbiased, "blind" scoring procedure. These blind ratings were subjected to the statistical evaluation reported below. In order to get an estimate of the reliability of the ratings, the senior author also rated the dreams and the percentage agreement between the 2 raters was calculated.

RESULTS

For the 240 dreams the raters agreed as to the presence or absence of a "masochistic element" on 229 of the dreams, which is slightly in excess of 95 per cent agreement. This indicates that the scoring procedure is highly reliable. The

TABLE 2. FREQUENCY OF "MASOCHISTIC" DREAMS OF MATCHED DEPRESSED AND NONDEPRESSED PATIENTS

| Pair | Number of dreams out of 20 scoring "masochistic" | |
	Depressed	Nondepressed
A	13	1
B	9	3
C	14	3
D	13	3
E	7	3
F	9	2

$p < .025$ (one-tailed test).

results of the comparison between the two groups are listed in Table 2.

It will be seen that there is no overlap between the groups. Over one-half of the dreams (54 per cent) of the depressed patients contained 1 or more "masochistic elements," whereas in the nondepressed group, one-eighth (12.5 per cent) of the dreams contained 1 or more.

DISCUSSION

The obtained differences between the depressed group and the control group are statistically significant and clear-cut. On the basis of these results the hypothesis that the depressed patients show a greater incidence of dreams with "masochistic" content than the nondepressed patients appears to be clearly confirmed.

Several qualifications of the scope of these results should be stressed, however. The smallness of the sample, the use of dreams of females only, and the restricted socioeconomic and IQ ranges represented by these private patients all limit the possible generalizability of the present findings. Further, although the present dream sample was not explicitly used as a basis for construction of the rating scale, it is probable that some aspects of the rating scale are at least partly based on the dreams of patients in the present sample, since these dreams were known to the senior author when the scoring manual was developed. It is clear that both cross-validation and multiple-validation studies are necessary to confirm these findings and allow a specification of their generalizability.

Collection of data for these essential studies, including the use of dream samples of different therapists both in private and institutional practice, is now being undertaken. The present findings may, therefore, be viewed as tentative pending results from these further studies.

THEORETICAL CONSIDERATIONS

Assuming that the dream is an expression of the important motivations and the interplay of defenses as manifested by the dream work, we could speculate that the "masochistic" dream theme is the representation of self-punitive tendencies. This is consistent with the psychoanalytic view that the depressed person turns his hostility against himself. It is also consistent with the formulation that the depressed person feels guilty about his ego-alien drives and punishes himself for them. Examples of the self-punishment are evident in the dreams of not getting food that is requested, of things turning out wrong, of being rejected, etc.

It seems likely that the "masochistic" dream content is an expression of the habitual defensive pattern of the ego rather than of the depressed state per se. The senior author has observed "masochistic" dream content frequently in patients who are notably masochistic in life but not depressed. There is some suggestion, moreover, that some persons who become depressed have an enduring masochistic orientation even during their nondepressed periods. If this is so, then one might anticipate that masochistic inidividuals are more prone to develop depressions than other individuals without this particular configuration.

Further studies are contemplated to elucidate this problem. One study will follow depressed patients (who have not received psychotherapy) after remission to determine whether they continue to show a persistence of "masochistic" dreams. Another study will set up behavioral rating scales for masochism and attempt to correlate the results on these rating systems with the frequency of "masochistic" dreams.

SUMMARY

1. In the course of the psychoanalytic treatment of patients with neurotic-depressive reactions, it was noted that there was a high incidence of dreams with unpleasant content. This unpleasant content was of a particular kind; namely, the dreamer was the recipient of rejection, disappointment, humiliation, or similar unpleasant experiences in the dream content.

2. A rating scale was constructed for the objective identification of these unpleasant themes, which were labelled "masochistic." This rating scale was applied to the first 20 dreams in treatment of 6 patients who had the diagnosis of neurotic depression and to the dreams of 6 nondepressed patients. The 2 groups were matched as closely as possible on the basis of sex, age, and estimated degree of psychopathology.

3. The total sample of 240 dreams was randomized and then subjected to a "blind" scoring by the junior author. The dreams were also scored by the senior author for a reliability check, and 95 per cent agreement was obtained.

4. The depressed patients showed a significantly higher number of dreams with "masochistic" content than the nondepressed patients ($p < .025$). Cross-validation and multiple-validation studies are necessary to confirm these findings.

5. These results appear to be consistent with the psychoanalytic concept of inverted hostility in depressed patients. Future studies will attempt to establish whether there is any correlation between other clinical manifestations of masochism and the occurrence of "masochistic" dream content.

REFERENCES

1. Abraham, K. "Notes on the Psychocanalytical Investigation and Treatment of Manic-depressive Insanity and Allied Conditions." In *Selected Papers on Psychoanalysis.* New York, Basic Books, 1953.

2. Alexander, F., and Wilson, G. W. Quantitative dream studies: A methodological attempt at a quantitative evaluation of psychoanalytic material. *Psychoanalyt. Quart.* 1935, *4,* 371.

3. Bellak, L. *Manic-Depressive Psychosis and Allied Conditions.* New York, Grune & Stratton, 1952.

4. Cohen, M. B., *et al.* An intensive study of twelve cases of manic-depressive psychosis. *Psychiatry* 1954, *17,* 103.

5. Doust, J. W. L. Studies of the psysiology of awareness: the incidents and content of dream patterns and their relationship to anoxia. *J. Ment. Sc.* 1951, *9,* 801.

6. Freud, S. "Mourning and Melancholia." In *Collected Papers.* London, Hogarth, 1946.

7. Gero, G. The construction of depression. *Internat. J. Psycho-Analysis* 1936, *17,* 423.

8. Gibson, R. "Comparison of the Family Background and Early Life Experience of the Manic-depressive and Schizophrenic Patient." Final report on Office of Naval Research Contract, Nonr-751 (00), May, 1957. Washington School of Psychiatry.

9. Jacobsen, E. Depression, the Oedipus complex in the development of depressive mechanisms. *Psychiatric Quart.* 1943, *12,* 541.

10. Rado, S. Psychosomatics of depression from the etiological point of view. *Psychosom. Med.* 1951, *13,* 951.

11. Saul, L. Utilization of early current dreams in formulating psychoanalytic cases. *Psychoanalyt. Quart.* 1940, *9,* 453.

12. Saul, L., and Sheppard, E. An attempt to quantify emotional forces using manifest dreams: A preliminary study. *J. Am. Pschoanalyt. A.* 1956, *14,* 486.

13. Sheppard, E., and Saul, L. An approach to a systematic study of ego functions. *Psychoanalyt. Quart.* 1958, *27,* 237.

14. Siegel, S. *Nonparametric Statistics for the Behavioral Sciences.* New York, McGraw-Hill, 1956.

The Symptoms of Involutional Psychosis

J. R. WITTENBORN AND CLARK BAILEY

THE present study comprises an evaluation of the descriptive efficacy of two different diagnostic procedures for mental hospital patients. One of the procedures is the conventional diagnosis of the psychiatrists. The other procedure has been described elsewhere (*3*) and is based upon a scoring of a standard set of symptom rating scales. The rating scales may be scored with respect to nine different symptom clusters in much the same manner as a Bernreuter Personality Inventory is scored. This new procedure has been described as a quantified multiple

Reprinted by permission from the *Journal of Consulting Psychiatry,* Vol. 17, No. 1, 1952.

psychiatric diagnosis to distinguish it from the psychiatrist's conventional diagnosis which is not quantified and may or may not be multiple in nature.

The criterion for evaluating these two descriptive procedures is the pattern of symptomatic similarities and dissimilarities revealed by a factor analysis of the intercorrelations among a sample of patients. The required correlation coefficients between each patient and every other one were determined by the similarity or dissimilarity between the patients revealed by a standard set of 55 symptom rating scales (*4, 5, 6*). The set of standard symptom rating scales which provided the basis for correlations between patients is also the set of rating scales upon which the quantified multiple diagnostic procedure is based. This set of symptom rating scales was developed in collaboration with a large number of psychiatrists and may be considered as a good and representative sample of the kinds of symptoms which psychiatrists currently consider to be important in the study of mental hospital patients with functional disorders.

Since other studies have indicated respects in which the quantified multiple diagnostic procedure is descriptively superior to the conventional diagnostic labels of psychiatrists (6), the present investigation was designed in a manner calculated to favor the descriptive value of psychiatrist's diagnosis and to reveal limits in the descriptive value of the quantified multiple diagnostic procedure. The sample of patients was selected with a common diagnosis—involutional psychosis. Although the common primary diagnosis for these patients implies symptomatic homogeneity within the group, there was for each patient a secondary diagnosis so that symptomatic diversity within the group could presumably be designated by the secondary diagnostic label. The final diagnosis was approved by a diagnostic staff conference in which the examining psychiatrist as well as other psychiatrists, psychologists, and social workers participated. The patient group comprised 20 consecutive admissions to the Connecticut State Hospital with this diagnosis.

If important symptomatic differences among the involutional patients are revealed by the factor analysis and if the symptom cluster scores of the quantified multiple diagnostic procedure indicate these differences in a manner superior to the way in which they are indicated by the psychiatrist's diagnosis, a relative superiority could be claimed for the quantified multiple diagnosis. Inasmuch as the quantified multiple diagnostic procedure is based on symptom clusters which were revealed in large samples of quite heterogeneous patients,

one would not expect the cluster scores of this diagnostic procedure to reveal numerous differences within a relatively homogeneous diagnostic group. (There is no certainty that the symptom clusters within such a special homogeneous group would be the same as those found among the large heterogeneous groups and it seems plausible that the symptom clusters for this special group should correspond with the secondary diagnosis.)

The present investigation, incidentally, was expected to be of interest in respects additional to its evaluative purpose. It was hoped that the present analyses would contribute to our knowledge of the involutional psychosis.

The first step in our procedure involved a factor analysis of the intercorrelations among our sample of 20 patients. It was assumed that the major similarities and dissimilarities among these 20 patients would be revealed by the factor analysis of their intercorrelations.

The factor analysis shows that there is no important general factor which indicates a consistent major similarity among all these patients. The absence of evidence for an important general factor suggests that the diagnosis of involutional psychosis is not particularly useful from a purely descriptive standpoint, i.e., it appears to have no consistent descriptive implication from patient to patient. In addition, the factor analysis shows that six factors are necessary to account for the intercorrelations among the patients. This finding suggests that the three different secondary diagnoses employed by psychiatrists in describing (or in diagnosing) the present sample are not sufficient to account for important diversities among patients. If the general diagnosis, involutional psychosis, used in combination with three secondary diagnoses, specifically, "paranoid," "melancholia," and "other types," were sufficient to account for the principal symptom patterns manifested by the present group, one would expect to find an important general factor and three broad group factors. Ideally, one would have expected to find in each of the patients a factorial complexity of two so that the intercorrelations among the patients would be due to the degree to which they resembled the total group of patients and the degree to which they resembled the hypothetical subgroup which the secondary diagnosis implies. Such is not the case, however. Nevertheless, it should be noted that all the patients with a secondary diagnosis of paranoid have high loadings

the patient groupings are more characteristic of one sex than of the other.

Since the psychiatrists' diagnoses failed in several important respects to anticipate the pattern of similarity and dissimilarity revealed by the analysis of the intercorrelations among the patients, the descriptive efficacy of the multiple quantified diagnostic procedure becomes of particular interest. Accordingly, the nine symptom cluster scores (3) were prepared

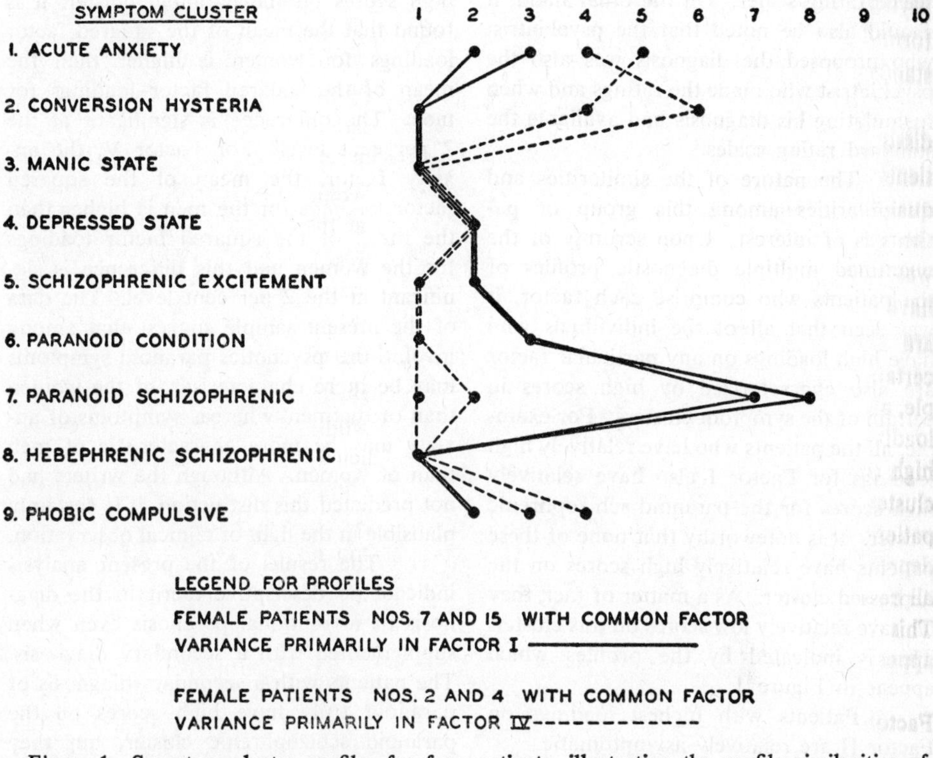

LEGEND FOR PROFILES

FEMALE PATIENTS NOS. 7 AND 15 WITH COMMON FACTOR VARIANCE PRIMARILY IN FACTOR I ———————

FEMALE PATIENTS NOS. 2 AND 4 WITH COMMON FACTOR VARIANCE PRIMARILY IN FACTOR IV------------

Figure 1. Symptom cluster profiles for four patients, illustrating the profile similarities of patients with similar factorial compositions.

for the first factor. Seemingly, the psychiatrist's diagnosis has the greatest descriptive sufficiency for the involutional patients of a paranoid type.

The records of the patients who clustered together to form each of the various factors were examined. There was no evidence that the factors were a result of rater differences. Interestingly enough, however, there is evidence that certain of

for each member of the sample and the profiles such as illustrated by Figure 1 were drawn. The patients with similar factorial compositions were found to have similar quantified multiple diagnostic profiles. The nature of this similarity for two groups of patients is shown in Figure 1. The symptom cluster scores may be used to classify the patients in the same way as they are classified on the basis of these factor analyses. With the limitations imposed by the present sample of patients and by the standard set of 55 symptom rating scales, it is concluded that patients with a general diagnosis of involutional psychosis may be better described by the quantified multiple diagnostic procedure than they are described by secondary psychiatric diagnosis. It should be noted that the criteria (the factor analysis) and the quantified multiple psychiatric diagnosis are based on the same data, i.e., a standard set of rating scales. On the other hand, it should also be noted that the psychiatrist who proposed the diagnosis was also the psychiatrist who made the ratings and when formulating his diagnosis had available the standard rating scales.

The nature of the similarities and dissimilarities among this group of patients is of interest. Upon scrutiny of the quantified multiple diagnostic profiles of the patients who comprise each factor, it was seen that all of the individuals who have high loadings on any particular factor are also characterized by high scores in certain of the symptom clusters. For example, all the patients who have relatively high loadings for Factor I also have relatively high scores for the paranoid schizophrenic cluster. It is noteworthy that none of these patients have relatively high scores on the depressed cluster. As a matter of fact, they all have relatively low scores on this cluster. This is indicated by the profiles which appear in Figure 1.

Patients with highest loadings on Factor II are relatively asymptomatic.

Factor III is of particular interest because all of the patients who have high loadings on this factor have high scores on both the depressed cluster and the excited cluster, and may be considered to give the symptomatic picture of an agitated type of depression.

Those patients who have high loadings on Factor IV have relatively high scores on both the hysterical and the anxiety clusters, whereas those patients who have relatively high loadings on Factor V

have their highest scores for the anxiety symptom cluster.

Factor VI also has a compound symptomatic significance in the sense that patients with highest loadings on this factor are those who have high scores on both the paranoid schizophrenic cluster and the excited cluster.

There is some evidence that factor pattern is in part determined by the sex of the patient. Specifically on Factor I, the factor which is due to individuals with high scores on the paranoid cluster, it is found that the mean of the squared factor loadings for women is higher than the mean of the squared factor loadings for men. The difference is significant at the 2 per cent level. For Factor V, the anxiety factor, the mean of the squared factor loadings for the men is higher than the mean of the squared factor loadings for the women and this difference is significant at the 2 per cent level. The data of the present sample suggest that among involutional psychotics paranoid symptoms may be more characteristic of the women than of the men, whereas symptoms of anxiety may be more characteristic of men than of women. Although the writers had not predicted this distinction, it is certainly plausible in the light of clinical observation.

The results of the present analysis indicate no descriptive merit in the diagnosis of involutional psychosis even when supplemented with a secondary diagnosis. The patients with a secondary diagnosis of paranoid truly have high scores on the paranoid schizophrenic cluster, but they are without conspicuous evidences of depression and also somewhat varied with respect to other types of symptom cluster scores. The patients with a secondary diagnosis of melancholia seem quite varied from the standpoint of the symptom cluster scores; patients who have high factor loading on Factor IV and on Factor V have this secondary diagnosis, but the patients who have high factor loadings for these two factors are respectively quite different from each other symptomatically. For example, patients who have high factor loadings on Factor IV are without appreciable symptoms of depression, whereas those with high loadings on Factor V have relatively marked symptoms of depression, i.e., they have relatively high scores on the depression cluster. It should also be noted that all of the patients who have high loadings on Factor II are relatively asymptomatic, but they have the secondary diagnosis of melancholia as do a number of the patients who have relatively high loadings on Factor III.

SUMMARY AND CONCLUSIONS

The present report describes a study of the symptomatic similarities and dissimilarities among a sample of 20 patients with a diagnosis of involutional psychosis. The 20 patients were intercorrelated on the basis of their ratings on a set of 55 symptom rating scales and the resulting intercorrelations were factorized by Thurstone's centroid method. As a result of this analysis certain conclusions are offered subject to the limitations of the present sample of patients and symptoms:

1. The patients are symptomatically heterogeneous. Some are practically asymptomatic, others are without important symptoms of depression, and still others are characterized by all combinations of important scores on symptom clusters other than depression. This suggests an important descriptive limitation for the diagnosis of involutional psychosis.

2. Instead of there being one important general factor to account for the intercorrelations among the patients, there were instead six group factors. The secondary diagnoses of "paranoid," "melancholia," and "other types" are insufficient to designate the diversities among the patients. Nevertheless, the groups of patients respectively designated by the factors were found to be relatively homogeneous with respect to certain of the cluster scores which comprise the quantified multiple diagnostic procedure.

3. Patients with the secondary diagnosis of paranoid are all found to have very high scores for the paranoid schizophrenia symptom cluster.

4. For the present sample of patients, it may be claimed that the symptom cluster scores (the quantified multiple diagnoses) provide a relatively efficient and economical means for describing the principal similarities and dissimilarities which may be revealed by the standard set of 55 symptom rating scales.

REFERENCES

1. English, O. S. Observations of trends in manic depressive psychosis. *Psychiatry*, 1949, *12*, 125–134.

2. Good, R. Depression. *Brit. J. med. Psychol.*, 1945-46, *20*, 344–375.

3. Wittenborn, J. R. A new procedure for evaluating mental hospital patients. *J. consult. Psychol.*, 1950, *14*, 500–501.

4. Wittenborn, J. R. Symptom patterns in a group of mental hospital patients. *J. consult. Psychol.*, 1950, *15*, 290–302.

5. Wittenborn, J. R., & Holzberg, J. D. The generality of psychiatric syndromes. *J. consult, Psychol.*, 1950, *15*, 372–380.

6. Wittenborn, J. R., Holzberg, J. D., & Simon, B. Symptom correlates for descriptive diagnosis. *Genet. Psychol. Monogr.* (In press)

7

Psychophysiological Methods, Psychosomatic Syndromes, and Behavior Pathology

ONE of the most thoroughly worked research areas is psychosomatics, the study of the relationship between psychological stress and somatic illness. Sufficient evidence has been accumulated to support the general hypothesis that anatomical lesions and physiological dysfunction may follow prolonged stress. Specifications of the theory, however, are troublesome. The focus of current research activity may be phrased as a question: Under what conditions (social, geographical, psychological, biochemical, etc.) will the experiencing of stress produce somatic illness? Within this question lies an even more difficult problem: the definition of stress. It would take us too far afield now to enter into a discussion of how stressors should be defined and classified. In the readings of this section, the stressors used are defined but the results of each experiment cannot readily be generalized to stressors not included in the experiment.

The paper by King and Henry is one in a series designed to study the effects of experimentally induced stress. A significant finding in an earlier study was the relationship between type of emotional reaction (aggression or anxiety) and the pattern of cardiovascular response. In the present study, the investigators addressed themselves to a further question: Are the emotional or cardiovascular reactions associated with type of parental discipline and control? The answer to the question directs us toward an analysis of the effects of different modes of social learning and is an important step toward solving the jigsaw puzzle of psychosomatic illness.

Malmo, Shagass, Bélanger, and Smith attack the problem of motor control under experimentally induced stress. They test the hypothesis that a nonspecific stressor increases motor disturbance in psychoneurotic patients. The data give support to the hypothesis and to the folk belief about the association of "nervousness" (improper motor regulation) and psychopathology. Consider the implication of the finding that performance on perceptual tasks under stress conditions does not discriminate between psychoneurotic patients and normals. If we take this finding seriously, we should question the widespread use of perceptual tasks in diagnostic procedures. Since defective motor regulation seems to be a property of psychoneurotics, it would seem appropriate to ask why motoric tests are not used in diagnostic settings. Some interesting theoretical questions are raised by the findings. Is defective regulation constitutional? Or is it acquired through inconsistent or special socialization techniques? Is the lack of motor control a discharge phenomenon, which allows the patient an opportunity to reduce tension?

The paper by Mednick, Garner, and Stone reports the results of an investigation that attempted to confirm a specificity theory of psychosomatic illness. Their point of departure was Alexander's theory, which relates specific symptoms, such as ulcer, to specific personality configurations, such as dependency conflict. The theory was translated into a set of experimental hypotheses in which success and failure experiences were manipulated. Findings were negative and raise an important problem for behavior pathologists: How can we resolve the conflicting evidence produced by the clinically derived specificity hypothesis and the experimental inability to confirm this hypothesis?

Kepecs, Robin, and Munro conducted their study with a sample of diagnosed psychosomatic patients suffering from skin disorders, arthritis, asthma, or hypertension. They observed emotional responsiveness to various kinds of stimuli. Emotional responsiveness was estimated by rating drawings made by the subjects following each stimulus presentation. Employing the framework of psychoanalytic theory, the authors exhibit the various types of content elicited by sensory stimulation to diagnosed psychosomatic patients. The interpretation that persons with certain types of disorders are fixated at different levels of the socialization continuum gives some support to a "specificity" treatment of psychosomatic theory.

The highly original paper by Weiner, Thaler, Reiser, and Mirsky deals with some of the factors responsible for duodenal ulcer. Their study is unique in that they obtained data *before* the patients showed the somatic lesions. Measures of gastric secretion were taken and various psychological tests were administered before the subjects (draftees) were placed in a real stressor situation. Gastric and psychological tests were repeated after eight to sixteen weeks of basic military training. The highly significant association between rate of gastric secretion and personality type is a finding that raises complex questions to students of behavior. Questions such as the following are posed: Do constitutional differences in biochemistry contribute to the development of enduring personality traits? Do the subtle influences of early socialization produce shifts in rate of biochemical processes? How do these factors interact, and under what conditions?

Aggression and Cardiovascular Reactions Related to Parental Control over Behavior

STANLEY H. KING AND ANDREW F. HENRY

THIS study examines certain relationships among three factors: the degree to which behavior is required to conform to the expectations of parents, the direction of the expression of aggression,

Reprinted by permission from *The Journal of Abnormal and Social Psychology*, Vol. 50, No. 2, 1955.

and cardiovascular reactions during experimentally induced stress.

Funkenstein and King (2) studied the relationship between the direction of aggression and cardiovascular reaction during experimentally induced stress. They divided the emotional responses during stress into the following categories: (a) anger-out, (b) anger-in or anxiety, and (c) miscellaneous (anger equally in and out, anger and anxiety equal, or no emotion). They found that the response of anger directed outward was associated with a specific type of cardiovascular reaction. This reaction they termed "nor-epinephrine-like" because it was similar to that produced by an injection of nor-epinephrine. The responses of subjects (Ss) responding with anger directed against the self, or with anxiety and fear, were associated with a different type of cardiovascular reaction, one termed "epinephrine-like," that is, similar to one that can be produced by an injection of epinephrine. Table 1 shows the relationship which they found between emotion and cardiovascular pattern, obtained from a two-year study of Harvard College students.

It is to be noted that they faced two measurement problems. First, some of the cardiovascular patterns could not be classified as either epinephrine-like or nor-epinephrine-like, and had to be placed in an unclassified category. Second, the scoring of the emotional response during stress had to depend on the subjective response of S, with the danger that subjective response may not always reflect S's true feeling. Despite these measurement difficulties, the association between cardiovascular reaction and emotional reaction was significant beyond the .001 level.

Earlier research by Funkenstein and Greenblatt (1) established a positive relationship between seriously depressed states and the secretion of an epinephrine-like substance. Results of their study have proved fruitful in predicting the therapeutic results of electric shock therapy in cases of severe depression. These two relationships, the one between depression and epinephrine-like secretion, and the one between aggression directed against the self or anxiety and epinephrine-like cardiovascular response, are mutually supportive. Psychoanalytic theory (4) has further suggested a relation between psychological depression and the expression of aggression inwardly against the self.

The relation of a third variable to those already discussed in the background presentation became apparent when extensive questionnaire data from Ss tested by Funkenstein and King were analyzed. This variable was concerned with the discipline and control function of the parents as reported by Ss. Our purpose in this paper then is to relate this variable to the variables of cardiovascular reaction and emotional reaction during experimentally induced stress.

PROCEDURE AND RESULTS

There were three questions in the questionnaire which were relevant to the disciplinary roles of the parents. These were:

1. Who was the principal disciplinarian in your family?
   a. Mother
   b. Father
   c. Mother and father equally
   d. Other (specify)
2. In disciplinary matters is your father:
   a. Stern
   b. Mild
3. In disciplinary matters is your mother:
   a. Stern
   b. Mild

TABLE 1. EMOTIONAL AND CARDIOVASCULAR REACTION DURING EXPERIMENTALLY INDUCED STRESS

Emotional reaction	Cardiovascular reaction			
	Nor-epineph-rine-like	Epineph-rine-like	Unclas-sified	Total
Anger directed outward	24	6	4	34
Anger directed inward or anxiety	7	35	10	52
Total	31	41	14	86

Note.—$\chi^2 = 29.93$, $p < .001$; epinephrine-like and unclassified added together, $\chi^2 = 26.68$, $p < .001$.

The first question unfortunately does not provide a measure of the relative amounts of discipline administered by the father and mother. But when seen in relation to the answers to the second and third questions, a rough measure of the degree of control imposed by the parents upon S is possible.

The first step in procedure was to combine questions 2 and 3 into three categories: both parents stern, one parent stern, and both parents mild. These two questions, thus categorized, are presented together with question 1 and data on cardiovascular reaction in Table 2.

When the relationship between dominance in discipline and strictness in discipline is considered, it can be seen that when both parents were strict the father was inclined to be dominant. There were no cases of mother dominant when both parents were described as strict. When one parent was strict, one half of the Ss checked father as dominant while about one quarter checked mother as dominant. However, when both parents were checked as mild only about one fifth of the Ss checked father as dominant. The positive association between strictness of parents and dominance of the father was significant at the .01 level.

The next relationship to be considered was that of parental dominance in discipline and cardiovascular reaction. Here it was apparent that when father was checked as dominant Ss tended to have nor-epinephrine-like reactions. This relationship was significant at the .001 level but it was complicated by the distribution of unclassified reactions. The distribution of the unclassified cases was significantly different (at the .01) level from the distribution of the nor-epinephrine-like cases, but did not differ significantly from the distribution of the epinephrine-like cases.

The relationship between strictness of the parents and cardiovascular reaction was not significant, but it was in the predicted direction, that is, the proportion of nor-epinephrine-like cases was highest when both parents were strict.

Analysis of the data to this point indicated that Ss who reported father as dominant in discipline tended to have nor-epinephrine-like reactions. This relationship held in all three of the strictness categories. Further analysis showed that all

of the 14 nor-epinephrine-like cases in the "father dominant-one parent strict" category reported that it was their father rather

TABLE 2. PARENTAL DOMINANCE IN DISCIPLINE, STRICTNESS-MILDNESS IN DISCIPLINE, AND CARDIOVASCULAR REACTION

Cardiovascular reaction	Father domi- nant	Parents equally domi- nant	Mother domi- nant	Total
Both parents strict				
Nor-epinephrine-like	6	3	0	9
Epinephrine-like	1	2	0	3
Unclassified	1	1	0	2
Total	8	6	0	14
One parent strict				
Nor-epinephrine-like	14	3	1	18
Epinephrine-like	9	7	8	24
Unclassified	1	4	4	9
Total	24	14	13	51
Neither parent strict				
Nor-epinephrine-like	6	4	5	15
Epinephrine-like	2	13	7	22
Unclassified	0	2	5	7
Total	8	19	17	44
Total				
Nor-epinephrine-like	26	10	6	42
Epinephrine-like	12	22	15	49
Unclassified	2	7	9	18
Grand total	40	39	30	109

Note.—Dominance and cardiovascular reaction, $\chi^2 = 21.51$, $p < .001$; dominance and cardiovascular reaction, adding the unclassified and epinephrine-like cases toegther, $\chi^2 = 18.93$, $p < .001$; dominance and cardiovascular reaction, omitting the epinephrine-like cases, $\chi^2 = 11.00$, $p < .01$; dominance and cardiovascular reaction, omitting the nor-epinephrine-like cases, $\chi^2 = 2.33$, not significant at the .05 level; parental strictness and cardiovascular reaction, $\chi^2 = 5.54$, not significant at the .05 level; parental strictness and cardiovascular reaction, adding the unclassified and epinephrine-like cases together, $\chi^2 = 3.52$, not significant at the .05 level; parental strictness and dominance in discipline, $\chi^2 = 14.87$, $p < .01$.

than their mother who was the strict parent. This suggested that the interrelationship of strictness of father, dominance in discipline, and cardiovascular reaction should be investigated. This procedure may be justified on two grounds. First, the measurement of strictness of mother did not distribute our Ss over the range of the variable since only about one quarter of the mothers were reported as strict. Second, the association between strictness of the father and relative dominance of the father was significant beyond the .001 level.

242

Table 3 shows that strictness of the father was associated with nor-epinephrine-like reactions at the .06 level. When strictness of the father was held constant, the strong relationship between dominance of the father and nor-epinephrine-like reaction was maintained.

TABLE 3. PARENTAL DOMINANCE IN DISCIPLINE AND STRICTNESS-MILDNESS OF FATHER IN DISCIPLINE

Cardiovascular reaction	Father dominant	Parents equally dominant	Mother dominant	Total
Father strict				
Nor-epinephrine-like	20	5	0	25
Epinephrine-like	9	8	2	19
Unclassified	2	5	0	7
Total	31	18	2	51
Father mild				
Nor-epinephrine-like	6	5	6	17
Epinephrine-like	3	14	13	30
Unclassified	0	2	9	11
Total	9	21	28	58
Grand total	40	39	30	109

Note.—Parental dominance and strictness-mildness of father, $\chi^2 = 35.45$, $p < .001$; strictness-mildness and cardiovascular reaction, $\chi^2 = 4.74$, $p = .06$.

Twenty of the 25 nor-epinephrine-like cases who reported father as strict also reported father as the dominant disciplinarian. Of the 51 cases who reported father as strict, over one half, or 31, also reported father as dominant. However, of the 58 cases who reported father as mild in discipline only nine reported him as dominant. This table shows, as already reported, a very high correlation between

TABLE 4. COMBINED MEASURE OF PATERNAL CONTROL AND CARDIOVASCULAR REACTION

Cardiovascular reaction	Strict control	Medium control	Lenient control	Total
Nor-epinephrine-like	20	11	11	42
Epinephrine-like	9	13	28	50
Unclassified	2	5	11	18
Total	31	29	50	110

Note.—Paternal control and cardiovascular reaction, omitting unclassified category, $\chi^2 = 11.21$, $p < .01$; paternal control and cardiovascular reaction, adding together the unclassified and epinephrine-like categories, $\chi^2 = 14.76$, $p < .01$.

strictness of the father and dominance by the father in discipline. Further, Ss reporting strict and dominant fathers tended to have nor-epinephrine-like reactions, while Ss reporting mild and nondominant fathers tended to have epinephrine-like reactions.[1]

Accordingly, questions 1 and 2 were

TABLE 5. COMBINED MEASURE OF PATERNAL CONTROL AND CARDIOVASCULAR REACTION, HOLDING EMOTIONAL REACTION CONSTANT

Cardiovascular reaction	Strict control	Medium control	Lenient control	Total
Anger directed outward				
Nor-epinephrine-like	12	3	6	21
Epinephrine-like	0	1	4	5
Unclassified	0	2	2	4
Total	12	6	12	30
Anger directed inward or anxiety				
Nor-epinephrine-like	3	2	2	7
Epinephrine-like	6	9	16	31
Unclassified	2	2	4	8
Total	11	13	22	46
Miscellaneous reaction				
Nor-epinephrine-like	5	6	3	14
Epinephrine-like	3	3	8	14
Unclassified	0	1	6	7
Total	8	10	17	35
Grand total	31	29	51	111

combined and categorized in the following way: *strict:* Father the dominant disciplinarian and strict (31 cases); *medium:* Father the dominant disciplinarian but mild —Father strict but not the dominant disciplinarian (29 cases); *lenient:* Father mild and not the dominant disciplinarian (50 cases). This combined measure was then related to cardiovascular reaction as shown in Table 4. A test for association yielded a chi square of 11.21 when the unclassified cases were omitted. It is to be noted that the unclassified reactions were again distributed in the same manner as the epinephrine-like reactions. When the epinephrine-like and unclassified cases were combined and compared with the nor-epi-

[1] Ten of the 11 Ss who reported that their mothers were both stern and dominant in discipline but that their fathers were mild had epinephrine-like or unclassified cardiovascular reactions. This suggests that for these Ss control imposed by the father is more predictive of nor-epinephrine-like cardiovascular reaction than control imposed by the mother.

nephrine-like reactions, the chi square was 14.76. Both were significant at less than the .01 level.

The final step in the analysis, as presented in Table 5, shows the relation between the combined measure of control and emotional reactions of Ss during stress. The relation between control and emotional reaction was in the predicted direction but was not significant. The relation between cardiovascular reaction and control, however, "stood up" when the effect of the emotional reaction was held constant.

DISCUSSION

The results show that Ss who reported father as the principal disciplinarian and also stern in discipline had norepinephrine-like reactions (during stress), whereas Ss who reported father as the non-dominant disciplinarian and mild in discipline had epinephrine-like reactions. Whereas the relation between the direction of expression of aggression and cardiovascular reaction was strong, as shown by Funkenstein and King, the relation between reported control by the father and the direction of aggression was in the predicted direction, but not significant.

It is again necessary to note the measurement problem. This occurred in three places. First, there was the assessment of the Ss' emotional reactions during stress, which depended on subjective report. Second, there was the problem of the cardiovascular reactions that could not be typed either as epinephrine-like or norepinephrine-like. The unclassified cases were distributed more like the epinephrine-like cases. Third, there was the problem of the measurement of parental control in discipline. Better measurement of this variable is clearly needed.

An additional problem of the measurement of degree of control must be made explicit. This measure was derived from S's perception of the degree of control to which he was subjected, as reported in answers to items on a questionnaire. We

have no evidence on the question of the degree of correspondence between S's reported perception of this control and the amount of disciplinary control which was in fact imposed by the parents.

Granting these limitations of measurement, we suggest that these data have implications for the relationship of social and family factors during childhood and later physiological reactions during stress. We have not attempted to spell out any of these implications in this paper, being of the opinion that they need to be set in a wider theoretical framework. Such a framework is beyond the scope of this paper.[2]

From the empirical data presented here certain further lines of research are suggested:

1. Is the control of the father still operative for the subject in the external world, and if so how does it relate to the reactions to a frustrating stress-inducing situation?

2. What is the relation between the perception of childhood control and discipline by the parents and the actual amount of control?

3. Is there a tendency for cardiovascular reaction during stress to become habitually nor-epinephrine-like or epinephrine-like as a function of childhood control, remaining relatively constant thereafter?

4. What is the effect of experimentally induced control on cardiovascular reaction and emotional response, holding constant the amount of control imposed by the parents in childhood?

5. What is the relationship of these findings with other "psychological" determinants of the direction of expression of aggression, such as "superego" strength, the effect of projection, and identification with the aggressor?

6. Would the same result be obtained from a similar experiment involving a group of female subjects?

[2] An interpretation of these findings can be found in Henry and Short (3).

SUMMARY

The type of cardiovascular reaction of Ss during experimentally induced stress was related to questions about childhood discipline and control by parents.

The Ss describing their fathers as strict and dominant disciplinarians experienced a nor-epinephrine-like cardiovascular reaction during experimentally induced stress whereas Ss describing their fathers as mild and nondominant disciplinarians experienced an epinephrine-like reaction.

REFERENCES

1. Funkenstein, D. H., and Greenblatt, M. Nor-epinephrine-like and epinephrine-like substances and the elevation of blood pressure during acute stress. *J. nerv. ment. Dis.*, in press.

2. Funkenstein, D. H., King, S. H., and Drolette, Margaret. The experimental evocation of stress. In *Symposium on stress*. Washington, D. C.: Walter Reed Army Medical Center and Army Medical Service Graduate School, 1953.

3. Henry, A. F., and Short, J. F., Jr. *Suicide and homicide*. Glencoe, Ill.: The Free Press, 1954. Pp. 101-119.

4. Rado, S. Emergency behavior. In P. H. Hoch and J. Zubin (Eds.), *Anxiety*. New York: Grune & Stratton, 1950. Pp. 150-175.

Motor Control in Psychiatric Patients under Experimental Stress

ROBERT B. MALMO, CHARLES SHAGASS, DAVID J. BÉLANGER,
AND A. ARTHUR SMITH

CLINICAL evidence of disordered physiological activity is frequently encountered in the psychoneuroses. It is also known that phenomena such as trembling, palpitations, and excessive sweating are most likely to occur in the psychoneurotic when he encounters some form of stressful stimulation. These physiological changes under stress constitute objective data for the experimental approach to the problems of psychoneurosis. By recording physiological events under controlled stress in the laboratory it is possible to determine the characteristics of physiological response in psychoneurosis and to infer something about the central processes involved.

Among experimental investigations of psychoneurosis, Luria's (8) contribution is noteworthy. Luria's method of recording finger movement simultaneously with the classical word association technique stimulated several investigations of skeletal-motor activities in emotion (*1, 2, 3, 4, 5, 6, 7, 9, 11, 12, 13, 14, 15*). Further, his results served to emphasize the important role of the skeletal-motor system in psychoneurosis and in the field of emotion generally, a role largely neglected as a consequence of attention directed toward study of autonomic function (*9*).

Luria's recording techniques were used by Ebaugh (*4*) and Barnacle, Ebaugh, and Lemere (*2*) in clinical studies of psychoneurosis. From the therapist's knowledge of the patient's history, he chose particular words whose emotional significance for the patient he knew to be high. Other words which he chose referred to items in the history which were of doubtful significance. It was claimed that the Luria technique was helpful in assessing the significance of such items and in facilitating psychotherapy.

We have applied the term "specific

Reprinted by permission from *The Journal of Abnormal and Social Psychology*, Vol. 46, No. 4, 1951.

stress" to the patient's experience of responding to such words chosen with special reference to certain sensitive areas in his case history. The stress value of such words depends upon *specific* events in the past history of the particular individual. Now there are forms of stress which appear to be nonspecific in the sense that all individuals find them stressful, despite wide differences from individual to individual in life history. As an example of nonspecific stress, we may cite painful stimulation, which is stressful to all persons with intact pain sensibility and which would hardly be expected to bear any closer relation to specific life experience in a group of psychoneurotics than in a group of normals.

In comparing physiological reactions of psychoneourotics and normals on a group basis, use of specific stress is usually not feasible, principally because adequate case histories are not available for the normals. Actually, the methodological emphasis on specific stress stems from a tacit assumption which may be invalid. It is assumed that degree of physiological disturbance is mainly a function of stress intensity. We do not deny the possible heuristic value of proceeding under this assumption in certain studies. But there is a further assumption about psychoneurotics' physiological disturbance in relation to stress intensity which, if held to rigidly, may lead to serious neglect of another aspect of the general problem of psychoneurotic mechanisms. We refer to the assumption that in a particular psychoneurotic, as a product of his own individual life experiences, certain situations (or words, say, in the association-experiment) have acquired such high stress intensities that they produce a marked physiological disturbance. Strong emphasis is laid on the stress intensity, and the amount of physiological disturbance is viewed as commensurate with the degree of stress. This view (in its extreme form) does not consider the possibility of defective motor mechanisms. It assumes that the observed motor disturbance represents the reaction

of "normal" motor mechanisms to stress of extremely high intensity.

Methodologically, and from the point of view of avoiding shaky assumptions, use of nonspecific stress in investigation of the psychoneuroses appears preferable to specific stress. A standardized series of painful stimulations has been employed in our laboratory (*9, 11*) in physiological investigations of psychoneuroses. These investigations have led to the conclusion that under this form of nonspecific stress (pain), psychoneurotics were particularly characterized by disturbances in motor function, as evidenced in impaired motor control and excessive muscular tension.

These results suggest that the most important distinguishing features of psychoneurosis may lie in defective motor mechanisms rather than in individual susceptibility to specific stresses. In these findings there is the implication that the psychoneurotic will manifest disproportionately increased motor disturbance in response to *any* stress. In opposition to the stress intensity hypothesis, the "motor hypothesis" may be stated as follows: *Psychoneurotic disorders involve defective motor regulation manifested by abnormally increased motor disturbance under any stressful condition.*

The present experiment was designed to provide further data bearing on this hypothesis. Our main purpose was to test this hypothesis in a situation of nonspecific stress different from the pain stress employed previously. In designing the stress situation employed here we also attempted to provide simultaneous and independent measurements of perceptual performance in order to determine whether motor disturbance was related to accuracy of perceptual performance.

METHOD

In an attempt to reproduce the essential features of the Luria method (combining speech with finger movement, including the feature of stress, but excluding the feature of emotion-producing verbal cues specific to any individual's system of associations), we employed a test involving speeded size discrimination, which we have called the Rapid Discrimination Test (RDT). The RDT was given following the administration of our Pain-Stress Test.

The subject (*S*), seated in a darkened room, viewed a screen 18 inches by 24 inches on which were projected six circles, like those shown in Figure I. The task was to choose the largest circle and to call out its number before the next set of six circles appeared on the screen. If *S* made an error (called out the wrong number) or failed to respond in time, a buzzer was sounded by the examiner. There were 20 sets of circles, like the set shown in Figure I. In the first part of the test, each of the 20 sets was presented for 5 seconds: the first set of six circles came on the screen, 5 seconds later the second set of six circles came on the screen, and so on. In the second part of the test the same 20 sets were presented in the same

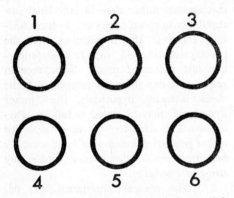

Figure 1. One of the sets of circles used in the size discrimination test

order, but presentation time was shortened to 3 seconds, and in the third part of the test, presentation time was still more rapid (2 seconds). Between presentations there was a 30-second rest period. The total administration time for the test was 4 minutes 20 seconds.

In addition to calling out the number of the largest circle, *S* was required to press with his right forefinger on a button (at the time of the verbal response). Both left and right forefingers rested on buttons which were attached to Rochelle salt crystals whose outputs were fed into two channels of an Offner electroencephalograph. These provided ink tracings (Luria-type records) of finger movement throughout the test.

A team of operators was required for the present experiment. The examiner, who was seated in the room with *S*, gave instruc-

tions to *S* before the test, and during the test kept a record of *S*'s responses and sounded the buzzer following errors or omissions. The other operators were stationed in the adjoining control room. One was required to operate the projector, and the others were engaged with the physiological recordings.

The slide projector was operated manually in rhythm with flashes from a pilot light on an electronic interval timer. The relay which closed the light circuit also served to activate a signal marker on the polygraph used for physiological recording.

The recording amplifications were adjusted so that a slight "normal" tremor was just visible in the left finger record, while the right finger record was taken at a level below that required to observe "normal" tremor. As noted before, a signal marker served to indicate on the record the time of each single stimulus presentation. Sounding of the buzzer was recorded as a 60-cycle oscillation.

Test Reliability

Reliability of discrimination accuracy was estimated in two ways: (I) Test-retest reliability was 0.86. This represents the rank-order correlation coefficient for 10 *S*s tested two different occasions, a week or more apart. (2) Item consistency was estimated in the following way. The mean number of errors for each of the 20 items was computed separately for the group of 21 control *S*s and the group of 15 anxiety-patients. The two mean values for each item were paired and the rank-order correlation determined for the 20 pairs was 0.95.

Validity of RDT as a Stress Test

An objective indication of stressfulness is provided by the lymphocyte count. The RDT produced a statistically significant drop in number of circulating lymphocytes. As might have been expected, because of its brevity and absence of noxious stimulation, the amount of drop in lymphocytes was less than that found in association with the Pain-Stress Test (*II*).

Treatment of Finger Movement Data

Three aspects of the records were selected for quantitative treatment. These were (1) regularity and duration of voluntary right-finger pressure, (2) frequency and magnitude of left-finger activity occurring synchronously with right-finger pressure, (3) the frequency with which left-finger activity occurred during times when no voluntary finger pressure was taking place. In order to obtain measures of each aspect of motor disturbance, simple rating methods involving clearly objective criteria were employed. All ratings were carried out by a technician from whom the nature of the case was concealed. The following measures were employed:

1. *Right pressure-quality.* Pressure-quality was rated on a four-point scale. A smooth, regular, single pressure-response was given a rating of 1, whereas a disorganized response containing at least four major oscillations of the pressure line was rated 4. Figure 2 shows examples of all four ratings.

2. *Left synchronous finger movement (SFM).* This was rated on a three-point scale. The rating was zero if no synchronous move-

were made. Because the number of voluntary pressures was not the same from S to S, mean ratings for each series and for the whole test were determined by dividing the total of the ratings by the number of pressures in each case. This procedure ruled out the influence of differing frequency of pressure for the various Ss. The LFI ratings which were not dependent upon the occurrence of voluntary pressure were simply added (for each series and for the whole test) in computing the LFI scores.

Statistics

The chi-square test was employed to test the reliability of group differences. The test

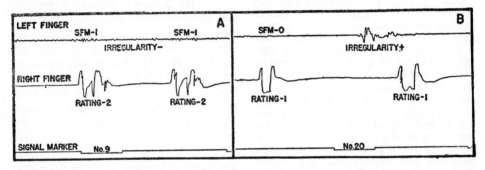

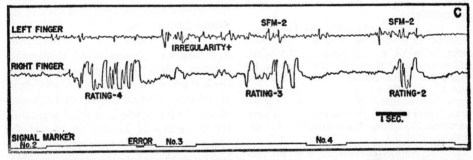

Figure 2. Illustration of rating methods by reference to sample recording of synchronous finger movement. Note that left-finger irregularity is scored + or −, and that SFM and right-finger pressure are rated in terms of numbers.

ment was apparent in the left-finger line at the time of right pressure. If a slight movement was visible, a rating of 1 was assigned; if a large oscillation occurred, a rating of 2 was given (see Fig. 2 for examples).

3. *Left-finger irregularity (LFI).* This rating was made on a plus-or-minus basis. If clearly visible oscillation, beyond that of natural tremor, was present during periods of no voluntary pressure, a plus rating was assigned (see Fig. 2).

Pressure quality and SFM could be scored only when voluntary pressure responses

was applied to fourfold distributions made by selecting the division point as close as possible to the median of the total subject group.

For various technical reasons parts of the data were not available in a few cases. The N's are presented in the tables.

Subjects

The original group consisted of 21 normal controls and 76 psychiatric patients. The patients were (1) psychoneurotics and (2) acute psychotics from the psychiatric department of a large general hospital, and (3) chronic schizophrenics from a mental hospital.

1. *Psychoneurotic group.* There were 45 patients in this group, 20 males and 25 females. Mean age was 37.6 years, with a range from 17 to 60. Anxiety was a prominent symptom in nearly all cases, but only 15 (5 males and 10 females) presented clearly predominant anxiety states in the absence of other equally prominent clinical features (such as depression, hysterical features, alcoholism). Mean age for this group of 15 cases was 31.1 (range from 17 to 52).

This group of 15 cases will be referred to as the "anxiety-patient group." The remaining 30 patients will be called the "mixed neurotic group." The separation into subgroups was made entirely on clinical grounds and was entirely independent of the patient's performance in the RDT. The distinction here is similar to the one of Malmo and Shagass (9) except that *all* psychotics were omitted from the present mixed group.

2. *Acute psychotic group.* Mean age for the 14 patients in this group was 33.4 years, ranging from 19 to 61. There were 8 males and 6 females. Schizophrenic symptoms were present in 11, 2 were paranoid states, and 1 was an endogenous depression. None had ever required prolonged commitment to a mental hospital, and none showed deterioration.

3. *Chronic schizophrenics.* The 17 patients in this group were all males. Age varied from 19 to 37, with a mean of 28.5 years. Mean time since onset of symptoms was 4.5 years, and mean duration of hospitalization was 3 years. Only 1 patient had shown any prolonged remission since the start of his illness. Types of schizophrenia represented were paranoid, 10; simple, 4; catatonic, 2; unclassified, 1.

4. *Normal controls.* This group contained 7 males and 14 females. Mean age was 26.0 years, ranging from 18 to 39. Most of these *S*s were employed during the day and enrolled for night classes in a small urban college. As a group, adjustment was about average as determined by the Cornell Selectee and Seitz-McFarland inventories.

Inasmuch as it was not possible to match these groups exactly with respect to factors of age and sex, the possible influence of these factors was assessed separately for each of the factors involved. For blood pressure, factors of age and sex were partialed out by means of *T*-scores. With the exception of left synchronous movement, in which male scores were reliably higher than female scores, no significant sex differences were found, and

except for the cardiovascular measures there were no significant correlations with age.

RESULTS

Accuracy in Discrimination

Table 1 and Figure 3 present data showing that controls, psychoneurotics, and acute psychotics made size discriminations with about equal accuracy. Actually, although the differences were not statistically significant, these patients were slightly more accurate in their discriminations than were the controls.

The number of erroneous responses was about the same in all groups, including those chronic schizophrenics who were cooperative enough to attempt the discriminations. The 12 chronic schizophrenics who fell into this category omitted significantly more responses than any other group. Omissions rather than erroneous responses were responsible for their fewer correct responses. With respect to the mean number of correct responses, statistically significant differences were found between the chronic schizophrenics and each of the three other groups.

The evidence which we have from item analysis indicates a fair relationship between difficulty of the item and failure in the schizophrenic group. Mean number of all errors (including omissions) from each of the 20 items was computed separately for the group of 21 control *S*s and the group of 12 chronic schizophrenics. The two mean-values for each item were paired, and the rank-order correlation determined for the 20 pairs was .77. It should be noted that this value is lower than that obtained when the anxiety-patient group was paired with the control group (.95). This difference suggests that inattention may have been an important contributing factor in the schizophrenics' lower score.

Measures of Motor Disorganization

We may now proceed to a comparison of the groups with respect to the measures of motor disorganization. Measures

TABLE 1. ACCURACY IN DISCRIMINATION PERFORMANCE

Group	N	Mean no. correct responses series			Total test	Mean no. omissions series			Total test
		I	II	III		I	II	III	
Controls	21	14.6	13.2	11.6	39.4	1.4	2.6	5.4	9.4
Psychoneurotics	44	15.5	14.3	11.9	41.7	1.8	2.6	5.0	9.4
Acute psychotics	14	14.9	14.6	11.8	41.3	1.6	2.4	5.6	9.6
Chronic schiz.	12	11.2	10.2	8.2	29.6	4.3	5.7	8.8	18.8

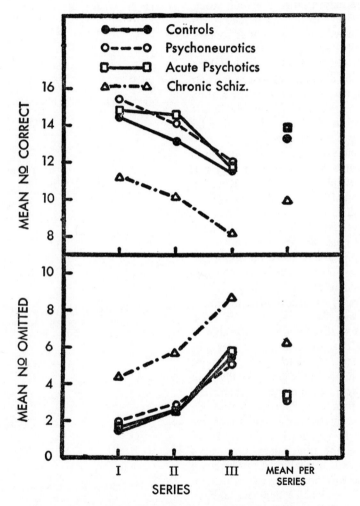

Figure 3. Graphs comparing the groups with respect to perceptual performance. (Note that curves for psychoneurotics, acute psychotics, and controls are practically identical.)

from all groups except chronic schizophrenics may be directly compared without the necessity for taking the factor of dis-criminative accuracy into account. In the case of chronic schizophrenics, however, caution must be exercised in the interpretation of their motor records, because of their poorer co-operation in this test.

Right pressure-quality. Table 2 presents the median values for ratings of voluntary pressure with the right forefinger. The superiority of the controls is very evident. Their lower median ratings signify more discrete, better coordinated (less disturbed) pressures than those of the patients. One may arrange the four groups in order of severity of the psychotic disorder (from least to greatest) as follows: (1) controls, (2) psychoneurotics, (3) acute psychotics, and (4) chronic schizophrenics. The differences between the control group and each of the other three groups were all statistically significant. There were no significant differences between any two patient-groups.

Because of procedural limitation of response duration occurring in Series II and III (particularly in Series III), no importance should be attached to the general trend (in all groups) toward lowering of rating values from one series to the next.

Left synchronous finger movement. The lower the rating score the more discrete the response in the sense that response was limited to pressure with the *right* forefinger, without the left forefinger being involved. Reference to Tables 4 and 5 again reveals that response in the control group was characterized by greater discreteness than that in the patient groups. Patients' voluntary pressures with the right forefinger were accompanied by more left forefinger pressures than controls. Although showing the same pattern as for right pressure-quality, intergroup differences among the three diagnostic groups were small and unreliable. The difference between patients and controls in this instance is of questionable significance, however, because of the sex factor. Frequency of LSM was greater in males than in females, and the proportion of males to females is higher in the patient group than it is in the control group.

Left-finger irregularity. Of the three motor measures this one resembles most

the measure of finger movement which Malmo and Shagass (9) found to be highly correlated with severity of anxiety. It is, therefore, of special interest to find in the present study that of the three motor measures, this measure was the only one which yielded a reliable difference between anxiety patients and mixed neurotics (see

TABLE 2. MEDIAN RIGHT PRESSURE-QUALITY RATINGS (FOUR-POINT SCALE)

Group	N	Series			Total test
		I	II	III	
Controls (C)	21	1.63	1.48	1.31	1.48
Psychoneurotics (PN)	42	1.95	1.80	1.63	1.77
Acute psychotics (AP)	13	2.15	2.10	1.55	1.90
Chronic schiz. (CS)	9	2.75	2.65	1.95	2.50
All patients	64	2.12	2.02	1.68	1.92

TABLE 3. P-VALUES FROM CHI-SQUARE TEST OF DIFFERENCES IN RIGHT PRESSURE-QUALITY RATINGS

Groups	Series			Total test
	I	II	III	
C vs. PN	.13	.07	.04	.04
C vs. AP	.03	.02	.11	.05
C vs. CS	.05	.03	.03	.03
C vs. All patients	.04	.02	.02	<.01

TABLE 4. MEDIAN RATINGS OF LEFT SYNCHRONOUS FINGER MOVEMENT (THREE-POINT SCALE)

Group	N	Series			Total test
		I	II	III	
Controls (C)	20	0.80	0.93	1.00	0.92
Psychoneurotics (PN)	42	1.50	1.40	1.40	1.37
Acute psychotics (AP)	13	1.63	1.63	1.43	1.45
Chronic schiz. (CS)	9	1.83	1.50	1.70	1.65
All patients	64	1.65	1.43	1.43	1.45

TABLE 5. P-VALUES FROM CHI-SQUARE TEST OF DIFFERENCES IN LEFT SYNCHRONOUS FINGER MOVEMENT

Groups	Series			Total test
	I	II	III	
C vs. PN	<.01	.04	.08	.02
C vs. AP	.02	.03	.03	.03
C vs. CS	<.01	.21	<.01	.02
C vs. All patients	<.01	.02	<.01	<.01

TABLE 6. MEDIAN NUMBER OF LEFT-FINGER IRREGULARITIES

| Group | N | Series | | | Total test |
		I	II	III	
Controls (C)	20	5.2	2.7	2.8	12.8
Psychoneurotics (PN)	44	8.3	4.8	4.9	18.0
Acute psychotics (AP)	13	8.5	5.8	3.5	15.3
Chronic schizophrenics (CS)	15	8.3	6.2	7.3	21.0
All patients	72	8.3	4.8	5.4	18.4
Anxiety patients	15	12.5	8.3	5.4	29.0
Mixed neurotics	29	5.6	4.1	3.9	12.5

Tables 6 and 7 and section on "Subjects"). It should also be noted that the *only* statistically reliable difference for Series I was that between these two groups. This suggests that in anxiety, overreaction during the initial period of a task situation is more inclined to occur as abrupt breaks in the regularity of "tonic" or background motor activity. It will be noted that, with the

TABLE 7. *P*-VALUES FROM CHI-SQUARE TEST OF DIFFERENCES IN LEFT-FINGER IRREGULARITIES

| Groups | Series | | | Total test |
	I	II	III	
C vs. PN	.10	.30	.02	.05
C vs. AP	.18	.08	.21	.19
C vs. CS	.17	.04	<.01	.05
C vs. All patients	.08	.09	<.01	.03
Anxiety pt's vs. Mixed neurotics	<.01	.19	.12	.03

exception of the anxiety-patient group, the most reliable differences between patients and controls were found in Series III. There were no reliable differences between acute psychotics and controls.

Physiological Data

A detailed account of these data are to be presented elsewhere. Muscular tension, as measured electromyographically, was found to be significantly lower in controls than in patients. Psychoneurotics and acute psychotics were higher in systolic blood pressure than normals and chronic schizophrenics.

Intermeasure Correlations

Discriminative accuracy vs. movement ratings. From the finding that controls showed consistently superior motor performance, but not greater discriminative accuracy, when compared with psychoneurotics, we may infer that the correlation between these two variables is probably low. In order to obtain further data on this point, correlation coefficients were computed.

The correlations between discriminative accuracy and each of the three movement ratings were (*a*) with right pressure-quality, .05; with left synchronous movement, .14; and with left-finger irregularity, .27. These correlations are all low. The correlation of .27 is barely significant statistically, indicating a slight tendency for accuracy to be associated with left-finger irregularity. These data are consistent with the conclusion that motor disturbance was practically independent of discriminative accuracy.

Intercorrelations among the three movement-ratings. As might have been expected, the highest correlation was that between the two measures involving the left hand (.38). The lowest correlation (.02) was obtained with right pressure-quality and left synchronous movement. Correlation between right pressure-quality and left-finger irregularity was .26. These intercorrelations indicate a high degree of independence among measures.

Correlation between right pressure-quality and muscular tension in the right arm. Correlations with right pressure-quality were .04 for muscle potential level and .19 for muscle potential change, indicating a high degree of independence between the pressure ratings and muscular tension. This means that we are not justified in speaking of finger-movement measures as tension measures.

Qualitative Observations

Some interesting features of the records could not be completely incorporated in the quantitative scores employed in the present study. Figure 4 presents two phenomena of this sort. In Figure 4*A* a full left pressure is "substituted" for the usual right pressure, when toward the end of the most rapid series (No. III) the subject was making numerous errors and omissions. From the record it appeared that when blocking occurred in execution of right-finger pressure, the action sequence was "completed" by the left finger.

more instances of this kind of correlation between discriminative performance and motor activity. However, our statistical tests, carried out in several ways, failed to show reliable evidence of greater motor disturbance occurring after error (or omission). One reason for these negative statistical results may be noted in the fact that the subject of Figure 4*B* made no further errors during the period of motor disturbance shown in the figure.

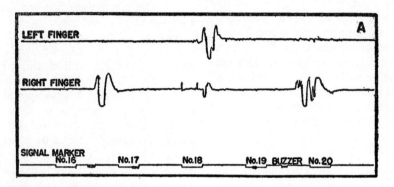

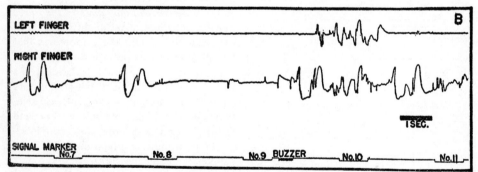

Figure 4. *A*. Full left pressure "substituted" for usual right pressure. *B*. Sudden change from regular, well-coordinated pressure to a disorganized state of activity.

Figure 4*B* shows a sudden transition from regular, well-coordinated pressures to a disorganized state of activity involving both hands. This is the kind of disturbance which Luria found associated with emotion-producing stimuli. Our subject may very well have been reacting to his failure to respond to item 8, which was his first error in Series II. The buzzer sound which followed this omission appeared to "trigger off" the motor disturbance. Actually, we expected to find many

DISCUSSION

The present study was designed to provide further data bearing on the hypothesis that psychoneurotic disorders involve defective motor regulation manifested by abnormally increased motor disturbance under any stressful condition. The results support the hypothesis. All measures of motor activity recorded during performance of speeded size discrimination yielded reliable differences between patients and controls. In every instance there was evidence of greater physiological disturbance in the patients. The measures employed may be distinguished as skeletal-motor (motor control, muscular tension) and autonomic (systolic blood pressure).

These differences in motor activity were manifested even though psychoneurotics, acute psychotics, and controls were practically identical with respect to perceptual performance. These results lead us to question the neglect of motor aspects of behavior in most studies dealing with personality and, especially, with its pathological manifestations in psychiatric disorders. The strong emphasis on perceptual aspects of behavior (as in the Rorschach test) in the field of personality analysis has undoubtedly been amply justified, but it would seem that more attention should be directed toward motor phenomena in this field.

In our laboratory, evidence of regulatory deficiency in motor systems has been obtained under three different conditions of nonspecific stress.[1] This consistency of findings under varied conditions of stress strengthens the "motor hypothesis" (as distinguished from the "stress intensity" hypothesis).

The nature of these probable regulatory deficiencies remains a problem for future research. But considering the recent findings of Malmo, Shagass, and J. F. Davis (10), it may not be too early to suggest that the current neurophysiological work on the brain stem and thalamic reticular systems may reveal the neural basis of this motor regulation which seems defective in psychoneurosis.

[1] Malmo, R. B., and Shagass, C. Studies of blood pressure in psychiatric patients under stress. *Psychosom. Med.* (in press).
Malmo, R. B., Shagass, C., and Davis, J. F. Electromyographic studies of muscular tension in psychiatric patients under stress. *J. clin. exper. Psychopath.*, 1951, *12*, 45-66.

REFERENCES

1. Albino, R. C. The stabile and labile personality types of Luria in clinically normal individuals. *Brit. J. Psychol.*, 1948, *39*, 54–60.

2. Barnacle, C. H., Ebaugh, F. G., and Lemere, F. Association-motor investigation of the psychoneuroses. *Amer. J. Psychiat.*, 1935, *91*, 925–937.

3. Burtt, H. E. Motor concomitants of the association reaction. *J. exp. Psychol.*, 1936, *19*, 51–63.

4. Ebaugh, F. G. Association-motor investigation in clinical psychiatry. *J. ment. Sci.*, 1936, *82*, 731–743.

5. Gardner, J. W. An experimental study of the Luria technique for detecting mental conflict. *J. exp. Psychol.*, 1937, *20*, 495–506.

6. Huston, P. E., Shakow, D., and Erickson, M. H. A study of hypnotically induced complexes by means of the Luria technique. *J. gen. Psychol.*, 1934, *11*, 65–97.

7. Krause, L. S. Relation of voluntary motor pressure disorganization (Luria) to two other alleged complex indicators. *J. exp. Psychol.*, 1937, *21*, 653–661.

8. Luria, A. R. *The nature of human conflicts.* New York: Liveright, 1932.

9. Malmo, R. B., and Shagass, C. Physiologic studies of reaction to stress in anxiety and early schizophrenia. *Psychosom. Med.*, 1949, *11*, 9–24.

10. Malmo, R. B., Shagass, C., and Davis, J. F. A method for the investigation of somatic response mechanisms in psychoneuroses. *Science*, 1950, *112*, 325–328.

11. Malmo, R. B., Shagass, C., Davis, J. F., Cleghorn, R. A., Graham, B. F., and Goodman, A. J. Standardized pain stimulation as controlled stress in physiological studies of psychoneurosis. *Science*, 1948, *108*, 509–511.

12. Olson, D. M., and Jones, V. An objective measure of emotionally toned attitudes. *Ped. Sem.*, 1931, *39*, 174–196.

13. Reymert, M. L., and Speer, G. S. Does the Luria technique measure emotion or merely bodily tension? A re-evaluation of the method. *Character & Pers.*, 1938-39, *7*, 192–200.

14. Runkel, J. E. Luria's motor method and word association in the study of deception. *J. gen. Psychol.*, 1936, *15*, 23–37.

15. Shagass, C. Word association tests for pilot selection. *Bull. Can. psychol. Ass.*, 1945, *5*, 81–82.

A Test of Some Behavioral Hypotheses Drawn from Alexander's Specificity Theory

SARNOFF A. MEDNICK, ANN MARGARET GARNER, AND HERBERT K. STONE

ALEXANDER's theory regarding the correlation of specific personality organizations with certain somatic conditions (1) has been the subject of much discussion in the literature. In an attempt to make this theory more accessible to experimental test it has been translated into more strictly and unequivocally behavioral terms.[1] Table 1 presents a summary statement of this translation. As may be seen, it is hypothesized that upon encountering a problem situation the peptic ulcer patient will tend to feel optimistic regarding his chances of success, tend to

consistently along comparable continua. Where the ulcer patient is optimistic, the ulcerative colitis patient is hopeless; where the ulcer patient persists to accomplishment, the ulcerative colitis patient gives up; where the ulcer patient stresses his own role in his efforts, the ulcerative colitis patient projects blame.

As a first test of the hypotheses expressed in Table 1 it was decided to compare these two groups with each other and another "nonpsychosomatic" chronically ill group of orthopedic cases. A technique was developed in which S was confronted with

TABLE 1. HYPOTHESES ABOUT ATTITUDES TOWARD PROBLEM SITUATIONS

	Initial attitude	Behavior	Afterreaction
Ulcerative colitis	Hopeless: devil-may-care	Gives up, or fantastic, unreal performance	Projection
Ulcer	Optimistic	Persists to accomplishment	Denial of dependence
Hypertension	Persistent, stubborn	Realistically struggles to impossible goals	Bitter, fatalistic
Dermatitis	Compulsion to fail conspicuously	Fails	Self-punitive if successful

work on the problem until it is completed, and to deny or minimize any help he may have received. While none of the listings under the category headings is completely dimensionally independent of any other, two of the conditions seem to vary most

[1] These behavioral hypotheses were formulated by Alexander. They grew out of findings most frequently reported by staff members of the Institute for Psychoanalysis, Chicago, regarding cases manifesting psychosomatic complaints. Their source is lengthy, detailed, analytically oriented case material. Predicting from this set of data to a limited problem-solving situation is difficult; the hypotheses were offered in the interest of objectifying the investigation of the specificity problem, and must be regarded as tentative.

Reprinted by permission from the *American Journal of Orthopsychiatry*, Vol. 29, 1954.

ambiguous behavioral situations which he could interpret in line with his hypothesized mode of reaction.

Hypothesis 1. In an ambiguous situation, the ulcer S will tend to predict that he will be successful while the ulcerative colitis S will tend to predict that he will fail.

The situations were then allowed to become less and less ambiguous and more and more in conflict with S's hypothesized mode of reaction. The S's tenacity in clinging to this now inappropriate mode of reaction was taken as a measure of the strength of his hypothesized tendency.

Hypothesis 2. In a situation where it becomes increasingly clear that S will fail, ulcer Ss will tend to resist seeing this longer than the ulcerative colitis or orthopedic patients. In a situation where it becomes increasingly clear that S will succeed, ulcerative colitis Ss will tend to resist seeing this longer than the ulcer or orthopedic patients.

Hypothesis 3. Ulcer patients will persist longer at a task in which they are apparently failing than will the orthopedic or ulcerative colitis patients.

Hypothesis 4. On a postexperimental situation questionnaire the ulcer Ss will check more items denying dependence than will the other groups. The ulcerative colitis Ss will check more items projecting blame than will the other groups.

METHOD

Apparatus. The apparatus confronting S was a confusing array of dials and wires. The only aspect of it that S was concerned with was a Miles pursuit rotor (a turntable with a small brass target which S follows with a hinged stylus). The remainder of the apparatus was intended to enhance the brass instrument character of the situation, disguise the purpose of the study and promote S's cooperation.

Subjects. Three groups of Ss were tested. Group U was composed of 20 outpatients of the Gastrointestinal Clinics of Michael Reese Hospital and Montgomery Ward Clinic, Northwestern University Medical School (both of Chicago, Ill.), all of whom had an X-ray-confirmed clinic diagnosis of peptic ulcer. The average age and education of this group were 42.8 and 8.6 years, respectively. Group C was composed of 17 outpatients of the Gastrointestinal Clinic of the University of Illinois Hospital, Chicago, all of whom had a proctoscopic and X-ray-confirmed clinical diagnosis of ulcerative colitis. The average age and education of this group were 33.8 and 10.0 years, respectively. Group O was composed of 20 hospitalized orthopedic patients of the University of Illinois Hospital.

The average age and education of this group were 33.2 and 10.3 years, respectively.

Subjects were recruited during one of their regular meetings to the clinic or in the case of the orthopedic patients during hospital rounds. Inasmuch as the clinic patients were waiting to be seen by their physician, less than 10 per cent of those invited to participate refused.

PROCEDURE

Initial attitude. The pursuit rotor apparatus was briefly described and demonstrated by E. The E then said, "We have found that the average person your age can keep the pointer on the disk for one tenth of a second out of ten seconds on the first try. I want to see how well you can do. Do you think you'll be able to do as well as the average person your age?" The S was then given a ten-second trial and was told he was successful.

Strength of initial attitude. The E then said, "We have found that the average Air Force man, after twenty-four trials of practice, can keep the pointer on the disk for seven seconds out of ten. Do you think that after twenty-four trials of practice you will be able to do this?" This was further explained if necessary to ensure S's understanding. The S's answer was recorded and the trials were begun. The S was informed of his score after each trial during the 20-second rest between trials. At the end of every even-numbered trial E said, "On your last trial, which was the .... th, you got a score of .... seconds. Do you think you'll be able to make a seven out of ten score?"

Two specially prepared lists of scores, rather than S's true scores, were reported to S. The Ss were alternately assigned to two lists. List S (Success) was meant to give S the feeling that he would succeed. The progression of the scores was markedly negatively accelerated. List F (Failure) was meant to give S the feeling that he would fail and was markedly positively accelerated. Each list consisted of 24 scores. At the very end of both lists Ss were told they had succeeded in meeting the criterion.

To provide material for the later questionnaire all Ss were told (after the fourth trial), "It usually helps if you stand on the balls of your feet and rotate your whole body instead of just your arm." After the eighth trial all Ss were told, "Since the trials are so short you might find it helpful if you hold your breath for the ten seconds. This will prevent your chest muscles from interfering with your arm and shoulder muscles." When, owing to some mishap, an S did very poorly he was told that he "did not do so well on this trial." All Ss seemed to accept the reported scores as true.

One reason the pursuit rotor was employed is the inherent interest which the task seems to have for people from all walks of life. The Ss of this study seemed completely absorbed in the situation. They seemed to regard it as a game of skill, became deeply involved in their performance and satisfied at their ultimate success.

Test of persistence. After a few minutes of rest, Ss were told, "I am going to turn up the turntable speed so that it will be much harder to keep up with. With the faster speed I want to see if you can get good enough to keep the pointer on the disk for twelve seconds out of fifteen. If you think you will be able to make it, just keep going. However, since we are a bit rushed for time (here E looked at his wristwatch) you can stop at any time, whenever you think you won't be able to make twelve seconds out of fifteen." The S was then asked whether he thought he would make the criterion, and the first 15-second trial was run. After the second trial and every even-numbered trial thereafter, E reported a score to S from a previously devised list. All Ss were read the same list of scores. The list was constructed to be extremely discouraging. After reading the score E said, "Well, you're not doing so well, are you? Remember, if you don't think you will make it you can stop at any time and we can go on to the last part of the study."

"Projection" and "Denial of Dependence" scores. After S indicated that he felt he could not attain the criterion he was given a questionnaire and asked to answer all questions. The questionnaire consisted of 18 items designed to tap tendencies toward projection and/or denial of dependence. Each tendency was represented by 9 items drawn from a larger pool of items submitted to 15 judges (psychologists and psychiatrists of advanced training). On most items selected there was unanimous agreement. An item with less than 90 per cent agreement was rejected. The items may be found in Table 2.

RESULTS

Initial attitude. When asked initially whether they thought they could do as well as the average person their age most Ss said "yes" (70% of Group O, 95% of Group U, and 82% of Group C). The intergroup differences were not significant (chi square = 3.93, 2 df).

Strength of initial attitude. It will be recalled that in this task S was asked on alternate trials whether he felt he would reach the criterion. Two methods of analyzing the resultant data will be presented. The first is a count of the total number of times S answered affirmatively. This might be termed an "optimism" score. Scores could and did range between 0 and 12. It would be predicted that the ulcer group would score highest on this measure. Table 3 presents an analysis of variance of these data. The differences between the U, C, and O groups were not significant, indicating that disease group could not be used to predict the optimism score. The S and F treatments did not influence the optimism score, suggesting that idiosyncratic factors were predominantly producing the variability.

Another method of analyzing the data is a count of the number of consecutive trials, counting from the last trial, that S affirms he will reach the criterion. This response may run consecutively through all the trials or may come as late as the twenty-second trial. It may be termed an "assurance score," i.e., the point at which S is sure he will make the criterion. The scores could and did range between 0 and 12. It would be predicted that the ulcer group would score highest on this score. Table 4 presents an analysis of variance of these data. A t test disclosed no significant difference between sexes on this score (t = .13, 35 df) so that this variable was not included in the analysis of variance. The results repeat those of Table 3.

Persistence score. In this section of the study S was asked to quit when he felt he would not be able to reach the criterion. Here the scores could and did range from 1 to 24 trials. The higher the score the greater the persistence. It would be predicted here that Group U would persist longest, getting the largest scores, while the ulcerative colitis group would give up earliest. A t test between sex groups disclosed no significant difference (t = .67, 35 df). Table 5 presents an analysis of variance of these data. The difference between the U, C and O groups was not significant, indicating that disease group could not be used to predict the persistence score.

Projection score. An individual's projection score was the number of "Projection" items on the questionnaire he marked as "True." This score could range from 0 to 9, but actually ranged from 0 to 7. It would be predicted that the ulcerative colitis group would have the

that Group U would have the highest denial of dependence score. Table 7 presents an analysis of variance of the denial of dependency score data. The differences were not significant.

DISCUSSION

As pointed out by Streitfeld (2), the specificity hypothesis has been well received in clinical literature. However, experimental studies which have utilized

TABLE 2. ITEMS COMPRISING THE "PROJECTION AND DENIAL OF DEPENDENCY" QUESTIONNAIRE

Projection

1. The turntable did not maintain a constant speed and this sometimes threw me off.
2. The examiners made the goals too high.
3. The connections of the clock weren't working well on my trials because a few times I was on target longer than the clock said.
4. The examiner talked too much and this tended to lower my score.
5. Having a hinge in the middle of the pointer made it too hard to handle and cut down on my score.
6. On the last part I felt that the examiner wanted me to quit.
7. I can't put my finger on it but something was wrong with the equipment and this kept confusing me.
8. A person should be allowed to do the task while sitting.
9. The hint which the examiner gave me about holding my breath cut down on my score.

Denial of Dependency

1. You learn to do something better when you learn it by yourself.
2. The hint which the examiner gave me about holding my breath may be helpful to some people but did not particularly help me.
3. I have always preferred to work on my own where I do not have to depend on other people.
4. The hints which the examiner gave me about rotating my whole body may be helpful to some people but did not particularly help me.
5. If the examiner had just let me work on my own, I would have done just as well.
6. The rest period between trials may be helpful to some people but I did not feel they were particularly necessary.
7. The advice of the examiner about the way to hold the pointer may be helpful to some people but did not particularly help me.
8. I think I could have done just as well without the examiner's instructions.
9. In general I thought I did well, but especially when I was working on my own.

---

highest projection score. Table 6 presents an analysis of variance of the projection score data. The differences were not significant.

Denial of dependence score. An individual's denial of dependence score was the number of such items on the questionnaire he marked as "True." This score could range from 0 to 9, but actually ranged from 0 to 8. It would be predicted

adequate control groups have tended to fail to clearly support the hypothesis. In view of the fact that the hypothesis deals mainly with unconscious processes, it was never clear that any individual investigative technique adequately tapped the hypothesized conflict. In this instance Alexander and his colleagues have attempted to translate their hypotheses into immediately behavioral terms. The test of this particular

TABLE 3. ANALYSIS OF VARIANCE OF OPTIMISM SCORES

Source	df	MS	F	P
Diagnostic groups	2	.880	—	n.s.
Failure-Success schedules	1	.02	—	n.s.
Sex	1	.02	—	n.s.
D X F *	2	.405	—	n.s.
D X S	2	2.51	—	n.s.
F X S	1	4.37	1.41	n.s.
D X F X S	2	2.215	—	n.s.
Error	45	3.09		

* In this and the following tables, D X F denotes the interaction of Diagnostic groups with Failure-Success schedules D X S denotes the interaction of Diagnostic groups with Sex, etc. The abbreviation n.s. stands for "not significant."—Ed.

TABLE 4. ANALYSIS OF VARIANCE OF ASSURANCE SCORES

Source	df	MS	F	P
Diagnostic groups	2	.2137	—	n.s.
Failure-Success schedules	1	.0004	—	n.s.
D X F	2	2.715	1.14	n.s.
Error	51	2.338		

TABLE 5. ANALYSIS OF VARIANCE OF PERSISTENCE SCORES

Source	df	MS	F	P
Diagnostic groups	2	2.0532	—	n.s.
Failure-Success schedules	1	.0032	—	n.s.
D X F	2	1.92	—	n.s.
Error	51	6.43		

TABLE 6. ANALYSIS OF VARIANCE OF PROJECTION SCORES

Source	df	MS	F	P
Between diagnostic groups	2	.68	—	n.s.
Within diagnostic groups	54	2.77		

TABLE 7. ANALYSIS OF VARIANCE OF DENIAL
OF DEPENDENCE SCORES

Source	df	MS	F	P
Between diagnostic groups	2	2.38	—	n.s.
Within diagnostic groups	54	4.57		

translation does not support the hypotheses put forth regarding the ulcer and ulcerative colitis groups.

The utter lack of positive results or even suggestive trends deserves comment. It is fairly clear that the hypothesized attitudes and behaviors did not manifest themselves in this experimental situation. A possible explanation might state that these hypothesized attitudes and behaviors were learned in highly interpersonal, social stimulus situations. When *S*s are brought into the laboratory, which is social in a very minor way, these attitudes and behaviors are not elicited. This explanation points up the importance of considering both dynamic and stimulus-response aspects in theoretical analyses and prediction of psychological events.

SUMMARY AND CONCLUSIONS

In the interests of greater precision and clarity, Alexander has translated the specificity hypothesis into concrete predictions of the behavior of "psychosomatic" groups in a problem situation. The predictions concerning the ulcer and ulcerative colitis groups were tested by means of a behavioral projective technique and questionnaire. The results do not support the predictions.

REFERENCES

1. Alexander, F. "Psychological Factors in Gastrointestinal Disturbances," in F. Alexander and T. French (Eds.), *Studies in Psychosomatic Medicine*. New York: Ronald Press, 1948.

2. Streitfeld, H. S. Specificity of Peptic Ulcer to Intense Oral Conflicts. *Psychosom. Med.*, 1954, *16*, 315–326.

Response to Sensory Stimulation in Certain Psychosomatic Disorders

JOSEPH G. KEPECS, MILTON ROBIN, AND CLARE MUNRO

How does stimulation through senses other than vision and hearing influence and interact with the central personal elements of the person who is stimulated? The visual and auditory spheres, relating to the highest levels of cognition and sensory organization, have been extensively studied in many ways, such as by tachistoscopic presentations and projective tests. What can be learned from studying the central effects of stimulation of less highly intellectualized senses? More specifically, can we learn something about psychosomatic disorders through studying sensory modalities which

Reprinted by permission from *Psychosomatic Medicine*, Vol. 20, No. 5, 1958.

are presumably intimately related to them? Is there value to Wisdom's statement: (*19*) "A purely psychological disorder is one in which the imagination conducts basic conflicts in terms of projective images; a psychosomatic disorder is one in which the imagination conducts basic conflicts in terms of tactile or kinesthetic sensations."? Reusch (*16*) expresses a similar notion when he says, in referring to those infantile personalities who tend to get psychosomatic disorders, "In the process of perception, undue weight is placed upon proprioceptive stimuli, while certain exteroceptive stimuli are neglected. Information derived from perceptions to the chemical and mechanical sensory end organs is given more weight than information derived from the perception through the distance receivers. Apparently the shift from the *proximity* to the more complex distance receivers, which usually occurs in the course of progressive maturation, is absent or delayed." Having unsatisfactory means of self-expression and a preference for proximity receivers, there is "an overemphasis upon somatic signs and signals and a neglect of verbal or gestural signs and signals." Is there a specific tendency for particular sensory modalities to be linked to particular psychosomatic disorders? If so, what is the nature of this linkage? The experiments described below have to do with these and related questions.

EXPERIMENTAL PROCEDURE

Our present work grew out of previous studies in skin stimulation (*11, 12, 15*) in which we had been interested in peripheral manifestations of the central (emotional) state of the individual. We now are interested in both central and peripheral effects of sensory stimulation and in interrelationships existing between them at preconscious levels.* Influenced by recent studies by Fisher (*6*) and others in the visual area, we devised the following procedures:

SENSE STIMULATION

Three sensory modalities of each subject were stimulated.

Skin Sensation

This was elicited by 2 minutes of stroking the forehead with a bit of cotton wool. In previous studies using the same cotton test we found that most subjects felt a brief initial period of tickle or itch, followed by sensations of stroking, rubbing, or touching. This response we termed normal adaptation. Some individuals felt tickle, itch, or irritation throughout the test period; others reported only stroking

---

* For convenience, the immediate, consciously reported response to stimulation will be called peripheral; the preconsciously aroused affective and cognitive responses will be called central. We are aware that both types of responses are really central.

---

or touch sensations. We observed that normal adaptation occurred in persons whose emotions were well controlled; all itch-tickle responses occurred in emotionally labile individuals; all touch responses were in persons attempting excessive control of affects.

Proprioception

This was stimulated by requesting the subject to hold his arm (left arm in right-handed subjects) horizontal for 1 minute.

Smell

This was tested by handing the subject a strip of filter paper such as perfumers use, one end of which had been dipped into a special mixture of jasmine and skatol,† and requesting him to smell it. During each type of stimulation the subject was requested to give a running account of his sensations, which was recorded. This reporting concentrated his attention upon his sensations.

DRAWINGS

Each subject was tested with skin, muscle, and smell stimulation. This was done in more or less random order except that smell was usually tested last because the odor of the stimulus tends to persist in the room and thus might contaminate other stimuli. After each stimulus, the subject was asked to make a drawing. The only direction was: "Draw anything that comes to mind." Sometimes considerable encouragement was needed to get the per-

---

† Formula for JS (for convenience this mixture is referred to in text as JS):

	Parts by weight
Jasmin no. 49[a]	18
Skatol crystals[b]	2
Civet 40[b]	4
Indol @ 10% in alcohol[b]	4
Alcohol	252
TOTAL	280

[a] Fleuroma, Inc., New York.
[b] Givaudan-Delawanna, Inc., New York.

son to draw. After each drawing was made he was asked to tell what it was. When the three stimuli had been given and the three drawings were collected, the examiner discussed the drawings with the subject as follows:

Inquiry 1

Each picture was shown individually to the subject. He was asked to look at it, tell what it looked like to him, what it reminded him of, if he could regard it in any other way, etc. Finally he was asked: "Why did you draw this particular picture?"

All three drawings were then spread out on a desk before the subject and he was asked which one he liked best and which he liked least.

Inquiry 2

Again each picture was shown to the subject, but now he was told the particular stimulus which had immediately preceded his drawing the picture and asked if he could see any connections between what he had drawn and the stimulus. All three drawings were again spread out before the subject and he was asked which was most closely related to the preceding stimulus.

Our subjects consisted of four groups of patients. (1) asthmatics, (2) patients who suffered from atopic dermatitis (and 2 cases of localized neurodermatitis), (3) rheumatoid arthritics, and (4) hypertensives. Some of these patients came from the private practices of cooperating physicians, others from clinics at Michael Reese Hospital and the University of Illinois. Prior to testing, a brief interview was conducted to discuss the person's medical history and to obtain an account of his life and personal problems. This served to gain some information and the subject's cooperation. The test was explained as being based on our wish to know whether patients with various medical conditions feel things differently. The interview and testing were conducted by one of us (J.K.),

while one or both of the others (M. R. and C. M.) were in the room in almost all cases. The observers watched particularly for evidence that the examiner might be trying to bias the results of testing in accordance with our previously conceived hypotheses.

INITIAL ASSUMPTION

A. Our general assumption is that there is some characteristic association or connection between the effects of stimulating a particular sensory modality and the particular disorders from which the person suffers. Thus we expected that dermatitis patients would respond more emotionally to skin stimulation than to muscle or olfactory stimulation. We expected similar relationships between muscle stimulation and arthritis and between smell and asthma. We chose the hypertensive group for comparison, as there is no reason to expect to find a relationship between any of the sensory modalities tested and hypertension.

B. We wished to obtain information as to the central effects of peripheral stimulation. In almost every instance, the subject expressed no conscious awareness that the drawing he had made was in any way influenced by the immediately preceding stimulation. This question of conscious awareness was regularly tested in Inquiry 1 by asking why this particular drawing was made, and in only 4 instances out of a total of 135 drawings did the subject consciously relate the drawing to the stimulus. So, we consider that, taken as an entity, the process of sensory stimulation, central effect, and peripheral visual-motor response (the drawing) was a function of the periphery of consciousness or preconscious. (The subject was perfectly aware, e.g., of being tickled, of having some ideas and images, of making a drawing, but not that the images and drawings were influenced by the preceding stimulation.) By asking the subject to make a drawing, we ask him to translate the central effects of the peripheral stimulation into the visual-cognitive field, where it becomes accessible to objective regard and verbal description.

Two types of evidence indicate that sensory stimulation does have a considerable effect on what is drawn. One is the numerous times where, on the second Inquiry, subjects and examiners readily recognized a clear-cut and unquestionable relationship between stimulus and drawing; for example, after the muscle test a figure is drawn with an outstretched arm. The other line of evidence is the significant relationship between the responses on the inquiries to the drawings and the specific disorder the subject had. We believe these could not exist if there were no regular connection between the sensory stimulus and the drawing with its attendant associations.

CLINICAL EXAMPLES

ASTHMA

Mrs. I. N., a 43-year-old white woman, has suffered from asthma for 3 years. She relates the onset of asthma to trouble with her husband, from whom she is separated, and to the surgical removal of a needle from her thumb. "Whenever my husband would yell at me and pull me out of bed at night I'd get so scared I'd shake inside. I'd be mad, but as much as possible, I tried to keep quiet." This woman has 4 children. She has no other illnesses, no skin or gastrointestinal symptoms, no arthritis. She weeps easily as she discusses her troubles. (For convenience to the reader, all the responses to a particular type of stimulation will be presented together, though, as the description of our technical procedure indicates, they were not obtained in this order.)

1. Cotton Test. There were no tickle responses. She felt touch throughout the test period.

Drawing. "A boy fishing." She says, "This is the first thing that came to mind. Recently I helped my little girl make a picture like this for homework."

Inquiry 1. [What does the picture remind you of?] "My older boy—he likes to go fishing. If he stayed too long I'd worry about him. I always do stay home with my children. I worry if they don't come home when they are supposed to, but if they're having a good time I don't blame them for it. I never cared for fishing. I'd rather sit in the sun on the beach." [Why did you draw this?] "It came to mind because I was helping my daughter make a picture like this."

Inquiry 2. [You drew this after I stroked your forehead with cotton. Do you see any connection between this and your drawing?] "The way the hair hangs down would make me think of cotton, just like a little ball of cotton hanging down there."

2. Left arm held horizontal for 1 minute. She describes a feeling of strain through the elbow. The fingers feel a bit cold.

Drawing. "A house. Tables, chairs, windows, curtains." She says "This test sort of gets me nervous."

Inquiry 1. "The house. I'm always in the house. Seldom get out. My house is not the way I'd like it. This is how we drew houses as kids." [Why did you draw this?] "House—home—first thought in my head." [Do you have any feeling about it?] "No, I'm numb to it. I stay in the house and I do what I can."

Inquiry 2. [Any relationship to holding your arm up?] "I still get very tired in the evening after working in the house. It's all upset—not a neat drawing. My house is upset."

3. Smell test. "Sort of like moth balls; like disinfectant which are formed like a moth ball that you use in the bathroom. A sort of perfumey smell in them."

Drawing. "A little girl walking in the garden grass—flowers."

Inquiry 1. "I always would like to have a house where I would have a yard, flowers, grass. I wish my children could have a little yard to play in, but they never did." (She begins to weep.) [Why draw this?] "The only reason is because my children never had a yard with flowers and grass to play in. We always lived in a poorer section." (Weeping has been continuing. She tries to hold back her sobs and appears on the verge of an attack of asthma.)

Inquiry 2. [You drew this after smelling something like moth balls?] "Perfumey-like—makes me think of flowers. (Weeps.) Roses, peonies. Sometimes I get a running nose from flowers. I can't stand liquor and cigarette smoke. I never did smoke myself."

Comment

The strong emotional response to the drawing elicited by the smell stimulus is evident. An asthmatic attack was almost precipitated by it. The patient perceived both elements, the floral and the skatol, in the stimulus, and attempted to handle the perception of the skatol by reaction formation (or perhaps it might be better called a condensation), referring to the smell as of moth balls or disinfectant—the enemies of dirt. The content of the response to smell stimulation has to do with her own dependent needs and this is most directly elicited by the smell stimulus.

RHEUMATOID ARTHRITIS

Mrs. Y. D. is a 32-year-old white woman who has had rheumatoid arthritis for almost 6 years. Its onset was during her second pregnancy. She states that now the least fatigue or worry starts her joints hurting. She describes herself as a great worrier. She likes to scrub and clean to relieve tension, but this work will cause arthritic pain. She is disturbed if any tasks are left incomplete. Apart from arthritis she is in good health, though she has what has been diagnosed as a psoriatic patch on one hip, which is constant, never spreading or getting smaller. She has no respiratory disorders.

1. Cotton test. Some irritation, but quick adaptation.

Drawing. "A house." Facetiously she says, "Beautiful drawing."

Inquiry 1. "Just a home. We're going to build a home next year, and I certainly hope it's prettier than this one." [Why did you draw this?] "I probably knew I could draw a house."

Inquiry 2. [What is the relationship of the cotton test to the drawing?] "I don't see any relation. I can't see any connection to a home in that."

2. Left arm held horizontal for 1 minute. She describes a feeling of stiffness and then says she feels nothing except that her arm is out in the air.

Drawing. "A boat. My children draw better than I."

Inquiry 1. "Picture of our houseboat. I like it." [Why?] "Relaxing—fun to go on. Not a phone or anything out there. Get away from it all." [Why did you draw this?] "I thought I could draw a boat."

Inquiry 2. [Is there any relationship in this between having your arm out and making this drawing?] "I can see a connection there (she says emphatically). My arm wasn't relaxed and the boat is relaxing. This is the only thing it brings to mind." (After the entire test was completed, she said spontaneously, "The boat is the only place I can feel free of worry. I get sleepy as soon as I get on the boat.")

3. Smell test. "Lilacs. Perfume." [Is it a pleasant smell?] "Sweet."

Drawing. "A tree."

Inquiry 1. "Poem lovely as a tree." [Do you have any feeling about this?] "No." [Why did you draw this?] "I just think of trees and drawing."

Inquiry 2. [Any connection to smell stimulus?] "None, unless the smell of lilacs reminded me of the country, trees, and so on. I like the country."

Comment

A clearly recognized connection between stimulus and drawings was found only in the muscle test. The drawing this elicits has a strong dependent regressive affect, away from tension. The failure to perceive and react to the skatol note in the JS mixture contrasts sharply to its recognition in the asthma patient.

DERMATITIS

Mrs. N. E. is a 56-year-old white woman who has had a localized neurodermatitis on her right leg for 16 years. She was orphaned early in life and "raised myself," and in addition to 11 of her own children, has raised 14 orphans. However, if children "do the least thing to aggravate me, or don't mind me, my nerves are tore up and I have to throw whatever I have in my hand, or go off and cry. If I get to worrying, like about bills, I get nervous and this leg aggravates me. It burns and hurts. I work all day and then find myself scratching. It helps to relieve the nervousness."

1. Left arm held horizontal for one minute. She describes a little tingling feeling and then that she feels her heart beating in her arm and then in her hand.

Drawing. "House. Looks like the old house I was born in, that's why I made it."

Inquiry 1. "Looks like the little old place where I was born: Lacks a couple of trees. It was a log cabin. I was telling (while giving the history) this is where Mother died. It made me think of this." [Why did you draw this?] "That was all that came to mind."

Inquiry 2. [Relationship to arm held out?] I don't see any connection."

2. Smell test. "Doesn't smell good." (Wrinkles nose) "Smells like glue. This don't smell good—it was like I smelled flowers then."

Drawing. "A doll."

Inquiry 1. "I just draw them all the time for the children."

Inquiry 2. [Relationship to smell?] "I had children on my mind when I drew the doll."

3. Cotton test. Patient described irritation throughout the 2-minute test period.

Drawing. "A box."

Inquiry 1. "Another thing that the children ask: Mom draw me a box. That's all it brings to my mind. There's so many boxes home on the floor. I should be home cleaning my house. I never want to think of boxes. I lost two little children. I'll never forget how they brought the caskets in. I had a nervous breakdown after I lost my two children. (She is close to tears at this point.) They died 22 years ago from TB meningitis they got from my sister-in-law."

Inquiry 2. [Connection to cotton test?] "I see no connection."

Comment

Because she became quite disturbed on the first inquiry in regard to the skin stimulus, Inquiry 2 was not pressed. The strong affective responses connected with the skin stimulation is in her major area of interest, children. In contrast to the asthmatic who perceived and tried to handle the skatol note by reaction formation, and the arthritic who did not perceive it, this patient perceived it rather undefensively. While her peripheral responses were quite intense, only the skin stimulus evoked a strong central response, indicated by the drawing and association to it.

HYPERTENSION

Miss T. Y. is a 40-year-old white woman, who has hypertension which was first discovered 14 years ago. For 9 years she has had severe headaches and nausea. A right nephrectomy produced only transient results. She lives with a schizophrenic sister who is difficult to get on with but, "As a rule I get on fairly well with everybody." The patient does not complain of nervousness or depression, does not think she has a hot temper. At present she is receiving Serpasil for hypertension, which produces some nasal congestion.

1. Left arm held horizontal for 1 minute. She emphasizes having little feeling in the arm. There is some feeling of heaviness toward the end of the 1-minute test period.

Drawing. "Sort of a tree. Birds. Sort of a bush like. Thinking of spring."

Inquiry 1. "My sister's place—lots of trees and bushes. I like to go there on the week-end and help her with planting. I like the out-of-doors and plants, now that everything is getting green." [Why did you draw this?] "I didn't know what else to draw."

Inquiry 2. [Connection to holding arm out?] "Planting is hard work. This line is the earth as sort of an arm maybe?" [And the tree?] "Sort of like fiingers—more or less like fingers—something extending." (Subject and interviewer both count five fingers as represented by the five branches of the tree.)

2. Smell test. "Perfume or cologne. A sweet smell."

Drawing. "Sort of a house door, picture window."

Inquiry 1. "More or less my sister's home—a poor imitation. I go out there a great deal. I like it there." [Why?] "I enjoy being there." [Why did you draw this?] "I don't know."

Inquiry 2. [Relationship to smell?] "I don't see any connection. My sister's home is nice to me. The perfume was a bit too sweet, a heavy nauseating scent. It smelled more like perfume to me and I prefer cologne. I wouldn't associate a sweet smell to the house. The only sweet-smelling things out there is the flowers when they bloom."

3. Cotton test. Quick adaptation to the cotton, but the patient seemed rather annoyed and upset during the test.

Drawing. "Sort of a railroad track."

Inquiry 1. "The railroad reminds me of taking a train to my sister's place. I like the train ride when I have somewhere to go." [Why did you draw this?] "I don't know."

Inquiry 2. [Connection to cotton test?] "I don't see any connection unless the jar of the train—sometimes it's a smooth ride—sometimes not."

Comment

Unlike the other subjects, no strong emotional responses were elicited by the stimuli or in the associations to the drawings that they stimulated. There was a good representation of the arm stimulus in the drawing of the tree, but this was not accompanied by any particular affect.

GENERAL RESULTS

The representative subjects described above are members of the population of 45 individuals who were all tested by the same methods (Table 1). The subjects' responses to the first and second inquiries were typed on file cards. The responses were numbered 1 and 2, indicating first and second inquiries. No data identifying either the stimulus or the subject's disease were included on the cards. These responses were then rated in two ways. In one, the cards were presented in random order to the raters. Rating on a 6 point scale of affectivity from 1 to 6, was done by the three authors of this article independently and by one independent rater unconnected with the project. In the other type of rating the three cards from each subject, representing his responses to

TABLE 1. POPULATION

Disorder	N	Age range	Age mean[a]	Race		Sex	
				W	N	F	M
Arthritis	11	17–50	36.36	7	4	9	2
Hypertension	11	34–53	45.73	7	4	9	2
Asthma	10	14–43	32.90	6	4	8	2
Dermatitis	13	16–56	26.16	12	1	10	3

[a] Difference in mean ages significant (0.001). However, over-all level of responsivity is not significantly different between groups (see Table 4).

the three stimuli, were grouped together. The raters were then asked to decide which of the three responses was the most strongly emotional. This rating was done by two of the authors independently, and by two independent raters unconnected with the project. (The independent rater on the 6-point scale was not one of the two independent raters of each subject's strongest response.) The reliability of agreement between the raters, which is high, is demonstrated in Table 2.

TABLE 2. RELIABILITY OF RATINGS
(4 RATERS)

Scale	Reliability
Six-point scale of affectivity	0.94[a]
Each subject's strongest response	0.78

[a] This figure represents the reliability of agreement between raters, and is based on all items, including those in which there was widest disagreement. After this figure was obtained, 21 items in which the raters differed by two or more points were considered too ambiguous to rate and were discarded. There was no significant difference in the number of ambiguous statements by sex, race, or test. On the remaining 114 items, the scores of the four raters were averaged.

Neither the order in which the tests were given, nor the individual characteristics of the different stimuli, significantly affected the intensity of response (Tables 3A and 3B). Indicating the stimulus on the second inquiry did not significantly alter the level of affect.

Rating of affective response on the 6-point scale supports our hypothesis that stimulation of the sensory modality related to the particular disorder arouses more affect than stimulation of other modalities

tested (Table 4A). It will be noted that the hypertensive group has no peak of intensity as do the other groups. Table 4B indicates that the specific response to muscle stimulation of arthritic patients and of dermatitis patients to skin stimulation is highly significant, and, while the variance of the smell response is such that no statistical calculations are valid, the tendency of asthmatics to respond affectively to smell is suggested by the results.*

The rating of each subject's strongest affective response (Table 5) is highly significant for all groups and shows again how arthritics respond most emotionally to muscle, asthmatics to smell, and skin patients to skin. Hypertensives, when a rating is required, as it is in this instance, appear to respond more to smell than to other modalities, but even here the tendency of this group not to respond is evidenced by the two hypertensives who showed so little response in all tests it was impossible to rate them.

ANALYSIS OF RESPONSES TO STIMULATION

Two of us (C. M. and J. K.) independently rated: (1) the subject's initial response (how the subject described the odor as he smelled it; how much tickle irritation he felt as the skin was stroked; how he described the feelings of his outstretched arm), and (2) the content of responses in association to the drawings. Following Stein and Ottenberg (17), we used a simple classification based on the classic developmental phases described by psychoanalysis—the oral, anal, and genital. Dependency corresponds to the oral period, responses emphasizing cleanliness and/or uncleanliness to the anal, responses of sex, perfume, personal adornment (romance) to the genital. In addition to these affective

* The fact that the asthmatics did not show a statistically significant difference from the other groups on the 6-point scale may be due to two factors: (1) the universality of conflicts about smell due to toilet training compared to the nonuniversality of conflicts with regard to skin and muscle; (2) it is impossible to test an asthmatic in an acute attack, unlike skin and arthritis patients.

responses, we have classified as stimulus representation responses which are essentially cognitive, representing either the form or sensation of the stimulus. For example, a figure with outstretched arm is drawn in response to the muscle test; a figure whose hair is described as being like a cotton ball in response to skin stimulation. Stimulus-representation responses are elicited when

the subject is informed of the stimulus on the second inquiry. Our two independent ratings were in almost complete agreement, so we conclude that the nature of the responses is ratable in a useful way. The number of itch-tickle responses is quantitative (Table 7) and is derived from the fact that during the 2-minute period of stroking with cotton a notation was made every 15

TABLE 3A. EFFECT OF TEST UPON LEVEL OF AFFECT[a]

Test	Mean intensity
Muscle	2.74
Skin	2.90
Smell	3.01

[a] Analysis of variance not significant.

TABLE 3B. EFFECT OF ORDER UPON LEVEL OF AFFECT[a]

Order	Mean intensity
1st test given	2.57
2nd test given	3.15
3rd test given	2.96

[a] Analysis of variance not significant.

Tests were presented in modified random order to rule out the effect of sequence of tests. There is no significant difference in mean intensity of tests. The order in which tests were given did not affect results.

TABLE 4A. AFFECTIVE RESPONSES TO ALL STIMULI RATED ON A SIX POINT SCALE

Disorder	Muscle	Skin	Smell	Total mean
Arthritis	3.84	2.06	2.75	2.88
Hypertension	2.40	2.13	2.83	2.44
Asthma	2.67	2.61	4.00	3.02
Dermatitis	2.39	4.36	2.88	3.11
	F 3.69 ($F_{0.95} = 2.88$)	F 8.04 ($F_{0.99} = 4.42$)	F 1.33 ($F_{0.95} = 2.88$)	Not sig[a]

[a] No difference in over-all level of responsiveness. Although sex and color affect the over-all level of responsiveness in this situation (0.05 and 0.001 significance respectively), Negro, white, male, and female groups all vary in the same directions as the total groups for each disorder.

TABLE 4B. χ^2 TEST OF GROUPS SHOWING SIGNIFICANCE ON ANALYSIS OF VARIANCE

Test	Groups	Significance
Muscle	Arthritis-other	0.001
Skin	Dermatitis-other	0.001

TABLE 5. EACH SUBJECT'S STRONGEST AFFECTIVE RESPONSE

Disorder	Muscle	Skin	Smell	Total
Arthritis	9	1	1	11
Hypertension	3	0	6[a]	9
Asthma	0	2	8	10
Dermatitis	1	10	2	13
TOTAL	13	13	17	43

[a] Two hypertensives showed so little response on all tests, it was impossible to rate them. Probability of this distribution occurring by chance <0.001.

seconds as to the subject's reported sensation. The classification of responses is found in Tables 6, 7, 8, and 9A.

TABLE 6. INITIAL RESPONSES, MUSCLE TEST

Disorder	M	H	P	U	N	Total[a]
Arthritis	9	3	1	0	1	14
Dermatitis	5	0	7	0	0	12
Dermatitis-respiratory	4	1	2	0	0	7
Asthma	6	0	6	1	1	14
Hypertension	8	1	2	0	7	18
Total	32	5	18	1	9	65

[a] When responses were rated as having components of two categories, each was scored in the appropriate category. This accounts for the fact that total number of responses is greater than total number of patients in group. M = muscle sensations (tiredness, shaking, tension); P = parasthesias (burning, tingling, numbness, etc.); H = pain; U = unclassified; N = subject emphasizes having no feeling in outstretched arm.

TABLE 7. MEAN TICKLE—ITCH RESPONSES[a]

Disorder	Mean
Arthritis	3.00
Dermatitis and dermatitis-respiratory	4.45
Asthma	3.10
Hypertension	2.27

[a] Analysis of variance not significant.

TABLE 8. INITIAL RESPONSES, SMELL TEST[a]

Disorder	A	R	U	Total
Arthritis	2	8	1	11
Dermatitis	3	5	0	8
Dermatitis-respiratory	2	2	1	5
Asthma	6	3	1	10
Hypertension	2	8	1	11
Total	15	26	4	45

[a] A = clean-unclean responses; R = sex, perfume, personal adornment; U = unclassified.

TABLE 9A. CONTENT OF RESPONSES IN ASSOCIATION TO DRAWINGS[a]

Muscle	D	A	R	S-R	U	Total
Arthritis	6	3	0	0	2	11
Dermatitis	1	0	2	3	2	8
Asthma	0	1	0	4	5	10
Hypertension	2	1	0	3	5	11
Dermatitis-respiratory	0	0	0	3	2	5
Total	9	5	2	13	16	45
Skin						
Arthritis	2	0	0	8	1	11
Dermatitis	6	0	2	0	0	8
Asthma	2	1	1	5	1	10
Hypertension	3	0	0	2	6	11
Dermatitis-respiratory	3	1	0	1	0	5
Total	16	2	3	16	8	45
Smell						
Arthritis	5	2	3		1	11
Dermatitis	1	2	5		0	8
Asthma	2	7	0		1	10
Hypertension	1	4	2		4	11
Dermatitis-respiratory	1	3	0		1	5
Total	10	18	10		7	45

[a] D = dependency and passivity; A = anal (cleanliness, uncleanliness, and the like); R = romance (sex, perfume, personal adornment, etc.); S-R = stimulus representation; U = unclassified, frequently little observed connection with the stimulus.

OBSERVATIONS ON THE SPECIFIC DISORDERS STUDIED

Asthma

On ratings of individual affect 8 asthmatics reacted most strongly to smell stimulation, 2 to skin stimulation, and none to muscle. On the 6-point scale of affec-

tivity the direction is the same, though not to a statistically significant degree. Asthmatics react most strongly to odor of any group tested. As a group they reacted more to the anal components in the JS mixture than did any other group. Their initial responses tended to be compromises, of which moth balls was most frequent.* This moth ball response we considered to represent an awareness of dirt and the reaction against it. Dermatitis patients with a respiratory complication, e.g., chronic rhinitis, and uncomplicated dermatitis patients showed the next most frequent anal responses. This corresponds to the generally close association between asthma and dermatitis somatically (the asthma-eczema complex) and psychologically. On the other hand, arthritics and hyptertensives reacted least to the anal component in the JS mixture and emphasized the floral odor, seeming to repress the other components (Table 8).

On other peripheral tests, asthmatics emphasized skin sensations (paresthesias) in the muscle test (Table 6) and tickle-irritation on the skin test (Table 7) second in both instances to skin patients, again pointing to the relatedness of these two groups.

The drawings and associations elicited from asthmatics by the JS test most characteristically refer to conflicts concerning cleanliness-uncleanliness (Table 9A). For example, a drawing of flowers and a hovering butterfly on further scrutiny is thought by the subject to look more like a moth than a butterfly. Attendant associations then are to moths destroying clothes, to dirt, etc. Muscle stimulation produced either responses representing the stimulus, or unclassifiable responses. Skin stimulation produced predominantly stimulus-representation responses, but there was a scattering of responses in the dependency, anal, and romance categories.

Discussion: Asthmatics' tendency

* Of a total of 8 moth ball responses, 5 occurred in asthmatics, 1 in a dermatitis-respiratory patient, 1 in a dermatitis patient, and 1 in an arthritic.

to emotional response to odor is in accord with a number of observations by others, such as Dunbar (3) and Fenichel (4). Bacon (1) suggests that asthmatic attacks occur when "nascent excretory aggression arouses fears of excretory aggression from the outside world." The patient expects his respiratory apparatus to be attacked in talion manner for his excretory aggression with its olfactory component of bad smell. Wilson (18) discusses a closely related respiratory disorder—hay fever, as being the result of unsuccessful olfactory repression. In his patients visual-sexual curiosity was displaced to the olfactory sphere, and he suggests that this unrelieved olfactory curiosity may be a source of constant irritation to the nasal mucosa. Knapp and Nemet (13) indicate that in 50 per cent of 40 asthmatic patients nasal-olfactory conflicts are among the sources of tension. These include "worry over, or preoccupation with, nose, nasal secretions, or drainage, 'colds' or rhinorrhea lasting for more than a month, or more frequent than four times per year," and "unusual awareness or sensitivity to odors, or feeling of being harmed by them."

Stein, Ottenberg, and their associates (17) point out that many asthmatics relate odors to the precipitation of their attacks, and the majority (74 per cent) of the substances reported as precipitating the attacks are in the cleanliness-uncleanliness category. They also found that when a number of odors were sequentially presented to 20 healthy subjects and to 20 asthmatics, all of whom were asked to describe their associations following each odor, in both groups the largest number of responses were in the cleanliness-uncleanliness category, and the only significant difference between the groups was that the asthmatics showed more associative blocks than the control group: i.e., sometimes they could not smell the odor or they had no associations after smelling it.

Perceptual blocking of the anal odor in our asthmatic subjects was much less than in any of the other disorders

tested, though it did occur in a few patients. Perhaps the introduction of the pleasant jasmine note made the asthmatics less defensive than Stein and Ottenberg's patients. What was notable was the tendency of the other groups to block perception of the anal component.

Dermatitis

On both the 6-point scale and the individual affect ratings, dermatitis patients responded with most affect to skin stimulation. As a group, the skin patients responded with more tickle-irritation to the cotton test than did the other groups (Table 7). Skin patients more than any other group responded to muscle stimulation with sensations referable to the skin or of a hysterical character (paresthesias): i.e., they tend to feel even the outstretched arm mainly in skin terms (Table 6). To smell stimulation (Table 8) skin patients responded to the anal component second in frequency to the asthmatics, pointing to the interrelation between these disorders. It was necessary to divide the skin patients into those complicated by respiratory disorders and those free of such disorders, because the dermatitis-respiratory patients show responses to smell stimulation similar to the asthmatics.

The affect stirred up, as obtained from drawings and associations to them, indicate that skin patients respond mainly with dependency feelings to skin stimulation. To muscle stimulation they react either with unclassified responses or at a cognitive level of stimulus representation. Olfactory stimulation stirred up anal conflicts in some, particularly the mixed dermatitis-respiratory group, but repression of the anal component and a pure romance response is frequent.

Discussion: The passive-dependent meaning of desires for skin stimulation appears here. Exhibitionistic wishes may be inferred from the large number of romance responses in skin patients (Table 9B). But these responses were predominantly elicited by stimulation of other modalities than the skin.

Arthritis

Arthritic patients responded with highest affectivity to muscle stimulation as measured by the 6-point and the individual-affect scales. On muscle stimulation they had predominant muscle sensations—for example, tiredness, tension, and shaking. They had less tickle-irritation responses than the dermatitis patients, slightly less than the asthmatics, and a little more than the hypertensives. To JS stimulation they gave predominantly romance responses, repressing the anal component to the same degree as did the hypertensives.

TABLE 9B. TOTAL CONTENT OF RESPONSES

Disorder	D	A	R	S-R	U	Total
Arthritis	13	5	3	8	4	33
Dermatitis	8	2	9	3	2	24
Asthma	4	9	1	9	7	30
Hypertension	6	5	2	5	15	33
Dermatitis-respiratory	4	4	0	4	3	15
Total	35	25	15	29	31	135

pr. <0.001.

TABLE 9C. TOTAL CONTENT BY TEST

Test	D	A	R	S-R	U	Total
Muscle	9	5	2	13	16	45
Skin	16	2	3	16	8	45
Smell	10	18	10	0	7	45
Total	35	25	15	29	31	135

pr. <0.001.

The affect stirred up by muscle stimulation, as reflected by drawings and associations, was predominantly of a dependent nature. There were some anal and pain responses, too, and, significantly, no stimulus-representation responses (cognitive), which were frequent in the other groups. The dependency response to muscle stimulation did not appear in any of the other groups to any extent. In other groups, where there was less affective response to muscle stimulation, the stimulus representation (cognitive response) was frequent. Thus, affective preconscious responses tend to stand in reciprocal relation to cognitive preconscious processes.

To skin stimulation, arthritics reacted predominantly with stimulus-representation responses. Odors, in which the anal component was mainly repressed on immediate perception, resulted in a considerable number of dependent responses in the arthritics.

Discussion: As in the other two groups, the specific modality produced the emotionally specific response. Skin patients react with dependency to skin stimulation; arthritics react similarly to muscle stimulation, though with some qualitative differences. The peripheral suppression of anal odor perception (Table 8) and the central response of dependency to odor stimulation (Table 9A) suggest that arthritics tend to handle anal conflicts by regression to dependency.

Johnson, Shapiro, and Alexander, (10), in their study of rheumatoid arthritis, suggest that a chronic, inhibited, hostile, aggressive state is present as the reaction to the earliest masochistic dependency on the mother and is carried over into other human relationships. Hostility is discharged through masculine competition, physical activity, and serving others and dominating the family. Interruption of these means of discharging hostility causes increased muscle tonus from inhibited aggression and the defenses against it, which somehow precipitates attacks of arthritis. Another point of view is expressed by McLaughlin *et al.* (14), who describe rheumatoid arthritics as follows: "without exception the patients revealed marked passive dependency upon key persons in their environment." They describe these patients as very guarded and remote, without much expression of feeling. Our own findings also emphasize the passive dependency of the arthritics rather than their hostility. This may be connected with the fact that there were very few directly hostile associations elicited by any of the tests that we are using. By designating any reference to anger, irritation, meanness, or destructiveness as hostility, we found only 12 hostile responses in our total of 135. And, as is to be expected, 7 of these were stimulated by the smell test.

Hypertension

Hypertensives were chosen as a control group because we do not know of any specific sensory modality connected with their disorder and therefore we expected that they would respond differently from the other groups. On the 6-point scale, stimulation of one modality produced no notably more intensive affective responses than stimulation of any other. On the individual affective ratings this flatness of response is indicated by the 2 patients whose responses were so limited it was impossible to rate them. In responses which were ratable, the strongest responses were most often to smell and next to muscle. Peripheral responses of the hypertensive group to muscle showed an interesting tendency to "nothing" response; i.e., when asked to describe the feelings in the outstretched arm, a number of hypertensives emphasized feeling nothing. Seven such responses occurred in hypertensives and only 2 in all other groups. There is, thus, a tendency to deny or suppress muscle or perhaps body feeling in this group. This goes along with the fact that to skin stimulation hypertensives showed the lowest number of tickle-irritation responses. To smell, they showed the same degree of suppression of anal recognition as did the arthritics.

Central responses to muscle and skin stimulation (Table 9*A*) were mainly stimulus representation or unclassified. To smell there were 4 anal responses, 2 romance responses, 1 dependency, and 4 unclassified. Thus, hypertensives tend not to respond affectively to these types of stimulation, except for several anal responses to smell. Their reactions to smell were, however, much less direct, prominent, or frequent than in asthmatics.

Discussion: Gottschalk, Serota, and Shapiro (*9*) report that electromyographic tracings in patients with rheumatoid arthritis and patients with hypertensive cardiovascular disease both had a "definite propensity to divert excess psychological tension into somatic muscular tonus." A control group without disease and a group of arthritics in psychoanalytic therapy showed less muscle tension. Our findings support their conclusion to a limited extent. Both arthritic and hypertensive groups showed an approximately equal number of initial responses of muscle sensation to the outstretched arm test (Table 6). However, the groups differ in the fact that arthritics tend to have more emotional responses (Table 9) aroused by muscle stimulation than do hypertensives, and hypertensives tend to minimize their initial muscular response (*N* response in Table 6).

Finally, the general nature of the tests and what they elicit (Table 9*C*) is of interest. Skin evokes most dependency responses, smell the largest number of anal responses. Smell does not evoke cognitive (stimulus-representation) responses. The total number of responses in each category indicates the predominance of pregenital feelings in the disorders tested.

DISCUSSION AND CONCLUSIONS

1. In patients having a particular disorder, stimulation of the sensory modality most closely related to that disorder arouses more emotional response than does stimulation of another modality. The connection between stimulation and emotional response is preconscious.

2. There is a consistent tendency for stimulation of the sensory modality most closely related to the particular disorder to produce what might be called heightened conscious perception of the stimulus. Thus, (*a*) on skin testing, skin patients had more tickle-irritation responses than did the other groups; (*b*) on the muscle test, arthritic patients had more responses indicating awareness of muscle sensations than did the other groups; (*c*) on the smell test, asthmatics and other patients with respiratory disorders responded more directly and immediately to the unpleasant anal component of the stimulus than did the other groups.

3. Thus, both responses pertinent to a particular disorder, the immediate

conscious perception and report and the preconscious arousal of emotion, move in the same direction—of increase.

4. But the amount of increase in response seems to be more significant in the central preconsciously aroused emotional effect than in the peripheral consciously reported perception of the stimulus. (For example, we have quantitative data only on the tickle-irritation response, which is highest in skin patients, but not at a level of statistical significance, whereas the strong central affective response of the skin patients to the skin stimulation is highly significant.)

5. An important difference between the peripheral and central responses is this: in both, preconscious linkages to other events and feelings occur. However, in the peripheral response the request to describe and report what is happening focuses attention on the preconscious and limits the extension of preconscious connections. Consciousness and cognition, the secondary process, are emphasized. In the central response there is much less interference with preconscious functioning and the extension of its connections to even deeper layers because the connection between it and the sensory stimulus is not recognized. The relatively smaller amount of intrusion of the secondary process in the central response perhaps accounts for the higher significance of the central response than of the peripheral.

6. When the peripheral stimulus did not give rise to an affective central response, the most frequent classifiable sort of preconscious central effect was what we term stimulus representation. Here, either the form or sensation of the peripheral stimulus is represented, without affective admixtures. Stimulus-representation responses could be considered as the result of greater cognitive or secondary-process influences, both peripherally and centrally. The fact that some central responses are essentially cognitive and others are essentially affective, though both exist at preconscious levels, demonstrates the separate

pathway of ideas and affects originally described by Freud (8).

7. Our clinical experience causes us to assume that the passage from periphery to center which we have demonstrated is often reversed, and that disturbances in peripheral perception, e.g., itching, may proceed from central disturbances.

8. Thus, we are dealing with a holistic complex, periphery-center, which may be modified or affected as a unit by the ego. Thus, if periphery is influenced by the ego, this influences center at the same time that center is directly influenced by the ego, and, if periphery is less influenced by the ego, this results in a lesser cognitive influence on the center. At the same time a diminished direct effect on center by the ego facilitates central affective response.

This interrelationship between periphery and center was recognized by Ferenczi (5), who states: "Such a reciprocity of central and peripheral excitations is known to us in other directions. For instance, a skin wound can itch, but a purely central itch can lead to scratching; in other words to an inflicting of skin wounds on the itching surface, and give rise, therefore, to a kind of self-injury."

In discussing the somatic sources of dreams, Freud (7) presents a similar design of interaction indicating that psychosomatic and somatopsychic are essentially one system. He states that some anxiety dreams have somatic sources—for example, heart disease (periphery), and others are psychically (centrally) determined. "In the one case the somatically determined anxiety calls up the suppressed ideational content, and in the other the ideational content . . . calls up a release of anxiety."

Summary

1. Groups of patients suffering from asthma, atopic or localized neurodermatitis, arthritis, and hypertension were tested. Each subject received three types of sensory stimulation—cutaneous, muscular, and olfactory, in modified random order.

2. Following each type of sensory stimulation the subject was requested to make a drawing of anything that came to mind. The subjects were then requested to describe and associate to their drawings.

3. It was found by independent rating that cutaneous stimulation produced the strongest emotional responses in dermatitis patients, muscle stimulation in arthritics, and olfactory stimulation in asthmatics. Hypertensives did not react with outstandingly strong affect to stimulation of any of the sensory modalities tested. Thus, stimulation of the sensory modality appropriate to the particular psychosomatic disorder produces stronger affective responses than stimulation of other sensory modalities. As subjects rarely consciously recognized a connection between the stimulus and the drawings and associations to them, the linkage between them is considered to be at preconscious levels.

4. Certain differing characteristics of the four groups studied, as elicited by these tests, have been discussed. General ideas concerning the relation of peripheral sensory stimulation and central responses to this stimulation have been suggested.

REFERENCES

1. Bacon, C. L. The role of aggression in the asthmatic attack. *Psychoanalyt. Quart.*, 1956, *25*, 309.

2. Ebel, R. L. Estimation of reliability of ratings. *Psychometrica*, 1951, *16*, 407.

3. Dunbar, F. Psychoanalytic notes relating to syndromes of asthma and hay fever. *Psychoanalyt. Quart.*, 1938, *7*, 25.

4. Fenichel, O. *The Psychoanalytic Theory of Neurosis.* New York, Norton, 1945.

5. Ferenczi, S. Disease or Patho-neuroses. In *Further Contributions to the Theory and Technique of Psychoanalysis.* London, Hogarth, 1950.

6. Fisher, C. A study of the preliminary stages of the construction of dreams and images. *J. Am. Psychoanalyt. Assn.*, 1957, *5*, 5.

7. Freud, S. *The Interpretation of Dreams.* New York, Basic Books, 1955.

8. Freud, S. Repression. In *Collected Papers: IV.* London, Hogarth, and Institute of Psychoanalysis, 1950.

9. Gottschalk, L. A., Serota, H. M., and Shapiro, L. B., Psychological conflict and neuromuscular tension. *Psychosom. Med.*, 1950, *12*, 315.

10. Johnson, A., Shapiro, L. B., and Alexander, F. Preliminary report on a psychosomatic study of rheumatoid arthritis. *Psychosom. Med.*, 1957, *9*, 245.

11. Kepecs, J. G., and Robin, M. Studies in itching: I. Contributions toward an understanding of the physiology of masochism. *Psychosom. Med.*, 1957, *9*, 245.

12. Kepecs, J. G., and Robin, M. Studies on itching: II. Some psychological implications of the interrelationships between the cutaneous pain touch systems. *Arch. Neurol. & Psychiat.*, 1956, *76*, 325.

13. Knapp, P. H., and Nemetz, S. J. Sources of tension in bronchial asthma. *Psychosom. Med.*, 1957, *19*, 466.

14. McLaughlin, J. T., *et al.* Emotional reactions of rheumatoid arthritis to ACTH. *Psychosom. Med.*, 1953, *15*, 187.

15. Robin, M., and Kepecs, J. G. Studies on Itching: III. The effect of topical hydrocortisone on pruritis. *J. Invest. Derm.*, 1957, *29*, 91.

16. Ruesch, J., *Disturbed Communication.* New York. Norton, 1957.

17. Stein, M., and Ottenberg, P. Role of odors in asthma. *Psychosom. Med.*, 1958, *20*, 60.

18. Wilson, G. W. A study of structural and instinctual conflicts in cases of hay fever. *Psychosom. Med.*, 1941, *3*, 51.

19. Wisdom, J. O. A general hypothesis of psychosomatic disorder. *Brit. J. M. Psychol.*, 1953, *26*, 15.

Etiology of Duodenal Ulcer

I. Relation of Specific Psychological Characteristics to Rate of Gastric Secretion (Serum Pepsinogen)

HERBERT WEINER, MARGARET THALER,
MORTON F. REISER, AND I. ARTHUR MIRSKY

THE life history of a clinical syndrome and the various factors that contribute to the predisposition and precipitation of the syndrome in any particular person are usually inferred from data obtained after the clinical disorder has developed. Such inferences are frequently biased by the investigator's particular orientation. Thus, there are those who claim that the development of duodenal ulcer is determined solely by "organic" factors, (11) whereas others claim that "psychic" factors are the sole determinants (8). Such polar attitudes are inevitable when the data being considered is *post hoc* in nature. The ideal approach for evaluating the determinants responsible for precipitating any clinical disorder is to study the subject who is going to develop the disorder before he does so. This *propter hoc* approach requires criteria that will permit the selection of individuals who are susceptible to the development of the particular syndrome.

Previous studies have established that the concentration of pepsinogen in the blood is dependent upon the rate of pepsinogen production by the stomach (15). In 87 per cent of patients with duodenal ulcer, the pepsinogen concentration is greater than the mean of values found in subjects without duodenal or other gastrointestinal disturbances (16). This observation is consistent with the general consensus that patients with duodenal ulcer tend to secrete more gastric juice, hydrochloric acid, and pepsin than do healthy subjects (10). The fact that the high concentration of pep-

sinogen in the sera of such patients was found to persist even after the duodenal lesion was healed (16), as does also the increased rate of gastric secretion (13), suggested that gastric hypersecretion is an essential but not the sole determinant in the development of the lesion.

The concentration of pepsinogen in the blood of 14 per cent of subjects without any gastrointestinal disturbance is greater than the mean of values found in patients with duodenal ulcer (16). Presumably, the stomachs of such "healthy" subjects are hypersecreting pepsinogen. If gastric hypersecretion is an essential determinant in the development of duodenal ulcer, it may be postulated that the high pepsinogen secretors represent that segment of the population with a maximal secretory capacity (9) that is most likely to develop duodenal ulcer when exposed to those circumstances responsible for precipitating the sequence of physiological events that result in the characteristic lesion. In accord with this hypothesis is the observation that apparently healthy subjects, without any previous history of gastrointestinal derangement, but with serum pepsinogen values in the range of those of patients with duodenal ulcer may go on to develop the lesion without any further significant increase in the concentration of pepsinogen in the blood (16, 17, 18).

The precise circumstances responsible for the precipitation of duodenal ulcer remain unknown. The consensus, however, is that psychic tension initiated by exposure to some environmental event is a prepotent factor. Although numerous studies have established that various manifestations of

Reprinted by permission from *Psychosomatic Medicine*, Vol. 19, No. 1, 1957.

psychic tension can be related to a variety of gastrointestinal changes, no clue to the source of the tension became apparent until Alexander and his colleagues applied psychoanalytical principles to the study of patients with peptic ulcer (*1, 2*). Such studies by Alexander and others (*2, 12, 19*) led to the generalization that patients with duodenal ulcer have in common a conflict related to the persistence of strong infantile wishes to be loved and cared for, on the one hand, and the repudiation of these wishes by the adult ego or by external circumstances, on the other hand. This psychic conflict is postulated to be responsible for initiating a sequence of physiological changes that result in the development of the duodenal lesion. Yet, as Alexander (*1*) and others (*12*) have stressed, similar psychodynamic patterns can be demonstrated in subjects without any gastrointestinal disturbance or in subjects with some other derangement. Consequently, as Alexander indicated, psychic conflict, specific or otherwise, cannot be the sole determinant in the precipitation of duodenal ulcer.

It is generally acknowledged that the response to some environmental event is a major factor in initiating the process responsible for the precipitation of peptic ulcer. Yet, there is nothing specific about the social situation that so frequently precedes the precipitation of duodenal ulcer (*20*). The only inference than can be made is that the specific meaning of the environmental event to the particular individual determines whether or not the event is responded to as a noxious one.

From the preceding it would appear that there are three parameters which may contribute to the precipitation of duodenal ulcer: a physiological parameter, which determines the susceptibility of the duodenum to ulceration; a psychological parameter, which determines the relatively specific psychic conflict that induces psychic tension; and a social parameter, which determines the environmental event that will prove noxious to the particular in-

dividual. Accordingly, a duodenal ulcer should develop when an individual with a sustained rate of gastric hypersecretion and the aforementioned psychic conflict is exposed to an environmental situation that mobilizes conflict and induces psychic tension.

This report deals with part of a study designed to evaluate the role of the three parameters* in the precipitation of duodenal ulcer. The degree of gastric secretion gauged by the concentration of three pepsinogen in the serum comprised the physiological parameter; subjects with serum pepsinogen values beyond one standard deviation of the mean were regarded as hypersecretors, and subjects with pepsinogen values below one standard deviation of the mean were regarded as hyposecretors. The selection of subjects representative of those with the highest and lowest concentrations of pepsinogen in the blood permitted one group to serve as a control for the other. The style of interpersonal interactions that could be inferred from projective and other psychological techniques comprised the psychological parameter. The exposure to 16 weeks of basic training comprised the environmental situation that might prove noxious to some and not to other subjects.

METHOD

A total of 2073 draftees between the ages of 17.5 years and 29.2 years were chosen at random while being processed at induction at an army camp. Before entering service all had resided in the northeastern United States. Ten ml. of blood was drawn from each man. The sample was identified by code number, refrigerated, and sent to one of us (IAM) for analysis. The concentration of pepsinogen in the serum was determined by a method described in an earlier paper (*15*). The Cornell Medical Index (*5*), the Saslow Screening Inventory (*21*), and a sociologi-

[* Strictly speaking, these are variables rather than parameters.—Ed.]

cal rating scale were administered to each man. Approximately 300 men were processed per week.

At the end of each week, the code numbers of 20 men were returned to the research group at the Induction Center without their levels of serum pepsinogen being revealed. These numbers identified men who were chosen for more detailed study because they were in the range of the highest and lowest values obtained in the group of men tested during the previous week. At the end of seven weeks, a total of 120 men had been selected for special study.

During the second week the 20 men who had been selected at the end of the first week were given a battery of psychological tests (Rorschach Test, Blacky Pictures, and Draw-A-Person Test). Each man was interviewed briefly by a psychiatrist and social worker, and each man was given a complete gastrointestinal roentgenological examination. The psychological tests were administered by a technician, and the test material was then sent to three of us (MT, HW, and MR) for evaluation.

After these studies were completed the men were sent to the basic training area. Subsequently, all but 13 men were again given the psychological tests and roentgenological examinations some time between the eighth and sixteenth week of the basic training period.

The Rorschach results were submitted both to a formal scoring (3) and to that devised by DeVos, which divides content into various categories and subcategories "concerned with the symbolic expressions of affect" (6). Each drawing from the Draw-A-Person Test was classified as primitive, distorted, boyish, masculine, or adult. The Cornell Medical Index (5) Saslow (21) and Blacky (4) tests were scored as recommended by their originators. In addition, Card II of the Blacky Test was scored as to whether Blacky was seen as openly expressing anger or whether the expression of such affect was denied, rationalized, or ignored.

RESULTS

Figure 1 illustrates the normal distribution of the values for the concentration of pepsinogen in the sera of the population of 2073 men who were screened. The hypersecretor group selected for special study consisted of 63 of the 300 men who comprised those with the upper 15 per cent of the serum pepsinogen values. The hyposecretor group selected for special study consisted of 57 of the 179 men who comprised those with the lowest 9 per cent of the serum pepsinogen values.

The first roentgenological examination revealed evidences of a healed duodenal ulcer in three, and of an active ulcer in one of the 63 men with gastric hypersecretion. Of these four men with evidence of duodenal lesions at the outset, one became a disciplinary problem and was confined to the stockade, one went "absent without leave," one went throught his basic training without incident, and the fourth man, who had the active duodenal lesion, was discharged from the service.

The second roentgenological examination at the eighth to sixteenth week revealed evidences of active duodenal ulcer in an additional five men who had no evidences of a gastrointestinal derangement at the outset of the study. All the subjects who had or developed evidences of duodenal ulcer were found among the 63 individuals with high blood pepsinogen values (Fig. 1).

With no knowledge of the pepsinogen levels or roentgenological findings, we evaluated the psychological test material to test the hypothesis that the hypersecretor could be differentiated from the hyposecretor and that men with or prone to duodenal ulcer could be identified. These hypotheses were based on clinical observations that suggested that the hypersecretor, like the patient with duodenal ulcer, would exhibit evidences of intense infantile oral dependent wishes, marked "immaturity," tendencies to please and placate, and difficulties revolving particularly about the management of oral impulses and hostility

(17, 18). Similar clinical observations suggested that the hyposecretor, like the patient with pernicious anemia, would exhibit evidences of pseudo-masculine defenses and paranoid trends *(17)*. Accordingly, in order to categorize those who might belong among the hypersecretor group, the psychological test material was examined specifically for the presence of strong direct references to the acts of feeding, of being

swers, that many records might be characterized by depressive associations, and that the drawings would be those of boys, or primitive and gross, or asexual.

To categorize those who might belong to the hyposecretor group, special attention was paid to indications of problems referable to activity and passivity, submissiveness and assertiveness, femininity and masculinity, as evidenced by responses

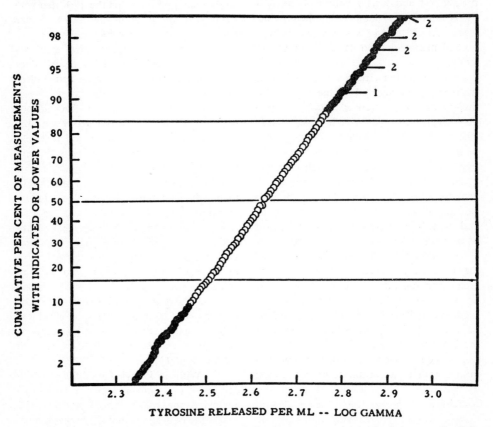

Figure 1. Distribution of blood serum pepsinogen concentrations: the frequency distributions of the logarithm of the concentration of the pepsinogen in the serum plotted on a probit scale. The subjects selected for special study were among those designated with closed circles. The numerals refer to individuals wtih duodenal ulcer.

fed, and of incorporation. Indirect or inferred oral symbolism such as talking, smoking, kissing, blowing, etc., and responses referable to heat and cold (e.g., snow, people warming themselves, flowers growing in the snow) were also sought. It was anticipated that the hypersecretors would reveal diffuse anxiety in their an-

suggesting conflict over sexual identification, passive sexual longing, and anal symbolism. It was postulated that the test material of the hyposecretors, in contrast to the hypersecretors, would show little or no oral, depressive, or anxiety content and a paucity of indications of a need to please and placate.

Using the above criteria, one psychologist and two psychiatrists independently rated the test records to determine whether the subject belonged to the hypersecretor or hyposecretor group. On the basis of a majority opinion, 61 per cent of the 120 men—71 per cent of the hypersecretors and 51 per cent of the hyposecretors—were correctly designated on the basis of the postulated traits.

It had been anticipated that the psychological test material and social histories would permit the prediction of the way in which each individual would react to the social situation represented by the period of basic training. This anticipation, however, proved incorrect since no technique could be devised *post hoc* to permit the selection of individuals who would react to the situation as if it were a noxious one. Consequently, based on previous experience with test patterns from patients with duodenal ulcer (*23*) and on inferences derived from psychoanalytical and other clinical observations of such patients (*1, 2, 7, 12, 14, 17, 19, 20, 22, 24*), an attempt was made to predict which individual would develop a duodenal ulcer during the 16 weeks of basic training. It was postulated that the subject most likely to develop an ulcer during the period of basic training would show all the characteristics of the hypersecretor but with a much greater intensity than the individual who was not likely to develop the lesion. Accordingly, the psychological test material of the inductees was evaluated *before* the biochemical and roentgenological data became available.

Ten men were selected as those most likely to develop an ulcer because their test material not only suggested that they belong to the group of hypersecretors but also showed evidences of intense needs to maintain relationships with others. Their anxieties centered around a fear of expressing hostility lest there be a loss of supplies for their needs; they went out of their way to rationalize, deny, and displace such feelings. The need to please and placate authority figures as potential sources of affection was particularly striking. The predictions were accurate in seven out of the ten. Of the three who did not have or did not develop an ulcer, two were hypersecretors.

Post hoc studies revealed that all of the nine men who had or developed a duodenal ulcer during the period of basic training had been classified correctly as belonging to the group with high serum pepsinogen values on the basis of the psychological criteria given above. Other than the intensity of their attempt to maintain relationships, no criterion was found to distinguish the hypersecretor who developed an ulcer from the hypersecretor who did not.

The attempt to differentiate the hypersecretors from the hyposecretors on the basis of clinical impressions of the available psychological test material indicated that the criteria used for such differentiation were inadequate. To develop a more accurate diagnostic tool, a variety of criteria from the test material of the hypersecretors and hyposecretors were analyzed statistically. Only those criteria that were significant at less than the 5 per cent level of confidence were used for a final classification. By means of a cluster of 20 such criteria it was possible to distinguish the two groups to the extent that 85 per cent of the 120 men could be assigned accurately to their group at a 0.001 level of confidence. Thus, of the 120 men, only 6 hypersecretors and 12 hyposecretors could not be correctly classified on the basis of the cluster of psychological test criteria.

The twenty criteria that permitted the relatively correct differentiation of the hypersecretor from the hyposecretor are listed in Table 1. No single criterion permitted the separation of the two groups with an accuracy exceeding 64.2 per cent, but all were significant at the 5 per cent level of confidence or better. The combinations of items, however, permitted the more accurate designation.

The overall impression of the psychological makeup of hypersecretors gained from the use of these scoring criteria was one of marked dependency in their relationships to others, of compliance, and of passiveness. Thus the affect of a greater number was childishly toned (criteria 1 and 2); they gave more texture responses (criterion 3), suggesting a greater awareness of, or need for tactile contact with others. A greater incidence of responses symbolizing oral needs (criterion 4) and dependency on authority figures (criterion 2) were given by the hypersecretors. This group also displayed a greater incidence of immature body images on human drawings (criterion 5).

The majority of the hypersecretors gave responses symbolizing the expression, explicit or implicit, of anxiety (criterion 6) the source of which appeared to be

TABLE 1. CRITERIA DISTINGUISHING SUBJECTS WITH HIGH AND LOW
CONCENTRATION OF PEPSINOGEN IN THE BLOOD

Criterion	Responses: Cut-off score	Serum pepsinogen concentration		No. correctly classified	% of total corr. classified	χ^2	P level
		High	Low				
1. Rorschach: Color-form	Present	31	17	71	59.2	4.684	<.05
	Absent	32	40				
2. Rorschach: Childish and authority-dependency	Present	37	21	73	60.8	5.741	<.02
	Absent	26	36				
3. Rorschach: Texture	Present	33	18	72	60.0	5.299	<.05
	Absent	30	39				
4. Rorschach: Oral symbolism	31% or more	35	19	73	60.8	5.971	<.02
	30% or less	28	38				
5. Draw-A-Person: Boyish drawings	Present	24	8	73	60.8	7.67	<.01
	Absent	39	49				
6. Rorschach: Openly symbolized anxiety	3 or more	27	14	70	58.3	5.010	<.05
	2 or less	36	43				
7. Rorschach: Per cent hostile responses	24% or less	50	30	77	64.2	9.624	<.01
	25% or more	13	27				
8. Blacky Test: Anger on Card II	Absent	32	18	71	59.2	4.546	<.05
	Present	31	39				
9. Blacky Test: Denial of aggression, Card IIIb	Present	29	16	70	48.3	4.119	<.05
	Absent	34	41				
10. Saslow Test: Anger expressed (N = 110)	No	36	22	66	60.0	4.296	<.05
	Yes	22	30				
11. Rorschach: Per cent small details	8% or more	36	20	73	60.8	5.849	<.02
	7% or less	27	37				
12. Rorschach: Poorly perceived responses	20% or less	31	14	74	61.7	7.755	<.01
	21% or more	32	43				
13. Cornell Medical Index: No. of items	15 or less	46	26	75	62.5	9.153	<.01
	16 or more	16	29				
14. Saslow Text: Anxiety expressed (N = 109)	No	30	14	67	61.5	6.64	=.01
	Yes	28	37				
15. Rorschach: Hostile-sado-masochistic content	Absent	52	37	72	60.0	4.853	<.05
	Present	11	20				
16. Rorschach: Feminine identification	Absent	52	37	72	60.0	4.853	<.05
	Present	11	20				
17. Rorschach: Anxious face details	Absent	62	49	70	58.3	5.010	<.05
	Present	1	8				
18. Rorschach: Hybrid combinations	1 or less	62	47	72	60.0	7.335	<.01
	2 or more	1	10				
19. Rorschach: Per cent unpleasant content	39% or less	33	18	72	60.0	5.299	<.05
	40% or more	30	39				
20. Rorschach: Per cent neutral content	35% or more	33	18	72	60.0	5.299	<.05
	34% or less	30	39				
Total Classification (20 Criteria)	10 or more	57	45	102	85.0	....	<.001

ness of, or need for tactile contact with others. A greater incidence of responses symbolizing oral needs (criterion 4) and dependency on authority figures (criterion 2) were given by the hypersecretors. This group also displayed a greater incidence

hostile impulses (criterion 7) that they felt must not be revealed or directly expressed (criteria 8, 9, and 10). This was inferred from the resulting formal evidences of depression that were evident in the Rorschach scores (criteria 11 and 12).

The hypersecretors had relatively few complaints about bodily symptoms, be they of discomfort, physical illness (criterion 13), or of the anxiety reaction (criterion 14). It is noteworthy, however, that the Rorschach associations of some individuals indicated both the presence of anxiety (criterion 6) in freely associated material, and a tendency not to complain of its physical concomitant and not to be aware of and/or acknowledge its presence on direct questioning (criteria 13 and 14). Thus, of the 27 individuals with high serum pepsinogen levels who gave anxiety associations (criterion 6), 12 denied that they felt anxious on the Saslow questionnaire. Yet anxiety associations (criterion 6) were given by 14 hyposecretors, 11 of whom admitted their anxiety openly (criterion 14).

Although the above features, so common to many of the hypersecretors, were also present in 12 of the hyposecretors, the incidence of such features was insignificant among the latter (criteria 1, 2, 4, and 5). The greater "immaturity" of the hypersecretors, when compared with the hyposecretors, is also revealed in the fact that they consistently showed two of the three categories which best reveal juvenile traits (criteria 1, 2, and 5) when these criteria were combined to evaluate this feature.

Another distinction between the two groups was that the hyposecretors showed high hostility scores (criterion 7) in which sadomasochistic associations figured prominently (criterion 15), or they openly expressed their anger (criteria 8 and 10).

To test the consistency with which the hypersecretor group appeared to avoid or evade the evidences of the expression of hostility, responses to criteria 7, 8, 9, 10, and 15 were combined. Using a simple majority tally as a cut-off score, the direct expression of hostility was found to be rarer among the hypersecretors than among the hyposecretors ($P < 0.001$).

Bodily preoccupation (criterion 13) and more complaints about bodily symptoms generally characterized individuals in the group with low serum pepsinogen concentrations. The hyposecretors gave a mean of 19 complaints, whereas the hypersecretors gave a mean of 12 complaints. Furthermore, using Brodman's criterion of 30 or more complaints as an indicator of potentially inadequate military performance (5), there were 4 hypersecretors and 15 hyposecretors who gave 30 or more of these answers; the difference is statistically

TABLE 2. CHECK LIST OF "DISTURBED" RECORDS

Sign	Responses: Cut-off score	Serum pepsinogen concentration		No. correctly classified	% of total (120) corr. classified	χ^2	P level
		High	Low				
1. Formal Rorschach. N-33							
a) P [popular] %	12% or less	8	7	20	60.0	....	N. S.
	13% or more	6	12				
b) F minus [poor form] % and i % combined	49% or more	9	9	19	57.0	....	N. S.
	48% or less	5	10				
c) W [whole] %	20% or less	9	8	20	60.0	....	N. S.
	21% or more	5	11				
d) Feminine on Card 3	Absent	14	12	21	63.0	4.417	<.05
	Present	0	7				
e) Elaboration	Absent	14	10	23	69.0	6.76	<.01
	Present	0	9				
2. DeVos Scoring:							
f) Ahyb [weird hybrids of human and animal parts]	1 or less	13	13	19	57.0	....	N. S.
	2 or more	1	6				
g) AA and Aa combined [direct and indirect anxiety]	2 or more	13	6	26	78.0	9.874	<.01
	1 or less	1	13				
h) Oral	2 or more	10	6	23	69.0	4.515	<.05
	1 or less	4	13				

TABLE 3. OVER-ALL CLINICAL JUDGMENT OF
            RORSCHACH RECORD

DeVos index no. of responses	Hypersecretors		Hyposecretors	
	Not disturbed (49)	Disturbed (14)	Not disturbed (38)	Disturbed (19)
0	32	4	22	5
1	12	1	9	3
2 and more	5	9	7	11
	$\chi^2 = 8.75$		$\chi^2 = 7.399$	
	$p < .01$		$p < .01$	

significant ($P < 0.01$).

Twenty of the 57 hyposecretors drew very masculine and adult figures on the Draw-A-Person Test, but 20 of these had an apparent difficulty in sexual identity, revealed by their identifying the figures on the third Rorschach card as women or by giving only female human content on the entire test.

That a small number of hyposecretors handle their anxiety by focusing on profile details on the Rorschach test is indicated by criterion 17. Other subjects gave two or more autistic and hybrid combinations of humans and animals (criterion 18).

In the overall group of 120 soldiers, there were 33 (14 hypersecretors and 19 hyposecretors) whose test records on inspection indicated sufficient psychological difficulties to rate the protocols as "disturbed" (6). The contrast between "disturbed" hyper- and hyposecretors was consistent with the inference drawn above for the entire group. In fact, the "disturbed" records of hypersecretors revealed that their anxieties were the product of variants of primitive oral impulses in dependent relationships. The hyposecretors, in contrast, evidenced marked somatic preoccupation, predominantly projective defenses, and an elaborate form of thought disorder.

DISCUSSION

In the present study, the criterion chosen as an index of the susceptibility to the development of duodenal ulcer was the concentration of pepsinogen in the serum. This criterion was selected because

long-term studies still in progress have indicated that duodenal ulcer develops only in those with high serum pepsinogen concentrations (17, 18).

The data reported herein reveal a remarkable correlation between the concentration of pepsinogen in the serum and specific personality characteristics of a group of young men inducted into the army. The group of subjects with high serum pepsinogen concentrations show intense needs that are principally "oral" in nature and which are exhibited in terms of wishing to be fed, to lean on others, and to seek close bodily contact with others. Satisfaction of these needs for external support and external sources for satiation is attempted by many means. When such attempts fail, the resultant frustration arouses anger that cannot be expressed lest there ensue a loss of supply for their needs. Consequently these subjects usually do not make complaints or express any feelings of anger.

In contrast to the above, the subjects with low concentrations of pepsinogen in the serum exhibit fewer problems about and less dependency on external sources of supply and support. They are more narcissistic and exhibit more problems relative to internal, bodily discomfort, and react to the sources of the discomfort with intense hostility which they express relatively freely. They show evidences of a disturbance in language style that is characterized by elaboration and pretentiousness. Some of the subjects show a hostile feminine identification which they defend themselves against by a masculine overcompensation. Projective defenses against anxiety are common.

In accord with the hypothesis stated at the outset, the men who had or developed a duodenal lesion were among those with high concentrations of pepsinogen in the circulation; that is, among the hypersecretors. Further, the personality characteristics of those who did develop a duodenal ulcer are essentially the same as most of the subjects comprising the hypersecretor group. Although the predictions were accurate in seven of nine subjects who had or developed duodenal ulcer, it proved impossible in the present study to use the available data to determine why only some of the hypersecretors reacted as they did to the social situation or developed the duodenal lesion. In another study in which psychoanalytically oriented anamnestic interviews were conducted, however, it has been possible to predict the character of the social situation that would prove noxious to the specific individual, and subsequently to observe that when such exposure occurred, a duodenal ulcer ensued. These observations, as well as the mechanism whereby exposure to a social event that is noxious to the individual induces the development of a duodenal lesion, will be described in another communication.

The present study does not provide an explanation for the high correlation between the serum pepsinogen concentration and the relatively specific personality characteristics. Studies on siblings and twins reveal that the secretory capacity of the gastric mucosa as gauged by the serum pepsinogen concentrations is genetically determined (18). Even at birth, the concentration of serum pepsinogen is distributed normally with some newborn infants having values that are beyond the mean of patients with duodenal ulcer. Consequently, it is improbable that the psychological characteristics described above are responsible for the physiological state of the stomach. Although the psychological development of the infant is largely dependent upon his human environment, the secretory capacity of the stomach with which the child is born may play a significant role in his relationship with that environment (17). Studies on the manner in which the quantitative aspects of a physiological system influences the child-mother unit and thereby the child's psychological development are in progress and should provide data that may clarify the mechanisms involved.

Although it is possible to postulate that the inherited secretory capacity of the stomach plays a role in determining not only the psychological development of the

infant but also his physiological predisposition, it does not account for the marked individual differences that characterize the manner in which the needs described above are handled. Study of these individual differences suggest that the vagaries of each person's life experiences determine the manner in which impulses and wishes are mastered, whereas the hypersecretor's persistent wishes for support and succor from the external environment are determined by early childhood factors. The manner in which he handles these wishes is determined by all his life experiences, that is, by the factors that determine his integrative capacity.

SUMMARY

1. Serum pepsinogen was determined for each of 2073 army inductees. Sixty-three with values in the upper 15 per cent and 57 with values in the lower 9 per cent of the blood pepsinogen distribution were selected for special study. Each of these was given the Rorschach, Blacky, Draw-A-Person, Cornell Medical Index, and Saslow tests, and a complete upper gastrointestinal roentgenological examination before being sent to basic training.

2. One hundred and seven subjects were reexamined between the eighth and sixteenth week of basic training. The first roentgenological examination revealed healed duodenal ulcers in three subjects and an active ulcer in one. The second roentgenological examination revealed active duodenal ulcers in five additional men. All nine subjects with peptic ulcer were in the upper 15 per cent of the blood pepsinogen distribution, eight of them being in the upper 5 per cent. Thus, 15 per cent of men in the top 5 per cent developed peptic ulcer.

3. Independent evaluation of the psychological data revealed that subjects with peptic ulcer displayed evidence of major unresolved and persistent conflicts about dependency and oral gratification, the characteristics of which are described.

4. Classification of the selected test population into two groups on the basis of

criteria derived from the psychological tests was found to correlate (85 per cent) with the two groups (hyper- and hypo-pepsinogen secretors) derived from the physiological tests.

5. The study indicates that neither a high rate of gastric secretion nor a specific psychodynamic constellation is independently responsible for development of peptic ulcer. Together, however, these two parameters constitute the essential determinants in the precipitation of peptic ulcer on exposure to social situations noxious to the specific individual.

References

1. Alexander, F. The influence of psychologic factors upon gastrointestinal disturbances: General principles, objectives and preliminary results. *Psychoanalyt. Quart.* 1934, *3,* 501.

2. Alexander, F. *Psychosomatic Medicine.* New York, Norton, 1950.

3. Beck, S. J. *Rorschach's Test.* New York, Grune and Stratton, 1947.

4. Blum, G. S. Revised scoring system for research use of the Blacky pictures. (Male form—1951). Ann Arbor, Mich., Univ. of Mich., 1951.

5. Brodman, K., Erdmann, A. J., Jr., Lorge, I., Deutschberger, J., and Wolff, H. G. The Cornell Medical Index — Health Questionnaire VII: The prediction of psychosomatic and psychiatric disabilities in army training. *Am. J. Psychiat.* 1954, *111,* 37.

6. DeVos, G. A quantitative approach to affective symbolism in Rorschach responses. *J. of Proj. Tech.* 1952, *16,* 133.

7. Gildea, E. G. Special features of the personality which are common to certain psychosomatic disorders. *Psychosom. Med.* 1949, *11,* 273.

8. Garma, A. Internalized mother as harmful food in peptic ulcer patients. *Internat. J. Psycho-analysis* 1953, *34,* 102.

9. Hunt, J. N., and Kay, A. W. The nature of gastric hypersecretion of acid in patients with duodenal ulcer. *Brit. M. J.* 1954, *2,* 1444.

10. Ivy, A. C., Grossman, M. I., and Bachrach, W. H. *Peptic Ulcer.* Philadelphia, Blakiston, 1950.

11. Jones, F. A. The problem of peptic ulcer. *Ann. Int. Med.* 1956, *44,* 63.

12. Kapp, F. T., Rosenbaum, M., and Romano, J. Psychological factors in men with peptic ulcer. *Am. J. Psychiat.* 1947, *103,* 700.

13. Levin, E., Kirsner, J. B., and Palmer, W. L. Twelve-hour nocturnal gastric secretion in uncomplicated duodenal ulcer patients: Before and after healing. *Proc. Soc. Exper. Biol. Med.* 1948, *69,* 153.

14. Minski, L., and Desai, M. M. Aspects of personality in peptic ulcer patients. *Brit. J. M. Psychol.* 1955, *28,* 113.

15. Mirsky, I. A., Futterman, P., Kaplan, S., and Broh-Kahn, R. H. Blood plasma pepsinogen: I. The source, properties, and assay of the proteolytic activity of plasma at acid reactions. *J. Lab. and Clin. Med.* 1952, *40,* 17.

16. Mirsky, I. A., Futterman, P., and Kaplan, S. Blood plasma pepsinogen: II. The activity of the plasma from "normal" subjects, patients with duodenal ulcer, and patients with pernicious anemia. *J. Lab. and Clin. Med.* 1952, *40,* 188.

17. Mirsky, I. A. Psychoanalysis and the biological sciences. In Alexander and Ross, *Twenty Years of Psychoanalysis.* New York, Norton and Co., 1953.

18. Mirsky, I. A. In preparation.

19. Ruesch, J. The infantile personality. *Psychosom. Med.* 1948, *10,* 134.

20. Ruesch, J., Christiansen, C., Dewkes, S., Harris, R. E., Jacobson, A., and Loeb, M. B. Duodenal ulcer, a sociopsychological study of naval enlisted personnel and civilians. Berkeley, Cal., University of California Press, 1948.

21. Saslow, G., Counts, R. M., and Dubois, P. H. Evaluation of a new psychiatric screening test. *Psychosom. Med.* 1951, *13,* 242.

22. Streitfeld, H. S. Specificity of peptic ulcer to intense oral conflicts. *Psychosom. Med.* 1954, *16,* 315.

23. Thaler, M. B., Weiner, H., and Reiser, M. F. An exploration of the doctor-patient relationship through projective techniques. Presented at 111th Annual Meeting, American Psychiatric Association, Atlantic City, N. J., May 12, 1955.

24. Zane, M. Psychosomatic considerations in peptic ulcer. *Psychosom. Med.* 1947, *2,* 372.

8 | *Behavioral Consequences of Cerebral Disorders*

THE disorders of thinking and overt conduct associated with various forms of organic brain damage have been the focus of intensive study for a long time. In the practical setting, when a patient is found to have cerebral damage or disease, the diagnostic question is: to what extent is the disordered behavior that brings him to the attention of the diagnostician a consequent of organic damage or disease? To answer this question psychologists and neurologists have devised various diagnostic tests. This section presents three research reports that illustrate a variety of approaches to the topic. The investigations by Reitan and by Milgram are addressed to the problem of identifying the psychological variables that differentiate "organic" patients from other patients and from normals. The paper by Talland and Ekdahl focuses on a specific disorder—Korsakoff's psychosis.

Reitan employed in his study a battery of tests developed by Halstead. It is important to note that the tests were not verbal paper-and-pencil instruments but performance and perceptual tests. One of the criticisms of earlier work in this area points to the limitation of generalizations resulting from failure to select representative samples of patients and nonpatients. Reitan achieved representativeness with his pathological sample by using persons with a wide variety of diagnoses of brain damage. The control group also met the criterion of representativeness by being composed of a wide assortment of persons without brain damage. Results showed that the sensitivity of the battery based on performance and perceptual tests in discriminating patients with organic brain damage was extremely high.

Milgram approached the problem in a different fashion. His interest was less in establishing a diagnostic procedure than in demonstrating the usefulness of the concept of role-taking in psychopathological research. Both schizophrenic and brain-damaged persons exhibit gross defects in the ability to perceive and enact social roles. Milgram introduces a relatively new procedure to obtain his raw data. This procedure demands that the subject adopt the role, or take the perspective, of a person different from himself in some recognizable way, such as age or sex, and perform a task from this perspective. Analysis of the data demonstrated that two components of role-taking

283

differentiate schizophrenic and brain-damaged patients. Schizophrenics are deficient in "empathic" role-taking and the brain-damaged are deficient in "cognitive" role-taking.

The report by Talland and Ekdahl analyzes in considerable detail the memory for narrative material of patients with Korsakoff's psychosis as compared to normal controls. One of the findings is contrary to the clinical lore about Korsakoff's psychosis. Confabulation is supposed to be a primary symptom of the disease. However, the data collected by Talland and Ekdahl demonstrate that normal subjects also confabulate, and in much the same manner.

In interpreting the results of this article, we should keep in mind these questions: Which deficiencies are in the original learning of the narrative material? Which deficiencies are in the retention or storage of the material? Which deficiencies are in "access" to learned and retained material?

Investigation of the Validity of Halstead's Measures of Biological Intelligence

RALPH M. REITAN

The whole theory of learning and intelligence is in confusion. We know at present nothing of the organic basis of these functions and little enough of either the variety or uniformities of their expression in behavior. The concepts are so poorly defined that it has not been possible even to imagine a program of physiological research which seemed likely to reveal more than superficial relationships (8).

SINCE Lashley wrote these words, in 1929, a large-scale attack, sponsored primarily by psychologists, has been directed toward elucidation of the learning process (6), and a tremendous amount of time and energy has gone into the construction and standardization of formal scales of psychometric intelligence (11, 12). The "organic basis of these functions" in human beings, however, remains nearly as unclear as before.

A number of investigators have attempted to devise special tests for studying relationships between brain functions and

Reprinted by permission from the *A.M.A. Archives of Neurology and Psychiatry*, Vol. 73, 1955.

behavioral potentialities (1, 2, 3, 4, 5, 7, 9, 10). Most of these researchers have recognized the value of objective and standardized test situations which yield quantitative results, not only as a basis for comparable general use of their tests, but also to permit replication and possible verification of the findings. Objective and reliable measurement has long been viewed as a fundamental tenet of science.

Independent evaluation of the validity of most of these testing procedures, unfortunately, has generally produced equivocal conclusions. The most likely explanation of this is that the original investigator's samples of subjects differed in certain unknown but relevant ways from the samples used in subsequent studies, even though brain damage may have been present in appropriate groups in each study. This is not surprising, of course, since it is usually impossible for a researcher to know completely all the variables pertinent to his measurements. The problem of controlling the influence of irrelevant variables through experimental design or methodological techniques would be theoretically possible, although likely very difficult, provided they had been identified. In addition, technical problems in measurement, such as the reliability of measures and equivalence of scaling units, add to the difficulties in experimental validation of original findings. Nevertheless, the search continues for behavioral tests selectively sensitive to the organic condition of the brain, because without such tests even partial fulfillment of the hope for elucidation of comunnicable relationships between brain function and behavior seems remote.

In 1947 Halstead (5) described and presented results for a battery of tests used with brain-damaged and control subjects. The results indicated that patients with predominantly frontal brain damage (unilateral or bilateral) did more poorly on most of the tests than did patients with nonfrontal damage. The group with nonfrontal damage, in turn, generally performed more poorly than the control group, composed of patients without brain damage. The results were very striking, mean intergroup differences in many instances being sufficiently large with relation to variability of the scores to have occurred less than 1 time in 1,000 on a chance basis. While it would seem highly unlikely that chance was responsible for the intergroup differences, the possibility remains that unknown factors differing systematically between the groups may have been responsible, rather than brain damage. The present study is concerned with possible validation of Halstead's results, using the same tests administered in the same way, but with entirely different patients and in a different geographic locale.

MATERIAL AND METHODS

Fifty patients with proved brain damage or dysfunction composed one group. A second group consisted of 50 persons who had received neurological examinations before testing and showed no signs or symptoms of cerebral damage or dysfunction. Thorough histories relating to head injuries and diseases possibly involving the brain were obtained from each patient. None of the control subjects had positive anamnestic findings.

The patients in the two groups were individually matched on the basis of color and sex, and as closely as possible for chronological age and years of formal education. Means and standard deviations on the latter variables are presented in Table 1. Neither of the differences in central tendency or variability approached statistical significance. There were 35 men and 15 women in each group.

Each patient was interviewed before testing was begun. Only those were included in the study who were sufficiently alert and in contact with reality to provide detailed anamnestic information. None of the brain-damaged patients was acutely ill at the time of testing. Although many were examined postoperatively, testing was delayed until these patients had received maximal benefits from hospitalization and were ready for discharge. No attempt was made to control either the location or the extent of brain damage. The patients ranged from one having a surgical excision of a cortical tumor approximately the size of a thumbnail to a patient with complete agenesis of the corpus callosum. The diagnostic distribution of patients in each group is given in Table 2. It should be obvious from the types of brain damage that the results of this study will have no significance with respect to either location or extent of brain damage.

The inclusion of a substantial proportion of paraplegic and neurotic patients in the group without brain damage was done as a conservative procedure. Although several of the paraplegic patients had received traumatic spinal cord injuries, none had ever been unconscious from a head injury. The neurotic subjects were all sufficiently disturbed to be hospitalized for psychiatric treatment. These patients were included to minimize the possibility that differences in the test results for the brain-damaged and the control group could be attributed to hospitalization, chronic illness, and possible affective disturbances.

The Halstead battery of neuropsychologic measures was administered individually to each subject, in nearly all instances by a person other than myself. All tests were finally scored immediately after testing of each patient had been completed and before the groups were composed or the subjects matched on the controlled variables. Matching of the subjects was done without reference to the variables which were to be compared. Intergroup statistical comparisons of mean differences were made on the 10 "discriminating" tests (those which Halstead proposed as being sensitive to the effects of frontal lobe damage). In addition, a graphic presentation of the difference scores on these tests was prepared.

RESULTS AND COMMENT

Mean scores on each test and the Halstead Impairment Index are presented graphically for each group in Chart 1. Before the intergroup comparisons are commented on, the design of the Chart should be explained. The norms for this profile chart were developed in Halstead's laboratory on the basis of a large group (N-451)

Index as an example. The percentile rank of 56 on this variable for the brain-damaged group, above the criterion line, indicates that the mean score was at a level poorer than 56% of Halstead's patients who scored in the brain-damaged range on this variable. The group without brain damage had a mean Impairment Index which was better than that obtained by 38% of Halstead's subjects who scored in the normal range.

In order that the meaning of these results may be understood with respect to

TABLE 1. MEANS AND STANDARD DEVIATIONS FOR CHRONOLOGICAL AGE AND YEARS OF FORMAL EDUCATION FOR GROUPS WITH AND WITHOUT BRAIN DAMAGE

	N	Mean age, yr.	S.D.	Mean education	S.D.
Brain-damaged group	50	32.42	10.61	11.56	3.08
Non-brain-damaged group	50	32.36	10.78	11.58	2.86

TABLE 2. DIAGNOSTIC DISTRIBUTIONS OF PATIENTS INCLUDED IN STUDY

Patients with brain damage		Patients without brain damage	
Brain Tumor	17	Paraplegia	13
Epilepsy	6	Depression	17
Closed head injury	6	Acute anxiety state	6
Penetrating head injury	6	Obsessive-compulsive neurosis	2
Cerebral vascular accident	4	Normal	12
Degenerative cerebrovascular disease	3		—
Cerebral atrophy	3		50
Cerebral abscess	2		
Subdural hematoma	1		
Dementia paralytica	1		
Developmental anomaly	1		
	—		
	50		

composed of individually tested brain-damaged and control subjects. The heavy horizontal midline represents the criterion level for each test which Halstead found to differentiate best his control and frontal-brain-damaged subjects. A test performance above the criterion line indicates a performance similar to those characteristic of Halstead's subjects with frontal brain damage, and a score below is in the control range. Deciles above and below the criterion level are indicated along the vertical axis.

Interpretation of the results in Chart 1 will be illustrated, using the Impairment

the types of impairment which occur with brain damage, the tests should be described individually. A more detailed description of each test, together with its rationale, may be found in Halstead's book (5), "Brain and Intelligence: A Quantitative Study of the Frontal Lobes." Significant mean differences were obtained with each measure except Tests II and III (Critical Flicker Frequency and Critical Flicker Frequency —Deviation).

The Impairment Index is a composite score based upon the 10 "discriminating" tests and is determined for an individual subject merely by counting the number of tests which fall above the criterion level. The mean difference between our brain-damaged and control groups was tremendous with relation to variability of differences. Statistical analysis indicated that chance alone could account for the difference in less than 1 in 10,000 repetitions

stimulus material. The subject is required to "abstract" principles based upon variables such as size, shape, number, position, brightness, and color around which to organize his responses. Halstead's (5) factor analysis of his results, as well as a subjective interpretation, suggests that this test

PROFILE CHART

MEAN PROFILES FOR 50 BRAIN DAMAGED AND 50 NON-BRAIN DAMAGED SUBJECTS

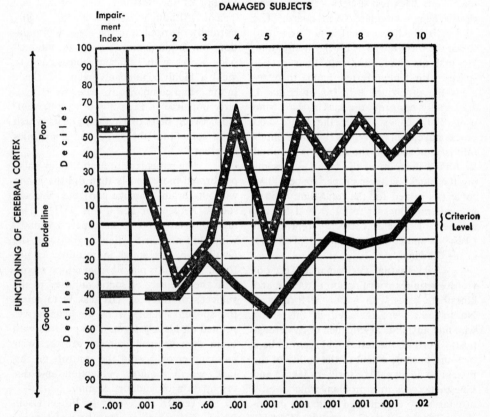

Chart 1.—Graphic presentation of mean values for matched brain-damaged and non-brain-damaged groups on Halstead's Impairment Index and 10 "discriminating" tests. *I*, Category Test; *II*, Critical Flicker Frequency; *III*, Critical Flicker Frequency—Deviation; *IV*, Tactual Performance Test—Time Component; *V*, Tactual Performance Test—Memory Component; *VI*, Tactual Performance Test—Localization Component; *VII*, Rhythm subtest—Seashore Tests of Musical Talent; *VIII*; Speech-sounds Perception Test; *IX*, Finger Oscillation Test; *X*, Time Sense Test—Memory Component.

of the experiment. These results indicate strongly that the Impairment Index measured a striking and consistent difference in our two groups.

The Category Test (Test I) utilizes a projection apparatus for presentation of

measures primarily abstraction ability. The nature of the problems posed seems to require the ability to group the stimulus material in accordance with proposed criteria, to recognize recurrent, and possibly significant, similarities in successive stimulus exposures in spite of the presence of pronounced dissimilarities, and to recognize the significance of stimulus details with relation to the overall pattern or principle that is being developed. The brain-damaged group was strikingly deficient in comparison with the control patients in these respects.

Tests IV, V, and VI represent various components of the Tactual Performance Test. This test utilizes a modification of the Seguin-Goddard form board. The subject is blindfolded and is not permitted to see the form board or blocks at any time. He first fits the blocks into their proper spaces with his preferred hand, then repeats the procedure with his other hand, and finally performs the task a third time using both hands. After the board and blocks have been put out of sight, the blindfold is removed and the subject is required to draw a diagram of the board representing the blocks in their proper spaces. The subject is scored for the total time needed to place the blocks (Test IV) and for the number of blocks correctly reproduced (Test V) and correctly localized (Test VI) in his drawing.

The Tactual Performance Test obviously requires coordination of tactile and kinesthetic cues with motor performance. No patients were included in this study who had any clinical evidence of dystereognosis. Further, the test would seem to be a measure to some extent of the ability of the patient to adapt satisfactorily to tactile and kinesthetic cues in a problem which would ordinarily be coordinated primarily by vision. The Memory Component (Test V) of this test is based upon the number of blocks correctly reproduced in the drawing of the board, and the Localization Component (Test VI), on the number correctly localized. Although the brain-damaged subjects required twice as much time to place the blocks, and thus were exposed to the board on the average twice as long as the controls, they were able to reproduce and localize significantly fewer of the shapes. While Tests V and VI are un-

doubtedly in part measures of incidental memory, Halstead's results suggest that they also are measures of abstraction ability. The brain-damaged patients apparently are impaired in the ability to relate the specific sensory cues they have obtained during the course of placing the blocks to an over-all concept of the appearance of the board.

Test VII represents the Rhythm Subtest of the Seashore Tests of Musical Talent. Although this measure is roughly normally distributed in the general population, our brain-damaged subjects obtained poor scores with sufficient consistency to yield a highly significant mean difference in the group comparisons. They were regularly impaired in their ability to differentiate between pairs of rhythmic beats which were sometimes the same and sometimes different.

The patients with brain damage also performed more poorly than did the group without brain damage on the Speech-sounds Perception Test (Test VIII). This test consists of 60 spoken speech sounds, which are nonsense syllable variants of the *ee* digraph, presented in multiple choice form. The test is played from a tape record with the intensity of sound adjusted to the subject's preference. His task is to select the spoken syllable from the alternatives printed on his test form. The patients with brain damage made almost exactly twice as many errors as did the controls on this task, which requires perception and discrimination of auditory stimuli.

Test IX represents the Finger Oscillation Test, which is a measure of tapping speed, the subject using the index finger of the preferred hand. Although clinically significant ataxia or impairment of motor control of the upper extremities was not present in either group, the mean difference in favor of the group without brain damage was sufficiently large to have occurred considerably less than 1 time in 1,000 on a chance basis.

While significant statistically, the difference between the group with and the group without brain damage on Test X, the Time Sense Test—Memory Component, does not reach the extreme levels of confidence of the tests reported above. This test requires the subject to depress a key which permits a sweep hand to rotate on the face of a clock. The subject's task is to permit the hand to rotate 10 times and then to stop it as close to the starting position as possible. The Visual Component of this test is scored as the amount of error in 40 trials. The Memory Component is the error on 20 trials, interspersed among the visual trials in series of 10, when the fact of the clock is turned away and the subject is asked to duplicate the visually controlled performance as closely as possible by memory. The mean error score of the brain-damaged subjects was nearly twice as great as that for the controls, but variability in both groups was great. Only on this test was the mean for the control group above the criterion level in Chart 1, although this level was approached in several other instances. This result is in accord with our deliberate attempt to include persons in the control group with recurrent hospitalizations, chronic illnesses, and neurotic disturbances.

Test II and III, Critical Flicker Frequency and Critical Flicker Frequency— Deviation, failed to differentiate between our group with and our group without brain damage. This result is consistent with Halstead's findings on patients with nonfrontal lesions, as compared with his control group. Although his results approached significance in the CFF comparison, the 0.05 probability level was not quite reached. Halstead did find that CFF was significantly lowered in his patients with frontal lobectomies, and the deviation on successive trials was also less in comparison with both the nonfrontal-brain-damaged and the control group. The types of brain damage included in the present study obviously do not permit any comment on Halstead's findings in his frontal lobectomy group. It should be noted, further, that the present results with CFF are not directly

comparable, because of apparatus differences, to many of the reports which have appeared in the literature. An electronic instrument (Strobotac), with a short flash duration, housed in a specially constructed, soundproof apparatus, was used in this study. The instrument and testing conditions were strictly comparable to those used by Halstead.

A procedure for graphic comparison of the efficacy of these tests in differentiating the patients with and without brain damage was worked out, and the results are presented in Chart 2. The frequency distribution for each test is based upon difference scores for the 50 paired brain-damaged and control subjects. To permit direct comparison of frequency distributions, the difference scores for each test were converted to T-scores, which have a mean of 50 and a standard deviation of 10. Further, the location of each frequency distribution on the horizontal axis is determined by the position in the distribution of the difference score of zero, or the point at which no difference was present in the scores of matched brain-damaged and control pairs. This point is indicated by the heavy vertical line which runs through the various distributions. The scales are so arranged that scores to the right of this line indicate brain-damaged subjects who have done more poorly than their matched controls. Scores to the left of the line indicate, on the contrary, deviations from the expected finding, or instances in which the control subject of the pair has done more poorly. The differentiating ability of any of the measures is thus apparent at a glance by comparing the areas under the curve to the right and the left of the zero, or "no difference" point (heavy vertical line).

The curve for the Impairment Index indicates that not a single patient with brain damage did better than his matched control, although there were six pairs who did equally as well. The quantitative magnitude of the Impairment Index would have permitted classification of the 50 pairs of patients into their diagnostic categories

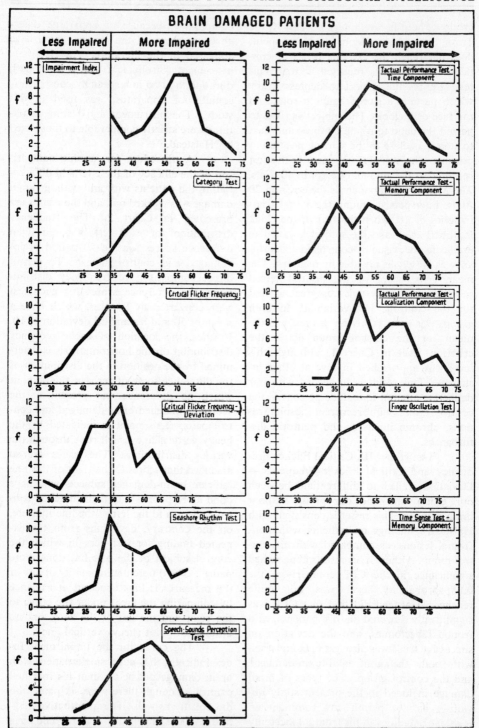

Chart 2. Graphic comparison of efficacy of Halstead's tests in differentiating paired patients with and without brain damage. Area to right of continuous vertical line indicates brain-damaged patients who performed more poorly than did paired patients without brain damage. Raw difference scores for each variable were converted to a T-score distribution having a mean of 50 and a standard deviation of 10.

(brain-damaged or control) without a single reversal, leaving six pairs unclassified. The Category Test, which is principally a measure of abstraction ability, does nearly as well in differentiating the pairs according to diagnosis. With this test there were only three reversals, and these were of relatively small magnitude. While the mean differences were highly significant on the remaining tests, with the exception of the two measures based on flicker fusion, it is apparent from Chart 2 that they do not approach as closely a perfect job of classification as do the Impairment Index and the Category Test.

The results of this study indicate more consistent differences between the group with and the group without brain damage than were found generally by Halstead in his original comparison of non-frontal-brain-damaged and control groups. Halstead's patients with frontal lobectomies generally performed as poorly as, or somewhat more poorly than did our brain-damaged patients. The magnitude and consistency of the differences in this validity study between the brain-damaged and the control patients constitute convincing evidence of the pertinence of results upon these tests to the organic condition of the brain. The results are particularly striking, for most attempts at verification of other testing procedures have resulted in equivocal conclusions.

The Halstead Impairment Index appears to be almost specifically sensitive to brain damage. Although our patients were matched in pairs on the basis of color, sex, age, and education, the paired subjects certainly must have differed in many ways besides the presence or absence of brain damage. No attempt was made to hold constant such variables as occupation, socioeconomic status, psychometric intelligence, or personality factors. Nevertheless,

in no instance was the aggregate influence of such variables of sufficient weight to cause the control to have a higher Impairment Index than the brain-damaged patient with whom he was paired. There is probably no other measure of the psychological effects of brain damage for which such striking evidence of validity could be cited. No direct conclusion can be drawn regarding the possible influence of variables such as occupation, socioeconomic status, and I. Q. on the test results, since these factors were not systematically varied; but the results suggest that their effect is negligible as compared with that of brain damage.

SUMMARY AND CONCLUSIONS

Fifty brain-damaged patients were individually matched on the basis of color, sex, chronological age, and years of formal education with 50 patients having no neurologic or anamnestic evidence of brain damage or disease. Intergroup statistical comparisons were made of results on the Halstead Impairment Index and 10 "discriminating" tests. Each of these measures, except two based on critical flicker frequency, showed significant differences. The magnitude of the mean differences with relation to variability was even more striking than in Halstead's original report. On the Impairment Index, for example, not a single brain-damaged person did better than his matched control, although six pairs had equal scores. The Category Test differentiated the groups according to diagnosis nearly as well as did the Impairment Index.

Although further validity studies are necessary, the present results suggest that the Halstead battery is sufficiently sensitive to the effects of organic brain damage to provide an objective and quantitative basis for detailed study of relationships between brain function and behavior.

REFERENCES

1. Babcock, H. An Experiment in the Measurement of Mental Deterioration. *Arch. Psychol.*, 1930, *No. 117.*

2. Benton, A. L. Visual Retention Test for Clinical Use. *Arch. Neurol. & Psychiat.*, 1945, *54*, 212.

3. Goldstein, K., and Scheerer, M. Abstract and Concrete Behavior: An Experimental Study with Special Mental Tests. *Psychol. Monogr.*, 1941, *No. 239*.

4. Graham, F. K., and Kendall, B. S. Performance of Brain-Damaged Cases on a Memory-for-Designs Test. *J. Abnorm. & Soc. Psychol.*, 1946, *41*, 303.

5. Halstead, W. C. *Brain and Intelligence: A Quantitative Study of the Frontal Lobes.* Chicago, University of Chicago Press, 1947.

6. Hilgard, E. R. *Theories of Learning.* New York, Appleton-Century-Crofts, Inc., 1948.

7. Hunt, H. F. A Practical Clinical Test for Organic Brain Damage. *J. Appl. Psychol.*, 1943, *27*, 375.

8. Lashley, K. S. *Brain Mechanisms and Intelligence.* Chicago, University of Chicago Press, 1929.

9. Piotrowski, Z. The Rorscach Ink-Blot Method in Organic Disturbances of the Central Nervous System. *J. Nerv. & Ment. Dis.*, 1937, *86*, 525.

10. Shipley, W. C. A self-Administering Scale for Measuring Intellectual Impairment and Deterioration. *J. Psychol.*, 1940, *9*, 371.

11. Terman, L. M., and Merrill, M. A. *Measuring Intelligence: A Guide to the Administration of the New Revised Stanford-Binet Tests of Intelligence.* Boston, Houghton Mifflin Company, 1937.

12. Wechsler, D. *Measurement of Adult Intelligence.* Baltimore, Williams & Wilkins Company, 1939.

Cognitive and Empathic Factors in Role-Taking by Schizophrenic and Brain Damaged Patients

NORMAN A. MILGRAM

THIS study investigates deficiencies in role-taking on the part of schizophrenic patients and nonpsychotic brain damaged patients. Cronbach (7) and others (2, 14) have cited the theoretical and methodological problems encountered in research on role-taking and interpersonal perception. The definitions and operations employed in this study were selected in an effort to avoid such difficulties. Role-taking is defined as an implicit, empathic process whereby a person predicts the behavior in a given situation of another person or persons. According to Taft (27) role-taking is said to involve two different types of empathy, *individual empathy* and *mass empathy.* The former is an intuitive process by which one experiences the thoughts and feelings of another person. The latter is an inferential process whereby one uses socially shared, conventional frames of reference about groups and group members as a basis

for predicting their behavior. The present study is concerned with the analytic judgments required in mass empathy, and investigates the ability of subjects to identify the verbal responses of men, women, adults, and children in multiple-choice word association tests.

Previous studies in this area (6, 9, 25, 31) have shown a positive relationship between empathic ability and psychological adjustment. A number of theorists (4, 8, 10, 17, 26) have suggested that schizophrenia in particular is characterized by a breakdown in role-taking skills. Several studies (12, 16, 19, 25) have borne out this assertion.

These investigations have not considered, however, the possibility that both *cognitive* and *empathic* abilities are required for an effective role-taking performance. In the typical role-taking test, the subject is called upon to give his own idiosyncratic responses on one form of a preference test and to simulate the answers of another person or persons on the same

Reprinted by permission from *The Journal of Abnormal and Social Psychology,* Vol. 60, No. 2, 1960.

or a second form of the test. It would appear that the cognitive ability to shift from giving one's preferred or dominant responses to deliberately giving the non-dominant responses that characterize another is a prerequisite to simulating the responses of another. A second cognitive ability is the forming of concepts as measured by the ability to select the terms that are normally connoted by a conceptual label, and the rejection of terms that are not. In the present study where Ss are instructed to choose the verbal responses that men, women, adults, and children characteristically give to certain stimulus words, these Ss must have, as a cognitive minimum, the ability to attach relevant connotations to these conceptual headings, *men, women,* etc.

It has been generally agreed that brain-damaged patients suffer some degree of cognitive deficit (*18*). With respect to cognitive deficit in schizophrenia, some theorists (*15*) maintain that schizophrenic patients demonstrate cognitive deficits not unlike those observed in brain-damaged patients. Others (*3, 26*) argue that what is lessened or lost in schizophrenia is not cognitive abilities, but the intent or the ability to take the role of the other as a guide to effective communication with others.

Hypothesis I. *Schizophrenic patients and brain damaged patients are deficient in role-taking in comparison with normals.*

Hypothesis II. *Brain damaged patients are deficient in cognitive abilities in comparison with schizophrenic patients.*

Hypothesis III. *Schizophrenic patients are deficient in role-taking in comparison with brain damaged patients when differences in cognitive abilities are taken into account.*

METHOD

Subjects

Three male groups consisting of 32 schizophrenic patients, 30 brain damaged patients, and 20 normal Ss were used.

Criteria for selection of the schizophrenic group included the following: (*a*) all patients had been given a psychiatric diagnosis of schizophrenia, the diagnostic breakdown showing paranoid (24), hebephrenic (2), Catatonic (2), and chronic undifferentiated (4); (*b*) no patient had neurological involvement, had undergone somatic therapy (electric shock or insulin coma) within the past six months, or had ever undergone a lobotomy.

Criteria for selection of the brain damaged group included these observations: (*a*) all patients had been given a neurological diagnosis of damage to the cerebral cortex, these diagnoses including vascular disease (9), degenerative disease (12), chronic brain syndrome (9); (*b*) no patient had a previous history of severe mental disturbance or was known to be psychotic at time of testing.

The three groups were selected with attention to age, IQ (as measured by the Vocabulary Subtest of the Wechsler-Bellevue Form I), and education. The data are summarized in Table 1. Differences in age and IQ were not significant. A statistically significant but small difference in years of formal education between normals and the two patient groups was observed.

Role-taking Tests

Multiple-choice word association tests were chosen as measures of role-taking performance because the various responses to each stimulus word could be precoded as to the age or sex group into which they fell. More important, normative data were available as to the empirically observed word association preferences of these groups.

TABLE 1. AGE, IQ, AND YEARS OF FORMAL EDUCATION

Group		Age	IQ	Education
N	M	44.6	116.2	12.0
	SD	15.2	10.0	2.7
S	M	43.1	114.9	10.8
	SD	13.4	15.7	3.2
BD	M	45.6	110.5	11.5
	SD	15.2	17.7	3.2

Terman-Miles Masculinity-Femininity Word Association Test (28). Ss were instructed to choose the verbal associations characteristically given by men on one form of the test and by women on the other. Each form contained 60 items. In any given item, there was a stimulus word printed in capital letters and four response words in lower case. One or more of these responses had been empirically demonstrated to be chosen more frequently by men, one or more by women, and the remaining responses were nondiscriminating. Masculine responses were scored $+$, feminine $-$, and neutral zero.

Abstract-Concrete Word Association Test. The paradigm for this test was taken from Flavell (*12*) and was based on empirical evidence in the literature (*32*) and in pilot studies supporting the assertion that adults choose abstractly related associations (synonym, superordinate, and subordinate) in preference to concretely related associations (part-whole, adjective, verb, concrete context) and children do the reverse. Each form of the test contained 48 items. All stimulus words were nouns. Response words were nouns, adjectives, and verbs. In any test item, the stimulus word bore an abstract relationship to one of the response words and a concrete relationship to the other, e.g., DOG—animal (superordinate), bark (verb). The score was the number of abstractly related associations chosen under each of two sets of instructions, i.e., to take adult and child roles.

Cognitive Tests

Mental Set Shifting Test. This test, taken from Appelbaum (*1*), involved three presentations of 50 words from the Kent-Rosanoff list (1938). On the first presentation, free associations were obtained; on the second, *S*s were asked to respond with the same word they had given previously; on the third, *S*s were instructed to give responses different from the previous ones. The score was the number of different responses on the third presentation. The rationale for this measure is that *S* is called upon to inhibit his own dominant responses and to adopt and sustain the mental set to give nondominant responses. An analogous cognitive process is required in role-taking.

Concept Forming Test. This test, adapted from Capps (*5*), involved a discrimination between relevant and irrelevant associations to a stimulus word. *S*s were instructed to select 3 of 7 response words which went with the stimulus word in some way. The score was the number of items (25 in all) in which all 3 related words were selected. This measure is analogous to a second cognitive requirement of role-taking, i.e., that of selecting the terms that are normally connoted by a conceptual label and rejecting the terms that are not.

Procedure

*S*s were tested individually, usually in one session. The Mental Set Shifting Test was administered first in order to obtain each *S*'s normally dominant responses. Two alternate forms of the Terman-Miles and of the Abstract-Concrete Word Association Tests were administered next with instructions to choose the associations of men and women on the first pair and of adults and children on the second. The Concept Forming Test and Vocabulary Subtest followed.

RESULTS

Hypothesis I. Means and standard deviations of the role-taking scores for the three groups are presented in Table 2. It is evident that the difference between instructions was much greater for the normals than for either of the two patient groups. Since the over-all interaction between Instruction and Groups was significant and in the predicted direction (Table 3), Hypothesis I was confirmed. Comparison of the three groups on the separate scores shows that normals were superior to both

TABLE 2. MEANS AND STANDARD DEVIATIONS OF ROLE-TAKING SCORES

Measure	Group	M	SD	D	p^a
Male	N	6.60	6.00		
	BD	−.50	6.79	7.10	<.001
	S	−4.28	8.14	3.78	<.05
Female	N	−15.05	7.53		
	S	−11.35	8.87	3.70	.13
	BD^b	−8.93	9.28	2.42	.28
Adult	N	35.85	6.27		
	S	32.91	6.63	2.94	.11
	BD	28.90	5.56	4.01	<.02
Child	N	20.05	8.00		
	S	23.41	7.72	3.36	.10
	BD^b	26.23	6.83	2.82	.12

^{a} All statistical tests are two-tailed.
^{b} Normals were superior to the brain damaged group on this comparison beyond the .02 level.

TABLE 3. ANALYSIS OF VARIANCE OF ROLE-TAKING SCORES

Source	df	Male-female Mean square	p	Adult-child Mean square	p
Groups	2	224.43	—	5.48	—
Subjects	79	81.38		60.84	
Instructions	1	5071.61	<.001	2987.80	<.001
Instructions × Group	2	740.24	<.001	1029.63	<.001
Subjects × Instructions	79	45.19		27.19	
Total	163				

TABLE 4. MEANS AND STANDARD DEVIATIONS
OF COGNITIVE TESTS

Measure	Group	M	SD	D	p[a]
Mental Set Shifting	N	45.30	4.41		
	S	42.59	8.80	2.71	.15
	BD	32.46	12.08	10.13	<.001
Concept Forming	N	23.70	1.14		
	S	22.03	3.62	1.67	<.03
	BD	21.73	2.70	0.30	—

[a] The t test with Snedecor's Correction for heterogeneity of variance was used (20). With respect to Concept Forming scores, value of H from Kriskal-Wallis analysis of variance scarcely approached significance and the differences between Normals and patient groups are of questionable significance.

TABLE 5. ANALYSIS OF COVARIANCE: MENTAL
SET SHIFTING[a] ON ROLE-TAKING SCORES

Measure	Source	Before adjustment df	Before adjustment Mean square	Before adjustment p	After adjustment df	After adjustment Mean square	After adjustment p
Male	Between	1	221.58	.05	1	718.41	<.001
	Within	60	56.53		59	43.73	
	Total	61			60		
Female	Between	1	89.96	.25	1	2.00	.89
	Within	60	82.22		59	80.16	
	Total	61			60		
Adult	Between	1	248.52	<.02	1	227.03	<.02
	Within	60	37.46		59	37.89	
	Total	61			60		
Child	Between	1	123.75	.11	1	11.31	.88
	Within	60	45.55		59	43.44	
	Total	61			60		

[a] An Arcsin transformation (29) was used to make the variances homogeneous as a necessary condition for covariance adjustment.

patient groups on male scores, but only to the brain damaged group on female scores. Normals were superior to the brain damaged group on both adult and child scores, but were not significantly different from the schizophrenic group on either.

Hypothesis II. Means and standard deviations of scores on the cognitive tests are presented in Table 4 and show that the hypothesis is confirmed with respect to mental set shifting. The difference in concept forming between the two patient groups was not significant.

Hypothesis III. Hypothesis III held that the mean role-taking score of the brain damaged group is greater than that of the schizophrenic group when a correction is made for differences in cognitive abilities (i.e., mental set shifting). This assertion was confirmed for male scores only. The data on analysis of covariance of mental set shifting scores and the four role-taking scores are summarized in Table 5. Analyses of covariance for female and child scores revealed no significant differences between the patient groups, although the adjustment was in the predicted direction. With respect to adult scores, the schizophrenic group was superior both before and after covariance adjustment.

DISCUSSION

Hypothesis I. Experimental findings have confirmed the hypothesis that schizophrenic and brain damaged patients are deficient in role-taking performance. These findings are consistent with interpersonal theory (3), which states that schizophrenics are deficient in taking the role of the other, and with cognitive theory (15), which states that brain damaged patients do poorly in role-taking tasks because of their deficits in the cognitive abilities required for effective role-taking.

The specific deficiency of the schizophrenic group in taking the male role is also consistent with the psychoanalytic theory of a relationship between paranoid schizophrenia (24 of the 32 schizophrenic patients were paranoid) and feminine identification (13). It is worthwhile noting that the use of the Terman-Miles Word Association Test to discriminate between normals and paranoid schizophrenics has singularly failed until now. Musiker (22) cites a number of studies, including his own, to make this point. In these earlier studies, the test was administered with instructions "to choose the word that goes best or most naturally with the stimulus word." Male Ss tended to choose both male and female responses with the latter in the majority by a narrow margin. In the present study where Ss were specifically instructed to discriminate male and female responses, normals were successful in this deliberate effort, but schizophrenics were not.

Hypothesis II. Results on the Mental Set Shifting Test suggest that the inability to inhibit one's dominant or preferred mode of response is a specific characteristic of thought pathology in organic brain damage. Schizophrenics as a group were not significantly different from normals. The few schizophrenics who did poorly on this test tended to be older, chronically ill patients. Their "brain-damaged-like" performance may have been related either to chronicity of illness, to the mental deterioration that presumably accompanies senescence (*30*), or both. Rank order correlation coefficients between age and mental set shifting were .46 for the brain damaged group and .61 for the schizophrenic group. The higher correlation for the schizophrenic group may reflect a compounding of chronicity of illness and age. The older schizophrenic patients had been hospitalized for many years (up to 40), whereas the brain damaged patients, regardless of age, had all had fairly recent onsets of illness and hospitalization.

It is felt that the Concept Forming Test failed to support the hypothesis because of its low ceiling of difficulty. Even the difference between the normals and the two patient groups was of questionable significance.

Hypothesis III. The magnitude of the correlations which obtained between mental set shifting and male-female role-taking scores confirms the original contention, that the role-taking task has cognitive as well as empathic requirements. The covariance adjustment of the male scores highlights the specifically *empathic* deficiency of the schizophrenics in taking the male role.

Several explanations come to mind to account for the failure of the brain damaged group on the adult-child role-taking polarity. This task implicitly requires a discrimination between abstract and concrete word relationships. Considerable evidence has shown that brain damaged patients are especially deficient in this

discrimination (*21*); hence, they are penalized by an additional cognitive requirement which does not apply in the male-female role-taking task. Moreover, in the male-female polarity, an *S* is aided in his choices by specific knowledge about the habits, interests, feelings, and attitudes of men and women; on the adult-child polarity, a subject is called upon to identify a subtle quality of thinking that is reflected in language usage. Such a task, requiring a discrimination between the thought characteristics of adults and children, may be especially difficult for the brain damaged group.

At any rate, the performance of the brain damaged group on the adult-child polarity was so poor as to recommend the test as a little understood but highly interesting diagnostic tool. If 7 is taken as the cutoff point for each *S*, then three normals were misdiagnosed because of their failure to shift at least 7 points from adult to child score, whereas only two brain damaged *S*s were misdiagnosed because they shifted more than 7 points.

Implications for future research extend in several directions. The present study should be supplemented by testing the ability of female schizophrenics to take male and female roles. Theoretically, an underlying masculine indentification would result in a poor performance on female role. A second study should deal with the adult-child polarity in children. It would be interesting to learn at what age a child follows the adult pattern of preference for abstract relationship in his free associations and in his taking the role of adult. This study would provide a clue to the relationship between role perception and role enactment. Finally, the diagnostic implications of the various cognitive and role-taking tests employed herein merit further study.

SUMMARY

The purpose of this investigation was twofold: to study the nature of role-taking performance in schizophrenic and brain damaged patients, and to contribute thereby to an understanding of thought pathology in these patient groups. Schizophrenic and nonpsychotic brain damaged *S*s were administered four multiple-choice word association tests which required shifting from the male to female role on one pair and from the adult to child role on the other. The latter, for which empirical norms were obtained, required an implicit discrimination between abstract and concrete relationships of stimulus and response words. The most relevant cognitive aspect of the role-taking performance was tapped by a task requiring the ability to inhibit one's preferred response in favor of another.

When role-taking scores were ad-justed for differences in this cognitive ability, the brain damaged group was superior to the schizophrenic group on the male-female polarity, chiefly because of the schizophrenics' inability to take the male role. The brain damaged group failed completely on the adult-child polarity to discriminate the abstract from the concrete relationship with the result that the schizophrenics were superior in the shift from adult to child role. Both patient groups were deficient in comparison with normal controls on both role-taking polarities. Results were interpreted as indicating that lowered role-taking performances in schizophrenic and brain damaged groups were related to empathic and cognitive deficiencies respectively.

REFERENCES

1. Appelbaum, S. Automatic and volitional processes in the verbal responses of brain-damaged and normal subjects. Unpublished doctoral dissertation, Boston Univer., 1958.

2. Bronfenbrenner, U. The study of identification through interpersonal perception. In R. Tagiuri & L. Petrullo (Eds.), *Person perception and interpersonal behavior*. Stanford Univer. Press, 1958, Pp. 110–130.

3. Cameron, N. Deterioration and regression in schizophrenic thinking. *J. abnorm. soc. Psychol.*, 1939, *34*, 265–270.

4. Cameron, N. The paranoid pseudo-community. *Amer. J. Social.*, 1943, *49*, 32–48.

5. Capps, H. Vocabulary changes in mental deterioration. *Arch. Psychol., N. Y.*, 1939, No. 242.

6. Cline, V. Ability to judge personality assessed with a stress interview and sound-film technique. *J. abnorm. soc. Psychol.*, 1955, *50*, 183–187.

7. Cronbach, L. Proposals leading to analytic treatment of social perception scores. In R. Tagiuri & L. Petrullo (Eds.), *Person perception and interpersonal behavior*. Stanford Univer. Press, 1958, Pp. 353–379.

8. Dunham, H. The social personality of the catatonic-schizophrene. *Amer. J. Social.*, 1944, *49*, 508–518.

9. Dymond, Rosalind. Personality and empathy. *J. consult. Psychol.*, 1950, *14*, 343–350.

10. Faris, R. Reflections of social disorganization in the behavior of a schizophrenic patient. *Amer. J. Sociol.*, 1944, *50*, 134–141.

11. Flavell, J. Thought, communication, and social integration in schizophrenia: An experimental and theoretical study. Unpublished doctoral dissertation, Clark Univer., 1955.

12. Flavell, J. Abstract thinking and social behavior in schizophrenia. *J. abnorm. soc. Psychol.*, 1956, *52*, 208–211.

13. Freud, S. Psychoanalytic notes on an autobiographical account of a case of paranoia. *Collected papers.* Vol. III. London: Hogarth, 1924.

14. Gage, N., and Cronbach, L. Conceptual and methodological problems in interpersonal perception. *Psychol. Rev.*, 1955, *62*, 411–423.

15. Goldstein, K. Significance of psychological research in schizophrenia. *J. nerv. ment. Dis.*, 1943, *97*, 492–507.

16. Helfand, I. Role-taking in schizophrenia. *J. consult. Psychol.*, 1956, *20*, 37–41.

17. Hoskins, R. *Biology of schizophrenia.* New York: Norton, 1946.

18. Hunt, J., and Cofer, C. Psychological deficit. In J. Hunt (Ed.), *Personality and*

the behavior disorders. Vol. II. New York: Ronald Press, 1944, Pp. 971–1032.

19. McGaughran, L., and Moran, L. "Conceptual level" versus "Conceptual area" analysis of object-sorting behavior of schizophrenic and nonpsychiatric groups. *J. abnorm. soc. Psychol.,* 1956, *52,* 43–50.

20. McNemar, Q. *Psychological statistics.* New York: Wiley, 1949.

21. Milgram, N. Preference for abstract versus concrete word meanings in schizophrenic and brain-damaged patients. *J. clin. Psychol.,* 1959, *15,* 207–212.

22. Musiker, H. Sex identification and other aspects of the personality of the male paranoid schizophrenic. Unpublished doctoral dissertation, Boston Univ., 1952.

23. Rosanoff, A. *Manual of psychiatry.* (7th ed.) New York: Wiley, 1938.

24. Sarbin, T. Role theory. In G. Lindzey (Ed.), *Handbook of social psychology.* Vol. I. Cambridge, Mass.: Addison-Wesley, 1954, Pp. 223–258.

25. Sarbin, T., and Hardyck, C. Conformance in role perception as a personality variable. *J. consult. Psychol.,* 1955, *19,* 109–111.

26. Sullivan, H. The language of schizophrenia. In J. Kasanin (Ed.), *Language and thought in schizophrenia.* Berkeley: Univer. of California Press, 1944, Pp. 4–16.

27. Taft, R. The ability to judge people. *Psychol. Bull.,* 1955, *52,* 1–23.

28. Terman, L., and Miles, Catherine. *Sex and personality.* New York: McGraw-Hill, 1936.

29. Walker, Helen, and Lev, J. *Statistical inference.* New York: Holt, Rinehart and Winston, 1953.

30. Wechsler, D. *The measurement of adult intelligence.* Baltimore: Williams & Wilkins, 1944.

31. Wittick, J. The generality of the prediction of self reports. *J. consult. Psychol.,* 1955, *19,* 445–448.

32. Woodrow, H., and Lowell, Frances. Children's association frequency tables. *Psychol. Monogr.,* 1916, *22* (5, Whole No. 97).

Psychological Studies of Korsakoff's Psychosis

IV. The Rate and Mode of Forgetting Narrative Material

GEORGE A. TALLAND AND MARILYN EKDAHL

DEFECTIVE retention is the most prominent symptom in Korsakoff's psychosis. This syndrome presents such extreme cases as those described by Gruenthal and Stoerring (8) and Conrad (6), in whom all memory of personal experiences as well as of other information vanished within a minute, though without seriously impairing the availability of long-established habits. As the neurological symptoms and the confusional state of the acute phase clear up the amnesic disturbance shows little improvement. Earlier memories tend to be recalled with fair reliability, but information imparted, events observed, or even experienced with some measure of personal involvement after the onset of the disease are at the most recol-lected vaguely, inaccurately, and more often completely forgotten.

The extent of the memory disturbance is by no means uniform in all its manifestations. For example, one of the patients studied in the present research, who was never able to report the title or any of the contents of the book she had been reading and was holding at the time of questioning, could describe her daily activities with reasonable accuracy. Another patient who appeared to have no idea of what her daily routine consisted of, was capable of recalling in some detail a conversation she had overheard several hours earlier. A third patient's amnesia typically extended to the name of the experimenter who had seen her some forty times and had told her his name on as many occasions, yet she invariably recognized him as some-

Reprinted by permission from the *Journal of Nervous and Mental Diseases,* Vol. 29, 1959.

one she had met before, sometimes in the "hospital" but more often, and with remarkable consistency over the years, as having seen him "calling at the Flanagans," one-time neighbors of hers whom he had never visited. Yet another of these patients both recognized the experimenter by name and correctly placed him in his setting, but in other respects displayed very severe amnesic defects, for she was unable to relearn eight lines of a nursing rhyme she remembered having known as a child, and could not retain the gist of a simple story after a few minutes. Neither could these patients be relied on to perform consistently in a specific memory test on repeated occasions; some of them showed a tendency to improve, while most of them fluctuated.

These apparent inconsistencies cannot be accounted for in the absence of an adequate theory of remembering, but may indeed contribute to the formulation of one. Clearly, the damage is not simply a general diminution of some capacity, whether it be registration, retention, or recall, neither does it result from an abnormally severe susceptibility to interference as demonstrated by an experiment (11) in the reproduction and recognition of both meaningful words and nonsense syllables; nor can it be attributed to motivated repression. The argument for the latter explanation could hardly be sustained in the face of the very extensive amnesic defect characteristic of Korsakoff patients, and of their tendency to forget emotionally neutral impressions as fully as they do painful, disturbing or perplexing experiences. Betlheim and Hartmann's experimental study (4) with three Korsakoff patients would support the relevance of the motivational factor to their memory disturbance but, as will be reported below, their findings could not be reproduced in our study. Moreover, these authors themselves considered repression to be but one of the several circumstances which constitute the total amnesic condition in Korsakoff's psychosis.

An adequate assessment of the memory disturbance in Korsakoff's psychosis presupposes a survey of performances both in the course of clinical interviews and in the experimental laboratory, varying the content as well as the conditions and operations of recall. The present report is limited to one segment of this study, for it deals only with recall of meaningful narrative material presented in the form of several short stories to be memorized. Recall was tested after intervals of varying length, by means of both reproduction and recognition. Two specific hypotheses tested concerned the tendency toward symbolic distortion observed by Betlheim and Hartmann, and the interference effect of redundant or insignificant information. Tests of recall also raised the question of confabulation, which will be considered without attempting a systematic analysis of the phenomenon in this paper.

METHOD

Subjects

The experimental group consisted of 22 patients of the Boston State Hospital, diagnosed by neurologists as having Korsakoff's psychosis, who at the time of their first testing had been at that hospital for periods ranging from one year to over twelve years. They all had a history of alcoholism prior to their hospitalization, and had been under observation for the neurological symptoms of Wernicke's encephalopathy in the acute phase of their disease. Their cultural background was predominantly that of the lower class of Irish extraction; their I.Q. was in the average range as tested by the Wechsler Bellevue Intelligence Scale (12), with a mean of 98.5 (SD = 12.2); in age they ranged from 31 to 74 at the time of their first testing, with a mean of 53.4 (SD = 9.8). In most of the studies here reported the Korsakoff patients served as their own controls. For two of the tests, however, control groups were used. One consisted of 14 alcoholic patients who were receiving psychotherapy in an out-patient clinic and of eight hospitalized neurological patients who were receiving physiotherapy. The second control group was composed of ten psychiatric in-patients and six neurological out-patients. Both control groups were matched for age with the Korsakoff group.

Material

Five narrative passages were used in the tests. These included Franz's (7) *cowboy story* which has been extensively employed in psychological studies of neurological diseases:

A *cowboy*[1]/ from *Arizona*[2]/ went to *San Francisco*[3]/ with his *dog*,[4]/ which he *left*[5]/ at a *friend's*[6]/ while he *purchased*[7]/ a *new* suit of *clothes*.[8]/ Dressed finely,[9]/ he *went back*[10]/ to the dog,[11]/ *whistled* to him,[12]/ *called him* by name[13]/ and *patted* him.[14]/ But the dog would *have nothing to do* with him,[15]/ in his new *hat*[16]/ and *coat*,[17]/ but gave a *mournful*[18]/ *howl*.[19]/ *Coaxing* was of no effect/[20]; so the cowboy *went away*[21]/ donned his *old garments*,[22]/ whereon the *dog*/[23] *immediately*[24]/ showed his wild *joy*[25]/ on *seeing his master*[26]/ as he thought he *ought to be*.[27]/

The tendency towards symbolic distortion was tested by one of Betlheim and Hartmann's own short stories (B) and a control text (C) matched for length and information but free from disturbing sexual content:

(B) "When the mother left the house,/ the father locked himself up in a room/ with his daughter,/ threw her on the bed,/ and raped his own child."

(C) "When the mother left the house,/ the daughter stole into the pantry,/ took down a box of cookies from the shelf,/ and ate the lot,/ so that none was left."

Lastly, the interference effect of redundant information was tested by two versions of two passages from a morning paper, the longer ones somewhat embellished, the shorter couched in a terser style than the reporter's.

(D/long) Mailmen/ are frequently asked questions that have little to do with postal matters./ Paul Callahan/ was covering his route/ in the Inman-St. section/ of Cambridge,/ and was stopped by a woman/ in her twenties,/ wearing a brown dress,/ who had a worried expression on her face/ when she asked him: "Can you tell me where I could borrow some money/ without having to ask my husband to sign a paper?"/ "I don't know offhand" the mailman replied,/ "but I would not advise it,/ for he will find out about the loan/ when the payments are due."

(D/short) When a woman/ asked a mailman/ in the street/ where she could borrow money/ without her husband's knowledge,/ he replied he didn't know/ and would not advise it/ because the husband would find out/ when the payments are due.

(E/long) In a city/ in India/ several thousand school children/ paraded/ in the main square/ to celebrate the sixty eighth birthday/ of the prime minister./ While reviewing the parade/ the prime minister released/ a number of doves,/ the symbols of peace,/ from the cages in which they had been kept./ The white doves flew over the heads/ of the young marchers./ One of them, however, perched atop the prime minister's head/ while he took the salute.

(E/short) The prime minister/ of India/ released white peace doves/ over the heads of several thousand school children/ who were parading/ to celebrate/ his sixty eighth birthday,/ but one dove perched on his head/ while he took the salute.

The strokes indicate the units into which the stories were divided for quantitative analysis of recall. The division of the *cowboy story* follows the original design which broke it down into 27 sections for verbatim reproduction. When the instruction was for recall of content, only certain significant words or phrases within each of these sections were scored, those in italics above. Suitable synonyms or substitutes were accepted, *e.g.,* "bought" (but not "got") for "purchased," "did not recognize him" or "did not know him" for "would have nothing to do with him," "put on his old clothes" for "donned his old garments," "happy" or "pleased" instead of "showed his wild joy," "seeing him" for "seeing his master." Items 10 and 11, 16 and 17, 18 and 19 were paired into single units, so that *e.g.,* "mournful howl" counted as one point only. A second reference to the new

clothes, in place of "dressed finely" did not add to the score, neither did a repeated mention of the old clothes or of a cowboy outfit in place of the last section.

The same principle applied to the scoring of the other stories; the content of each unit counted, no matter how loosely phrased or how far out of its original position in the sequence of sections, as long as its referent was unmistakably correct. A "lady" or merely "she" was accepted instead of a "woman" in the *mailman story,* "flew down on", "sat on" or "lit upon" in place of "perched atop" in the report from India, "crackers" or "candies" for "cookies" in *story C.* The single sentence stories (*B* and *C*) each divided into five sections, the shorter versions of *D* and *E* into nine, the longer into 16 units.

---

1. Whom is the story about?	Farmer Cowboy Carpenter Sailor
2. Where was he from?	Chicago Mexico Arizona Florida
3. What did he take with him?	His daughter His car His guitar His dog
4. Where did he go to?	San Francisco New York Canada California
5. What did he do with the dog?	Kept him with him all the time Asked his wife to look after him Left him with a friend Locked him up in the kennel
6. What did he go out to do?	Take a girl to a dance Buy some clothes Buy a new radio See a movie
7. What happened on his return?	Had he forgotten about the dog? Did he pick up the dog? Did he call the dog by name? Had the dog disarppeared?
8. What did the dog do?	Did he jump on him? Did he howl mournfully? Did he snap at him? Did he growl at him?
9. Why did the dog not recognize his master?	Because of the strange place Because he wore new clothes Because he was a very old dog Because he was very hungry
10. What did his master do to be recognized by the dog?	Coax the dog Give him a bone to chew Put on his old garments Stroke the dog's neck

Recall of the *cowboy story* was also tested by means of recognition, presenting the ten questions listed on page 301 with a set choice of four answers to each.

PROCEDURE

All the stories were presented with an instruction to memorize them. In every instance but one the experimenter read the stories aloud in a clear loud voice and at an even rate. The reason for choosing this procedure was that the task of reading, particularly of texts longer than a single sentence, creates additional difficulties for Korsakoff patients who, as other studies (*10*) have shown, were likely to react as if faced with two separate tasks simultaneously, the one to read and the other to remember, and their performance in the latter would have suffered as a consequence. *Stories B* and *C,* however, since they each consisted of one sentence only, were presented to the subjects to be read aloud by them, the experimenter helping or correcting them if necessary.*

The *cowboy story* was read to the Korsakoff patients on three occasions. At first they were instructed to try and remember it word by word, and were tested for verbatim reproduction immediately after the experimenter completed his presentation of the material. All 22 Korsakoff patients and the first control group of 22 participated in this test. After the lapse of some 18 to 20 months a second test of reproduction was given to 20 members of

the Korsakoff group. Their instruction was to reproduce the content of the story immediately after its presentation, and the experimenter helped with a few prompting questions. This procedure was followed immediately by a test of recognition presenting the ten forced choice questions. After 24 hours, and again a week following the reading of the text, recall was tested first by means of unaided reproduction and subsequently by recognition. Only 10 of the original 20 subjects were available for the two repeat tests. Last, after a further interval of ten months, the story was read once again to 16 members of the Korsakoff group. Recall was tested by unaided reproduction, first immediately following the presentation of the material, and subsequently after one hour, two hours, and three hours. Finally, after the fourth test of reproduction, the forced choice questionnaire was presented for further tests of recognition. The first hour was occupied by a standard procedure of psychological experiments, most of the second hour by EEG recordings, and the third hour was a rest period. Our second control group of 16 was tested for recall by reproduction both after the short and longer delays, *i.e.* after intervals of one, two, and three hours, 12 of its members also a day later, and ten after a week's interval. The control subjects were occupied with psychological experiments during the first two hours. It will be noted that, owing to the somewhat different experimental conditions of the two groups, the control data for delayed recall are not completely comparable with those of the Korsakoff patients. In no instance were the subjects warned that further tests of recall would follow, whether an hour, a day, or a week later.

Stories B and *C* were given to 14 Korsakoff patients only, each on a separate day. Test of recall was by reproduction of content five, 15 and 45 minutes after reading the story. *Stories D* and *E* were presented so that the longer version of one and the shorter version of the other were read on one occasion, the alternate versions

---

* [In a personal communication, Dr. Talland writes:

"Since writing that paper, I have had the opportunity to complete two supplementary experiments, the results of which are relevant to that report.

"Briefly, stories D or E (long version) were presented to 14 patients under three conditions on different occasions: (a) read by the experimenter as in the earlier procedure; (b) read by the experimenter six times in succession; (c) read by the subject, always with instruction to remember contents.

"The results show a slight but statistically not significant increment under (b) as compared with (a) both on immediate testing and after an hour's delay; a statistically significant increment between (c) on the one hand, and (a) and (b) on the other on immediate testing, but not after an hour's delay."

Thus, these results support, in part, those findings by Talland (*10*) reported above.—Ed.]

several weeks later. The sequence of long and short version of the same story and of the long and short story within one session alternated among the subjects. Tests of recall was by reproduction of the content a few seconds following the reading of each story. Seventeen Korsakoff patients formed the experimental group in this study. No control group was studied under the same conditions, but a parallel experiment was conducted with 21 staff members of the Department of Psychiatry of the Massachusetts General Hospital, who reproduced the stories serially, *i.e.* one sub-

QUANTIFIED RESULTS

Under conditions of immediate verbatim recall the Korsakoff group reproduced a mean of 3.97 of the 27 units of the *cowboy story*, as compared with the control group's 8.32. With $t = 5.51$ the difference is significant at the .01 level. Both groups tended to reproduce the first few items of the story more accurately, no doubt because these hardly lend themselves to changed phrasing. The controls also scored fairly highly on the last sentence, as would be expected in accordance with experiments in rote learning; the Korsakoff pa-

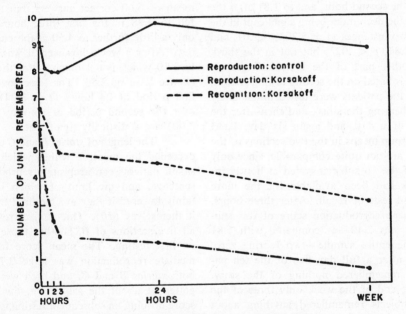

Figure 1. Forgetting curves: Cowboy Story.

ject having read the stories, wrote down a day later what he remembered of them, read this to a second subject, who in turn reported his recollection of the stories to a third person after a day's delay, and the last member of the chain also waited for a day before writing down his report. The purpose of this experiment was to investigate the qualitative changes in recall which arise from the cumulative effects of omission and distortion characteristic of this procedure.

tients, in contrast, reproduced none of the last five items.

With the number of units reduced from 27 to 24, the Korsakoff group's immediate recall score for content, giving a mean of 5.82, was signifiacantly higher than their score for verbatim reconstruction ($t = 2.51$, $p < .02$). For the controls the increment under these conditions was much smaller and statistically not significant; their mean score for reproducing content, 9.56, however, was significantly higher than the Korsakoff group's ($t =$ 5.22). Prompting questions helped to increase the Korsakoff group's immediate recall score to 9.30, a mean significantly higher ($t = 5.37$) than for reproduction of content without such helpful questions as "Where did he come from?", "What did he do?", "Then what happened?"

Figure 1 shows a composite forgetting curve for the Korsakoff patients as tested by reproduction, the first section representing the progressive decrement in their recall of content in the third testing session. Their reproduction score dropped from 5.82 to 3.62 in the first hour, to 2.44 after the second hour, and to 1.81 after the third, the decrement being significant in the first two instances ($t = 5.20$, $p < .01$, and $t = 2.84$, $p < .02$), but not in the third. The other part of the Korsakoff group's curve is based on the second testing session, when the patients were tested immediately after hearing the story, and then after the lapse of a day, and again six days later. The group means in the two sections of the curve are not quite comparable, since only ten of the 16 subjects tested at hourly intervals had been available for the more delayed tests of recall. After three hours, the mean reproduction score of this subgroup was 2.40—as compared with 1.81 for the entire sample—two scoring zero, while after a full day five of the ten patients remembered nothing of the story. At the end of the week only three of the ten subjects remembered anything about the story, two reproducing one, and the third three sections of its content. The control group forgot at a much steadier rate, dropping from 9.12 on immediate reproduction to 8.12 after the first hour, and to 8.00 after the second, and retaining this mean after the third. After 24 hours their mean score rose to 9.75, and still reached 8.75 after a week. The paradoxical gain shown by the control group after a day as compared with immediate testing is an example of reminiscence (2), an occurrence which accounted in part for their slow rate of forgetting in the first two hours. With 16 Korsakoff patients there were only four instances of reminiscence, i.e. the re-emergence of information missing from an earlier test of recall; in the control group of the same size this phenomenon occurred on 25 occasions.

The recognition test confirmed the finding based on the reproduction scores, that in the Korsakoff syndrome the rate of forgetting is rapid in the first few hours, and then tapers off. These results also illustrated the argument that the patients' retention defect does not fully account for their amnesic symptoms. Their score on immediate testing was fairly high, with a mean of 6.60 correct answers, but then it fell to 4.88 in the first three hours, and only a little further to 4.60 at the end of a day. After a week, however, it was down to 3.10 which is not much better than the chance level of 2.50. The losses over the first period of 24 hours ($t = 3.04$), and over the second period of six days ($t = 3.00$) are statistically significant.

The length of *stories B and C* clearly exceeded the measure within which Korsakoff patients can accurately reproduce a sentence, and the limit of which is certainly lowered if they are required to read it themselves (*10*). One subject reported all five sections of *B*, another those of *C* on first testing. The mean score for immediate reproduction was alike 2.71 for both *stories B and C,* and both were forgotten at about the same rate, the recall score droping on subsequent testing to 2.00, 1.57, and 1.00 for the one, to 1.86, 1.43, and 1.07 for the other. Prompting in many instances helped to recover some detail omitted in the spontaneous report, more particularly in delayed recall, *e.g.* "When did it happen?": "When the mother left the house;" "Who did it?": "The father" in place of "he," "the daughter" instead of "she." Only two instances of reminiscence occurred, one after five, the other after 15 minutes. After five minutes every subject remembered the gist of both stories; one completely forgot *story B* after 15, and four others after 45 minutes, yet another subject could recall nothing of *story C* after 15 minutes, and a seventh after 45 minutes. Mean differences of individual recall scores were significant ($p < .01$) between immediate and delayed testing after five minutes, and also between retesting after five and 15 minutes.

Stories D and *E* were both presented in a long and a short version, the former including seven additional items of information of minor importance for the incident reported. Mean units recalled were 4.1 alike for the two versions of *story E* and 5.2 for the longer, 4.8 for the shorter variant of *story D*. The seven additional items of the longer version accounted for a score of only one in the total group record of 17 Korsakoff patients in *story E*, and for seven in *story D*. Unimportant details were evidently neither remembered, nor did they noticeably interfere with the recall of the central theme.

In view of the numerous reproductions of all the stories given in the briefest and barest phrasing, it is at least arguable that details of a story serve as cues for recalling other details, as Cameron (5) suggested in his distinction of two types of memory defect in amnesic patients. The omission, or only very scanty sketching of the setting in which the events reported took place, corresponds to the perceptual limitations observed by several students of the Korsakoff syndrome, while the distortions and elaborations of the core content recalled are suggestive of the verbal behavior often referred to as confabulation.

Discussion and Analysis of Content

The foregoing quantitative analysis of recall performance has shown that, when faced with the task of memorizing some comparatively simple and short narrative material, Korsakoff patients are impaired in the amount of information they can take in at first, and then forget at a faster rate than control subjects. They retain very little, and many of them retain nothing after a period during which controls show virtually no memory loss. They tend to recall information given at the beginning of the story more accurately than details or phrases which occur at the end. Data which bear little relevance to the central theme do not seem seriously to interfere with the amount or the clarity of the essential information registered and reproduced on immediate testing; in the absence of reminiscence effects, they are therefore unlikely to increase the rate of forgetting. The recall scores for the single sentence stories (*B* and *C*) also suggest that within 15 or at most 45 minutes even a unitary narrative text presented in the starkest phrasing attenuates into a skeleton statement, such as "he raped her" or "she ate the cookies."

Although test of recognition indicated a higher level of retention at every phase, the rate of forgetting was rapid in the first three hours. This method of testing recall, as with prompting questions, points out that the spontaneous process of reproduction imposes an additional burden on the Korsakoff patients. So does, of course, the requirement of verbatim recall, and to a greater extent than for the controls. Completely accurate reproduction, as demonstrated by Bartlett (3), is the exception, the limiting instance of recall, so it is somewhat surprising that the control group which worked under instructions to repeat the story verbatim performed about as efficiently as the group instructed to reproduce the content of the story. As remarked above, certain items of the *cowboy story* could either be remembered verbatim or not at all, and this is one reason for the negligible difference in performance between the two control groups; the immediate test of recall is another. Such words or phrases as "donned," "coaxed," "howled," "showed his wild joy" occurred repeatedly in the records of the control group, but hardly at all in the many more protocols of the Korsakoff patients, and the last of these, like the two final units of the story, not once.

The omissions, distortions, embellishments, and elaborations introduced by the Korsakoff patients into their reproductions of the stories, and any progressive trend in these are of interest in view of the general attribution of the symptom of confabulation to this syndrome. Apart from the various modes of impoverishment of the content, the changes which occurred in reproduction divide into five general types.

The first of these implies no error, merely a loosening or *levelling* of some item of information. The most frequent example in the *cowboy story* occurred at the beginning, when the central figure would be reported to have gone "to town," to "California," or "out west." This type of alteration of the content was quite common with the controls as well as with the Korsakoff patients, though only the latter referred to him simply as "a man." Another instance of levelling provided by this group was "the dog didn't like him" for "would have nothing to do with him."

A second type of content change involved some *error*. The control and Korsakoff subjects between them listed a fair sample of the south-western states in lieu of Arizona (correct), and the opening words of a control subject, "A sailor from Wisconsin . . ." was nicely matched by a patient who began his story with, "A sailor from Illinois . . .".

The third type of change consisted of some *elaboration* of an incident, some gratuitous embellishment of the original text. Examples from the records of the control group are "A cowboy left his ranch . . .", ". . . the dog barked at him when he came out of the store," ". . . the dog ran to him and licked him," ". . . the dog yelped at him;" from those of the Korsakoff group "Nobody knew him he was so dressed up, even his neighbors did not recognize him," ". . . the man was very poorly dressed, so he bought . . .", "purchased new clothes, and then bought some food." Several members of both groups seemingly had formed the impression that the central character had gone to San Francisco in his cowboy's outfit and

there replaced it with civilian clothes, a plausible enough conclusion though not warranted by the text of the story.

The fourth type of change did not affect the content, but was merely a *comment* on the part of the narrator. The most typical instance of this modification was induced, quite reasonably, by a glaring improbability of the text. Dogs are not at all likely to rely on a visual recognition of their master, and this evidently perplexed several members of both groups, so that they either made some comment to this effect and thus questioned the verisimilitude of the story, or tried to explain this apparent contradiction by suggesting that the new clothes had not yet absorbed the master's scent. One member of each group made an attempt with this rather feeble argument.

Lastly, there were instances of *fabrication,* of inserting a complete unit from a different context into the story, or of substituting an entirely different narrative for it. In this type of change the two groups differed quite markedly, and the examples given by the Korsakoff patients are of considerable interest in the context of their syndrome. The only instance provided by a control subject which might fit into this category (though it might more properly be termed an *elaboration*) is: "If the dog did not recognize him he would not take him back with him to Arizona." One example drawn from the Korsakoff records, in turn, is perhaps merely a case of a jesting *comment*: "The gentleman went to town to get himself some things and came back with a new suit he had not intended to buy. At least he got himself a nice birthday present." This was all the patient recalled after three hours, though an hour earlier she still remembered the theme of the story and reported it with a score of 4. A clear case of fabrication was the following: "A man from Texas went on a mission to visit some boy schools. He took his dog with him, bought some new clothes, and then continued on his mission." Another example was produced by a patient who after the first hour reproduced the barest skeleton of the story; an hour later introduced a "fence" into her report, and after yet another hour, forgetting the cowboy theme altogether, produced this: "When the dog went near the fence someone tapped him on the shoulder —had to prevent him from going near the fence. He was afraid he might get hurt." The same concern emerged earlier in the testing session when this patient was shown a picture of some children walking out from Sunday school and a line of cars at the edge of the road, a father waiting in each. The picture depicts no fence, nor is there any likelihood of a child rushing thoughtlessly into the road, for the close array of stationary cars forms a solid barrier. Yet, when asked to describe this scene, the same patient also introduced a non-existent fence which had to be there to guard the children from the dangers of the road traffic. As far as could be ascertained, the patient had no personal experience which would account for this theme; her own children were certainly beyond school age at the time she was first hospitalized.

The most remarkable case of *fabrication* was the following story recited on immediate testing: "A farmer went to the market with cows to sell, and to buy some finery for his wife. He sold the cows, shopped for the wife, built a new barn, bought cows. I forget the rest." The following day the same patient recalled what she had heard 24 hours earlier in these words: "Farmer story—went to market, did a lot of shopping, bought cows and some finery for his wife. Bought some paint for his barn which he was going to paint, to get ready for the spring." This much is not particularly striking; the patient presumably confused the story she was given to remember with some other story, and slightly elaborated the latter in the intervening 24 hours. Ten months later the original story was read to her again, and on immediate testing she reproduced it with considerable embellishment,

much omission and a few errors. The story, however, was recognizably about a cowboy and his dog. After an hour it became a story about a farmer who went to the market and left his dog behind, and this was thus further elaborated by the time two hours had elapsed: "Farmer went to the market. Left his dog at home. Did not know he would be so long, he stayed in the market till the sun went down. When he went home the dog ran up to him barking, showing he was happy." Admittedly, this time a core of the original story carried through the reproductions, in a much distorted form, but again it set off the theme of the farmer going to the market. This was not a unique occurrence, for the same patient misperceived a tachistoscopically presented figure in the same way on two occasions over a year apart. Another patient twice distorted the *cowboy story* in much the same manner on immediate testing, though ten months had passed by between the two occasions. Her reproductions were these: a) "About a man and a dog; he took the dog for a walk, the dog ran off. The man kept calling, the dog would run off, and so the man would have to keep on calling;" b) "Fellow went out with the dogs, called them and whistled to them, but they would not come back, because he was dressed in different clothes. Dogs go by scent." In this instance again the second attempt retained more of the original text, but the same extraneous content crept into it as on the first occasion. These full quotations exemplify the most thoroughgoing distortions of the original story, and they also provide as good an instance of progressive embellishment as any of our records. Their main interest, however, is not so much in the extent to which they altered the original story, but in suggesting that a standard input of information can undergo much the same distortion in coding on repeated occasions, without the intervention of any other ascertainable agency than the patient's brain damage.

Betlheim and Hartmann, of course, have a psychological explanation for this phenomenon, though their own reference system would hardly regard a farmer as a stable symbol for a cowboy, a market for a clothing store, or a happy dog for a surly one. Nonetheless, it is quite possible that the same mechanism which produces instances of symbolic reproduction also mediates these other distortions which recur with such striking uniformity over long gaps of time.

Our Korsakoff patients furnished little or no evidence in support of Betlheim and Hartmann's thesis. They recalled test story B as acurately as the control text C, and on immediate testing each patient reproduced the word "raped" and mentioned "father" and "daughter" as the parties involved. This was also true of the reproductions after five minutes, although one patient phrased it this way: "The father entered the room where his daughter lay, and attacked her." However, when the experimenter remarked that attack was not quite the right word, the patient reproduced the original phrasing.

There were very few instances of elaboration or distortion in the reproductions of either stories B or C. One patient referred to a "little girl" in her first reproduction of story B, though not in the later attempts; another reported after 15 minutes that "some gentleman seduced his secretary—his daughter," and reverted to "man raped his daughter" on the last test. The only instances suggestive of symbolization were these: "When the mother left the home, the father threw his daughter on the bed, and she had a child by him," and "When the mother left home, father climbed the stairs and raped his own child." The former, however, is probably more a case of deliberate euphemism, and the latter hardly qualifies as symbolization since the act which is supposed to be symbolized was named in full. The rape story visibly upset two or three women patients and seemed to embarrass a few others, but not to such an extent as to prevent their repeating it. Several of them, however, appended some censorious or exculpatory

comment to their report, e.g. "ought to be shot" or "took advantage of her, did not know better." One comment of this kind also followed a report of the control story, a patient remarking on the girl's taking the cookies, "that was larceny."

Stories D and E, although they were tested only for immediate recall, produced many distortions of the five types listed above. Examples of levelling were the substitution of a mere "man" or "stranger" for the mailman, or the suggestion that borrowing money without the husband's knowledge "wouldn't do," "could not be done"; "populace" for the parading children, "leader" for the prime minister; "doves turned up" or "A group went to India to see the prime minister. They had birds there" for the carefully staged peace ceremony. Story E gave one patient the opportunity to demonstrate the process of sharpening, by correctly calling the prime minister Nehru.

Crude errors of fact were few in the mailman story, e.g. placing the event in Inman Square or Central Square, but more frequent in the reproduction of the Nehru story, particularly as the result of confusing or condensing incidents, such as references to him as a "maharajah" or "the minister responsible for children," to the occasion as "a man and wife celebrating his 68th birthday" or as a "parade to celebrate peace," mentioning "5000 children" by number, transferring the symbolic gesture to "the spectators who released doves." There were several errors of reasoning of the non sequitur type, more particularly in the explanation given the woman why she should not borrow without letting her husband know, e.g. "because he would see the mail and know she had borrowed it," or the mailman "didn't know because the husband would find out." This section of story D also allowed for all kinds of elaboration and for comments, mostly spoken through the mailman's mouth, e.g. "it would get her into trouble," "husband would be awfully mad," "why not go to husband?" "bad policy," "people who borrow without permission easily get into trouble." In some instances the mailman's answer was radically misinterpreted, as in the case of the patient who believed that "the mailman thought it was a good idea," or of another who recalled his suggesting "she should go and ask someone else." One patient thought the woman asked the mailman to tell her where her husband could borrow some money. This was the most serious distortion of the original text, for story D did not give rise to any *fabrication*.

In reproducing story E, *elaborations* occurred most commonly in the description of the prime minister's part in the ceremony which, according to the original text, consisted of reviewing the parade, releasing some doves, and taking the salute. Several patients thought that he was delivering a speech, one of them making the specious though somewhat trivial remark that "he addressed them in his native tongue," another believed he told the children that "the doves were the symbols of peace"; one patient thought the "prime minister was preaching," and another that he "gave prayers over the children." The doves were reported to have "circled around" or to "have gone out to spread peace." The one *comment* on the story concerned the dove's felicitous choice of a landing stage: ". . . it lit on his head—to show appreciation, I should imagine" and again by the same patient several weeks later ". . . in appreciation, I suppose." There were some examples of *elaboration* which, perhaps, amount to *fabrication*. This class may include a couple of suggestions about the children's response to the final incident of the story: ". . . and the children watched the dove on the prime minister's head until it flew away;" "The assembly, especially the children, cheered. The prime minister thought they were cheering him, they were actually cheering the dove." Confusion which almost amounts to *fabrication* was exemplified by this report: "Maharajah of India came on a visit and brought some doves with him, one of which landed on the prime minister's head, thereby endowing

peace on the world." Lastly, a clear case of *fabrication*, though still retaining some elements of the story: "Prime minister had 68 doves to celebrate his birthday. When he went to count the doves, one was missing, as it was perched on his head."

Before labeling these instances of distortion as examples of the processes customarily described as confabulation, it may be of interest to look at the content of the serial reproductions of intelligent and neurologically sound subjects, made under the conditions of ambiguity and delay characteristic of the experimental procedure employed. Since distortions and elaborations tend to be cumulative, only examples from the final, *i.e.* third, report in each chain will be listed. In the *mailman story* they mentioned a "William Connolly", a woman who is "excited" and asks the postman to "help her steal some money," the woman's "husband being sick," a "young girl, married who lived in Inman St.," or a "young blond 'dish' who walked up to a postman." They also included such remarks as, "she somehow thought the postman could arrange it for her" or a final *comment:* "The woman told him that he was right, she hadn't thought of that," and this example of distortion: "A very anxious woman walked along a street in North Cambridge. She finally spotted a policeman by the name of Callahan. She proceeded to tell him her troubles and then felt much better." The *Nehru story* produced such exact data as "2000 pigeons," "64 white doves," and as many as "30,000 school children who were excused from classes to attend." The central figure is "a maharajah" as it was for one of the Korsakoff patients, or "the prime minister of Islam," the occasion a "large party for children," or a celebration which it is "customary for the prime minister of India to give"; the people honor Nehru . . . with fireworks," who "makes a speech and is disturbed" by the final episode. One version retains no more of the original than this: "A great crowd gathered in India. They all began to cheer. A flock of birds swooped down and then up again. This was a sign of good luck." In one instance there is the typical *comment* "must have looked amusing," in another an exact parallel of the Korsakoff group's most characteristic example of *fabrication*: "In honor of this occasion he released a flock of doves, 44 in number; 43 turned up, the 44th he couldn't find, for it was perched on his head." The Korsakoff patients, on the other hand, produced nothing to match this ending of the story: "During the course of the celebration one or more doves were released, and one of them laid an egg which hit Nehru on the head."

These examples of distortion in serial reproduction have been listed in detail because they directly bear on the question of confabulation. Should we call them, or some of them, instances of confabulation, and if we do is it right to regard confabulation as a primary symptom of a disease, or is it merely a manifestation of a state of confusion, indirection, ambiguity? If we accept the latter definition, the fact that Korsakoff patients typically confabulate in talking about themselves rather than in reporting extraneous events has no particular significance, for when they do so they are clearly also confused about their whereabouts and about the temporal sequence of preceding events. Their personal experiences have become as disjointed, as bereft of stable cues as the impersonal story which has passed from one healthy person to another after he had reconstructed it as well as he could from memory. By referring to this state as one of indirection, and presenting it as the situation in which confabulaiton arises, the problem of this symptom has obviously not been given adequate examination. A detailed analysis of it cannot be attempted in the context of the present report, but will be given in another paper in the light of clinical as well as experimental observations of the Korsakoff patients reported on in this study. Here we only wish to point out that the processes of omission and levelling, of substituting erroneous data,

and of elaborating the content so as to make it more plausible, more dramatic, or a more rounded tale, of rationalizing and commenting, of introducing extraneous incidents, are all familiar phenomena in the verbal and pictorial reproduction of normal persons (*1, 3, 9*). The characteristic difference of certain classes of neurological patients is that conditions conducive to these processes occur more commonly, under objectively less severe strain, and over shorter time intervals.

SUMMARY

The memory of Korsakoff patients for narrative material was studied by asking them to recall several brief texts after intervals ranging from a few seconds to one week. Short and longer term forgetting curves were thus determined for performance by reproduction and recognition.

These patients miss and distort much of even short and unitary stories at the phase of first hearing or reading, and forget more and at a steeper rate than control subjects. Since their recall is less faulty under conditions of recognition and in reply to prompting questions than in unaided reproduction, it is likely that one of the processes damaged by the disease is that of establishing connections between self-contained units of information, and consequently of isolating groups of interdependent units within the universe of impressions.

As in most instances of faulty remembering, loss of information, by omission and levelling of content, is not the only defect which characterizes the Korsakoff patients' recall of narrative material. They also substitute erroneous data, and tend to introduce extraneous material, explanatory remarks and evaluative comments into the narrative context. While most of these errors appear to be unsystematic, in a few instances the same or similar incorrect narrative or phrase was reported in place of the original text after an interval of several weeks or months, thus suggesting a defect in the original coding rather than in retention.

The study failed to support the case for motivated forgetting with instances of symbolization as conceived in psychoanalytic theory. Neither did it furnish evidence for the hypothesis that in the amnesic syndrome irrelevant or inessential information interferes with the retention of significant information.

The problem of confabulation was considered in the light of elaborations and distortions in the Korsakoff patients' reproduction of the narrative material. Since, under experimentally created conditions of ambiguity and delay, normal subjects tended to distort and elaborate the stories in much the same manner, it was suggested that confabulation may more properly be regarded as an effect of the Korsakoff patient's state of indirection than as a primary symptom of his disease.

REFERENCES

1. Allport, G. W. and Postman, L. *The Psychology of Rumor*. Holt, Rinehart and Winston, New York, 1947.

2. Ballard, P. B. Obliviscence and reminiscence. *Brit. J. Psychol.* Monogr. No. 2. 1913.

3. Bartlett, F. C. *Remembering*. Macmillan, New York, 1932.

4. Betlheim, S. and Hartmann, H. On parapraxes in the Korsakow psychosis. In *Organization and Pathology of Thought*, Rapaport, D., ed., pp. 288–307. Columbia Univ. Press, New York, 1951.

5. Cameron, D. E. Impairment of the retention phase of remembering. *Psychiat. Quart.*, 1943, *17*, 395–404.

6. Conrad, K. Über einen Fall von "Minuten Gedächtnis". *Arch. Psychiat.*, 1953, *190*, 471–502.

7. Franz, S. L. *Handbook of Mental Examination Methods*. 2nd ed. Macmillan, New York, 1919.

8. Gruenthal, E. and Stoerring, G. Über das Verhalten bei umschriebener völliger Merkunfähigkeit. *Mnschr. Psychiat. Neurol.*, 1930, *74*, 254-269.

9. Talland, G. A. Cultural differences in serial reproduction. *J. Social Psychol.*, 1956, *43*, 75–81.

10. Talland, G. A. Psychological studies of Korsakoff's psychosis: II. Perceptual functions. *J. Nerv. & Ment. Dis.*, 1958, *127*, 197–219.

11. Talland, G. A. The interference theory of forgetting and the amnesic syndrome. *J. abnorm. soc. Psychol.*, 1959, *59*, 10–16.

12. Wechsler, D. *The Measurement of Adult Intelligence*. 3rd ed. Williams & Wilkins, Baltimore, 1944.

9 | *Prognosis in the Social Context*

BEHAVIOR pathologists and others have given a great deal of attention to the problem of forecasting the behavior of disordered persons who come to the attention of hospitals, clinics, and other institutions. The practical value of being able to predict outcome of hospitalization needs no great elaboration. If, as is usually the case, a mental hospital is so understaffed that only a portion of the patients can receive specific therapies, it is important that we identify those patients who are most likely to respond to treatment efforts. A related question is: How can chronicity be predicted?

Since many patients who are discharged from mental hospitals as recovered or improved find their way back to the hospital, another important question is raised: How can we predict which patients will remain in the community? When we discover that variables such as social class membership and marital status are significant correlates of outcomes of treatment, and further, that the type of community available to the patient upon discharge is significantly correlated with outcome, then we must perceive behavior disorders as something more than occurrences within the organism.

The three papers in this section all deal with problems of prediction, or prognosis of behavior. The paper by Freeman and Simmons is a carefully conducted study that illustrates how the survey method and the structured interview may be used to obtain significant knowledge about probable outcomes. These investigators directed their attention to the effects of a patient's role within the family with which he resides. Not only do these data provide additional factors for prognosis, but they give us some important leads for the study of the relationship between social roles and tolerance of deviance.

Their data support the thesis that differences in family structure, attitude, personality, and behavior of members of the patient's family are associated with his level of performance in the community. This report contains some provocative information concerning the difference in attitude of a wife and mother toward an adult male with mental illness. Some of the data challenge the belief that a patient will perform better if he is returned to the parental family.

312

The paper by Lindemann, Fairweather, Stone, Smith, and London illustrates how a few items of information obtained at the time of admission to a hospital may be used to predict which patients will be chronic and which well leave the hospital. It is important to note that the prognostic index developed by these investigators was composed of demographic variables and therefore did not include variables that demand intensive psychological or medical examinations. Such an easily available index can be extremely useful in the proper placement of patients or admission. This is an example of "file research" in which meaningful predictions are made from information contained in the files of a hospital or other institution.

Membership in social class is a potent variable in sociological analysis. Its importance in studies of behavior pathology is becoming more and more recognized. The paper by Hardt and Feinhandler demonstrates a highly significant relation between social class membership and the risk of long-term hospitalization. The relationship between discharge rates and social class reinforces the notion that perhaps we are not dealing with "illness" as traditionally defined by medical science but with the products of socialization. Additional research is needed to locate the exact factors linked to social class that are responsible for these findings.

Mental Patients in the Community: Family Settings and Performance Levels

HOWARD E. FREEMAN AND OZZIE G. SIMMONS

SHORTER periods of hospitalization and longer periods of community living between hospitalizations are among the notable trends in the treatment of psychotics, particularly those with functional disorders. Although the extensive employment of tranquilizing drugs has discernibly increased the length of community experience of patients, the largest proportion of those ever exposed to hospital treatment remained in the community for substantial period of time, even prior to the advent of tranquilizers.[1]

There is considerable evidence, however, that improved functioning is not a necessary requisite for "success," i.e., remaining in the community. The clinical impression that former patients frequently reside in the community while actively psychotic and socially withdrawn is supported by studies employing modes of interpersonal performance as criteria of level of functioning.[2] As Clausen has noted, some released patients are "fully as ill as many patients currently in hospitals" (3).

Explanation of the continued existence in the community of a large number of patients who are less than well must be made with reference to the nature of their interpersonal relations in the posthospital situation. Patients are able to avoid the hospital when the interpersonal performance is within the range of behaviors expected by those with whom they interact. Tolerance of deviant behavior, on the part of the patient's "significant others," is a key factor affecting the process of posthospital experience and crucial to whether or not the patient succeeds in remaining in the community.

By tolerance of deviant behavior we

[1] Adler, for example, found that one year after release from a state hospital, almost three-fourths of the patients in her cohort were still in the community. (1)

Reprinted by permission from the *American Sociological Review*, Vol. 23, No. 2, 1958.

[2] For example, in Adler's cohort, less than one-fourth of the patients were regularly employed and socially active one year after release. *Ibid.* (1)

mean the continued acceptance of the former patient by his significant others even when he fails to perform according to the basic prescriptions of his age-sex roles, as these are defined by the society. In our society, access to status is very largely determined by occupational achievement, and the strong emphasis on this factor, and to a lesser extent on other instrumental orientations, tends to be reasonably constant in American society (6). Consequently, whatever the areas in which deviant behavior is likely to become a critical issue between the patient and those who comprise his world, instrumental performance is one of the most strategic, and acceptance of *non-instrumental* performance may be said to constitute substantial evidence of high tolerance of deviance.[3]

The familial network in which the patient resides and his status within this network thus assume considerable importance. Not only is tolerance by other household members directly related to "success" in remaining out of the hospital, but since familial expectations affect the patient's participation in other interpersonal networks, acceptance of the patient as a deviant restricts his exposure to others usually less tolerant of non-instrumental performance.[4] If those with whom the patient resides place little emphasis upon his being gainfully employed and, moreover, make few demands upon him to be socially

active, he can exist as if in a one-person chronic ward, insulated from all but those in the highly tolerant household.

Investigation of the relationship between level of performance and structural and status variations in the residential settings of successful patients was a major purpose of a pilot investigation of a small number of patients and their families (4). One of the principal findings of this exploratory study was that low levels of interpersonal performance are most tolerated in parental families where the patient occupies the status of "child." When patients were divided by level of performance into high and low groups, high level patients clustered in conjugal families or non-familial residences, while those with low levels were concentrated in parental families.[5] Further analysis indicated that this correlation between family type and performance level was not an artifact of associations between family types and either prehospital psychiatric state or psychiatric state at the time of release.

The finding was amplified by comparing, within the same cohort, those low level patients who were successful with those who were rehospitalized. Among the rehospitalized group, about as many came from parental families as there were low level patients living with parental families in the community. In contrast, there were four times as many returned to the hospital from conjugal families or non-familial settings as there were low level patients living in such settings in the community.

The finding that patients with a low level of performance who succeed in remaining in the community cluster in parental families is consistent with the fact that the role of the child in the parental family is the only social-biological role without expectations of instrumental performance.

[3] In the longitudinal studies of rehabilitative process that constitute one of our principal research activities, we are working with a much broader concept of deviance than that implemented in the survey research reported in this paper. We are here concerned only with the tolerance of non-instrumental performance in role relationships where instrumental behavior is ordinarily prescribed. The objectives of our processual studies are to discern, along a time axis, what becomes viewed as deviant behavior on the part of the patient, by the patient himself as well as by his significant others; how much of this is viewed as problematic and by whom; the ways in which the problems are handled; and the thresholds or points at which deviance is no longer tolerated and cannot be handled within the network. It would be inappropriate to elucidate this statement here, but a paper on the conceptual analysis of deviance for purposes of our research is now in preparation.

[4] This observation is an illustration of the point advanced by Merton that the social structure may tend to insulate the individual from having his activities observed by those who would normally be his peers. Such insulation obviously results in a reduction of pressures for prescribed performance. (5)

[5] The patients were dichotomized so that those rated high: (1) worked full time or were solely responsible for the care of the home; (2) participated in informal and social activities about as often as other family members; (3) were able to relate well in the interview situation (as judged by a clinically sophisticated interviewer); and (4) were reported by their relatives to be recovered, active in the life of the family, and without such symptoms as periods of depression or hallucinations.

The child's role, regardless of age, consists largely of affective relations with parents and, compared with other family roles, is less concerned with instrumental performance.

To the extent that the grown-up "child" in the parental family has specific prescriptions built into his role, the structure of such families usually provides for alternate actors who can replace or supplement his performance when it is below expectation. Unlike spouses or those who live in non-familial settings, "children" are free of many of the stresses that accompany every other kin or household status.

On the basis of these findings, as well as upon differences in attitudes found to exist between relatives of patients with high and low levels of performance, a large-scale survey of female relatives of successful male patients was undertaken. In this paper, the first report of the survey, we report replication of the association between structural differences in the family settings of patients and performance levels.

METHODOLOGY

The female informants interviewed were all relatives, predominantly wives and mothers, of male patients who have succeeded in remaining in the community since their latest release from a mental hospital sometime between November, 1954 and December, 1955. Every male patient with the following characteristics was included in the potential drawing group: between 20 and 60 years of age; white; native-born; living in the Boston area at the time of release; hospitalized more than 45 days prior to release; not physically handicapped to the extent of being unemployable; not addicted to narcotics; and not hospitalized primarily for acute alcoholism. By diagnosis, all were psychotics with non-organic, functional disorders, the majority diagnosed as schizophrenic. Each patient selected was last hospitalized in one of thirteen hospitals in the Boston area, of which nine are State, three Veterans Administration, and one private.

Preliminary screening of the pa-

tients was accomplished by examining the discharge forms at the State's central reporting agency. The hospital records of all patients who initially met the criteria were thoroughly reviewed. From this more detailed source of information, it became clear that a number of patients who appeared eligible on the State forms actually did not meet all the criteria, and the drawing group was reduced to 294. We planned to interview a female relative in the household of each patient.[6] Except in cases where the hospital record clearly indicated that the patient was not living with his family, attempts were made to locate a female relative.[7]

Interviews were attempted in 209 of the 294 cases. The remaining cases consisted of five patients who lived in all male households, 64 who lived in non-familial settings, and 16 where the location of neither the patient nor his family could be discovered. It is probable that most of these 16 patients, even if living with families, no longer reside in the interviewing area, which comprises the whole of metropolitan Boston. Of the 209 interviews attempted, 182 were completed. Thus 88 per cent of the attempted interviews were completed and, even if the 16 cases that could not be located are included, the loss rate is still under 20 per cent.[8]

Interviews averaged two hours and were conducted with a standardized sched-

6 The difficulty of rating instrumentality of the "homemaker" role was only one of the reasons for restricting the informants to female relatives of male patients. These requirements also reduced variability in terms of both informants and patients. In addition, as survey research studies indicate, females are more likely to be at home and less likely to refuse to be interviewed.

7 The informants were notified in advance by mail that they were to be interviewed. The letters were sent ordinary mail but the envelopes were stamped "Postmaster: DO NOT FORWARD, RETURN TO SENDER." Each one returned to us was sent out certified mail with a request for the new address. In this way it was possible to reach all cases in which there was a forwarding address on file. A second source of locating cases was the social service exchange.

8 This loss rate is exceptionally low. In our exploratory study it was 45 per cent and in other cases of interviewing patients and their families, loss rates over 50 per cent are not unusual. Our refusal rate compares favorably with those encountered in studies of normal populations and in marketing research.

ule which contained items to elicit social data, particularly regarding family structure; attitudes toward mental hospitals, treatment and illness; and "personality" measures such as the "F" scale. In addition, the schedule included items to obtain information about the patient's pre- and posthospital work history and social life. For each of the 182 completed cases, the data available from the interview and hospital record occupy nearly 1,000 IBM columns. For all the cases, information on 15 background variables is available. There are no differences on these 15 variables between the 182 cases completed and the 27 refusals.

PERFORMANCE LEVEL AND FAMILY SETTING

The relationship between family setting and performance level uncovered in the exploratory study is clearly substantiated in this survey. Two separate measures of performance are employed which are modifications of work and social participation scales originally developed by Adler (1). The high end of the six-point work performance scale includes those patients who have been continuously employed since their release, the low end those who have never worked since their release. As Table 1 indicates, patients who are husbands are almost exclusively concentrated on the high side and, conversely, patients who are sons cluster on the low side.

When social participation is employed as the measure of interpersonal performance, the same results occur. The highest category is composed of patients who belong to one or more voluntary associations and attend their meetings regularly, and who visit and are visited at least twice a month and at least as often as the rest of the household. Former patients in the lowest category do not belong to any voluntary associations, visit and are visited less than once a month and less frequently than other household members. Once again the results are striking, particularly when the cases are dichotomized.

The Pearsonian correlation between

the work and social participation ratings of interpersonal performance is .51. The magnitude of this correlation indicates that the two ratings are manifestations of a more general mode of interpersonal performance.[9] This is evident when the two ratings are dichotomized and then combined.

TABLE 1. RELATIONSHIP BETWEEN LEVEL OF WORK PERFORMANCE AND FAMILY SETTING

Level of performance		Family setting*			
		Parental		Conjugal	
		N	%	N	%
(High)	1	20	20.0	45	66.2
	2	11	11.0	14	20.6
	3	7	7.0	2	2.9
	4	5	5.0	4	5.9
	5	13	13.0	1	1.5
(Low)	6	44	44.0	2	2.9
	Total	100	100.0	68	100.0
	$r_{pbs} = .83$				

* 14 cases living with siblings not included.

Our thesis regarding the relationship between the differential tolerance of family members and variations in levels of performance of patients who succeed in remaining in the community receives additional support when we consider patients from the cohort who were released during the same time period but subsequently rehospitalized. In the course of collecting information on the successful patients in the cohort, a record check was made of the "failures." These failures, it should be noted, include only patients released to the

[9] For purposes of future, more quantitative aspects of data analysis, distributions on the work and social participation ratings have been normalized, added together, and distributed into categories. The intercorrelations of either the raw or normalized work and social participation scores with this combined, standardized level of performance measure range between .80 and .90.

We wish to stress, however, that this study deals with level of performance as defined in terms of performance in work and social participation. The relationship between performance as so defined and the level of functioning of the patients from a psychiatric viewpoint has not been assessed. But it is our belief, based on our exploratory study where patients as well as relatives were interviewed and on the field work experience and judgments of our clinical staff, that the bulk of the "low" patients would be judged seriously disturbed by a psychiatrist, although we cannot present empirical evidence of this.

community and returned to the hospital after having been dropped from the hospital's books. Most of the patients not voluntarily committed are so dropped only after leaving bed and successfully remaining on trial visit in the community for one year

TABLE 2. RELATIONSHIP BETWEEN LEVEL OF SOCIAL PARTICIPATION AND FAMILY SETTING

Level of performance		Family setting*			
		Parental		Conjugal	
		N	%	N	%
(High)	1	2	2.0	4	5.9
	2	16	16.0	23	33.8
	3	9	9.0	18	26.4
	4	18	18.0	8	11.8
	5	13	13.0	5	7.4
	6	11	11.0	4	5.9
(Low)	7	31	31.0	6	8.8
	Total	100	100.0	68	100.0

$r_{pbs} = .53$

* 14 cases living with siblings not included.

TABLE 3. RELATIONSHIP BETWEEN COMBINED WORK AND SOCIAL LEVEL OF PERFORMANCE AND FAMILY SETTING

Level of performance		Family setting*			
Work	Social	Parental		Conjugal	
		N	%	N	%
High (1–3)	High (1–3)	19	19.0	43	63.2
High (1–3)	Low (4–7)	19	19.0	18	26.5
Low (4–6)	High (1–3)	8	8.0	2	2.9
Low (4–6)	Low (4–7)	54	54.0	5	7.4
	Total	100	100.0	68	100.0

$r_{pbs} = .60$

* 14 cases living with siblings not included.

There are other variations in the release practices of hospitals. For example, patients whose prognosis is doubtful are sometimes released on extended leaves of absence and then discharged if they succeed in remaining in the community. However, if they "fail," it is not reflected in the records used to select the cohort. The failures whose records are available thus consist of the "best" of the failures in the sense that patients officially discharged are in the community the longest time of all

hospitalized patients given an opportunity to "leave bed." [10]

In Table 4, the family settings of the low level patients are compared with the settings at the time of rehospitalization of the official failures. Many more patients who last lived with conjugal families are back in the hospital in comparison with successful low level patients presently living with wives. In contrast, few patients whose last residence was with parents are back in the hospital in comparison with low level patients presently living in parental families. Table 4 presents these findings for each rating of performance level.

TABLE 4. FAMILY SETTING OF PATIENTS REHOSPITALIZED AND THOSE WITH LOW LEVEL OF PERFORMANCE WHO REMAIN IN THE COMMUNITY

	Family setting				
	Parental		Conjugal		
	N	%	N	%	r
Work Rating					
Low Level in Community (4–6)	62	65.3	7	25.9	
Rehospitalized	33	34.7	20	74.1	
Total	95	100.0	27	100.0	.33
Social Rating					
Low Level in Comunity (4–7)	73	68.9	23	53.5	
Rehospitalized	33	31.1	20	46.5	
Total	106	100.0	43	100.0	.15
Combined Work-Social Rating					
Low Level in Community	54	62.1	5	20.0	
Rehospitalized	33	37.9	20	80.0	
Total	87	100.0	25	100.0	.35

These results are consistent with our introductory remarks regarding more tolerant expectations toward those who occupy the status of "child." Over time it

[10] The problem of the use of legal definitions as criteria has been amply evaluated by the criminologist, whose comments are directly applicable to the field of mental health. It was possible, in our definition of success, to employ the more realistic one of the date the patient "left bed." It was more difficult to distinguish "failures" from patients not ever returned to the community. The hospitals are required to indicate the "left bed" date only when the case is officially "dropped" from the books.

appears that a greater proportion of patients are returned to hospitals from conjugal families. In their entirety, these findings support the earlier exploratory study.

INFLUENCE OF PRIOR CONDITIONS

Considering the replicative nature of the investigation and the magnitude of the correlation, it is quite certain that the relationship between performance level and family setting is a stable one. Explanation of the differential performance of former patients, however, in terms of tolerance of deviance on the part of their significant others could represent an overemphasis upon the posthospital situation and a neglect of prehospital and hospital conditions. Our analysis of the influence of prior conditions has to depend upon hospital record data and retrospective information from the relative interviewed. Within the limits of accuracy and reliability of these types of data, our explanation of tolerance is not vitiated by this additional information.

Information from the hospital record eliminates the possibility that differences in hospital experience offer a satisfactory alternative explanation. There are no significant differences in performance level which can be accounted for in terms of such variables as type of hospital, diagnosis, type of psychiatric treatment, and ward mobility.

The influence of the prehospital condition of the patient presents a more complex set of relationships for analysis. There is considerable evidence that patients from parental families are more ill when hospitalized than those from conjugal families. Without reference to the data of this study, the argument can be advanced that marriage serves a screening function and "sicker" persons cluster in parental families before hospitalization since the "healthier" of the mentally ill are more likely to marry. Actually, in terms of similar measures of level of performance employed in the previous section of our analysis, but with reference to prehospital history, patients from parental families do have a lower performance level than do those from conjugal families.[11] Furthermore, the obvious point that patients "sicker" when hospitalized are generally "sicker" after release is confirmed by the correlation among patients studied between pre- and posthospital level of performance. On the basis of these findings, is the relationship between level of posthospital performance and family setting perhaps an artifact of differences in prehospital level of functioning of the patients?

While differences in prehospital levels of performance partly explain our findings, several considerations strongly support the relevance of differential tolerance of deviance as a key variable in accounting for the range of variation in performance of successful patients during the posthospital period. First, the magnitude of the correlations between prehospital level of performance and family setting are substantially lower than those between posthospital level of performance and family setting. Second, if low level patients do cluster in parental families before as well as after hospitalization, a higher proportion of patients should be rehospitalized from parental as compared with conjugal families, unless rehospitalization is associated with differential conditions in posthospital settings. The same proportion are rehospitalized from the two types of settings, however, supporting our explanation of tolerance of deviance on the part of family members in the posthospital period. Moreover, as already reported in Table 4, the number of failures in relation to the number of patients rated "low" is much higher among those from conjugal settings.

Finally, when prehospital level of performance is controlled in the cross-tabulations, posthospital level of performance remains associated with family type,

---

[11] Differences in number of times hospitalized and number of months hospitalized since first admitted to a mental hospital also suggest that patients from parental families tend to have lower prehospital levels of performance.

within prehospital level of performance groups, indicating that prehospital functioning, in itself, is an insufficient explanation.

Actually, the correlation between prehospital level of performance and family setting is support for our contention that tolerance of deviance is a key variable. While of special significance during the posthospital period, undoubtedly the importance of the tolerance of family members is not unique to this period but crucial to understanding the process of hospitalization as well as rehospitalization. Mothers, compared with wives, are more likely to tolerate deviant performance before the admission of the patient to the hospital, as well as between subsequent readmissions.[12] The person with a low level of interpersonal performance is probably less likely to be hospitalized if living in a parental family, as well as less likely to be rehospitalized if returned to the community in a similar state.

CONCLUSIONS

In this survey of families of male mental patients living in the community, we have found a high correlation between level of performance and family setting. Unlike the exploratory study upon which this survey is based, we have attempted to control variations which might account for the relationship. This replication, with its added controls, convinces us of the stability of the finding. However, several qualifications regarding its generality should be noted:

1. With the exception of the few cases where an interview was refused, the results are based upon all cases in a preselected cohort of patients. Unlike most survey research, where a sample is interviewed and findings generalized to a population, our findings are limited, in the strict sense, to the cases at hand.

2. Clearly, generalization to groups of patients excluded from the cohort—such as Negroes, foreign-born, and psychotics with organic disorders—is precarious. Athough female patients were not included in this research, they were considered in the earlier, exploratory study. On the basis of the results of the earlier study, we believe that the present findings and their implications also apply to female patients.

3. A number of patients who do not live with their families succeed in remaining in the community. Of male patients whose social background and diagnosis are similar to those studied here, probably only seventy or eighty per cent live with their families. Questions regarding the relationship between performance level and residential setting of some twenty to thirty per cent remain unanswered. Nevertheless, we believe that nonfamilial settings provide functional equivalents in the form of surrogate mothers and wives, and that patterns would be found similar to those depicted in this study of patients with families.

Future reports of the analysis of the survey will amplify the data discussed here by specification of structural distinctions *within* parental and conjugal settings. Though we have confined this report to structural differences, data processing has advanced considerably further. The additional analysis supports the basic proposition underlying the survey, namely that differences in family structure and attitudes, personality, and behavior of family members are associated with level of performance of mental patients who succeed in remaining in the community.

We believe that the findings reported here, in themselves, are of considerable interest from both a psychiatric and

---

12 The tolerance of wives, compared with mothers, probably decreases after the patient's first hospital experience. Wives, emancipated from the patient during hospitalization, are more likely to find, in terms of complementary systems of emotional gratification as well as everyday activities, that they can get along as well or better without their mates. Mothers could not as easily move to such a position. Clausen and Yarrow imply that wives are likely to regard the behavior of husbands, after release, without much tolerance, and the recurrence of the husband's illness as "the last straw." (*3*)

sociological point of view. The relationship between family setting and performance level should be of concern to practitioners associated with mental hospitals in planning the release of the patient and in prognosticating his posthospital behavior. If the goal of treatment is only the permanent or semi-permanent separation of hospital and patient, the release of patients to parental families would appear to be an efficient practice. While effective in freeing a hospital bed, however, releasing the patient to the tolerant milieu which tends to predominate in the parental family may be the most inadequate community setting if movement toward instrumental performance is a desired outcome of hospitalization. Return of the patient to the parental family, where there is less likely to be an expectation of instrumental performance, may well occasion regression from, rather than movement toward, better functioning, and eliminate any gains of a therapeutic hospital experience.

The findings are particularly relevant for the sociological study of deviance. In terms of our measures of instrumental performance—work and social participation—the question can be raised whether differences between mothers and wives in tolerance of deviance is peculiar to the perception of the person as a mental patient. Are mothers and wives of, e.g., drug addicts, alcoholics, and the physically handicapped differentially distributed in degree of tolerance when the definition of deviance is with respect to instrumental performance?

Finally, we are convinced that it is the differential *quality* of the role relationships which is critical to understanding the influence of significant others in the posthospital experience of the patient. For example, with respect to the role of the patient in the family, there is the question of the availability of functionally equivalent actors to occupy the normally prescribed roles. Patients who are husbands probably are tolerated more often in noninstrumental roles when there are other adult males in the household to occupy the instrumental roles. Conversely, sons who are patients are probably least tolerated in the parental family when no other male actors are available to take instrumental roles. Such speculations can be partly verified and assessed by further analysis of our survey data, but problems of this order also require longitudinal investigations that employ repeated interviewing. Our research strategy includes cross-sectional surveys, of the kind reported here, and processual studies for observation and assessment of change. Both are necessary for systematic inquiry into the posthospital experience of former mental patients.

REFERENCES

1. Adler, L. M., Patients of a State Mental Hospital: The Outcome of Their Hospitalization, in Rose, A. (ed.), *Mental Health and Mental Disorder,* New York: Norton, 1955, 501–523.

2. Clausen, J. A., *Sociology and the Field of Mental Health,* New York: Russell Sage Foundation, 1956, p. 9.

3. Clausen, J. A., and Yarrow, M. R., Further Observations and Some Implications, *J. Soc. Issues,* 1955, *11,* p. 62.

4. Davis, J. A., Freeman, H. E. and Simmons, O. G., Rehospitalization and Performance level of Former Mental Patients, *Soc. Prob.* 1957, *5,* 37–44.

5. Merton, R. K., The Role Set: Problems in Sociological Theory, *Brit. J. Soc.,* 1957, *8,* 106–121.

6. Parsons, T., *An Analytical Approach to the Theory of Social Stratification, Essays in Sociological Theory: Pure and Applied,* Glencoe Ill.: Free Press, 1949, p. 174.

The Use of Demographic Characteristics in Predicting Length of Neuropsychiatric Hospital Stay

JAMES E. LINDEMANN, GEORGE W. FAIRWEATHER, GIDEON B. STONE, ROBERT S. SMITH, AND IRA T. LONDON

THE ever-increasing number of chronic neuropsychiatric patients represents perhaps the foremost problem in the field of mental health today. Despite recent advances, notably in the fields of chemotherapy and rehabilitation, the burden of the chronic population grows, threatening to overwhelm existing hospital facilities and available professional personnel. This study was conceived as the first step in a three-part plan to: (a) develop an index predictive of chronicity; (b) attempt to isolate and study the determinants of chronicity; and (c) develop and test the effectiveness of retaining programs based on the defining characteristics of the chronic population.

The possibility of a predictive index was suggested by a study previously completed at the Perry Point Veterans Administration Hospital (2). An analysis of the time sequence of discharge rate for the patient population revealed that 61% of admitted patients left the hospital during the first 90 days, 25% during the next 15 months, and only 2% during the remaining 24 months covered by the study. A predictive index, based on demographic characteristics ascertainable at the time of hospital admission, would permit a comparison of the characteristics of the "quick discharge" population with the potential chronic population. In addition, it would facilitate the early, comprehensive study of the potential chronic population so that the characteristics of those who finally did leave the hospital could be compared with those who remained indefinitely. Such an early study, before the leveling effect of

Reprinted by permission from the *Journal of Consulting Psychology*, Vol. 23, No. 1, 1959.

hospitalization on social characteristics and attitudes became operative, was deemed particularly desirable.

The extensive literature (see, for example, 5) on the prognosis of length of hospitalization was reviewed and the following variables selected for study:

1. Number of previous hospitalizations
2. Age at first neuropsychiatric hospitalization
3. Age at time of current hospitalization
4. Service-connection of disability (per cent)
5. Length of military service
6. Age entering service
7. Months service prior to first NP hospitalization
8. Education
9. Religion
10. Marital status
11. Number of children
12. Combat experience (Yes or No)
13. Neuropsychiatric diagnosis in service (Yes or No)
14. Diagnosis
15. Severity of external precipitating stress
16. Predisposition
17. Degree of incapacity
18. Secondary diagnosis (NP—Yes or No)
19. Legal competence (Yes or No)
20. Alcoholism (History of—Yes or No)
21. Occupational classification level

METHOD

Data for this study were derived from the clinical record folders of all male neuropsychiatric patients admitted to a large Veterans Administration hospital during the period from July 1, 1954 to December 31, 1954. With the exception of length of hospital stay, the criterion, all of the information used in the index was obtained from the initial psychiatric summary, which is completed within three weeks of admission, and from demographic data which are recorded immediately upon admission. The final total sample for the 1954 period consisted of 248 cases. A small percentage (less than 5%) of the clinical record folders were unavailable because they had been transferred to other hospitals or because they were otherwise unobtainable. Where patients had been admitted more than once during the period, data from the first admission only were included in the sample.

Information on the 21 variables that had been selected for study was recorded and the sample was divided into those who were hospitalized for 90 days or less (Short Stay group, $N = 120$) and those hospitalized for 91 days or longer (Long Stay group, $N = 128$). The high frequency of discharges found during the first 90 days in the earlier study (2) suggested that this cutting point might have psychological, as well as statistical, significance. The two groups were then examined for differences within the 21 categories, and the significance of differences between groups evaluated by chi square.

RESULTS

Of the 21 variables, four served to differentiate the two groups beyond the .001 level of confidence. These were: diagnosis, degree of incapacity, legal competence, and alcoholism. Marital status differentiated the two groups beyond the .01 level of confidence[1] and combat experience beyond the .05 level. A seventh variable, per cent of service connection, differentiated the groups between the .05 and .10 level of confidence. Finally, an eighth variable, occupational classification, significant beyond the .30 level, was retained in the original predictive index because of the special significance that has been accorded it (1).

A score for each item within the eight variables was computed following a

[1] Two other variables significant beyond the .01 level, external precipitating stress and predisposition, were eliminated because of their high correlation with diagnosis, which was retained in the index.

method devised by Moran, Fairweather, Morton, and McGaughran (4). This method essentially involved computing for each item the probability of a patient's falling in the Long Stay group. The log of each probability value was then ascertained. Each patient was then assigned a score which was the sum of the eight log values that applied to him.

Scores thus computed for all cases ranged from $\bar{5}.75$ to $\bar{2}.25$. Below an arbitrary cutting point of $\bar{4}.25$ were 75 cases. Of these, 85.3% were in the Short Stay group. Above a cutting point of $\bar{2}.75$ were 89 cases. Of these, 85.4% were in the Long Stay group. This index, then, served to predict long or short stay for 66.1% of the sample with a high degree of accuracy. In addition, it allowed for the specification of those cases for which accurate prediction could not be made.

Prediction for this group of 1954 admissions might have been spuriously high, of course, since the index was constructed from the very cases being predicted. Therefore, the index was cross-validated on a sample of 1955 admissions.

Cross-Validation

Data were collected for all male neuropsychiatric patients admitted to the same hospital during the period January 1, 1955 to June 30, 1955. The same scoring procedures and cutoff points were employed with this sample of 209 cases. Below the cutting point of $\bar{4}.25$ were 69 cases. Of these, 87% were in the Short Stay group. Above the cutting point of $\bar{2}.75$ were 76 cases. Of these, 78.9% were in the Long Stay group. Thus the index, based on 1954 admissions, could have predicted length of stay for 69.4% of the 1955 admissions with 82.8% accuracy.

In calculating the differential power of the individual variables of the cross-validation sample, it was found that three of the eight variables did not reach the .05 level of significance. These were: occupational classification, service connection, and combat experience.[2] Accordingly, these variables were not included in the final, revised form of the index.

The Revised Index

The final form of the index was based on a combination of both samples, embracing all admissions during the period July 1, 1954 to June 30, 1955. Scores on the final form were derived from the remaining five variables exactly as in the original form. The individual probabilities furnished by each variable are given in Table 1.

for every case by cutting above and below 2.5, in which case the index would yield 77.2% accuracy. Cutting scores might be established below $\overline{2}.1$ and above $\overline{2}.9$. In this case, 172 Short Stay cases would be predicted with 84.3% accuracy, and 153 Long Stay cases would be predicted with 87.6% accuracy. Thus 71.1% of all cases could be predicted with 85.8% accuracy. If homogeneity rather than size of sample is emphasized, cutting scores might be established below $\overline{3}.7$ and above $\overline{1}.1$. In this case, 102 Short Stay cases would be predicted with 91.2% accuracy, and 116 Long

TABLE 1. PROBABILITIES OF LONG STAY GIVEN BY EACH OF THE VARIABLES IN THE REVISED FORM OF THE INDEX

Variable	N^a	Chi Square p	Cutting points	Probability of long stay	Log values
Marital status	454	.001	Married and widowed	.40*	9.59988–10
			Separated and divorced	.43	9.63548–10
			Single	.66	9.81624–10
Diagnosis	447	.001	Organic	.39	9.59550–10
			Psychotic	.78*	9.89321–10
			Neurotic	.30	9.48287–10
			Character disorder	.10	9.01703–10
Degree of incapacity	445	.001	None, mild, moderate	.38	9.58320–10
			Severe	.82*	9.91169–10
			Not part of diagnosis[b]	.10	9.02119–10
Legal competence	444	.001	Competent	.33*	9.51983–10
			Incompetent	.88	9.94498–10
Alcohol	449	.001	Yes	.37	9.56585–10
			No	.65*	9.81023–10

[a] N differs for each variable because occasionally information on one item is "unknown" for a particular case. In such instances, the score used in the index is the log of the modal p value of that item, which is indicated here by an asterisk.

[b] In the case of Degree of Incapacity, "not part of diagnosis" refers to those instances, notably alcoholism and personality disorders, where this is not included in the formal diagnosis.

The scores of each group distribute as shown in Fig. 1.

The validity of this index, i.e., the relationship between scores and short and long stay, clearly depends on the cutting points selected. Predictions might be made

[2] Two of these variables, service connection and combat experience, were ones in which there was an unusually high number of "unknowns." In such cases modal scores were assigned. It is suggested that these variables may prove significant in future studies involving veterans where the data may be gathered with a higher degree of precision than was possible in this "file" study.

Stay cases would be predicted with 91.4% accuracy. Thus prediction is possible for 47.7% of the sample with 91.3% accuracy. The validity of the index might also be expressed directly in terms of the correlation between index scores and short and long stay. A biserial correlation of .759 was obtained.

DISCUSSION

By means of this index, samples of a given size and with a given probability of

long or short stay may be selected from the patients entering the hospital under study. Generalization of these results to other neuropsychiatric hospitals must, of course, await further cross-validation studies. It should be pointed out that none of the variables in the final form of the index are restricted to a veteran population, and that it has potential applicability in any neuropsychiatric hospital.

The value of this index for research lies in its usefulness for the economical preselection of stratified samples for intensive study during the course of hospitaliza-

to be completed on the Admissions Service, could be instituted without delay for those patients in the Short Stay group.

In addition to the usefulness of the index for prediction, the variables themselves allow for certain speculations concerning their psychological implications. The finding that length of stay for single patients exceeds that for others suggests a possible differentiating adaptive factor. The other group, which would include the married, widowed, separated, and divorced persons, have at some time in their lives attracted and formed a relationship with an-

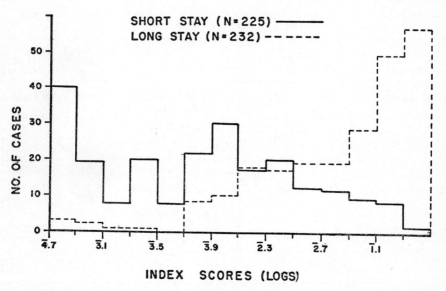

Figure 1. Distribution of scores for short-stay and long-stay cases on the revised index.

tion. Homogeneous populations of potential long or short stay patients may be selected for immediate study or for assignment to treatment programs for evaluative purposes.

The index is also seen to have immediate service value. In those hospitals where an intensive continued treatment program is available, those patients who fall in the Long Stay group could be transferred to such a program immediately upon completion of the routine admission procedures. Correspondingly, short-term therapeutic and counseling procedures, designed

other person, and thus may possess greater personal resources. An alternative explanation is that the single patients are less likely to have an established setting in the community to which to return. However, this explanation fails to account for the fact that separated and divorced patients achieved approximately the same probability of short stay as did married and widowed.

It should be pointed out that history of alcohol was scored in the study wherever it was mentioned as contributory to the current need for hospitalization, as well as where it was an established diagnosis. Several possible explanations can be advanced for the highly significant relationship between alcoholism and "short stay." In part, in may reflect a group of patients who ordinarily maintain adequate integration, but whose defenses can be temporarily weakened by alcohol, necessitating short-term hospitalization. On the other hand, it may reflect the inappropriateness of current hospital treatment for the alcoholic. A further theoretical interpretation might be that the use of alcohol as a means of handling anxiety is generally not associated with the development of perseverant psychotic symptoms.

It is of interest that although psychiatric diagnoses have been shown to be of doubtful reliability (3), their implications for length of hospital stay have been demonstrated to be valid predictors in this study. This is seen in three of the final variables (Diagnosis, Degree of incapacity and Legal competence) which reflect the diagnostic judgments of psychiatric observers. In this case these judgments seem to reflect two underlying determinants: severity of illness of psychotics and the previously mentioned inappropriateness of treatment in the general neuropsychiatric hospital for alcoholics and character disorders. While the argument could be raised that these initial judgments merely predetermined the patients' course of hospital treatment (short or long), the accuracy of their predictive value suggests the more parsimonious explanation that the judgments genuinely reflect the patients' need for treatment in a neuropsychiatric hospital.

SUMMARY

The potential value for research in chronic mental illness of an instrument for the early prediction of length of hospital stay was indicated. Data on 21 demographic variables, available within three weeks of hospitalization, were gathered from clinical record folders. Five variables were found to predict significantly for the initial and cross-validation samples. Based on the combined samples ($N = 457$), an index was devised which predicted Short Stay (under 90 days) and Long Stay (91 days or more). The validity of the index depends on the cutting point selected. Prediction can be made for the entire sample with 77% accuracy, or for approximately one-half the sample with 91% accuracy. Potential uses of the index and the psychological implications of the significant variables were discussed.

REFERENCES

1. Frumkin, R. M. Occupation and major mental disorders. In A. M. Rose (Ed.), *Mental health and mental disorder.* New York: Norton, 1955. Pp. 136–160.

2. Giedt, F. H., and Schlosser, J. R. Movement of patients through a neuropsychiatric hospital. Unpublished manuscript, Medical Library, VA Hospital, Perry Point, Maryland, 1955.

3. Mehlman, B. The reliability of psychiatric diagnosis. *J. abnorm. soc. Psychol.,* 1952, *47,* 577–578.

4. Moran, L. J., Fairweather, G. W., Morton, R. B., and McGaughran, L. S. The use of demographic characteristics in predicting response to hospitalization for tuberculosis. *J. consult. Psychol.,* 1955, *19,* 65–70.

5. Zubin, J. Role of prognostic indicators in the evaluation of therapy. In R. W. Gerard and J. O. Cole (Eds.), *The proceedings of the conference on the evaluation of pharmacotherapy in mental illness.* (September, 1956.) Washington, D. C.: National Academy of Sciences, in press.

Social Class and Mental Hospitalization Prognosis

ROBERT H. HARDT AND SHERWIN J. FEINHANDLER

Many studies in the field of mental health epidemiology have focused on the relationship between socio-environmental characteristics and the prevalence of mental illness (16). Until recently, however, relatively little attention has been directed toward the discovery of social characteristics of mentally disordered persons which arc related to differential outcomes of mental illness. While there is considerable disagreement among mental health specialists about an appropriate definition of recovery or cure (19), one aspect of outcome which may be determined fairly readily is the duration of the hospitalized phase of the illness. This particular criterion of "recovery" has a certain amount of face validity since hospitalization is recognized as a severe social disability and is implicated in both legal and public definitions of mental illness.

The duration of hospitalization becomes a crucially important factor in evaluating the social and personal costs of one of the major mental illnesses: schizophrenia. In comparison with other patients, schizophrenics tend to have a longer duration of hospitalization. The longer time is accounted for by diagnostic differentials in the length of stay per admission, rate of readmissions, and longevity. An illustration of the cumulative effect of these influences, is the discrepancy between the following pair of figures: schizophrenics composed only 28 per cent of first admissions but 57 per cent of resident patients in New York State mental hospitals in 1955 (2).

Among schizophrenics, however, considerable individual variability is to be found in the duration of hospitalization. The factors, including socio-environmental conditions, which are responsible for differ-

Reprinted by permission from the *American Sociological Review*, Vol. 24, No. 6, 1959.

ent outcome experiences are largely undetermined. This paper reports on the relationship between the patient's social class position and the duration of the initial hospitalization of male schizophrenics. Specifically, we examine the hypothesis that the higher the social class position, the lower the proportion of patients who experience continuous long-term hospitalization.

This study reflects a convergence of interest between the fields of mental health epidemiology and sociology. In the first field, the investigations most pertinent to the purposes of this investigation have been conducted by Kramer at the Warren State Hospital (12) and by Malzberg in the New York State hospital system (13). These studies are generally concerned with an examination of duration differentials displayed by various age, sex, and diagnostic groups. The sociological field is represented by the growing number of researches on the relationship between social variables and rates of community prevalence and hospitalized incidence, as well as other aspects of mental health concern such as public information and attitudes about psychiatric services (5).

The research in the area of social psychiatry most directly relevant to the present investigation is the New Haven study conducted by Hollingshead and Redlich (10). In one phase of that inquiry, the relationship between social class and the treatment process was examined, with the data demonstrating rather conclusively that, among psychotic patients in general and among schizophrenics in particular, the lower the class level of the patient, the higher the proportion of chronic patients. Similarly, a preliminary report on recent hospital experience in Britain suggests the presence of a rather marked relationship between duration of initial hospitalization and occupational level (1). Also, Dunham has reported a slight association between duration of hospitalization and the patient's educational and economic status (7).

However, there is considerable lack of consensus about the generality of the relationship between hospital duration and such indicators of social class as education and occupation. For example, in a recent study of discharge rates from one large Canadian mental hospital, it was found that "educational attainment did not in any way influence the probability of discharge," and that "male probabilities of discharge differed little among the various occupational categories" (17). Furthermore, a recent analysis of discharge experience from Louisiana mental hospital led Whatley to conclude that "if the case for a sociological dimension of prognosis were rested on such status variables, the findings would be almost entirely negative. The conclusion would then follow that social factors play a negligible role in prolonging behavior pathology" (18). On the basis of a general review of the literature on prognostic indicators in schizophrenia, Zubin reported only two significant findings in regard to socio-economic variables (20). Favorable outcome experiences were obtained by clerical and skilled workers in one study, and in another study by females with limited education. Although there are differences in the nature of the patient populations and procedures in these various investigations, the cited findings demonstrate the present lack of general agreement about the implications of social class factors for the prognostic criterion of duration of hospitalization.

PROCEDURES

The study population was defined as consisting of patients who met the following criteria: (1) males; (2) first admitted to a registered or licensed hospital in New York State between January 1, 1944 and March 31, 1950; (3) dementia praecox (schizophrenia) diagnosis; and (4) residents of New York State exclusive of New York City.

Data on duration of hospitalization were obtained by collating reports of discharge and death as submitted by the hospitals with information reported at the time of initial admission. The sets of information were checked for consistency, and discrepancies were reconciled by referring to more detailed records available in the central departmental files.

Patients who were not discharged by the hospital within the first 24 months following their initial admission are referred to below as "long-term patients." Patients who were discharged "alive" within this period are called "short-term patients." This definition involves a discharge from the care and the responsibility of the hospital; the period of duration includes both the time spent in the hospital and in supervised convalescent care. Those patients who died within the hospital prior to a stay of 25 months are not included in either of these groups, or in the following analysis. With other minor exclusions, the eventual study sample consisted of 3,943 patients.[1]

The decision to select 24 months as the cutting point was influenced by certain findings obtained in previous studies. The patient's experience in the first two years appeared particularly crucial in studies made at the Warren State (12) and Ontario (19) hospitals. Zubin also concluded that "immobility during the two years following first admission is one of the better prognostic indications of eventual outcome" (20).

In addition, rather marked similarities in discharge probabilities by the end of two years were reported for these various studies. The research at Warren State Hospital indicates that 38 per cent of the

---

[1] All admissions to Syracuse Psychiatric Hospital and from the county (Onondaga) in which the hospital is located were excluded because of: (1) the distinctive character of observation service provided by the hospital, which was utilized primarily by the residents of this county; (2) variations in the procedures for recording short-term admissions to the hospital.

schizophrenics had been hospitalized for two years following their first admission (12). Similarly, the Ontario hospital study disclosed that 38 per cent of the study

TABLE 1. OCCUPATIONAL AND EDUCATIONAL DISTRIBUTION OF PATIENTS BY SOCIAL CLASS INDEX WEIGHTS (N = 3943)

Weights	Occupation	%	Education	%
5	Prof., Mgrs.	10.3	College	9.6
4	Clerical, sales	8.5	12th grade	15.2
3	Craftsmen	12.1	9–11 grades	29.6
2	Operatives	15.0	8th grade	15.4
1	Service			
	workers	6.6	7th grade	13.0
0	Laborers	28.0	7 & unknown	17.2
*	Unknown	19.5		
	Total	100.0	Total	100.0

* For this group, class scores consisted of double the educational weight. This group consists of those with occupation unknown, no occupation, and students.

sample remained within the hospital for two years after first admission (19). In our study population, approximately 42 per cent of the schizophrenics fitted this definition of a long-term patient.

The social class index used here was derived from the reports on the educational level and past occupation of each patient, obtained at the time of admission. (Since most females were not employed and the occupations of other family members were not listed, the present study is limited to males.) Weights ranging from zero to five were assigned to the various occupational and educational categories. The distributions of patients by categories are presented in Table 1. The pair of weights obtained by each patient were added to obtain the social class index. For those patients without an occupational listing, the weighting of the educational category was doubled.

In this study, the term "social class" refers to an arbitrarily defined stratum of individuals who have relatively similar index scores. The patients were grouped into six social classes on the basis of their scores. The highest class, I, includes ap-

proximately nine per cent of the patients, while the lowest class, VI, includes about eleven per cent. Classes II, III, IV, and V include, respectively, 15, 25, 24, and 16 per cent of the patients. Thus the distribution of patients by social class is roughly normal. No assumption should be made about the exact equivalence of class assignment procedures in this and other stratification studies.[2] However, it is assumed that the index used here and other "objective" indicators of class position would be highly correlated (3).

FINDINGS

The relationship between social class position and the percentage of long-term patients is presented in Table 2. These data permit an evaluation of the principal prediction that the lower the social class, the higher will be the percentage of male schizophrenics who are continuous long-term patients. The major hypothesis is clearly supported. The percentage of long-term patients increases consistently from a low of 23.6 in Class I to a high of 63.6 in Class VI.

Some differences in the age distributions of the various social classes were observed. Since chronological age tends to be positively associated with duration of stay, the social class percentages were age-adjusted by the indirect method; these adjusted rates are presented in the last column of Table 2. A comparison of the crude and age-adjusted rates reveals that age differences in class composition account for only a fraction of the class differences in length of stay. Thus the present findings are in accord with the generalizations made by Hollingshead and Redlich (10).

In the present report, however, this general finding has been subjected to a

[2] The variation between the class distribution of patients in this and the New Haven study is viewed as resulting primarily from a slicing of the stratification continuum at different points as dictated by somewhat divergent objectives. A major interest in the New Haven study, but not in the present report, was the discovery of the incidence rate of treated schizophrenia by social class.

more intensive analysis through the use of additional information on the patient. Can the linkage between class and length of hospitalization be accounted for by the influence of class factors on the admission process? Lower-class patients were more likely to enter state hospitals than private or Veterans Administration (VA) hospi-

TABLE 2. PER CENT OF LONG-TERM PATIENTS
BY SOCIAL CLASS

| | | Percent over 24 months | |
Social class	No. of patients all durations	Crude	Age adjusted
I	369	23.6	24.7
II	601	31.3	32.6
III	990	36.8	37.7
IV	935	42.6	42.8
V	630	54.6	52.7
VI	418	63.6	57.6
Total	3943	41.8	41.8
χ^2		212.62	146.54
P value		< .001	< .001

tals, and to be admitted on the basis of a court certification rather than on a voluntary basis.[3] Furthermore, the admission characteristics more typical of the lower class were also associated with a greater risk of a long-term hospitalization. Since such admission aspects antecede the actual term of stay, it was regarded as important to examine whether or not the original finding would appear to be spurious when these characteristics were taken into account.

Together, state and VA hospitals received almost 95 per cent of the patients. The relationship between social class and duration within each of these hospital systems is presented in Table 3. Within each system, the general relationship between social class level and rates of long-term stay prevails although it is more marked and consistent in the state system.

[3] The association between class level and type of hospital—state, private, VA, and criminal—is significant at the .001 level ($\chi^2 = 306.14$, 15df). The relationship between class position and type of certification—court, voluntary, medical, and other procedures—is significant at the .001 level ($\chi^2 = 142.31$, 15df).

A similar analysis was conducted controlling for various admission procedures. Patients certified to the hospitals through different methods varied markedly in discharge rates. Nevertheless, it may be observed in Table 4 that for each type of

TABLE 3. PER CENT OF LONG-TERM PATIENTS*
BY SOCIAL CLASS AND HOSPITAL TYPE

Social class	State		Veterans	
	%	N	%	N
I	25.9	(201)	32.0	(97)
II	32.0	(372)	37.2	(183)
III	37.7	(664)	37.2	(277)
IV	43.4	(668)	40.6	(234)
V	55.2	(475)	51.2	(129)
VI	66.3	(332)	50.8	(59)
Total	44.0	(2712)	40.1	(979)
χ^2	150.36		12.41	
P,5df	< .001		< .05	

* In Tables 3 and 4, percentages refer to patients not discharged within 24 months of first admission. Numbers in parentheses indicate the denominator population, that is, patients of all durations.

admission procedure, a highly significant relationship persists between social class and discharge rates.

Patients labelled as schizophrenic are far from a homogeneous group in their clinical manifestations. Certain specific clinical factors have previously been reported to be associated with differential outcome (20). If certain of these clinical characteristics were concentrated disproportionately in different social classes, this intervening relationship might account for the relationship between social class and duration. This possibility was tested by utilizing the following items of information on the clinical characteristics of the patients: (1) diagnostic sub type—catatonic, paranoid, hebephrenic, and other; (2) behavior type—depressed-suicidal, disturbed-destructive, quiet-idle, and employed; (3) duration of onset of the illness prior to hospitalization as grouped into the categories of less than six months, seven to 24 months, and over two years. For each of the three items, significant differences in the proportions of long-term patients existed among the various categories.[4]

The only one of these variables which is significantly related to social class is behavior type (P < .001, χ^2 = 41.64, 15 df). Upper class patients tend to be over-represented in the depressed-suicidal category, and lower class patients in the quiet-idle and disturbed-destructive categories. For each of the four major behavior types, however, class and duration demonstrate a highly significant relationship (P < .001). A similar analysis was made for

TABLE 4. PER CENT OF LONG-TERM PATIENTS BY SOCIAL CLASS AND TYPE OF ADMISSION CERTIFICATE

Social class	Court		Medical*		Voluntary		Other	
	%	N	%	N	%	N	%	N
I	39.2	(130)	20.3	(69)	10.3	(136)	23.5	(34)
II	42.6	(258)	24.2	(95)	21.5	(200)	25.0	(48)
III	46.7	(469)	28.8	(139)	21.5	(289)	46.2	(93)
IV	52.1	(461)	38.0	(150)	24.2	(227)	46.4	(97)
V	61.6	(359)	45.0	(109)	31.5	(92)	64.3	(70)
VI	69.8	(235)	60.3	(78)	44.2	(52)	60.4	(53)
Total	52.6	(1912)	36.1	(640)	22.7	(996)	46.8	(395)
χ^2	25.17		40.40		30.49		29.09	
P,5df	< .001		< .001		< .001		< .001	

* Includes physicians and health officers' certificates.

TABLE 5. CONDITION AT TIME OF DISCHARGE BY SOCIAL CLASS FOR PATIENTS DISCHARGED WITHIN TWO YEARS OF ADMISSION *

Social class	Recovered	Much improved	Improved	Unimproved	Total	N
I	20.6%	33.5%	33.8%	12.1%	100.0%	281
II	19.4	38.8	31.7	10.1	100.0	407
III	19.2	39.7	30.5	10.5	99.9	619
IV	14.1	39.6	35.4	10.9	100.0	523
V	18.8	41.7	30.8	8.7	100.0	276
VI	17.4	34.0	34.7	13.9	100.0	144
Total	18.1	38.6	32.6	10.7	100.0	2250

* Excluding 38 elopements and 5 family care placements.
χ^2 for entire table: 13.08, 15 df. P > .50.

[4] Due to space limitations, the basic data tables for these variables are not included, but will be supplied by the authors upon request. Definitions of these clinical categories are presented in *Statistical Guide,* N. Y. State Department of Mental Hygiene, Utica: State Hospitals Press, 1943. Although these clinical data were collected routinely for admistrative purposes and probably possess only moderate reliability, the three clinical items did display predictive utility in relation to hospital outcome. A given degree of random error in classification in testing for group differences is likely to be less serious the larger the size of the sample. With a sample of the present size, a more critical question is the extent to which each variable is measured independently of the others. Specifically, to what extent does the initial process of assigning a given label to a patient operate independently of the patient's actual behavior to determine the hospital response to the patient? That is, in typical clinical practice, the contribution made by the self-fulfilling prophecy is undetermined. For further discussion of this point, see (*14*).

each of the four categories of diagnosis and for the three periods of onset duration. Again, a highly significant relationship obtains between class and discharge rates within each of these seven categories (P < .001).

Conceivably, the entire series of findings could result from the application of different discharge criteria to patients of different social classes. It might be assumed that patients of higher class positions would tend to receive discharges at lower levels of improvement than other patients since their personal and family financial resources would be viewed as more adequate for assisting in their readjustment to the community. The data presented in Table 5 do not support this speculation. The level of improvement at discharge is not significantly related to class level among those patients discharged prior to a two-year hospitalization. But the extent to which class differences in discharge rates are a function of differential improvement has not been fully established. To answer this question, information would also be required on the improvement level of those patients who were not discharged.

CONCLUSIONS

The linkage between social class and the duration of hospitalization reported by Hollingshead is confirmed by the findings of this study. The present data also indicate that the relationship cannot readily be attributed to such factors as class differences in admission policies, clinical characteristics, and level of improvement at time of discharge.

The present findings suggest the feasibility of making actuarial predictions of hospital discharge probabilities on the basis of relatively objective social characteristics. Research is now in progress on the development of a predictive instrument. Additional social and clinical variables will be included and a more complex statistical technique of multivariate analysis will be used. It is believed that the refinement of an efficient and economical prognostic instrument should provide a useful tool for the clinician, experimentalist, and epidemiologist in the attack on the costly problem of chronicity among schizophrenics.

Additional research is also needed to locate class-linked variables such as different patterns of interaction, information, and attitudes which may be more directly related to patient improvement and discharge.[5] Some leads have been furnished by the New Haven studies. Hollingshead

and Redlich report that a more active course of treatment in public mental hospitals was received by higher class patients (10). Myers and Roberts indicate that middle-class schizophrenics tended to respond more favorably to treatment, such as electroshock (15). Substantial class differences in attitudes toward mentally ill patients were also discovered in a community survey conducted by Cumming and Cumming (16). Class differences in such attitudes were found among schizophrenic patients and their families by Myers and Roberts, who indicate that lower-class families are more likely to respond to hospitalization by a virtual abandonment of the patient.[6] Such behavior may have serious consequences for outcome; a recent British study reports that schizophrenics who had not received hospital visits from friends or relatives had a very unfavorable chance of obtaining an early discharge (4).

While the accumulating weight of evidence suggests that social factors may play an important role in the discharge process, there are serious gaps in our knowledge. Deserving more careful exploration are the relative contributions to the discharge decision made by behavioral changes in the patient, differences in the pattern of family support and intervention,

---

[5] An interesting example of a successful specification of a social class-health practice linkage in terms of an intervening psychological state is provided in (9).

[6] Myers and Roberts (15), p. 217, and Appendix Table 22, p. 285. Another team of investigators has offered a different and partly contrasting interpretation of class differences in attitudes toward the mentally ill. They suggest that "middle class families are less tolerant than others of deviants and more likely to exclude them from their midst." (8) It should be recognized that, within the framework of their paper, the quoted statement has the status of a postulate and not that of a directly tested hypothesis. In making such a test, we would suggest a careful study of the nature and intent of the responses to the deviator, as well as to different definitions of deviant acts. We would propose that, once an act of deviation is recognized, there would be a greater tendency for the middle-class person to respond in a manner calculated to reduce the recurrence of the act, while the lower-class person would more frequently reject or reduce his involvement with the "deviant." Some evidence for this postulate has been provided in the area of parent-child relations by Kohn who points out that middle-class parents value more highly the understanding of the child and his misbehavior. Even in the area of task performance, where failure should be highly threatening to middle-class parents, he indicates, "when the child does poorly in school, they often try to be supportive, while working-class parents are likely to respond negatively" (11).

and staff variations in defining such phenomena as "discharge readiness" and "overcrowding." Studies of contrasts in the natural history of hospitalization as experienced by patients from markedly different class levels could be useful in leading to the specification of those conditions responsible for different outcomes.

REFERENCES

1. *"A National Study of Schizophrenic Patients in Relation to Occupation,"* Medical Statistics Branch, General Registrar's Office; London (mimeo), 1958, p. 8.

2. Annual Report of the Department of Mental Hygiene, State of New York, Albany: *Legislative Document No. 98,* 1956.

3. Boek, W. E., Yankauer, A., and Sussman, M. B., *Social Class, Maternal Health and Child Care,* Albany: New York State Department of Health, 1957.

4. Brown, G. W., "Social Factors Influencing the Length of Hospital Stay of Schizophrenic Patients," *British Medical Journal* (in press).

5. Clausen, J. A., *Sociology and the Field of Mental Health,* New York: Russell Sage Foundation, 1956, pp. 13–36.

6. Cumming, J., and Cumming, Elaine, *Closed Ranks: An Experiment in Mental Health Education,* Cambridge: Harvard University Press, 1957, 57–58.

7. Dunham, H. W., and Meltzer, H. B., Predicting Length of Hospitalization of Mental Patients, *Amer. J. Soc.,* 1946, *52,* p. 126.

8. Freeman, H. E., and Simmons, O. G., Social Class and Posthospital Performance Levels, *Amer. Soc. Rev.,* 1959, *24,* p. 346.

9. Hochbaum, G. M., *Public Participation in Medical Screening Programs: A Socio-Psychological Study,* Public Health Monograph N. 572, Washington: U.S. Government Printing Office, 1958.

10. Hollingshead, A. D., and Redlich, F. C., *Social Class and Mental Illness,* New York: Wiley, 1958.

11. Kohn, M. L., Social Class and the Exercise of Parental Authority, *Amer. Soc. Rev.,* 1959, *24,* p. 366.

12. Kramer, M., Goldstein, H., Israel, R. H., and Johnson, N. A., *A Historical Study of the Disposition of First Admissions to a State Mental Hospital,* Public Health Monograph *No. 32,* Washington: U.S. Government Printing Office, 1955.

13. Malzberg, B., *Cohort Studies of Mental Disease in New York State: 1943-49,* New York: National Association for Mental Health, 1958.

14. Miller, S. M., and Mishler, E. G., Social Class, Mental Illness, and American Psychiatry, *The Milbank Memorial Fund Quarterly,* 1959, *37,* p. 188.

15. Myers, J. K., and Roberts, B. H., *Family and Class Dynamics in Mental Illness,* New York: Wiley, 1959, p. 216.

16. Rose, A. M. (ed.), *Mental Health and Mental Disorder,* New York: Norton, 1956.

17. Wanklin, J. M., Fleming, D. F., Buck, C., and Hobbs, G. E., Discharge and Readmission among Mental Hospital Patients, *A.M.A. Archives of Neurology and Psychiatry,* 1956, *76,* 664–665.

18. Whatley, C. D., *Reference Groups and Recovery from Mental Illness,* Tulane University, unpublished Ph.D. thesis, 1957, p. 139.

19. Zubin, J., Evaluation of Therapeutic Outcome in Mental Disorders, *J. Nerv. and Ment. Dis.,* 1953, *117,* 95–111.

20. Zubin, J., Burdock, E. I., Sutton, S., and Cheek, F., Epidemiological Aspects of Prognosis in Mental Illness, presented at symposium of the Amer. Assoc. for the Advancement of Science, N. Y. City, Dec. 27, 1956.

GLOSSARY

Adrenergic	Acting like adrenalin, activated or stimulated by adrenalin. Producing increased blood pressure, increased cardiac output, decreased vasomotor resistance, and an increased pulse. (See *Epinephrine.*)
Affect	A widely used term that may refer to one or a combination of the following: feeling, emotion, mood, temperament.
Agnosia	Loss of ability to recognize or identify familiar objects.
Anamnesis	Personal and family history as recalled by the patient. Adj: anamnestic.
Anorexia	Lack of appetite.
Associative interference	Interference in the establishment of a new associative bond by an already existing association.
Ataraxic	Tranquilizing.
Autistic	Thinking or perceiving that tends to be strongly influenced or distorted by one's needs and wishes.
Autokinetic effect	Perceived movement of a small nonmoving spot of light seen in darkness.
Brain stem reticular formation	A neural network in the brain stem that has an arousing or activating effect upon wide areas of the cerebral cortex. To be contrasted with the specific sensory impulse from the receptor organs.
Cathected	(Adj.) An object, idea, or action invested with emotional energy.
Chi square (χ^2)	A statistical test used to estimate whether the obtained results of an experiment differ from expected values to such an extent that evidence is given for the operation of nonchance factors.
Cholinergic	Stimulated or activated by acetylcholine. An adjective describing a set of bodily reactions that are to some extent the opposite of adrenergic reactions. (See *Adrenergic.*)
Chronicity	The degree of permanence of a disorder. A chronic disorder would be a long-persisting, more or less permanent one.
Cohort	All the cases of a given description; not a sample, e.g. "men over 25," "unemployed females, over 45."

Colitis	Inflammation of the large intestine, especially of its mucous membrane.
Confabulation	The production of false recollections of actually forgotten events.
Conjugal	Pertaining to marriage and marital relations.
Critical flicker frequency	The frequency at which an interrupted light stimulus is perceived as nonflickering; the perception of continuous light takes the place of the perception of flicker.
Critical ratio	A measure of significance that indicates the likelihood of the obtained statistic being affected by chance. It is obtained by dividing a statistic by its standard error.
Demography	The study of human populations, vital statistics, geographic distributions, causes of increases and decreases in populations, etc.
Dreams, manifest and latent contents of	Manifest content: What is remembered of the dream. Latent content: The repressed wishes that are indirectly and symbolically represented in the manifest content.
Dystereognosis	Disordered perception by touch of objects or forms.
Epidemiological	Pertaining to the origins and course of disease or disorders that affect many persons in a community (epidemics).
Epinephrine	A synonym for "adrenalin." An "epinephrine-like" reaction could include such responses as: increased heart rate, rise in blood pressure, dilation of the pupils, and increased blood supply to the skeletal muscles.
Etiology	The study of causes or origins.
Extrapunitive	A reaction to frustration in which one blames others for the frustration.
Factor analysis	A multidimensional method of statistical analysis by which scores and correlations of scores from a number of tests can be interpreted. In brief, the method helps one to reduce a great number of dimensions to as few as possible—i.e., to factors.
Figural after-effect	An alteration in the perception of a figure after prolonged inspection of a previous figure that occupied the same region in the visual field.
Foot-candle	A unit of illuminance equal to the illumination on a surface, every point of which is one foot away from a light source of one standard candle.
F ratio	A value used to determine whether the difference between two variances is statistically significant.

Generalization, stimulus	After a certain stimulus elicits a certain response, other similar stimuli then are able to elicit the same response.
Generalization, response	After a certain response is elicited by a certain stimulus, this stimulus becomes effective in eliciting similar responses.
Generalized other	An individual's abstracted concept of others. The average or pooled conception of the expectations one has of multiple others.
Genetically	Sometimes used to refer to the history and development of an individual, and sometimes to the effects of genes.
Galvanic skin response (GSR)	A measure of the change of skin resistance. It is regarded as an indication of emotional response or arousal.
Heuristic	Leading to further thinking and investigation.
Hypermnesic	Enhanced or unusual memory ability.
Hypnagogic	Pertaining to drowsiness or a sleep-like or trance-like state.
Intropunitive	A reaction to frustration in which one blames oneself.
Kendall's tau	A measure of the correlation between ranked scores.
Inverted hostility	Hostility directed towards the self.
Korsakoff's psychosis	A mental disorder often characterized by falsification of memory and disturbance of orientation, brought about through long-term and excessive consumption of alcohol.
Labile	Unstable, changeable, quickly shifting from one emotion to another.
Learning, instrumental	Learning that is instrumental in reaching a goal; often used in contrast to Pavlovian conditioning.
Leptokurtically	A leptokurtic frequency curve is *peaked* in the region about the mode.
Mann-Whitney test	A nonparametric test of the significance of the difference between means for unmatched groups.
Median	The point in a ranked distribution at which half the cases fall above and half fall below.
Mean difference	The mean of the differences between two sets of scores.
Milieu therapy	A system of therapy in which the patient's environment—especially all contacts between patients and hospital personnel—is designed to be therapeutic.
Modal personality	The "typical" personality in a given culture.
Multiple correlation (R)	The correlation between one variable (often called the "criterion variable") and two or more variables (often called "predictor variables").

Nociceptive	Painful.
Nonparametric	Statistical methods that do not assume any particular parameter, especially those that do not assume a normal distribution.
Nor-epinephrine-like reaction	Similar to the epinephrine-like reaction in that it includes an elevated blood pressure, but *differs* in that it involves an *unchanged* or *decreased* cardiac output, an *increased* peripheral-blood-system resistance, and a *decreased* pulse.
Nosology	The classification of diseases.
Null hypothesis	A statistical term for a statement hypothesizing that no difference exists between conditions. It is proposed in order to be rejected. The alternative hypothesis, which is the experimenter's research hypothesis, may be accepted if the null hypothesis is confidently rejected.
One-tailed test	A statistical test in which *direction* of a difference is predicted. For example, the prediction is made that $A > B$, or that $A < B$, but not that A shall merely differ from B. See *Two-tailed test*.
Operant conditioning	Usually refers to the control of behavior obtained by carefully arranging the consequences of the responses, the consequences usually being termed reinforcements. From a simple reinforced response, a complicated series of responses may be brought "under experimental control."
Operational	Referring to an operation or procedure. An operational definition is a definition in terms of the actual operations or procedures employed.
Orthopedic	Concerned with treatment of bone injuries, fractures, and disorders.
P *(or p)*	Represents the probability of the obtained results of an experiment being due to chance. The expression ($p = .05$) means that the obtained results of an experiment would occur less than five times in a hundred if only chance factors were operating.
Parameter	A term employed in statistical inference. It refers to a statistic, having an exact value, calculated from the total observations possible on any particular variable.
Paramnesia	Incorrect recollection or recognition.
Partial out (partial correlation)	(Verb) The correlation remaining between two variables, after the influence of one or more other variables on their correlation has been allowed for or eliminated.
Pathognomic	Distinctive of a certain disorder.

Phi-phenomenon	The perception of motion produced by stationery stimuli, such as two lights, flashed in rapid succession.
Placebo	A pill or other preparation containing only non-active substances.
Porteus maze	A paper-and-pencil maze.
Premorbidity	Previous to the disease or morbidity.
Prepotent factor	A factor that has ascendency over all other factors acting at any one time in controlling behavior.
Prognosis	Prediction of the duration, course, and/or outcome of a certain process or activity, especially of a disease.
Proprioception	The perception of the position and movements of the body and its members.
Protocol	The original record of the responses of a subject in a testing situation or experiment.
Putative	Commonly thought or supposed.
Q-sort	A personality assessment device in which a person sorts a considerable number of statements.
Regression equation	A formula for predicting the most likely value of one variable to be obtained from the known values of another variable. If it is a "multiple regression equation," the prediction is from two or more variables.
Reliability, coefficient of	A general term for measures of the dependability of observations, tests, etc., using correlation coefficients.
Remitting schizophrenic	A person previously diagnosed as schizophrenic in whom no symptoms of schizophrenia are present at the moment.
Rho	A coefficient of correlation.
Role-position	A position in a social structure as defined by expected actions of the occupant of the position.
Somaesthetic	Refers to sensations of the body, and includes *kinesthesis* which refers only to sensations of position and movement of the body.
Suppressor variable	An influence (variable) that reduces the effect of one or more other variables.
Symbiotic	Literally, living together. A reciprocal relationship, sometimes equated to mutual parasitism.
Syncretic	Usually refers to a type of perception or cognition in which there occurs diffuse, global, and undifferentiated responses. Syncretic behavior is often said to be characteristic of severely regressed schizophrenics and young children.

t Test

A statistic used to test the significance of the difference between two sample means when the number of cases or subjects in the sample is small.

Tachistoscope

A device that provides very brief timed exposures of visual material.

Two-tailed test

A test for the statistical significance of a difference in which it is assumed that the difference may be in *either* direction. A two-sided hypothesis.

Validation, cross and multiple

In general, validation refers to the extent to which an instrument has measured what it purports to measure. Cross-validation refers to the extent to which the instrument makes the same discriminations on one sample that it makes on similar samples. Multiple validity extends the notion of cross validation to include the reproducibility of an instrument's discriminatory power when used with dissimilar samples.

Variance, analysis of

A method used to analyze the variance (variability) in an experiment in which the influence of one or more independent variables upon the dependent variable is assessed.

Z Score

A statistical term referring to a new score obtained by transforming an original raw score. Because distributions of z scores have the same means and standard deviations, they are known as standard scores.

Index

339